Austro-Thai:

Language and Culture,
with a Glossary of Roots

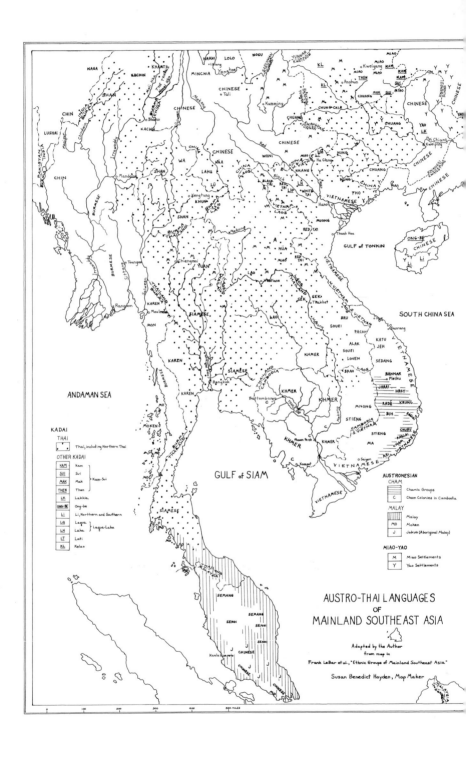

AUSTRO-THAI LANGUAGES
OF
MAINLAND SOUTHEAST ASIA

Adapted by the Author
from map in
Frank LeBar et al., "Ethnic Groups of Mainland Southeast Asia."

Susan Benedict Hayden, Map Maker

AUSTRO - THAI

LANGUAGE AND CULTURE

WITH A GLOSSARY OF ROOTS

PAUL K. BENEDICT

with a foreword by
WARD H. GOODENOUGH

HRAF PRESS
1975

ABOUT THE AUTHOR

Paul K. Benedict is a linguist by nature, an anthropologist and Orientalist by education and training (A.B., University of New Mexico, M.A. and Ph.D., Harvard University; Arnold and Harvard-Yenching Fellow, Harvard, fieldwork in Southeast Asia). He is also a clinical and research psychiatrist (M.D., New York Medical College), with a special interest in ethnopsychiatry.

LIBRARY OF CONGRESS CATALOG CARD NUMBER: 67-30152

INTERNATIONAL STANDARD BOOK NUMBER: 0-87536-323-7

© 1975

HUMAN RELATIONS AREA FILES, INCORPORATED

DEDICATION

TO THE MEMORY OF CLYDE KLUCKHOHN

Contents

Foreword

Ward H. Goodenough

In 1942, Paul K. Benedict presented evidence for a radical revision of the then accepted phylogenetic grouping of languages in Southeast Asia and the Pacific ("Thai, Kadai, and Indonesian: A New Alignment in Southeastern Asia," *American Anthropologist 44:* 576-601). He proposed that the Thai family of languages be taken out of the Sino-Tibetan phylum and, together with a group of four languages from South China, which he called Kadai, be joined in a phylum with the Indonesian family of languages. He presented very strong evidence for the latter relationship as the basic one for the Thai and Kadai languages.

His reclassification was accepted by some scholars, but was ignored or rejected by others. Little was done with the lead Benedict had provided until his own return to the subject twenty-five years later with a series of articles published in 1966-67 in *Behavior Science Notes.* There he presented a large body of further evidence in support of his original thesis, to which he has added even more in this expanded version of those articles. That so much more evidence could be produced is itself an important fact in support of Benedict's earlier thesis.[1] There can now be no question that the Malayo-Polynesian or Austronesian phylum (including Indonesian) is itself part of a larger phylum, Benedict's Austro-Thai, which includes the Thai and Kadai languages and apparently, as Benedict now suggests, the Miao and Yao languages as well. There is room for all kinds of argument about the details, but not about the fact of relationship.

This fact puts into new perspective the problem of the homeland of the Austronesian family of languages. The assumed mainland location of the Proto-Austronesian languages has been questioned in the past decade in consequence of the results of Isidore Dyen's massive lexico-statistical study (Dyen 1963a).

ix

Because of the concentration in Melanesia of the most distantly related languages and groups of languages, it seemed that northern Melanesia might have been the homeland of the Austronesian languages (Dyen 1962a, 1962b; Murdock 1964). Later, Dyen (1963b, 1965) argued on phonological grounds that Formosa might have been the Austronesian homeland. In his published work, however, he has not considered the relationship of the Thai and Kadai languages to Austronesian and the possible implication of that relationship.

To follow the steps taken by Benedict in relating the Thai and Kadai to the Austronesian languages, the reader is advised to start with his earlier paper of 1942 (see Appendix I). Taking the mostly disyllabic forms of Proto-Indonesian, as reconstructed by Dempwolff (1934-38) and as amended by later scholars, Benedict set out to show how they can be transformed into the monosyllabic forms of the Thai and Kadai languages. Thus Proto-Indonesian *mata, "eye," corresponds to Proto-Thai *ta, derived from a presumed older *mta, just as Proto-Indonesian *balik, "turn," corresponds to Proto-Thai *blik. Such would result naturally from the development of a strong stress accent on the final syllable of the original disyllabic form. Given such a process, comparative study requires working out the phonological shifts of what had become consonant clusters in the Thai and Kadai languages. In these languages some clusters are preserved, providing strong support for the basic working hypothesis.

From the correspondences worked out between the consonants of the Thai and Kadai languages and pairs of consonants in Proto-Indonesian, Benedict then observed that some additional Thai and Kadai forms might be seen as cognate with Proto-Indonesian ones if there had been consonant clusters in the earlier parent language from which Proto-Indonesian itself was derived, these clusters having disappeared in Proto-Indonesian. Thus the pattern of Thai and Kadai correspondences with the Proto-Indonesian *təlu, "three," one that involved the cluster *tl, also occurred in the Thai and Kadai word for louse, suggesting the reconstruction of an Austro-Thai form *katlu, which became Proto-Indonesian *kutu. He similarly reconstructed (in the 1966-67 articles) Austro-Thai *matla,* "eye,"[2] and *pitlu,* "seven" (cf. Proto-Indonesian *mata* and *pitu*).

There are many doublets in the Thai and Kadai languages, and many doublets have been reconstructed by Dempwolff for Proto-Indonesian (e.g. *nipit'* and *tipis',* "thin," *dalan* and *d'alan,* "path"). These doublets pose a major problem of interpretation. The usual view is that doublets are indicative of borrowings of cognate forms from closely related languages or dialects in which there have been different histories of phonological change. Thus in Gilbertese we find the doublet *oŋo,* "hear," and *roŋoroŋo,* "news." The original initial consonant has been lost in Gilbertese proper, but it was preserved as /l/ or /r/ in the Polynesian languages. The word for "news" is demonstrably part of a sizable corpus of borrowings into Gilbertese from a Polynesian source. Borrowing back and forth among related dialects has produced significant numbers of doublets in many Austronesian languages (Goodenough 1962). Biggs (1965) has shown how large a role such borrowing has played in the history of Rotuman. I had to take account of this process in order not to reconstruct far too many consonant phonemes for Proto-Nakanai in New Britain (Goodenough 1961). It is also possible that doublets with different initial consonants in Dempwolff's Proto-Indonesian reflect older initial consonant clusters that were differently reduced in different daughter languages with subsequent back-borrowing among them. Benedict has chosen to make such interpretation. Doublets can also result from old patterns of morphophonemic variation. To find evidence that clearly points to any one of these possibilities as against the others remains a fundamental problem in Benedict's method. The possibility of differences among scholars in the interpretation and consequent use of doublets does not invalidate Benedict's conclusions about the cognation of words, but opens the way for disagreement regarding the reconstruction of ancestral forms.

In the process of reducing older disyllabic and trisyllabic forms to monosyllabic ones in the Thai and Kadai languages, sometimes the first syllable and sometimes the final syllable, depending on the location of stress, was the part that was preserved.

Thus Austro-Thai *katlu, "louse," gave rise to Ong-Be kat and Proto-Thai *[t]hraw. If one adds this consideration to the idea that Proto-Indonesian itself has lost some original Austro-Thai consonant clusters, it becomes conceivable to relate Shan ta:k, "small leech," and Thai pliŋ, "leech," to Proto-Indonesian *lima-(n)[t]ek, "small leech," from a presumed Austro-Thai *pliŋwant-[r]a(a)k, as Benedict did in his 1966-67 articles. Here, of course, we cannot be sure that we are not reconstructing a compound of two distinct words, both of which were semantically linked with leeches and blood-sucking, and Benedict has since withdrawn his earlier suggestion (see present Glossary).

At this point the game becomes tricky. In the example just cited, the Proto-Indonesian form provides a possible bridge between the Shan and Thai forms. But there is no such bridging form that justifies seeing the Proto-Indonesian forms *γumah, "house," and *baruŋ, "hut," as having been joined in a trisyllabic Austro-Thai *ba[γr]uŋwaa-, an earlier suggestion that Benedict has also now withdrawn from his present glossary. That both γumah and *baruŋ have cognates in the Thai and Kadai languages, however, is clear.

The foregoing comments indicate both the strengths and the weaknesses of what Benedict has done. By making certain bold and insightful assumptions about the change processes by which the Thai and Kadai languages have become progressively differentiated from the related Austronesian languages, he has managed to recover a large number of cognate or possibly cognate forms and to make a strong case for a phylogenetic relationship between these language stocks. At the same time, he has pushed the method to the limit and, in my view, pushed it too far in places. But that is, perhaps, as it should be. Better to go too far and have one's excesses corrected later than to be overly cautious and fail to make a significant advance that opens up possibilities for exploration and study.

Benedict has without question made such a significant advance. His conclusions regarding the influence of Austro-Thai speakers on the ancient Chinese are startling, to say the least; yet equally startling, recent archeological discoveries are consistent with these conclusions (Solheim 1971). Scholars will be reviewing the materials, arguing the pros and cons, and refining and correcting what Benedict has begun. But one thing is certain, as he himself states: "It is no longer a question as to whether these languages are related, but rather as to just how we are to reconstruct the ancestral forms."

NOTES

[1] In an effort by implication to discredit Benedict's work, Dyen (1970), with tongue in cheek, has offered a body of evidence in favor of a relationship between Indo-European and Austronesian languages. The evidence he can muster is paltry by comparison with Benedict's, which is of a different quality and a different order of magnitude.

[2] Now reconstructed by Benedict as Austro-Thai *mapḷa (see Glossary).

REFERENCES

Benedict, Paul K.
    1942   "Thai, Kadai, and Indonesian: A New Alignment in Southeastern Asia," *American Anthropologist*, n.s., *44*, 576-601.
    1966   "Austro-Thai," *Behavior Science Notes, 1:* 227-61.
    1967a "Austro-Thai Studies: 1. Material culture [and 2. Kinship terms]," *Behavior Science Notes, 2:* 203–44.
    1967b "Austro-Thai Studies: 3. Austro-Thai and Chinese," *Behavior Science Notes, 2:* 275-336.
Biggs, Bruce
    1965   "Direct and Indirect Inheritance in Rotuman," in G. B. Milner and E. J. A. Henderson, eds., *Indo-Pacific Linguistic Studies,* Part I, pp. 383-415, Amsterdam, North Holland Publishing Co. (published also in *Lingua, 14,* 383-415).
Dempwolff, Otto
    1934- *Vergleichende Lautlehre des Austronesischen Wortschatzes,* 3
    38   vols. Berlin, Dietrich Reimer (Ernst Vohsen) A.G.
Dyen, Isidore
    1962a "The lexicostatistical classification of the Malayo-Polynesian languages," *Language, 38:* 34-46.
    1962b "Comment on 'Oceanic Linguistics Today,'" *Current Anthropology, 3:* 402-05.
    1963a *The Lexicostatistical Classification of the Austronesian Languages,* New Haven.
    1963b "The Position of the Malayopolynesian Languages of Formosa," *Asian Perspectives, 7:* 261-71.
    1970   "Background 'Noise' or 'Evidence' in Comparative Linguistics: The Case of the Austronesian-Indo-European Hypothesis," in G. Cardona, H. M. Hoenigswald, and A. Senn, eds., *Indo-*

European and Indo-Europeans, pp. 431-40. Philadelphia, University of Pennsylvania Press.

Goodenough, Ward H.
    1961   "Migrations Implied by Relationships of New Britain Dialects to Central Pacific Languages," *Journal of the Polynesian Society,* 70: 112-26.
    1962   "Comment on 'Oceanic Linguistics Today,'" *Current Anthropology,* 3: 406-08.

Murdock, George Peter
    1964   "Genetic Classification of the Austronesian Languages: A Key to Oceanic Culture History," *Ethnology,* 3: 117-26.

Solheim, William G., II
    1971   "New Light on a Forgotten Past," *National Geographic,* 139: 330-39.

Preface

Austro-Thai had a humble origin in the early 1940s as a modest linguistic undertaking by the author, who was faced with the problem of disentangling the complex language relationships in Southeast Asia. The dim outlines of a hypothetical language ancestral to Thai and Austronesian first took shape at that time (1942 article), but this proto-language was not dignified by a name until much later (1966 article), when material from Kam-Sui and other mainland languages made possible a huge expansion of the original thesis. It soon became evident from a consideration of the lexical material that the Austro-Thai speakers were by no means the culturally primitive people that the author had envisaged, but rather were the bearers of a fairly sophisticated culture (1967 article). At about the same time, the author also belatedly realized that numerous key items in the culture of the ancient Chinese must be assigned an Austro-Thai origin on the basis of loan-word analysis, with similar early influences also at work in the Tibeto-Burman area (1967bis article). Dr. Frank LeBar, of the Human Relations Area Files, suggested that these articles be reprinted under one cover, and the author pulled together his material in the form of a *Glossary* of Austro-Thai "roots" and an *Introduction,* to appear under the same cover in 1968/1969.

In the spring of 1968, however, the author began to re-examine available material on the Miao-Yao languages, which had long resisted his efforts to link with other language groups. The newly created Austro-Thai proved to be the key to this puzzle, and in June 1968, he informed Dr. LeBar that Miao-Yao appeared to be another branch of Austro-Thai. The author at first felt that he might be able simply to "slip" some of the relevant Miao-Yao material into the existing manuscript, but it soon became evident that extensive alteration would be required. These changes resulted in a major recasting of the manuscript, especially with the availability of Purnell's reconstruction of Miao-

Yao (1970), with consequent delay in publication. The addition of Miao-Yao also entailed a basic change in the attempted reconstruction of the parent Austro-Thai language, the earlier conjectural "two-legged" base (Austronesian and Kadai) having now been replaced by a linguistic tripod (Austronesian, Kadai, and Miao-Yao), yielding a much firmer substructure, as might be anticipated. As a consequence, the original *Introduction* was greatly expanded so as to include a virtual comparative phonology of Austro-Thai.

Austro-Thai has come a long way from its humble origin, with every promise of supplying essential keys to an array of problems in the early history of Southeast Asia, and with possible ramifications as far afield as the Americas (see *Introduction*). Together with the startling archeological finds by Solheim and others, it enables us to establish Southeast Asia as a focal area in the emergent cultural development of Homo sapiens. It now seems likely that the first true agriculturists anywhere, perhaps also the first true metal workers, were Austro-Thai speakers.

The author is indebted to Dr. LeBar for his encouragement, support, and patience throughout the several years that this book has been "in process." Elizabeth P. Swift, also of Human Relations Area Files, has been of invaluable assistance in editing the manuscript, both of this book and of the earlier articles, and has also displayed unusual patience with the author in his perpetual revisions of the manuscript. The author is further indebted to Professor Ward Goodenough of the Department of Anthropology, University of Pennsylvania, for his kindness in supplying the *Foreword* for this book and for his encouragement over the years. He also wishes to express his gratitude to Mr. Raleigh Ferrell, who spared no effort in assembling Formosan material for the author's use; to Dr. Herbert Purnell, Jr., who furnished him with a copy of his doctoral dissertation on Miao-Yao and further aided him in working with this difficult language family; also to the many scholars who have furnished him with Austro-Thai materials: Inez de Beauclair, B. Biggs, A. Capell, K. Chang, I. Dyen, S. Egerod, W. Gedney, G. Grace, A. Haudricourt, F. K. Li, and H. Mohring. Additional Austro-Thai materials were made available through the generosity of Professor Marvin Herzog of the Department of Linguistics, Columbia University, and the staff of the Columbia University Library. A special note of thanks is due Marilyn Benedict, who contributed to the task of compiling material and who suffered as a wife throughout the many years that this book was coming into being. Finally, in the dedication of this book the author acknowledges his deep indebtedness to the late Professor Clyde Kluckhohn, gifted teacher of anthropology at Harvard University, who many years ago first guided his footsteps toward the East.

AUSTRO-THAI   AT

Austronesian   AN

  Indonesian   IN
    Hova   Ho.
    Javanese   Ja.
    Malay   Ml.
    Ngaju-Dayak   NgD.
    Toba-Batak   TB.
    Tagalog   Tg.
    Yami (Botel Tobago)

  Cham group
    Cham
    Jarai
    Radé

  Oceanic   (PO = Proto-Oceanic)
    Fiji   Fi.
    Sa'a   Sa.
      Ulawa dial.   U.

  Polynesian (PPN = Proto-Polynesian)
    Futuna   Fu.
    Samoa   Sm.
    Tonga   To.

  Southeast Papua   SEP

  Formosa   Form.

  East
    Ami
    Bunun   Bun.
    Favorlang [extinct]   Fav.
    Kuvalan (= Kavalan)   Kuv.
    Paiwan   Pai.
      Makazayazaya dial.   Mak.
    Pazeh   Paz.
    Puyuma   Puy.

Rukai   Ruk.
  East Rukai   E. Ruk.
  West Rukai   W. Ruk.
Saisiat   Sai.
Siraya [extinct]   Sir.
Thao

Tsouic
Kanakanabu (= Kanabu)   Kan.
Saaroa   Saa.
Tsou

Atayalic
Atayal   Ata.
  Squliq dial.
  Ci'uli dial.
Sedik   Sed.

Kadai   KD

Thai   T

Southwest   SW
  Ahom [extinct]
  Black Tai   BT
  Khamti   Kh.
  Lao
  Shan
  Siamese   Si.
  White Tai   WT

Tho-Nung (= Central)
Nung
Tho

Northern   N. Thai
  Cao-lan/Ts'un-lao   CT
  Chuang
  Dioi (cf. Yay)
  Po-ai
  Sek
  Wu-ming
  Yay (cf. Dioi)

Kam-Sui **KS**
    Kam (= Tung)
    Mak
    Sui
        Jungchiang dial. Sui-J.
        Li-Ngam dial. Sui-LN
        Pyo dial. Sui-P.
    Then (= T'en)

Lakkia Lk.

Ong-Be (= Be) OB

Li
  Southern Li S. Li
  Northern Li N. Li
  (Savina)
  Basadungli Bas.
  Dogang Dog.
  Double Cloth Loi DC Loi
  Mefuli Mef.
  Shaved Head Loi SH Loi
    Five Fingers Mt. dial. FF Loi
    Liamui dial.
  Small Cloth Loi SC Loi
  White Sand Loi WS Loi
  White Sand Li WS Li
  (Wang)
  Bupäli (transitional) Bup.

Laqua-Laha
  Laqua (= Ka Beo) Lq.
  Pu-peo dial.
  Laha Lh.
    Than-Uyên TU
    Ban Bung BB
    Noong Lay NL

Lati Lt.
  Ban-Phung dial. BP
  Man-P'ang dial. MP

Kelao Kl.
 Northern Kelao N. Kl.
 Mulao
 Southern Kelao S. Kl.

Miao-Yao (PMY = Proto-Miao-Yao)
 Miao (PM = Proto-Miao)
  Eastern Miao (PE = Proto-Eastern)
   Tai-kung Miao MTK
   K'ai-li Miao MKL
   Lu-shan Miao MLS
   T'ai-chiang Miao MTC
   Cheng-feng Miao (= Kanao) MCF
   Phö Miao
   Jung-chiang Miao MJC
  [Northern Miao]
   Hua-yuan Miao MHY
  Central Miao (PC = Proto-Central)
   Lung-li Miao MLL
   Kwei-chu Miao MKC
  Western Miao (PW = Proto-Western)
   Li-po Miao (= Hei "Yao") MLP
   Wei-ning Miao MWN
   Kwang-shun Miao (= I Miao, Yi Miao) MKS
   West A (PWA = Proto-West A)
    Petchabun Miao (= White Miao) MPT
    Tak Miao (= Green Miao, Blue Miao) MTT
    Su-yung Miao (= Magpie Miao) MSY
    Ch'uan Miao MCh.
    Hua-chieh Miao MHC
  Pateng group
   Pateng PT
   Yung-ts'ung Miao (= Tahua "Yao") MYT
  Miao-fang Pei-lan vocabulary ("Kelao" list) MFPL
 Yao (PY = Proto-Yao)
  Iu Mien (PIM = Proto-Iu Mien)
   Chiengrai Yao (= Highland Yao) YCR

Hsing-an Yao   YHA
Taipan Yao   YTP

Kim Mun   (PKM = Proto-Kim Mun)
Haininh Yao   YHN
Ling-chun Yao   YLC
Paip'ai Yao   YPP

ABBREVIATIONS

AA Austroasiatic
AD *Analytic Dictionary* (Karlgren 1923)
AN Austronesian
Anc. Ancient [Chinese]
Arch. Archaic [Chinese]
AT Austro-Thai
AT *Austro-Thai* (Benedict 1966, 1967, 1967bis)
Ata. Atayal

B, bro brother
Bas. Basadungli
BB Ban Bung [Laha dial.]
b.l. back-loan
Bon. Bonifacy
BP Ban-Phung
BT Black Tai
Bun. Bunun
Bup. Bupäli

C cousin
Cap. Capell
cg. cognate
Ch child
Ch. Chinese
CL Capell and Lester (1945-46)
CT Cao-lan/Ts'un-lao
cw. in composition with

D daughter
DC Double Cloth [Loi dial.]
Demp. Dempwolff
Dog. Dogang
d.t. different tone

E. East [Rukai]
Eg. Egerod

F, fa father
Fav. Favorlang
Ferr. Ferrell
FF Five Fingers Mt. [Loi dial.]
Fi. Fiji
Form. Formosa
Fu. Futuna

g great [kinship comb. form]
Ged. Gedney
gr grand [kinship comb. form]
GSR "Grammata Serica Recensa" (Karlgren 1957)

Haud. Haudricourt
Ho. Hova
h.t. high tone

ic. in composition
IN Indonesian

J. Jungchiang [Sui dial.]
Ja. Javanese
Jer. Jeremaissen

Kan. Kanakanabu
KD Kadai
Kh. Khamti
Kl. Kelao

KN kin numerative (Benedict 1945)
KS Kam-Sui
Kuv. Kuvalan

Laj. Lajonquière
LCG Likely Cognate Group (*Introduction*)
Lh. Laha
Lk. Lakkia
LN Li-Ngam [Sui dial.]
Lq. Laqua
Lt. Lati
l.t. low tone

M, mo mother
Mak. Makazayazaya
MCF Cheng-feng Miao
MCh. Ch'uan Miao
Mef. Mefuli
MFPL *Miao-fang Pei-lan*
MHC Hua-chieh Miao
MHY Hua-yuan Miao
MJC Jung-chiang Miao
MKC Kwei-chu Miao
MKL K'ai-li Miao
MKS Kwang-shun Miao
Ml. Malay
MLL Lung-li Miao
MLP Li-po Miao
MLS Lu-shan Miao
MN Melanesian
MP Man-P'ang
MPT Petchabun Miao
MSY Su-yung Miao
MTC T'ai-chiang Miao
MTK T'ai-kung Miao
MTT Tak Miao
MWN Wei-ning Miao
MY Miao-Yao
MYT Yung-ts'ung Miao

N nephew/niece
N. Northern [Kelao, Li, Thai]
n.a. not analyzed
Ne nephew
NgD. Ngaju-Dayak
Ni niece
NL Noong Lay [Laha dial.]

o older [kinship terms]
OB Ong-Be
Og. Ogawa
Og.-As. Ogawa and Asai (1935)

P parent
P. Pyo [Sui dial.]
Pai. Paiwan
Paz. Pazeh
PC Proto-Central [Miao]
PE Proto-Eastern [Miao]
PIM Proto-Iu Mien [Yao]
PKM Proto-Kim Mun [Yao]
PM Proto-Miao
PMY Proto-Miao-Yao
PN Polynesian
PO Proto-Oceanic
PPN Proto-Polynesian
PT Pateng
Puy. Puyuma
PW Proto-Western [Miao]
PWA Proto-West A [Miao]
PY Proto-Yao

reg. regularly
Rob. Robert
Ruk. Rukai

S son
S. Southern [Kelao, Li]
Sa. Sa'a
Saa. Saaroa
Sai. Saisiat
Sav. Savina
Sb sibling
SC Small Cloth [Loi dial.]
Sed. Sedik
SEP Southeast Papua [Capell]
SH Shaved Head [Loi dial.]
Si, si sister
Si. Siamese
Sir. Siraya
Sm. Samoa
Sp spouse
ST Sino-Tibetan
s.t. same tone
SW Southwest [Thai]

T Thai
TB Tibeto-Burman

TB. Toba-Batak
Tg. Tagalog
To. Tonga
TU Than-Uyên [Laha dial.]

U. Ulawa

VT Vocalic Transfer
v.t., v.tr. transitive verb

W wife
W. West [Rukai]

WS White Sand [Li, Loi dial.]
WT White Tai

xC cross-cousin

y younger [kinship terms]
YCR Chiengrai Yao
YHA Hsing-an Yao
YHN Haininh Yao
YLC Ling-chun Yao
YPP Paip'ai Yao
YTP Taipan Yao

Austro-Thai:

Language and Culture, with a Glossary of Roots

Austro-Thai[1]

Paul K. Benedict[*]

Some quarter of a century ago the writer proposed that the languages of Southeast Asia be reclassified as follows (schema from Benedict 1942):

Proto-Austric —
{ Thai
Kadai
Indonesian

{ Mon-Khmer
Annamese

?Miao-Yao

Chinese

Sino-Tibetan { Tibeto-Burman
Karen

This schema completely removes Thai from its traditional association with Chinese and Tibeto-Burman (TB) and places it in a supergrouping with Indonesian (IN). Thai features such as monosyllabicism and tonality are explained as the product of an early, profound influence from Chinese upon the Thai languages, at that time (1st millennium B. C. or earlier) spoken in southern China. The Thai numerals and some other lexical elements are also attributed to this influence, whereas the more nuclear root affinities are considered to lie with Indonesian. Kadai was created as a grouping for several residual languages of the area: Li (Hainan), Laqua and Lati (China–North Vietnam border) and Kelao (small, scattered groups in south-central China). These languages were shown to have striking IN correspondences in the numerals and elsewhere, along with Thai features, and were described as transitional between Thai and

* Paul K. Benedict is a linguist by nature (but studied with Sapir), an anthropologist and Orientalist by education and training (A.B., University of New Mexico; M.A. and Ph.D., Harvard University; Arnold and Harvard-Yenching Fellow, Harvard, field work in Southeast Asia). For the past fifteen years he has been a clinical and research psychiatrist (M.D., New York Medical College), with ethnopsychiatry as one of his main interests (collaborating editor of *Schizophrenia*, New York: Logos Press, 1958, and contributor of the section on "Social and Cultural Factors in Schizophrenia").

IN. A general historical thesis was advanced, viz. that the ancient center of dispersion for these several languages and/or linguistic complexes was the South China area, and that the Cham and Malay language areas on the mainland could best be regarded as enclaves rather than as possible points of departure for the IN peoples.

The basic hypothesis advanced in 1942 has fared rather well over the years, especially in view of the violence that it did to the traditional scheme of things. The writer has contented himself with studies in related fields (see References) which tend to support his earlier conclusions without making any significant advance in the field. The Kadai grouping has won favor from most scholars, including Coedès (1949) and Capell (1945), and Haudricourt (1962) has even elevated this lowly tribal conglomeration to the role of a veritable linguistic "cross-roads" of Southeast Asia, connecting not only Austronesian (AN) and Daic (Thai) but even Austroasiatic and TB! The most influential advocate, however, has probably been Greenberg (1953), whose diagram of relationships is often reproduced (Capell 1962, Suggs 1951) along with the minor error in it.[2] Most recently, *Ethnic Groups of Mainland Southeast Asia* (LeBar et al. 1964) presented Thai and Kadai as a group but retained Malayo-Polynesian as a separate unity, along with a note as to the possible relationship with Thai. The writer was willing to accept this as representing a cautious approach until he noted that in this same work Miao-Yao is unabashedly placed in the Sino-Tibetan family, along with such legitimate members as Chinese and Tibeto-Burman. This led him to a review of the whole problem, with the feeling that a stronger case might be made for the original hypothesis as a whole. His goals were extremely modest: to strengthen a point here or there, to come up with a few lexical correspondences previously not noted. He was totally unprepared for the mass of material which he uncovered, partly with the aid of new key factors which will be described. After all, he had already announced in the original paper his belief that "most of the important lexical correspondences have been uncovered," and he had seen no reason, over the years, for changing this view. What is more, his colleagues appear to have believed him, since virtually no new comparative material has been brought forward to this time. It would appear that this unfortunate statement, which surely must be ranked with the most egregious overstatements of our times, contributed to a veritable standstill in this field.

The Kadai languages had always seemed to the writer to be of critical importance if new advances were to be made in the field, and it has been a disappointing fact that no new sources on any of these languages have appeared since the publication in 1937 of Stübel's monumental work on the populations of Hainan. A previously overlooked source on Lati (Robert 1913) has been uncovered, however, and we now have two dialects of this language (Man P'ang and Ban Phung), the former often tying in more directly with material from the other Kadai languages, especially in the numerals (see the discussion below). An early Chinese source on Kelao, a word list from the *Miao-fang Pei-lan*, has been made available (in Chinese) by Ruey Yih-fu (1956), but this material presents more problems than solutions. On the Indonesian side, Dyen has made important contributions to the reconstruction of the parent speech (Dyen 1947a, 1947b; 1951; 1953a, 1953b), but no systematic comparative study of all IN lexemes has yet appeared, and we must largely content ourselves with the basic work by Dempwolff (1930), especially as modified by Dyen. As for the wider field of Austronesian, the recent review by Capell (1962), to which are appended lengthy comments by outstanding scholars in the field, highlights the sharp disagreements by these experts at almost every point and on every level. They agree perhaps on only one point, viz. that "someone" should do for AN what Dempwolff did for IN, in providing for it a comparative phonology and a corpus of roots.

We must turn now to the more positive aspect of our search for new tools or "keys" with which we may pry into hitherto inaccessible areas, and we find that two such sets of material have been supplied to us:

(A) F. K. Li has described and recorded in detail a new group of languages, the Kam-Sui (including also Mak and Then), spoken in various villages in Kweichou and Kwangsi provinces, in south-central China (see References). He has published (in Chinese) a complete study on Mak, has contributed perceptive linguistic analyses relating to Kam-Sui and

Thai, and has promised a complete study of Sui. He reports
the appearance of a Kam dictionary (apparently in Chinese),
and it seems in general that before long we shall have very
substantial materials on the Kam-Sui group as a whole. The
writer (1942) had predicted that new languages would be uncovered in this area, but had visualized rather languages of
Kadai type. The Kam-Sui (KS) languages, which might be
considered para-Thai, retain complex initials, e.g. ʔ*b* and ʔ*d*,
hm and *hn*, which have been lost in the modern Thai languages,
and they also present a number of highly distinctive features,
notably a separate post-velar or uvular series of consonants.
With this material in mind, the writer reviewed the word list
and sentences long ago recorded by Jeremaissen (1892) for the
Ong-Be (OB), also known in the literature as Shu-Li, one of
the many populations on the island of Hainan, and found that
this language exhibits specific Kam-Sui affinities and can be
placed in this general para-Thai framework. In general, these
languages both confirm our reconstructions of the parent Thai
speech, as Li has pointed out in detail, and also present a maze
of new forms and lexemes which bridge the gap between Thai
and IN and/or Kadai at many critical junctures. One striking
illustration will suffice here: the writer had not even included
IN **kutu*, Thai (T) **hraw* "head louse" in his list of possible
correspondences, but the KS forms (Sui *tu*, Mak *təu*, Then *tiu*)
led him to reconstruct T **[t]hraw*, and he was delighted to un-
cover OB *kat* "lice"; he was then able to interpret the already
recognized Li cognate *sau~su* as a development from a **tl*-
initial cluster, exactly paralleling IN **təlu* "3"; Li *śu~su*, and
on this basis was able to reconstruct Austro-Thai (AT) **kut(a)lu*.
Other important inferences are to be drawn from the same illustration, both as to the importance of the stress factor in determining development (**'kutu*>*kat*, but **ku'tu*>*tu*) and with
regard to the simplification of consonant clusters in IN (see
further discussion below).

(B) In 1951 Haudricourt pointed out the existence of a distinctive series of labio-velar consonants in New Caledonia, the
Solomons, and the Gilberts and Carolines, and Goodenough
(1962) has extended this to Fiji. This made available, for the
first time, a body of data regarding some specific aspect of AN

as opposed to IN and thus provided a test case, so to speak, for evaluating the claim that Thai and Kadai are directly related to this ancestral AN language. As will be shown below, the correspondences for these labio-velar consonants are remarkable in their scope and establish the general thesis beyond any possibility of rebuttal.

The original paper (1942) presented a list of 30 roots common to Thai and IN, with several additional comparisons added in footnotes.[3] One of these must now be rejected: T *ʔ*duuk* "bone"; IN *ta(n)duk* "horn" (one of only two of the original group involving any semantic shift). We now have three separate bits of information for this rejection. The long (phonemically geminate) vowel normally leads to replacement of *-k* by *-ʔ* in IN (see below). The initial ʔ*d-* shows three separate sets of correspondences in KS, as established by F. K. Li (1965). Inasmuch as we have excellent IN correspondences for several of the roots involved, it will repay us to study this material in some detail:

TABLE I

	GROUP I (F. K. Li ʔd-)		GROUP II (F. K. Li ʔl-)	
	winnow	raw	plant, v.	bone
IN	*ta(m)pi*	*hudip*	*pandəm*	[t]*ulaŋ*
(reconstr.)	*traŋkwi*	*hublip*	*pandlam*	*tulak*
Thai	ʔ*doŋ*	ʔ*diip*	ʔ*dam*	ʔ*duuk*
Sui-LN	ʔ*doŋ*	ʔ*dyup*	ʔ*dam*	ʔ*dak*
Sui-J.	*doŋ*	*dyup*	*lam*	*lak*
Sui-P.	ʔ*doŋ*	ʔ*dyup*	*lam*	*lak*
Mak	ʔ*doŋ*	ʔ*dip*	ʔ*dam*	ʔ*dook*
Then	*loŋ*	*lip*	*zam*	*zaak*
S. Li	*duŋ yau*	*diep*	*dom*	*drüʔ*
N. Li		*fiep*		*füök*

Notes to Table I: "winnow": see below for the IN reconstruction as to the final; for the initial, T has a root *k(h)röŋ*, represented also by Si. *tăkrɛ:ŋ* and Dioi *raŋ* "sift; sieve, winnowing basket"; Mak has *jiŋ* as a doublet to ʔ*doŋ* "winnowing basket," and this is the general Thai and KS as well as Li meaning; the second part of the basic root is found in Dioi *wi*< *hwi* "clean grain with winnowing basket," probably also in T *wi* "fan; to fan" (Dioi *bi*) and Mak *pəi* "fan," *pəi pəi həu* "winnow rice (*həu*)"; *"raw"*: IN "live"; T "raw, green, alive"; *"plant"*: IN "bury," with the form cited by Dyen, who extricated it from scattered material

cited by Dempwolff under IN *pǝ(n)dǝm* "close the eyes";
Nung has "plant rice," but the general T meaning is "dive"; KS
"plant young rice plants"; *"bone"*: for AT we can reconstruct the
doublet **tulaŋ ∼ *tulak*, fitting a type encountered in other roots
(cf. "areca" below); the vocalism of the Thai form is explained
by the KS series with medial *-aa-*, the whole closely paralleling
T **luuk* "child"; KS **laak*, giving a reconstructed form **lwak*
(F. K. Li); here the reconstructed form is **ʔdwak*, through influence exerted by the preceding vowel.

TABLE II
Group III (F. K. Li ʔn-)

	black	nose	numbed	salty
IN	*i(n)tǝm*	*ʃug'uŋ*	[*dd*]ǝŋǝn	*ʔapdaŋ*
(reconstr.)	**i(n)tam*	*⎨ig'uŋ*	**dangan*	(Formosa)
Thai	*ʔdam*	*ʔdaŋ*	*ʔdaaŋ*	*ʔdaŋ*
Sui-LN	*ʔnam*	*ʔnaŋ*	*ʔnaŋ*	*ʔnaŋ*
Sui-J.	*nam*	*naŋ*	*naŋ*	*naŋ*
Sui-P.	*ʔnam*	*ʔnaŋ*	*ʔnaŋ*	*ʔnaŋ*
Mak	*nam*	*naŋ*	*naan*	*ʔdaŋ*
Then	*nam*	*naŋ*		*laŋ*
Ong-Be	*lam*	*löŋ*		
S. Li	*dǝm*			
N. Li	*dam*		*duŋ ∼ ŋan*	
Laqua	*dǝm*	*taŋ*		
Lati	*ńǝ*	*ńǝ*		

Notes to Table II: "numbed": **[dd]ǝŋ ǝn* "stunned" (TB "sad-
dened"; NgD. "deaf"; Fu., Sm. "silent"); T "numbed (as with
cold)"; Mak "numbed, unknowing" (the final from *-n/g*); Li:
these dial. forms, both meaning "stupid (*dumm*)" are derived
from either "end" of the root (cf. discussion below).

The above material all relates directly to a single T root:
*ʔduuk "bone," which must be grouped with IN **[t]ulaŋ*, id.
rather than with IN **ta(n)duk* "horn," as in the 1942 presentation. Several basic points are illustrated here:

(1) The KS material, along with our understanding of the
development of velo-labial clusters (as in "winnow"), affords
us an opportunity to reconstruct in some detail. It is no longer
a question as to whether these languages are related, but rather
as to just how we are to reconstruct the ancestral forms.

(2) Our corpus of common roots has expanded, only half the roots in the above tables having been cited in 1942. Actually, the expansion has been on a tremendous scale—roughly tenfold —and the writer tends to add a root or two every time he pokes about in his array of materials.

(3) The huge increase in material available for comparative materials indicates an even greater complexity in the ancestral AT language than had previously been suspected. This involves initial or medial consonantal clusters in particular, and many difficult problems remain to be worked out. In the above tables, for example, we have reconstructed *pandlam* rather than *pandram* precisely on the basis of this parallelism with the root for "bone." IN has a series of retroflex consonants (incomplete) consisting of *t̪*, *d̪*, and *z̪* (the last as reconstructed by Dyen). These consonants, which are not found elsewhere in our material, appear to have been derived from stop+*r/l* clusters (or *sr-*, *zr-*, *sl-*, *zl-*), but it has not yet been possible to establish the details here with any precision. IN also has ʟ, as reconstructed by Dempwolff, but Dyen writes *r* here, and the most common correspondence in Thai is with *r-*, as previously noted in the 1942 paper: IN *t'aʟaŋ*; T *raŋ*; Mak *sən<*srən/g-* "nest." In Table II we are struck by the parallelism shown by the roots for "black" and "nose," extending even to Laqua and Lati, but strangely excluding IN itself. In the former case, the true IN cognate is perhaps *tidəm* "dark" (NgD. "black"), *dədəm*, id., as suggested previously (1942), and this would indicate an original complex initial. The latter case involves *g'*, written by Dyen as a simple affricate (*j*), relatively rare in our material but with two excellent correspondences in addition to "nose," viz. IN *ag'an* "name"; Sui ʔ*dan*~*dan*; Mak ʔ*daan*; Then *laan* (reflexes as in Group I of F. K. Li); IN *lag'a* "plait or weave mats"; Thai and Mak *do*, id. Here the Thai-Mak cognates belong to an entirely different (nonglottalized) series of voiced stops (along with *b-*), which the writer in 1942 had speculated might be part of a later stratum of the language (Thai), partly because these initials appear in certain Chinese loan-words. This no longer appears to be the case, even though the preglottalized stops (ʔ*d* and ʔ*b*) are the typical reflexes (in nonfinal position) of IN *d* and *b*, sometimes also of *t* and *p*. In the present root

("plait") there appears to be a relationship with IN *ḍan-ḍan* "plait cables"; T *saan* "weave (baskets, mats), plait"; Mak *saan*, id., with the suffixed verbal affix *-n* (see below). This strongly suggests the presence of an original consonantal complex, as elsewhere in roots with initial *d-*, notably IN *bə(n)təŋ* "belly"; T *dooŋ* and KS *loŋ*, id.; IN *dalan~*d'alan* "road"; T *daaŋ*, a doublet formation with *xron*, id.; KS: Sui *khwən~khun*; Mak *khun*; Then *khen*; OB *sun*; Li *kuon*, dial. *kwan~kun*; N.Kl. *ken*. It is possible that these and similar correspondences present virtually insoluble problems in reconstruction because the original root was of a complex trisyllabic nature (see the discussion below).

(4) As shown by the root "salty," the marginal and often quite aberrant languages of Formosa sometimes provide us with root correspondences not found in Dempwolff (but perhaps present in IN material not included in that work). Ogawa and Asai (1935) have published (in Japanese) extensive word lists on a wide range of Formosan languages and dialects, and recently Egerod (1965) has published a word list of Atayal, but the basic comparative work remains to be done. The most important correspondences uncovered to date include the following: *tumay* (Paiwan *tumai~ćumai*, Tsou *ćmoi*) "bear"; T *hmi*; Lao also has *hmüay* "bear (large sp.), large ox"; Dioi *mɔi*; Mak *mui<*hmui* (this resemblance noted by Haudricourt, 1962, who stressed the importance of Formosa); Paiwan (Makazayazaya dialect, by R. Ferrell) *laulau* "fat, grease, oil" (this language apparently preserves both initial *l-* and final *-au*); T *laaw* "fat, grease"; Nung *la:u* "fat, lard"; Dioi *la:u~lɛu* "fat (of man and some animals)"; S.Li *duoi*; N.Li *ui<*luoi* "fat"; Atayal *abau* "leaf"; T *ʔbaü*; Li *böü*, but Saisiat *bira*, Rukai *biya*, Puyuma *bira~viraʔ*, all suggest a complex form, possibly *birahwa/n*, underlying the IN triple forms: [*ḍḍ*]*awən~*dahən~*daʔun*, and KS: Sui *wa~va*, Mak *va*, Then *wa* (all h.t.); Paiwan (Mak.) *biloŋ* "cave"; Atayal *bliŋ* "hole, cave"; T *plooŋ* "to be pierced with a hole; hole" (Si. "hole, tube, funnel; hollow, natural cave"); Mak *pyoŋ* "tubular, pierced." One must also go to Formosa for an explanation of the IN root *buɣaw* (Dyen reconstructs *buɣəw* "put to flight, chase, hunt"), represented in Thai by Tho *thau<*ph[rl]aw* "go hunting"; Nung *tik phiau* "hunt"="catch (some-

thing)," paralleling *tik pia* "fish"="catch fish (*pia*)"; also N.Li
(Bupäli dial.) *dop hau* "hunt"="catch (something)," *dop hlou*
"fish"="catch fish (*hlou*)." The "something" here is neatly supplied by Paiwan *biau~viau*, Rukai *biau*, Puyuma *biao~viao*
"spotted deer" (Chinese *hua lu*); cf. also Atayal *mhiau* "run after,
chase, pursue"; Sui *pyau*, Mak *ywaau* "run"; Li *dau*<**rau*, id. An
important root with an entirely peripheral—and by inference,
early—distribution is represented in Formosa by **s-ma* "tongue,"
found in all three primary groups: Atayalic *hama-, he:ma, xamma
~humma*; Paiwanic: *sima, sma, mama*; Tsouic *umo*<**uma*; cf.
the general SEP root **maya*; also KS **ma* (but not traced in Thai
or Kadai). An earlier root meaning is apparently preserved in Saisiat, Bunun *komis*, Ami *kumis~komis* "pubic hair," corresponding to IN **kumit'* "beard," **gumi*, id.; the latter is directly cognate with T **hmooy* "hair (pubic, axillary)" (Shan also "beard"),
Dioi *mi*<**hmi*, id. As in the case of the root for "leaf," Formosa
languages supply key forms in the following complex root: IN
*tuma<**tum(u)la* "louse (of body, clothes)"; Formosa: Puyuma
timula~hatimula, Saaroa ʔatimula, Ami *atimula*, Tsou *timuyo*
"flea"; T **mlen~*mlön*<**m(u)la/n* "louse of body, clothes"
(BT, WT also "flea"); Mak *nan*<**mlan* "body louse"; also T
*ray<**m[rl]a/i* "louse (of birds, fowl)" (Si. "louse, general
term"); Dioi *rwi* "lice of fowls"; KS: Sui *myai~byai*, Mak *byai*,
Then ʔbai<ʔm(b)[rl]ai "chicken flea." Finally, two Formosan
languages appear to have retained a unique reflex for a medial
cluster *-nl-* in the root for "water"; here Dioi has *r-*, as also in
one root with *-tl-*; cf. the following:

Table III

	water	bird	fart
IN	[*dd*]*anum*	*manuk*	*kə(n)tut*
(reconstr.)	**danlom*	**manluk*	**ka(n)tlut*
Thai	*nam*	*nok*	*tot*
Dioi	*ram*	*rok*	*rat*
Kam-Sui	*nam*	*nok*	*tut~tət*
Ong-Be	*nam*	*nok*	
S. Li	*nom*	*tat*	*thuot*
N. Li	*nam*	*tat~sat*	
Laqua		*nuk*	
Kelao		*ńie*	

Notes to Table III: "*water*": most Formosan languages show forms such as *janum, źanom, lanum, nanum*, directly comparable with IN *danum, but Saisiat has *ralum*, Paiwan (all dialects) has *zalum*, requiring a reconstruction with *-*nlum*, since both these languages regularly retain medial -*n*- in all other roots; N.Li regularly has *t*- for *n-, as in S.Li *nom*, N.Li *tom* "six" (IN *ənəm), hence a special reconstruction such as -*nl*- is needed to explain its retention here; "*bird*": the Li forms are quite inexplicable in terms of a root such as *nok or *manuk, and apparently have evolved via an intermediate *matlat (*mathlat>*sat*); S.Kl. *ñie* probably has developed via *nyo<**nlok;* "*fart*": Thai also has *tuut "horn, trumpet, bugle" (Si. "anus"); Li *thuot*< **tluut;* cf. *thu* "seven"<**pitlu.*

The rich material uncovered in Formosa in a most cursory survey leads one to wonder just what might be the eventual scope of the non-IN material in the greater Oceania area. Milke (1962) estimates that this "special Oceanic vocabulary" might be of "nearly the same magnitude as that shared with the Indonesian group." This suggests that our present body of comparative material represents only a fraction of the potential harvest, especially since IN itself has still been only partially explored from this point of view. We can anticipate with some confidence that this non-IN material will show many points of contact with Thai, Kam-Sui, and the Kadai languages. Milke cites as one of the "unexplained phonemic irregularities" in the Oceanic group the form *suɣi "bone, thorn," where IN has **[dḍ]uɣi*. The mainland forms are most unusual here: T *sian "thorn," but Dioi has ɔn (d.t.), a most irregular form, while Mak has *dun* (cf. the alteration of *s*- and *d*- in "plait," above) and Li has *hüön*, as if from an initial velar. Clearly we are dealing with a complex, possibly trisyllabic root here, of a form approximating that of *tulaŋ "bone," with which it is commonly merged or confused; cf. Formosa: Saisiat *tatolöŋ* "thorn." Further afield, in the Papua area, Capell (1943) has indicated in an appendix of "Unplaced Words" a number of roots which appear to be Austronesian but not Indonesian. These forms are phonetically abraded and difficult to interpret, but at least two roots are of interest here: SEP *poa "cloud"; T *füa~*fa "cloud"; Dioi *wüö*<*hwüa "cloud, cloudy"; also T *va~*wa (Tho) "sky" (all these forms on s.t.); KS: Sui *wa*~*fa*, Mak *va*<*hwa "cloud"; OB *pha* "heaven"; S.Li *pa;* N.Li *fa* "sky"; Bupäli dial. *bou* "cloud"; Lt.

vo~mbo "sky"; SEP *siwi~*sihi* (also *tsipi* and *n-sibe*) "cloth-ing (men's), girdle" (also "cloth" and "waist-cloth"); T *sii̇a* "clothing (general term, or for upper part of body)"; also T *sin* "skirt, petticoat" (Lao *zin* "robe"); Mak *fin* "skirt"; OB *vɛ* "skirt (woman's)"; Li *vɛŋ*; dial. *viaŋ~wiaŋ* "clothing"; Lq. *pĭie* "apron"; Lt. (*pu*) *ve* "clothing"; all apparently related to IN *tapih<*tapiik* "apron, piece of clothing" (Tg. "apron"; Ja. "up-per garment of women"; Ml., NgD. "lower garment of women"; Ho. "clothe oneself"); Formosa: *k-piŋi* but Puyuma *kipiŋ~ kavaŋ*, Paiwan *kava~ʔava;* this root appears to have been the main AT root for "clothing," but the reconstruction is uncertain at present. Another important and widespread early AT root presenting similar difficulties is represented by IN *huma* "gar-den (crop-land)"; Thai *suan;* KS: Sui *fyan~fiən~hyan*, Mak *fiin*, Then *wyaan* (F. K. Li reconstructs *swyaan*); the root here is perhaps AT *qwungwa* or *saqwungwa*, initial *q-* regularly yielding *h-* in IN. SEP also makes an important contribution to our analysis of the root for "shame(d)." IN has *malu*, but Capell cites *mala* as the deviant SEP root, then includes some examples with final *-i*, indicating a suffixed variant of the root: *mala/i.* Tregear had connected this root with Kayan *mala* "white," but Capell notes, "Shame, however, does not turn the face white, but red, presumably even in New Zealand." Thai has the doublet forms: *raay<*m/raay*, and *ʔaay<*mʔaay;* Li has *dei<*rei* or *lei;* the root clearly seems to be part of an extensive root-complex for "red," represented at its simplest level by such forms as IN *iɣah* "red," and Sui *xa<*xra*, id. In the same general region, Fiji offers kinship terms which are of unusual interest.

As indicated above, much remains to be worked out with regard to phonological details of AT reconstruction, and no attempt will be made here to present this material in any depth. The Kam-Sui data, in particular, will be required before any major effort can be undertaken here, and one still hopes that some reasonably full vocabularies of the Kadai languages will appear, as well as a major publication on AN (as opposed to IN) roots. In the interim, we must make do with what we have, and with this reservation in mind we shall briefly review the main features in phonology:

(1) Thai and KS have as consonant finals only the simple

series: -*p*, -*t*, -*k;* -*m*, -*n*, -ŋ; -*w* and -*y* (these pattern phonemically as consonants; can follow geminate vowels). The Kadai languages, especially Lati, tend to reduce all to vocalic finals. IN has a richer range of finals, including also -*t′* (=*s*), -γ, -*l*, -ʟ (=*r*) , and rarely -*b* and -*d*, but significantly not -*g*. The mainland languages, including Chinese and most Tibeto-Burman as well as Miao-Yao, exhibit the same pattern of reduction of consonantal contrasts in syllable-final position, and we must reconstruct AT with the fuller set of finals. In some roots IN -*t′* appears to be an added element (cf. "hair," above) but in general it forms part of the root and is represented in Thai by -*t;* cf. IN **pat′pat′* "shake, clean," but NgD. "broom; sweep"; T *pat "sweep, dust" (these forms are the simplest elements of a complex root). As noted in the 1942 paper, Thai also has -*t* for IN -*t* in medial (but syllable-final) position; cf. IN **put′uh* "heart," but Ja. "lungs"; T *poot and Mak *pət* "lungs"; IN **but′uγ* "bow"; Formosa: Paiwan (Mak.) *vit/ilatan;* Lao *fot*<*vot "bough, branch" (app. isolated in Thai); Li *va:t* "bow, crossbow"; Bas. dial. *wat* "bow"; Lakia dial. *vat* "shoot a bow." Thai, which shows palatalizing tendencies elsewhere (see below), has -*n* for -ŋ in some roots, especially with the vowel *i:* cf. IN *taŋgiliŋ "pangolin" (<*giliŋ "roll up"); T *lin~*hlin (Lao); Mak *lin;* IN *iliŋ<*ibliŋ "pour"; T **rin;* Tho *rin*, also *diŋ*<**ʔdiŋ;* Mak *ʔdiŋ;* IN **t′umbiŋ* "notched"; T *ʔbin "notched"; also Si. *win* "cloven" (ic. "hare-lip"); Mak *biŋ* "notched"; Li *vɛŋ* "notched" (ic. "hare-lip"). After back vowels Thai exhibits the opposite tendency; cf. "round" (below); also IN *γumun "den, lair"; T *muŋ.

(2) Thai generally has -*n* for both -*l* and -ʟ (=*r*); cf. IN **t′aŋkal* "handle"; T **k(h)an*~*gan "handle, stick, stem, peduncle"; Mak *ŋan*<**ŋ(k)al* "peduncle (stem of fruit)"; IN *puŋku[ʟ] "hind-part"; T *kon* "buttocks." Thai also has -*n* for -γ in most roots, as in "thorn" (above), but γ occasionally appears simply to have been dropped; cf. the doublet in the following root: IN **t′a(m)buγ*~*tabuγ~**ha(m)buγ* "sprinkle," but NgD. "squirt"; T *bon~*ʔbon (Shan var.)~*bun (Lao var.) "eject from mouth, squirt"; also *bo (s.t.) "spring, well"; KS *ʔbən "well, spring." Replacement of -γ by -*i* also occurs in association with palatalization, notably in the following: IN *dənəγ (Dyen reconstructs *dəŋəγ*) "hear"; Thai *ŋin~**ńin;*

Dioi *ńin* (ic.) ~*ńε*<*hńε;* Sui *hŋai,* Mak *hai.* In some intervocalic positions, especially *-aγa-,* the fricative is absorbed; cf. **baγa* "shoulder"; Thai ***ba;* OB *wia;* Mak *ha;* Kl. *gö*<AT **gwara* (see discussion under "axe," below), but Li has *va~van* (ic.), showing the doublet treatment of final *-γ;* cf. also "hew" (below).

(3) Final *-b* and *-g* are reconstructed by Dempwolff for only a few IN roots, and little comparative data are at hand. The best correspondence for IN *-b* is found in the complex root for "cover" (below), where there is alternation with IN *-p.* The two correspondences for IN *-d* both suggest that it follows a long vowel (*uu*): IN **tuᵖud* "knee"; Li *khuoi* "kneel" (with *-i* perhaps from *-d*); IN **udud* "smoke (tobacco)"; T ***duut* "suck, smoke"; Lao also has *ᵖut,* as if from a root **ud/ud.* It might be argued that IN *-b* and *-d* are simply variants of *-p* and *-t* after long (geminate) vowels, the length feature itself having been lost in IN. In this view, final *-g* does not exist in IN simply because final *-k* is also missing here after long vowels (see section 4, below).

(4) In addition to the above finals, IN also has final *-h* as reconstructed by Dempwolff. As already noted (1942), this corresponds in two basic roots ("ten," "blood") to Li or Thai final *-t* (see below), but the most frequent correspondence is with Thai final *-k* in roots with long (geminate) vowels: IN **babah* "mouth"; T **paak;* OB *pak;* IN **taγah* "hew (smooth)"; T **thaak* (with *h* possibly as a reflex of *γ*); IN **bintih* "kick"; Lao **tiak* (app. isolated in Thai, where the general SW root is **thiip*); Li *thiᵖ*<**thiik.* IN **mu(n)t'uh~*mət'ah* "enemy"; T **sük~*sök* "enemy; war, battle" would seem to run counter to this scheme, but IN doublets of this type appear to have been derived from *-ua-,* so that we must reconstruct AT **m-suak* or **m-suᵖak,* with a long vowel effect. Dyen has reconstructed this final as *-ᵖ* rather than *-h,* and this neatly fits with the historical evidence that we are concerned here with the replacement of *-t* and *-k* with glottal stop after long vowels (N.Li and some dialects of Dioi show the same pattern after long vowels, but only before *-k*). Final *-g,* if ever present, has disappeared without trace in the following: IN **pi[y]a* "to desire" (Fi. *via/kana,* Sm. *fia/ᵖai* "hungry"="desire to eat"); T ***yaak* "to desire; to be hungry (also thirsty)"; Sui *ᵖyak* "hungry"; cf. also the roots for "urine" and "mortar" (below), which present some evidence for a possible

final -g in AT. Finally, IN also seems to have -ay in a few roots, notably *[ḍḍ]ahay "forehead"; T *phraak (usu. cw. *hna "face"); KS *pyaak; OB tui; Li la da:u<*ra:u (rather than the anticipated *raʔ), all suggesting a possible reconstruction: AT *brahaag.

(5) Although Dyen's final -ʔ seems preferable to Dempwolff's final -h, as analyzed above, his medial -ʔ- appears generally to be at a disadvantage; cf. "forehead" (above) and *pahit "bitter, pungent"; T *phet "pungent," but the point must still be considered a moot one. The glottal stop apparently serves as an (original) morpheme boundary marker in roots such as IN *daʔat "crowd"; T ʔat "condense(d), compresse(d), close"; Li a:t "close (serré), dense (dru), thick (touffu)" (as cloth; as method of planting rice); note also IN *bəyat (but Dyen bəγʔat) "heavy"<AT *[gk]waγʔak, which has yielded T *hnak, but KS ʔzan~zan; OB khon; Li khün; N.Kl. khen (all with -n< -γ). Finally, the function of ʔ is not at all clear in the following set of roots showing a remarkable parallelism: IN *diŋin "cool"; T *ʔyen, id.; OB phon (ʔ); S.Li gan; N.Li an<ʔŋan (ʔ); N.Kl. ka yin, all meaning "cold"; IN *diŋdiŋ "dried meat" (TB "smoked meat"); T *ʔya(a)ŋ "smoke, dry (meat, fish, rice)"; IN *diγi "stand," also *tə(n)dəγ "stand up" (Capell); T *ʔyüün, id.; KS *ʔyuən; OB ćun; Li ćuon.

(6) As might be anticipated, the reconstruction of the AT vowel system presents great difficulties. IN has a very simple four-vowel schema: i, u, a, ə, without any indication of length. Thai has a much richer scheme, with the mid-high vowels e and o as well as the back unrounded vowels ü and ö, with a distinction between short and long (geminate) in most cases. Vowel clusters such as üa and ui are prominent, and in some cases these can occur before -y and/or -w (üay, iaw, etc.). The Mak-Sui languages in general show somewhat simpler versions of the Thai system. The analysis of finals (above) has yielded evidence that AT had some length distinction in vowels, and the variety of correspondences already uncovered makes it seem probable that this distinction will play an important role in any eventual reconstruction of AT. IN tends to have medial -u- corresponding mainly to -o- and/or -a- elsewhere (as in all three roots in Table III), and the original value here is quite uncertain.

(7) Although the vowels present great problems in analysis, some of these difficulties can be resolved by the recognition of consonant clusters with *w* and/or *y*, as shown for Thai and KS by F. K. Li (1965); cf. the discussion of "bone" (above), also correspondences such as Mak *kwap* "frog"; T **kop*. It has also become increasingly evident that palatalization has played a major role in the development of the Thai system. As shown above, final **iŋ* is frequently shifted to *-in*, and vowel shifts to *e* or *i* before dental finals are also in evidence; cf. IN **tanah~ **tanəh* "earth"; T **ʔdin;* Dioi **dən;* Li *dan~den;* IN **ka~ **kaʔən~**kaʔi* "eat"; T **kin<**ka/n;* KS *tsyan, tsye, tsin, siin,* etc. (KS palatalizes to a greater degree than does Thai); OB *kon;* N.Li *khan;* Lq. *küön,* Kl. *ka~kə;* Lt. *kho* "eat, drink"; IN **kulat* "mushroom"; T: SW **hret,* Nung *vit<**ku(w)at;* Dioi *rat* (Dioi shows less marked palatalization in general); cf. also "hear" and "louse, flea" (above).

(8) The diphthong *üa,* a prominent feature of Thai phonology, appears to represent a kind of palatalization, with back position under the influence of a "labial environment," and these Thai forms are directly equivalent to the KS forms reconstructed by F. K. Li; cf. Table IV.

TABLE IV

	IN	Thai	Kam-Sui	Li
hand	*lima*	*mü*	*mya*	*möü*
boat	*paʟahu*	*rüa*	*ʔdwa~zwa*	*da*
cat	*pusa[h]*	*süa*		
poison	*tuba*	*ʔbüa*		
disgust	*iba/y*	*ʔbüa*	*bya*	
house	*rumah*	*rüan*	*ryaan*	*düön*
moon	*bulan*	*ʔblüan*	*nyaan*	*ńa:n*
forest	*hutan*	{*thüan* / *wan*	*wyaan*	*śun*
worm	*[t]u[n]a*	*ʔdüan*	*zan*	*hen*
blood	{*daɣah* / *ẓuɣuh*	*lüat*	*phyaat*	*da:t~tla:t*
rind	*u(m)pak*	*plüak*		

Notes to Table IV: "hand": cf. "five" (below); "boat": KS: Mak "raft"; "cat": IN "cat," but Ho. "cat-like beast of prey"; T "tiger";

Si. also has the doublet *saaŋ*, indicating an original *saaŋk-*; "*poison*": IN "name of plant used for stupefying fish, fish poison"; T "poison," but Nung and Dioi "to poison fish"; "*disgust*": also "nausea"; from the same root: *iba/n* is derived T *ʔüan* "nauseous odor (as of sweat)"; Li *en~voan* "sweat" (cw. "water"); "*house*": IN *rumah*<*ruŋwaa-* (see below); "*forest*": T also "wild, savage (=of the woods)"; Lao "forest, meadow, pasture," also *wan* "forest"; Sui "field"; Mak "dry field" (*vi:n*); Li "brushwood, forest"; cf. also Kl. (*pu*) *tiə* "forest"; "*worm*": IN "eel," but TB *goia/tuna* "large worm"; T and KS both "earthworm"; Li "gnawing worms; worms of rotten meat"; cf. also OB *nu* "worm" (this root app. had a complex initial); "*blood*": IN *[dd]ayah* "blood"; also *d'uɣuh* "liquid (syrup, sap, broth)," but Tg. "blood" and *duɣuh*, id. (Dyen reconstructs the last two roots as *ʒuruʔ*); S.Li *da:t*; N.Li *tla:t*, dial. *hlat*<*phlat*; Lq. *khə*<*xlat* (?); Kl. *plə*; Lt. *pio*<*plat*; OB *baʔ*<*[bp]lat*; all from AT *bluɣa(a)t* (?); "*rind*": IN *u(m)pak*<*u(m)plak* (see below); T "rind, bark, peel, shell, hull."

(9) The AT initials included labial, dental, velar, and perhaps post-velar series, but the palatals are poorly represented and can scarcely be reconstructed for the ancestral language. IN *g'* (written *j* by Dyen) does not occur as an initial, and (like *ḍ*) is rare as a final and was excluded from the above discussion of finals. One comparison has been found, however, viz. IN *pu'təg'* "navel"; T *ʔdü*; KS *ʔdwa* (Type 1–Table I), suggesting an initial *bl-* in this root: AT *publaj* (?). The corresponding surd, *k'*, does occur as an initial, but the two good correspondences uncovered are both with Thai consonant clusters: IN *kəŋk'əŋ~*ɣə(n)[t]əŋ* "stretch tight"; T *greŋ* "tight; stretch, tighten"; Sui *xaŋ*<*xraŋ* "tight"; Li *küŋ*<*kyaŋ* "tight"; IN *kə(ŋ)k'iŋ* "urine odor" (Ml. "urinate," Ho. "odor of dead body"); T *klin*<*kliŋ* (see above for this shift) "odor (good or bad), but Dioi *kiɛn~kian* "odeur de sauvage (of urine of wildcat)." IN lacks *z*, but Thai has a fairly substantial number of roots with initial *z-*, which must be postulated for AT. The one excellent comparison available indicates that IN has replaced this sound with *s-*: IN *t'ut'un* "pile up" (TB., Ja., Ml. "piled up"; Tg. "doubled"; Ho. "doubling"); T *zoon* "place one upon another, superpose; double." Initial *ń-* seems to be indicated for the following root, with simple loss in IN: cf. IN *uyah* "salt"; OB *nyiau*; Li *ńa:u*; Lq. *ńuŋ*<*ńu/ńu* (?); Kl. *nyö~ńu*;

Lt. *a ńu;* perhaps also T *°klüa<°k-nywa,* and Sui *kwa,* Mak *ćwa<°klwa<°k-nywa;* this would yield AT *°k-ńuyaa-* or *°k-nyuyaa-.* Other evidence for initial *°ń-* is presented below (see "urine" and "3rd pr. prn."). Dempwolff cites initial *ń-* for several roots, but no correspondences have been found for any of these in the mainland languages, and they may well represent secondary formations. Both IN and Thai appear to show loss of medial *-ń-* in the following root: IN *°payah* "difficult" (Ja. "wearied"); T *°yaak* "difficult, laborious, hard, poor, miserable"; Dioi *dya~ dyak<°ya(a)k* "difficult, laborious; bad, wicked"; Sui *hńak-hńan* "rough, coarse"; Mak *yak* "laborious"; Li *ya°~tek<°nyaak* "bad, wicked, cruel, difficult"; T also has *°hńaap* "hard, difficult, coarse, rude"; Dioi *ńat~ńɛt* "laborious, difficult; ill-tempered"; AT *°pańaak.*

(10) Post-velar consonants are represented in Sui by *q, qh,* and *ʀ,* and F. K. Li concludes that this series must be postulated for the ancestral KS language. The aspirated stop is represented by *qha* "ear," apparently connected with the widespread IN root *°taliŋa,* as if from an original *°taliŋqa,* but Thai has *°hru* here, and reconstruction is most uncertain. Excellent correspondences are at hand, however, for *q* and *ʀ;* see Table V. For "thigh," F. K. Li suggests an original labialized post-velar, but the *p-* forms perhaps are another "echo" (cf. the notes) of the first element (*°paŋ*) of this root. Li's suggestion of the voiced post-velar stop, *ɢ,* for the root "excrement" (note the low tone) also appears to fit here, especially to explain the different reflex in OB. Both roots in *ʀ-* are on high tone, but this is often found in KS and Thai after the loss of initial stop consonants (syllables), with *h-* standing for the lost consonant, as in T *°hret* "mushroom."

TABLE V

	thigh	excrement	chin	mushroom
IN	*paha*	*tahi*	*baɣ°aŋ*	*kulat*
(reconstr.)	*°pa(ŋ)q(w)a*	*taɢ[°]ay*	*°baʀ°aŋ*	*kuʀa-*
Thai	*kha~xa*	*khi~°e*	*ɣaaŋ*	*hret*
Dioi	*ka*		*haŋ*	*rat*
Sui-LN.	*qa* (h.t.)	*qe* (l.t.)	*ʀaŋ* (h.t.)	*ʀa* (h.t.)
Sui-J.	*pa*	*qe*	*ʀaŋ*	*ʀa*

(continued on next page)

TABLE V (*continued*)

	thigh	excrement	chin	mushroom
Sui-P.	*pa*	*će*	*ʀaŋ*	*ʀa*
Mak	*ka*	*će*	*gaaŋ*	*ga*
Then	*pa*	*ʔe*	*ʔaaŋ*	*ʔa*
Ong-Be	*wa*	*kai*	*ŋaŋ*	
S. Li	*ha*	*hai*	*ha:ŋ*	*dit*
N. Li	*ka~ha*			

Notes to Table V: "*thigh*": IN "thigh, stalk" (Fi. "bone"); IN also has doublet *°pahi*, possibly as a reflex of the post-velar; T *°kha*, but WT has *pa:n xa~xa pa:n;* Tho has *pa:ŋ kha*, apparently as an "echo" of the original root; cf. Li *pɛŋ* "thigh" and (in IN) Bugis *paŋ* "thigh"; OB *wa* "bone," *mai-wa* "thigh"; KS "leg"; S.Li "num. adj. for trousers," but N.Li dial. "thigh"; the IN root appears to be related to *°[dd]ahan<°[dd]aha/n* "branch" (=bifurcation) and related roots; "*excrement*": T *°khi* "excrement; defecate" (general root); *°ʔe* "excrete (urine, feces), discharge (semen)" (Shan, Tho, Nung only); OB "stool"; "*chin*": IN *°baγʔaŋ* (Demp. has *baγaŋ*, but Dyen reconstructs with ʔ) "molar teeth," but Ja. "jaw"; T "chin, jaw"; Li "jaw" (ic. "chin"); "*mushroom*": Nung has *vit<°ku(w)at* (see also below for this root); Li *dit<°rit*.

(11) Initial consonant clusters of stop + *r/l* are best preserved in Si. and Ahom, of the Thai group, in the N.Li dialects, and in Kelao. IN does not have clusters of this type, and simplifies in various ways, as with merging in *d* or *g'* (see examples above), also simply by dropping the second element (cf. "louse," above). IN simplifies *°pl* in either of two ways: loss of the first element, or loss of the second after an initial (*u-*); see Table VI:

TABLE VI

	fish	leech	rind	shed, v.	bud
IN	{ *laʔuk* { *iwak*	{ *lintah* { *limantɔk*	*u(m)pak*	*upaw*	*upih*
(reconstr.)	*°pla(i)wak*	*°pliŋ-*	*°(u)plak*	*°(u)plaw*	*°(u)plii-*
Thai	*pla*	*pliŋ*	*plüak*	*plaw*	*pli*
Ong-Be	*ba*	*beɛŋ*			
S. Li	*da*	*diŋ*		*la:u*	
N. Li	*tla*	*biaŋ*		*pla:u*	

Notes to Table VI: "fish": IN *la?uk* also "mixture, side-dish," but NgD. and Sm. "fish"; the second element appears to be basically identical with **?iwak* "fish"; Li dial. *hla,* apparently the earlier form, from **phla*; this root present in all the Kadai languages: Lq. *peu,* Kl. *lü,* Lt. *a hli~a li,* all from **pla;* "leech": see below for a discussion of this complex root; "rind" (from Table IV); "shed": IN "shed hair, feathers" (T "bald"; Ho. "moult"); T "empty, vacant, vain"; T also has **plüay* "naked" (WT "bald"); Li "blind" (cf. T **vaaŋ* "blind," also "empty").

(12) Inasmuch as Thai has reduced to monosyllables, it does not sharply distinguish between original clusters and "secondary" clusters derived from disyllabic forms, although in general these tend to be better preserved (esp. in N.Li and Kelao). Thai lacks initial **tl-*, and shifts **təl-* to **kl-*, as shown in Table VII. Table VIII illustrates three separate sets of reflexes in the mainland languages for IN initials of the type: **bəl-*, indicating three different types of initials in AT, the distinctions perhaps having involved preglottalization as well as stress.

TABLE VII

	IN	Thai	Kam-Sui	Other
skin	*kulit*	*klet~klat*	*kyat~kyen*	
dark	*kələm*	*klam~kam*	*qam~kam*	
roll, v.	*galiŋ*	*kliŋ*		
cylindrical	*təluŋ*	*klooŋ*	*kyuŋ*	Li: *loŋ*
middle	*tələŋ*	*klaaŋ*		
swallow, v.	{ *təlun* { *lunlun*	{ *klüün~dun* { *nün~?ün*	*?dun*	OB: *lun*

Notes to Table VII: "skin": **kulit* "skin" (To. also "rind"); IN also has **kaʟah<*kaʟaat* "shell" (esp. tortoise-shell, mother-of-pearl)"; T **klet* "scales, scab," but Dioi *kyat<*klat* "scales"; Mak *ćat<*klat* "fish scales," but Sui and Then show variant **klen;* KS also has a root represented by Sui *ʀa~ha,* Mak *ja* "skin," suggesting a reconstruction AT **kuʀaat* "skin, shell," with the possibility that *l~ʟ* variation in IN reflects AT **ʀ;* "dark": cf. "black" (Table II); T **klam~*kam* "dark-colored (red, purple, black)" suggest the possibility of an original infixed form: **k/l/am;* Sui has *qam* "dark (red)"; Mak *kam* "black," suggesting an original **qlam* or **q/l/am;* "roll": IN also **giliŋ~*guliŋ~*guluŋ;* both IN and T roots mean "roll (up, over)"; "*cylindrical*": T "tube, pipe, barrel (gun); throat," also (d.t.) "drum, tambour"; Mak *ćuŋ* < *kyuŋ "drum"; Li "tambour"; "*swallow*": T: SW *klüün ~ *ʔ*ün* (Kh., Shan); Tho and Nung *nün* ~ **nön;* Dioi *dun* < **dun,* all these variants app. reflecting the original complex **təl-*.

TABLE VIII

	IN	Thai	Kam-Sui	Li
moon	*bulan*	ʔ*blüan*	*nyaan*	*ńa:n*
flower	*bulak*	ʔ*blook*	*nuk* (Sui)	
spotted	*bəlaŋ*	ʔ*blaaŋ*	*naaŋ* (Mak)	
turn	*balik*	*blik*		
fling	*{ balaŋ / buliŋ }*	*{ phleeŋ / bluŋ }*	*{ peeŋ / boŋ }*	*{ phɛŋ / daŋ }*
separate	*{ bəlah / bilah }*	*bla(a)t*		
buy	*{ bəli / bili }*	*{ zü / rü }* (Tho)	*dyai*	*{ sau / döi }*
grasshopper	*balaŋ*	*{ tak / ya:ŋ }* (Nung)	*dyak*	
bamboo	*buluh*	*{ took / phio:k }* (Nung)	*dyuk*	
round	*bəluγ*	ʔ*duaŋ* ~ ʔ*den*	ʔ*duun*	*{ pluon / luon }*

Notes to Table VIII: "*flower*": IN: Tg. *bulaklak;* Bisayan *bolak* "flower," from a root *lak "unfold, develop," part of a rootcomplex in AT involving also *laaki "child, man, male"; "*spotted*": T also "piebald"; Mak "small-pox"; "*turn*": IN "turn upside down; reverse side"; T "turn (change direction)"; "*fling*": IN *balaŋ "fling"; Formosa: Atayal *buliŋ* ~ *sbuliŋ* "throw"; T *bluŋ "throw (esp. long objects), fling, leap"; *phleeŋ "throw" (Si. also "shoot arrow"); perhaps also Si. and Lao *ńiŋ* "fling, throw, shoot"; Mak *boŋ* "throw (stick)," *pe:ŋ* "throw, shoot (arrow)"; Li *daŋ* < *laŋ "fling, throw," *phɛŋ* "throw (in air)"; "*separate*": IN *bəlah "split" (Tg., Ja. "half"; NgD. "part," n.), *bilah "chip (splinter)," from an original **b-laat;* T **bla(a)t* "separate" (Dioi "pick by hand"; WT "break up, as embers"); "*buy*": Li *sau lüöŋ* "buy back" (*lüöŋ* "return"), but N.Li dial. has *döi* "buy"; "*grasshopper*": T *tak (usu. ic. *tak *teen); this perhaps influenced the shift in final from -ŋ to -*k,* but Tho preserves the

nasal final; "*bamboo*": IN *buluh* < **buluuk* "species of bamboo";
Formosa: Rukai *balu-balu* ~ *valo-valo* "bamboo"; T and Nung, also KS, all "bamboo withe (strip)"; "*round*": IN "round (esp. cylindrical)"; T "round (esp. globular)," with -ŋ rather than -n, app.
influ. by the vowel *u* (cf. "den," above); Dioi has the regular
-n (**?den*); "round (circular)."

(13) This discussion of consonant clusters is appropriately
concluded with a note on the two basic roots for "eye" and
"die," the parallelism of which so impressed this writer in 1942.
He arrived at this conclusion, with a very simple "explanation"
of the aspiration shown in Tho and Nung, by eliminating those
forms in Kadai which seemed not to belong. This no longer
appears to be justifiable, and we now present these two roots
in toto:

TABLE IX

	eye	die
IN	*mata*	*matay* ~ *patay*
Thai	*ta*	*taay*
Tho-Nung	*tha* ~ *ha*	*tha:i* ~ *ha:i*
Kam-Sui	*da*	*tay*
Ong-Be	*da*	
S. Li	*sa* ~ *śa*	*ta:u* "die"; *hau* "kill"
N. Li	*sa*	*thui* "die"; *hau* "kill"
Bupäli (Li)	*dou*	*lo:d* ~ *la:d*
Laqua	*te*	*tie*
N. Kelao	*tau*	
S. Kelao	{ (*bu*) *mo kho* / *tu*	*ple u*
Lati (BP)		*pien* (Rob.)
Lati (MP)	*mću*	*pe* (Rob.), *phi* (Bon.)

Notes to Table IX: "*eye*": Formosa: Atayal *loziŋ*; N.Kl. *tau*,
but MFPL cites a form with initial *k*: *kai mei*; S.Kl. *bu mo kho*
(*bu* found in other terms for parts of body) "eye," but *tu* ic.
"blind"; "*die*": Formosa: Atayal *mhoqil* (also *hoqil, hqilan*) "die,"
phoqil "kill"; N.Li *thui* "die"; Shaved Head Loi dial. *hau* "kill."

For "eye," the most likely reconstruction now appears to be
*matla or **mat-la* (intervening unidentified vowel), explaining

Li *śa~sa* as from *thla (as in "10" and "louse," see above); the
vowels in Kadai indicate an original *-a* (see the 1942 paper),
but Kl. *mo kho* remains a problem, possibly<*mokhlo<**mothlo;*
Atayal perhaps retains a reflex of the *tl* cluster, but the phonology of this aberrant IN language remains to be worked out.
The root for "die" is even more of a puzzle, and one is tempted
to reject all forms which do not fit the Thai-IN pattern, but
Kelao preserves clusters in some roots, and the *u* and *l* elements
in Li appear to tie in with this; this might also have been a
trisyllabic root of the type *mat-play, a possible source also for
the synonymous S.Li term *dom*, via. **-to(m)play.*

(14) Continued study of the AT materials has indicated that
many of the reconstructed roots eventually will prove to be
trisyllabic, of the type represented by IN *taliŋa "ear." As indicated at the beginning of this paper, stress differences appear to have played the significant role in determining whether
the first or last element of a root is retained in any given case,
e.g. AT **kut(a)lu* "louse" has yielded both OB *kat* (fore-stress)
and T **[t]hraw* (end-stress). The root for "weep" furnishes an
outstanding illustration here: IN **taŋit'*<**taŋi/s* (with *-s* as an
added element here; cf. "beard"~"pubic hair," above); T *hay
<*hŋay, but Dioi *tai;* KS **ʔŋe;* OB *ŋai;* Li *ŋei;* Lt. *ćuŋ*<*taŋ
(cf. "eye"); perhaps also Lq. *dek*<*dak<*daŋ. In this root,
the Dioi form had been suspected of being related to the general Thai root because of the concordance of finals, but the
initials could not be reconciled; many other cognates probably
remain isolated from their respective roots because of lack of
knowledge of the di- or trisyllabic root needed to tie them together. The variability shown in many roots indicates that the
longer roots persisted, along with variable stress, to a much
later date than one might have suspected, e.g. the ancestral
Thai (incl. Dioi) speech must have included a disyllabic root
such as *taʔŋay "weep." Another example is provided by IN
*ḍabuk "ashes"; Thai *daw, strikingly parallel to the root IN
*mabuk "drunk"; Thai *maw (both show *-b->-w-*). The IN
root is simply part of a complex root meaning "ashes, dust, gray
(ash-colored)," with several IN forms: **abu,* **kul/abu,* **ləbu,*
**abuk,* *ɣabuk and *ʟabu (TB *aek rabu* "wet ashes"); Thai
has *daw here, but Nung, the conservative Thai speech in this

respect, has *piau,* pointing to an original **blaw* or the like (cf. seventeenth-century Annamese *blo* "ashes," part of the early Thai stratum in that language); Li has *pau* "ashes (of tobacco), flour (of rice)," tending to confirm the nature of the complex initial in this root. One might think from all this that the mainland languages had retained only the first element of this root, yet Mak has *vuk* "ashes," showing that the whole root was retained to a fairly late period, the AT root having been something like **b-labuuk* (long *u* because of tendency for *-k* to be lost in IN).

(15) Related problems are at times encountered in analyzing the evolution of trisyllabic roots, since various possibilities must be kept in mind. A striking example here, and one of great significance for Oceanic studies in general, is furnished by the following: IN **banu[w]a* "land, mainland," but MN: "land, settlement"; SEP "village" (Capell 1943: 117); Thai **ʔbaan* "village"; Mak *ʔbaːn;* Li *bau* "village"; dial.: Bupäli *vun;* Loi (various) *fa~fan~au;* perhaps also Lt. *li mia,* all meaning "village." The Li development has been either from the first part of the root, as in Thai, or from the first and third parts: **ba(nu)wa.* This makes the relationship of these forms even more certain, and we cannot escape the conclusion that the SEP meaning is *original* and not secondary, as Capell had supposed, hence must have been derived directly from non-IN sources (rather than via IN). Capell points out, however, that Friederici traced *banua* "people" to Buru and Minahassa, and *banua* "village, place" to Buru and the Moluccas; note that the PN cognate, *fanua,* has the IN meaning ("land").

(16) The complexities involved in trisyllabic root evolution are reflected by IN **lintah* "leech," *lima[n][t]ək* "small leech." The most obvious comparison here, and the one first made by the writer, is with T **da(a)k* "leech (esp. land leech)"; Shan has *taːk<*daak* "small leech, water leech," also *tɛk<*de(e)k* "land leech," the doublet formation suggesting an original complex initial **draak;* Dioi *ta<*da(a)k* (irreg. tone, as if with short vowel) "large leech of rice-fields"; the N.Li dialects also have the root: *thɛak~thɛk~thɛt~thɛ* (evidence of long vowel) "leech." With the consideration of velo-labial clusters in general, it became evident that the IN doublet has been derived

from an original *liŋwanta(a)k, with -k·replaced by -h after the long vowel. Further evidence brought forward about initial clusters (see Table VI), however, made it clear that the complete reconstruction should be *pliŋwant[r]a(a)k. Thai has taken from each end of the root, even developing a distinction in meaning: T *pliŋ* "leech (esp. water leech)"; Mak *piŋ* "leech"; OB *beɛŋ* "leech"; Li *diŋ*<*liŋ, dial. *biaŋ* "worm."

It seems probable that many AT roots were trisyllabic, but it is rare that the evidence is as clear as in the foregoing. One such root concerns IN *ɣumah "house," which the writer (1942) had speculated about as a possible cognate of T *rüan, id. Other mainland languages show forms similar to that of Thai, viz. KS *ryaan, OB *lan, Kl. (*du*) *hle*, also S.Li *düön*<*rüön, but the closely related N.Li has *ploŋ*, dial. *bloŋ~blaŋ* "house." The latter seemed to have been derived from the same root as IN *baʟuŋ "hut," and Laqua *neŋ* "house" also seemed to be related (cf. Laqua *nen* "moon"; IN *bulan). Thai has the reciprocal kinship term *ʔdooŋ "parents of son- or daughter-in-law"; Si. *kiau ʔdooŋ* "allied, of the same kindred" (=allied houses); cf. the N.Li dial. phrase *pha-bloŋ* "father (of the house)," apparently cognate with these words for "house." The puzzle was solved by the publication by Goodenough (1962) of a brief list of Oceanic words with velo-labial clusters, including *(y)uŋwa "house" (my rough reconstruction). We can now safely reconstruct AN *ɣuŋwaa- or *ɣungwaa-, whence Thai *rüan et al., and can further link this with *baʟuŋ in a trisyllabic root *ba[ɣr]uŋwaa-; IN *[ḍḍ]aŋaw "hut, house" might be another derivative from this root. Many more syntheses of roots of this kind can be expected as our knowledge of AT roots expands.

As shown in the above analyses, the recognition of velo-labial clusters opens up many new vistas in this field. We are now able, for example, to recognize the relationship of IN *[t]amit' <*taŋwit', *manit' and *mamit'<*maŋwit' "sweet" with *ta(m)baɣ<*ta(ŋ)gwaɣ "without aftertaste, flat, sweet (water)," the latter corresponding closely to the mainland roots: T *hwaan "sweet"; KS: Sui *qhan~fan*, Mak *khan*, Then *khan~xwaan*, yielding the reconstruction AT *ta(ŋ)qwaaɣ. This root does not appear in the lists published by Haudricourt or Goodenough, and the roots found there are not usually so easy to analyze, but it is amply clear that they are distinctive as a group and are derived from an AN level earlier than anything seen in IN itself. The following material is of interest here, although much remains uncertain in the interpretation of it:

Class I: *gw- type*:

gwara (-ala, -aca) "old (persons), weak, unable, loose," cf. the IN doublet *tuha~*tuwa* "old (persons)"; Thai *thaw,* id. (both IN and Thai words often used in kinship terms), possibly from AT *tuqwa.*

gwele (-ere, -ori) "earth, mud, dirt": cf. IN *[dd]aki* "body (skin) dirt"; T γlay, id., but Nung kai~nai; Dioi hi~i; KS: Sui and Mak zai<*γwai<*γlay* "dirt" (Mak also "mud"); complex initial, reconstruction uncertain.

gwoni (gwo/ni) "odor; smell (v.t.)": IN *baʔu* "odor" (PN: all "fish odor"); T *γr(i)aaw~*xriu* (s.t.) "raw (fetid, putrid) odor (esp. of fish, flesh, sweat)"; Mak ṅəu (h.t.)<*hṅəu* "odor, scent," ṅəu ju "raw flesh odor" (ju perhaps cg. with *xriu); Li ha:i<*γa:i* "stink, smell bad," also (d.t.) "smell, sniff," v. tr.; another complex initial, poss. *ŋraaw.*

gwengi (gweŋi) "night": IN *bəŋ[i]<*gwaŋi; T *γüün; KS *γyan; Li fen "evening"; all dial. fan; reconstr. *γwan/gi.*

gwau "head": IN *ha(m)baw~*babaw~*[t]i(m)baw* "top, high, above" (Tg. tibao "crowning"); Haudricourt adduces IN *batuk* "cranium" (Sa. "head"); T *klaw* "head, top of head; topknot"; Dioi kyau<*klaw* "head, end, extremity; chief"; Dioi also has mau "head," app. related to Nung bau<*ʔbaw, id.; KS *kyau<*klaw* "head"; OB hau "head"; S.Li dau; N.Li fo~o; dial. ŋo~giu~vo~wau~wou "head"; N.Kl. ka; Lt ic. khe~kha "head"; reconstr. *glaw.*

nagwuk "mosquito": IN *ṅamuk~lamuk* "gnat"; T: SW *hlüak* "gadfly"; Nung küök<*klüak, id.; Dioi nö<*(h)nüak* "certain flies with flat bodies which sting cattle and dogs"; KS: Sui qak "kind of flies"; Mak nak<*hnak* "gnat"; reconstr. *laqluk~*laqlak* (redupl. form).

(h)maguuk "wasp": cf. the foregoing, also IN *ləbah* "bee"; reconstr. *(ma-, la-)gwaak*.

gwala "taro field": IN *t'abah* "irrigated rice-field"; T *ɣan* "dike of rice-field"; KS *yan* (h.t.), id., also *ɣa* "rice-field"; reconstr. *saɣwa-*.

gwat "bijou en (plante)" (Ponape *pmet* "tortoise-shell"); cf. AT *kuʀaat* "skin, shell," as reconstructed above (Table VII).

pagwun "grandson": T *hlaan* "grandchild; nephew, niece"; KS: Sui *khan~han;* Then *laan<*hlaan* "grandchild"; Mak *laan* <*hlaan* "grandchild; nephew or niece"; Li *han* "nephew or niece"; reconstr. uncertain.

*Class II: *kw- type:*

bekwa "bat": IN *labaw* "rat"; Si. *gaaŋ-gaaw* "bat"; cf. also Shan *ʔbaaw;* Si. and Lao *(h)wa(a)w* "kite (paper)"; Dioi *wa:w* "bat," also (d.t.) "rat"; Mak *təkau wa:u* "bat" (*təkau* "horned owl"); reconstr. *gwa(a)w*.

kway "bivalve": IN *t'igay* "shellfish." T *hooy* "shellfish" (WT and Nung also "snail"); KS: *qhui;* Mak *ćhui;* Then *khuei* "snail, shellfish"; S.Li *huoi~hui;* N.Li *khoi* "lime" (=powder of shells, as in Si. *puun hɔi* "chaux de coquillage"); Li also has *sei* as generic term for "shellfish," and Loi dial. has *sei-nom-kai* "bivalve" (app. combines both elements of root, along with *nom* "water"); reconstr. *sayqhwaay*.

hakwelin "cross-cousin": cf. T *hlen~*hlin* "great-grandchild; great-nephew or -niece"; for the semantics here, cf. the writer's papers on kinship.

kwa(n)jelan "near": IN *hampiʟ;* T *k(h)laü;* also *ćam* and *ćuan* (only in SW); KS: Sui and Mak *phyai<*phlai;* S.Li *löü;* N.Li *plöü* "near," also *kui* "near, on the point of"; app. a trisyllabic root, reconstr. uncertain.

*Class III: *ŋw- type:*

ŋwaane "man, male; boy; brother; sibling (opp. sex)"; cf. IN *ɣani* "courage, manliness"; SEP *manay* "male; husband;

spouse; wife"; T *gon~γon "man (homo)"; KS Sui zən~zen, Mak jin, Then ?yin, id.; reconstr. *(n)gwan.

*(y)uŋwa "house": see discussion above.

*(u)ŋwuta "vomit": cf. SEP *mutah, preferable to *m/utah in view of forms such as Motu mumuta<*ma/mutah; IN *u(n)tah; cf. also *luwah "vomit, spit up" and *ludah "spittle"; T *raak "vomit"; Dioi ruö<*rüak "vomit"; T *γraay (Ahom khrai) "spit up, vomit"; KS: Sui će~ći, Mak gaai (all l.t.) "to spit"; Li e?<*eek "vomit"; complex root which app. included an element *ŋraak.

*ŋwata "snake": SEP *ŋata~*mwata; T *ŋu; Dioi ŋöö; Si. and Lao also *ŋiaw; Si. also ŋot "sp. of snake (lycodon)"; KS: Sui hui~fui, Mak zui, Then thuei; OB ŋia; S.Li ya, N.Li tha; dial. ya~ja<*ńa or *ŋya; Lq. ŋü; Lt. kuŋ<*ku/ŋ(u); reconstr. uncertain, poss. *ŋuiata.

Class IV: *khw- type: (only one root cited)

*khwət (khwot, khwor) "hole (nose, mouth)"; cf. Li khɛt "nose"; dial. khat~kat~hoet<*khwat.

The above material amply illustrates the thoroughgoing relationship of these languages at a pre-IN or non-IN level, as well as the complexity of the phonological problems that are raised. It is quite clear that the Oceanic velo-labial clusters come from a variety of sources in AT, including velar $+r/l$ clusters as well as velar $+w$ clusters. A detailed investigation of the Oceanic material should greatly aid in throwing light on this matter.

Further clarification, when compared with the 1942 findings, has come in other areas, mainly as a result of our improved knowledge of comparative phonology and the huge expansion in the corpus of roots. As noted in the earlier study, the Thai and Kadai (also Kam-Sui) languages have a significant basic agreement in syntax with Indonesian (and Austronesian in general) in placing modifying elements (including nouns) after the modified element. Only in the case of Li, which has been heavily influenced by Chinese, has this been modified to the degree that Li has alternative phrases such as *hun sa∼sa hun* "eyebrows" (eye-hair); *nei fa* "this man," but *mau nei* "this year." The mainland languages have rarely retained affixed elements, as in Thai *kin, Sui *tsyan, OB *kon, N.Li *khan, Lq. *küön, all from a root such as IN *kaʔən, from a basic root IN *ka. Strangely enough, Thai has retained what appears to be the basic affix itself in the form *an, defined in Si. as "la chose que" (Laj.) and used as a preformative for abstract nouns. Thai apparently has derived a number of forms from roots with suffixed -*n*, notably in verbal formations; cf. IN *i(m)pi∼*nupi "dream"; Thai *fan; IN *kita "see"; Formosa: Atayal *ktan∼kitaʔ*; T *hran∼*hren; S.Li *lai<*ra/i* "see"; N.Li *fan* "look at"; Lq. *thəi<*thla/i; N.Kl: MFPL *tsai<*tla/i; Lt. *to<*tla* "see." As in the above root, Thai also makes use of the affix -*i*, which is frequently encountered in the Oceanic area (cf. "shame," above). Infixed -*l*- is perhaps preserved in a few roots; cf. "dark" (above) and the following: IN *tu(ŋ)kup∼*ta(ŋ)kub∼kubkub∼*kəb-kəb "cover (various: lid, a cover, shell, crust; also v.)"; T *kap "sheath"; *kaap* "sheath, husk, shell; *klup* "large bamboo or leaf hat"; *kleep* "husk; scab"; *kliip* "petal, skin, scale, scab"; Mak *kup* "close (mouth, door), cover"; Li *kap∼khap* "cover (roof with tiles)." Very little material is available on this point, however, because of the loss of consonant clusters in most languages aside from Siamese.

The original paper cited the 1st pr. prn. as one of the basic roots (no. 29): IN *aku "I"; Thai *ku∼*kaw (complementary distribution); OB *hau;* Li *həu;* Lq. *khəu;* Mulao (Kl. dial.) *sou<*khou;* Lt. *ki∼ku* (subj.), *kui* (poss.); AT *ak(h)aw. Note was also made of the distinction in Thai between inclusive and exclusive forms of the 1st pr. pl. prn., as in IN. We must now add basic correspondences in the other two persons: IN *kamu "you" (Windstedt: Ml. also "thou"); SEP *kamiw "you" (also "thou" in Mekeo, Pokau); T: SW *maü∼*müŋ; C: *(h)maü∼*(h)mü; Dioi *möŋ "thou; you (latter only with plural modifiers)"; OB *mö "you" (unspecified); S.Li *mü "thou, you"; N.Li *möü, id.; Lq. *mi "thou"; AT form uncertain, but it probably was nonspecific for number; IN *iya<*ñiya "3rd pr. prn.," *iyan<*ñiya/n "that"; SEP *-na "3rd pr. prn. suffix"; T *nan "that (one, time, place)," *hnan (s.t.) "there," but Tho has yen<*ńan "that one," also ic. "there"; T also has *ʔyan <*ʔńa/n "extend, spread out"; *ʔyaan<*ʔńaa/n "distant, distance"; Li na "3rd pr. prn."

The numerical system has been subjected to further analysis with the aid of our advances in phonology, yielding important advances. The newly uncovered material on Lati (Man P'ang dial.) has tied this language closer to the others, e.g. nam "6" (for nə); cf. IN *ənəm; pət "10" (for pa); cf. Lq. pət, Li phuot~fuot, and IN *puluh<*puluut. The numerals for "4," "5," and "6" in general present no problems, that for "5" being identical or a variant with the root for "hand" (see Table IV). Li is deviant from the other Kadai languages, however, in having śau~śɔ and similar forms for "4," in the face of IN *ə(m)pat; most Formosa languages have a prefixed form of the type *spat (soʔat in one Rukai dialect, which regularly replaces p with ʔ in this position), and one Li dialect (Shaved Head Loi) shows a final -t (söt), hence we appear to have here an important link with the Formosan languages (cf. the discussion above). Inasmuch as replacement of medial -b- by -w- is not uncommon in Thai and other mainland languages (cf. "ashes," above), we can postulate a development such as *sapat>*sabat>*saw> sau. Li also is deviant in having an entirely separate root for "9," which can be reconstructed as *pal, apparently closely related to *puluut "10." These aberrations shown by Li in the numeral system are quite unexpected, since Li in general seems to stand closer to Thai than do the other Kadai languages.

The most important key to the IN (and AT) numeral system, however, is supplied by Laqua, which shows features which were described (in 1942) as "suggestive of a quinary system." Laqua has mö təu "7," mö dü "8," mö diə "9," with mö apparently identical with mö "5." Closer inspection, however, reveals that the təu of "7" is identical with təu "3," that the dü of "8" is virtually identical with de "2," and that the diə of "9" is simply a voiced variant of tiə "1." It thus is clear that we are dealing here with subtraction from "10," with mö standing for "10" (5 × 2). This feature is not found in Formosa, which commonly derives "6" from "3" and "8" from "4," but occurs in Cham (for "8" and "9"). Further study strongly indicates that

IN *pitu* "7" is derived from *pitlu*<*pitəlu*, with IN *təlu* "3" being simply an abbreviated version of the root. The IN root for "2" has presented difficulties, with Dyen (1947a) suggesting *dəhwa* for Dempwolff's *ḍuwa*. The initial ḍ- indicates an original consonant cluster, probably with *r*, and the root appears to be represented in Thai by *ra* "we" (Lao and WT) but "we two" in Kh. and Shan; perhaps also by T *raw* "we" and even *z(r)aaw* "score" (2 × 10). KS has retained the root in its numerical sense: Sui γ*a*, Mak and Then *za* (all h.t.) "2," reconstructed as *-γa* (preposed element to explain the h.t.). OB has *vön* "2," apparently from *völ(u)*, resembling IN *walu* "8." Kähler (1962) has pointed out "compound consonants" as correspondences for AN *w-*, citing here Chamorro *gwalo* "8," *hugwa* "2." The mainland evidence indicates that the common root for these two numerals was *gγahwalu*, the gγ- yielding gw- in Chamorro (cf. our discussion of velo-labials). Finally, IN *it'a* "1" appears to be an abbreviated version of *t'iwa* "9," the latter being cognate with T *ʔdiaw* "single, alone"; KS: Sui ʔ*dau~deu* "1"; Mak ʔ*de:u* "single (one of a pair)." The most likely reconstr. for the root is *tiyawa* or *itiyawa*. The Laqua numerals, with the same system of subtraction from 10 as that reconstructed for IN, place this feature definitely at the AT archaic level.

We shall conclude this review of AT comparative material with a note on the higher numerals. As pointed out in 1942, the Kadai languages have a root for "100" which appears to be entirely distinct from IN or Thai, viz. Li *dan*, Lq. *dön*, Kl. *jin~tsin* (but Lt. has *khre*). IN has *ratut'*, and Thai has *rooy*, which Coedès and Burnay (1926) have related ("string of coins") to the Thai root *rooy~*drooy* (Shan var.) "string (of anything); to put on a string (as beads, fish)"; cf. IN *tali* "string, cord" (cf. also Lt. *khre*). In view of the absence of a root for "100," the writer was astonished to find a well-developed root for "1,000," with forms developed from either end of the root: IN *Libu*<*rigwu*<*rigwa;* T *hriaŋ* (Ahom, Kh., Shan); Dioi *rɛŋ* "million"; Si. and Lao have *ban*<*gwan* (a rare but not unknown development in Thai); Li ŋ*uon*<*ŋwan;* Kl. *gɛ*<*gwa(n);* AT *ri(ŋ)gwa/n.*

In summary we shall make the following points:

(1) Thai, the para-Thai languages (Kam-Sui, Ong-Be), and Kadai, together with Indonesian and Austronesian in general, constitute a single, rather well-united family of languages (Austro-Thai).

(2) A corpus of some 400 roots is now in evidence, and systematic phonological correspondences can be worked out for many of these.

(3) The conclusion that the Austro-Thai-speaking peoples originated on the mainland, roughly in the South China region, seems to be irrefutable at this point.

(4) The limited study of Formosan materials available indicates that at least some of these languages are in part independent of IN, as suggested by Ferrell (1966).

(5) The evidence in general seems to show conclusively that IN stands somewhat apart from the main AN line.

CLASSIFICATION OF SOUTHEAST ASIATIC
LANGUAGES (revised)

1. Sino-Tibetan {
   Chinese

   { Tibeto-Burman
   { Karen

2. Miao-Yao {
   Yao

   { Miao
   { Paṭeng

3. Min-chia

4. Austroasiatic (Mon, Khmer, Palaung-Wa, Khasi, Sakai, et al.)

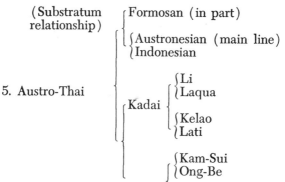

(Substratum relationship)   Formosan (in part)

                                  { Austronesian (main line)
                                  { Indonesian

5. Austro-Thai

                          Kadai   { Li
                                  { Laqua

                                  { Kelao
                                  { Lati

                                  { Kam-Sui
                                  { Ong-Be

                                  Thai

Notes on Classification Schema:

1, 2, and 3: frequently grouped under one heading, such as "Sino-Tibetan," but the nuclear group of roots in each stock appears to be distinct.

4 and 5: the reconstruction of roots for AT has not closed the gap between this stock and Austroasiatic. Some structural similarities, notably the substantial infix *-an-, along with a handful of significant root elements, especially *ka "fish" and *mat "eye," suggest that the relationship between the two stocks is of "substratum" type. As Capell (1943) has shown particularly well for SEP, structural (and especially syntactical) features tend

to be persistent in these situations. Here it would appear that, at a very early period (probably 2nd to 3rd millennium B.C.), the ancestral AT language was grafted onto a substratum stock of Austroasiatic affiliation, with almost complete replacement of the latter. Since the ancestral AT homeland can with considerable confidence be placed in southern China (generally), we can infer that the Austroasiatic language area formerly extended well to the north of its historic boundary, into southern and probably eastern China. Annamese (Vietnamese), which at one time probably extended north along the China coast (see Benedict 1947), seems to represent the old northeastern "anchor" of the Austroasiatic bloc, heavily overlain from early times with Thai elements, including the old Thai (and Chinese) tonal system. It therefore seems unlikely that Cham could represent an old extension of the AT stock along the coast, and the writer still favors the view that the Cham group, like Malay, is an old enclave on the mainland.

NOTES

[1] The writer is indebted to F. K. Li and Inez de Beauclair for providing him with source material, particularly in Oriental languages, and to Raleigh Ferrell, who generously supplied him with rich source materials on Formosa.

[2] The Hainan "Muslims" or "Mohammedans" listed as a member of the Kadai group are in reality a Cham colony on Hainan, which the writer described in 1941 ("A Cham Colony on the Island of Hainan," *Harvard Journal of Asiatic Studies, 6:* 129-34).

[3] The phonetic symbols are conventional, except for ü and ö, which represent the back unrounded vowels characteristic of many of the languages studied. L is the IN retroflex l (Demp.); *j* is the voiced affricate, equivalent to ʒ' in Demp. Abbreviations are as follows: AN Austronesian; AT Austro-Thai (our term for Thai-Kadai-Malayo-Polynesian; includes also Kam-Sui and Ong-Be); Bas. Basadungli (Li dial.); Bon Bonifacy; BT Black Tai; cg. cognate; cw. in composition with; Demp. Dempwolff; d.t. different tone; Fi. Fiji; Fu. Futuna; h.t. high tone; Ho. Hova; ic. in composition; IN Indonesian; Ja. Javanese; Kh. Khamti; Kl. Kelao; KS Kam-Sui; Laj. Lajonquière; l.t. low tone; Lq. Laqua; Lt. Lati; Mak. Makazayazaya (Paiwan dial.); MFPL *Miao-fang Pei-lan* (Chinese source on Kelao; vide Ruey Yih-fu); Ml. Malay; MN Melanesian; NgD. Ngaju-Dayak; OB Ong-Be; PN Polynesian; Rob. Roberts; Sa. Sa'a; SEP Southeast Papua (general term for area described in Capell, 1943); Si. Siamese; Sm. Samoa; s.t. same tone; Sui-LN, Sui-J., Sui-P. (Sui dialects; see F. K. Li); T Thai; TB Toba-Batak; To. Tonga; v.t., v. tr., transitive verb; WT White Tai.

EDITOR'S NOTE

Three additional sections of this article, on Austro-Thai cultural items and kinship terms and on the relationship of Austro-Thai and Chinese, will appear in a future issue of *Behavior Science Notes.*

Austro-Thai Studies:

1. Material Culture

Paul K. Benedict[*]

The Austro-Thai language family, as recently set up by the writer (1966),[1] includes Indonesian and the Austronesian languages in general, together with Thai, Kadai, and certain "para-Thai" languages (Kam-Sui, Ong-Be). The data presented in this study point to an origin on the Asiatic mainland, roughly in the South China region. The evidence also suggests that Indonesian (IN) stands somewhat apart from the main Austronesian (AN) line, and that the Formosan languages are in part independent of both IN and AN. Some attention was also paid to the AN material from Southeastern Papua (after Capell 1943), which at times show striking agreements with Thai as opposed to IN or AN. Certain Austro-Thai (AT) roots relating to cultural items were included in the 1966 study, but the bulk of this material was reserved for the present study. Some of the roots relate to aspects of material culture, such as agriculture and weaving, while others, to be considered separately, relate to kinship terminology. A third group of roots show significant correspondences with forms from Archaic Chinese as well as Thai, and these will be analyzed in a concluding section.[†]

[*] Paul K. Benedict is a linguist by nature (but studied with Sapir), an anthropologist and Orientalist by education and training (A.B., University of New Mexico; M.A. and Ph.D., Harvard University; Arnold and Harvard-Yenching Fellow, Harvard, field work in Southeast Asia). For the past fifteen years he has been a clinical and research psychiatrist (M.D., New York Medical College), with ethnopsychiatry as one of his main interests (collaborating editor of *Schizophrenia*, New York: Logos Press, 1958, and contributor of the section on "Social and Cultural Factors in Schizophrenia"). The first section of the current study, "Austro-Thai," appeared in *Behavior Science Notes 1* (1966): 227-61.

[†] Part 3, "Austro-Thai and Chinese," will appear in a forthcoming issue of *Behavior Science Notes,* and will include a list of the Chinese characters referred to in both sections.

In addition to the sources previously listed (1966), the present study has been able to draw upon an important new source of basic comparative materials for the AT languages, viz. Haudricourt's elaborate analysis of the Be (Ong-Be) manuscript prepared by Savina around 1930 (Savina 1965). This Ong-Be material supplements our hitherto skimpy knowledge of this important language, which was previously known largely from the account by Jeremaissen (1892), and reflects certain changes in the language over a span of roughly forty years, e.g. the confusion of initial *b-* and *w-* as *v-* (distinct in Jer.). Haudricourt presents numerous comparative tables in which he lists forms for Kam (Tong), from a Tong-Chinese dictionary published in 1959. In addition, he presents comparative material for Sek, a language of Northern Thai (Dioi) type, spoken in the Thakhek region of Laos.[2] Sek is remarkably archaic in certain respects, e.g. it retains the form *ʔblian* "moon," almost identical to the Thai root *°ʔblüan* as reconstructed by the writer (1942), and it has initial *pr-* in the "eye" and "die" pair of roots.[3] Even more surprisingly, Sek has final *-l* in a number of cases, and this can be shown in some cases to correspond to IN *°-γ* (see *SOW* and *FIREPLACE*, below). Haudricourt now has in publication material on another remarkable language, apparently also of Northern Thai type, viz. Lakia,[4] which has *pla* "eye," *plei* "kill," also *mlok* "bird," corresponding to Kam *mok*, AT *°manluk* (*AT*, Table III). The writer has also made use of a Chinese source on the White Sand dialect of Li (Wang 1952), included also in Haudricourt's material. We can only hope that before long material will become available on the mainland Kadai languages (Laqua, Lati, Kelao), still known only from older and incomplete sources.[5]

AGRICULTURE

This basic area is well represented, with several roots for "field" and "garden," including the concept of irrigation or wet field. There is also a root for "seed" as well as roots for such basic concepts as "plough," "sow," "winnow," and "mortar" and "pestle." The Sui-Thai root *°ʔdam* "to plant young rice plants," however, appears to have been a relatively late development from a basic root for "bury/dive" (*AT*, Table I); Ong-Be (Sav.) also has a cognate: *zom*<*ʔdam/lam* "repiquer."

FIELD

1. Oceanic *gwala* "taro field"; IN *tʼabaʔ*<*sagwaa-* "irrigated rice-field"; T *ɣan*<*g(w)al/a* "dice of rice-field"; Sui and Mak *yan*, id. Cf. also KS *ʔɣa* "rice-field"; perhaps also S. Kl. (*thü*) *bo*, id.

2. IN *bəna* "low-lying land, flooded land"; T *na*; OB *nea*; S. Li *na*; N.Li *ta*; Lq. *ne*<*na*; Lt. *nu*<*na*; all meaning "rice-field" (wet-field type). Thai has a separate root *ray*, Dioi *ri*, for the upland field for dry cultivation, apparently distinct from the above root, although T *r-* sometimes corresponds to KS *ɣ-*. This root is part of the Thai stratum in Vietnamese: *rây* "land covered with underbrush." The Kadai languages, which for the most part show concord with Thai in the root for "wet field," have divergent forms for "dry (upland) field": Li *oŋ*; Lt. *ɔu*<*ɔŋ*(?); Lq. *ləu*; S. Kl. (*thü*) *lə*, the latter pair possibly cognate with the following root.

3. IN *talun*<*talu/n* "fallow land" (Sm. "young underwood"), apparently from the root: *talu* "conquer" ("conquered land"); T *hlaw* "upland field, jungle" (WT also "young underwood"); Dioi *lau*<*hla*(ə)*w* "fallow land"; BT has *la:u*<*hlaaw* "to clear (mountain rice-field)," possibly related to T *hlaw* (s.t.) "coax, persuade."

GARDEN

IN *tʼuwan* "digging stick" but TB "to plant," To. "to clear a field," Sm. "to turn over the soil"; T *suan/thrüan* "garden." The latter variant is from the Northern Thai languages (Tsʼun-lao and Cao-lan) of North Vietnam, recently described by Haudricourt (1960)[6]. The doublet is reflected also in Lao *thin*<*th[r]in* "garden" and Shan *thön*<*th[r]üan* (s.t.) "to harrow; a harrow"; Ahom *thun* "plough; to plough." KS also reflects the doublet: Sui *fyan*~*fiən*~*hyan*, Mak *fiin*, Then *wyaan* "garden" (F. K. Li reconstructs *swyaan* for Sui-Thai), but Sui *wya:n*, Mak *vi:n* "field (cultivated)" (*contra AT*, Table IV, notes). The root is also represented by OB *buon*~*büön*<*wuan* (see above) "garden"; S. Li *vien*<*wian;* WS Li *ku:ŋ*<*ku:n* (regular shift) <*kwan,* id. The alternative comparison, with IN *huma* "garden" (*AT,* 237), seems to be ruled out by the Thai doublet form, but it presents a significant semantic analogy, since in Sm. and frequently in SEP this root has the meaning "to clear land." The core meaning of both roots was perhaps "to dig (as with a digging stick)." Si. retains an element of this meaning in *suan* (same tone as for "garden") "to thrust into the anus," and it has *suan* as a modifying element in the phrase *na suan* "rizière repiquée" (Laj.).

MORTAR

IN *lət'uŋ*<*ləkruŋ;* Formosa: Puyuma *losoŋ* "mortar," *lisok* (dial. *lasok*)<*ləkrok* "pestle" (cf. the root below); T. *grok* "mortar"; Mak *sok*<*grok* "pound in a mortar"; reconstruction: AT *-kroŋ/krok/grok.* The N. Thai or Dioi group of languages have what appears to be a distinct although similar root: *qrum* (Haudricourt 1960).

PESTLE/MORTAR

IN *halu* "pestle"; Formosa has forms of the type: *qa/su/lu* with infixed *s;* Li *drau* "mortar"; Bas. dial. *rɔ,* id. S. Li *dr-* regularly corresponds to clusters with *l* (see *COOK,* below); cf. Li *drüʔ*<*drüük* "bone," IN *tulak* (*AT,* Table I), also the exactly parallel root: IN *lipan*~*halipan* (Capell) "centipede"; T *xlep;* Dioi *sip* "large venomous centipede"; Mak *sip;* Li *drip*~*dip*: AT reconstructions: *qal(a)u* "mortar," *qalip/an* "centipede."

PLOUGH (CULTIVATE)

IN *buhat*<*buhlat* "to produce"; Ml. "to produce, cultivate"; Fi., Fu., Sm. "harvest"; also the doublet: *ulaʔ*<*buhlaat* "production"; T *hret*~*ret*~*yet* "do, work, make; cultivate, plough"; also *thlay*<*phla(a)d*<*phla(a)t* "to plough, plough"; KS: Sui *čoi,* Kam *khay* "plough," Mak *čwai* "plough, to plough," but *čha:i* (d.t.) "to harrow a field"; OB *lei*<*lai;* S. Li (*dau*) *lai;* Bupäli (N.Li) *thei;* Lq. *thəi,* S.Kl. *dzɛ və;* Lt. *hle,* all meaning "plough."

This important root illustrates some basic phonological phenomena in AT. The IN doublet is the product of variable stress:

*buhlat>*buhat with fore-stress, but *buhlat>*wulaat>*ula?
with end-stress and associated vocalic lengthening (the replacement of final -t after long vowel with -? is regular; see *AT*, 239).
The Thai and KS (Mak) doublets apparently correspond directly to that of IN, so that this stress factor can be placed in
the precursor AT language (cf. also *AT*, 230 and 248). Thai
*hret~*ret~*yet show palatalization before the dental final
(*AT*, 241) and the equation of Thai r with IN l, paralleling the
root: IN *kulat "mushroom," T *hret, id. (*AT*, 243, 244, and
Table V). The second Thai form (*thlay) illustrates replacement
of final -d with -i (see *AT*, 239) and the replacement of labial
by dental stop in clusters with r/l (*AT*, 246 and Table VIII;
also the discussion in Note 3 and the reconstructions of initial
clusters in Li 1954); note (*AT*, Table VIII) that the Thai initial
stop is characteristically unvoiced in these correspondences. A
close parallel, but with unaspirated initial, is furnished by: IN
*buluŋ "foliage," T *tlooŋ "large leaf, esp. of banana" (see
BANANA, below).

SEED/GRAIN

IN *bəni?~*bini?<*(ŋ)gwanii- "seed"; T *van~*ban (Si.,
Lao); Dioi hɔn (s.t.)<*khwan; Li fen<*khwan, all "seed." OB
has zean<*y(e)an, probably from the same root via *gwyan
(palatalized). A prenasalized version of the same root shows a
semantic development along the lines of "grain," viz. T *hŋuay<
*hŋ(g)wa(n)i (Ahom, Kh., Shan)~*hnuay (Si., Lao)~*hmuay
(Tho, Nung) "seed, grain; num. adj. for small spherical things";
Mak ŋui "fruit, seed, kernel; num. adj. for grain."

SOW, v.

IN *t'əba[L]<*səgwar; T *hwaal, the final -l reconstructed
on the basis of Sek va:l; OB bien (for *vien, see above)<*wian;
Li viet<*wiat, apparently from *wian/wiat.

WINNOW

IN *ta(m)pi<*qra(ŋ)kwi; T *qraŋ/khrüŋ "winnow, sift;
winnowing basket, sieve" (Haudricourt 1960); Mak. ji:ŋ (h.t.)
<*kri:ŋ "winnowing basket." For the initial cluster, cf. IN
*taliŋa "ear," but Formosa *ṭaliŋa (see Note 3); T *qhru/ru;

KS *qha<*qhra; OB sa<*qhra; S. Li yai; N. Li thai~tsai~čai <*qhra/i; Lq. rö; N. Kl. rau; Lt. lu<*la (contra the end-stress analysis suggested in AT, 243).

An apparent doublet form is represented by T *ʔdoŋ; KS *ʔdoŋ or ʔloŋ (AT, 231 and Table I); Li duŋ yau, all "winnowing basket"; also OB zoŋ<*ʔdoŋ or ʔloŋ "winnow," perhaps from a form *ʔɢroŋ (not traced in IN).

ALCOHOL

LIQUOR/WINE

IN *laʟu<*laru "means of clarifying fermenting liquids": TB raru; Ja., Ml. laru "sap for clarifying palm wine"; Ho. laru "means for stupefying fish"; Formosa: Puyuma ʔrao, Atayal quowao (Egerod: quau), Paiwan wawa~vava, Ami ʔpah, Rukai bawa~bva; T *hlaw; KS *qlaaw;[7] OB jan (Jer.), zon (Sav.)< *ron/lon<*rar/lar; Li ŋa:u<*ŋla:u, dial. bian~biaŋ<*gwar(u) <*glaru, Mefuli dial. po; N.Kl. pa "whiskey"; reconstruction: AT *(ŋ)qlaru, with several instances of the development: *ql- >*qw->p/b-.

DRUNK

IN *mabuk "psychic abnormality"; TB "stupefied"; Ml. "drunk"; NgD. mabok "violent," mauk "drunk"; T *maw "drunk; dizzy"; N. Thai mi; OB moi (Jer.), mei (Sav.); S. Li mui; N. Li pui. The development -b->-w is paralleled by IN *ḍabuk "ashes," T *daw/braw (AT, 248 and 255).

ARECA (TRAIT)

All the main aspects of the areca trait-complex appear to be included in our group of basic AT roots: "areca," "betel," "lime," and "betel-chewing."

ARECA

Two roots, ultimately related, with complex semantic interchange: "fruit"~"jackfruit"~"areca"~"betel." These are diagramed below, with the writer's reconstructed forms in brackets:

ROOT #1

	fruit	areca	betel
Indonesian	*buha?* [*bluhaak*]		
Formosa	*boa* (Puyuma)	(*a*)*buwa?* (Yami)	
Southeast Papua			
I. Pokau	*vua*	*buakau*	
II. Motu	*huahua*	*bua-tau*	
III. Kiriwina	*uwa*	*bua*	
13th-century Siamese	(*hmaak*)		
Modern Siamese		(*hmaak*)	
Thai languages			
Ahom and Shan		*mlu* [*mblu*]	*blu*
Si., Lao,			
BT, WT			*blu*
Tho			*myau* [*mblau*]
Nung			*dau* [*blau*]
17th-century Vietnamese			*bləu*
Southern Li		*ləu* [*blau*]"chew areca"	

Notes on Root # 1

For *b-<bl-* in IN, cf. *PLOUGH* (above) and *BEE* (below).
The Formosa languages show three or four roots for "fruit,"
including Puyuma *boa~voa?*, Atayal *bowai~boai*, Saisiat *bowai*.
Yami is distinctive in having this root in the meaning "areca,"
and since Yami (on Botel Tobago) in general stands closer to
certain (Philippine) IN languages than to Formosan languages
proper, it seems likely that this semantic interchange is also to
be found elsewhere in IN, although not noted in Dempwolff.
The most widespread Formosan root for "areca," represented
by Rukai *sabiki~saveke*, Paiwan and Bunun *saviki* et al., perhaps also belongs here via a form such as **sa/bu(a)k/i.*
The Chinese transcription *pin-lü* "betel (quid) for chewing"
apparently reflects this root: **p-liu.†*
SEP: Capell assigns the meaning "fruit" to Movement I, since
it occurs in most SEP areas and shows regular sound shifts, e.g.
initial *b-* regularly drops before *u* in Kiriwina. The meaning

"areca" (Capell: "betel"), on the other hand, shows irregular phonetic features and is restricted to the three SEP areas illustrated in the above table, hence Capell assigns it to the later Movement II. Capell remarks, apropos this root, "it bears every mark of being a foreign word, for neither in Papua nor in SES [Southeast Solomons] does it obey the phonetic laws," yet he dismisses it as simply a specialized use of the word for "fruit," without specifying the loan source.

T *hmaak* "fruit"; OB *mak* ic., id; this meaning is also retained in the thirteenth-century (Siamese) Rama Khamheng inscription, but Modern Siamese has "areca" (Lao has both meanings). There is a possible connection with the main root; cf. also IN *d'ambay* < *d'ambaag* (?) "areca."

S. Li *ləu* "chew areca," also "eat, drink" (no distinction).

Vietnamese *bləu* (*blâu*) "betel" in the seventeenth-century dictionary of Rhodes (Modern Vietnamese *trâu*), part of the Thai stratum in that language; Vietnamese *kau* (*cau*) "areca" appears to be distinct.

ROOT #2

	jackfruit	areca	betel
Indonesian	*naŋka*	*pinaŋ*	
Formosa		*poran* (Puyuma)	
13th-century Siamese	*laaŋ*?	*laaŋ*?	
Modern Siamese		*liŋ*	*hmiaŋ* [*hmliaŋ*][8]
Thai languages Ahom, Shan	*laaŋ*		
BT, WT, Tho, Nung		*laaŋ*	
Southern Li		{ *luoŋ* [*pluaŋ*] { *lɔŋ*	

Notes on Root #2

IN *pinaŋ* is apparently derived from *pi(n)laŋ*, IN showing a tendency to shift medial -*l*- to -*n*- in a "labial environment"; cf. IN *anak* "child," from the root represented by IN *lak* "develop," *bulak* "flower" (*AT*, 246 and Table VIII).

The Chinese transcription *pin-laŋ* "betel-nut [areca]" (general term) can be explained on the basis of the above reconstruction; Swatow (S. China dialect) has an irregular initial *n*- in the second element of this transcription, but this might well represent a "back reading" or "dictionary pronunciation."

Formosa: Puyuma *poran*<*polan*<*polaŋ* (the latter shift is unexplained). The only other Formosa occurrences of this root are: Atayal *ipnaŋ*, Saisiat *puniŋ*. Note that IN *buhaʔ* "fruit" and *pinaŋ* "areca" have precisely the same pattern of occurrence in Formosa, with a center in Atayal-Saisiat (Atayalic group) and extension to Puyuma (Paiwanic group).

The thirteenth-century Siamese form *laaŋ* is from the Rama Khamheng inscription; it is tentatively translated "jackfruit" by Coedès, but might well stand for "areca" (later to be replaced by *hmaak*).

Siamese also has *hmaak liŋ* (s.t.) "wild areca" (Laj.), as well as the phrase *hmiaŋ hmaak* "betel and areca" (Laj.).

S. Li initial *l-* regularly corresponds to N.Li *pl-* (*AT*, Tables VI and VIII) and in at least one root can be shown to correspond to an IN consonant group of *bl-* type: IN *bəluɣ* "round"; S.Li *luon*; N.Li *pluon*. The word for "areca" is not cited in any of our N.Li sources (including Wang), however, hence the reconstruction here remains in some doubt.

To summarize the material on this pair of complex roots, there is evidence of a doublet of the type: *bluhaak/bluhaaŋ* or *buhlaak/buhlaaŋ* "fruit" for AT, with partial specialization in the meaning "areca." This development must have been early, in view of the peripheral distribution: Formosa (Botel Tobago), SEP, and the mainland. Thai has also shown a tendency to shift the meaning to "betel" (cf. the confusion in English "betel-nut") as well as to associate one root with the phonetically similar root for "jackfruit" or to replace it with a third root (*hmaak*) of uncertain affiliation.

BETEL

There is evidence for a general root for "pepper (plant, spice)," with later development in IN of the specialized meaning "betel pepper." On the mainland, the specialization has been in the direction of "pimento, chili," the meaning "betel" having already been developed from the root for "areca" (above).

IN *tʼiLiʔ*<*tiriit/pririit* "betel pepper": Tg. "pepper"; Ja., Ml. "betel pepper"; NgD. *sirih* "betel pepper," *ńihi* "piquant (of spices)"; T *brit*~*brik* (Si., Lao) "pepper, pimento, chili"; Lao also has *hrüat*<*phrüat* (?) "pimento, all-spice"; Li *drit* <*trit/prit* "piquant (pimento)."

44 *Austro-Thai*

Thai also has *phet<*phret (?) "pungent, piquant" (Nung *ma:k phet* "pimento"), apparently cognate with IN *paʔit "bitter"; both forms appear to belong with the above root, but the reconstruction is uncertain. The Formosa languages supply further evidence for an original consonant group of *pl-* type: Rukai *mapilil*, Puyuma *apilil* "bitter."

CHEW (BETEL)

IN *mamah "chew" (Sa. "betel-quid"); SEP generally in meaning "chew betel" (assigned to Movement II), but in Fiji usually "chew kava." T *hmam/hmaam/mam and *hñam/ñam "chew soft foods (esp. as infants or edentulous persons)"; Lao *hñam "chew (as tiger), chew betel"; Si. *kin hmaak yam yam* "chew areca" = "eat betel *yam yam*" (*yam*<*ñam). This root, definitely part of the original trait-complex, refers to a specific type of chewing associated with areca (and kava in Fiji).

LIME

IN *kapuɣ~*apuɣ: Ja. *apuʻ* "lime," *n/apur/an* "betel quid"; Formosa: most forms cited are from roots for "ashes," but Ami *hapor~apor*, Bunun *apuʟ*, Kanakanabu *apuru*; SEP: only in groups I and II (assigned to Movement II); Si. and Lao *puun* (not elsewhere in Thai). The basic AT root can be reconstructed as */kwuɣ, represented also in Thai by the following doublet: *khun "dust; manure"; *fun (s.t.) "dust, powder; manure"; Mak *vən* "ash dust; powder"; OB *phon*<*khwon "excrement, manure."

DOMESTICATED ANIMALS

The evidence from root reconstructions indicates that both cattle and water buffalo had been domesticated by the early AT period, and it suggests that the goat was domesticated at a later period, the mainland cognate referring only to the wild goat. There is also a very complex root involving "bees (wasps, hornets)," but the degree of domestication is questionable. A similar problem obtains in the case of "rabbit," the root here showing a specific tie-up with Formosa. The evidence for "dog" and "pig," probably the two earliest domesticated animals, involving Chinese data, is presented in Part 3.†

BEE/WASP/HORNET

IN *tabuʔ/an* "animal that makes a drumming noise," but Ja. *tawon*<*tawu/an* "bumble-bee"; NgD. *tabuan* "wasp," derived by Dempwolff from *ta(m)buʔ* "drumstick." The generalized basic form can be reconstructed as *tabluuk/tabluuŋ-an*, yielding three lines of development, as follows:

1. *(ta)blu/bluuk*: Formosa: Rukai *vulo~valo~halu~walo*, Puyuma, Sedik, Saisiat *walo*; Saaroa *ʔaʟoʔo* "honey bee"; T *to*<*pro*<*blo* "hornet" (Si. "kind of wasp"); Mak *ʔdəu*<*blu* "kind of large bee"; Kam *ʔla:u*<*ʔbla:u* "bee"; Li dial.: Small Cloth Loi *blou*, WS Li *fok*<*ʔblok* "bee."

2. *tabl(u)an*: Formosa: Paiwan *tainan* "honey bee"; T *teen/preen*<*bleen* "wasp" (Shan "small hornet," BT "bee"), Dioi *dün*<*blüün* "wasp"; Mak *din*<*brin* "wasp."

3. *(ta)bluuŋ*: Formosa: Tsou *teyoŋo*<*tebloŋo* (?) "honey bee"; T *phrüŋ/thüaŋ*: Ahom *prüŋ* "honey," but SW generally *phüŋ* "bee" (*nam phüŋ* "honey," *khi phüŋ* "wax"); Lao *phüŋ~phöŋ* "wax," *to phöŋ* "large wild bee" (this phrase combines two forms from the same basic root); BT *füöŋ~föŋ* "wax," but the Tho-Nung group shows the characteristic Thai shift from labial to dental stop in clusters of this kind: Tho *thüöŋ* "bee"; Nung *thö:ŋ* "sugar," *me:ŋ thö:ŋ* "bee" (cw. "insect"); OB *saŋ* (Jer.), *soŋ* (Sav.)<*phraŋ* "bee" (cf. Note 3).

BUFFALO (WATER)

IN *kəbaw*: Ja. *kĕbo*, but Tg. *kalabao*, Tb. *horbo*; Ml. *kĕrbao*; also Fi. *karavau* "cattle" (Demp. analyzes the *l* as an infix); T *γwaay/*γrwaay*<*glwaay*, the initial cluster demonstrated by Ahom *khrai*; KS *gwəi*: Sui *kwi~kui*, Mak *həi*, Then *wei* (all l.t.); Mak also has *həi ʔdoŋ* "wild ox" (ic. "forest"); OB *tai*<*kwai/qwai*; Li *tui*<*kwui* (regular shift), dial. also *toi~čoi*; Lq. *həi* (but *khɛ* in Laj.); N.Kl. *wu* (*ni wu* in MFPL); S.Kl. *ŋi uə*; Lt. *ko~kua*. The *l* appears to have been part of the AT root, with shift to *r* in Thai, as shown also by Müöng *klau*, seventeenth-century Vietnamese (Rhodes dictionary) *tlau* (Modern *trâu*) as well as by the early loans in Tibeto-Burman (see Pt. 3). The indicated reconstruction is *kala(ŋ)gwaw*, yielding *klwaay/glwaay* through dissimilation of the final. The original ŋ in this root is reflected in Formosa: Ami *koloŋ* "cattle," also "buffalo," Rukai *goŋ~xoŋ* "cattle," Paiwan *goŋ~guŋ~loaŋ*, id.

CATTLE

IN *ləmbu<*ləŋgwu;* Formosa: see forms cited above; T *ŋwa,* with the rare cluster *ŋw-* as reconstructed by F. K. Li (1956), reflected in three different forms: *ŋua* (general in SW, but Ahom has *hu<*hŋua*); *wua* (Shan and Si. variant); *mo <*ŋwo* (Tho and Nung); Mak *pho<*khwo* (cf. Mak *pha* "right," T *khwa/xwa*); Lt. *mmo<*ŋwo.* In addition to the end-stress root, Thai also shows a fore-stress doublet root: Ahom *liŋ* "cattle," Lao *hiŋ<*hriŋ* "buffalo."

This root for "cattle" is simply an abbreviated version of the longer AT root for "buffalo": *ləŋgwu=*/la(ŋ)gwaw,* as suggested by the frequent semantic interchange.

GOAT

IN *kambiŋ<*kaŋgw(ay)iŋ;* Formosa: Yami *kagulin* (analysis uncertain); the root does not appear to be represented in Formosa proper; T *ñüaŋ/yüaŋ<*ŋyaŋ* through palatalization: Shan "goat antelope," Lao "wild goat," WT "wild goat, attaining the size of a small deer; sp. of ibex with small horns"; OB *toaŋ <*kwaŋ/gwaŋ* (cf. *BUFFALO*, above) "goat, sheep." Li *ya:ŋ* "goat, sheep" can be identified as a "back loan" from Chinese (see Pt. 3).

RABBIT

Formosa: *tok/tuk*: Atayal, Saisiat *rotok,* Rukai *rotoko~lutuk,* Tsou *yutuka,* Paiwan *lut'uk~lot'ok,* Kanakanabu *lituka,* Bunun *autok;* T *tho/tho?,* with limited distribution: Nung *thɔ,* Dioi *ñut tɔ,* but Si. and Lao *tho?* (a rare final in Thai). S: also has *kăta:i* "rabbit," related to Shan and Kh. *pa:ŋ-ta:i<*/taag* (?). Li *thoa* can be identified as another Chinese "back loan" (see Pt. 3).

DOMESTICATED PLANTS

The outstanding feature in this category is the presence of several roots, fairly well differentiated, for "rice." This evidence, together with that presented above under *AGRICULTURE,* points to rice cultivation as a central factor in the early AT agricultural economy. The presence of a root for "sugarcane," probably the second most important cultivated crop in early times in Southeast Asia, is also noteworthy. The roots for "yam" and "banana" are less well represented, but the latter has an important tie-in with Archaic Chinese (see Pt. 3). There are additional roots for "coconut," "ginger/pepper," "gourd/cucumber," and "sesame," the last-named previously noted in Benedict 1942.

BANANA (PLANTAIN)

IN *pit'aŋ, with a central type of distribution (TB, Ja., Ml., NgD.); T *hyuak, Dioi šiɛ<*šiɛk<*šiak "wild banana" (as opposed to T *kluay "cultivated banana"); S.Li vaʔ<*waak, N.Li weŋʔ, dial. veak~vɛk (WS Li veʔ hau); perhaps also Lt. hin. The reconstruction is uncertain, possibly *thrwak/thywak, corresponding to an IN doublet form: *pit'aŋ/pit'ak. This comparison is greatly supported by the presence of a direct transcription loan-word in early Chinese (see Pt. 3).

A second IN root for "banana," *pun[t]i, which has a more peripheral distribution (Ho., MN, PN, Movement I in SEP) and is presumably the earlier of the pair, appears to have no cognates on the mainland but can be compared with Formosa forms: Saaroa tabulu/bulu, Kanakanabu tabunu/bunu, Bunun bun/bun, but elsewhere: blu/blu, bul/bul, vul/vul; cf. also the following specialized root:

IN *upiʔ "leaf-sheath" (Ml.: of banana); T pli "bud or flower of banana (plantain)"; for the initial cluster, see AT, Table VI.

The following root has been developed into a generic term for "wild banana" in WT:

IN *buluŋ "foliage," but TB. "leaf," Ho. "young (= large) leaves"; T *tlooŋ "banana leaf (large leaf, used for wrapping, etc.)"; Dioi rɔŋ "large leaves of certain plants (banana, taro), used in wrapping"; WT tɔŋ "leaf of banana tree (domestic or wild, detached from the trunk to be used)," kɔ tɔŋ "wild banana tree," maʔ tɔŋ "flower of wild banana tree (edible)"; Mak tuŋ "coir palm leaf used as wrapper"; Kadai: Lq. tɔəŋ, S.Kl. gi ti <*tuŋ, Lt. li lu<*luŋ, all meaning "leaf."

COCONUT

IN *niyuɣ; Thai has two apparently isolated forms, showing different reflexes of final *-ɣ: Shan ʔun<*(y)uɣ, Tho yüa<

°yu(γ); OB (*mai-*)*ĭia* (Jer.), *zea* (Sav.); S. Li *un*, N.Li *dun*, dial. *ĭun*<*nyun*. The Tho and OB forms are perhaps "back loans" from Chinese (see Pt. 3). The IN root was long ago compared with Nicobarese (Austroasiatic) *oyau* "coconut tree," *niyau*~ *yinau* "coconut not ripe" (Schmidt 1906).

GINGER/PEPPER

Two roots are in evidence here:
1. IN *°t'a?aŋ*<*°saqaŋ* "sharp (tasting)": Tg. "strong (of wine)," Ml. "pepper," NgD. "Spanish pepper"; T *°xiŋ* "ginger"; KS: all *siŋ*, id.; OB *kiaŋ*; S.Li *khüöŋ*, WS Li *khüŋ*, id. The OB and Li forms are possible "back loans" from Chinese (see Pt. 3). The Thai and KS forms represent heavily palatalized developments (*AT*, 241); cf. the following:

	IN	Thai	Mak	Ong-Be	Li
eat	*ka/ən*	*kin*	*si:n*	*kon*	*khan*
ginger/ pepper	*°saqaŋ*	*xiŋ*	*siŋ*	*kiaŋ*	*khüöŋ*

2. IN *°liya* "ginger": SEP also "chili; pepper"; Sui *lyan* "hot, as pepper," Mak *li:n* "pungent, pepper"; reconstruction: AT *°liya/n*.

GOURD/CUCUMBER

IN *°balu?*<*°baluuk* "gourd"; T *°teeŋ/preeŋ* "cucumber," but WT "generic name for gourds," Dioi *tiaŋ* "cucumber," Sek *priaŋ*, id.; WS Li *piaŋ* "gourd"; for the initial cluster, see Note 3; cf. the following (see *AT*, Table VIII):

	IN	Siamese	Nung	Wu-ming (N.Thai)	Sek
gourd/ cucumber	*balu?*	*teeŋ*	*phe:ŋ*	—	*priaŋ*
bamboo/ withe	*bulu?*	*took*	*phio:k*	*ruk*	—

Mak shows a divergent correspondence in the above pair, with *pi:ŋ* "cucumber" but *duk* "bamboo withe."

The indicated reconstruction is AT *°baluaŋ/baluak*, with the Thai vowels showing palatalization.

RICE

Several distinct roots are represented here, with some indication of specialization of meaning: "rice as a cereal" (No. 3), "prepared (husked, cooked) rice" (No. 4), "rice plant or seedling" (No. 5), "rice as grain" (No. 6), and "rice as a meal" (No. 7). No. 1 shows a surprising extension (in OB and Li) to "sugarcane," the interpretation here being supported by a similar extension (in Hova) in root No. 5. This extension, which appears to be amply established by the above data, actually involves a greater semantic shift than the further extension in root No. 1 to "tree" via "bamboo" (Shan), since sugarcane grows in clumps to heights of over twenty feet, is segmented in nodal fashion, and is often described as being similar to bamboo. There are other extensions to "millet" (Nos. 1 and 3) and to "maize" (No. 4); for the latter, cf. also *SUGARCANE* (below). Finally, a separate root exists specifically for "rice bran."

1. IN **imay* "rice" (TB: in husk; Ml.: cooked); T **may* "tree, wood," but Shan also "bamboo"; OB *moi* < **mai* "sugarcane"; S.Li *mai*, WS Li *maːi* "sugarcane." Bupäli (N.Li dialect) *böi* < **möi* "rice (unhusked)"; *böi lob* "husked rice" probably also belongs here, but the possibility of "back loans" from Chinese (see Pt. 3) creates a problem here, e.g. WS Li *mai* "rice" (listed in category of foods, along with Chinese loan-word for "wine," etc.) appears to be such a borrowing, also N.Kl. *me* "cooked rice," yet the MFPL cites *tsou mou* "rice" (unspecified), which could be derived from a form such as **ma/i;* cf. also Lq. *mö* "millet."

2. Formosa: Yami *mugis* "rice" (general, also cooked); OB *mök* (Jer.), *mok* (Sav.) "paddy"; S.Li *mok* but N.Li *kok*, id.; Lt. *kuk ŋu* (MP dial.) but *mu* < **muk* (BP dial.), id. N.Li dial. forms *koʔ* < *kok* "paddy" were also recorded by Jeremaissen, but there is the possibility of borrowing from Chinese *kuk* "cereal" (general term) (see Pt. 3), as in WS Li *kuː?*, id. Lati *kuk/muk* shows a similar alternation of initials, however, and there is additional support for this in Chinese (see Pt. 3). Tho *khau kɔk* "paddy" is the only possible representative of this root in Thai, with the following forms appearing to be distinct:

Ahom *khau kak* "rice not properly husked"; WT *khau kaʔ* <

*kaak "paddy"; Mak *həu ka:k* "spiked millet," all in composition
with **qʀaw* "rice, millet."

Mak has *həu mo<*hmo* "wheat," perhaps related to Chinese
xmog "kind of millet or rice" (see Pt. 3).

3. IN **d'awa<*ɢʀawa* "millet"; T **xaw<*xraw/qraw* "rice,"
also "cereals" in WT and Dioi; N. Thai **ɣaw>*ɣraw* "rice"
(F. K. Li, 1957); Sek *ga:w* "rice"; OB *ŋao<*ʀao,* id.; KS: **qʀaw*
"rice": Sui *ʔau,* Mak *həu,* Then *xau,* Kam *ʔəu;* Mak *həu* is fully
defined as "rice, paddy [used before names of the five cereals]."
This root rather surprisingly has not been traced in any of the
Kadai languages. WT regularly has *x-* (literally *kx-,* possibly an
uvular affricate) for T **x-,* but has *kh-* in this root, perhaps because of the original cluster. OB *ŋao<*ʀao* is paralleled by OB
ŋa:ŋ "chin," IN **baɣʔaŋ<*baʀʔaŋ* (*AT,* 244 and Table V). The
unusual uvular cluster in this KS root has been reconstructed
with the aid of a strikingly parallel series for the root meaning
"inside," in which Sui shows the alternation *ʔau~ʀau.*

4. IN **bəɣat'<*bəɣa/s* "husked rice"; Si. *kăbrau<*bra/w*
"unhusked rice" (apparently isolated in Thai); Mak *həu pya*
"corn, maize" (cw. *həu,* No. 3); OB *phia<*phra* (Jer.), *tea*
(Sav.) "cooked rice"; Li *tha<*phra* "cooked rice," dial. *tha~
ta~ha,* id., also *ta* used in various phrases for "paddy" as well
as "cooked rice"; Lt. *yi* (MP dial.), *ye* (BP dial.)*<*ya<*ɣa*
"paddy." The connection of the Li forms is shown here by the
parallel development in the neighboring OB, which in the course
of some forty years, from Jeremaissen (ca. 1890) to Savina (ca.
1930), assimilated the labial cluster to a dental; cf. *mia* "come"
(Jer.), *nea* (Sav.). The final */s* in IN is paralleled in Formosa
in the root for "sugarcane" (see below). The Mak and OB forms
are in the same tonal series, but high and low, respectively, suggesting OB **phra<*bra.* The connection of the Si. form is uncertain, particularly in view of the semantic distinction, and it
is possible that this form belongs under root No. 3.

5. IN **pag'ay<*pagla/i* "rice plant, paddy" (Ml. *padi*), but
Ho. *fari* "sugarcane," *tsimpari/fari* "wild rice"; T **kla* "rice seedling," but BT "rice plant"; Sek *tla<*kla,* id.; OB *la<*kla* "rice
plant, rice seedling"; KS **kla* "rice plant"; N.Li dial.: Double
Cloth Loi *kɛi<*kai<*klai* "rice (row)" (growing), perhaps
also WS Loi *tsai* "corn." For the development of affricates or

spirants in IN from original clusters of velar + *r/l* type, see *AT*, 242. The N.Li form indicates that the added element /i in this root is of considerable antiquity.

6. IN *bə[t]iʔ* "roasted rice"; Lt. (both dialects) *ti* "rice in grain."

7. IN *ba[L]i* "rice as food (a meal of rice)," but Ho. "rice"; S.Li *bui* "cooked rice," perhaps related to *pui* (d.t.) "cooked" (of vegetables, meat, rice). This correspondence, like the preceding, is doubtful because of its highly restricted occurrence.

8. IN *ʐəɣami* "hay, rice-straw, stubble" (Dyen 1951); T *ram* "rice bran," but Ahom *ram* "rice," *ram mu* "powdered chaff."

SESAME

IN *ləŋa*; T *ŋa*, but Dioi and Wu-ming *ra*; KS: Sui ʔŋa~ŋa, Mak *ŋa*, Then *ŋya*; S.Li *ŋöü*; reconstruction: AT *lə[ʔ]ŋra*.

SUGARCANE

IN *təbu<*tagwu*; Formosa: *təbu/s*, with added /s as in IN *bəɣa/s* "rice"; T *ʔooy<*/wu/y* (dissimilation); Dioi has *ɔi* (l.t.), suggesting a lost nasal initial, perhaps *ŋwooy*; KS ʔoi generally, but ʔui in Jungchiang dialect of Sui; Mak has the phrase: *thoŋ ʔoi*, as if reflecting an original *thaŋʔui*; Li *ɔi* "maize," a semantic extension comparable to the interchange between "rice" and "sugarcane," the root for "rice" (No. 1) filling the "gap" in Li created by this shift.

YAM/SWEET POTATO

The sources show general confusion with "sweet potato," and there is much interchange also with "taro." The two most likely correspondences are as follows:

1. IN *ubi* "yam," the widespread root in IN and in Oceania in general, but "curiously limited" in SEP (Capell assigns to Movement IIA); S.Li *va:i* "sweet potato." These are regular phonetic correspondences, but the AT root can be reconstructed either as *ub(a)y* or *ugw(a)y*. The latter root, in nasalized form: *uŋgway*, is comparable with Oceanic: *ŋwaci~gwaci* (*ŋwadi, ŋwasi*) "a kind of yam" (Goodenough); cf. also Formosa: Sedik *buŋa*, Puyuma *boŋa*, Ami *voŋa~koŋa*, Atayal *ŋahi* (Egerod) "sweet potato"; Li dial. *ŋo~ŋou* "potato"; OB

(*ma-*)*phau*<***ʔŋau** (?) (cf. OB *phon* "cold," *AT*, 240), perhaps also Mak *za:u* "yam."

2. Formosa: *buɣasi "sweet potato": Rukai *boraθe*~*boraθi*~ *urasi*, Puyuma dial. *vurasi*, Paiwan *vorasi*~*vorati*; T *phrüak, variously defined as "yam" (Si., Lao, also Wu-ming dial. of N. Thai), "sweet potato" (Tho), "kind of potato" (Nung), "kind of edible root" (Ahom), "kind of tuber" (Shan), and "taro (tubercle)" (Dioi); KS: Sui *ʔɣak*~*ɣak*, Then *zyaak*, Kam *ʔya:k*, but Mak *pə:k* "taro";[9] OB *sak*<*phrak "taro"; Lq. *rɔ* "sweet potato." The indicated Sui-Thai reconstruction is *p[ʔ]*ɣaak*, showing general agreement with the Formosa form, but we should anticipate *p[ʔ]*ɣaat* for *b(*u*)*ɣat*<*buɣas(*i*); the indicated shift of final -*t* to -*k* after the glottal stop is paralleled in IN *bəɣʔat "heavy," T *hnak (see *AT*, 240), but Kam preserves the -*t* here (*hńə:t*).

The tendency to equate these cultivated plants with "tuber" or "root" is also found in IN *aka[L]~*waka[L] "root," but Sa. "wild yam"; cf. also Yami *wakai* "sweet potato," with possible relationships to T *raak "root" (via *ŋraak) and to forms cited above.

FOOD PREPARATION

This category is well represented, with a general term for "firewood/fireplace," with terms for utensils, such as "vessel," "dipper," and "ladle," and with additional terms for a number of very highly specialized kinds of food preparation: cooking in a bamboo container, cooking with steam, smoking/drying meat, pickling, and ripening fruit artificially.

COOK (IN BAMBOO CONTAINER)

IN *ləməŋ; T *hlaam; a very specific root not found elsewhere.

COOK (WITH STEAM)

IN *da(*n*)*daŋ* "to heat": Tg. "heated," TB. "singed," Sm. "roast," but Ja. and Ml. "steam pot"; T *thruŋ "cook (boil, steam)": Ahom "boil," Lao "distil, cook by steam," Nung "cook (as rice)," Dioi "cook in water," Cao-lan *thoŋ* "cook rice" (Haudricourt 1960), Sek *ruŋ*, id.; OB *hoŋ*<*throŋ "cook (rice), distil (alcohol)"; KS: all *tuŋ*<*truŋ "cook (boil) rice"; S. Li *da:ŋ*

"cook (rice)," *dra:ŋ* (d.t.) "roast (meat)," N.Li *lɔŋ* "cook (rice)";
reconstruction: AT *troŋ/droŋ* and *dra(a)ŋ*, with basic meaning "cook with steam or water," and "roast" as a later development (for the correspondences, see Pt. 3, Table V).

Thai has a root of closely similar meaning: *hnüŋ* "cook with
steam," Dioi *naŋ* "to stew, cook with steam," probably another
derivation of the same basic root via a form such as *bloŋ<
droŋ (cf. *BAIT*, below).

DIPPER (FROM COCONUT)

IN *tabu* "dipper": Tg.: made from coconut shell; Ja. *tawu*
"scoop up water," *tabon<*tabu/an* "coconut-shell"; T **?buay*
~*?büay* (Lao var.) "water-dipper made from coconut," but
WT *bu* "sort of pitcher (of bamboo, for drinking water)"; Si.
has a prefixed form: *kăbuay;* Mak *?be* "gourd," *?be tak nam*
"gourd for ladling water" (the vowel is irregular here); Li dial.:
Mefuli *peu* "dipper (of coconut shell)."

The following, with very restricted distribution, is an apparent
derivative of this root: Lao *?buaŋ* "spoon, ladle," BT *?buoŋ*
"spoon," yielding Vietnamese *muoŋ* "spoon" (*m-* for **?b-* is regular), an element of the old Thai stratum in that language.

FIREWOOD/FIREPLACE

IN *dapuγ<*dakwuγ* "fireplace": IN generally "fireplace,
kitchen," but MN: Sa. "leaves in which cooking is done"; PN:
To. *faka/?afu* "prepare the kitchen," Fu. *?afu* "to be hot," *faka/
?afu* "sit at the fire," Sm. *?afu* "to be hot," *fa?a/afu* "lay ready
the firewood"; T *vüül* "firewood," Dioi *fɛn*, Sek *vul*, id., yielding the reconstruction of final *-l* and showing correspondence
with IN *-γ*; OB *vön* (Jer.), *büön* (Sav.) "firewood"; S. Li *ŋun*,
N.Li *kun<*ŋun*, id.

The reconstruction here is AT *da(ŋ)kwuuγ*, as indicated
especially by the Li forms, with support for the final also from
Sek. Additional support comes from Vietnamese-Müöng, where
this root occurs as part of the early Thai stratum: Vietnamese
*kui (cui)<*kul;* Sach *kul*, Nguon *kun<*kul* "firewood."

The above forms all show end-stress development: *da'kwuuγ.*
Fore-stress: *'dakwuuγ* could have yielded the following:

T *taw* "fireplace, kiln," from *tab-<*tagw-.*

KS: Sui *dyət~dyet,* Mak *dit,* Then *zet,* Kam *tyət* "firewood," from **d(y)ak,* with final *-t* for *-k* after the front vowel; cf. *IRON/ SPEAR,* below.

LADLE

IN **k'i(n)ḍuk* "ladle" (Ml. "ladle out"), **t'anḍuk~*t'u(n)du* "ladle"; T **tak* "draw, dip up (water, rice)"; Mak *tak* "ladle," v., n.; OB *sak<*t(h)rak* "dipper"; reconstruction: AT **trak/ drak.*

PICKLE

IN **pəlaŋ,* based on Batak *poloŋ* "sour preparation from palm wine or gherkins and lemons, fermented with yeast from rice and fish" (cited in Wulff); T **ʔblooŋ* "to pickle, let become sour (various vegetables, also often with some maceration)"; for the initial cluster, see F. K. Li (1954); the indicated reconstruction is AT **palooŋ/balooŋ.*

RIPEN (ARTIFICIALLY)

Three sets of forms, all apparently related, can be distinguished here, with semantic associations for "warm" and "shut up, cover":

1. IN **pə[ʟ]əm* "ripen fruits artificially"; T **pom:* Tho *pom* "warm."

2. T: SW **ʔbom~*ʔbum* (Lao var.) "ripen fruit": Shan "cover over, as when plantains are ripened in the ground," Si. "shut up fruit, in order to ripen it."

3. T **ʔum/ʔo(o)m,* represented by Ahom *ɔm* "to bask a little in the sun," Shan *ɔm* "to warm oneself by the fire," Si. *kɔ:ŋ ʔɔ:m* "kind of ragout," Lao *ʔɔm* "macerate, make ripe in water, make simmer," also *ʔum* (d.t.) "cook slowly, let simmer," Nung *um* "to shut up (bananas) to make them ripe," Dioi *ɔm* "heavy heat (of weather); to ripen (as fruit)," also *um* (d.t.) "to warm up gently something covered or enveloped" (*um kyɔi=ɔm kyɔi* "ripen bananas"); cf. also WT *ɔm* "action of putting children to bed and to sleep"; Mak *ʔum* "spoiled, over-ripe"; OB *um da* "to cover the eyes (*da*)"; Li *üöm* "to warm oneself by the fire."

For AT we must reconstruct an infixed root: **p/ol/om~ *b/ol/om* "warm (oneself, something)," with specialization in the meaning: "ripen fruit artificially."

SMOKE, DRY (MEAT)

IN *ḍiŋḍiŋ* "dried meat" (TB. "smoked meat").

T *°ʔyaaŋ~°ʔyaŋ* (Lao) "smoke, dry (meat, fish, rice)," but Nung has *yɛŋ<*yeeŋ* "fumé" (of fish), *diɛŋ<*°ʔdiaŋ* "boucanée" (of meat); OB *teaŋ* "boucanée" (meat); reconstruction: AT *°ʔdyaŋ* (?) For the initials, see *AT*, 240; for the vocalism, see the analysis of "elephant" in Pt. 3.

VESSEL (CONTAINER)

IN *baŋa~*b/al/aŋa* "pitcher, pan, pot"; T *°ʔaaŋ* "basin, pitcher, jug, jar, pan." The prefixed form must be postulated here for the AT level, since the root without infix could have yielded only forms of the type *baŋ* or *ŋa*.

HUNTING AND FISHING

Less than half a dozen roots can be established in this category, but these few roots are of considerable interest. The general root for "hunt," with possible semantic association with "deer," has already been discussed (*AT*, 234-35), but in addition to this we have only a poorly represented root for "trap." For "fishing," on the other hand, there is no general root, but there is a root for the very specific method of "poisoning fish" (*AT*, 241 and Table IV), also two roots for "fishhook" and one for "bait," so that fishing can be considered an integral part of the AT cultural complex.

BAIT

IN *umpan<*umpla/n* (for initial, see *AT*, 244), also *pa/ən* (Dempwolff analyzes as "that which serves as food"); SEP *(m)panay*: Paiwa *vani*, Wedau *bani* "bait," but Dobu and Bwaidoga *bani* "hook." The basic meaning is "meat," maintained in Formosa: Rukai *bola/bola/i* and derived forms with infixed /t/, apparently also Tsou *beyia-*, Kanakanabu *ala-*, and Saisiat *bori*; the reconstructed form for Formosa is *b(u)la/i* "meat (flesh)," corresponding to IN *umpla/n* "bait."

The semantic interchange between "meat" and "bait" is also very much in evidence in Thai. The Thai root *hñüa* "bait" (in Shan, Kh., Si., Lao) has the meaning "flesh, meat" in BT and WT, which have "borrowed" this meaning from the widespread

Thai root: *nüa* "flesh, meat (esp. deer meat)." WT also has the curious pair: *ńam* "bait" and *ńam* (d.t.) < *hńam* "meat." The problem is further complicated by Si., which has the unusual doublet: *ʔbüa~nüa* "meat, deer," apparently matched by only one other in the language (see discussion of "urinate" in Pt. 3). The closest parallel in Thai is with the alternation *ʔb-~ʔd-*, for which the writer (1942) suggested the reconstruction *ʔbl-*, as in *ʔblüan* "moon" (Sek *ʔblian*). A possible reconstruction here is *ml-*, but this characteristically yields *m-*, *n-*, or *l-* in Thai (see the analysis of "louse" in *AT*, 235). To explain the *ʔb-* we must reconstruct the initial cluster as *[ʔ]m(b)l-*, with the diphthong *üa* developing in this "labial environment" (*AT*, 241). The reconstruction of this root for Thai thus becomes: *m(b)la/n* "meat," *ʔm(b)la/n* "bait," with /n/ > /m/ through assimilation.

The root as thus reconstructed throws much light on the curious forms for "meat" in N.Thai and elsewhere. Most N.Thai (Dioi type) languages have *no*, but Sek, which is archaic in its initial clusters, has *mlo*, in close agreement with our reconstructed form. KS *naan*, OB *nan* reflect the added /n. S.Li *mam*, N.Li *am*, dial. *xam~ham* show an assimilation of this element, as in WT, and alternative simplifications of the initial cluster. This simplification is carried even further in Kadai: Lq. *yeu*; N.Kl. *a*, but MFPL has *ya* ic. "eat," S.Kl. *hə*; Lt. *ho~o*.

Forms for "bait" are not available for these languages, so that it is not possible to determine whether the association with "meat" found in IN and Thai prevails everywhere, yet it does appear again in early Chinese loans from AT (see Pt. 3).

FISHHOOK

Two closely similar roots can be distinguished, and must be reconstructed for AT:

1. IN *kawit* "hook" (general term); T *ʔbet* < *g(a)wet* "fishhook," but Lao and WT "fishing line"; Mak *se:t* < *k(aw)et*, id. Thai has *ʔb-* for *gw-* under conditions as yet undetermined; cf. T *ʔba* "shoulder" < *gwaɣa* (see analysis under AX, below). Mak regularly assibilates velar stops (see *GINGER*, above); cf. also Mak *se* < *g(w)i* "ride a horse" (see Pt. 3).

2. IN *kawil* "fishing gear (Angel)"; OB *tin~tien* < *kwil*

"fishhook"; apparently isolated in OB, for which these are regular changes; cf. OB *tai*<*kwai/gwai* "buffalo."

HUNT

IN *buγəw* "put to flight, chase, hunt" (Dyen); T *praw* "hunt": not in SW Thai; N.Thai dialects have *tau*, but Tho *thau*, Nung *tik phiau* "hunt" (cf. *tik pia* "fish"="catch fish"); N.Li dial.: Bupäli *dop hau* "hunt" (cf. *dop hlou* "fish"="catch fish"). The parallelism with "fish" in both Nung and Li suggests that this root might refer basically to "something" that is hunted or caught (*AT*, 235), and this missing element is supplied by forms from Formosa: Paiwan *biau~viau*, Rukai *biau*, Puyuma *biao~viao* "spotted deer" (Chinese *hua lu*). Both the Nung and Li phrases might have been developed through analogy with "fish," however, from a basically verbal root; cf. also Formosa: Atayal *mhiau* "run after, chase, pursue" (Egerod); Sui *pyau*, Mak *ywaau* "run"; Li *dau*<*rau*, id.; perhaps also the Si.-Lao form *bra:n* "hunt; hunter."

POISON FISH

IN *tuba* "name of plant used for stupefying fish, fish poison"; T *ʔbüa* "poison," but Nung and Dioi "to poison fish." For the development *üa*<*a*, see *AT*, 241 and Table IV.

TRAP

IN *t'əlu*<*səru* "trap (as for rats)," but Ja. "fish-weir." T *h[r]aaw* "trap for animals" (Shan: for transfixing wild animals); reconstruction: AT *sər(a)u*. A palatalized doublet of this root is perhaps represented by T *reew* "snare, trap, net": Ahom "snare for a bird, piece of bamboo bent and tied in form of a snare," Si. "nets, snares," Lao "noose-trap for catching game," WT "trap for catching animals."

TOOLS ET AL.

This category is also represented by very few roots, but again the material is of unusual interest.

ARROW/GUN

IN *panah*: Tg., Ja. "arrow," Ml., NgD. "firearm"; MN: Fi.,

Sa. "shoot"; PN: To. *kau/fana* "bow," Fu. *fana,* id., Sm. *fana* "shoot," *au/fana* "bow"; Formosa: Ami *pana?,* Puyuma, Saisiat *papana?* "arrow"; T **püün* "arrow" (generally), but Si. "gun, cannon, firearm," Lao "gun; arrow." Thai has medial *-üü-* for **a/ə* in several roots, including **klüün* "swallow" (*AT,* Table VII), **?yüün* "stand" (*AT,* 240), **phüün* "flat" and **ʄüün* "lead," n. (both discussed in Pt. 3); cf. also the following, with the short (single) vowel: IN **t'akay<*saka/i* "climb, ascend"; T **xün<*xü/n,* Dioi *hen;* KS **kha;* OB *kan<*ka/n;* Li *khan <*kha/n.*

End-stress forms of this root are represented by Dioi *ńɛ<*nya* (palatalized) "poisoned arrow of crossbow"; Li *ńöü<*ńaü* "arrow." These forms supply evidence that a disyllabic root persisted to the proto-Thai period.

Schmidt (1906) made much use of the seeming correspondence between IN **panah* and the Mok-Khmer root represented by Mon *pah~poh* "hurl stones with a bow," *pnoh* "bow," analyzing the IN form as containing a "frozen" infix: **pa/na/h.* The present evidence makes this comparison unlikely, however, since one would have to postulate that both IN and Thai-Li *independently* evolved the meaning "arrow" from a basic meaning "bow/shoot" preserved in MN and PN.

The following correspondence is also of some interest:

SEP **takwana/tukuara* "arrow"; Capell compares Mota *tiqa* "shoot at a mark," Buruwe (Bougainville) *tek* "spear"; PN **teka* "dart"; Lakia (Li dial.) *teek* "arrow"; possibly also T **thuuk/thüük* "hit (target)."

AX

IN **bali[y]uŋ<*gwal/* "ax, hatchet"; Dempwolff defines it as "Schlichtbeil" (polishing hatchet), but Shellabear cites Ml. *běliuŋ* "the large Malay axe"; SEP **kira,* apparently related, but the phonetic development not clear; T **khwaan/xwaan;* KS **kwa(a)n;* Lt. *khu la* perhaps also belongs here. The indicated reconstruction is AT **qwal/ɢwal* or **kwal/gwal.*

The root cannot be analyzed further, but one is tempted to reconstruct it as **gwala/yuŋ* (with *a>i* before the *y*) and compare it with the similar root for shoulder: IN **baγa<*gwaγa;* T **?ba;* Sek *va;* Mak *ha<*gwa* (cf. Mak *həi* "water buffalo," T

grwaay); OB *wia* (Jer.), *bea* (Sav.); S.Li *va~van*, WS Li
va:ŋ<*va:n*<*gwa:l*; cf. also the further analysis of "ax/shoul-
der" in Pt. 3. The SEP form, if related, would point in this direction (*l~γ* alternation). One would thus hope to find an ultimate derivation for the root for this tool in the "shouldered
adze" so familiar to archaeologists in Southeast Asia.

BOARD/PLANK/TABLET

IN *papan* "board, plank" (Fi. "canoe planks"), but Ho. "writing slate"; T *peen* "flat; board, plank"; *pheen* "num. adj. for
flat things: planks, cloth, fishnets, mats": WT "side planks of
canoe"; *phüin* "num. adj. for flat things: books, mats, skins,
nets, clothes," Dioi *pɛn~bɛn* "num. adj. for flat things"; Mak
pa:n "flat"; OB *bien* "plank," *phan* "num. adj. for nets, mats;
spread (a mat)"; Li *pen* "num. adj. (clothes, paper)."

BOAT/CANOE

IN *baŋka*[ʔ]<*gwaŋkaak*: Tg. "boat," Fi. *mbaka/nava* "canoe without hollow space, log (single tree-trunk) canoe (Ein-
baum)," Sa. "boat, stranger"; also the following, a kind of doublet
form: IN *waŋkaŋ*<*ŋwaŋkaŋ* (?) "boat," but Fi. and all PN:
"canoe"; Formosa shows only the former root, in an unusual
pattern of occurrence: Tsou *apaŋu*, Kanakanabu and Saaroa
abaŋu, Rukai (western dialects only) *avaŋu*.

Li *yüöŋ*<*gwiaŋ* "num. adj. for boats." This root, which
stands for the simpler type of boat, has not been uncovered in
any of the mainland languages proper, yet it is found as an
early loan in Chinese (see Pt. 3). Li, an island language, has
retained another "maritime" root not found elsewhere: IN *kima*
"giant mussel"; Li (*sei*) *ma* "large shellfish, called benitier"
(this root has meaning "fishhook" in some SEP languages).

BOAT/RAFT

IN *paʟaʔu* "boat," the general term (Ml. *prau*), analyzed as
para/ʔu, probably a derivative of IN *paʟa* "framework" (possible reference to structure of more elaborate type of boat);
Formosa: Paiwan *baro/kor~varo/kor~varu/kur*, Rukai (eastern)
varo/kor, Saisiat *palo/no*, perhaps also Ami dial. *tsi/far* and
lo/nan; T *rüa*<*(p)ra* (see AT, Table IV); Dioi *ruö*, Sek *rua*,

all "boat"; Mak *ʔdwa~zwa* "raft," Kam *ʔlo<*plo* "boat"; OB *zoa<*roa,* id.; S. Li *da,* WS Li *fa<*bla/pla* (cf. the initial correspondences in *AT,* Table I—Group I).

BOW, n.

This root, like that for "arrow," reflects the effect of contrasting types of stress. It is minimally represented on Hainan or the mainland, the general Thai root **koŋ* "bow" being a derivative of the general root **koŋ* "bent, curved," Arch. Ch. showing a similar series, with *kı̆uŋ* "bow."

1. (fore-stress) IN **but'uγ* "bow"; Formosa: Ami *vutsir~futsir,* Bunun *buşul,* Rukai *buşu,* Tsou *fusuyu,* but Paiwan has heavily affixed forms of the type: *ti/vu/la/t/an,* indicating an analysis **but'/uγ* for the IN root (cf. also *AT,* 237 for final *-t'=-t*); Li *va:t* "bow, crossbow," WS Li *vat,* dial. *wat~wad* "bow," but Lakia dial. *vat* "shoot a bow." The *v(w)-=b-* correspondence is regular; cf. *YAM,* above. The single possible Thai cognate here is Lao *fot<*vot* "bough, branch."

2. (end-stress) Si. *son* "bow" (general term), written *sor* (Laj.) as if a loan-word, but an apparent doublet of *kăsun* "bow to shoot earthen balls" (Laj.). Si. also has written final *-r* (pronounced *-n*) in the general Thai root phrase **xraw-saan* "husked rice," which can now be reconstructed **-saal* on the basis of the Sek cognate: *gaw-sa:l* (no IN correspondence has been uncovered, but the root was borrowed by Chinese; see Pt. 3). This evidence suggests that Si. maintained a final liquid in the form *-r* until the very beginning of the historic period (thirteenth century), when it was replaced by *-n*.

In addition to the above, there is evidence for a root **p(h)leeŋ* "shoot an arrow" at the proto-Sui-Thai level; cf. Ahom *phriŋ* "throw off," Si. *phlɛ:ŋ* "muster all one's strength, as in shooting an arrow"; Sui *peŋ<*pleŋ* "shoot (arrow)" (from text in F. K. Li 1949). This root is a derivative of the general AT root: **balaŋ/buliŋ/bluŋ* "throw, fling" (*AT,* Table VIII).

SPEAR/IRON

IN **t'uligi<*t(h)uligi* (?) "spear"; T **hlek* "iron," but Dioi *riɛ<*riɛk* in the phrase *riɛ hao* "tin" (="white iron"); KS **khlet:* Sui *khət~hyət~set,* Mak *lit,* Then *let* (with assimilation of the final stop, and with initial *khl-<*thl-; (AT, 245 and Table VII); perhaps also Lt. khɛ<*khlɛk. The case for this correspondence is greatly strengthened by the presence of a precise parallel within AN, viz. IN *bət'i "iron," but Fi. *vesi* "name of spear." One would have to suppose that "spear" was the earlier meaning, at least in the IN-Thai correspondence. The root has been borrowed by Miao-Yao (Taipan Yao *hliet* "iron") and apparently also by Chinese (see Pt. 3).

STAIRS/LADDER

IN *aṇḍa<*andla "upward," but Ja. "ladder"; T *ʔday< *ʔdla/i "ladder, stairs," Si. kădai, Kh. hok-ka lai "wooden or bamboo steps leading up to the house," Shan kho lai "stairs," Tho duei<*ʔdwai<*ʔdlai, id.; Dioi lai "stone steps in front of a house," Wu-ming loi, Po-ai ai lai (cf. F. K. Li 1954). There is also a doublet root, without the added /i: *dra:

Ahom ša "ladder," Shan sʻa<*za~*dra "ladder formed of a single bamboo with pieces inserted horizontally for the feet"; Li ta~tha<*tra "ladder."

WEAVING ET AL.

This final group of roots indicates that weaving, plaiting, and similar household arts were already well developed at a proto-AT epoch.

EMBROIDER/KNOT

IN *ikət "twist, knot together" (the Ml. *ikat* technique).

T *koot "embrace," but Si., Lao "enlace"; *xoot "knot, tie in a knot": WT also "embroider" (type of Tai embroidery made with small rings in relief).

INDIGO

IN *taɣum; T *[t]hroom; Kh. and Shan have a variant *ron for the same plant (Ruellia); Mak yom "large-leafed indigo tree"; Li sieŋ. The variant final -n in Thai and the final -ŋ in Li suggest an original trisyllabic root of the type *taɣun/gw-. The initial t- has been reconstructed here (cognates are lacking in the Tho-Nung group, which is critical for this point), but a perfect parallel exists in the following curious series:

IN *tiɣəm* "oyster"; T *thram* "testicle"; Si., Lao *kăham*<
kăhram; Li *sa:m~śa:m;* Lq. *dəm,* both "fruit." The Li-Laqua
meaning is probably original; for the Thai semantics, cf. the
Western U.S.A. phrase "mountain oysters" (sheep testicles).

NEEDLE

IN *daɣum;* Formosa: generally from the IN root, with analysis indicated as *da/ɣum;* cf. Atayal *raom* but Sedik *qom/i;*
some Paiwan dialects show a distinct root: *ligim* (one dialect
has both *ligim* and *daom*), indicating a basic doublet root of
the type: */ɣum/gim.*

Thai and KS have developed their forms for "needle" from
different members of the doublet: T *khem/xem,* *khim/xim,*
but KS *khum:* Sui and Mak *sum<*khum,* Then *tshem,* Kam
thyəm. For the contrast between IN *daɣum/khum* (KS) "needle"
and IN *zəɣami/ram* (Thai) "rice bran," cf. Dyen (1953), who
presents evidence that IN *ɣ derives from two or more distinct
sources.

PLAIT/WEAVE

IN *lag'a* "plait or weave mats"; T *do* "weave," but Dioi
"twist (as thread)"; Mak *do* "plait"; perhaps also Lt. *so* "weave."
The following with added /n are also to be compared (*AT,*
233-34):

IN *dandan* "plait (cables)"; T *saan* "weave (baskets, mats),
plait"; Mak *saan,* id.

The indicated reconstruction is AT *dla/dla/n,* yielding *dwa
>*do* in Thai, paralleling the development *tulak>*ʔdwak
>*ʔduuk* "bone" (*AT,* 232 and Table I). The variant *dra/dra/n*
yielded *zaan>*saan* in Thai, which typically shows initial *dr-
~z-* alternation.

RATTAN/WICKER (BASKET)

IN *uway* "rattan"; T *hwaay;* Sek *va:y;* OB *boi<*wai.*

IN *ka[ʟ]and'aŋ* "wicker basket," a derivative of *[ʟ]and'aŋ*
"wicker-work"; T *zooŋ* "basket (loosely woven)": Ahom "cage,"
Shan "basket loosely woven with large meshes, generally long
and of small diameter," Si. "sheathe, envelope," Dioi "cover (of
lid), wicker jacket (of jar), basket (for carrying pigs)"; Tho-

Nung shows a variant: **troŋ/soŋ*: Tho *tuŋ* "trap (cage, basket, for birds)," *suŋ* (s.t.) "cage, basket (for birds, fowl)," Nung *soŋ* "cage"; another variant is represented by Kh. *thüŋ<*thraŋ* "large wicker basket"; Shan *üŋ<*(dr)aŋ* "large wicker basket, four cornered at the bottom and round at the top"; reconstruction: AT **droŋ/troŋ* and **draŋ/traŋ*.

The root is distinct from the following:

IN **kaʟuŋ* "bag," but Ho. "basket"; T **khlooŋ/klooŋ* "basket (esp. the suspended type)": Wu-ming (N.Thai) *kloŋ* "basket" (F. K. Li 1954).

SEW/EMBROIDER

IN **d'aʔit* "sew": Formosa has the same root, both prefixed: **m/taʔit*, and infixed: **t/im/aʔit;* IN also has **t'uŋkit* "to pick": Ho. "work with a sharp instrument," NgD. "embroidery," Sm. "thread a needle, embroider."

T **khwit∼*kwit* (Lao var.) "pierce, thrust in," but BT *tam huʔ khwit* "sew (in making designs)" (*tam huʔ* "weave"), Lao "thrust in, embroider." The initial **khw/kw-*, unusual before front vowel in Thai, perhaps reflects an original post-velar, as indicated by IN ?, yielding the reconstruction: AT **/q(w)it*.

T **tam* "prick" is another possible derivative of this root via an infixed form such as that cited for Formosa: **tam=*tim/;* cf. below under *WEAVE*.

SEW/PLAIT

IN **añam* "plait"; T **ñap∼*ñep∼*ñip* "sew"; Li *ñop*, id. The final *-m* is retained in the early Chinese loan (see Pt. 3). The affiliation of KS: Sui, Mak *tip,* Then *tiep* "sew"; Lq. *thɛm*, id.; S.Kl. *(dü) thɛ,* id. is uncertain, but an original cluster in this root is a possibility.

WEAVE

IN **tənun;* Formosa: Bunun *tinun*, but elsewhere the root generally appears with the characteristic Formosan *-m-* infix, the vowel varying: Atayal *taminun/təminun*, Yami and Sedik *tuminun*, Paiwan *timinun;* T **tam* (d.t. from **tam* "prick," above under *SEW*); Mak *tam*. This is the most likely instance of the incorporation of this infix, and as such tends to tie the mainland language closer to Formosa (although this infix is not restricted to this area in IN). For a similar instance of infixed -*l*-, see *AT*, 254.

2. KINSHIP TERMS

The 1942 paper included in its list of common Thai-Indonesian roots only one kinship term (grandfather), but we are now able to present a substantial number of such terms. In the present study, special attention is given to the material from Capell and Lester (CL) on Fiji (listed simply under this heading), since this area offers striking parallels to the Thai kinship system (see discussion below). Abbreviations follow the system previously employed by the writer.[10]

CHILD

IN *anak<*alwak*, from root *lak* "to develop"; also *laki* "man, adult (married man)" (but in Formosa generally "child"); Fiji *luve*, Bulu (Celebes) *lowai* (cited from CL).

T *luuk<*lwak* (*AT*, Table I); KS *laak*; OB *lök-*; S.Li *lek*, N.Li dial. *hlok~hlök*; Lq. *zio<*lyok*; N.Kl. *lə ye<*lyak*; S.Kl. *hla*; Lt. *li i~le e*, all for *(h)lak*.

FATHER

IN has three different roots here, and all are represented on the mainland, although No. 1, the widespread term in AN, is present only in one language. The common mainland root is related to No. 2, which is mainly an IN root.

1. *ama*; Kl. *ba<*ma*; ə *ba<*a ma*; this development appears to be indicated by the earlier MFPL citation: *a ma*, directly comparable with the IN root.

2. *bapa*; OB (*nö-*)*ba*; S.Li *fa<*pha*, N.Li *ba*: dial. *pa~ba*; Lq. *pe<*pa*; Lt. *pu<*pa*. The Thai and KS terms for "father" appear to have been developed from the root for "grandfather" (below).

3. IN *ayah* (Demp. cites IN forms only); T *ʔaay* "eldest son or brother," but BT and WT "father"; also T *ʔüay* "eldest female (esp. sister)." The original root meaning here was perhaps "eldest," with partial specialization in meaning "father."

GRANDCHILD

Oceanic *pagwun* (Haudricourt); Formosa: Rukai (eastern) *agani;* (Western) *aganu, haganu, taganu* (?); T *hlaan* "grCh, N"; KS: *qhlan* (see Note 7): KS *qhan~khan~han,* Then *laan* (h.t.) "grCh," Mak *laan* (h.t.) "grCh, N," but then further defined as "SiCh, DCh" and as "FSiD" (the cross-cousin preferred in marriage—see discussion below); Li *han* "N"; reconstruction: AT */q(h)lan,* whence Oceanic *gwun.*

GREAT-GRANDCHILD

Oceanic *hakwelin* "xC"; T *hlen~*hlin* "ggrCh, gN." For the semantics, cf. the above root (and the discussion below).

GRANDPARENT

Two different roots are in evidence, one with very limited distribution both on the mainland and in Oceania (Fiji), the other with broad extension and complex semantic differentiation.

1. Fiji *tai:* Western term applied to all gPs; in southwest, applied reciprocally to grCh. CL analyze it as a derivative of *ta + i* "father of" (either M or F), hence consider its extension to female relatives (gM) as "entirely illegitimate." The Nadrau term, *tatai* "FM," is the source of some anguish for these authors, who in effect explain that they cannot explain it. In Thai, however, Dioi and Nung have *tai* "MM," suggesting that the original meaning of this root might have been "grM" rather than "gF," thus affording some contrast with the following root. Possibly related are the Thai terms *ta* "MF" and *naay* "MM"; the first of these is also represented by Lq. *te<*ta* "grF"; Lati *tö* (*le*), id.

2. IN *pu* "sir" (app. the basic root, preserved here only as a term of respect); *ə(m)pu* "grandparent, grandchild (reciprocal term)," but NgD. "parents-in-law"; *makəmpu* "grandchild" (Fi. and PN); *[t]umpu* "ancestor; sir" (Sm. "king").

SEP: Capell cites only forms derived from *əmpu* "ancestor," which he divides into two groups (i) without initial vowel: limited in SEP to Motu *bubu* "term of address to elders." This is also said to be the normal word for "gP" (vocative) in Malekula and other parts of the New Hebrides, but Fiji has *mbu* "grM" (ii) with initial *a*: Paiwa *yavu,* Mukawa *abu,* Ubir *avu,*

Wedau *avu,* Wagawaga *au,* all "MB." These are described as "Philippine forms" and are assigned to Movement IIA, whereas those under (i) are said to belong to a different stratum of the language, and one that in IN is more general.

Fiji: **tubu,* analyzed as *t/ubu* (*t-* prefixed element found in other kinship terms there, e.g. *t/ama* "F"), used generally in reciprocal sense: "grP, grCh," as in IN **ə(m)pu,* but in some systems (Lau, Bau) applied only to females. CL also note, as "a very important, although rare, variant of this use," the application of this term to "MB" and/or "MBW," in two parts of Vanua Levu (Macuata and Bua). They further point out that the same root is also found in the meaning "MB" in Florida and in southern Ysabel (Bogotu and Nggao) of the Solomon Islands. They further point out that all these areas are (or have been) matrilineal, and remark, "it cannot be without significance that they [these specialized meanings] occur just in these regions," but they make no attempt at explanation (see discussion below for this).

T **pu* "FF"; W.S. Li *phəu* "grF"; Kl: MFPL *a wu* "FF."

T **ʔaaw<*awu<*abu<*apu* "FyB" (see above for medial *-w-<-b-* in Thai); cf. the analysis in Benedict 1943. Thai also has the root **ʔa* (phonemically *ʔaa*) "FySi," although in Siamese the two forms have merged (*ʔaa*).

T **phua* "H"<**phu/a* appears to be from the same root; cf. T **mia* "wife"<**mi/a* (see below).

T **bo* "F" appears to be another derivative of the basic root, in view of the apparently cognate KS form: **bu* "F."

IN-LAW

There are two roots here, each applied at times to affinal relatives (Ego's generation or younger, rarely older) of either sex:

1. **hipaγ<*hikwaγ* "related by marriage": Tg., Ja., also Sa. "B-in-law," Ml. "related by marriage" (Shellabear cites *ipar* "B-in-law, S-in-law"), Fi. *ra/iva* "HSi." CL add, "The western Fijian dialects have *iva* in its original sense [related by marriage]."

T **khüay~*khöy* (Si.)~**güay* (Dioi) "male affinal kin," applied to PySiH, SiH, DH, NiH, grDH (Benedict 1943). Lao defines the term itself as "marry, marriage," and WT as "serve as a son-in-law" (matrilocal residence); the root appears to be a semantic extension of T *göy (s.t.) "to be familiar with, acquainted with." The final shows replacement of -γ with -y, as in other roots (see above). Li *töü*<*kwiya* "S-in-law" is definitely cognate, since Li has initial *t*- for *kw*- (cf. *BUFFALO*, above). The KS root is perhaps distinct: Sui *hau*, Mak *zaau*, Then *thaau* "S-in-law."

2. IN *t'awa* "spouse"; *bayaw* "relationship by marriage" (Demp. cites only Tg. *bayao*, TB. *bao*); apparently from a trisyllabic root *sab(w)ayaw*.

SEP *sawa* (often with prefixed *ka*-), usually in meaning "wife."

Fiji: *ćawai* "WP, WM," but Vuda has "WF, DH, SW." CL comment, "It ought, phonetically, to answer to IN *sawa*, but original IN *t'awa* is 'spouse,' not spouse's parents or any other affinal. So the equation must be rejected." In view of the Thai data, this rejection now seems premature. Note also that the SEP root has a final -*i* that cannot be explained on the basis of *sawa* itself, but which is readily explained in terms of the longer root *sa(b)wayaw*.

T *baü*~*sabaü* (Si.) "female affinal kin," applied to PyBW, BW, SW, NeW, grSW (Benedict 1943). It is the precise feminine equivalent of the Thai term under No. 1 above. Thai final -*aü* at times appears to be a reflex of *-aya*, so that the reconstructed form for this Thai root is *sabaya*. This is an apparently unique example of the retention of a trisyllabic form (reconstruction) in Thai.

T *ʔbaaw*: generally defined as "young unmarried man," also "sweetheart," but also "fiancé" in Lao, while Si. has the additional meaning "bridegroom." This appears to be another derivative of the same basic root, with medial -*y*- simply dropping: *-ba(y)aw*.

The nature of the original distinction between these two affinal terms is not clear; possibly No. 1 was originally "affinal kin (general)," while No. 2 was "spouse."

MOTHER

IN *ina* "M," *binay* "W"; KS *ni; Kl: MFPL *a nai* "M." Note that Kl. (MFPL) has preserved the most common roots for "F" and "M."

In general, the mainland languages have forms with initial

m- and front vowel *i* or *e; cf.* T *me "M," *mia<**mi/a* "W"; OB *mai* "female" (M, W); Li *mei* "female (all living things)," also "W"; Lq. *məi* "woman, mother" (also used as feminine suffix); S.Kl. *i mie* "woman"; Lt. *mia* "M" (also used as feminine suffix)," *ni mia~li me* "wife, girl."

SIBLING

The roots involved here are difficult to analyze, but the following pair can be postulated:

1. Fiji: not clearly represented in Fiji itself, but CL discuss the terminology of central-marginal Polynesia, which has *huŋavai* for "affinals of the senior generation," as contrasted with *hunoŋa* "affinals of the younger generation." This suggests that *huŋavai* must be analyzed as *hun/gavai*, with *gavai having a general meaning, such as "elder."

T *bi<**gw(a)y*<*gaway "older sibling"; KS *khwaay or *xwaay, id.: Sui *fai*, Mak *va:i*, Then *xwa:i*. On the basis of the Thai development, we can also identify as probable cognates: OB *böi* "oSi"; Li dial. *bɛi*, id.; Lq. *pəi*, id.

This root is perhaps related to the Oceanic root for "old" (above).

2. IN *a(ŋ)*g′i*: generally "ySb" in IN, MN, PN, but Tg. "aunt"; *ha(ŋ)*g′i*: NgD. and Sa. "Sb of other sex"; To. *fa/ʔahi* "kin," *ta/ʔahi/ne* "D in relation to the M"; reconstruction possibly **(h)a*(ŋ)*gli*.

T *ʔeeŋ*: represented only by Lao *ʔɛŋ* "F," Tho *ɛŋ* "young" (*luk ɛŋ* "Ch").

OB *eŋ(-tok)* "yB" (Jer.), *eŋ-ne* "oB" (Sav.); S. and N.Li *ɛŋ* "oB," but one Loi dialect has *eŋ* "oSi," *eŋ-hoaŋ* "ySi." Annamese has *anh*<*iŋ "oB," analyzed as part of the old Thai stratum in that language (Benedict 1947).

The vocalism of the mainland forms probably represents a form of assimilation to the front vowel of the second element of the root. The original meaning seems to have been "younger sibling" or "younger kin," with some reciprocity, as in To., thus explaining seemingly unrelated meanings such as Tg. "aunt" and Lao "F."

3. IN *bətaw "Sb of the other sex" is perhaps to be interpreted as originally meaning "of the same birth"; cf. *tawu "man"; also

*bətu "appear," but some forms of the root have meaning "to be born" in Southeast Solomons (Capell 1943); Dioi *tau* "to be born, go out," but Lao *tau* "Ch," Si. *luuk tau* "sons and daughters, family" (*tau* "paps"); S.Li *təu* "give birth," but N.Li *tləu*, indicating an original complex cluster for this root. The Formosa material definitely points to an original cluster in the word for "man," with Puyuma having a retroflex stop in this series (cf. Note 3):

	IN	Paiwan	Puyuma	W. Rukai
eye	*mata*	*matsa*	*maṭa*	*matsa*
man	*tawu*	*tsau/tsau*	*ṭao*	*utsao*

WOMAN (MARRIED), WIFE, AUNT

Fiji *lewa~*lewe* "woman; wife."

T *lua~*liau* "female affinal kin": BT *lua* "aunt"; Ahom *lu* "oBW," *liu* "FSi"; Nung *lua~lu~liu* ic. "D-in-law; married woman; bride"; Dioi *me lea:u* "FyBW," *ya lea:u* "yBW."

Mak *li* "D-in-law," *a:u li* "take a wife."

Li (*dü*) *liu* "D-in-law," *kɛʔ liu* "take a bride."

SUMMARY (ON FIJI)

We are not at this time in a position to attempt a reconstruction of the AT system of kinship terms, but should like to call attention to the remarkable parallelism between the Fiji system (with its many variations) and the Thai pattern, as described in detail in Benedict 1943. Five different points can be made in this connection:

1. Four grandparent terms are a feature of the Thai system, a feature which sets it off from other systems in Southeast Asia. CL emphasize their finding that four terms here are also basic to the Fijian system, although there have been drastic modifications in these terms.

2. Reciprocity is a noteworthy feature of the Fijian system, and is prominent in IN generally, as reflected in some of the roots presented above. This is particularly seen in the "grP— grCh" terminology, and an unusual example of this is found in Thai, viz. Ahom *lin* "ggrF," from the root *hlin* "ggrCh" (see above).[11]

3. Both the Thai and Fijian systems have special terms for "parents of in-laws" (reciprocal), the Thai root being *?doŋ, possibly from a root for "house" (AT, 250).

4. Thai equates "N" with "grCh," creating a kind of "skew" in the system. The writer (1943) interpreted this as simply a reflection of the equation of PSb with gP, e.g. if Ego calls his uncle "grF," his uncle must call him "grCh," since the relationship is a reciprocal one, and he presented some data on this equation in Thai. He compared this with similar phenomena in the Tibeto-Burman terminologies, particularly Tibetan and Lushei, and put forward a suggestion that an earlier pattern of unilateral xC marriage and teknonymy might have given rise to these findings (for a full discussion of this complex subject, see the writer's papers on Tibetan and Chinese, also on the Annamese system). With continued teknonymy in the kind of framework described, the xC (equated with Sb-in-law) also becomes identified as "gF" or "uncle," and the Oceanic *hakwelin "xC" apparently represents this type of semantic development. The SEP and Fijian equation of "gP" with "MB," which CL have presented without explanation, is simply one aspect of this over-all process.

Teknonymy is very prominent in the Thai system (Benedict 1943), but no reference to preferred xC marriage in this group has yet been uncovered. The closely related Mak language, however, shows the full semantic development: la:n "grCh, N," but then further defined as "SiCh, DCh" (the unilateral or skew feature) and finally as "FSiD" (the xC). F. K. Li, who recorded this key language, has included the significant phrase: ?a:u la:n "to marry a FSiD (very common)" (transl. from Chinese). This affords strong support for our theory of an original unilateral xC marriage pattern for Thai (and KS and Kadai).

We come now to Fiji, which has been regarded as one of the "homes" of xC marriage ever since the days of Lewis H. Morgan (CL). CL tend to minimize this as an original or ancestral trait, although they note the association with the equation "gF"="MB" (above). The striking fact is that in Bau and Nadrau, and in eastern Fiji generally, the *prescribed* form of marriage for a man is with FSiD, e.g. "Bauan custom limits the type marriage to the *davola*—who is Ego's FSiD, though allowing him to marry the MBD as a second best." Thus we have in Fiji an exact replica of the mainland feature.

5. Thai makes a basic distinction in siblings between "older" and "younger" rather than "B" and "Si," and CL conclude that this type of distinction is also basic in Fiji (and AN generally).

6. Thai has an unusual, highly specific, set of PSb terms, which has hitherto defied explanation:

(Feminine)	(Common)	(Masculine)
pa PoSi	*na* MySb	*luŋ* PoB
ʔa FySi		*ʔaaw* FyB

Note that the collaterals are merged in the terms for PoSi and PoB but distinguished in the PySb terminology, with a careful distinction between FyB and FySi. As we have seen above, the term $**ʔaaw$ FyB appears to be a derivative formation: $**ʔapu$ or $**ʔabu$, from the versatile root for "gF." The strange Thai PSb terminology in fact seems to have come about in response to a need for a specific term for FyB. Now the FyB has a very specific function in the levirate, and this has been described for two different Thai groups, the Shan and the Nhang (see the citations in LeBar et al.), as well as for the Lati (Bonifacy 1906). The levirate, known as *curuyada*, also formed part of the Bauan (Fiji) practice (CL), and has been reported for the Li of Hainan, who show Indonesian cultural traits not found among the mainland Kadai groups (Cheng and Liang 1945).

The Oceanic word *tabu,* of unknown etymology, is perhaps to be explained simply as $*t/abu$=FyB (perhaps also other kin covered by the ubiquitous root $*pu$~$*bu$), with prefixed *t-* as in $*t/ama$ "F." In Colo West (Fiji), for example, the compound term *o qu tabu* "my avoided person" is applied by a woman to the HB, and the origin of the term *tabu* may well have been in the magically charged environment of kinship practices, especially avoidance rules related to incest.

SUMMARY ON KINSHIP TERMS

This analysis of the kinship terms of the mainland languages and the related AN languages, especially in Fiji and SEP, strongly suggests that an archaic kinship system with very specific features, as delineated above, underlies the present terminologies found in this broad area. One might argue that the structural features, although very similar in several details, could be the results of independent development or convergence. In the present case, however, we are also confronted with a substantial number of kinship terms shared by these several languages and/or language-complexes, hence the hypothesis in general seems difficult to refute.

NOTES

¹ Phonetic symbols are used here as in the 1966 article, referred to as *AT*, except for ? for Dempwolff's medial and final *h*, and *h* for his medial ' (following Dyen). The following corrigenda are to be noted for the AT article:

p. 238, line 14: read: for IN *-t'*
p. 239, line 6: read: Final *-b* and *-d*
p. 240, line 8: read: and IN **pahit*
p. 241, line 10: read: Dioi **?dən*
p. 242, line 6: read: in **γumah*<**γuŋwaa- waa-*
p. 245, line 3: read: with **iwak* "fish"
p. 247, line 6 from bottom: read: with initial *m*
p. 248, line 1: read: as in "3" and "louse"
p. 252, line 18: read: KS: Sui *khui~qhui*
p. 254, line 6: read: IN **ka* "eat"
p. 256, line 15: the *-hw-* yielding
p. 259, line 29: read: to *g'* in Demp.

For REFERENCES, add Milke. Comment in Capell 1962.

² The Sek are incorrectly classified as Mon-Khmer in LeBar et al. 1964, according to William Gedney of Michigan University (personal communication), who is now preparing a full study on this language.

³ This new evidence from Sek and Lakia speaks strongly in favor of reconstructions for AT of the type: **mapra* "eye" and **maprai* "die," the latter tying in directly with S.Kl. *ple u* (*AT*, Table IX). The distinctions made by the Kadai languages as well as by Kam-Sui in these two roots perhaps reflect morphophonemic factors, since the forms for "die" are derived from original prefixed forms. The writer agrees with F. K. Li (1957) in rejecting the suggestion by Haudricourt (1956): *mata*>*mda*>*pda*>*pra*, but he follows the latter in giving full value to early recordings, e.g. in Laj. (1906), showing initial *p(h)y-* in these roots; both Li and Haudricourt appear to have over-

looked the form *rem pia* "eye" cited by V. K. Ting (1929) for a Chuang group in N. Kwangsi. It is now clear from recent work by Japanese linguists (see Haudricourt 1965) that Paiwan and Puyuma (Formosa) distinguish a class of retroflex stops: *ṭ* and *ḍ*, which have fallen together with *t* and *d* elsewhere in IN and Oceania, and that these retroflex stops appear to correspond to clusters previously reconstructed by the writer (1966), e.g. Formosa *maṭa* "eye," **matla* (AT, 247); Formosa *kuṭu* "louse," **kut(a)lu* (AT, 230). The validity of this general line of reconstruction appears to be amply supported, although the details of the clusters remain to be worked out. The writer and Haudricourt are in complete agreement as to the need to grant to at least some of the Formosan languages a separate classification from IN and from the Oceanic languages in general, and this more recent material would appear to settle this point beyond any doubt.

[4] Haudricourt (personal communication) has completed an article on Lakia, based on a Chinese publication of 1959, to appear in BSLP, 1967. The few forms provided by Haudricourt show that this language (also written Lakkia) is entirely distinct from the Lakia dialect of Li, recorded almost a century ago by R. Swinhoe (1871) (this dialect cited below, under BOW).

[5] Abbreviations are as in Benedict 1966. The following are in addition: Anc. Ancient; AD *Analytic Dictionary* (Karlgen 1923); Arch. Archaic, AT Austro-Thai (also, italicized, stands for "Austro Thai" article, Benedict 1966); Ch. Chinese; CL Capell and Lester (1945-46); GSR *Grammata Serica Recensa* (Karlgren 1957); Jer. Jeremaissen; Sav. Savina; SW Southwest group of Thai languages (Ahom, Khamti, Shan, Si., Lao, BT, WT), ST Sino-Tibetan; TB Tibeto-Burman; WS White Sand.

[6] Haudricourt sets up a special "Eastern Tai" group for these languages, but the writer follows F. K. Li in placing them in the Northern Thai group, along with Dioi.

[7] The Li-Ngam dialect of Sui (abbreviated SLN) has a few pairs in which Li has initial *qh-* for Ngam *kh-*, and these appear to be derivatives of **q(h)l-*, as in *qhau~khau* "wine," *qhan~khan* "nephew" (Pt. 2); cf. also Lakia *khyau* "alcohol," *khyan* "grandson" (see Note 4).

[8] This Si. form is related to Lao **hmiəŋ* "tea, evening repast (of monks)," Shan and Kh. *neŋ<*hmliaŋ* "tea" (generic term, also used alone in sense "fermented tea"). This "fermented tea" trait-complex has apparently replaced an earlier areca-betel

complex; cf. Frank M. LeBar, "Miang: Fermented Tea in North Thailand," *Behavior Science Notes*, 2 (1967), 105-21.

⁹ See F. K. Li 1954, for this root, the reconstruction being supported by Wu-ming *plüak* "yam" (Wu-ming lacks *r*). Sui has a parallel form in **ʔɣum* "lean," T **phroom*, id., contrasting with *pyam* "hair," T **phrom*, id.

¹⁰ Kinship abbreviations are as follows: B brother, C cousin, xC cross-cousin, Ch child, D daughter, F father, g great, gr grand, H husband, M mother, N nephew/niece, Ne nephew, Ni niece, o older, P parent, Sb sibling, Si sister, S son, Sp spouse, W wife, y younger. These are directly combined, e.g. MM mother's mother, SpB spouse's brother, etc.

¹¹ The first reasonably complete list of kinship terms for any Kadai language has now been made available, for White Sand Li (Wang Li), and this shows reciprocity of precisely the same kind as that encountered in Indonesian: *phəu* "grF" but *pəu* "grS" (grF speaking), from the AT root **pu*. There is also a parallel set of terms: *tśa:l* "grM" but *źa:l* "grS" (grM speaking), with equivalent phonological alternation of initials. These terms are used in combination with *hlök* "Ch," and are distinct from *hlök a* "grCh" (someone else's). We can now with confidence reconstruct reciprocity of this type for the AT kinship system, with indicated general loss in Thai.

Austro-Thai Studies:

3. Austro-Thai and Chinese

Paul K. Benedict[*]

We come now, finally, to the fundamental question as to the nature of the relationship between Austro-Thai and Chinese. The problem is a highly complex one, and the writer has come to his present view through a succession of stages, as follows:

1. When the writer entered the field in the late 1930s, first as a student of Chinese and later of TB, a very simple scheme of relationships obtained, diagramed as follows:

$$\text{Sino-Tibetan} \begin{cases} \text{Western Division} \begin{cases} \text{Tibeto-Burman} \\ \text{Karen} \end{cases} \\ \text{Eastern Division} \begin{cases} \text{Chinese} \\ \text{Thai} \end{cases} \end{cases}$$

The real problem about this schema is why anyone with more than a smattering of linguistic training ever believed in it. Chinese and Thai are both tonal and essentially monosyllabic, to be sure, but on this basis they might equally well be grouped with similar languages in West Africa or Mexico. They have the same subject-verb-object syntactical arrangement, but in Chinese the determinant precedes, while in Thai it follows (as in IN and Kadai; see *AT*, 253-54). When the "nuclear"[1] lexical elements are studied, they are found to be neatly divided, with Chinese and TB on one side, Thai and IN on the other:

---

[*] Paul K. Benedict's two previous articles appeared in *Behavior Science Notes 1*(1966): 227-61 and *2*(1967): 203-44. The first was entitled "Austro-Thai," and the second, "Austro-Thai Studies," included sections on (1) "Material Culture" and (2) "Kinship Terms." The current article completes Dr. Benedict's study. All three of the articles, plus a complete glossary of Austro-Thai terms, will be published in book form by HRAF Press early in 1968 under the title "Austro-Thai."

Table I

	TB	Arch.Ch.	Thai	IN
eye	*mik/myak*	*mĭôk*	*ta/pra*	*mata*
die	*si/s*	*sĭər*	*taay/praay*	*matay/patay*
louse	*śrik*	*şĭɛt*	*thraw*	*kutu*
eat	*dza[?]*	*dˊˀɪ̯ək*	*kin*	*ka/ən*
fire	*hwar/bar*	*xwâr*	*vay*	*apuy*
weep	*khrap*	*kˊĭ̯əp*	*tay/hŋay*	*taŋi/s*

The results of attempting to put together two languages thus "unequally yoked" are manifest in Shafer's paper (1940-41) on the vocalism of ST (in which he includes Thai); the tables of comparisons consist largely of those between Chinese and TB on the one hand and Chinese and Thai on the other, surrounded by large white spaces representing the gaps. Apart from the numerals, the roots bridging these gaps are almost exclusively on the order of "tea," "cards," and "gluel" The writer must confess that he too became involved in this hopeless task, as can be seen from random comparisons in his earliest studies (1939, 1940).

2. About 1940 the writer, having unsuccessfully wrestled with this problem for some time, attempted to fit some of the other languages of Southeast Asia into the picture. He came upon four languages, poorly recorded and little known (Li, Laqua, Kelao, and Lati), which he was finally able to put loosely together into a single language stock (Kadai). The best known of these languages, Li (Hainan), has numerals which are unmistakably related to IN numerals, as well as some other IN elements, along with much Thai material. The writer at first thought that he was dealing here with a basically IN language which had come under Thai influence, but it soon became apparent that many of the "nuclear" elements occurred in all or most of these languages, and that a Thai-Kadai-IN language complex must be postulated. All now seemed straightforward, and this "new alignment" appeared in an article in 1942. In this paper, Thai is presented as a language basically of Indonesian (and Kadai) affiliation, which has been deeply affected by Chinese, from which it has borrowed a sizable number of roots (mainly of "cultural" type), a complete tonal system,[2] and monosyllabic speech

habits. So firmly was the reigning "China doctrine" ensconced in the writer's view of the world (Southeast Asia) that he did not even mention the *possibility* of any cultural flow in the other direction!

3. The writer went happily along in this state of error until 1965, after the appearance of *Ethnic Groups of Mainland Southeast Asia* (LeBar et al. 1964), which accepted the Thai-Kadai linkage but hedged about IN. This led him to a review of the whole matter and eventually to the setting up of an AT language stock, including the Kam-Sui (KS) languages described by F. K. Li, with attempts to work out some of the basic phonology (Benedict 1966). In the course of this research, and entirely as a by-product, he noted that certain of the "Chinese loan-words" apparently had AT origins! The root for "cattle," for example, had always created a problem, since the Chinese form, *ŋiəu< *ŋu, should have yielded Thai *ŋaw rather than the actual Thai root: *ŋwa, and it would scarcely serve to explain forms like Mak *pho< *khwo. If we begin with AT forms such as *ləngwu/ la(ŋ)gwaw (see Part 1),† however, we can readily explain the Thai and Mak forms as well as the Chinese, with the latter obviously representing the "end of the line" in the diffusion process. The writer gathered together several such roots, placing primary emphasis on the culturally important roots for "cattle," "goat/ sheep," "rice," "sugarcane," and "plough." He concluded that the early Chinese had, after all, borrowed a few important items from their AT neighbors to the south, and that the process had not been simply a one-way affair. This view was embodied in the first draft of the present paper, completed in the fall of 1966.

4. The present stage, like the preceding, was forced upon the writer, and it emerged while he was reworking the draft. He had long ago been "programed" for Chinese, and he found that Chinese comparisons kept coming up in his mind as he worked on the Thai-IN cultural items presented in Part 1. It then became evident that many of the most basic Chinese terms could readily be explained in terms of Thai and IN, and that these terms largely had to do with various important aspects of culture. The writer now, for the first time, fully appreciated a fact that he had managed to overlook for some quarter of a century, viz.

that practically none of the so-called "Chinese loan-words" has
any TB affiliations, as surely would have been the case had the
cultural flow in fact been from Chinese "outward." He had long
been misled by the numeral system, unmistakably of TB affiliation and clearly borrowed by Thai, and by a superficial (and
later) veneer of roots for "paper," "ink," "cards," and the like.
Even the numerals, when studied more closely, show a pattern
of "core" lower numerals of ST origin plus "peripheral" higher
numerals with AT affiliations. The absence of ST correspondences on the one hand and the presence of AT correspondences
on the other, plus weighty phonological evidence of various
kinds, combine to make it evident that the ancient Chinese were
not the donors but the borrowers, and that they borrowed from
a language (and culture) that was technologically far superior
to their own. These linguistic acquisitions, after becoming "naturalized" in Chinese, were then in many cases "exported" to
various groups in Southeast Asia in the form of "back loans,"
most notably in the case of "indigo" (see below).

This general argument will be documented by a presentation
of Chinese terms considered to be early loans from AT, arranged
under various categories, as in Part 1. Certain points are best
considered separately, however, and these will be reviewed first.

The writer, as an old student of the TB languages, had long
been aware of occasional correspondences with Thai (see WA-
TER BUFFALO) as well as various curious similarities of one
kind or another, most of which he tended to dismiss (see COP-
PER). He had found one basic correspondence (*pu* "grandfather") in the kinship terminology (TB, Thai, and IN), but
had been hard pressed to find common elements, the following
being a rare example: TB *pur~*pir* "to fly"; Ch. *pĭwǝr;* T
**?bil* (generally *?bin,* but Sek has *?bwil*). He was not prepared
to find the large number of apparent early loans in TB, often
disguised in some manner (see SUGARCANE), most of which
had previously been overlooked or ignored. An attempt has
been made to present these findings in the material offered
below, but not all possible comparisons are included, notably
TB *mrok/brok* or *mlok/blok* "monkey" (Burmese *mrauk,*
Intha dial. *mrok~mlok,* Bhramu *pǝyuk,* Chepang *yuk,* Bahing

moro, Digaro *tə/myu*, Gurung *ti/myu*); IN **bəʟuk<*bəruk* "a kind of ape"; OB *ma-lu* "monkey"; Li *nu:k<*blu:k*, id. Many of these findings still remain unexplained, and there are certain curiosities, e.g. the following pair of roots: Burmese *khrwe<* **khrwi* "shellfish; cowry"; Kachin *khoi* "shellfish"; Burmese *khro<*khru* "dove"; Kachin *khru;* Garo *kru;* Lushei *t'u-<*khru;* Burmese also has *khu* "pigeon," corresponding to Ch. *kḭəu;* for "shellfish," cf. Ch. *klwâ/glwâ* "snail" (a variant meaning in AT).

	Oceanic	IN	Thai	Kam-Sui	TB
shellfish	*kway*	*t'igay*	*hooy*	*qhui*	*khrwi*
dove	—	*daʟa* (?)	*khraw*	*qwaw*	*khru*

It is difficult to regard these parallel roots as simply the product of coincidence in TB, and it is therefore tempting to reconstruct initial **q(h)r-* for both, implying of necessity great antiquity (cf. also BEE below).

The AT and Chinese correspondences occasionally exhibit phonological features of peculiar interest, as illustrated by the following:

Ch. *nieu<niog* "urine; urinate"; T **ńiaw~*niaw*, had always seemed to present a straightforward correspondence, and Mak *ne:u* also fitted here. A possible comparison was noted, however, with IN **ihə[ʔ]* "urine," since initial **ń-* appears to drop in IN (*AT*, 242-43) and the indicated lost final stop (**ńihək*) seemed to find an echo in Arch. Ch. The OB and Kadai forms, however, point to an initial cluster with *l*: OB *lou<ʔdou* or *lou;* S. Li *dəu*, WS Li *tou;* Lq. *ŏi;* S.Kl. *ŏü tu*, Lt. *i hle* (cw. "water"), all "urine." It was then discovered that Si. has a doublet: *ʔbau~* *yiau* (*<*ńiau*) "urinate," similar to the doublet for "bait/meat" (Part 1), suggesting a reconstruction of the type: **m(b)law/* *m(b)liaw*, yielding a clue also to the development in OB and Kadai (**bl->d-*, etc.). We now have further support for a cluster in this root in the Arch. Ch. doublet form *ṣiog<*ṣlo(g)/ṣro(g)* (cf. "louse," Table I).

In at least two basic respects, TB appears to have retained original ST features which became modified in Arch.Ch. under AT influence. TB has object/verb word order, which in Chinese has become verb/object (as in AT), the shift having not yet

Austro-Thai

become complete in the Early Archaic period (Dobson 1962). TB shows *w and *y, both as initial and final, corresponding to Arch.Ch. *g and *d, and the writer (1948) has attempted to show that these were secondary in Chinese. It would now appear that AT might have played a major role in bringing about this sound shift, which was presented as one aspect of a general phonological transformation. Occasional early Ch. forms also exhibit signs of "contagion" from AT, notably the following:

Ch. *tieu<tiog* "bird" presents a "riddle" (Karlgren) in the fact that all modern dialects have *niao* or its equivalent rather than the anticipated *tiao. The root has apparent cognates both in Karen (*tho) and the Barish group of TB (*dau), so that borrowing seems to be ruled out as a possibility here, especially since this is not a normal "cultural" item. We must infer influence exerted by the AT root **manuk/manluk*, on the initial and indirectly also on the final. Miao-Yao also has this root: Hmong *noŋ*, Kanao *nau*, Yao-mien *nok*, Yao-mun *noʔ*; Miao-Yao **noŋ/nok* (Haudricourt 1966).

The numeral system is the one general area of the lexicon in which an ST origin can be demonstrated beyond question. Table II presents the TB roots (as reconstructed by the writer), Anc.Ch. forms, Thai roots, a column of the Si. representatives of Thai kin numeratives (KN) after Benedict (1945), Kam-Sui roots, and Ong-Be forms. The following points should be noted:

Table II

TB	Anc.Ch.	Thai	KN	Kam-Sui	Ong-Be
1. *it*	*iĕt*	{*ʔet* {*(h)nüŋ*	—	{*ʔ(y)ət* {*ʔdiaw*	{*it* {*au*
2. *g/nis*	*ńi*	{*ni* {*sooŋ*	*ńi*	{*ńi* {*γa* (h.t.)	{*ŋei* {*vön*
3. *g/sum*	*sâm*	*saam*	*saam*	*saam*	*tam*
4. *b/li*	*si*	*si*	*sai*	*si*	*ŋa*
5. *(b-)l/ŋa*	*ŋuo*	*ha*	*ŋua*	*ŋo*	*ti*
6. *d/ruk*	*liuk*	*hrok*	*lok*	*lyok*	*sok*
7. *s/nis*	*tshet*	*čet*	*čet*	*śet*	*sit*
8. *(b-)g/ryat*	*pwat*	*peet*	*peet*	*peet*	*bɛt*
9. *d/ku*	*kĭəu*	*kaw*	*čaw*	*č(ə)u*	*ku*
10. *gip*	*zĭəp*	*sip*	—	*zip*	*töp*

1. The Thai and other systems definitely reflect the Chinese variety of the ST system, as seen particularly in the forms for "4," "7," and "8."

2. The regular Thai numerals show two definitely pre-Archaic features, indicating that they were borrowed at a period antedating the sound shifts involved, viz. "5": Ch. ŋuo<ŋo<*ŋa (regular shift after velars), but Thai *ha<*hŋa, reflecting also the lost prefix; "6": Ch. liuk<liôk<*ruk (regular shifts), but Thai *hrok, again reflecting the prefix.

3. One feature appears to reflect a dialectical distinction in early Chinese. Arch.Ch. has sǝm "3," a regular development from *sum, but the later Anc.Ch. shows an irregular sâm, probably of dialectical origin, and all these numeral systems faithfully follow Anc.Ch. here (with lengthening of the vowel).

4. The KN of Siamese are closely similar to Anc.Ch. forms (ŋua stands for ŋuo), showing only palatalization of the numeral for "9" (as in KS), and they can be assigned to that general historical period (see also the discussion in the summary).

5. The KS numerals in general resemble the Thai system, but are independent to some degree, notably in the preservation of the voiced initial in the numeral for "10." Thai lacks z-, and has shifted this sound to s-; cf. Ch. ziuk "ripe"; KS *zok, but Thai *suk.

6. The Ong-Be numerals show the *s->t- shift which is characteristic of this language in the numerals for "3," "4," and "10," but they also include some archaic forms, notably ŋa "5," sok "6" (already shifted to lok in Sav.) and ku "9." This material in general shows that OB borrowed its numerals independently of Thai but from the same Chinese dialect (pre-Archaic).

7. Thai, KS, and OB all preserve original numerals for "1" and "2" alongside numerals of Chinese origin, the latter typically being restricted to phrases such as "11" and "20." Thai *(h)nüŋ is isolated, but *sooŋ "2" corresponds to IN *pat'aŋ<*pasaŋ "pair," the latter meaning being preserved in the early Ch. loan: sɔŋ "pair." A perfect phonetic parallel is furnished by the following: T *sooŋ "light (give light), glitter"; IN *ga(n)t'aŋ "kindled (easily)": To., Sm. "glowing hot." For the KS and OB

roots for "1" and "2," which have AT affiliations, see the discussion in *AT*, 255-56.

An analysis of the higher numerals is highly illuminating. Chinese has three common numerals here, also a fourth uncommon numeral, and they present some uncommonly complex relationships:

"100": Ch. *păk;* probably related to Tibetan *b/rgya,* Burmese *ra* (cf. "8" in Table II); borrowed by most Thai languages, with typical vowel lengthening (**paak*), but Si., Lao, BT, and WT have a separate root **rooy,* apparently related to T **rooy/drooy* "string (as of coins)," with the possible IN cognate: *tali* "string, cord" (*AT*, 256).

"1,000": Ch. *tsⁱien;* apparently an early loan from an old AT root for "100"; cf. S.Li *da:n,* N.Li *va:n;* WS Li *va:ŋ<*va:n< *zra:n* (?); Lq. *dön;* N.Kl. *ɟin~tsin;* IN **ɣatut';* reconstruction: **zrat/zran* (*contra AT*, 256, where this root is overlooked). This relationship appears to be demonstrated by the remarkable parallelism with the root for "vein, artery, nerve, tendon":

	IN	Thai	S.Li	N.Li
vein/ nerve	*uɣat*	{*sen* {*ʔen~ńen*	*deu~dieu*	*van*
100/ 100,000	*ɣatut'*	*seen*	*da:n*	*va:n*

To make the parallelism even more complete in this pair of roots, the γ of each IN root has been identified by Dyen (1953) as his R2. Thai **seen* generally has the meaning "100,000," but BT "10,000" and WT "million"; cf. Tg. *gatos* "million" from IN **ɣatut* "100." The Thai development has been **sen<*san* (fronting of vowel before *-n; AT*, 241)*<*zan* (unvoicing)*<*zran.* The initial **zr-* of this root apparently alternated with **zl-,* producing the Thai (SW only) doublet: **laan* "million" (but Ahom "one lac" = "100,000"). The Ch. loan reflects a later version of the Thai order, with unvoicing and with fronting of the vowel. This was the original AT root for "100," retained in Kadai but displaced upward in the other languages.

"10,000": Ch. *mïwăn;* T **hmüün,* id. (SW only); Li *ŋuon<*

*ŋuan<*ŋwan "thousand"; S.Kl. *gɛ<*gwa(n)*, id.; IN ʟibu<
rigwu/ri(ŋ)gwa/n, id.; for initial *m-<*ŋw-*, see Tables IV and
VI. Again the original meaning ("thousand") is preserved in
Kadai, the Chinese (borrowed) meaning having been "moved
up" one step, precisely as in the foregoing numeral, to make
room for the intrusive numeral "100." Remarkably enough, Thai
has doublet forms here preserving the original meaning, making
up a triplet with the above form: *ban<*gwan* "thousand"
(Si. and Lao only); *hriaŋ*, id. (Ahom, Kh., Shan), but Dioi
rɛŋ "million" (the latter is a fore-stress form).

To complicate matters further, Ch. also developed a fore-
stress form, as in Thai: *lyi* "thousandth" (as of an ounce, or an
acre), with a variant reading *rin (= Ch. *lin*) in Sino-Japanese,
pointing to an ancient doublet: *lyi/lyin*, based on syllable division: *lyi<*ri/ŋgwu*, but *lyin<*rin/gwu*. Note the phonetic
of this character: *lyi* "mile" (the *li* or Chinese mile, about a third
of an English mile), probably the original stepped off distance
(approximately a thousand ordinary steps).

"Billion": *ku* (not in early texts in this meaning), from an
original *rigwu/rikwu*, with *w* dropping (Table VI).

TB has a distinct root for "thousand," of limited occurrence:
Tibetan *stoŋ*, Burmese *thauŋ<*stoŋ*. Tibetan *'bum* "100,000"
has been compared with Ch. *mĭwăn* "10,000" (above), but the
phonological analysis (Forrest 1964) is generally faulty, although
there is a possible line of development via *gwun* (with assimilation of the final). Tibetan also has *k'ri* (also *k'ri-k'rag* and
k'rag-k'rig) "10,000; myriad," which is enigmatic even for Tibetan, since it bears a general resemblance to the above root
as fore-stressed (cf. T *hriaŋ*) and has a strange echo in Lt.
khre "100."

Before leaving the numerals, it should be noted that Miao-Yao
has also borrowed most of its numerals above "3" from ST or
perhaps from an early stage of TB itself. This contrasts sharply with the situation described above, and places this language
stock definitely west of the AT peoples at an early period.[3]
Table III gives the forms for four numerals in normalized transcription for Taipan (TP) Yao and Lantien (LT) Yao, Black
Miao (BM), White Miao (WM) and Pateng (PT).

Table III

	TP	LT	BM	WM	PT
four	$\begin{cases} plei \\ piei \end{cases}$	*piei*	$\begin{cases} plau \\ plo \end{cases}$	*plau*	*pi*
eight	*hiet*	$\begin{cases} yet \\ yiet \end{cases}$	*ya*	*yi*	*yi*
nine	*dua*	*du*	$\begin{cases} kio \\ čio \end{cases}$	$\begin{cases} kua \\ čua \end{cases}$	*ko*
ten	*tsiep*	$\begin{cases} tsap \\ sap \end{cases}$	$\begin{cases} kiu \\ čiu \end{cases}$	*kau*	*ku*

Four sets of data referring to some of the more common animals and metals must concern us before we proceed to a study of the several categories in Part 1. The first concerns fowl and such; the second: elephants, tusks, and ivory; the third: horses, dogs, and pigs; the fourth: metals.[4]

FOWL ET AL.

Roots for "fowl," "duck," and "goose" cannot be established with certainty for AT, the most likely candidates being the following:

IN *baliwit'* "wild duck"; T *pet "duck" (general term); cf. Ch. *ap* (not in GSR). Other AT languages reflect one or the other form (borrowed?): Sek *pit;* Kam *pət;* OB *bit* (Jer.), *bot* (Sav.); WS Li *pet,* Li dial. *bet∼bit;* N.Kl. *bö*<*böt,* but Mak *ɛ:p;* S.Li *ɛp.* These forms appear to represent different syllabicizations of an original root such as *balap(w)it':* *bala/pit'*> *pet/pit,* but *bal/ap/it'*>*ap/ɛp.* Burmese has *bai* "duck," apparently from a fore-stressed variant with *r* for *l:* *bar/apit';* cf. Burmese *khai* "lead, tin," Tibetan *'khar-ba* "bronze" (see below).

The AT root *manluk* "bird" (AT, Table III) has been commonly semanticized as "fowl" in IN (Tg., TB., NgD.) and Yami (Botel Tobago), and as "animal" in MN (Fi.) and PN (generally); SEP: generally "bird," but "ant" (living creature) in Nuakata; in Thai and the AT languages of Hainan and the mainland, the meaning "bird" is uniformly retained.

Thai and the related languages have a distinct root for "fowl":
T *kay; KS *qaay; Li and Lq. khai; N.Kl. kai or qai (inexact
description), but Lt. ka is probably a loan from Vietnamese ga.
Formosa shows onomatopoetic forms such as koka and kuka;
cf. IN *kukuk "cackle," gukguk "animal cry"; T *kuk "cackle."
The root *k(h)a, possibly related, is found in TB: Takpa and
Nung kha "fowl," Newari kha "cock," am-kha "pheasant"; cf.
also Burmese kha "partridge"; Ch. ko<*ka, id. T *kaay corresponds in a regular manner (Wulff) with Ch. kiei "fowl," and
has always been dismissed simply as a loan from Chinese. We
must now reconstruct this root with initial q- (*qay), however,
and this places the whole matter in an entirely different light.
Chinese k- would predictably be the reflex for *q-, since it lacks
this series of consonants, and Ch. does have k- here and in the
loan-word for "ginger" (below) as well as the following: T
*kaat "mustard"; KS *qaat; Ch. kai<kad, id. The final -d is
perhaps a secondary development after the long vowel; cf. IN
*put'uʔ "heart" (Ja. "lungs"); T *poot "lungs"; Mak pət, id.;
Ch. pʽiwəi<pʽiwăd, id. The evidence is thus most persuasive that
all three roots were borrowed by the Chinese, not by the AT
peoples. A similar argument must be made in the case of "gold"
(below) as well as several other roots, notably the following:
T *ka "price"; Sui ʀa; Ch. ka; reconstruction: *ʀa. T *ya "cangue";
Ch. ka; reconstruction: *ya (or ɢa). Sui qe (l.t.)<*ɢe "market";
Ch. zi<dʽiə; also borrowed by Burmese: dzʽe<*(d)zi; reconstruction: *ɢ(a)y, in view of the probable relationship to the
following: T *khaay/xaay "sell"; KS *qwe: Sui qe~pe, Mak će,
Then pe, id.; Ch. kuo<ko "sell, buy." This appears to be an
end-stress form of the AT root represented by IN *dʽuhal<
*dʽuqal "sell," with replacement of final -l by -i (cf. AT, 238);
cf. also OB ven (Jer.) "sell" (but Savina has bean<*vean "buy"),
Lt. va, id., both apparently from a form such as *u(q)al, and
the fore-stress Li forms: S.Li diu, N.Li dial. ʄiu, but Small Cloth
Loi ʄoaŋ<*ʄoan (reg. shift)<*ʄo(q)al, id. This correspondence
furnishes important additional evidence for the equation: Ch.
k- = AT q-; both the KS and Chinese forms reflect secondary
labialization under the influence of the preceding u: *dʽuqal>
*/qwai>*qwe, and>*/qwa(l)>*kwa>*ko.

The root for "goose" shows definite ST correspondences: Tibetan ŋaŋ<*ŋan (through assimilation) "goose" (in his dictionary of 1834, Csoma de Kórös noted that the domestic goose and the breeding of it were not known at that time, i.e. in Western Tibet); Burmese ŋan "goose" (general); Ch. ŋan "wild goose," as opposed to ŋâ "domestic goose"; Thai *haan<*hŋaan (cf. "5" in Table II) "goose" (general); Sui and Mak ŋaan; OB *phon* (Jer.), *büön* (Sav.)<*ŋ(w)an; WS Loi boŋ<*bon (cf. OB), but S.Li ŋe, Small Cloth Loi ŋɛ (cf. Chinese). The Ch. doublet ŋâ/ŋan strongly indicates an original root of the type *ŋal (see Table V), hence the origin of this root remains in some doubt.

The egg itself perhaps came with the chicken; cf. the following root: IN *təluɣ "egg"; T *khray, id. via *khlay<*khlaɣ, with k(h)l-<tl- (AT, 245) and final -i<-ɣ (AT, 238); Ch. has the apparent doublet (Wulff): lwân and dʻân "egg," requiring a reconstruction such as *dl(w)an<*dl(w)aɣ (but Wulff regarded this as an infixed root).

ELEPHANTS, TUSKS, AND IVORY

Thai and Chinese show the following pair of correspondences, traditionally interpreted as loan-words from the latter language:

Thai *ǰaaŋ "elephant"; Ch. zĭaŋ<dzĭaŋ "elephant; ivory."

Thai *ŋa "tusk, ivory"; Ch. ŋâ "tooth (general sense); tusk, ivory"; also an old Thai loan in Vietnamese: ŋa "ivory."

The former root is represented in TB by Burmese tshaŋ "elephant," also in Jili (extinct Kachin dialect recorded by Brown 1837) tsaŋ, possibly also Lepcha tyaŋ-mo, but it scarcely can be considered an established TB root. The latter root is even more isolated, the single likely cognate being represented by Taungthu (Karen) tə/ŋa "tooth."

This material, although sparse in comparisons, would appear to make a case for the traditional view, especially since *ŋa "tooth" appears only in Chinese in the general sense, yet both roots present problems in phonology. Ch. regularly has -o<*-a after velar initials (cf. "5" and "partridge," above), with the vowel -a appearing only in special circumstances, e.g. ŋâ as a

doublet of ŋ*an* "goose" (above), and ŋ*á* "I" as a functional variant of the regular form ŋ*o* "I"; TB *ŋa. In the case of the root
for "elephant," the initials do not agree, since Thai regularly has
s- for the closely related initial *z*- (see discussion under "10,"
above), while Ch. has *i-*<*di*- for Thai *ʄ*- (see TIN/LEAD,
below). We might still be in doubt, however, were it not for
the occurrence of the "real" ST root in Chinese, viz. TB *m/(g)wi*
"elephant": Kachin *gwi~măgwi*; Nung *məgö*<*məgui*; Southern
Kukish *m/wi*, all "elephant"; Ch. *ywie*<*gwia*, borrowed in the
meaning "make, do," but Karlgren (GSR) notes, "The earliest
form shows a hand at the head of an elephant (possibly referring
to the handicraft in ivory, so prominent in Yin time)." The graph
also might be said to suggest the domestication of the elephant at
that period. Boodberg (1937, note 68) also takes note of this
obsolete root for "elephant," which furnishes evidence for initial
g- in Arch.Ch.

If, as now certainly appears to be the case, Chinese replaced
the old ST root for "elephant" with a loan from AT, the question
of the origin for this loan naturally arises. AT has *gadiŋ* "ivory,"
perhaps the original meaning (cf. its retention in Chinese),
possibly also replaced in an original meaning "elephant" by the
loan-word *gad'ah* (Dempwolff). This appears to be the IN
cognate of our root for "elephant," via a form such as */dyaŋ;*
cf. the following:

	IN	Thai	Anc.Ch.
elephant/ivory	*gadiŋ*	*ʄaaŋ*	*zĭaŋ*
smoke(d) meat	*diŋdiŋ*	*ʔyaaŋ*	*śiaŋ/sĭăk*

HORSES, DOGS, AND PIGS

These three animals, none of them represented in our category
of DOMESTICATED ANIMALS, are conveniently considered
together because of the nature of the material (Chinese). This
analysis is best introduced by considering the following well-
known set of correspondences, again traditionally considered
loan-words from Chinese: T *ma* "horse"; Ch. *ma,* id. T *an*
"saddle"; Ch. *ân,* id. T *khwi/gwi* "ride (a horse)"; Ch. *g'yie*<
g'ia.

These roots appear to be "floating" in the sense that clues as to the direction of borrowing cannot be established from any apparent cognate forms in other languages. Tibetan has *rta* "horse," with only local spread (e.g. to Nung dialects), but Burmese *mraŋ* is the prefixed representative of a TB root found also in Kachin *kumraŋ* (also borrowed in Nung) and in West Himalayish *$sraŋ* "horse": Bunan *śraŋs*, Manchati *hraŋ*, Kanauri *raŋ*. IN has *$ad'al/an* "horse," from *$ad'al* "learn": i.e. the "learned" animal.

The root for "saddle" is not helpful, but that for "ride" supplies important phonological data. In Thai *$khwi/gwi* "ride," the medial *w* is lost in the SW group generally (although kept as a doublet in BT and WT) but well preserved elsewhere; Dioi has the voiced forms: *$gwoi~$güi*; KS has voicing plus palatalization: Sui *$dyi*, Mak *ze*; Sek *khoy<$khui* also show the medial *w*, while the OB forms show this same element plus voicing: *$güöi~$gai*. This is also an old loan-word in Vietnamese: *köi* (*cöi*). As will be shown below (Table VI), the ancient Chinese loans from AT characteristically show loss of the medial *w*, hence we have a strong argument here for reversing the orthodox view as to the direction of borrowing in this whole set of correspondences.

This root occurs in TB only in Burmese *či* "ride (horse)," a palatalized version of the earlier *ki* found in the inscriptions; this again has been derived from *$gi*, as shown by the correspondences in various Burmese-Lolo languages, which tend to maintain voiced initials: Lisu *dzi*, Ahi and Lolopho *dze*, Nyi Lolo *de*. These languages maintain velo-labial clusters, e.g. Burmese *khwe* "dog," TB *$khwi*, hence we must infer that this early Burmese-Lolo loan was made either from Anc.Ch. or from the donor AT language itself, with characteristic loss of medial *-w-*. There is no general TB root here, but Tibetan has *zon-pa*, related to Kachin *jon*, Nung *zun*, all meaning "mount, ride."

The derivation of the Thai-Chinese root *$ma* "horse" itself remained a puzzle until a re-examination was made of F. K. Li's study (1945) of the *ti-chih*, or series of twelve calendrical terms. These terms appear in the earliest Chinese inscriptions (the oracle bones of the Yin dynasty) and are still used, in conjunction with the similar *t'ien-kan*, to enumerate various divisions of time, including the years. They are also known to several Thai peoples, including the Dioi of Kweichow, the Lü of Yunnan, the Lao, and the Ahom (an extinct Thai language of Assam). The phonological correspondences have been studied in detail by Li, who treats them as loans from Chinese and dismisses lightly the traditional Chinese association of these terms with various animals. This study illuminates certain critical aspects of the reconstruction of Arch.Ch. (see discussion under BOAT, below), but Li does not carry the analysis further. If now we consider the possibility that at least some of these terms did in fact stand for animal names in some non-Chinese language, we arrive at the following array of material, for "dog" and "pig" as well as for "horse":

Table IV

	horse	dog	pig
Chinese	*ma*	—	—
Thai	°*ma*	°*hma*	°*hmu*
Sui[5]	*ma*	*hma*	*hmu*
S.Kelao	ŋ*üə*	*xmə*	*xmüə*
Li (Hainan)	ŋ*a/ka*	*ma/pa*	*mau/pau*
Vietnamese	ŋ*üa*	—	—
ti-chih	ŋ*o*	*śiuĕt*	*g'əi/g'əg*
(reconstr.)	°*zŋa*	°*sm(w)et*	°*gəy/guy*
Indonesian	[°*t'aŋa*]	°*at'u*	°*babuy*
AT reconstr.	[°*saŋa*]	°*asuma/t*	°*ba(ŋ)gwu/y*

Notes to Table IV: "horse": the *ti-chih* ŋ*o*<°ŋ*a* shows regular shift for Arch.Ch. (see above); the initial reconstruction is by F. K. Li, on the basis of Ahom *si-ŋa*, Lü *sa-ŋa*, but in a low tone series. The indicated development has been °*ma*<°ŋ(*w*)*a*, without the need for reconstructing a form such as °*m-ŋa* (Shafer 1957). This root is not pre-aspirated, because of the previous assimilation: °*zŋa*<°*sŋa*. IN °*t'aŋa* "to stand apart, be forked, be branched"; Li ŋ*a* (d.t. from ŋ*a* "horse") "to open" (anything hinged: door, umbrella, mouth, eyes); the reference is to the animal ridden "forkedly" (cf. French: *à califourchon*); "*dog*": the *ti-chih s̆iuĕt*, reconstructed with initial *sm-* on the basis of its use as a phonetic in *m̆iat* "destroy," et al. (F. K. Li). This reconstruction neatly explains the Thai forms here: Lü *set*, Dioi *söt*, but Ahom *mit*. The labialization of this root can be explained by influence from the preceding *u*, while *smet<*smat reflects a standard Thai shift before final *-t* (*AT*, 241). The final *-t* is a problem, but this alternation between vocalic and *-t* final is found elsewhere, e.g. "mushroom" (*AT*, Table V); it perhaps reflects an archaic group of affixed dental elements: /n, /t, /s, /i(y); "*pig*": the reconstruction: AT *ba(ŋ)gwu/y, as clearly indicated by the *ti-chih*, provides for a ready understanding of many hitherto puzzling forms for "pig" in Southeast Asia, in addition to tying together the Thai and IN forms via the shift: *hmu<*(ph)ŋwu/y. Capell (1943, 137) assigns this root to Movement II, and quotes the opinion of Speiser (1934, 145) to the effect that the earliest AN movement did not possess the pig. The suggested reconstruction explains some of the IN forms without the added /i, also the development traced through Halmahera and Mysol *boh* with the common MN *bo, quo, qoe*. It further explains certain forms from Formosa, which generally show the root *babuy in the meaning "wild boar" as well as "pig," but Rukai (western) *buku~buku?u* "pig" (eastern) *bö:ki* "pig" (vs. *baboi* "wild boar"), perhaps also Yami *kuś* "pig, wild boar." On the mainland, this same archaic root surprisingly can now be seen as the source, via *bag/wu/y (non-nasalized) of the widespread TB root *bak "pig": Tibetan *phag*, Mikir *phak*, Empeo Naga *gə/bak*, Burmese and Garo *wak*, Kachin *wa?*< *wak. In addition, with different syllabic division: *ba/gwu/y, the same root serves as the source for the Miao-Yao forms without final *-k*: Hmong *mpua*, Hmu *pa*, Kanao *pa* (reconstructed *mpaih by Haudricourt 1966). Chinese has a similar form: *pa* "pig, sow," also the end-stress form: *ka<kɔ* "male pig, boar" (with regular loss of medial *-w-*). The latter through palatalization yielded the regular Chinese word for "pig," viz. *tĭo*, although the former term remained current in the northeastern dialects, according to the *Fang Yen* (Boodberg 1937, note 29).

As in the case of "horse," the calendar term ($*g^\prime \partial i$) reflects a distinct AT tradition. *Contra* Speiser (cited above), it seems evident that we must assign the pig to the very earliest AT level in Southeast Asia, with diffusion of the root to TB, Chinese, and Miao-Yao.

METALS

The terms for five important metals: gold, silver, copper, iron, and tin/lead, all show correspondences between AT and Chinese, and again the weight of evidence (except for "silver") indicates borrowing by the Chinese.

GOLD T *γam (SW only); Ch. *kǐəm* "gold" (but only "metal, bronze" in the early texts); S.Li *göm* < *$*gam$ (?); Lt. *kha* < *$*kham$ (?). Relatively recent Chinese "back-loans" are encountered in most of these languages, including Thai itself (Nung *kem*, Dioi *kim*, and Si. has the doublet *kim*); OB *kim*. TB has no general root for "gold," but tends to equate this with "yellow" or "red" (Benedict 1939), e.g. Tibetan *ser* "yellow," *gser* "gold"; Dimasa *gǎjau* "red," also "gold" (and cf. "copper," below): cf. also IN *$*uwaŋ$ "money" and Ch. *$\gamma waŋ$* < *$*g^\prime waŋ$ "yellow"; also, for the Thai-Chinese root, the AT root *$*k/l/am$ or *$*q/l/am$ "dark-colored (red, etc.)" (*AT*, Table VII). The correspondence in the initials in this Thai-Chinese root is precisely the same as that for "cangue" (see above, under FOWL ET AL.), and on this general basis we can postulate a borrowing on the part of Chinese.

SILVER Tibetan *d/ŋul* "silver"; Burmese *ŋwe* < *$*ŋui$ < *$*ŋul$, id.; perhaps also Abor-Miri *ə/ŋün* "gold"; Ch. *ŋǐĕn* "silver"; T *$*ŋön;$ Li *ŋen;* N.Kl. *nyin*, all "silver." The Burmese-Lolo languages commonly equate "silver" with "white" (Benedict 1939); cf. also IN *$*piʟak$ < *$*pirak$ "silver"; T *$*phüak/phrüak$ "white," the latter form being indicated especially by the Lao doublet: *yuok* < *$*yuak$. The TB distribution of the root is restricted to those languages which commonly show loans from AT, hence a loan cannot be excluded as a possibility in this case, but the evidence favors an ST origin for this root, with borrowing by Thai.

COPPER This root has always been treated as a simple loan from Chinese to Thai, but the evidence now points conclusively to an AT origin. The Thai root is not *$doon$ but *$dloon/dluan$, in view of Dioi $luan$; Sek and Mak also have forms with initial l-, and Lq. $t'un$ suggests an earlier *$tlun$, so that the initial cluster here is certain. Table V presents a comparison of this root

Table V

	copper	stairs	steam, v.
AT reconstr.	$dloon/dluan$	$?dla$-i/tla-i	$\begin{cases} tron/dron \\ dra(a)\eta \end{cases}$
Ahom, Shan	$doon$	$\acute{s}a \sim \acute{s}^{\imath}a <$ *za	$hrun$
Thai (main)	$doon$	$?day$	$thrun$
N.Thai (Dioi)	$luan$	lai	run
Sek	$luon$	ray	run
Ong-Be	hon	$lei <$ *lai	hon
Mak	$lu{:}n$	$\check{c}e <$ *kle	tun
Sui	don	kle	tun
S.Li	$duon$	$ta/tha <$ *$thla$	$dra{:}n \sim da{:}n$
N.Li	—	—	bn
Arch.Ch.	$d'un <$ *$dlun$	$t'i\partial r <$ *$t'lay$	$\begin{cases} dion <$ *$yon \\ t'i\partial n <$ *$tran \end{cases}$

with two other roots having similar initial clusters. The Thai root generally has the meaning "copper" (Ahom "brass"), but in Si. the root meaning is "gold," modified by "red" (copper) and "yellow" (brass). There may be a relationship with T *$hlüan$ "yellow." Ch. $d'un$ "bronze, copper" has always been considered simply a semantic extension of $d'un$ "to join" (sense of alloy), as in Benedict (1939), who rejected the equation (by Simon) of this form with Tibetan $zans$ "copper." We are now able to reconcile these seemingly divergent forms: $d'un <$ *$dlun$, but $zan/s <$ *$dran/zan$ (as in the common Thai alternation)$<$ *$dl(u)an$. In addition to local borrowings from Tibetan (Nung dial. zan

mer "red copper" for Tibetan *zaŋs dmar*), the root also appears to be represented by Kachin *ɟaŋ* "bronze"; Burmese *saŋ-twai* "verdigris, acetate of copper" (unanalyzed compound), as well as by the following curious series, possibly reflecting the original cluster in this root: Tibetan *rag-* "brass," *rag-skya* "white copper, German silver" (cw. "white"); Burmese *hraŋ-sam* "platinum" (cw. "iron"); Lushei *raŋ-va* "tin," *raŋ-gačak* "gold" (latter cw. root for "red").

IRON IN *°t'uligi<°t(h)uligi* (?) "spear"; T *hlek* "iron"; KS *°qhlet*, id.; Ch. *t'iet<°t'liet* (Arch. form not known, but *t'l-* occurs in Arch. Ch.; cf. "ladder," Table V); Tibetan *lčags<°hlyag/s*, id.; for the initial here, cf. Tibetan *lče<°hlye* "tongue," from the general TB root: *°m/lay~s/lay* (Garo *sre*, Dimasa *salai*); this parallelism indicates an extremely early period of borrowing for this term; the *a* vocalism is characteristic of many early loans in Tibetan, and is suggestive of a tendency in Arch. Ch. to shift higher vowels to (*i*)ə (Benedict 1940). The Ch. form parallels KS in the shift to dental stop after the front vowel, a phenomenon also found in roots of ST origin (Benedict 1940); the character here (not analyzed by Karlgren) appears to have as phonetic *t'ieŋ/d'ieŋ* (GSR, No. 835), indicating an old doublet *°tiek/tieŋ*. Chinese alone maintained the dental + *l* cluster in this root. There are two other possible derivatives here: Ch. *tsiet<°triet<tliet* (?) "ax; iron block" (GSR: "chopping utensil"); Ch. *ts'iek<°thriek* (?) "battle-ax" (cf. the IN meaning).

TIN/LEAD IN *°timah<°tiŋwaa-*; T *°ɟüün~°ɟin* (Si., Tho)<*°dyan/gwaa-* "lead," but Lao "tin"; cf. also T *°ɟüam* "solder"; Anc.Ch. *iwän<diwan* "lead." The most likely reconstruction here is *°dy(w)an/ty(w)an*, with Thai developing the variant *°ɟin* through typical fronting of the vowel before final *-n* (*AT*, 241); for IN *°tiŋ/<°tyaŋ/*, see the discussion of "elephant," above. Ch. *siek* "tin," which has the same meaning as the IN term, may be related to this root through the doublet: *°tyaŋ/tyak* or *°tiŋ/tik*. Tibetan again has a highly distinctive form, if indeed it is at all related to this root: *za-nye* "lead," *za-dkar* "tin" (cw. "white").

It is a striking fact that none of these last three roots for metals is represented in Burmese or elsewhere in TB apart from Tibetan itself, except for a doubtful comparison for "copper"; cf. the quite distinct Burmese terms: *kre*<*gri "copper" (Tibetan *gri* "knife"); *sam* "iron" (Nung *śam* "iron, sword," Rgyarong *śom* "iron"); *khai* "lead, tin" (Tibetan *'khar-ba* "bronze").

We now present, under the several categories used in Part 1, the Chinese forms which we have identified as early loan-words from AT; for complete details on the AT material, the reader is referred back to Part 1.

AGRICULTURE

FIELD

These roots do not appear to be represented in Ch., but there are two isolated instances of possible borrowing in TB:

Tibetan *na~na-ma* "meadow," *neu-*(γ)*siŋ* "grass-plots on high mountains, alpine pastures"; cf. AT */*na* "low-lying flooded land, ricefield"; Kachin and Nung have *na* "ricefield" as a direct loan from Shan.

Burmese *lai* "ricefield"; cf. Thai *ray "upland (dry) field."

GARDEN

Ch. *ģiwǎn*<*ɣwan<*drwan "garden"; Ch. *ďien*<*dlien "field, cultivated land; to cultivate field"; IN **t'uwan* "digging stick" (also "turn over soil," etc.); T **suan/thrün* "garden"; KS has doublet: "cultivated field." The Ch. forms, although seemingly quite distinct, appear to reflect a basic doublet very much like that found in Thai and KS.

TB has an ancient loan represented by Burmese *thwan* "harrow," n., v., Tibetan *thoŋ*<*thwaŋ "plough," n. Houghton (1896), who originally noted the Burmese-Tibetan correspondence, adduced an Upper Burma dialectical form: *thwaŋ*, but it would now appear that the final -ŋ in Tibetan is secondary in this root. The TB loan is closest to the Thai forms: Shan *thön* "harrow," Ahom *thun* "plough."

MORTAR

Ch. g'ĭəu<g'ĭôg "mortar"; T *grok; IN */kroŋ/krok. This form supplies evidence for final -g in Arch.Ch., and also indicates the shift *gr->*g- in the donor language (cf. SALT). Both points are further confirmed in the Tibetan borrowing: *dgog-tiŋ* "pestle" (only in native dictionaries), corresponding to the colloquial *gog-tun*; the second element here also appears alone, as *γtun* "pestle," the first element presumably standing for "mortar." Both languages follow Thai in voicing the initial (Tibetan final -g stands for -k, agreeing with Thai rather than with Chinese).

In addition to the above, Ch. *śiuŋ* "to hull grain with a pestle" (ancient graph shows two hands with a mortar and pestle) appears to represent a separate loan from another form of this root, represented in IN *lət'uŋ "mortar" (see discussion in Part 1); Sui *tyuŋ* "to hull (rice)"; T *klooŋ<*krooŋ, represented only by Ahom *klɔŋ* "to husk paddy," Si. *khau klɔ:ŋ* "rice partly shelled" (*khau* "rice"). This apparent loan indicates a development of IN type in the donor language: *kr->*ś-, contrasting with *gr->*g-.

Tibeto-Burman has a possible ancient loan-word here: TB *ts(h)um "mortar," represented by Burmese *tshum*, Nung *sumphaŋ*, Kachin *thum*, Lushei *sum*, Garo *sam*<*tsum*; cf. the variant N.Thai root: *qrum, cited in Part 1; Mak *ćum toi* "mortar" (*toi* "pestle, pound"); cf. also T *zoom "to clean rice by pounding, husk rice with a pestle." The indicated shift in initial here: *qhr->*ts(h)- must again be postulated for the donor language (probably distinct from that above).

PLOUGH

Ch. *liei<lĭər*, and *lyi<lĭər* "plough"; *lywi<lĭwər*, and *luâi <lwər* "plough stem, plough" (Arch. graph depicts primitive type of same); both these doublet forms were derived from *bl(w)əi/bl(w)əd/bl(w)ər, the initial *b-* regularly dropping in clusters of this type; corresponds closely to AT *buhlat/buhlaat via *buhlaad (as in Thai), the root presenting evidence for final -d in Arch.Ch.; the variable *w* in the Ch. forms reflects the *u* of the preceding syllable.

Burmese has the apparent Thai loan-word: *thai* "plough." In
addition to the above, Ch. also has *b'a* "rake, harrow," corresponding to T *phüa* "harrow"; OB *p'a*, id. (probable back-loan).
The direction of borrowing here is indeterminate.

SEED

Ch. *zwi* < *z*(ŋ)*gwəi*/*z*(ŋ)*gwəd* "ear of grain"; Karlgren notes
the "curious combination of phonetically not cognate initials in
this phonetic series" (GSR, 533), with velar as well as dental
initials, and adds: "The Archaic initials are obscure." The above
reconstruction seems to be required, however, and agrees closely
with Thai *hŋuay* < *sŋuay*, which has developed semantically
along the same lines as "grain."

Tibetan has a closely similar form: *snye-ma*∼*snyi-ma* "ear of
corn; corn forming ears," which can be referred to an earlier
snye (cf. *nya* "fish"; TB *ŋya*; Ch. *ŋio* < *ŋia*). Tibetan also
has *sa-bon* "seed" (unanalyzed), a possible borrowing from the
AT root: *bon* < *bwan* < *gwan* (cf. IN).

SOW, v.

Ch. *puâ* < *pwâr* "sow"; also *ka* < *kar* (?) "sow; grain";[6] a doublet from a root *kwar*, closely corresponding to AT *səgwar*
(possibly unvoiced because of the *sə-*). This affords evidence
for final *-r* in Arch.Ch., which alternated with final *-n* as well
as with vocalic final (zero consonant).

This root is one of a remarkable series of several basic roots
with velar or uvular + *w* initial clusters, which tend to be preserved in certain Oceanic areas (*AT*, 250) but are in most cases
replaced by labial stop in IN and at times also in Thai (but
not in Mak). As shown in Table VI, Chinese typically has doublets for these roots, of *kw*/*pw*- type, but with the *w* tending
to drop after *k/g*-, and with *xw*- for *khw*-. This undoubtedly
reflects shifts that had already occurred in those northern AT
language(s) from which Chinese borrowed, since initial clusters
of this type are well maintained in Ch., e.g. Ch. *k'iwən* < *khwi/n*
"dog"; TB *khwi*; Ch. *xiwet* < *xwi/t* "blood"; TB *s/hwi*; Ch.
g'wo < *gwa* "fox"; TB *gwa* (Tibetan *wa*, Chamba Lahuli *gua*,
Bunan *gwa-nu*).

Table VI

	AT	IN	Thai	Arch.Ch.
sow, v.	/gwar ~qwar	t'əba[L]	hwaal	ka[r] pwar
ax	gwal ~qwal	baliyuŋ	qwaan ~khwaan	kwa[r] kiən piwo
shoulder	gwaɣ ~qwaɣ	baɣa	ʔba	kian
arm	—	—	qeen ~kheen	—
sleeve	—	—	kheen (khian)	kiwat mĭad
shellfish/ cowry	/gwoy ~qwoy	t'igay	hooy	xwəi/g kiwəi/d pwâi/d
dust/lime/ powder/ manure	/k(h)wuɣ	k/apuɣ	khon puun~fun hmon~mun	xwəi/g pĭwən
boat	gwaŋ/	baŋka[ʔ]	*gwiaŋ (Li)	g'âŋ pĭwăŋ
1,000/ 10,000	rigwu~ ri(ŋ)gwa/n	ʟibu	hriaŋ ban hmüün	liəi/g *liən ku miwăn

Notes to Table VI: The AT reconstructions are abbreviated for *gwar/kwar and *ɢwar/quar (there is evidence for both); for this comparison, Thai *x-* is written *q-* (after Wulff and Haudricourt). Thai generally has long (geminate) vowels in this series, but this may be a secondary process in part or in sum, and we have reconstructed AT roots with short (single) vowels. Mak (KS) has *k-, h-,* or *v-(u)* in this series: *ku:n* < *kuan "ax," *ha* < *gwa* "shoulder," and *hin* < *qin "arm" (cf. the Thai doublet); *čhui* < *qhui "shellfish"; *vən* < *gwən "dust; powder."

For "shoulder" see above under AX (Part 1) and add the following: T *qeen (xeen) "arm," but Dioi *k(h)een or *k(h)ian "arm; sleeve"; the development has been: *qeen < *qween, the *w* tending to drop before front vowels (cf. "ride," above) <

qwan, showing the regular Thai shift before final *-n* (*AT,* 241) <*qwaγ,* illustrating another regular Thai shift (*AT,* 238), contrasting with *ʔba*<*[ʔ]baγa* or *[ʔ]ba/γa.*

Ch. *kian* "shoulder" lacks the doublet form, but this appears to be supplied by the related words for "sleeve": *kiwat* and *miad* (Karlgren notes, "the same character has been applied to a synonymous word"); the final here probably developed via an intermediate form such as *kwal,* with *-l*>*-t* as in Sino-Korean (and cf. Li "sow").

For "dust" etc., see above (Part 1) and below, and add the following for Thai: *(h)mon*~*mun* "dust" (only in Dioi and Tho-Nung).

For "ax" and "boat," see the analyses below.

For "1,000" etc., see the discussion above, under numerals.

For "shellfish/cowry," see *AT,* 252, where the root is referred to Oceanic *kway;* cf. also above for the parallelism with the root for "dove." Ch. *pwâi*<*pwâi/d* "cowry" (graph depicts same), defined in Couvreur as the "name given to several species of shellfish (coquillages) of the sea, which have served as money since the reign of Ch'in Shih Wang (221-209 B.C.)," with the added definition: "precious objects"; *xwəi/g* "property, valuables; present, bribe"; *kiwəi/d* "precious; dear, expensive." The great importance of the cowry as a medium of exchange is well illustrated by the following: *pâu* "valuables" (graph shows jade, ceramics, and cowries under a roof); *mai* "buy" (graph shows the "catching" of cowries).

WINNOW

Ch. *iaŋ*<*dyaŋ*<*draŋ* "winnow"; AT *traŋ.* This early Ch. loan supports the indicated reconstruction for the AT root with initial *tr-* rather than *qr-* (as in Thai).

ALCOHOL

LIQUOR/WINE

Ch. *lâu*<*glâu* "spirits with sediment, wine"; AT *(ŋ)qlaru.* The standard Ch. word *tsiəu*<*tsiô/g* "spirits, wine" is a possible derivative (cf. "iron," "boat").

DRUNK

Not represented in Chinese, but Burmese has $mu<$ *$mo(u)$ "drunk; dizzy," agreeing closely with the Thai *maw both in form and in meaning.

Tibetan has the curious form: *ra-ro* "drunk," as if an "echo" of the AT root for "liquor" (TB *raru*), but it appears to be related to Kachin *šă/rui naŋ* "drunk," Lushei *rui*, id.

ARECA (TRAIT)

ARECA

Chinese has two different transcriptions here, corresponding to the two forms of the root: *pin-lü* and *pin-lâng* (see Part 1). The Thai root *hmliaŋ "fermented tea," which appears to be another form of the same root (retains meaning "betel" in Siamese), apparently has a curious "double echo" in the following pair of Chinese words, which are phonologically identical, even in tone—the graphs have the same phonetic—and show regular correspondences to the Thai root in the final rhyme: *mieŋ* "kind of tea" (Courveur: *thé receuilli dans l'arrière-saison*) and *mieŋ* "drunk," but defined by Couvreur as *"boisson obtenue en faisant chauffer du riz et de l'orge"* (neither word is in GSR).

BETEL

Ch. *lât* "sharp, biting; acrid, pungent" (not in GSR), from Arch. Ch. *dlât<*drât, as indicated by Ch. *t'ât*<*t'lât* "otter" from the same phonetic series (No. 272); AT **rit/ret/rat* "pepper, pimento/pungent, piquant." The various AT forms show clusters of **dr-* or **br-* type, the reconstructed Chinese form agreeing with the former, while the *â* vocalization is probably early (cf. Lao *hrüat "pimento"). The semantic development in Chinese has been similar to that elsewhere; cf. Modern Ch. *lachiao* "pepper, chili" (*la*<*lât).

LIME/DUST/MANURE

Ch. *xwəi/g* "ashes; dust; lime"; *pĭwən* "manure" and *pĭwən* (d.t.) "flour; powder"; IN */k(h)wuγ (Table VI).

DOMESTICATED ANIMALS

BEE/WASP/HORNET

Ch. *pʼiuŋ*<**pʼluŋ* "bee, wasp"; AT **bluuŋ*. Chinese has only the one borrowed form, used (with modifiers) for "hornet" as well as "bee" and "wasp," whereas Thai has three separate terms, each developed from a different form of the AT root.

Thai makes use of the compound "bee-water" for "honey," or equates "honey" with "bee" (Ahom). Chinese, however, has a primary term here: *mĭĕt* "honey," which has been regarded (Benedict 1942, note 40) as an ancient loan via Tocharian *mit* from Indo-European (Sanskrit *madhu*, English *mead*), comparable with the similar loan-word in IN (**madu*). In view of the early loan from AT for "bee," however, it is perhaps preferable (with Wulff) to regard Ch. *mĭĕt* as a related loan from AT **mit'*<**ŋwit'* (AT, 250) "sweet," as represented by IN **[t]amit'~*mamit'~*manit'* (for the **m-*<**ŋw-* shift in the donor AT language, see Table VI).

Tibetan *buŋ-ba* "bee" reflects an antecedent loss of *l* in the cluster **bl-*, since Tibetan maintains these clusters; the initial sonant also indicates an origin independent of Thai as well as Ch., both of which show unvoicing here. Tibetan also has *sbraŋ(-ma)*, used in the meaning "bee" as well as "fly," related to West Tibetan *bu-yaŋ* "bee"; Kanauri *yaŋ* "fly, bee"; Burmese *yaŋ* "fly, insect"; Ch. *iaŋ*<**blĭaŋ* "fly" (cf. "boat," below); ST **braŋ* (*contra* Benedict 1948) perhaps an archaic ST loan from the same root, with the typical *a* vocalism and with initial *br-* for the original unstable **bl-*.

Burmese, in addition to the above, provides the following possible correspondences:

AT **ta/blu* "bee"; Burmese *pya*, id., from Burmese-Lolo **bla* (Akha *bia*, Nhi Lolo *dla*), possibly via **ta/bla*.

Li dial. *kwai~kai* "bee," WS Li *kuai* "wild bee" (contrasted with *fok* "honey bee"; see discussion in Part 1); Burmese *kwai* "dammer bee"; Lushei *khuai~khoi* "bee, wasp" (Shafer 1957); cf. also Ch. *kwâ*<*klwâr* "kind of small wasp."

BUFFALO (WATER)

This root (*$kala$(η)$gwaw$) does not appear in Chinese, but it has been borrowed elsewhere in three different forms:

1. Mon *glau*, whence Karen *$glau'$ "water buffalo" (reconstruction by Haudricourt 1953).

2. Burmese *kywai*<*$klwai$, Lushei *loi*<*$lwai$, Siyin *loai*, Kachin $\eta\partial loi$<*$\eta\breve{a}/lwai$ (cw. "cattle," below) "water buffalo." This is of general Thai type, with the same treatment of the final, but preserves the *l* (shifted to *r* in Thai) and thus can be dated from a period somewhat antedating that of common Thai.

3. Tibetan *glaη* "ox, bullock," also "elephant." This distinctive and apparently very early loan, again with *a* vocalism, is directly comparable with the Formosa forms: Ami *koloη* "cattle; buffalo," etc.

CATTLE

Ch. $\eta\breve{i}\partial u$<*$\eta u/g$ "cattle"; AT */(η)gwu/(η)$gwaw$. The Ch. form is closer to that of IN, while the TB loan-words resemble rather the Thai root: *ηwa, viz. Burmese *nwa*, Nung $\eta wa\sim\eta a$ $\sim nwa$, Kachin and Moshang ηa "cattle"; Tibetan has *nor*< *nwa/r "cattle," but used mainly in the derived meanings of "property, wealth," and even "money."

GOAT

Ch. *ĭaη*<*$ya\eta$ "goat, sheep"; *g'wân* "goat, mountain sheep" (Shuowen; no text); AT /$\eta w(ay)i\eta$ "goat." The two Ch. forms appear to be two different attempts to handle a phonetically difficult root.

Tibetan *γyag*<*g/yak "yak" might well be an archaic loan from this root, paralleling Ch. *$ya\eta$. Tibetan has *skyin*<*$s/kwin$ "wild mountain goat (Capra ibex)," reminiscent of Ch. *g'wân*, suggesting an old doublet (loan) formation in this root.

RABBIT

Ch. *t'uo*<*$t'o$ "rabbit"; Formosa *tok/tuk. Thai has the unusual variant: *$tho?$ (Si., Lao), which appears to reflect the final -*k* of this root. Thai has another variant: *$taay$ (Kh. and Shan *pa:ŋ-ta:i,* Si. *kăta:i*), suggesting an original root of the type: **tooki/toogi/taagi.* In this event, the Ch.—and regular Thai—forms might represent nothing more unusual than a different point of syllabic division of the root: **too/ki,* etc.

ENCLOSURE (FOR ANIMALS)

Ch. *lâu* "pen, fold," also used in early texts in the derived meanings of "domestic animal" and "sacrifice of same," with "prison" as a later development (the graph has "ox" and a drawing of a pen, but in the Yin bone forms there is often a "sheep" instead of an "ox"); AT **ləbu/labu* "enclosure," as represented by IN **lə(m)bu* "enclosed" (Tg. "courtyard," NgD. "village"); T **law~*laaw* (Si. variant) "enclosure for various things, including animals (coop, sty), persons (prison), grain (granary)"; Mak *la:u* (defined by F. K. Li by the Chinese term; perhaps a back-loan). This root shows the development **-b->*-w,* as in the roots for "ashes" and "drunk" (*AT,* 248).

DOMESTICATED PLANTS

BANANA

Ch. *pɔ-tsïog* "banana" (not in early texts), apparently an ancient transcription for the root represented by IN **pit'aŋ,* T **hyuak;* Dioi *śiɛ<*śiak;* Li **waak/weŋ;* this transcription speaks in favor of a reconstruction such as **puts(y)ak/puts(y)aŋ,* with labialization produced through influence of the *u* of the initial syllable. An even earlier form, however, has only an initial *z-:* *i<*zïəg* "Plantago" (cited in the *Shih Ching*), as if for **/zyak.*

COCONUT

Ch. *ïa<*yo<*yor* "coconut" (not in GSR or the early texts); IN **niyuɣ.* The Anc.Ch. form *ïa* is a probable source, through "back-loans," of Tho *yüa* and OB *fia~zea.*

Shan *un* "coconut," isolated in Thai, is obviously the same form as Burmese *un,* id., but the direction of borrowing is uncertain.

GINGER

Ch. *kĭaŋ* "ginger"; IN *$^*t'a^{\jmath}aŋ < ^*saqaŋ$; T *$^*xiŋ$; KS *$^*siŋ$. OB *kĭaŋ* and Li *khüöŋ* < *$^*khiaŋ$ "ginger" are possible "back-loans" from Ch., although the aspirated initial of the latter form speaks against this view. For Ch. *k-* corresponding to AT *$^*q$-, see discussion under "fowl," above.

Burmese *khyaŋ* also appears to be a relatively early loan; the aspiration in this form and the Li form point to an alternative *$^*khiaŋ$ (doublet), from the original initial *q-*. Other TB forms are probably of Thai origin: Barish *$^*(hai-)\check{c}iŋ$; Meithei *siŋ*; Nung (*luŋ-*)*ziŋ*.

Again Tibetan presents a most unusual form, *sga* "ginger," similar in initial complex to the IN root: *$^*saqaŋ$, possibly a derivative of an archaic trisyllabic root such as *$^*sa/qa/ŋi$.

RICE

The AT terms for rice and related cereals appear to have been widely borrowed by Chinese and other languages from an early date (roots numbered as in Part 1).

1. Ch. *miei* < *miəi/r* "rice" (general term), also "millet" (= "little rice"); IN *$^*imay$.

This root appears in TB only in the Barish root: *$^*mai/mei$ "rice" (*$^*mai\text{-}roŋ$), "millet" (*$^*mei\text{-}si$); elsewhere it appears in the Karen root: *$^*me$ "rice."[7]

2. Ch. *xâu* < *$^*xmog$ (phonetic is *mog*) "kind of millet"; Yami *mugis* "rice"; Li *kok/mok* "paddy"; Lt. *kuk/muk* "cooked rice"; Tho *khau kɔk* "paddy." The Ch. form is of special interest because of evidence of a cluster (*xm-*) of the type indicated by the curious Li and Lt. alternations in initials. Ch. *mĭog* "barley" and *mwɛk* "wheat" perhaps also belong here, along with *kuk* "cereals; grain." Burmese *kauk* < *$^*kok/kuk$ "rice plant" is of Thai (Tho) type.

3. Ch. *dˊâu* < *$^*glâw/g$ (?) "growing rice, paddy"; AT *$^*\text{G}Rawa/qRawa$. This correspondence is most uncertain, in view of the rare nature of the AT initial cluster, but there is some evidence that initial clusters of this general type can be replaced with dental stops in Ch.; *dˊai* "moss" (not in GSR); T *$^*glay$, id.; Ch.

Austro-Thai

tieŋ "tripod"; T **gⁱliaŋ*, id.; KS has an unusual series for the latter root: Sui *kweŋ*, Mak *ćiŋ*, Then *ʔiŋ*, for which the most likely reconstruction is **ɢⁱliaŋ*, paralleling the indicated uvular element in the root for "rice."

4. Ch. *b'iwăn* < **b(w)ən* < **bəγ* "cooked rice; food"; IN **bəya/s* "husked rice"; OB and Li **phra* "cooked rice." The Ch. form shows a secondary *w*, as in "8" (see numerals, above), and final *-n* for *-γ*, as in "shoulder" (Table VI). This correspondence strongly indicates that the meaning "cooked rice" is of considerable antiquity.

Tibetan *'bras* "rice," which by Maspero and others has long been linked with this root (Malay *bĕras*) "husked rice," must regretfully be excluded as an imposter; it has a more general meaning of "fruit" (*'bras-bu*) and is a typical *b-* prefixed form from a TB root **ras*, as in Lushei *raʔ* < **ras* "to bear fruit."

5. Ch. *g'wâ* "growing grain"; *k'uâ* < *k'lwâr* "wheat, grain"; AT **kla/gla-i* "rice plant"; this equation, which is favored by the exact correspondence in meaning, indicates an alternative development of the cluster **gl/kl-* (cf. No. 3).

The only possible TB loan here is Tibetan *gro* < **grwa* "wheat."

An additional correspondence here is as follows: *sĭän* < **sĭan* "rice or millet" (Couvreur; not in GSR); T **saal* "husked rice" (cw. "rice") (in Dioi also applied to millet, maize); for the final *-l*, see the analysis under BOAT, below.

Burmese appears to have the same root: *tshan* "husked rice," *ă/tshan* "kernel," but the initial is unexplained.

SUGARCANE

Ch. *tśia* < **t'ĭăg* < **tăg* "sugarcane" (not in GSR); IN **təbu* < **təgwu;* id.; this is a perfect correspondence, and indicates an original analysis of the type: **tagʔ(w)u*, as shown also by T **ʔooy* and KS *oi~ui*. The complete Mak form is *thoŋʔoi* < **thaŋʔoi*, reflecting an archaic nasalized doublet: **tag/taŋ/*, the latter having given rise to Ch. *d'âŋ* "sugar" (not in GSR), a voiced variant.

Tibetan has the interesting term: *'dam-bu* "reed for thatching, writing," also "sugarcane," listed under *'dam* "swamp," as if indicating an analysis: "swamp product (*bu*)"; West Tibetan has *dam-bu/r* "sugarcane." This closely resembles a nasalized form of our root here: *tə(m)bu, and it is difficult indeed to credit this to coincidence, even in Tibetan; perhaps it represents an archaic loan-word which has been "naturalized" and in a sense etymologized. The Chinese and Tibetan forms, taken together, point to an archaic doublet with voiced initial: *taŋw-/daŋw-.

YAM

Although the above root does not appear to be represented in Chinese, this language does have two words in the early texts, each vaguely defined as "turnip" and each an apparent loan from an AT root for "yam" or "sweet potato":

1. Ch. *pʻiuŋ* < *pʻuŋ* "an edible plant (some kind of turnip?)"; cf. Formosa: E. Rukai *boŋa*, Ami *voŋa*, *koŋa*, Sedik *buŋa*, but Atayal *ŋahei~ŋahe* (analysis uncertain) "sweet potato"; T *ʔbuŋ: Tho *man buŋ* (cw. with root below) "potato"; Nung *man buŋ* "sweet potato" (Savina), *phiak buŋ bu* "kind of vegetable (*phiak*)," *phiak buŋ man* "sweet potato" (F. K. Li); cf. also Mak *muŋ* "a kind of potato (taro) with edible leaves" (this root not listed in *AT*).

2. Ch. *mwăn* "turnip" (only "creeping plants" in early texts); cf. T *man* "potato, sweet potato, yam" (generic root); KS *man* "yam"; N. Li (*som-*)*muon*, dial. *mon~man*, WS Li *maŋ* < *man* "sweet potato," all possibly from an AT root such as *ŋwa/n; cf. also Burmese *mun-la* "radish" (Tibetan *la-phug*).

TB has a root appearing to link up directly with the IN-Li root, viz. *k(y)wi or *g(y)wi: T *skyi* < *s/kwi* "medicinal plant," but *kyi-u* "potato" in the modern speech; Kiranti *k(w)i* "yam": Dumi *ki*, Sangpang *khi*, Limbu *khe*, Balali *khu*; Digaro *gi* "yam"; Nung *gi* "root, yam"; Burmese *kywe* < *k(y)wi* "wild yam"; cf. IN *ubi* "yam"; Li *va:i* "sweet potato," from an original *ub(a)y or *ugw(a)y. This correspondence, which "skips" Thai, favors the second of these reconstructions for AT and would yield a very early date for this root in Southeast Asia. Burmese also has *myauk* "yam (cultivated)," apparently from an earlier *bruk or

*brok, corresponding to the Sui-Thai root **p[?]γak* "yam, sweet potato, taro"; cf. Burmese *mrwe* < *mrul "snake"; Tibetan *sbrul*, and the root for "monkey" (see above).

FOOD PREPARATION

COOK (WITH STEAM)

Ch. has an ancient doublet here, with alternative vocalism; cf. Ch. *dĭoŋ* "hot air, steam, heat" (Archaic graph shows a vessel, suggesting a steam cooking process); T **troŋ/droŋ*; and Ch. *t'ĭəŋ* < *trĭəŋ "rising steam; to steam, distil," IN **da(n)daŋ*; Li *da:ŋ ~ dra:ŋ*. The initial correspondences here are presented in Table V.

This root also appears in Burmese *khyauŋ* < *khrauŋ < **droŋ/druŋ* "pot with perforated bottom" (used in cooking by steam); perhaps also Barish *soŋ "to boil"; Kachin *kă/čyoŋ* "to cook"; for the initial shift in Burmese, see the analysis under NEEDLE, below.

FIREWOOD/FIREPLACE

Ch. *d'âu* < *d'ôg* "kiln; pottery"; (latter meaning is derived; Arch. graph shows kiln containing pottery); also *dĭog "kiln" (not in GSR or AD; based on Mandarin *yao*); T *taw "fireplace, kiln"; IN *dapuγ < *dakwuγ. The Chinese form resembles the Thai fore-stress form in most respects, but has initial *d-* (as in IN), with the suggestion of a more complex initial, such as **dy-* (cf. Sui *dyət*, Mak *tyət* "firewood"). This complex initial has also yielded Ch. *tsâu* < *tsôg* "hearth, fireplace; cooking place, stove."

TB has a well-represented root which reflects the same fore-stress, with **kw->p-* (as in IN), viz. Tibetan *thab*, Kachin *dap*, Lushei *tap*, Barish *dap, all "fireplace"; TB **tap/dap*. This loan must necessarily be of some antiquity in TB, and as such demonstrates that the AT shift *kw > **p(w)* also occurred early (cf. Table VI).

TB also has an apparent loan-word for "ashes"; cf. IN **b-la/*

buuk (*AT*, 249); Burmese *pra*, but Barish *pla, Mikir p'əlo<
*phla, all "ashes." Shafer (1942) noted the resemblance between
Burmese *pra* and the Middle Vietnamese (17th century) *blo*
"ashes" (analyzed in *AT*, 249).

LADLE

Ch. *t'iăk*~*d'iăk* "ladle"; AT **trak/drak*.

TB has only Burmese *yauk*<**yok/yuk* "ladle," with vocalism
resembling that of IN **t'ənduk*, et al.

SALT

Ch. *iăm*<*griam (initial not reconstructed by Karlgren, but
the character is in the "indigo" series, GSR No. 609, with an
initial cluster of this type); IN *gaʟəm<*garəm, reconstructed
on the basis of Old Ja. *garem*, Ml. *garam* (cited in Wulff). Ch.
iəm<*iăm "to salt, pickle" (not in GSR) perhaps also belongs
here.

In addition to the above, which reveals a close correspondence
to the IN root, Chinese and Thai both show another (doublet)
form which reflects the *gr->*g- shift in the donor language
(cf. MORTAR): Ch. *γam*<*g'ɛm* "salt, salty," T *gem "salty,
salted." This Thai root must be considered a back-loan from
Chinese. The true Thai cognate is probably represented by the
following root for "bitter": T *xrom (Ahom *khrum*), Dioi *ham;*
Mak *kam;* Li *ha:m*, all apparently from an original **qarəm;* for
the semantics here, cf. Yami *ma/payit* "salty," cognate with IN
**pa?it* "bitter" (see BETEL); OB *hom* "brine" (ic.) and WS Li
huam "salty" are probably back-loans from Ch. *γam*.

In TB this root appears in a special sense: Tibetan *rgyam-
tshwa* "a kind of salt, like crystal" (*tswha* is the general term for
"salt"). The complex initial appears to be a metathesized cluster: *rgyam*<**gryam;* cf. Tibetan *brgya*<**b/grya* (= *băgrya)
"100," as indicated especially by the apparent Chinese cognate:
păk "100." This reconstructed form for "salt" is so close to the
Chinese word that it would appear to have been borrowed from
it. Burmese *yam* "saltpeter" (Nung *yam-sau*) perhaps also is a
loan from this root, possibly via the Anc. Ch. form (*iăm*<*iam).

In addition to these special loans, TB has a root for "salt" with fairly wide distribution, for which the writer (1948) suggested the reconstruction *ǰrum, but for which *gryum is also a possibility: Kiranti group rum~yum, Kachin ǰum~śum, Kadu sum, Moshang śum, Garo sum (obsolete), Dimasa sem, Meithei thum. The latter reconstruction would indicate an extremely ancient loan-word in TB, with assimilation of the vowel to the final -m.

SMOKE, DRY (MEAT)

Ch. śiaŋ (cited in Savina 1965); siăk "dried meat" (graph has "strips of meat" drying in the sun), pointing to an old AT doublet: *ʔdyaŋ/tyaŋ/tyak; another doublet is represented by t'ieŋ "slice of dried meat."

Tibetan has skam-saŋ "dried meat" (Ladak dial.), which shows an added skam "dry" to "explain" the borrowed term.

VESSEL

Ch. áŋ "bowl, basin, tub" (but no early text for these meanings); IN *b/al/aŋa; T *ʔaaŋ. There is also a doublet here: ěŋ "jar, vase"; T ʔeeŋ "pot, jar."

Burmese has the regular form: aŋ "earthen cup or bowl," probably a secondary loan from Thai or Chinese.

HUNTING AND FISHING

BAIT

Remarkably enough, Chinese has precisely the same association with "meat" as encountered in AT, with development of the complex initial closely resembling that found in Thai:

	Thai	White Tai	Arch.Ch.
meat	nüa	ńam	ńiốk < *ńo/k
bait	hńüa	ńam (d.t.)	ńiəg < *ńa/g

A different type of development, resembling that of Sek (mlo), is found in Burmese: hmya < *hmla "to catch with bait," ŋa-hmya "fishhook" (cw. "fish"), with semantics as in SEP; this is a kind of unit ("angling") in Burmese, serving as a base for the following: ŋa-hmya-sa "bait" (cw. "food"), ŋa-hmya-kro "fishing-line," ŋa-hmya-tam "fishing-pole."

In addition to the root for "bait," Chinese has another fishing term which is almost certainly of AT origin: mïwaŋ "fishing net; to catch with a net" (especially used of a casting net), apparently from an old AT root with velo-labial initial, represented also by N. Thai (Dioi) möaŋ "net" and Mak mə:ŋ "casting net" (Sui-Thai *müaŋ); BT mɔŋ < *mwaŋ "net," but WT has xwa:ŋ ~xa:ŋ "to fish with a net"; Shan and Lao wiŋ < *hwiŋ "hand net"; cf. also Si. muŋ, OB mɔŋ-deau, Li maŋ-dio "mosquito-net" (these may be later back-loans).

FISHHOOK

Not traced in Ch., but perhaps represented by Tibetan mčhil-pa "fishhook"; IN *kawil; OB tin < *gwil. Tibetan has ky- for *kw- (see YAM above), hence we must postulate palatalization of this root in the donor language.

HUNT

Ch. śĭŏg < *śyow/g "to hunt; great winter hunt"; ṣĭŏg < *ślow/g "hunting assembly in springtime" (for this initial, see Benedict 1948); IN buγəw; T *thaw/phraw. For the initial correspondence here, see BOAT, below.

TOOLS ET AL.

ARROW

There is no certain example of a loan in Chinese or TB for "bow" or for "arrow," but the following is of some interest: Arch.Ch. dïək "to shoot with arrow and string attached; arrow" (graph depicts this type of arrow); SEP Mota tiqa "shoot at a mark"; PN teka "dart"; Lakia (Li dial.) teek "arrow." Ch. has nuo "crossbow," corresponding to a widespread root: *(h)na of unknown origin: T *(h)na "crossbow" (only in Si., Lao, BT, Dioi) but Cao-lan nü; Sui hna "bow" (the only example of its use in this sense); Vietnamese na (distinct from no, the Sino-Vietnamese form); TB: Nung thə/na; Moso (Burmese-Lolo group in Yunnan) *tă/na*. The Ch. vocalism is irregular, since forms such as *°na* had already become heavily palatalized at an early period; cf. TB *°/na* "ear" (Tibetan *rna-ba*); Ch. *ńĭəg<°ńa/g*. In general, it would appear that this Ch. term has been borrowed from some AT source, partially replacing the term *d̑ắn* "shoot pellets (as at birds); pellet (of crossbow); crossbow" (last meaning not in early texts), corresponding to Kachin *ndan* "crossbow," dial. *kali ndan* "bow" (cw. regular term for "bow").

AX

Ch. *kĭən* "ax" (graph is picture); *kwâ<°kwâ[r]* "dagger-ax" (graph is picture); AT *°gwal/qwal*; for the correspondence, see Table VI; Chinese also has *pĭwo* "ax," apparently from this root; cf. Annamese *bua*, id., and T *°buo* and *°fu* (see Haudricourt 1960), perhaps "back-loans" from Chinese.

TB has the following root with restricted distribution: Barish: Garo *rua*, Dimasa *roa*; Kachin *n/wa~niŋ/wa*, all "ax," reconstructed as *°r/wa* (Kachin often has prefixed *n-* for *°r-*); possibly related to the AT root through a form such as *°qrwa/l* (cf. discussion of "shellfish" and "dove," above).

BOARD/PLANK/TABLET

Ch. *pwan<°pan* (labialized) "board"; also (diff. character) "board, tablet"; also (diff. character) "metal plate, plaque"; *pian* "flat and thin"; *p̑ĭan* "writing tablet"; *b̑ĭan* "board under body in coffin"; IN *°papan* (*contra* Benedict 1940).

BOAT

Chinese has forms corresponding to each of the main roots listed in Part 1 (227, 228). A Thai correspondence has now been uncovered for the first of these: Nung *bo:ŋ lü* "boat" (*lü <T °rüa*, id.); Tho *ba:ŋ* "tube; num. adj. for boats, canoes, rafts"; WT *ba:ŋ* "num. adj. of certain objects of concave shape (canoe, bowl, dish, etc.)"; Lao *ba:ŋ* "num. adj. for plates, cups, etc.," from T *°ʔbaaŋ/ʔbooŋ*; cf. IN *°baŋka* "boat, canoe." Thai has initial *°ʔb-* from the velo-labial *°gw-* in some roots (cf. discussions under AX, FISHHOOK), and in this case the similarity

with the IN root *waŋkaŋ "boat" suggests the reconstruction already offered. The Chinese loans are as follows:

1. Ch. *p̆iwăŋ* and *g'âŋ*, both defined in precisely the same way: "two boats lashed together; square boat"; AT *gwaŋ/*; for the correspondences, see Table VI. Burmese has *pauŋ~bauŋ* "a raft, float," probably from a distinct root for "float." Ch. *b'iwăt* and *p'iug* "raft" appear to be of similar origin ("that which floats"), but cf. T *be* "raft" (Ahom "raft, two boats tied together with a platform between").

2. Ch. *t'iəu<*plĭəu<*plau* "boat" (the main Ch. word here); Ch. *iu<*blĭu<*blou* "boat" (obsolete in this sense; Arch. graph depicts boat); cf. also Ch. *sâu~śĭəu* "boat; num. adju. for boats"; T *rüa;* IN *palɑʔu*. The Ch. loans reflect the final syllable of the IN root (lost in Thai), and also point to a doublet form with *b-*, as in Li *bla/pla;* they also afford important additional evidence for the loss or replacement of initial clusters in Arch.Ch. For *t'iəu<*plĭəu<*plau,* cf. the *ti-chih* (calendrical term) *t'iəu <*p'lĭəu<*p'lau* "ox,"[8] as shown by the archaic prototype still preserved in Thai *plau* (Li 1945). Again, for *iu<*blĭu,* cf. the simple loss of *bl-* in Ch. *iuĕt<*blĭuĕt* "writing stylus"; Ch. *iäŋ<*blĭăŋ* "full; fill"; TB *bliŋ* "full," *pliŋ* "fill." Despite the complex phonology here, the correspondence in this important root is unassailable.

Chinese has an additional correspondence, with Thai only, in the following root: Ch. *d'au<*dyau* "oar" (long oar, as contrasted with *zĭăd* "short oar"); T *čeew* "oar; to row" (Si. "long Siamese oar with which they row standing"), but Nung *ča:u* "row," with what seems to be the earlier *a* vocalism.

STAIRS/LADDER

Ch. *t'iei<*t'liei<*t'lay* "step, ladder, stairs"; AT *ʔdla-i/tla-i;* for the correspondence, see Table V.

Tibetan *skas-ka, skras-ka* (West Tibetan *śras-ka*) "ladder," *gya-śras* "stairs," and Burmese *hle-ka* "ladder, stairs" appear to be separate loans from this basic root, but the phonological development is not clear.

WEAVING ET AL.

EMBROIDER, KNOT

Ch. *g'wət* "knot; tassel" (not in GSR); if this is the early loan-word here, it suggests a reconstruction: AT **gwət/kwət* that might have yielded both IN **/kət* and T **koot*.

There is the additional correspondence: Ch. *sĭəu<*səu* "embroider"; T **seew*, id., with Si. retaining what may be a more archaic form: *siau* "prick with the beak, strike with the horns."

INDIGO

Ch. *lâm<glâm* "indigo"; IN **taɣum;* T **throom.* Several Thai languages (Si., Lao, WT, Nung) show a doublet root **graam* "indigo," an obvious "back-loan" from Chinese. The N. Thai (Dioi type) languages have *kyaam~śaam*, leading to the re-construction **ɣraam* (Li 1954). This yields a clue as to the prob-able origin of the initial *gr-* in Chinese, since there is just no evidence for prefixation as an active process at this period (*con-tra* Benedict 1942, note 42). The *gr-* stood for **ɣ-*, a non-Chinese sound at that time, so that we can date this loan from a period antedating the *gr->* *gl-* shift in Chinese. The vocalism also indi-cates that this was the same non-standard dialect of Arch.Ch. that had *ȧ* for *ə* before labial finals, hence we have a perfect parallel with the root for "3" (with lengthening of the vowel in Thai in each case):

		Arch.Ch. (standard)	Arch.Ch. (dialect)	Thai	N.Thai (Dioi)
three	*g/sum* (TB)	**səm*	*sâm*	*saam*	*saam*
indigo	*ta/ɣum* (IN)	**grəm*	*grâm*	*graam*	*ɣraam*

There is evidence of a doublet for the AT root: Kh. and Shan *ron<*dron* "indigo"; Li *sieŋ<*t(h)rien/gw-*. Precisely the same doublet appears in Chinese, namely *d'ien* "indigo"; this character has the phonetic *d'ieŋ*, pointing to an earlier "doublet of the doublet" based on syllabic division: *d'ien<*drien/gw-*, but *d'ieŋ* *<*drieŋ/w-*, all from an original trisyllabic root.

Tibetan *rams* "indigo" shows the added /s also found in *zaŋs* "copper," *lčags* "iron," of unknown function. The root also appears in Lepcha *ryom*<*d/ram* or *t/ram* (?), the form with "infixed" *y* suggesting a lost prefixed element (Benedict 1943 bis).

Chinese also has a correspondence with Thai, KS, and Li in the root for "dye": Ch. *ńiam;* T *ńoom;* Dioi *ńum;* KS: Sui *ʔyam*~ *yam,* Mak *ńum,* Then *yam,* Mak *ńum*~*ʔyam;* Li *vom*<*ńuom* (but apparently lacking in IN).

NEEDLE

Ch. *t'iəm* "needle"; the former character is in a phonetic series with velar initials (GSR 671), while the latter has *zïəp*< *d'iəp* "10" as phonetic, hence we can reconstruct an archaic doublet of the type: *kïəm/kïəp* directly comparable with AT */gim,* with the vowel shift as in *d'iəp* "10"; TB *gip* (Benedict 1940).

The TB forms are particularly interesting here. TB has the following root for "needle," with restricted distribution: Tibetan *khab,* Kanauri *keb,* but Burmese *ap,* from Burmese-Lolo *ɣap* (Phön *tə/ɣeʔ*<*ɣap,* Lisu *wɔʔ,* Ahi *woʔ*). This rare Tibetan-Burmese equation of initials is matched in the widespread TB root for "house": Tibetan *k'yim,* Vayu *kim*~*kem,* Miri *ă/kum,* Limbu *him,* Magari *im*~*yum,* Namsang *hum,* Moshang *yim*~ *yüm,* Meithei *yum,* Nung *kyim*~*čim*~*čum,* Burmese *im,* Kukish *im*~*in;* TB *ɣim/ɣum,* this reconstruction finding support in Karen *ɣĩ* (nasalized): Pwo *ɣaĩ,* Sgaw *hi,* Bghai *he.* We thus emerge with a totally unexpected correspondence directly with IN, despite diverse forms in Thai (possibly because of the doublet for "needle"):

	IN	Thai	TB
needle	*daɣum*	*khim/xim*	*ɣap*
house	*ɣumaʔ*	*rüan*	*ɣim/ɣum*

For "needle," the final -*p* reflects a doublet such as that indicated for Chinese, and the *a* vocalism is again typical of these ancient TB loans. The root for "house" shows a ŋw>m shift comparable with the *kw>p* shift already seen in the root for "fireplace." The data here can scarcely be explained without postulating an ancient loan for "house" from AT, at a proto-TB period, since certainly this is a root that has become completely "naturalized" in TB.

The story on "needle" is still not complete, however, since the same AT root (*daɣum/daɣup*) seems to have yielded a special TB root for "sew"; it has a restricted occurrence, and must date from the proto-TB period, as shown by the following parallelism:

	Tibetan	Gyarung	Burmese
six	*drug*	*tŏk*	*khrauk*
sew	*'drub-pa*	*tŭp*	*khyup<*khrup*

Magari has *rup* "sew," perhaps a loan from Tibetan, but the root is not general in TB. The regular Tibetan term is *'tshem-pa* "sew," another possible derivative of the root (cf. KS: Then *tshem* "needle"); *'drub-pa* means "embroider" as well as "sew," and perhaps retains something of an original meaning of "needle" in the phrase *'tshem-'drub* "needlework."

PLAIT/WEAVE

Ch. *ďâu<ďog<*dlow/g* "rope, string; braid, twist (rope)"; T **do*; Mak *do*. These latter forms have been derived from **dla/dla/n*, and there is also evidence of an initial cluster in this GSR series (No. 1047); cf. "kiln" (see FIREWOOD/FIRE-PLACE) and the following, from the same series: Ch. *ďâu<ďog<*dlow/g* "wash, cleanse" (not in GSR), but Couvreur defines it as "wash rice, minerals"; T **dlaaw/draaw* "wash" (esp. gold or silver; rice); IN **lu[t']aw* "rinse out"; Formosa: *sao* (widespread root) "wash (clothes, objects, body)."

The roots for "rattan" and "wickerwork" have not been traced in Chinese, but this language does have a term for "basket," conforming closely in all respects to Thai **droŋ*: *luŋ<*druŋ* (*dluŋ*) "basket, cage" (used for birds, etc.); the reconstruction is based on the phonetic series (GSR 1193), which includes initial *t'l-* as well as *l-*; contrast the development shown by Ch. *d'uŋ*<*dluŋ* "copper" (Table V).

The root for "basket" also appears as a loan in TB: Tibetan *droŋ-ma* "large basket or dosser, provided with a lid, and carried on the back"; Burmese *khyoŋ* "cylindrical basket" (see NEEDLE for the correspondence in initial cluster).

An additional woven or plaited cultural item is represented by the following root:

Ch. *d'âi* "bag, sack, pocket; envelop" (not in GSR); T *day* "bag, sack" (Nung also "pocket," perhaps through Chinese influence); Formosa: *kadai* (?) "woven bag": E. Rukai *kaʃai*, W. Rukai *kadai~kde* (defined as used by women), Yami *kalai;* also *kada/la/i* (?): Ami *kaladad~valasai*, Bunun *d'awad*, Saisiat *kawai*. OB *hoe* (Jer.) and Li *tai* "pocket" are probable backloans from Chinese. The meaning "pocket" appears to have been a specifically Chinese development.

SEW/PLAIT

Ch. *ñiəm~nïəm* "weave"; IN *añam* "plait." In this rare instance, the Ch. loan-word is closer both in form and meaning to IN than to the apparent Thai cognate: *ñap~ñep~ñip* "sew."

WEAVE

The most prominent IN root (*tənun*) has not been traced on Hainan or the mainland, but another AT root (not cited in *AT*) has now been uncovered, and this root has unmistakable loan associations with ST itself:

Cham *hrak* "loom"; T *thruuk*<*thrwak*<*th(u)rak* "loom (hand-loom); weaver's shuttle; warp" (often used in the phrases *tam thruuk* or *do thruuk* "weave"); Dioi *rɔ*<*hro:k* "warp of a fabric"; Sek *ro:k* "cloth" (?); Mak *tam di:k*<*dryak* (with typical palatalization) "weave" (cf. the Thai phrase); OB *huk* (<*thruk*) *hɔp* "weave" (cw. "cloth"; also used in general sense "do, make"); Li *sü*ʔ(<*thrüük*) *dop* "pass the shuttle back and forth on the loom" (cw. "cloth," directly cognate with the OB phrase); Lt. *so*<*thro(k)* "weave." The phonology of this root is closely similar to that of "bone" (*AT*, Table I and notes), with Thai medial °-*uu*-<°-*wa*-, as established by F. K. Li (1965):

	Cham	Thai	Dioi	Sek	Mak	Ong-Be	S.Li
bone	*tulaŋ* °*tulak*	ʔ*duuk*	dɔ	ro:k	ʔ*do:k*	zək	*drü*ʔ
loom	*hrak*	*thruuk*	rɔ	ro:k	di:k	*huk*	*sü*ʔ

The root has not been traced in IN proper, and the reconstruction from the Cham form is uncertain, probably °*thrak*. This is clearly the same root as the ST root represented by TB °*t(h)rak/drak* "weave": Tibetan '*thag-pa*, Magari *dak*, Kachin *da*ʔ<°*dak*, Garo *dak*, Lushei *ta*ʔ, Mikir *thak*, but Burmese (and Burmese-Lolo in general) *rak*, Nung *pɔ/ra*<°*rak*; Ch. *tïək*<°*t(r)ak*, id. This ancient loan appears to have been made at the ST period, before the separation of TB and Chinese, antedating even the loans for "house" and "wild yam" (not found in Chinese) and "pig" and "fireplace" (distinct forms in TB and Chinese).

SUMMARY AND CONCLUSIONS FOR PART 3

The AT loan-words in Chinese, when viewed as an ensemble, constitute the outlines of a substantial material culture: the higher numerals (above 100); the fowl and egg (and perhaps the duck); horse, saddle, and riding; elephant and ivory; the pig and rabbit (but not the dog); cattle and goat/sheep; the bee (curiously prominent in this material) and perhaps honey; garden and manure; plough; mortar and hull grain with pestle; seed, sow, and winnow; rice (various, including cooked rice) and sugarcane (whence sugar); banana and coconut; ginger and mustard; the dipper (made of a coconut or gourd), ladle, and vessel (container); salt; smoking (meat) and steaming (rice); bait (meat) and net; metals (gold, copper, iron, tin/lead); the ax; ladder/stairs; boat, rafts, and oars; washing (metals and rice); hunting (but not the bow or arrow); crossbow (but precise origin unknown); fireplace, kiln, and pottery; weaving and plaiting (twisting rope); the needle and embroidery; basket and bag; indigo; cowry (= money); market, price, and sell.

Three general lines of reasoning are employed in order to establish the direction of borrowing: by Chinese from AT rather than vice versa.

1. Most of the loan-words involve roots with cognates in IN and/or Formosa, Oceanic, or SEP. This permits of the reconstruction of AT roots, thus establishing the direction of borrowing. It should be noted that the meaning is *derivative* in certain cases, notably "iron" and "horse," e.g. Chinese borrowed *ma* "horse" from an AT language which had derived this from a root of the type **saŋa* "to be forked," and also borrowed (perhaps at a different time or from a different AT people) a calendrical system (the *ti-chih* and *t'ien-kan*), which included an earlier, "frozen" form (**zŋa*) of the same root. It seems evident, on historical grounds alone, that both "iron" and "horse (riding)" were cultural innovations in Southeast Asia of more recent date than the ancestral AT period, and indeed the linguistic data show that the terms for these items were developed quite independently from different roots in IN.

2. Phonological data have been employed at times to indicate the more likely direction of borrowing, e.g. Ch. *kai* < *kad* "mustard," corresponding to T **kaat*, KS **qaat*, where we can explain the initial *k-* as a simple substitute for **q-* (Chinese lacks the uvular series); if now we start with the Chinese word, we are entirely at a loss to explain the KS form.

3. In certain cases the direction of borrowing is suggested by indirect evidence, with or without phonological support. In the case of "elephant," for example, we must consider the fact that in early times in China the ST term: *ɣwie* < *gwia* (corresponding to TB **m/gwi* and **m/wi*) was already obsolescent, and what better reason for this need we offer than the supposition that it was en route to being replaced by the borrowed AT term: *ziaŋ* < *dziaŋ*? The closely related term: *ŋâ* "tooth; tusk, ivory" can be assigned the same direction of borrowing, especially in view of the phonological findings here (final *-â*, where we should expect an **-o* if this were in fact an old ST root). Similarly, Ch. *g'yie* < *g'ia* "ride a horse" (T **khwi/gwi*) reflects the loss of medial

-*w*- that has been shown to be typical of loan-words from AT (Table VI), and the close association of this root with that for "horse" further suggests an original AT source. The other closely related root here, *ân* "saddle" (T *°an*) can be assigned the same direction of borrowing, since one would be hard put to posit a cultural situation in which a reversal of direction might have occurred.

The early Chinese loans appear to have been made not from the ancestral AT language itself but rather from a later, otherwise unknown AT language (labeled here AT-x), not ancestral to Thai or any of the present-day mainland AT languages. This language had already simplified the initial cluster °*gr*- to °*g*-, as shown by the Chinese borrowings for "mortar" and "salt." More important, it had developed doublets of the type °*pw/k(w)*- for original velo-labial clusters, and these doublets are faithfully reflected in Chinese (Table VI). The recognition of this general line of development serves to clear up one of the knottiest problems in the analysis of Chinese script characters, viz. the appearance of 法 *pĭwăp* "law; model; style, fashion," with phonetic 去 *k'ĭab*, in a phonetic series (GSR No. 642), which otherwise has only the expected forms such as *k'ĭap, gĭap,* and *k'ap.* Here we can confidently reconstruct the doublet: °*pĭwăp/ kĭăp* and label it as a loan-word from AT-x. We can further recognize a parallel doublet with initial *b*- and final -*m*, represented by 範 *b'ĭwăm* "a mold; rule, law," with support for Karlgren's original (in AD) recognition of 己 *g'ăm* as a phonetic in this character: °*b'ĭwăm/g'ĭăm.* These typically palatalized Chinese doublet forms were borrowed from AT-x °*pwap/kap*<°*kwap* or °*kwakw*-, and °*bwam/gam*<°*gwam* or °*gwaŋw*-. The AT original might well have been a partially reduplicated, trisyllabic root of the type °*tə(ŋ)kwa(ŋ)kwa*, yielding IN °*tə(m)pa* <°*tə(ŋ)kwa* "form" (Ja. "model") as well as the indicated doublet in AT-x (the root has not been traced in Thai, KS or Kadai).

One might anticipate that Chinese would reflect "doublets" of another type, the result of borrowing a term from AT while at the same time retaining its ST equivalent, e.g. the AT loan-word *dzĭaŋ* "elephant" coexisted in the language for some time with its ST equivalent, *gwia,* before replacing it. In this instance, the AT term was successful, but there is one striking case in Chinese in which the ST term eventually won out. The archaic

graph for *sĭər* "die" is 死 , which is made up of 人 (man) and

歹 , the latter read as ŋât "fragment of bone," the whole making very little sense (Karlgren does not attempt to explain it in GSR). This second element has also been applied to a word *tâi* "bad," thus revealing another early reading (*tâi*), yielding clear evidence for a synonymous word *tâi* for "die," directly comparable with T **taay*, IN **matay/patay*. The fact of the borrowing itself is of considerable interest in view of other data relating to the ancestral cult (see below). In this instance, how-ever, the ST term (*sĭər*) persisted, whereas the AT loan-word (*tâi*) became obsolete.

As indicated above, our hypothetical AT-x language does not appear to have been ancestral to Thai or to any other present-day AT language. It can be reconstructed only on the basis of loans in Chinese, which reveal it to have been conservative in some forms, e.g. the retention of final **-m* in "weave" and of initial **d-* in "kiln, fireplace" (see above); cf. also Ch. *tśĭĕt<* **t'ĭĕt* "leech" (not in GSR), from an earlier **tik* (these are regular shifts for Arch.Ch.), an apparent early loan-word from AT, showing a correspondence in the *t-* initial with IN **lintah* and **lima[n][t]ək* as opposed both to T **daak/deek* and Li **thaak/theek*. It is also possible, of course, that AT-x preserved certain AT roots lost elsewhere, at least on the continent, and that these might be represented by Chinese loans. The most likely instance of this, and one of some cultural interest, is furnished by Ch. *tâu<tog* "knife," IN **pit'aw;* the most likely Thai cognate here is **ʔdaap* "sword"; Li *dau* "knife" appears to be a loan from Chinese, while Kl. *mi du,* id. is of uncertain affiliation; for the initials, cf. Ch. *d'âu<d'og* "wash," IN **lu[t'] aw* "rinse out" (see above, under PLAIT/WEAVE).

The AT loan material in Chinese, as presented above, relates for the most part to material culture. There are several highly

significant elements of another sort, however, and these are
listed below:

a. Fiji and western Polynesia show a root *ćaw/saw "chief"
(Capell and Lester 1945-46, who present a detailed discussion
of the institution involved). As in the case of much of the kinship terminology (Part 2), this root skips IN to reappear in the
AT mainland languages: T *ćaw "master, lord, chief," Mak
sau < *ćau "host, master." This appears to be the source, perhaps
via AT-x *ćow (see below for similar shift in TB borrowing) of
the basic Chinese term for a ruler: tśïu < t'ïu "master, lord, chief,
sovereign," also used in sense "to govern." The phonetic shape
of this Chinese term also suggests a later or loan origin (we
should expect a final *-g if this were from an ST source). As in
the case of other AT loans, Chinese has "exported" this back in
modern form, e.g. Mak has su < *ću (back-loan from Ch.) as a
doublet of sau < *ćau. This is, of course, a highly significant borrowing in Chinese, since it implies that AT political institutions
exerted a profound influence upon Chinese society. What is
more, the archaic graph for the character 主 tśïu probably
represents an ancestral tablet, and the same lexeme, written 祉 ,
was also semanticized as "ancestral tablet"; this suggests that
the ancestral cult, one of the most distinctive of all Chinese institutions, was also either borrowed from or, at least, deeply
influenced by a similar AT cultural institution (cf. also the discussion of "die," above).

b. As shown above, the basic Chinese term for "law": pïwăp
(Modern Ch. fa) can be identified as a loan-word from AT.
This borrowing, together with the above, makes an extremely
powerful case for the view that social organization and control
institutions at a very early level of Chinese culture were significantly modified, if not largely reshaped, as a result of contact
with an AT population.

c. Further evidence of AT influence upon Chinese is presented by the complex system of calendrical terms (ti-chih and
t'ien-kan), three of which have been analyzed above in some
detail (horse, pig, and dog). Here it seems quite clear that the
early Chinese people took over this system, foreign terms and

all, and "naturalized" it, maintaining only a tradition of the meaning of the terms of the animal cycle (*ti-chih*). The ultimate origin or origins of this cycle remain obscure, since it cannot be demonstrated that all the terms are of AT derivation. Coedès, who studied this cycle at some length, has shown that it is widely known in Southeast Asia in one form or another (but not to the Burmese, nor to the Mon in Burma). In the case of the Cham (southern Vietnam), the Vietnamese, and the Mon in Thailand, the ordinary terms in these languages for the various animals are employed in this cycle. The Cambodian (Khmer) cycle has a distinct set of terms, however, and Siamese has borrowed from this set. The entirely unanticipated finding by Coedès was that the Cambodians had borrowed this set of terms from the lowly Müöng, the unsophisticated "country cousins" of the Vietnamese! Actually, the terms reflect a proto-Müöng level, notably in the disyllabic forms: *msań* "snake" (Müöng *sań~t'ań*); *raka* "cock" (Müöng *ka~k'a~ga*). The term *roŋ* "dragon" (Müöng *roŋ~hoŋ*, Vietnamese *rôŋ*) is dismissed by Coedès with the notation: "*mot d'origine chinoise*," but this is more likely the source of the regular Chinese term: *lĭuŋ* "dragon" (cf. above, under BASKET). This cycle also has *tho*? "rabbit," which is the regular Thai and Chinese term, from an apparent AT (Formosan) source (cf. above). The two cycles perhaps have one term in common, viz. *raka* "cock" (above), comparable with Chinese *i̯əu<zĭôg*, Thai *°raw*, where F. K. Li (1945) suggests an original of the type *°rĭôg*, perhaps from an original doublet *°raka/rôga* (cf. also Burmese *krak* "fowl"). In any event, the evidence as a whole strongly suggests that the animal cycle originated in the general AT area (south-central China and probably parts of northern Indochina, including the old Müöng territory), with diffusion of the AT version northward to the Chinese, and of the Müöng version southward to the Cambodians (and later to the Siamese), with "stimulus" diffusion to other groups (cf. the discussion of the diffusion of kin numeratives in Benedict 1945).

    d. The key loan for "cowry," used as the basic medium of exchange (see the discussion above), also for "salt" (often with the same use), along with the loan-words for "market," "price," and "sell," all point to a fundamental indebtedness of early Chinese culture to AT in the economic (marketing) sphere. In addition, Anc.Ch. *mai* "buy," also (d.t.) "sell" may well belong here as another AT loan; cf. IN *bəli~*bili, T *zü*, Dioi *sɛ*<*ze, KS *dyai<*blai, all meaning "buy," from an AT root of the type *bəlay/bəley (for the initial, see *AT*, Table VIII). Karlgren has been unable to reconstruct the Archaic form for this word, but a derivation from a form with initial *ml- would be regular; cf. Anc.Ch. *măi* "bury," with phonetic *lyi*<*lïəg* "village," from Arch.Ch. *mlɛg*. The case for this as an early borrowing is greatly fortified by the presence of a parallel borrowing in TB: *b/re* "buy" (Kachin *mări*, Miri *re*, Garo *bre*, Dimasa *barai*).

e. Lastly, in the area of kinship, the writer (1942 bis) has already described the early Chinese system as reflecting a basic cross-cousin marriage pattern, with basic similarity to various TB systems. It does not appear that the AT cultural contacts had any significant influence on the over-all system, but there is a curious correspondence in the terms for oB and yB. Ch. *kâ* "oB" (Modern Ch. *ko-ko*) is late in the language (not in GSR), where it is written with an obsolete character for "sing," having replaced two earlier terms for oB; it appears to be a relatively late loan from the AT root represented by IN *kaka "oSb" (Fiji: "oB"). Ch. *d'iər* "yB" appears to have an ancient doublet *diər*, with indications of an original meaning "ySb" (Benedict *cit. supra*). This word, which is early in Chinese, appears to be directly comparable with IN *ha(ŋ)g'i~*a(ŋ)g'i, which basically has precisely the same denotation (ySb), thus greatly strengthening the view that this is in fact an ancient loan in Chinese (see Part 2 for fore-stress forms of the type *eŋ~*iŋ from the same root). Of greater significance, however, is the correspondence in the basic Chinese affinal term: *xuən* "take a wife, marriage; relatives by marriage" (also "bridegroom" in Modern Chinese); cf. IN *hipaγ<*hikwaγ "related by marriage"; T *khüay~*khöy~ *güay "male affinal kin" (Part 2, pp. 234-35). The Chinese term points to an original *khwəγ (see Table VI for other examples of *khw->*hw(u)-, *-γ>*-n). Karlgren reconstructs Arch. Ch. *xmwən (phonetic is *mïən*), indicating an old nasalized doublet form: *hŋ(k)wəγ. This correspondence again illustrates borrowing on the part of the Chinese of the more institutional aspects of AT culture.

The writer (1945) has also called attention to a system of kin numeratives ("No. 1 son," etc.), spread by "direct" as well as "stimulus" diffusion throughout Southeast Asia from an apparent Chinese source. He has since noted the occurrence of a numerical form of this pattern among the Vietnamese (Haut-Annam), and of a non-numerical form among the Palaung (Benedict 1947, 377 and note 18), while Egerod (1959)[9] has added to the Thai material, and an additional occurrence of the non-numerical form has been recorded for the Senoi (LeBar et al. 1964, 181). The earliest known form of this trait, however, is that of four *recurring* non-numerical terms, as encountered in ancient Chinese texts, and this precise pattern has been described for Bali (Belo 1936). In view of all the evidence at hand, there is now some question whether this Indonesian occurrence really represents an "independent focus" (Benedict *cit. supra*, 1947), and we must consider the possibility of an original AT source for this cultural item, with early "stimulus" diffusion to Chinese, followed by exportation to Southeast Asia of the later Chinese (numerical) elaboration of the trait.

To summarize the above discussion, the linguistic evidence as a whole points conclusively to an extensive cultural contact between the early Chinese and AT peoples. Aside from the lower numerals (1 through 100) and perhaps some other roots, notably those for "silver" and "goose," the process was essentially unidirectional, with the Chinese as the recipients rather than the donors. It would appear that the bulk of these loans were from an obsolete AT language, here labeled AT-x, not ancestral to any modern AT speech. For this reason, it is not certain whether the Chinese numerals were also taken over by AT-x, and it is possible that this "reversal" of borrowing occurred only at a somewhat later period and/or only in the ancestral Thai and related AT languages. In any event, the essentially recipient nature of the Chinese role in this general process is evident enough. It is also evident that many of these borrowed terms were then "exported" back to various groups in Southeast Asia. At a generally later period, of course, terms for such items as "tea" and "paper"

were diffused throughout the same region, this time as legitimate Chinese cultural loan-words.

The question now arises: How are we to interpret these linguistic findings? The core issue is whether the early Chinese had
all these cultural items and simply replaced their own terms for
them with AT loan-words, or whether they borrowed the cultural items along with the terms for them. Many of the agricultural and plant items, especially, have a southern "aspect," and
others (boats, cowry) have the look of the sea, so that we might
well imagine many of these items as diffusing inland from the
southeastern fringes of the continent. The root for "hunting" is
not so readily explained, however, and certainly we should not
expect to find the horse-riding complex here. The same might
be said for pottery and metal-working, though it should be noted
that for only one metal (tin/lead) do we have an IN cognate
specifically denoting a metal, so that presumably the use of other
metals (gold, copper, iron) was developed by the AT mainland
peoples subsequent to the archaic split from IN and the other
Oceanic groups. We know that the Chinese did have a term (of
ST origin) for "elephant," and yet borrowed a similar term from
AT, and perhaps the same process took place in the case of
"horse." It is also likely, however, that these borrowings reflected
the taking over of a more highly developed, more "sophisticated,"
aspect of the trait in question, e.g. a ceremonial or organized
hunt (note the Chinese meanings under HUNT); an elephant-
ivory (carving) complex; a horse-saddle-riding complex. The
writer finds it hard to reconcile the data with any assumption
other than that of a marked disparity in cultural development
between the early Chinese and the AT people or peoples from
whom they accepted so many basic cultural loan-words.

We must now consider the question as to the nature of the
contact between these two populations as well as the related
question as to where this might have occurred. Chinese culture,
as we know it historically, developed in the fertile valley of the
Huang Ho and its tributaries in northwestern China. The loan-
words in question are for the most part attested for the Archaic
Chinese period, dating from 1200 b.c. and earlier. The language
in which they are imbedded, Archaic Chinese, despite its an-

tiquity already shows marked phonological and morphological attrition when compared with its closest relatives, the TB languages, spoken generally far to the south and west of this Northwest China locus (Benedict 1939, 1940, 1948). It seems probable that the Chinese had arrived at that distant locus by moving generally north and somewhat east, thus skirting the south-central China region, the center of concentration of the ancestral AT populations. Somewhere along that line of migration, or perhaps at several points, these pioneering Chinese were subject to profound AT cultural influences—or had they already arrived at their promised land in the Huang Ho valley before experiencing this influence? This appears to be a moot question, at least as regards strictly linguistic evidence. The second alternative implies that the AT peoples actually moved as far north and west as that northwestern corner of China, but we know them to have been a highly vigorous and expanding stock, adventuresome even to the point of pushing off the mainland in the region of the South China coast, eventually to dominate all the island world of the Pacific. Also, in this same general context, can we speculate that the Chinese actually came under the suzerainty of some AT (presumably AT-x speaking) group? The fact that they were able to pass their basic numerals on to at least certain AT groups (the ancestors of the Thai, KS, and OB) appears to point in this direction, unless we posit a somewhat later (although still pre-Arch.Ch.) date for this "reversal" of borrowing, at a period when the Chinese had already attained a dominant cultural position.

Finally, it should be noted here in summary that the AT cultural influence extended also far to the west, providing many loan-words (and presumably cultural items) to the TB peoples in particular. These loan-words in TB are a curious and often puzzling lot. As might be expected, they are usually found in Tibetan and/or Burmese, often as isolated loans. Tibetan has probable or possible loans of this type for "iron," "tin/lead," "mortar," "goat," "field/meadow," "seed," "ear of corn," "sugar-cane," "wheat," "ginger," "dried meat," and "fishhook." The Burmese group of similarly isolated AT loan-words includes "field," "ladle," "bowl," "duck," "drunk/dizzy," "yam (cultivated)," "yam/

turnip/radish," and "bait/catch with bait," also the seemingly
more recent loans (from Chinese) for "market" and "ride," perhaps also "coconut" (from Shan). An additional example of
isolated occurrence, more difficult to explain, is that of the basic
root for "rice" in the Barish languages of Assam (and in the
Karen languages). Several loan-words are represented both in
Tibetan and Burmese, some with scattered representation elsewhere: "harrow/plough," "copper," "salt," "ladder/stairs," "basket," "needle," "sew"; in two instances, the specific forms are
quite distinct: "water buffalo" and "bee." Lepcha has two of
these loan-words, one shared with Tibetan ("indigo"), the other
with Burmese and Jili, an extinct Kachin dialect ("elephant")
—the latter are perhaps later loans from Thai. Several others are
found in Burmese and Kachin (but not Tibetan), usually with
representation also in Barish and/or Kukish: "shellfish," "dove,"
"cook with steam/steam pot," "ashes." Barish, in addition to the
isolated loan for "rice" (above), shares one possible loan-word
with Kachin ("ax"). In addition to the above, and to the even
earlier loan for "weave" (see above), four apparent AT loans
are basic TB roots with general distribution, viz. "house" (also
in Karen), "pig," "fireplace," and "wild yam" (as distinct from
"cultivated yam," an isolated loan in Burmese); "mortar" and
"salt" also perhaps belong here.

These loan-words in TB bear an entirely different stamp from
those found in Chinese and would appear to have been borrowed
from one or more AT languages distinct from AT-x and not
ancestral to any modern AT language. As pointed out repeatedly
above, these loan-words have a characteristic a vocalization, perhaps archaic in some cases ("iron"). They reflect a consistent
shift of velo-labial clusters to simple labials: $*kw>*p$ ("fireplace"); $*gw>*b$ ("seed," "sugarcane"); $*\eta w>*m$ ("house"),
somewhat as in the AT loans in Chinese. There is also one instance of $*-ow$ for $*-aw$ (Burmese "drunk"), paralleling the
shift found in the Chinese loan for "chief, lord" (above). The
simplification of initial $*gr-$ to $*g-$ ("mortar") also parallels the
shift found in Chinese. Two possible instances of palatalization
of $*k-$ before the vowel i are represented by the loans for "needle" (Tibetan "sew") and "fishhook" (Tibetan). There is some

evidence of interchange between *r* and *l* ("copper," "field"), especially after initial **b-* ("buy," "duck," "bee," "ashes"). Particularly striking is the indication of fore-stress and distinctive syllabicizing: Tibetan *za-* "lead, tin," AT **tyaŋwaa-/dyaŋwaa-* (syllabicized as *dya/ŋwaa-*); Tibetan *sga* "ginger," AT **saqaŋ-*; Burmese *bai* "duck," AT **balap(w)it′*; Burmese *pra*, Barish **pla*, Mikir *p′əlo<*phla* "ashes," AT **b-la/buuk*. One must posit phonological shifts of the above types for the AT language or languages from which the TB borrowings were made. The evidence from the distribution of terms within TB points to a long-continued contact or series of contacts, dating from the proto-TB period to relatively late (historic) times. Certain AT roots, notably those for "water buffalo" and "wild yam," were diffused to TB but not to Chinese. Apart from the curious group of basic TB roots which reveal an intimate contact at a very early period, however, the AT loans in TB appear to have been made sporadically and at a distance, so to speak, without the systematic, overwhelming cultural impact shown by the similar AT loans in Chinese.

NOTES

[1] See Benedict 1947, for an analysis of "nuclear" vs. "peripheral" as applied to a specific historical problem (the development of the Vietnamese kinship terminology).

[2] See Benedict 1948 for a comparative study of various tonal systems in Southeast Asia; the general observations made at that time are still applicable, since the origin of the principal tonal system remains a mystery. It may have arisen as the result of the Thai and Chinese mutual influence described below, and may have been later passed on to Miao-Yao and (through Thai) to Vietnamese.

[3] The writer still inclines to the view that Miao-Yao is basically a separate unity, despite loans of this kind as well as occasional correspondences with other groups, especially with Austroasiatic (this remains the most likely affiliation, if any is established, as noted in Benedict 1942).

[4] For Chinese, we follow Karlgren (1923, 1957) in all essential respects. Forms are noted either as Anc. or Arch., or left unmarked where the form has been consistent; forms marked with an asterisk are the writer's additional reconstructions.

[5] Sui generally stands for the KS group here, but Kam has a

most unusual group of correspondences, apparently of late origin: *ma* "horse" but *hŋwa* "dog" and *hŋu* "pig" (but cf. the AT root); cf. also Kam *hŋwat* "flea" for KS **hmat,* T **hmat,* but Kam *ma* "come," KS **hma,* T **ma,* and Kam *hma:n* "yellow," KS **hŋa:n.*

[6] Related to the basic Ch. term *ka* "house, home," which thus becomes "a place where one sows," although the graph shows a pig (this perhaps also a phonetic) under a roof.

[7] This extension to Barish is surprising; note that "bird" (above) has precisely the same pattern of occurrence as this root: Chinese-Karen-Barish. The Barish languages are unusual in some respects, e.g. they have many glottalized roots (this feature is not shown in our transcription) and they lack tones (personal communication from R. Burling); in general, they appear to represent an archaic "axis" overlain by more recent Kukish elements, so that the root for "rice" may be of considerable antiquity here. Burling and Bhattacharya (1956) have assigned a period of around 100 A.D. to this basic separation in the stock, but many definite cognates are marked as noncognate in this study (e.g. *ga/ham:nam/a* "good"), hence a much less early date is indicated.

[8] This *ti-chih,* **p'lau* "ox," was perhaps derived from the standard AT root: **kala(ŋ)gwaw* via **kwalaw* (metathesis) and **pwalaw* (this shift established as early in AT).

[9] A detailed analysis of Thai material on KN has been made by Søren Egerod (1959). The KN system in general furnishes an outstanding example, it would appear, of an originally borrowed trait (from AT) that then became "naturalized" in Chinese and later "exported" throughout Southeast Asia.

EDITOR's NOTE

Abbreviations and phonetic symbols are the same as those used in the two previous articles, referred to here as Benedict 1966, or *AT,* and as Benedict 1967, *AT-S,* Pts. 1 and 2. The following corrigenda are to be noted for *AT-S,* Pt. 1:

p. 204, line 10: read: as *b-*
p. 205, line 5: read: **γ(w)ala*
p. 220, line 10: read: **pu[ʔ]γaak*
p. 220, line 12: read: **pu[ʔ]γaat*
p. 223, line 10: read: affixed root
p. 224, line 2: delete: *<*hńam*

LIST OF THAI AND CHINESE TERMS

ân 鞍 saddle

âŋ 盎 bowl, basin, tub

ap 鴨 duck

b'a 耙 rake, harrow

b'ăk 帛 silk stuff

b'ïan 楄 board under body in coffin

b'ïuk 箙 quiver

b'ïwăm 範 mold; rule, law

b'ïwăn 飯 cooked rice; food

b'ïwăt 栿 raft

dïək 弋 shoot with arrow and string attached; arrow

diŏg 窯 kiln

diŏŋ 融 hot air, steam, heat

d'ai 苔 moss

d'ân 彈 shoot pellets; pellet (of crossbow); crossbow

d'ân 蛋 egg

d'âŋ 糖 sugar

d'âu 稻 growing rice, paddy

d'âu 陶 kiln; pottery

d'âu 繩 rope, string; to braid, twist (rope)

d'âu 淘 wash (rice, minerals), cleanse

d'iek/d'iôk 笛 flute

d'ïər 弟 yB

d'ien 田 field, cultivated land; to cultivate field

d'ien 淀 indigo

d'uŋ 同 to join

d'uŋ 銅 bronze, copper

d''au 櫂 oar (long)

d''ïək 食 to eat

dzïəd~ dzïwad 彗 broom
~g'ïwad

ěŋ 罌 jar, vase

gïwăn 園 garden

g'âŋ 航 two boats lashed together; square boat

g'əi 亥 pig (calendar term)

g'ïəu 臼 mortar

g'wâ 禾 growing grain

g'wân 莧 goat, mountain sheep

g'wən 魂 spiritual soul

g'wət 紇 knot; tassel

g'wo 狐 fox

g'yie 騎 ride (horse)

ɣăm 鹹 salt, salty

ɣwa 華 flower

γwaŋ 黄 yellow

i 改 Plantago

ĭa 椰 coconut

ĭak/dĭok 籥 flute

ĭäm 鹽 salt

ĭäŋ 盈 full; fill

ĭaŋ 蠅 fly, n.

ĭaŋ 羊 sheep

ĭaŋ 揚 to winnow

ĭəm 醃 to salt, pickle

ĭəu 酉 cock (calendar term)

ĭu 俞 boat (obsolete)

ĭuĕt 聿 writing stylus

ĭwän 鉛 lead, n.

ka 枷 cangue

ka 猳 male pig, boar

ka 賈 price

ka 家 house, home

ka 稼 sow; grain

kai 芥 mustard

kâ 哥 sing (obs.); oB

kian 肩 shoulder

kĭaŋ 薑 ginger

kĭəm 金 gold

kĭən 斤 ax

kĭəu 鳩 pigeon

kiei 鷄 fowl

kĭuŋ 弓 bow, n.

kiwat 袂 sleeve

kĭwəi/d 貴 precious; dear, expensive

klwâ/glwâ 蝸 snail

ko 鴣 pheasant

ko 沽 to sell

kɔk 角 horn

ku 彝 billion

kuk 稟 cereals; grain

kwa 瓜 gourd

kwâ 戈 dagger-ax

kwâ 螺 kind of small wasp

kwân 管 reed; tube, pipe; flute

kʻĭuən 犬 dog

kʻlĭəp 泣 to weep

kʻuâ 稞 wheat; grain

la-chiao 辣椒 pepper

lâm 藍 indigo

lât 辣 sharp, biting; acid, pungent

lâu 牢 pen, fold; domestic animal

lâu 醪 spirits with sediment, wine

liei~lyi 犁 plough

luŋ 籠 basket, cage

lwân 卵 egg

lyi 釐 thousandth

lyi 里 village; mile

lywi~
luâi 耒 plough stem, plough

ma 馬 horse

mai 買 to buy

mai (d.t.) 賣 to sell

mĭad 袂 sleeve

mĭan 綿 cotton-wool

mĭan 棉 cotton-tree; cotton

mĭat 滅 to destroy

miei 米 rice

mieŋ 茗 kind of tea

mieŋ 酩 drunk

mĭĕt 蜜 honey

mĭôg 麰 barley

mĭôk 目 eye

mĭwăn 萬 10,000

mĭwaŋ 網 fishing net; to catch
with a net

mwăn 蔓 turnip

mwəg 梅 plum

mwɛk 麥 wheat

nieu 溺 urine

nuo 奴 crossbow

ńĭam 染 to dye

ńĭəg 耳 ear

ńĭəg 餌 bait

ńĭəm~
ńĭəm 紝 to weave

ńĭôk 肉 meat

ŋa 牙 tooth; tusk, ivory

ŋan 雁 goose (wild)

ŋâ 鵝 goose (domestic)

ŋâ 我 I

ŋât 歹 fragment of bone

ŋĭăn 言 big flute

ŋĭəu 牛 cattle

ŋĭĕn 銀 silver

ŋĭo 魚 fish

ŋo 午· horse (calendar term)

ŋo 吾 I

pa 芭 pig, sow

păk 百 100

pâu 寶 valuables

pĭan 扁 flat and thin

pĭan 鞭 whip

pin-lâng 檳榔 betel-nut (areca)

pin-lü 檳蒟 betel (quid)

pïwăŋ 舫 two boats lashed together; square boat

pïwăp 法 law; model; style, fashion

pïwən 粉 flour; powder

pïwən (d.t.) 糞 manure

pïwər 飛 to fly

pïwo 斧 ax

pɔ-tsïog 芭蕉 banana

puâ 番 to sow

pwan 板 board

pwan 版 board, tablet

pwan 鈑 metal plate, plaque

pwo 布 cloth (esp. cotton cloth); currency, money

pwâi/d 貝 cowry

p'ăk 魄 animal soul

p'ïan 篇 writing tablet

p'ïug 桴 raft

p'ïuŋ 蜂 bee, wasp

p'ïuŋ 葑 kind of turnip

p'ïwəi 肺 lungs

sâu~

šïəu 艇 boat; num. adj. for boats

sĕŋ 甥 cousin (MBS, FSiS), nephew (SiS)

sĕŋ 生 live, be born

sĕŋ 笙 reed organ

sïän 私 rice or millet

sïăk 腊 dried meat

sïər 死 to die

sïəu 繡 to embroider

siek 錫 tin

sieu/
siôg 簫 pan-pipe

sïuĕt 戌 dog (calendar term)

sɔŋ 雙 pair

šïɛt 虱 louse

šïog 溲 urine

šïôg 蒐 hunting assembly in springtime

šïaŋ 鮈 smoked (meat) (cited in Savina 1965)

šïôg 狩 to hunt; great winter hunt

šïuŋ 舂 to hull grain with a pestle

tâi 歹 bad

tâu 刀 knife

ti-chih 地支 (calendar terms)

tieŋ 鼎 tripod

tieu 鳥 bird

tïo 猪 pig

t'ăt 獺 otter

t'iei 梯 step, ladder, stairs

t'ien-kan 天干 (calendar terms)

t'ieŋ 珽 slice of dried meat

t'iet 鐵 iron

t'uo 兔 rabbit

t'iăk~

d'iăk 杓 ladle

t'iək 織 to weave

t'iəm 鍼 and 針 needle

t'iəŋ 烝 rising steam; to steam, distil

t'iəu 舟 boat

t'iĕt 蛭 leech

t''iəu 丑 ox (calendar term)

tsău 竈 hearth, fireplace; cooking place, stove

tsiəu 酒 spirits, wine

ts'ien 千 1,000

tsĭa 蔗 sugarcane

tsĭu 主 master, lord, chief

tsĭu 祉 ancestral tablet

xău 耗 kind of millet

xmwəg 晦 dark, obscure

xuən 婚 take a wife, marriage; relatives by marriage

xwa 花 flower

xwâr 火 fire

xwəi/g 灰 ashes; dust; lime

xwəi/g 賄 property, valuables; present, bribe

xwiet 血 blood

yĭu/

gĭwo 竽 reed organ

ywie 爲 elephant (obs.); to make, do

zĭăd 枻 oar (short)

zĭaŋ 象 elephant

zwi 穗 ear of grain

zi 市 market

zĭəp 十 10

zĭuk 孰 ripe

Introduction to Glossary

The Austro-Thai (AT) language family, first tentatively joined together by the writer in 1942, then assembled in greater detail (and christened) in 1966 and 1967 (in the articles reprinted in this volume), has now grown even larger with the addition of the Miao-Yao (MY) group of languages of south-central China and Indochina. Although our comparative analysis of these languages is still at an early stage, it appears that they stand somewhat apart from the other AT languages. If now we group Indonesian, Cham, and the related languages of Formosa and Oceania under Austronesian, and Thai and the related languages of the mainland (Kam-Sui, Lakkia, Laqua, Kelao, Lati) and Hainan (Li, Ong-be) under Kadai (this extension of the writer's term proposed by Haudricourt 1967), we arrive at the following diagram of relationships:

As previously noted (*AT* 1966), there are indications of a very early linkage (less than a full genetic relationship) between AT and the Austroasiatic (AA) languages. Our present analysis confirms this linkage, with occasional forms of much linguistic interest, notably (provisional reconstructions) AA *sok "hair" (Kharia $sɔ^{?}$-; Bahnar $śok$, Khmer $sɔk$, Mon sok, Riang huk-, Sakai $sog \sim so^{?}$), IN *$buhuk$ <AT *$busuk$ or *$bosok$ (confirms the *s); AA *$^{?}(m)ba{:}r$ "two" (Santali bar, Juang $ambar$, Remo $^{?}mba{:}r$; Bahnar $^{?}ba{:}r$, Mon $^{?}ba$<$^{?}bar$ [inscriptions], Sakai $hmbar$ $\sim mar \sim ma$, Khasi $a{:}r$, Riang $ka{:}r$, Palaung $a{:}r \sim a$, Nicobarese q), AT *$(N)qa(m)bar$ "twin, double(d), two" (see GLOSSARY) (confirms the nasal + stop). Only very occasional correspondences of this kind have been noted, however, and we must still think in terms of a "linkage" or "substratum" rather than of a fully reconstructable language stock. The Min-chia language of southwest China (Yünnan province) is perhaps more closely related to AT, but it was inundated by loans from Chinese at an early period, and the remaining lexical material is too poorly known to permit of any definitive conclusion at this time. The remaining language stock in this part of the world, viz. Sino-Tibetan, must be regarded as quite unrelated, despite occasional remarks to the contrary in the literature; the doubter might profitably compare the assemblage of AT roots in the GLOSSARY with a similar collection of Tibeto-Burman (with modifications = Sino-Tibetan) roots in Benedict 1972, the correspondences being rare indeed (*AT* 1967bis).

The precise relationships within the AN and Kadai groups remain to be worked out; Miao-Yao, on the other hand, consists of two clearly demarcated divisions (Miao and Yao), the former including one aberrant language (Pateng; see Benedict 1942: note 58; not mentioned by Purnell), closely related to the Tahua "Yao" (= MYT) recorded by Chang (1947, 1953)—cf. BIRD; DOG; TWIN. Our previous emphasis (*AT* 1966 and 1967) on Formosa as a key area for the AN languages in general has been fully supported by our most recent comparative studies as reflected in the GLOSSARY, with Formosa repeatedly supplying critical phonological items (YELLOW: Siraya *ma/kuliaŋ) or lexical items (CULTIVATE/FIELD: Thao *buhat "field," *m/buhat "to work"<"to work the field"). On the basis of the linguistic evidence, Formosa must be regarded as the main "staging area" for the movements of the AT peoples from the mainland (South China coast) to the offshore islands and ultimately to the whole island world of Oceania and to Madagascar (the Hova). The Formosan languages fall into three distinct groupings, without any intermediate members: Atayalic (Atayal, Sedik); Tsouic (Tsou, Kanakanabu=Kanabu, Saaroa); East (Ferrell: Paiwanic) (Paiwan, Puyuma, Rukai, Ami, Bunun, Thao, Saisiat, Pazeh, Kuvalan=Kavalan and [extinct] Favorlang, Siraya). Dyen (1965) has presented some of the relevant evidence relating to the high degree of divergence shown by these languages, comparing it with the linguistic divergence found in Melanesia and New Guinea, and he makes the following comment: "thus there are at least two different homelands that can be proposed for the Austronesians: one in Formosa and one in Melanesia" (Dyen 1965: 287). This problem, which we shall term the "Dyen dilemma," is really only a "pseudoproblem," since the two areas present entirely different types of divergence. The divergence in the Melanesia-New Guinea area is on a superficial level, manifestly the product of the attenuation of AN lexical material at the edges of an expanding AN area as it gradually encroached upon non-AN areas. In Formosa, on the other hand, the divergence goes to the very core of the AN material, both lexically and phonologically, the latter to a degree that requires some basic alterations in our reconstructions of AN phonemes (see below), as recognized also by Dyen. Formosa was not the homeland, but it was only a giant step away from the true AN homeland on the continent. The two other major AT groups took the small step to the island of Hainan, one at an early period (the Li and Ong-Be), the other only in recent times (the "Miao" of Hainan, really a Yao group). Two AN peoples finally came back to the continent, far to the south (the Malay and Cham), and a small group of the latter actually came back off the continent to establish a colony on the southern coast of Hainan (Benedict 1941), thus completing a strange journey from China to Formosa to (unknown island/islands) to Vietnam to Hainan.

The GLOSSARY presents a series of LCG's (Likely Cognate Groups) drawn from comparative AT materials. Some of these (cf. EYE) are well defined phonologically, essentially universal in distribution in the stock, and might well qualify as AT "roots," while others (cf. SEIZE) exhibit considerable range in consonantism (mostly surd vs. sonant distinctions) and/or vocalism (especially $*a \sim *ə \sim *u$). In several cases (cf. DOG) it is not quite certain whether the various "pieces" actually do fit together (are cognate), but this material is included in the GLOSSARY nonetheless, in the hope that further study will shed more light on the subject. The GLOSSARY is replete with examples of "split cognates," often of a bizarre type, at times with no common element, e.g. Thai *maw and Lati *a/sŭ "drunk," from AT *ma/buśuk, the essential connecting links being supplied by other AT languages (see DRUNK). It is apparent that a number of accidental correspondences might well have slipped into our LCG's; it is equally apparent that many forms, now considered totally unrelated, will eventually be shown to be "split cognates," as we learn more of this complex process of syllabic reduction in AT.

The various forms under each entry in the GLOSSARY are grouped separately for the AN, Kadai, and MY divisions of AT, in that order. In those entries for which more than one reconstruction is indicated, or where more are required in the interest of clarity, the forms are further arranged under (I), (II), (III), etc. It is usually not clear at this stage whether we are dealing with doublet/triplet forms at the proto-AT level or whether our reconstructions simply are not sufficiently precise (work in progress).

A striking feature of the GLOSSARY, and one for which the writer was completely unprepared, is the very large number of "core" vocabulary items shared by groups so far apart as AN, Kadai, and MY. No attempt has been made at a lexicostatistical analysis of this material, but it would appear, even without such analysis, that the AT languages have preserved these basic items to a wholly unprecedented degree. It should also be remembered, however, that these languages were until recently considered unrelated, and indeed unrepentant scholars still inveigh against the AT hypothesis. These considerations must lead us, as comparative linguists, to the discomfiting possibility that our current lexicostatistical concepts are based to a considerable degree on faulty comparative acumen, with many AT families lying around waiting to become incarnate, so to speak. If this be so, we can anticipate extensive modifications of these concepts, with the introduction of totally new time scales.

The GLOSSARY material also contains surprises in the large number of very specialized items, the writer's favorite being perhaps PASS LENGTHWISE. It seems incredible that a root with so specific a meaning could have been preserved over so long a period of time, and it is understandable that the writer (1942: note 51), with reference to another root of this type (RIPEN FRUIT), described the correspondence as "semantically too specific to be trusted." In view of the large number of such correspondences in our GLOSSARY material, however, we can now afford to be more "trusting," and again it behooves us to reshape our linguistic view of the world.

We come now to the inevitable question of the selection of items to be included in the GLOSSARY. A number of possible entries have been excluded, at times with a sigh of regret, as being "possible" (50 per cent chance or less) rather than "probable" (more than 50 per cent chance) AT correspondences. Inasmuch as the question of the continental connections of the AN languages is of paramount importance historically, with few exceptions only LCG's having AN representation have been included in the GLOSSARY. This emphasizes the AN-Kadai and AN-MY connections at the expense of the MY-Kadai—but an occasional root having only MY and Kadai representation has been included because of special cultural and/or phonological interest (BEAN/PEA; FRAGRANT). The writer, as anthropologist turned linguist, does plead guilty to a bias of including roots of special interest to the ethnologist or the culture historian, hence the appearance of certain items of very restricted distribution (TUBER/SWEET POTATO) and perhaps the elaboration of kinship terminology (GRANDPARENT/GRAND-CHILD/ . . .) to a degree beyond that required for strictly linguistic purposes.

A final note must be devoted to the nature of the cultural material itself. The implications of much of this material are of staggering proportions, since they call for a radical reshaping of our current ideas of the early development of culture in Southeast Asia and the Far East in general.[1] These suggestions were developed at some length in earlier articles (*AT* 1967 and 1967bis), with particular attention to the apparent innovative role played by the ancestral AT people with respect to the Chinese. Striking confirmation has now come from archeologists working quite independently of the writer (Solheim 1967, 1969), who have uncovered in Thailand what appear to be the very graves of these ancestral AT people or peoples, with evidence of sophisticated bronze casting in the middle of the third millennium B.C., about a thousand years before the appearance of the celebrated bronzes of ancient China. We can even reconstruct

the very word for "copper/bronze" (AT *lu[y]aŋ) for this "Early
Bronze Culture" and trace the loan into Chinese and the back-
loans to Thai and Li (see COPPER/BRASS). The most recent
developments in the field of comparative Sino-Tibetan (Benedict
1972) have yielded a more precise knowledge of this "back-loan
influence" of Chinese upon the ancestral Thai and related Kadai
languages, as indicated here and there in the GLOSSARY, while
at the same time confirming the hypothesis that the essential
Chinese role vis-à-vis Austro-Thai was that of borrower rather
than lender. Some of the material presented earlier (*AT* 1967bis)
in this connection requires modification in the light of this more
recent knowledge of early Chinese forms, e.g. Ch. *ma* "horse,"
Anc. *ma*, Arch. *mɔ*, has now been derived from an original *mra
via *mwa, thus bringing it into (nongenetic) relationship with
TB *m/raŋ (both seen as very early loans from a non-ST form
such as *m[ ]raŋ[ ]) and keeping it apart from the *ti-chih* (calendar term) ŋo<*zŋa, from AT *tsaŋa, the two "horses" thus
symbolically meeting in ancient China. The associated term for
"ride a horse" remains firmly AT in origin (see CLIMB . . .
MOUNT), hence it would seem that whereas the Chinese first
learned of the horse from the west (presumably Central Asia
in the broad sense), they learned how to ride it from the AT
people, whose very term for the strange beast (*tsaŋa "fork")
apparently refers to its use in this manner (*AT* 1967bis). Another
recent finding in the field of Sino-Tibetan studies (Benedict
1972) is of critical importance for the culture historian. The
linguistic evidence, highly complex but quite unmistakable in
its implications, points to an AT source (see FIBER/BEARD)
for the Arch. Ch. doublet forms for "writing pen/brush" via
"feather/quill," with a further very early loan into Tibetan. Thus
writing itself must be reckoned as still another achievement of
the AT-speaking peoples, and we can anticipate the eventual
uncovering of AT inscriptions to go along with the bronze
artifacts.

The implications of this AT cultural material in other directions are equally surprising, and take us much further afield.
Much of the material presented earlier (*AT* 1967) has now
been substantially revised and should be checked against the

GLOSSARY forms—e.g. under AGRICULTURE, the basic root for CULTIVATE/FIELD/WORK (see GLOSSARY), represented in IN, Formosa, Kadai, and MY, is analyzed in a faulty manner, which fails to bring out the semantic connections of the root ("cultivate"~"field"). A strikingly parallel AT root for CULTIVATE/FIELD/WORK/YAM/SWEETPOTATO (see the GLOSSARY), with even broader representation, leads to the celebrated Polynesian (and Fijian) *kumala "sweet potato," with what appears to be an impeccable AT derivation (*Nqum/al/ah "the cultivated crop") and with apparently directly comparable forms on the continent (Thai *man "potato, sweet potato, yam," Dioi man "yams, potatoes," Sek man "yam," all from *mal) and on Hainan (Li *mwal<*(u)mal "sweet potato") and even apparent early loans in Sino-Tibetan; cf. Ch. mwăn "turnip" (AT 1967bis) and Burmese up-hmwàn "kind of potato," from */hmwàl~*/hmwàr (rather than Burmese mun-la "radish," as cited in the above source). This is all most surprising, since there is a consensus among ethnologists that the sweet potato, along with the term for it (kumala), was imported from South America into Polynesia. Perhaps, but the linguistic evidence speaks strongly against such a view, unless we are indeed involved here with a quite accidental, although highly specific, correspondence of sound and meaning. If we reject this explanation as unlikely, we must conclude that some early AT people, probably the forefathers of the Polynesians, reached the shores of South America with a highly developed knowledge of the cultivation of tuberous plants (but not the sweet potato, native to the Americas); that they applied one of their terms (kumala) to this welcome new plant which so resembled their yam, bringing it for the first time under intensive cultivation and thereby spreading the practice and the term regionally in South America; and, finally, that their descendants returned in time to Polynesia with their newly acquired plant (but not with the potato, too dissimilar from the yam to be acceptable). It is possible that another highly specific AT cultural term also found its way, by a similar route, to South America, viz. *(n)tu(m)ba "poison (for fish)" (see GLOSSARY); cf. the Tchikao (Carib-speaking tribe of the Upper Xingu, Brazil) timbo, id. A variety of cultural items, notably the blowgun, have long been pointed out by ethnologists as common to these two areas (Southeast Asia and South America), hence we should perhaps anticipate that specific lexical elements might also be involved in exceptional cases.

SOURCES

AUSTRONESIAN

Indonesian (IN): forms marked ** cited after Dempwolff (1930), with minor orthographical modifications (esp. *y* for *j*, *w* for *v*), along with changes proposed by Dyen (1947a, 1947b, 1951, 1953a, 1953b), notably ? for medial and final *h*, and *h* for medial '. Forms marked * are the writer's, based on forms from Dempwolff or occasionally from other sources (Shellabear for Malay, Tablan and Mallari for Tagalog), or are citations from other (named) sources; most of the modified reconstructions involve the substitution of *(*m*)*b* for **b*, almost always on the basis of *b* rather than *v* as a reflex in Javanese and/or Hova.

Yami: Ogawa and Asai (1935); Ferrell (1969).

Cham: Aymonier and Cabaton (1906) (written=early forms).

Proto-Oceanic (PO): forms marked ** cited after Grace (1969), with minor orthographical changes (? for *q*, γ for *R*). Forms marked * are the writer's, usually based on Fijian and Sa'a forms cited by Dempwolff (his MN=Melanesian), with the reconstitution of nasal + stop along the lines suggested by Biggs (1965), or are citations from other (named) sources, esp. Biggs. Fijian kinship terms are from Capell and Lester (1945-46).

Southeast Papua (SEP): based on material from Capell (1943), with the reconstitution of nasal + stop as for Proto-Oceanic (above).

Proto-Polynesian (PPN): forms marked ** cited after Walsh and Biggs (1966) or Biggs, Walsh, and Waqa (1970), without specification as to the precise level (PPN or later). There is some overlap here, since the PPN reconstructions are based in part on Fijian forms. At times there is an indication of a doublet reconstruction for PPN not cited in the above sources, and a few forms have been reconstructed on the basis of material from Dempwolff; these forms are marked *.

Formosa: Ogawa and Asai (1935) (in Japanese), with normalized phonetic orthography; Ferrell (1969), which includes a rich assortment of citations from early sources, some on extinct languages, notably from the Utrecht manuscript of 1650 (on Siraya); also Dyen (1965), which includes citations from recent workers in the field. Additional sources are Ferrell (1966bis) for Paiwan (Makazayazaya dialect); and both Ferrell (1967) and Egerod (1965, 1965bis, 1966, 1966bis, 1969) for Atayal. All reconstructions are by the writer.

KADAI

Thai: all reconstructions cited are by the writer, mostly from early work (see 1942 article, notes 27 and 28), based on forms from a number of primary sources: Borua 1920 (Ahom); Needham 1894 (Khamti); Cushing 1914 and Mix 1920 (Shan); Pallegoix 1896 (Siamese); Guignard 1912 (Lao); Diguet 1895 (Black Tai); Minot 1940 (White Tai); Diguet 1910 and Gordaliza 1908 (Tho); Savina 1924 and Li 1940 (Nung).

N. Thai: the Dioi forms are mainly from Esquirol and Williatte 1908, with Li 1957 as a secondary source; the forms for Yay, a closely related dialect, are from Gedney 1965, 1970. The Cao-lan and Ts'un-lao forms (CT) are from material presented by Haudricourt 1960. The N. Thai reconstructions are by the writer, largely following the analysis by Li 1954 and 1957bis; the forms cited for Wu-ming and Po-ai are from these articles or from Li 1957, 1965; other N. Thai reconstructions, cited as Chuang, are by Haudricourt (in Savina 1965), based on Dioi, Wu-ming (Chinese source) and Chuang (Chinese source) (op. cit., p. 13). Finally, the Sek forms are from Haudricourt (1963, 1963bis, 1967, or in Savina 1965) unless specifically credited to Gedney (1970, 1971), the latter from a somewhat different dialect spoken in the Nakhon Phanom province of Thailand (rather than inland from Thakhek in Laos).

Kam-Sui (KS): reconstructions cited are by the writer, following in part suggestions made by Li 1965, the source of many of the Sui, Mak, and Then forms. The same writer has supplied primary sources for Sui (Li 1948, 1949) and Then (Li 1966-67) and a major source for Mak (Li 1943) (in Chinese). The Kam forms are adapted from the reconstructed forms cited in Haudricourt 1967 and Savina 1965, based on a Chinese dictionary of the language (called Tung in Chinese) published at Kweiyang in 1959 (Savina 1965: 13).

Lakkia (Lk.): Haudricourt 1967, based on an anonymous work published at Peking in 1959 (see note 2 of this article), where source not cited; also Mao and Chou 1962.

Ong-Be (OB): Savina 1965, unless specifically credited to Jeremaissen 1892; the latter dialect is a "sister dialect," rather than directly ancestral to that recorded by Savina around 1930.

Li: Savina 1931, for Southern Li (S. Li) and Northern Li (N. Li), the latter almost identical with the Shaved Head Loi: Liamui forms in Jeremaissen (1892); Calder 1882, for Lakia (entirely distinct from Lakkia, above); Jeremaissen 1892, for the Loi (=Li) dialects: White Sand (WS) Loi, Shaved Head (SH) Loi (Liamui and Five Fingers Mountain [FF] dialects), Double Cloth (DC) Loi, Small Cloth (SC) Loi; Stübel 1937, for various dialects of N. Li type: Basadungli (Bas.), Mefuli (Mef.), Dakili, Dogangli, Ki, Ha, or for those of an intermediate type: Bupäli (Bup.); Wang 1952 (in Chinese), for White Sand Li (WS Li), very similar to WS Loi (above).

Laqua (Lq.): Bonifacy 1905, 1908 (with several discrepancies); also a few forms cited in Lajonquière 1906.[2]

Kelao (Kl.): Bonifacy 1905, cited as Kl. or S. Kl. (Southern Kelao); also a few forms cited in Lajonquière 1906; Clarke 1911, for Northern Kelao (N. Kl.), a quite distinct language; a few (mainly pronominal) forms for a Kelao language of N. Kl. type are cited in Beauclair 1946, while the citation for Mulao (see *Austro-Thai Pronouns: Notes*), also in the Kelao group, is from the writer's notes on a Beauclair manuscript (which has since disappeared).

Lati (Lt.): Bonifacy 1906 (similar to the Ban Phung dialect of Robert); also Robert 1913, for two dialects (reported to be mutually unintelligible): Man P'ang (MP) and Ban Phung (BP); also a few forms cited in Lajonquière 1906.

MIAO-YAO

Proto-MY (PMY) forms marked ** cited after Purnell 1970, with minor orthographical and other changes, notably *(m)p for **P, *(n)t for **T, *(n)d for **D, *(N)q for **Q, and with tone markings excluded. Forms marked * are by the writer, at times modifications of Purnell's forms, at other times based on reconstructions from other MY material (see below).

Proto-Miao (PM) forms marked ** cited after Purnell, who also reconstructs separately for Proto-Eastern (PE), Proto-Central (PC), and Proto-Western (PW) forms of Miao. PM forms marked * are by the writer, either modifications of Purnell's forms or based on reconstructions from other Miao material, mainly from Chang 1947, 1953 (for various Miao dialects); also Chang 1957, for I Miao or Kwang-shun Miao (MKS); Graham 1967, for Ch'uan Miao (MCh.), similar to the Su-yung Miao (MSY) forms cited by Purnell; Esquirol 1931, for Kanao or Cheng-feng Miao (MCF); Hosie 1897, for Phö (similar to MCF); Savina 1916 and Heimbach 1966, for White Meo or Petchabun Miao (MPT) (distinct dial.); also Bonifacy 1908, for Pateng. Finally, the MFPL citations under Miao are from the "Kelao" list in the *Miao-fang Pei-lan,* as made available (in Chinese) in Ruey (1956), now recognized as a word-list for Miao (exact affiliation uncertain) rather than for Kelao, despite the label (contra AT 1966).

Proto-Yao (PY) forms marked ** cited after Purnell, who also reconstructs separately for Proto-Iu Mien (PIM) and Proto-Kim Mun (PKM), corresponding closely to the distinction between YCR and YHN, respectively (below). PY forms marked * are by the writer or are credited to Haudricourt 1947-50, who had access to numerous Yao vocabularies, including two (Nos. 5 and 6 in his Mien material) showing rare or unique preservation of initial consonantal clusters. Mien or "Highland Yao" forms are cited from Lombard 1968, the record of a Yao speech in Chiengrai province, Thailand (Chiengrai Yao = YCR); Savina 1926 is the source for the Kim Mun forms, recorded in Haininh province, Vietnam (Haininh Yao = YHN), as well as for Taipan Yao (YTP), of the "Highland Yao" type; the Hsiang-

an Yao (YHA) and Ling-chun Yao (YLC) forms are cited from
Purnell (1970); the Paip'ai Yao (YPP) forms are cited from
Chang (1966).

RECONSTRUCTION

A provisional reconstruction of AT forms has been achieved
through fitting together reconstructions in each of the three
main divisions of the stock. As shown below, each of the three
has made its distinctive contributions toward the common end:
the AN forms are of special value in reconstructing finals, the
Kadai forms in reconstructing vowels and stop + *r/l* clusters,
the MY forms in reconstructing initials and stop + nasal units.
It should perhaps be stressed again that these are indeed provisional reconstructions, of a kind that might be labeled simply
"work in progress," and that they are presented here in order
to stimulate further interest in this difficult field, so that future
progress may be measured in years rather than in decades, as
at present.

Morphology

The syntactical features of the parent AT speech remain to
be worked out, but the subject + verb + object general arrangement appears to have been part of the scheme. The only
morphological process that can be established at the proto-AT
level is affixation, including infixation as well as prefixation and
suffixation. There is frequent alternation of sonant vs. surd at
the proto-AT level, e.g. EXCHANGE/ (AT *(m)bali~*pali~
*pali/t, as well as at the later levels, e.g. DIVIDE (IN *biyak
~*piyak), but it does not appear possible to attribute any morphological function to this alternation. The AN languages also
show frequent complete or partial reduplication, and at times
reduplicated forms can be reconstructed for AT on the basis of
lack of initial aspiration (PASS LENGTHWISE), voicing (CAR-
RY ON BACK), vocalic lengthening (FOOT; PILE UP; PLUCK),
or other special features (BLOW/; DIFFICULT; FROG; HORN;
LIVE; SUBMERGE) in the monosyllabic mainland languages,

with MY offering more concrete evidence in three roots (these show the typical MY initial stress):

	AT	Form: East	PMY
laugh	*(ma/)tla/tlaw[a]	*(ma/)taṭawa	*tlat
sew/plait/			
weave	*(m)pla/plaqi[s]	*ṭaṭaqis	*(n)tat
beat/wing	*(n)ta/tab	*tatab (IN)	*(n)taat

As in the case of the initial surd/sonant alternation, however, no specific function can be assigned to this process, although all three examples in the above table involve "repetitive action."

AT prefixes, as in the case of the other affixes, can generally be established for the proto-AT level only in those cases where there exists some example of inclusion in the final (reduced) Kadai or MY forms. A possible exception is furnished by the ubiquitous prefix AT *k/~*q/, often found with roots for parts of the body, regularly represented in bound forms by Thai *? before *d or *b, e.g. AT *q/baγa "shoulder," Thai *?ba=/?baa/ <*q/ba(γ)a, also by Thai *h (probably earlier *? on basis of Kam-Sui evidence) before continuants, e.g. AT *[q/][u]way "rattan," T *hwaay<*q(a)way. Siamese (and rarely Lao) exhibits another bound form *ka/, which appears generally to be from a much later level, e.g. it occurs before the above prefix in BONE (see GLOSSARY), yet it appears to correspond directly to the AT *k/ prefix in BAG, BAT/ and CATTLE/BUFFALO. In Miao-Yao, moreover, this AT prefix appears to be represented by prefixed ka/~qa/ found with words for parts of the body in Kanao (MCF), Phö, and other Miao speeches, with some evidence that it is not a completely bound form, e.g. Phö *hlie* "collar," *ka/hlie* "neck," from PMY *klaaŋ "neck/throat" (see BETWEEN/PART), but only two direct links with AN have been uncovered (CLOTHES; WATER[II]).

For other AT prefixes, the evidence is less conclusive, with the possible exception of AT *m/, which functions basically as a stative with verbal forms. This prefix, with *a* vocalism, is neatly represented in Thai *maw* "drunk," from AT *ma/busuk, and occasionally in other forms in Kadai and/or MY (RED). The basic contrast with the old causative $^*p/$ is classically represented by AT $^*m/play$ "die" $\sim$ $^*p/play$ "kill" (with lapsing of the distinction in IN as contrasted with most Formosan languages), the vocalism again being shown by Thai (by lengthening: $^*taay \sim$ $^*thraay$), but the prefixes themselves can only be inferred at the proto-AT level; PMY has $^*day$ "die," from $^*tay$ (unprefixed, with initial voicing); $^*tay$ "kill," from $^*(p/)tay$. The causative prefix appears to be preserved, however, in T $^*plian \sim$ $^*phrian$ "change, exchange," IN $^*liyan$ "to be changed," PMY $^*wian < $^*liyan$ "change" (see CHANGE/).

Several suffixed elements can be reconstructed at the proto-AT level, but the precise functions remain in doubt, and it would seem that some already existed in bound form at that level. There is some evidence for suffixed $^*/a(n)$ (GRANDPARENT; SPIRIT/; HEAD/HAIR; THORN), also for $^*/n$ (SHOULDER/ARM) and $^*/ən$ (EAT). In the absence of evidence from the mainland languages, it is difficult to determine whether certain AN forms had final $^*a$ as part of the morph or as the old suffix $^*/a$ (RABBIT). There is further comparative evidence for both suffixed $^*/i$ and $^*/t$ at the proto-AT level (CLIMB; DISGUST; EXCHANGE/; GNAW; THIGH) as well as for suffixed $^*/ts$ (HARD), all suggesting an original complete set of dental suffixes accompanying $^*/n$.

The proto-AT infix system probably included both $^*/m/$ and $^*/n/$ as well as $^*/l/$ and $^*/ḷ/$, perhaps also $^*/r/$ (rare, and difficult to differentiate from $^*/ḷ/$); (see BEAT/; BUFFALO; HUT/). Solid evidence for these is hard to come by, however, since we must secure comparative data from mainland languages. Infixed $^*/m/$, which is very common in Formosa, less so elsewhere, is perhaps represented in Kadai [Laqua and Kelao] in SEW/PLAIT/WEAVE; in MY in WEEP; SMELL/FRAGRANT. Infixed $^*/n/$, a more generally distributed element in AN, is represented in Kadai [generally] in FEMALE and in MY in OPEN/STAND OPEN. Direct correspondences between AN and Kadai and/or MY for infixed $^*/l/$ and $^*/ḷ/$ are infrequent, as in the case of the nasal infixes; for the Kadai evidence, see BRANCH/BROW (Thai), CHILD (gen. Kadai), JOIN/ (Thai), LIGHTNING/ (Thai), SKIN (Lati), WEEP (Kelao), and especially CULTIVATE/ (discussion above); for the MY evidence, see WEEP and especially FOUR (discussion below). The last named example, in which Atayal has infixed °/*l*/, underlines the apparently arbitrary nature of these AT infixes, which seem to have been inserted into various roots here and there with little if any attention to function, with the same infix or even a distinct infix appearing at times in another segment of the root (BUFFALO; WEEP). The various AT forms of the latter root (WEEP) nicely illustrate the complexities that arise from time to time:

AT	( )*pr/l,m/a*ŋ*/m,l/i(t)s*			
IN	*t*	*a*ŋ	*i t'*	
PPN	*t*	*a*ŋ	*i*	
Formosa: East	(*ṭ*)/	*m/a*ŋ	*i ts*	
Tsouic	(*t*)/	*m/a*ŋ	*i ts*	
Sedik	*l*	*m/i*ŋ	*i s*	[vocalic assim.]
Atayal		*m/a*ŋ/	*l/i s*	
Thai	*h*	[ŋ]	*a i* [*y*]	[vocalic transfer]
Siamese	(*h*)	ŋ	*e*	
Dioi/Sek	*t*	*a*	*i* [*y*]	
Kam-Sui	ʔ	ŋ	*e*	
Lakkia	*pi*	[ŋ]	*ę*	
Ong-Be	[*h*]	ŋ	*a i* [*y*]	
S. Li		ŋ	*e y*	
N. Li		ŋ	*a i* [*y*]	
Lati	*ć*	*u*ŋ		
Kelao			*l/i* [*y*]	
Miao-Yao	ʔ	*ń/m*		

PHONOLOGY

The basic AT syllabic structure was (C)(C)V(C)(C), with (C)(C) clusters limited to stop/nasal + *r/l/ḷ* types, perhaps only in syllable-initial position (see below). If the nasal/oral units are to be regarded as clusters (*mb, nd, ńj, ŋg, NG*), the above formula becomes (C)(C)(C)V(C)(C), these units not

occurring in final position. In polysyllabic shapes, all nonfinal
syllables were of "open" type, ending in (V) or *y/w, with
the exception of reduplicated forms with / as morph boundary-
marker, e.g. AT *til/til "foot."

The typical AT vocabulary morph (lexeme) was disyllabic,
with occasional trisyllabic (EAR) and rare monosyllabic (DIE/)
forms. In many but not all cases, the trisyllabic forms are sus-
ceptible of morphological analysis, suggesting ultimate derivation from shorter forms, e.g. AT *qraḷi[ŋ]a "ear," possibly from
*qraḷiŋ/a or *qr/aḷ/iŋa or even *qr/aḷ/iŋ/a. In AN gener-
ally, the trisyllabic forms tend to be replaced by disyllabic, e.g.
IN *t'urambi~*ambi "wing/addition (of house)" (see ROOM/
WING); Atayal bətunux~tunux "stone/head," from *batu/nux
(see STONE/GEM/PEARL). Cham and related languages on
the mainland show a marked trend to reduce disyllabic forms
to monosyllabic, with one language (Radé) having become completely monosyllabic, e.g. IN *təlu "three," Cham *klau*, Radé
tlâo; IN *tulaŋ "bone," Cham *tulaŋ*, Radé *klaŋ* (Haudricourt
1956). Reduction to monosyllables is the reigning motif throughout the Kadai and MY branches of the stock, very much as part
of an areal language feature, extending also to Vietnamese, which
has typically reduced disyllabic AA roots to monosyllables (Benedict 1942). All these languages, excluding the Cham group, have
also developed complete tonal systems, with a fundamental distinction between high (surd initial) and low (sonant initial)
tones. The AT material has not yet been systematically examined
for clues as to the factors making for the assignment of tones
to given morphs as they became reduced to monosyllables, but
it is assumed that such factors will ultimately be uncovered.[3]
There is some evidence that "paradoxical" h.gh tones with voiced
initials in Kam-Sui can be the product of earlier disyllabic forms
with unvoiced initial, e.g. AT *[k]a(n)tsaw "post/rafter/spar":
IN *kat'aw, Thai *saw, KS *[ ]zaaw (h.t.), from *(k)azaw<
*(k)ansaw. We do not have far to seek in attempting to explain
the linked monosyllabism/tonality areal features. The ST languages are monosyllabic and tonal ab origine, it now appears,
a two-tone system having recently been reconstructed for this

language stock (Benedict 1972). According to this same hypothesis, however, a third *sandhi* tone was developed in Chinese at a very early (Archaic) period, and it was this three-tone system that spread to the other tonal languages of the area, all with systems of three-tone type, typically with matching tones in the loanword material.

Apart from the development of tones, in which Kadai and MY resemble each other, these two branches of the AT stock tend to show divergent trends in reduction of AT forms to monosyllables. In Thai and other Kadai languages, as pointed out in the original paper (1942), the final syllable of the typical disyllabic form was usually maintained, indicating an original stress on the syllable, as in AT *(tsa)ran* "nest," Thai *ran*; AT *[b]əna* "field (wet, rice)," Thai *na*. The ə vowel in the latter root, which explains the palatalized cognate in Ong-Be (*nea*), is perhaps secondary; at any rate, there is much evidence throughout AT, particularly in the AN and Kadai branches, of the development of unstressed forms (with ə vowel) from stressed forms (typically with *a* vocalism), at times with doublet forms developed through assimilation, e.g. IN *bəli~*bili* "buy," from AT *(m)bali* (see EXCHANGE/BUY/SELL). Some of the exceptions to the rule for end-stress (or second syllable stress in longer forms) in Thai can be shown to be pseudofore-stress forms, e.g. IN *put'uʔ* "heart" (Javanese "lungs"), Thai *poot~*pot* "lungs," from AT *[ ]pots [oq]*, the unaspirated initial of the Thai form showing that it was derived from an earlier trisyllabic form, with the anticipated stress on the second syllable; IN *γakit* "pair, couple," Thai *ra* "we two," Kam-Sui *[ ]γa* "two," the high tones of the Kam-Sui forms indicating derivation from an earlier disyllabic form, yielding AT *( )γa[kit]*. It would appear, however, that "strong" initial syllables with an initial consonant cluster (or stop + nasal) or with long (geminate) vowel were stressed even in the normally unstressed initial position, e.g. Thai *glam* "feel/touch," from AT *glam[aq]*; Thai *pat* "gem/pearl," from AT *ba[]at[u]* "stone" (with normal unvoicing of the initial). Similarly, syllables with the "weak" vowel *i* were unstressed in favor of the initial syllable, e.g. Thai *thak* "plait," from AT

Austro-Thai

plaqi[s] (see SEW/PLAIT/WEAVE); Lakkia *lak* "man (male),"
from AT *lak[i]* (see MALE); Sek *vel* "left (hand)," from AT
weR[i]. In addition, syllables with secondary *w* (from AT *b*)
were unstressed in favor of an initial syllable with *a* vocalism,
e.g. Thai *maw* "drunk," from AT *ma/buśuk;* contrast Thai
ooy "sugarcane," from AT *[(n)t]obos* via *(o)woy<*(o)boy*.
Miao-Yao presents a clear contrast with Thai and other Kadai
languages in characteristically stressing initial rather than final (or
second) syllables, e.g. AT *luwaq* "vomit," MY *lo<*luw(aq)*,
agreeing with Sek *ruak<*rúwak*, OB *doak<*roak<*rúwak*,
rather than with Thai *raak<*rwak<*ruwák*, Mak *ʔo:k<
[r]uwák, S. Li *ɛʔ<*(ruw)áq;* note the existence of KD/MY
"split cognates," as illustrated by the following:

	AT	AN	KD	MY
louse/flea	*pru(m)baś*	*tumbaś*	*(u)(m)bat*	*ta(m)<pra(m)*
poison fish	*(n)tu(m)ba*	*(n)tu(m)ba*	*[ ](u)ba*	*dom<tom*
bear, n.	*kru(m)bay*	*krumay*	*[ ](u)may*	*krop<krob*
come/arrive	*da(n)təŋ*	*datəŋ*	*[ ](n)təŋ*	*daay<daat*

Miao-Yao distinguishes, however, between prefixed and non-
prefixed forms, as follows:

	AT	AN	KD	MY
die	*(ma/)play*	*matay*	*[ ]pla(a)y*	*day<tay*
kill	*[pa/]play*	*patay*	—	*tay<[p/]tay*
eye	*mapla*	*mata*	*[ ]pra*	*maay<maat*

The prefixed forms apparently served as a model for other
roots with original initial labial elements; cf. the following:

	AT	AN	KD	MY
bow/spear/ arrow	*[bo]tsoʀ*	*butsuʀ*	*son*	*tsɔ(ŋ)<[ ]tsoʀ*
cultivate/ field	*[bu]hat*	*buhat*	*het*	*ay<[h]at*
carry (on shoulder)	*(q/)(m)pekol*	*pikul*	*(q/)(m)pek*	*kw[ei]<[]kol*
eat/food	*[pa]ŋal*	*paŋal*	—	*ńan<ŋan*

The "splitting" of disyllabic or polysyllabic AT roots into curious pairs or groups of cognates also occurs, moreover, within
Kadai itself, with some tendency for sporadic retention of second or final syllable stress forms in Li and occasionally other
Kadai languages as contrasted with Thai, Kam-Sui, and Lakkia:

	AT	Thai/KS/ Lakkia	Kadai (other)
drunk	*ma/bu**ś**uk*	*maw* (Thai)	*möe~mei* (Ong-Be)
		mwi (N. Thai)	*mui~pui* (Li)
		mei (KS)	*a/sŭ* (Lai)
light (wt.)	*(n)sap[r,l]aqal*	*(n)sa* (KS)	*kho~khei* (Ong-Be)
			khƏ~kha:l (Li)
			kau (N. Kelao)
sweet/bee/ hornet	*(n)taboq*	*to* (Thai) *(n)to* (KS)	*fƆk* (S. Li)
snake	*(q/)uŋata*	*ŋu* (Thai)	*ŋia* (Ong-Be)
		ŋua (Sek)	*thya* (Li)
		ŋyie (Lakkia)	*ŋɨ* (Laqua)
			kuŋ (Lati)
right (hand)	*(N)q/(wa)nal*	*xwa* (Thai)	*nin* (Li)
		xwa (KS)	
		kyie (Lakkia)	

It is inferred that stress distinctions underlie the manifold
forms of "splitting" of the basic AT roots, but since both initial
and final stress forms exist side by side within each of the three
AT divisions, we must infer that the stress was variable at the
AT level;[4] cf. the following Kadai forms for NEW:

AT	*(q/)mbáʀo	*(q/)mbaʀó
Thai	*hmaɨ	—
Kam-Sui	*hmay	—
Lakkia	*wai*	—
Ong-Be	*na:u*	—
S. Li	*ma:n*	—
Dioi/Sek	—	*hmo
N. Li/WS Li	—	*no

CONSONANTS

The reconstructed AT consonant schema shows fundamental labial/dental/palatal/velar/postvelar/glottal contrasts as well as surd/sonant and oral/nasal contrasts, along with a highly distinctive nasal/oral unit (special type of cluster), as indicated in the following chart (doubtful reconstructions within brackets):

ORAL							NASAL/ORAL						NASAL
p	b					w	mp	mb					m
t	d	ts	dz	s	z	l	nt	nd	nts	ndz	ns	nz	n
ć	j		[ś]	[ź]	r	y	ńć	ńj			[ńś]	[ńz]	ńy ń
k	g		[x]	γ	ļ		ŋk	ŋg					ŋ
q	G			[R]			Nq	NG					N
[ʔ]				h									

As indicated above, the nasal/oral units do not occur in final position, while the palatal and postvelar stops and nasals are (except for *q) rare or lacking in this position.

Notes on Table of Austro-Thai Consonants (Oral)

The correspondences listed under Formosa are for the East Formosan (Paiwanic) group (Paiwan, Puyuma, Rukai, Ami, Bunun, Thao, Saisiat, Pazeh, Kuvalan, and [extinct] Favorlang, Siraya) and hold for all positions (initial, medial, final) except where otherwise noted (G, x). Tsouic and Atayalic, both of which present numerous problems in phonology, are of only occasional help in confirming basic distinctions, since they tend toward merger of some of the phonemes, especially in the dental series (for an exception, see Atayalic, under Consonant Clusters).

General features include the following:

1. Aspiration: KD and MY regularly aspirate initial surd stops (except for *t>PMY *d), producing a triple stop pattern similar to that found in many neighboring languages on the mainland, especially in the ST stock. There is also evidence here and there of secondary aspiration in medial position but conditions governing this have not yet been fully established.

2. Unvoicing: At the early level, KD shows regular unvoicing of initial *b, with occasional retention of voicing in redupli-

Austro-Thai Consonants (Oral)

AT	Form.	Indonesian Init.	Indonesian Med.	Indonesian Fin.	Kadai [>Thai] Init.	Kadai [>Thai] Med.	Kadai [>Thai] Fin.	Miao-Yao Init.	Miao-Yao Med.	Miao-Yao Fin.
p	p	p	p	p	ph/f	p/v	p	ph	p	p
b	b	b	b	b	p/b/v	b/v/w	p/w	p/b	p	p/w
t	t	t	t	t	th	t	t	d	-/y	t/y
d	d	d	d	dʼ	d	d/ø	t	d	t/-	t/-
ts	ts	tʼ	tʼ	tʼ	s/h	s/t	t	-	ts	t
dz	dz	dʼ	dʼ	-	z~s	-/d/ø	-	sy	y/ø	-
s	s	s>h	s>h	ø	s/h	s	y	s/h	-/y	y~ø
z	z	ḍ.	ḍ	ḍ.	ch	č	-	-	y	-
č	č	k̓	k̓	gʼ	-	i/d/-	y	-	č	t/y
i	i	-	gʼ	ø	s	s/y	t	-	-	-
[s]	s	ø	øɔ	øɔ	s	i/ø	-	-	-	?/k
[z]	z	-	z̃ɔk	-	-	k	-	-	-	y
k	k	k	k	k/ø	kh	k	k	kh~tsh	k~ts	?
g	g	gɔ	gɔ	gɔ	g[>x]	g/k/ø	y	qh	-	y
q	q	øɔ	gɔ	gɔ	q[>x]	G	k/?/ø	ø	q/?	?
G	q/g	hɔ	hɔ	rʔ/ʔ	G[>γ]	ʔ/ø	k	-	-	-
[ʔ]	ʔ	-	-	-	-	h/ø	-	h	ø	ø
h	h	hɔ	hɔ	øɔ	h	x/ø	h/ø	-	?	i
[x]	q/h	γ	γR	γR	x[>h]	γ/ø	ø	h	h/l/i	ŋ
γ	γ	-	R	R	γ[>r]	R/ø	l[>n/y]	-	-/l/ŋ	r
R	R~γ	r	r	r	-	r/ø	l[>n/y]	r	-	n/y
r	r	l	l	n	r	r/y/ø	l[>n/y]	l/w	l/w/n	n/y
l	l	l	n	n	l	l/y/ø	l[>n/y]	l	r/w/n	y
l	l	y	y	y	y	y/ø	y	y	y	w
y	y	w	w	w	w	w	w	w	w	
w	w									

cation (CARRY ON BACK; LIPS; MOUTH/; TURN/), while MY exhibits the same feature but in an irregular manner; this also appears to be an areal feature, Arch. Ch. showing precisely the same phenomenon (Benedict 1972: 166, n. 433). Unvoicing as a general feature is characteristic of later levels both in KD and MY, with tonality (suprasegmental) tending to replace voicing (segmental) as the critical distinctive feature, these languages thus conforming to the mainland areal pattern (Benedict 1948); yet unvoicing (without tonality) occurs in Formosa (Ami has the strange series: $*b>f$, $*d>t$, $*j>n$, $*g>k$) and is characteristic also of PO/PPN: $*b>p/f$, $*d>d/r$, $*j>s$, $*g>k$, with the dental again showing an aberrant development, as in MY (above).

3. Voicing: MY shows an entirely unexpected (and unexplained) shift of initial $*t$ to PMY $*d$, rather than the anticipated $*th$; the MY forms with initial $*th$- are largely Chinese loans (five of six PMY $*th$- roots cited by Purnell) or back-loans in Yao (RABBIT; LADDER/), but there seems to be one exception (APPEAR), perhaps also a loan, while this initial (PMY $*th$-) also can represent an original cluster (BURN/) (see below). Two very early Chinese loans (BAMBOO[II], BEAN/) present evidence that the initial $*t>d$ shift occurred not long before the PMY stage was reached.

4. Stop>nasal shift: typically found in AT in connection with nasal/oral units (see below), but appears also in several originally reduplicated forms in KD (CASTOR OIL; GNAW/; SPLEEN; WIND/); MY (BLOW/; COVER/; LIVE/; SUBMERGE/).

5. Intervocalic loss: characteristic of KD, dependent upon the stress pattern (weak stress$>\emptyset$), shown in table by $/\emptyset$, affecting largely the voiced phonemes, with the exception of medial $*b>w$, including $*y$ but not $*w$ (retained, or merges with $*u$). No instances of loss of medial $*z$, $*j$, $*g$, or $*G$ in this position are at hand, but it is likely that examples will in time be uncovered. MY appears to reflect this type of loss only sporadically, but here also we can anticipate that future research will disclose additional examples.

6. Procrustean and other loss: most of the remaining examples of consonant loss are of anticipated type, including loss of

initial *G in IN and MY, general loss of final *h, preserved only in Formosa (Ami, Paz., Sai.; Atayalic) and perhaps in a rare (originally) reduplicated form (BREAST[1]) in Thai and Yao, and of final *s in IN (and irregularly in MY), also loss of final *k in IN (after long vowel: DESIRE/; SPLEEN) and of final *q in KD (irregular, fluctuating with replacement by k or ꞏ); cf. PMY ꞏ for final *k (only after short vowel). In addition to these anticipated losses, however, several instances have been uncovered in which final consonants have been "chopped off" in a Procrustean manner simply because of the Thai/Kadai phonological pattern, which limits medial vowel clusters to /ia/, /ua/, and /ɨa/, not permitting /iu/, /ui/, or /aɨ/ in this position:

	AT	IN	Thai	Li
smell	kri[y]u[m]	k′iyum	khriw=khriu	–
blow/whistle	[iyu]p/iyup	piyup	phiw=phiu	viu
	t/iyup	tiyup	thiw=thiu	teu
flute	klu[l]i[ŋ]	t′uliŋ	khluy=khlui	tsui-
in-law	baya[w]	bayaw	(s-)baɨ<bayǝ	–

7. Labialization: characteristic of Kadai, which has *phw>f, *pw/bw>v under conditions not yet fully worked out but apparently always involving labialization by an (original) rounded vowel (*u, *o) or a labial consonant (*p, *b, *w), also secondarily labialized velars (CLIMB/; PIERCE; SPIDER) and postvelars (BARTER/; HORN[1]; THIGH/), as well as (rarely) *l (CHILD; LOUSE/FLEA[11]).

8. Palatalization: found at the early level only in MY, with dental affricates tending to replace velar stops, as one aspect of a general process of transformation of velars into dentals or palatals, followed by a shift of postvelars to velars, leading to the complete (Yao) or incomplete (Miao) loss of the postvelar series; at times doublets must be reconstructed at the PMY level (BRANCH; BOAT[11]; CLIMB/), the governing conditions remaining undetermined. At the later levels, palatalization is relatively uncommon throughout AT, with velar stops generally well

maintained even before front vowels, but occasionally shifting to the glottal stop (Pai.: Raisha Naibun Tamari *k>?, Sa. Sm. Hawaiian *g/k>?) or continuant (TB. *k>h, Ho. *g/k>h, Puy. *g>h), but the KS group has shifts similar to those in MY.

9. Dental shifts: the dental series as a whole tends to be unstable throughout the AT family (note the dental stop features under Nos. 2 and 3), with widespread merging, especially of the voiced phonemes. In Formosa, where the dental phonemes are best maintained, only Paiwan (most dialects) has consistently distinct reflexes for AT *dz (d') and *z (z), as opposed to *d (d); other Formosan languages tend to merge all three phonemes in d (as in Bunun and Pazeh), r (as in Saisiat), or ts~s (Tsouic), but Atayal appears to distinguish between AT *d/dz (r~ø) and *z (l). Formosan reflexes for the corresponding surd phonemes are more often kept distinct, but AT *ts>s or h, also *s>h, are common shifts, paralleling the shifts found in IN (*t' is represented by s in most IN languages), KD, and MY (*s>h before continuants in both). The IN reflexes are better reconstructed *ts (for Demp. *t') and *dz (for Demp. *d') than *s and *z (as Dyen and others would have it); this leaves *z (rather than Dyen's *ẓ) for those roots reconstructed by Dempwolff with *d/ḍ~d' doublets, as in RAIN; ROAD (Dyen 1951), apparently from an earlier *ndz; note that AT *z had already shifted to IN *d, tending to merge with AT *d>IN *d (HEAR), reflecting the same tendency toward development of a voiced stop for the continuant. AT *s, on the contrary, shifted to h in IN in initial/medial position, but was simply dropped as a final (with some alternation with AT final *ts, as in HAIR (BODY)/ and WEEP). Recently Blust (1969) has presented material indicating that AT *s was retained at the earliest level in IN before merging with AT *h, with the sibilant actually present in certain Borneo languages; cf. Lemiting and Long Kiput *sok* "hair," from IN *buhuk=*busuk (and see OVERFLOW/ and SUGARCANE). Dyen (1965) has shown that Formosa has several sets of sibilant reflexes corresponding to IN *h, reconstructed *s₁ . . . *s₆ at the AN level, but it does not appear that these distinctions also obtain at the AT level, hence

we provisionally reconstruct all as AT $*s$ (but make note of the Formosan set).

10. Palatal instability: the palatal series is poorly represented and clearly marginal with respect to the dental series, with both $*\acute{s}$ and $*\acute{z}$ only provisionally reconstructed. Formosa: East has a distinctive set of reflexes for AT $*j$ (Paz. j=Ruk. g=Pai. d=Puy. Thao δ=Sai. z=Ami Kuv. n=Bun. $\emptyset$) but AT $*\acute{c}$ is scarcely represented (provisionally reconstructed in RICE/: Paz. *sumai*, Puy. *ḷomai~rumai*, from $*\acute{c}umay$). IN $*\acute{c}$ and $*j$ are almost in complementary distribution (contrasted only as medials), and Kadai shows a similar pattern, with $*j$ after ? (<AT $*q$) shifting to d in the characteristic Thai cluster $*{}^{?}d$ (NOSE), paralleling the shift AT $*q/z$>Thai $*{}^{?}d$ (below). AT $*\acute{z}$ has been reconstructed in one root (POINT/FINGER[11]) on the basis of the distinctive Formosa: East series, with the various Paiwan dialects showing reflexes ($l~\emptyset$) for $*l$, while other languages of the group (Puy. Ami Sai.) show reflexes for $*z$, suggesting an earlier $*\acute{z}$, supported by the correspondences IN $*\acute{z}=*z$ (see above) and KD $*j$. In one group of roots lacking satisfactory Formosan cognates, however, the KD languages exhibit a distinctive set of correspondences after initial $*q$ or $*q/$; the indicated contrast is between AT $*q/\acute{z}$ (>Thai $*{}^{?}y$) and AT $*q/z$ (>Thai $*{}^{?}d$), the latter with good Formosan cognates, as shown in the following table:

AT $*\acute{s}$ has been reconstructed for those roots in which Formosa has a sibilant for IN $\emptyset$, the correspondences varying somewhat, designated by Dyen (1965) $*x_1$ (FIRE), $*x_2$ (FOUR) or X (THOU; DREAM); Dyen also reconstructs final X for "face" (see FACE/FOREHEAD[1]), but IN drops h in final position, hence we cannot differentiate from the $*s$ group of reflexes (under No. 9). KD has $*s$ for reflex as an initial (FOUR, in Li; see NUMERALS, below) and as a stressed medial (THOU, in Thai, Mak., and Lk.; see PRONOUNS, below). In addition to these roots, $*\acute{s}$ must also be reconstructed as a medial in DRUNK (IN $*mabuk$, Ata. *məbuśuk*), KD showing $*s$ again in stressed position (Lt. $a/s\breve{u}$), but $*y$ in unstressed intervocalic position (OB *mei*, Li *mui~pui*). Finally, KD appears to have

AT *ẓ and *ź

Form:	LIVE/	DARK/	CRUSTACEAN/	SMOKE/	COLD/	STAND/
AT	*quẓip	*qu(n)ẓæm / qu(n)ẓam	*qu(n)ẓaŋ	*(q/)źiaŋ	*(q/)źeŋen	*(q/)źaɣi / (n)ẓiɣi
IN	*ʔudip	*ḍeḍem	*ʔu(n)daŋ	*diŋdiŋ	*diŋin	*(n)diɣi
East	*quẓip	*/quẓmezb/	–	–	–	*[z]iɣi
Thai: SW	*ʔdip	*ʔdam	–	*ʔya(a)ŋ	*ʔyen	*ʔyɨn
Tho-Nung	*ʔdip	*ʔdam	–	*ʔdiaŋ / *ʔyeeŋ	*ʔyen	*ʔyɨn
Dioi	dip (h.t.)	–	–	dyaŋ (h.t.)	–	–
Sek	rip (h.t.)	ram (h.t.)	–	yuaŋ (h.t.)	–	–
Kam-Sui	*ʔdyip	*ʔnam	–		–	*ʔyun
Lakkia	–	lam (h.t.)	–		–	yun (h.t.)
Ong-Be (Sav.) (Jer.)	ẓɔp (h.t.) / –	ẓɔm (h.t.) / lam	zoaŋ	teaŋ	–	zun (h.t.) / ćun
S. Li	diep	ḍɔm	–	–	–	ćuon
WS Li	fip	tam	fiaŋ	–	–	ćuŋ
N. Kl.	–	laŋ	–	–	ka/yin	–

°y for final *°s* (CORD/; FACE/; HAIR (BODY)/; OLD/; SCRATCH/; STREAM/; SUGARCANE; WEEP), with possible preservation of the final *°s* in Li (reconstructed) in one root (WASH[11]), but *°t* for final *°ś* (LOUSE/FLEA[1]).

11. AT *°γ* and *°R*: as pointed out by Dyen (1953b), there appear to be four sets of correspondences for IN *°γ* as reconstructed by Dempwolff, with Truk reflecting a basic cleavage between one pair of these (*°γ₁* and *°γ₄*) as opposed to another (*°γ₂* and *°γ₃*). The situation is still far from clear, but a basic distinction appears to be reflected in Ja. *h~ø* contrasting with *r;* we have provisionally reconstructed IN *°R* (postvelar)>Ja. *h~ø*, IN *°γ* (velar)>Ja. *r,* for these two reflexes in view of the parallelism with AT *°G*>IN *°ø*. The evidence from Formosa is equally tenuous, but a few roots show departures from the regular set of reflexes for AT *°γ* (East: Kuv. *γ*=Paz. *x*=Sir. *g*=Puy. Ami *r*=Bun. *l*=Thao *l*=Pai. Ruk. *ø*), e.g. RICE[1] (Sir. *ø*, Ruk. *r*) and LEFT (Kuv. *l*, Pai. *r~R*, Ruk. *r*), the former corresponding to IN *°R*, the latter to an unusual reflex in Yami (*r* for the regular *y*); cf. also SIDE (OF BODY)/ (Yami *r*). The mainland evidence for the hypothetical AT *°γ* vs. *°R* distinction is also skimpy: KD appears to have unusual reflexes in one root (EMPTY/) for which Form. has *°R* (Ami *h*), while PM has AT *°γ*>*i* (DRY; HEAR) contrasting with AT *°R*>*ŋ* (LEFT; BOW/) in similar positions.

12. AT *°[x]*: the reconstruction schema for AT suggests the likelihood of a phoneme/pair of phonemes in this area as the surd counterpart of AT *°γ/R*, and there is some evidence in support of this; see EIGHT (under NUMERALS, below); HANG; HUSK/ and WHITE/MOON (all with *°x* as initial), also PUNGENT (as medial, stressed) and FEMALE/ (as medial, unstressed), also LEAF[11] (as final) and IRON (in *°xl* cluster, below). Dyen (1965) reconstructed *°Q₁* at the AN level for two of these roots (PUNGENT/ and LEAF[11]) on the basis of unusual Formosan correspondences to IN *°ʔ* (Form. *-h* in the latter); WS Li significantly has *x* in one of these (PUNGENT/), as well as in HUSK/ (corresponding to IN initial *ʔ*) and in EIGHT, with initial *°x[]w* fitting with IN *°kʷ* (under No. 16). IN appears to have lost an earlier initial *ʔ* in HANG (but *ʔ* preserved

in Atayal), but Thai has initial *h* here, presumably from an earlier KD *°x* (cognate lacking in Li). Finally, AT *°x* is indicated as the reconstruction in unstressed medial position in FEMALE/, with IN *°ʔ* (not *ø*, hence not to be assigned to final *H=°h*, contra Dyen 1965) corresponding to Form. *h*, KD *ø*.

13. Postvelar instability: a general feature throughout the AT family, affecting especially the sonant stop (*°G*), although it appears that this phoneme, preserved in KD but probably lost in MY (see SHELLFISH/ for poss. exc.), must be reconstructed (in initial position) for AN on the basis of the correspondence Form. *°q*=IN *°ø* (in medial position apparently replaced by *°g* in both groups). As indicated above (No. 8), MY tends to shift the whole postvelar series to velars, and Kadai reveals a similar trend at later levels, with Thai showing the developments *°q>°x* (preserved in Si. script, also *x* [h.t.] in WT)*>kh* (modern: all other) and *°G>°γ* (preserved in Si. script, also *x* [l.t.] in WT)*>k~kh* (modern: all other). Dioi and Sek both distinguish between *°qh>h* and *°q>k* (Haud. 1952), while Dioi has *°G>h* (l.t.), *°Gw>kw* (l.t.), and Sek has *°G>γ* (Ged.)*~g* (*=gγ*) (Haud.), *°Gw>khw* (l.t.).

14. Reduction of finals: both KD and MY share in an areal feature involving limitation of final consonants to surd stops and their homorganic nasals (excluding palatals) and the semivowels *y* and *w* (patterning as consonants, as shown by the system of medial vowels). In the KD division, however, Sek has final -*l*, and this final must also be reconstructed for Li (preserved in WS Li) and (rarely) for KS (STONE), with correspondences to AT medial or final *°γ* (HEARTH/); *°R* (LEFT; SLEEP; SPREAD OUT) and *°r* (FROG/; HAIR (BODY)/), as well as *°l* (EARTH/; FOREST¹; GRANDCHILD (-GREAT)/; LIGHT (WEIGHT); STONE; WORM/EEL; VILLAGE/) and *°ḷ* (BEAT/; CULTIVATE/; FLEA/). It would appear that all these AT phonemes were first merged in KD *°l* in final (or unstressed intervocalic) position, then replaced by *n* or *y*, a process now in evidence in Sek (final *l>n* among younger speakers; see Gedney 1970), but the conditions governing these shifts have not yet been determined; note also the irregular replacement (apparently under influence of *°u* vocalism) in Thai by final ŋ

(ROUND) and *m* (LIGHT/; SNAKE'; WIDE/), also in Laqua by final -ŋ (WATER"). The MY material, which is much more limited, indicates that final *r must be reconstructed in at least one root (TWIN/), but that replacement in general was of KD type, with final *l and *ḷ becoming *n* or *y*, with medial (unstressed intervocalic) and final *R going to ŋ (LEFT; BOW/). For the final voiced stops, KD and MY both tend to unvoice final *-b and *-d but to replace final *-g with -y and final *-j with either -t or -y (see TWIN for conditioning factor in Thai); note also final *-b>-w after vocalic length (YAWN/) and final *-G>-k (Thai)∼-ʔ/r (IN) (OUTSIDE). MY, which has an unanticipated *d* for initial *t, also under certain conditions has *y* for medial and final *t, apparently via secondary *d*; this shift occurs in unstressed intervocalic position, where it is associated with secondary vocalic lengthening (COME/; EYE; LIGHT), also in final (or equivalent) position, with *-at yielding -ay (CULTIVATE/) or (through palatalization) -ei (FOUR; LOUSE), *-ut yielding -wei (TAIL/); final *t is retained, however, after original vowels *i (EXCHANGE/) and *e (HOOK/), as well after secondary vocalic length (GLUTINOUS/; GNAW/; PULL LENGTHWISE/). MY also has *t* for medial *d (LICK/), *p* for medial *b (BEAN/; BEAR; FALL"), both in unstressed intervocalic position, presumably after both had become finals through loss of final syllable.

15. Glottal stop: provisionally reconstructed by Dyen (1965) for AN on the basis of Form. ʔ=IN ø, yielding *kaʔən "eat" and *ʔənəm "six"; it possibly marks a morpheme boundary in the former; cf. Thai *kin∼*in (Shan ʔin) (see EAT), but in general it appears to be simply a nondistinctive feature of vocalic onset, in Formosa as well as in KD and MY generally.

16. AT *y and *w: maintained throughout AT, with the single exception of Thai *y>ø in unstressed intervocalic position (under No. 5). Dyen (1962) has shown that Aloene (Piru: West Ceram) and Lau (Solomons) both have *kw* for IN initial or medial *w in certain roots; this unit or cluster, which we reconstruct *ʔw (Dyen: *kʷ), appears to have been derived from *qw, for an earlier *q/w or *q[]w (RIGHT; WATER" and [under NUMERALS, below] EIGHT; NINE). Dyen (1962) has

also shown that Niala (Piru: West Ceram) has *w*, at times corresponding to Chamorro (Marianas) *gw* (<*w*), in several roots with vocalic initial in IN, and here he writes *W* as a conventional symbol. Form: East, in which initial *w* is regularly represented by the correspondences: E. Ruk. Puy. Ami Bun. Sai. Thao Paz. Kuv. Sir. *w*=Bun. *w*~*v*=W. Ruk. *v*~*h*= Pai. ∅, has two different sets for two of these initial *W* roots, viz. *W₁atsu* "dog": Ami Paz. Kuv. *w*=Pai. *v*=W. Ruk. Bun. Sai. Thao Sir. ∅ (cf. Dyen 1965) and *W₂alak* "child": Ami *w*=Puy. *w*~∅=W. Ruk. *v*=Pai. Sai. Thao Sir. ∅ (not noted by Dyen); in a third root (*Waku* "I"), the Formosan evidence is of no help, but PM has initial *w* in an apparently cognate form (see PRONOUNS, below). We reconstruct simply *w* at the AT level, on the assumption that the AN phenomenon is secondary; note AT *Naw/al/ak* "child," yielding either *(Na)walak* or *(Naw)alak* through distinction in syllable division. In a fourth root (*Wapuy* "fire"), the labialization appears to have been secondary to the vocalism, since Form. has a sibilant (AT *śapuy*).

17. AT *l* and *ḷ*: this contrast between "front *l*" and "back *l*" (*ḷ*) is a highly distinctive AT feature. IN merges AT *l* with *ḷ* as initial, with *n* as medial and final, the latter leading Dyen (1965) into the error of setting up a contrast in Formosa between *n* (reflexes for AT *n*) and *N* (actually the reflexes for AT *l*), since some Formosan languages parallel IN in either complete (Bun. Kan.), nearly complete (Kuv.), or partial (Paz. Fav. Sir.) shift from AT *l* to *n*. In general, however, Form: East maintains AT *l* as *l* or *ł*, with some shifting to *d* (Ami: Taparon Tauran) or *ð* (Thao: final), and AT *ḷ* as *ḷ* (with some shifting to *r* or *y*>∅), while Tsouic has the contrasts *ł* and *l/r* (Saa.), *n* and *l/w* (Kan.) and *h* (<*hl*=*ł*) and *y* (Tsou) for AT *l* and *ḷ*, respectively, and Atayalic has *l* and *r/z/y/∅* (various conditioning factors) (Ata.), *l/d* and *ḷ/r* (Sed.) for the same contrast. KD generally has retained AT *l* while merging *ḷ* with *r*, but in secondary clusters *ḷ* tends to go to *l* rather than *r* (SPIDER; SPOTTED/) with some vacillation between *l* and *r* dependent upon aspiration (CHANGE/); note also Thai *l* rather than *r* for AT *r* or *γ* in similar situations, with Dioi

retaining *r* (COLOR(ED)/; SINK INTO/). The correspondences in MY are extremely complex, especially as regards secondary clusters, but it appears necessary to reconstruct both *°l*
and *°ḷ* for PMY. The key equation is found in Yao, with PIM
°l=PKM *°g* in one basic correspondence; Purnell reconstructs
PY *°r*, but this initial regularly stands for initial *l* in old Chinese
loans (cf. Haud. 1947-50), suggesting PY *°ḷ*; cf. the following
table of correspondences:

PMY	PM	PIM	PKM	PY	(Purn.)
°l	*°l*	*°l*	*°l*	*°l*	$(=°l^1)$
°ḷ	*°ḷ*	*°ḷ*	*°g*	*°ḷ*	$(=°l^2)$
°r	*°r*	*°l*	*°g*	*°ḷ*	$(=°r)$

In addition to the basic correspondences indicated above, an
AT *°ḷ>w* shift is noted before the high vowel cluster *°ia* in
EXCHANGE/ (PM and PY), SHINE/ (PY), and YELLOW
(PY), and an analogous *°ḷ>[w]>ø* shift before rounded vowel
in VOMIT¹ (PM and PKM), SKY, and CLOTHES (PM). A
parallel *°ḷ>w* shift must be reconstructed as a hypothetical intermediate stage in the curious transformation of initial dental
to labial stop in the following group of roots:

	AT		PMY	
three	*tuḷu/a*	*°twu/a*	*pua*	
fart	[]*t/ḷ/ot*	*°twot*	*pwot*	
bone	(*n*)*tuḷaŋ*	*°ntwuŋ*	*mpuŋ*	(PIM)
		°th[]luŋ	*tshuŋ*	(PM)
			suŋ	(PKM)

Note the divergent developments in the root for "bone," with
stress and nasalization playing key roles; the Li dialects show
striking parallels in their forms for "three," varying from *pu~fu
~vu* to *tsu~śu*. The following tables present the basic MY material on velar/postvelar and labial clusters, largely secondary
but including several examples of primary clusters preserved in
MY (HORN; DOG; EGG; BEAR; STRETCH(ED); also LICK/,
MONKEY, and BIRD); under the "Yao" columns, reconstructions by Purn. precede the /, followed by reconstructions by

Haud., based on dialects which in general show greater preservation of initial clusters. In the case of the velar/postvelar clusters, the distinctions among *kl, *kḷ, and *kr, etc., at the PMY level are based on comparisons of the PY and PM reconstructions; whereas in the case of the labial clusters the critical distinctions are based essentially on the PM reconstructions themselves, an unsurmountable problem for Purnell because of his failure to reconstruct *ḷ as distinct from *l. Note in both tables that AT *γ and *R form clusters much like AT *r and *l, merging in PMY; also note AT *k[]r>PMY *khḷ rather than the antici-

Miao-Yao Velar/Postvelar Clusters

	AT	Yao	PM	PMY
horn	kl-	ky/-	k	kl
penis	(N)qal-	ky/ky	q	ql
yellow	(N)quliaŋ			
	Guliaŋ	wiaŋ	Glɛŋ	Gḷiaŋ
dog	kḷ-	kl/ky	kl	kḷ
back/	k/ḷ-	kl/-	kl	kḷ
between/neck	kaḷ-	kl/ky	kl	kḷ
ashes/white	kuḷ-	—.	kl	kḷ
dark/	k/ḷ/	—	kl	kḷ
	(ŋ)k/ḷ/	gl (h.t.)	—	ŋkḷ
roll	(ŋ)guḷ-	kl (l.t.)	—	gḷ
egg	qḷ-	ky/kl	q	qḷ
dirt	(N)qaḷ-	kl/-	—	qḷ
head	qaḷ-	—	qhl	qhḷ
hoarse	q[]ḷ-	khl/-	—	qhḷ
shine/	NGilaŋ			
	(N)qilaŋ	gwiaŋ (h.t.)	—	Nqḷiaŋ
dark/	G/ḷ/	kl (l.t.)	—	Gḷ
bear	kr-	ky/ky	kl	kr
stretch(ed)/	(ŋ)kr-	gy (h.t.)	—	ŋkr
assemble/	kar-	khl	—	khḷ
enclose/	k[u/o]r-	[khḷ]	—	[khḷ]
rumble/	gur-	gl-	—	gḷ-
bite/cut	kəγ-	ky/-	—	kr
mussel	kaγ-	ky/-	—	kr
sink into/	qaγ-	khl-	—	qhḷ-

	AT	Yao	MKS	MPT	MWN	MHY	MCF	PT	PM	PMY
fruit/	b/l/	py/-	p	ts	ts	p	ć	p	pl	pl
monkey	bl-	b/bl	l	l	l	—	l	—	ʔl	ʔbl
face/	b[]l-	pl	—	pl	ndl	mr	n̄	—	bl	bl
lick/	(m)bl-	by/bl	mpl	mpl	—	ʔmr	ń	—	mbl	mbl
leech	(m)b[]l-	—	—	mpl	—	—	n	—	(ʔ)mbl	(ʔ)mbl
sky/	(m)bul-	b/bl	n	n	n	n	n	m	ml	m(b)l
bird	maml-	n	n	n	n	n	n	hm	hml	(h)ml
four	p/l/	py/pl	pl	pl	tl	pr	hl	py	pl	pl
stone	baḷ-	—/pl	—	—	—	—	—	—	—	pl̥
belly	bar-	—	—	—	—	—	—	—	—	—
run/	buʔ-	—/pl	—	pl	thl	—	—	—	pl	pl
exchange	paḷ-	—	—	pl	—	—	hl	—	pl̥	pl̥
empty/	(m)puR-	bl	mpl	phl	ndl	n	n	—	phl	phl
rice	(m)b[]l-	bl	—	—	—	—	n	—	mpl̥	mpl̥
glutinous	(m)buḷ-	bl	mpl	mpl	ndl	n	ń	—	mbl̥	mbl̥
leaf	(m)bul-	n	—	mpl	—	—	n	m	mbl	mbl
steal/	(m)boi-	n	—	ń	—	—	—	—	mbl̥	m(b)l̥
man/	maḷ(i)- / meḷ-	—	—	ń / ml	—	—	n / n	—	mly / ml	ml(y) / ml̥
hut/house	p/l/	py/pl	pr	ć	—	pr	[q]	py	pr	pr
palm/five	p/r/ / p/l/	py/pl / —	pr / —	ć / ńć	p / nts	— / mp (MLL)	ć / ń	py / by	pr / mpr	pr / mpr
blue/	mpir- / (m)bir-	by/pl	mpr	ńć	mp	mr	ń	by	mbr	mbr
fish	bul-	hn	hn	hn	hn	—	—	by	mbr	(m)br
smell/	(m)b[]r- / s/m/ar-	—	—	hn / ml	—	—	hn	—	hmr	hmr

Miao-Yao *hr=**xh¹ (Purnell)

	AT	PY	PM	PMY
high	s[u][l]aŋ	hḷ[a,aa]ŋ	hre(ŋ) hlaŋ	hraaŋ hḷaaŋ
liver	—	hḷaan	hri(ŋ)	hraan

Miao-Yao *sr=**xh² (Purnell)

	AT	PY	PM	PMY
centipede	s[a]lep	sap	—	s[r]ap

	Arch. Ch.	PY	PM	PMY
animal	śrĕŋ	sɛŋ	hri(ŋ)	srɛŋ
count	śriu	s[a,aa]w	hruɛ hrou	sraaw srou

Austro-Thai Consonants (Nasal/Oral and Nasal)

AT	Indo-nesian	Form: East	Kadai [>Thai]	Miao-Yao
mp	mp/p	b	b	mp(h)
mb	mb/b	mb~m	mb~m	mb
m	m	m	m	m
nt	nt/t	nt~d	d	nt(h)
nd	nd/d	n	n	nd
n	n	n	n	n
nts	nt'/t'	dz	dz~z	nts(h)
ndz	nd'/d'	—	n	ndz
ns	nh	ns	n/z	s
nz	nḍ/ḍ	n	n	ń
ńć	ńk'/k'	—	j	—
ńj	ńg'/g'	—	n	—
[ńś]	ń	—	z	ń~n
[ńź]	nẓ	—	ńj[>j]	ń
ńy	ń	—	ny[>ń]	—
ń	ń	ń	ń	ń
ŋk	ŋk/k	g	g	ŋk(h)~nts(h)
ŋg	ŋg/g	—	ŋ/ø	ŋg~ndz
ŋ	ŋ	ŋ	ŋ/ø	ń
Nq	(ŋ)k/k	ŋ~k	G[>γ]	Nq(h)
NG	ŋ(g)/g	—	N[>ń]	NG~ŋg
N	—	—	N	ŋ

pated *khr, apparently because of the aspiration. Finally, in the brief table on MY *hr and *sr, apparently all secondary, note AT *s[u]l>PMY *hr but *s[a]l>PMY *s[r], the latter reconstruction supported by two parallel PMY roots which appear to be very early loans from Arch. Ch. (see Benedict 1972: 170, n. 457 for the ST evidence concerning the *śr cluster in these Ch. forms: śrĕŋ "sacrificial animal"="living creature"="living," from ST *śriŋ "live, alive").

Notes on Table of Austro-Thai Consonants (Nasal/Oral and Nasal):

1. Nasals: generally maintained throughout AT, but KD has *ŋ>∅ in unstressed intervocalic position: COLD/ (Thai Kl.); SESAME (Dioi); SWIM/ (Thai KS Li), WEEP (Dioi); cf. LEAK(Y), showing *ŋg>*ŋ>∅ (Thai/Dioi); cf. also the Thai/ Dioi forms for the calendrical term for "horse": Ahom śi-ŋa, Lü sa-ŋa, Dioi sa<*za(ŋ)a, from AT *ts[a]ŋa (FORK/; see also Benedict 1967bis). Thai shows the assimilative final *ŋ>n shift after medial *i in NOTCHED/; ODOR; and POUR/, contrasting with retention of final *ŋ in MONKEY", LEECH", and ROLL, perhaps reflecting secondary vocalic length (*rin "pour," from *riin<*(i)liŋ), but KS and Li uniformly retain final *ŋ (NOTCHED/). PMY has the anticipated shifts from velar to dental and from postvelar to velar, paralleling the shifts in the oral consonants (above). The postvelar nasal is rare, but can be reconstructed for irregular initial series in Li (ROAR/) and Thai (CATTLE), each with corresponding initial *ŋ in PMY, while the Thai reconstruction (*Nua) in the latter root serves to explain the irregular initial series in the TB loan: Kachin and Moshang ŋa, Nungish ŋwa~ŋa~nwa (Trung ŋuŋ ŋua), Burmese nwà "cattle" (Benedict 1972: 50 and notes 164 and 165).

2. Nasal-orals: fairly well maintained in IN (medial position) and PO (Biggs 1965), as well as in MY (with velar>dental affricate and postvelar>velar shifts, as above) but generally not represented in Formosa, the scattered examples (from the East group) showing shifts closely paralleling the regular shifts found in KD. The main types of shifts are illustrated in the following table relating to the labial series:

Austro-Thai	*p	*mp	*b	*mb
Hova (IN)	f	(m)p	v	mb
Proto-Oceanic	*p	*mp	*p	*mp
Samoan (PN)	f	p	f	p
Dobu (SEP)	ø	b	ø	b
Tsou (Form.)	p	b	f	b
Pazeh (Form.)	p	b	b	m
Thai	*p	*b	*b	*m
Lao	p (h.t.)	p (l.t.)	p (l.t.)	m
Miao: PE	*p (h.t.)	*p (h.t.)	*p (l.t.)	*m
Yao: PY	*p (h.t.)	*b (h.t.)	*p (l.t.)	*b (l.t.)

Note the tendency in IN and PO for stops to be maintained (rather than shifting to continuants) in the nasal-oral units; note also the partial parallel to the Form./Thai shift in Miao: PE (but *mp>*p rather than *b) and the distinctive shifts found only in Yao. There is some evidence for preservation of AT *mb at the earliest level in Form: East, both in Saisiat (BORE/; GRASS) and in Bunun (BREATHE/; LOUSE/FLEA[1]), the latter corresponding to Thai *(m)b; also in KD, with Lati: BP apparently maintaining an original *mb in three different roots (GOAT; PIG; RAIN/); note also KS *mb in LOUSE/; SIDE. Shifts of Form./Thai type (voiced stop>nasal) occur on occasion in IN and/or PO under conditions not yet determined; cf. BEND/BENT (PPN *nd>n~l), HOLD/ (PO *ŋg>ŋ), RUMBLE/ (PPN *ŋg>ŋ), RIVER (IN *NG>ŋ); also BEAR, BREATHE/, CHANGE/ and HAIR (BODY)/, all showing the *mb>m shift in AN; in the case of BEAR, the reconstruction *mb rather than *m is possible only because of the MY cognate *(krop), both Form. and Thai showing the anticipated *mb>m shift. KD appears to retain *dz (<*nts) in CAT/ (Kl.) and WASH/ (Thai). Although the nasal-oral units ordinarily are of nasal + stop or nasal + affricate type, there is substantial evidence for the nasal + sibilant type: *ns (BLOW/; SEED), *nz (LIVE/; WATER[1]; WORM/), *ńś (SNAKE[1]), *ńź (POINT/), and even for nasal + y: *ńy (DIFFICULT). Haudricourt (1965) and others have considered the "prenasalized consonants" to be of relatively late origin in AN, particularly in view of their scarcity in Formosa, but Biggs (1965) has shown that they must be reconstructed for PO as a "nasal grade," often appearing in some but not all cognates, as in the related IN phenomenon (we follow both Demp. and Biggs in writing *(m)p for *p~*mp, etc). Blust (1970: 111 and n. 9) and others have made much of the presence of the cluster ŋs in certain roots, e.g. Ja. *lisa~liŋsa* "nit," which Dempwolff attempted to explain away as the result of dissimilation in setting up his system of homorganic nasal/orals for AN; rather we should regard this feature as evidence for an earlier cluster: IN *li(ń)t'a "nit," from *liŋkla, etc. It now appears that these nasal-oral units are even better represented in the mainland divisions, especially in MY, than they are in AN itself, and hence are to be reconstructed at the earliest AT level. Their ultimate origin remains in doubt, since it is not possible at this time to demonstrate that they are the accretion products of archaic prefixes or infixes, as commonly supposed (Haudricourt 1962; Biggs 1965). In given instances, the nasal element can be interpreted as the reflex of a final nasal in an earlier reduplicated form (HOLD/; OPEN/; PILE UP/); note also GLUTINOUS/, with IN *pulut and *dampul~*dəmpul, PO *mpulu[t], T *[br]ut<*mprut, PMY *mbḷut, as if from an original AT *dampuḷut (with secondary voicing by assimilation in PMY). The one nasal prefix (*m/) that can be established at the earliest AT level (above) perhaps plays a role in the development of the nasal-oral unit on rare occasions (FEAR; SEW/; WET/), but in general this prefix appears to be entirely unrelated, and on the whole it would seem that we must look toward ultimate explanations in terms of phonology rather than morphology.

CONSONANT CLUSTERS

The reconstructed AT schema shows a fairly symmetrical system of primary consonant clusters, which tend to be handled as units, e.g. they can enter into a nasal-oral combination (SEW: (m)plaqi[s]). The existence of clusters of this type was not even suspected when the writer first worked with these languages around 1940, since IN *mata and T *ta "eye," IN *matəy and T *taay "die" appeared to present no problem in reconstruction, the aspiration of the Tho-Nung forms (*tha~ha* "eye," *tha:i~ha:i* "die") being regarded as secondary (Benedict 1942). Somewhat later, however, F. K. Li (1954) reconstructed these Thai roots as *tra and *traay on the basis of N. Thai data (Wuming *ra* "eye," *rai* "die") while Haudricourt (1956), on the basis of different Thai data, suggested the reconstructions *pra and *praay. Haudricourt further indicated that one could not explain the IN forms (*mata and *matɘy) on the basis of Li's reconstructions, then postulated the following tortuous line of development: *mata>mda>pda>pra. Fortunately, a much simpler solution is at hand, since the Formosan languages, which regularly have *t corresponding to IN *t, show distinct reflexes here: East: Puy. *ṭ*=Ami Bun. Kuv. Sir. *t*=Pai. Ruk. *ts*=Fav. *ć*=Sai. Paz. *s*=Thao *θ*; Tsouic: Tsou Kan. Saa. *ts*; Atayalic: Ata. *s* (Dyen [1965] writes the conventional symbol *C). The writer (1966) first suggested the AT reconstructions *matla "eye" and *mat[]play "die," later (1967) changed to *mapra and *mapray, respectively, on the basis of the Thai evidence (Haudicourt 1956) and of the Sek (*pr*) and Lakkia (*pl*) reflexes in this pair of roots. This will not do, however, since both KS and Kelao/Lati make a distinction in the initials of the two roots, as shown in the following table, where they are paired with other roots, showing the same Formosan reflexes (but Tsouic has *t* rather than *ts* as initial), for which either Lati (SEW/PLAIT) or Sui/Mak (BURN/HOT) has the distinctive reflex; note also that Thai, which has *t as reflex in medial position, here distinguishes between *th and *phr as initial. The original AT distinction appears to have been between *pl and *pḷ, as shown in the table, to be differentiated from *pr (WEEP, in table), for which Sek has *t* rather than *pr,* and Lakkia has *pi=py* rather than *pl,* hence it can be seen that both these languages merged AT *pl and *pḷ, while keeping *pr distinct; whereas Lati merged *pḷ and *pr, while keeping *pl distinct. PMY parallels IN in a complete shift of these clusters to dentals, with details obscured by the special developments (above) shown by this division, e.g. initial *t>d (DIE/KILL).

On the basis of the above correspondences, we can reconstruct AT *pl in LIVER/, perhaps also in EXCREMENT, as well as

AT *pl, *pl and *pr

	SEW/PLAIT	DIE/KILL	BURN/HOT	EYE	WEEP
AT	*(m)plaqis	*ma/play, */pad/play	*plaluh, *pluluh	*mapla	*praŋits, *praŋis
IN	*tahi	ɦeɑpu	*tunu	*mata	*taŋit'
Form:					
East	*(m/)taqis	*matay, *patay	*tuluh	*mata	*taŋits, *t/m/aŋits
Tsouic	*t/m/aqis, *t/m/aqis	*matsay, */patsay	*ma/tuluh, */tsuluh	*matsa	*/taŋits, *t/m/aŋits
Atayal	s/m/aqis			/masa	
Thai: SW	*thak	*taay	*phraw	*ta	
Tho-Nung	tak (l.t.)	tha:i, ha:i	thaw	tha, ha	
Dioi		tai	plau	ta	tai
Wu-ming		rai	phraw	ra	tai
Sek		praai	dau (h.t.)	pra	piɛ
Sui/Mak		tai		da (h.t.)	
Lakkia		plei		pla	
Ong-Be	dɔʔ (l.t.)	dai (h.t.)	sau	da (h.t.)	
S. Li				śa~sa	
Laqua	them	tie		te	
Kelao	pe	ple u		/mokho	
Lati		pe~phi		mɕu	ćuŋ
PMY	*(n)tat, *taiʔ	*day, *tay	*thaw	*maay	

(m)pl̦ in FRAGRANT and *°pr* in LOUSE/; the situation is somewhat obscured when the prenasalization is more extensive, but a distinction evidently must be drawn between *°(m)pl̦* in EARTH and *°(m)pr* in BEE (see GLOSSARY for details).

As indicated above, the various clusters that have been reconstructed to date for AT make up a fairly symmetrical pattern (below), with the noteworthy absence of voiced stop+ *l̦* clusters as well as of nasal+ clusters except for *°ml;* these gaps appear to be systematic, but those in the *x*+ and postvelar+ series perhaps only remain to be filled in by later study in this intricate area.

	r	*l*	*l̦*
p	*pr*	*pl*	*pl̦*
b	*br*	*bl*	—
m	—	*ml*	—
t	*tr*	*tl*	*tl̦*
d	*dr*	*dl*	—
k	*kr*	*kl*	*kl̦*
g	*gr*	*gl*	—
x	—	*xl*	—
q	*qr*	—	*ql̦*

The AT consonant clusters, found only in initial or medial position, are represented fairly well at the earliest KD level, also (for dentals and velar/postvelars) in PMY, with the curious exception of AT *°bl,* yielding KD *°(h)l,* but PMY *°ʔbl* (a type of unvoicing). Throughout AT, however, at the earliest level in AN and at the later levels in KD and MY, there have occurred systematic shifts from clusters of all types to dental stops or affricates (retroflex stops in Form: East), although at the later levels in KD and MY there has more often been simple loss of *°r/l/l̦* in the velar/postvelar clusters, with Yao showing the "reverse shift": PMY *°tl>°k[l]>ky* (PMY *°tlat* "laugh," YHN *kyɛt,* YTP *kyat,* YCR *ćat,* but PPY *tut* retains the initial; see LAUGH). Atayalic appears to have retained velar stop + *r* clusters—BEAR; RICE (PLANT)—and Tsouic perhaps retained AT *°dr* (TWO), while the variation in reflexes shown by IN and by the three

AN divisions in Formosa suggests that at least some of the AT clusters survived into the earliest AN level, e.g. a development such as *pl>ts~t̯~t (all independent shifts) seems much more likely than *pl>*ts>*t̯>*t or the like.

Austro-Thai Consonant Clusters

FORMOSA

AT	Indonesian	East	Tsouic	Atayalic	Kadai[>Thai]	Miao-Yao
pr	t	t̯	t/-	—	p(h)r[>t(h)]	—
br	ḍ	ḍ	—	—	br[>d]	—
pl	t	t̯	t/ts	ts	pl[>t(h)]	d/t
bl	d~l	d~l	—	—	(h)l	ʔbl
ml	n	—	—	—	ml[>n]	[ml]>n
pḷ	t	ṭ	-/ts	ts	p(h)r[>t(h)]	t(h)
tr	-/t	t̯/t	-/t	-/t	t(h)r	—
dr	ḍ/z	ḍ/d	[dr]/-	d>r	dr	—
tl	t/ṭ	ṭ	ts/t	—	ty/t(h)l	tl
dl	-/ḍ	ḍ	—	[d]>r	-/dl	—
tḷ	t	ṭ	ts	—	t(h)ḷ	—
kr	k'	ṭ	ts	k[r]	k(h)r/kl	kr
gr	g'	j	y>ø	g[r]	—	—
kl	t'	ts	[ts]	[ts]>h	k(h)l	kl
gl	d'	—	—	—	gl	—
[xl]	t'	l	—	l	xl[>hl]	[hl]>hḷ
kḷ	t'	ts	[ts]	[ts]>h	[khḷ]	kḷ
qr	t	t̯	ts	—	qhr[>xr]	—
qḷ	t	t̯	ts	—	khr	qḷ

Notes on Table of Austro-Thai Consonant Clusters:

*pr/pl/pḷ: see discussion above; Atayalic *ts: Ata: Squliq s=Ci'uli ts=Sed. s (as final: Ata. t=Sed. ts~t); a cluster of this type appears in final position in some AN roots, but probably always represents a pseudo-final (BITE/), at times an apparent residue of partial reduplication (LIGHTNING/; SKIN/).

*br: see ASHES/; this reconstruction preferable to *bl̥, in view of Sek *br>th, paralleling *pr>t, although Lk. has *br>pl, *pr>pi=py; note Thai *br>*d~*b[r], with retention of voicing, but *b[]l>*p[]r (unvoicing of initial) >*t (BAMBOO/; LEAF¹; GRASSHOPPER), paralleling Laqua *b[]r>t (MONKEY¹).

*bl: see MONKEY¹¹; cf. also LICK/, with nasalization: *(m)bl.

*ml: see BIRD; SWEET/; occurs only in medial position, maintained in both roots in Lakkia, paralleling *pl>pl in this language; in BIRD the original *m appears also in KS (Kam mok) and MY (Pateng hmu).

*tr: see BODY/; COOK (WITH STEAM)/; SEE; STONE; TEN/THOUSAND (below, under NUMERALS); note Li *s in this series; Form. generally *t (SEE), but East *ṭ after *q/ (STONE in Pai.) and *k/ (TEN in Thao), paralleling AT *dr> ḍ as initial (below).

*dr: see COOK (WITH STEAM)/ (doublet of root under *tr); LADDER/; SAND; SUN/; TWO (below, under NUMER-ALS); IN *ḍ as initial (TWO), *ẓ as medial (LADDER/; SUN/), but *d in reduplicated form (COOK/); Form: East also *ḍ as initial (COOK/; TWO), but *d as medial (SAND; SUN/); Tsouic: Tsou y=Kan. ts=Sa. s (in TWO), but Tsou r~l in early sources, suggesting Tsouic *dr; note also *q/dr> Thai *ʔd (Thai lacks *ʔdr), Sek tr, Li *r (SUN/).

*tl̥: see LAUGH; SACK/; SMALL/; IN *t as initial (LAUGH), *ṭ as medial (SACK/; SMALL/) (IN *ṭ is marginal phoneme as initial); Tsouic *ts as initial (LAUGH), *t as medial (SMALL/) (the reverse of the reflexes for labial clusters); KD *ty as initial (LAUGH), reconstructed for Li, but *t(h)l as medial (SACK/; SMALL/).

*dl̥: see BAG/; SMALL/ (doublet of root under *tl̥); this poorly represented cluster appears to be differentiated from AT *dr by a distinct reflex both in IN (medial *ḍ rather than *ẓ) and in Form: East (medial *ḍ rather than *d).

*tl: see LOUSE; note IN *t, contrasting with *ṭ for AT medial *tr (above); these clusters (*tr and *tl) have the same reflexes in most KD languages, but appear to be distinct in Li, as shown in the following table, which includes the virtually identical Li reflexes for the secondary cluster in AT *tulu~*təlu "three":

AT *tr, *tl̩, and *t[]l̩

	BREAK/	STONE	LOUSE	THREE
AT	*trak *[mbə]trak	*(q/)(n)tril[ay]	*(ŋ)k[a]tlu̩ *qatlu̩	*tulu̩ *təlu̩
IN	*(m)bətak	—	*kutu	*təlu̩
Form:		*qatilay	*kutu̩	*tulu̩
East	—			*təlu̩
Thai	*thrak *trak	*thrin	*thraw	—
Dioi	rak	rin (h.t.)	rau (h.t.)	—
Sek	rak (h.t.)	riil (h.t.)	raw (h.t.)	—
Kam-Sui	*tyak	*d[r]i[l]	*t(y)u	—
Ong-Be	—	dien	kat	—
Li (recon.)	*sak	*siin	*traw	*tru
S. Li	śak	śien	śau	śu
SH Loi	—	sien	sou	su
WS Li	—	śiŋ	—	fu
DC Loi	—	sien	fou	fu
SC Loi	—	sien	fou	vu

*kr: see BEAR; ODOR; RICE (PLANT); SMELL; SPLIT; STRETCH(ED)/; Atayalic *k[r] on basis of Sed. k~s in BEAR (no Ata. cognate); KD *k(h)r as initial (SMELL: SPLIT) but *kl as medial (RICE; ODOR), on basis of Thai evidence, with variable aspiration in STRETCH(ED)/; it is possible that Thai secondarily shifted medial *kr to *kl, the most "natural" clusters in Thai being *khr and *kl (as opposed to *kr and *khl).

*gr: see RICE (PLANT), a doublet of root under *kr; Atayalic *g[r] on basis of Ata. g=Sed. ð~y, contrasting with Atayalic *j: Ata. r~s=Sed. ð~y, corresponding to Form: East *j (under No. 10); no comparisons have been uncovered for the anticipated *gr in KD and probably MY.

*kl: see HORN[II]; cf. also FLUTE, MORTAR/; and SALT, reconstructed with *k[l,l̩] in the absence of a cognate in MY, the only division of AT to retain the distinction between AT *kl and *kl̩ (see table on Miao-Yao Velar/Postvelar Clusters).

*gl: see FEEL (FOR)/; no comparisons have been uncovered for the anticipated *dz in Form. and probably *gl in MY.

*[xl]: see IRON.

*kl̩: see DOG; KD *[khl], based on Thai/KS *h(ma), Lk.

kh(*wą*), OB **h*(*ma*), Kl. **x*(*mə*) and Lt. **l*(*mu*), from KD
*khl[]*ma*.

   *qr: see EAR; the anticipated MY correspondence is **qr*.

   *ql: see EGG; KD **khr* for the anticipated **qhr* is unexplained; it is possible that a doublet AT root with initial **kl̦*
should be set up, but KD appears to have **khl* for AT **kl̦*
(above).

VOWELS

The basic AT vowel scheme is symmetrical, with distinctions
between front unrounded and back rounded vowels on high (**i*,
*u) and mid (**e*, **o*) levels (**e* and **o* rare as finals), along
with central **ə* vowel (only as medial) and low **a* vowel, as
follows:

It is not clear whether vocalic length (geminate vowel cluster)
must also be set up at the AT level in view of the all-pervasive
influence of Vocalic Transfer (below), but it does appear that
at least one true diphthong (*ia*) should be recognized. As shown
in the following table, AN simplifies to a four-vowel system
by merging AT **e* with **i*, **o* with **u*, while KD and MY
generally preserve the **e*~**i* and **o*~**u* distinctions but tend
to merge **ə* with **o*:

Notes on Table of Austro-Thai Vowels:

   AN **ay*>**əy*: as noted by Dyen (1949), Ja. and Ml. have
two sets of reflexes for IN final **ay* as reconstructed by Demp.;
Ja. *i*=Ml. *i* (Dyen reconstructs **əy*); Ja. *e*=Ml. *ai* (Dyen reconstructs **ay*); cf. DIE/ (Ja. Ml. *mati*~*pati*<**matəy*~**patəy*)
and RICE (PLANT) (Ja. *pari*, Ml. *padi*<**pag'əy*), as opposed to
MOVE BACK AND FORTH/ (Ja. *awe*, Ml. *ambai*<**a*(*m*)*bay*);
this distinction, which is not reflected in Formosa or elsewhere
in AT, conceivably represents an original AT length distinction
(**ay*~**aay*), but is more likely an IN innovation.

   KD and MY **a*>**e* before dentals: it appears that AT **a*

Austro-Thai Vowels

Austro-Thai	Austro-nesian	Kadai	Miao-Yao
a (final)	a	a	a
+ y	ay>əy	ay	ay
+ w	aw	aw	aw
+ labial	a	a	a
+ dental	a	a>e	a>e
+ velar	a	a	u
+ postvelar	a>i	a>e	a
[aa]	a	aa/a	aa
ə (medial)	ə	ə/ɨ/o	ə/o/ɔ
+ y	[əy]>i	ay	ay
+ w	əw>u	əw>aw	əw>u
o	u	o	ɔ
[oo]	u	oo=ɔ:	o
e	i	e	ɛ/a
[ee]	i	ee=ɛ:	e
u (final)	u	u	ou
(medial)	u	u	o
[uu]	u	uu	u
i (final)	i	i	ei
(medial)	i	i	i/e
[ii]	i	ii	—
ia (medial)	ia>i	ee=ɛ:	ia

was generally maintained before dentals at the earliest level in KD, in view of the sporadic retention here and there (MUSH-ROOM), also that *a was maintained before *ts (SWEEP/) and generally with vocalic length (BRANCH; FLESH/; GNAW/) (but cf. HARD/ for both); there were also shifts to *i under conditions not fully worked out (KNIFE/; MUSHROOM; RIGHT), perhaps including influence by earlier glottal stop: T *kin~*in "eat," from *kaʔən (above), with Li retaining the *a vocalism (N. Li kha:n). MY normally maintains AT *a before dentals, even in the *at>*ay shift noted above (CUL-TIVATE/), but when palatalized this secondary *ay (<*at or *as) is shifted to *ei (FOUR; LOUSE; STONE/).

MY $*a > *u$ before velars: there is good evidence for this unanticipated shift in MY before final $*ŋ$ (BONE; FLY/; SALTY/; SHARP (TASTING)/; SIDE; SKY), but note that $*a$ is preserved in the diphthong $*ia$ (below) and in secondary $*ua$ clusters (DEAF; SKY) as well as with vocalic length (BOAT; CUT DOWN/OFF/; MALE; SALTY/; VILLAGE); AT $*a$ before final $*k$ in MY is represented in only one comparison (COUGH/), which appears to show retention of $*a$ with vocalic length.

$*a > *i \sim *e$ before/after postvelars: AN $*a/i > *i$ after $*q$ at the earliest level in THIGH/, with the doublet $*paqa \sim *paqi < *paqa/i$ both in IN and Form. (Thao; Ata.); also at a late level in Form. (VOMIT[II]: Kuv. *muti?* $< *m/utaq$) and in IN after secondary $*q$ ($< *x$) in FEMALE/ (IN $*(m)babi < *(m)ba/ba?i$). KD apparently maintains $*a$ at the earliest level, but there has been some shifting to $*e$ before final $*q$ (DIP UP/; LEECH; VOMIT[1]) as well as to $*e$ and $*i$ (mainly in the combination $*ay$) after $*q/G$ (BEAR; CROCODILE; EARTH/; FACE/; OLD/; RED/; RIVER; SHARP (TASTING)/; WORM/) and original $*x$ (FEMALE/). There is no evidence for this kind of shift in MY, but note Yao $*a > *ə$ after an earlier $*G$ (FLESH/).

$*[aa]$: possibly secondary in all cases; see below under Vocalic Transfer.

KD $*ə > *ə/i/o$: it is possible that AT $*ə$ was maintained at the earliest level in KD in many or even all positions, since it apparently must be reconstructed before labial finals for Li, where S. Li o = WS Li o (S. Li *nom*, WS Li *tom* "six," from Li $*nəm < AT *ənəm$), contrasting with $*o$ for S. Li o = WS Li a (S. Li *nom*, WS Li *nam* "water," from Li $*nom < AT *(n)zalom$). Thai $*ə$ is rare and shows frequent interchange with $*i$ and $*ia$, both usually derived from $*ya$ (below), but the $*ə \sim *i$ doublet appears to stand for AT $*ə$ in one root (COME/), while $*i$ and $*o$ are the common replacements for AT $*ə$, the former apparently under special conditions not yet fully determined (BURY/; STRETCH(ED); STRETCH(ED)/; SUBMERGE/; SWALLOW; THICK/).

MY $*ə > *ə/o/ɔ$: MY has reflexes similar to those of KD, with $*ə$ to be reconstructed before labial finals for Yao where YCR

a=YHN ɔ (BITE/; COVER/; DARK/); Purnell reconstructs *ə in PMY *krəp "bear" (YCR e=YHN o), but this can be reconstructed *krop (YCR e for o after *r). As in KD, the normal shift in MY appears to be to *o, but to *ɔ as initial (CLOUD") and after *r (MIDDLE/; STRETCH(ED)/), the former showing a contrast with the regular reflex (*ntrɔŋ<*nt/l/əŋ, but *ntoŋ<*ntəŋ).

*[əy]>*i and *əw>*u: IN has final *əw>*u in "two" (Dyen 1947a), corresponding to *aw in Li, from AT *əw (below, under NUMERALS), but final *u corresponding to Li *əw in SAND, to MY *əw in DOG; IN *əy (above) seems rather to be a later innovation from AT *ay, and it is probable that AT *əy yielded AN and IN *i, KD and MY *ay (THIS/), paralleling the above shift.

KD *o>*o, *[oo]>*oo; *e>*e; *[ee]>*ee: these mid-height vowels, merged with AT *u and *i in AN, are best maintained in KD, especially in Thai. The long vowels are perhaps all secondary, as are *[aa], *[uu], and *[ii], often the result of Vocalic Transfer (below). Thai neatly filled in the three "vacant places" in the six-vowel scheme of AT (above), developing a high central vowel *ɨ (<*ə and *ya), as well as low front (*ɛ) and back (*ɔ) vowels from long (or geminate) *e and *o, respectively, followed by secondary length distinctions in all vowels:

i	$ɨ$	u
e	$ə$	o
$ɛ$	a	$ɔ$

MY *o>*ɔ; *e>*ɛ/a: MY also retains the basic AT distinction between *u and *o, *i and *e, but by lowering both sets of vowels to *o(u) and *ɔ, *e(i) and *ɛ, respectively. AT *o is retained after secondary labialization (FART; RAIN/) and initial *N (ROAR/); note also AT *ol>PMY *wei (CARRY ON SHOULDER/; SHELLFISH/). AT *e yielded PMY *ɛ before velar/postvelars (LEFT'; NOTCHED) but *a before labials (CENTIPEDE; DUCK) and dentals (HOOK/).

MY *u>*o(u); *[uu]>*u; *i>*ei and *i/e: cf. remarks above; AT medial *u>PMY *o, but when secondarily lengthened, by Vocalic Transfer (below) or reduplication, the high

vowel $*u$ is retained (COVER/; GLUTINOUS/; HEAD/;
GLUTINOUS/; LIVE; PULL LENGTHWISE/; RUB/; RUM-
BLE/; SKY/); contrast (without lengthening) $*ut > *wei$ (TAIL/).
AT $*i$ is retained in PMY before velars (LEECH[II]; MONKEY[II];
ROLL; STEAL/), but is lowered to $*e$ before labials (LIVE/)
and dentals (CUT/; LICK/).

$*ia > *i$ and ia/ee: this diphthong, which patterns as a unit,
ordinarily is found only before velar/postvelars (exception:
HINDER/; TWIN); it is represented by $*i$ in IN (the irregular
Ja. *binte* in KICK perhaps reflects this diphthong) and Atayalic
(THROW), but by $*ia$ in the single comparison available from
Form: East (YELLOW, in Sir.). Thai has a distinctive set of
three falling-stress diphthongs: $*ia/ia/ua$ (both medial and final
position), which appears to underlie vocalic systems in other
KD languages; these show frequent interchange with $*ee$ and
$*oo$, with stress apparently having played a basic role in the
development:

$$íya > ia \qquad\qquad (i)yá > ia \sim ya(a)$$
$$ia > ee$$
$$(y)ia > ia$$
$$úwa > ua \qquad\qquad uwá > wa(a)$$
$$ua > oo$$

As can be seen from the above table, T $*ia$ and $*ua$ do not
normally represent AT diphthongs, and in fact $*ua$ cannot be
reconstructed at the AT level. In both KD and MY, these vowel
clusters characteristically stand for AT $*iCa$ and $*uCa$ combinations, with C=voiced consonant (cf. discussion above), as in
LICK/ (T $*lia$, PMY $*mblia < $AT $*(m)bli[d]a/$). These clusters
also on occasion represent $*i/a$ or $*u/a$ morpheme boundaries
both in Thai (FEAR; THORN) and MY (FEAR). In Thai and
KD generally, there is frequent interchange with $*iya$, with
various possibilities illustrated in most of the following roots:
CHANGE/; CHOOSE; CRY OUT/; DESIRE/; DIVIDE/;
GOAT; HUT/; IRON; KICK; POINT/; SMOKE/; STICK/;
THROW; TWIN; YELLOW. PMY regularly has $*ia$ for both
AT $*ia$ (IRON; YELLOW) and $*iya$ (CHANGE/; STICK/),
but has $*ia > *i(i)$ in one root through assimilation to vowel i
in preceding syllable (KICK) as well as $*iya > *yia > *yua$ in

another root through vocalic transfer followed by dissimilation (GOAT).

Vocalic Transfer: KD and, to a lesser degree, MY exhibit a complex system of vocalic transformations which we have labeled Vocalic Transfer (VT). This is one aspect of the process of reduction to monosyllables and involves the transfer of the vowel in the first or preceding ("lost") syllable to the following syllable. The product is dependent primarily on the nature of the transferred vowel (VT vowel), secondarily on the consonants involved and on stress factors not yet fully understood. VT $*i$ normally leads to palatalization (Thai $*ya>*ɨ\sim*ɨa$), but can result in $*i+$ clusters (SHINE/ illustrates both); VT $*u$ leads to labialization and to $*u+$ clusters (including PMY $*u<*uu$, above); VT $*ə$ (which can be derived from other vowels through unstressing) leads to palatalization and to $*əə$ (Thai $*oo$) clusters; VT $*o$ and $*a$ (no examples of $*e$) lead simply to $*o+$ and $*a+$ clusters, respectively. Reduplication automatically involves VT, leading to geminate clusters, as in Thai in FOOT; PILE UP/; PLAIT/. The following table presents illustrations of VT of various types in Thai, Dioi, and Li; note the distinctions under SCALE OFF/ (in Thai and Li) and HAIR (BODY)/ (in Thai and Dioi) relating to presence or absence of stress, also under HAND/FIVE (in Li) relating to presence or absence of first syllable.

Vocalic Transfer

	Austro-Thai	Thai	Dioi	Li
disgust/nausea	*q/iba *q/iba/i *q/ipa/i	*ɓia	bə (h.t.) —	— — —
hand/five	*lima *ma	p̄hiay *mɨ	—	*ɲu *eu
fly/moth	*kuman	*muan moon (m)wan	wan	*mwal
cultivate/ yam/ sweet potato	*(N)qum/al/ah *(N)qøm/al/ah	*man	man	—
worm/penis	*q/uzay *q/øzay *q/ønzay	*ʔdi	duai (h.t.) dai (h.t.) nai (h.t.)	—
hair (body)/beard	*(N)qo(m)bis *(N)eb(N)biq	*hmooy	m̄i (h.t.)	—
grandparent/grandchild	*a(m)pu *e(m)pu	*pu	pau	*ɳed
support/lean on	*(m)bantu *(m)bəntu	*daw du	tau (l.t.)	—
scale off/scales	*qulap *qəlap	—	—	*luap
pierce/pick	*(n)tsu(ŋ)kit	*hliip *khwit kwit	kwit kwi	—
spotted/piebald	*q/balaŋ	*ɓlaaŋ	—	—
pickle	*(q/)(q/)(m)pelaŋ	*ɓblooŋ	—	—
leaf	*(m)boloŋ	*tooŋ	rɔŋ (h.t.) ruk	—
bamboo/withe	*(m)boloɡ	*took		

NOTES TO THE INTRODUCTION

[1] The suggestions made in this account now (1974) appear to be on the conservative side. Thermoluminescence analysis of early pottery from Northeast Thailand has yielded a date of about 4500 B.C., indicating that the associated bronze industry was by far the oldest in the world, around 1,500 years earlier than the Near Eastern. In the words of one leading authority (Froelich Rainey in the *New York Times*, August 25, 1974), ". . . the systematic excavation of Ban Chiang and other reports of ancient agriculture and pottery manufacture coming from East Asia already point to the conclusion: The Far East [*read:* Southeast Asia] may be the part of the world where the basic technology for civilized living first evolved." The linguistic evidence, of course, fits extremely well, pointing to an AT-speaking population as the creators of this technology. One puzzling bit of prehistory/linguistics remains. The AT *lu[y]aŋ "copper/bronze" root can now be reconstructed *(s-)luyaŋ on the basis of the early loan in Mon (*sluy*), an AA language, with prefixed *s/ also indicated for the early Chinese loan (Ch. *d-<*s/l-*; see COPPER/); while another, very early, loan must be posited to explain Proto-Munda (also AA stock) *luaŋ "iron," with a curious semantic shift (see Appendix II). The existence of a root of this type is only to be expected, in view of the known antiquity of copper/bronze. There is an additional AT root, however, equally well represented: *(m)baxliaq "iron," and yet the universal consensus appears to be that iron is much later, say by three millennia or so. One might argue that there is some semantic interchange here (note Proto-Munda "iron" for "copper/bronze," above, and Atayal [Formosa] "copper" as an added gloss for the AT "iron" root) and that the basic meaning of the "iron" root was rather "metal" (see the evidence for this from Formosa and Thai, under IRON), yet the stubborn fact remains that the "core" meaning of "iron" is consistent through-

out all three main branches (AN, KD, MY) of AT, appearing
also in the early Chinese loan (Anc. $t'iet < *xliet$). This suggests
that the knowledge of iron metallurgy was much earlier in
Southeast Asia than commonly believed, since the sound shifts
involved throughout the AT domain appear to rule out borrowing as a general explanation, except at an extremely early time
period.

   [2] Additional material on Laqua has recently become available
in a sketch of Laha, a closely related language spoken in North-
west Vietnam; see *Nhung Nhom Dan Toc Thuoc Ngu He Nam
A O Tay Bac Viet Nam* [*Peoples of the Austroasiatic Family of
Languages in Northwestern Vietnam*], by Dang Nghiem Van,
Nguyen Truc Binh, Nguyen Van Huy, and Thanh Thien (Hanoi:
Nha xuat-ban Khoa-hoc xa-hoi (Social Sciences Publishing House)
1972). [The author is indebted to Professor Dinh-Hoa Nguyen,
Southern Illinois University, and Mr. David Bradley, University
of London, for their generous aid in securing this material.]
Forms are cited for the Laha dialect of Than-Uyên (TU) and
for two Laha dialects of Thuân-Châu, viz. Ban Bung (BB) and
Noong Lay (NL) (the last-named is called Khla-phlao). Additional forms are cited, by way of comparison, for Pu-peo (Ha-
giang); these are for the most part identical with or closely
similar to Laqua forms recorded in the first decade of the century by Bonifacy (1905, 1908) and by Lajonquière (1906);
note that Pu-peo is the Miao (Meo) name for the people (Man
Laqua in Vietnamese), who call themselves Ka Beo (Benedict
1942). An analysis of the Laqua/Pu-peo material itself indicates
that three closely related dialects are involved, although that
recorded by Lajonquière is known from only a handful of forms.
The dialect recorded by Bonifacy resembles Li (Hainan), contrasting both with Kelao and with Lati, in lacking prefixes, with
the exception of $k/$ in a few forms (*kədəu* "man/person," *kəzio
kəpə* "boy" [*zio* "child," *pə* "man/male"], *kəzio kəmei* "girl" [cf.
məi "woman/mother"]). Lajonquière, on the other hand, cites
several $k/$ prefixed forms, mainly for body part words while
Pu-peo shows the same prefix in several forms; cf. the following
pair:

	Laqua: Bon.	Laqua: Laj.	Pu-peo
star	*luŋ*	*kʼaluoŋ*	*kaluoŋ*
mouth	*mɔn*	*kamu*	*kəmən*

	Laha: TU	Laha: BB	Laha: NL
star	*məluŋ*	*mluoŋ*	*kluŋ*
mouth	*mɔn*	*muol*	*mul*

Apart from the cluster *ml-* (BB "star"), prefixed *m/* appears only in Laha: TU, occurring in a number of roots which are unprefixed elsewhere: *matuk* "earth," *mətʼaŋ* "moon" (*tʼaŋ* "month"), *mətɛ* "sugarcane," *mətam* "egg," *məsam* "hair." Both prefixes appear to be innovations, although it is possible that prefixed *k/* reflects, at least in part, AT *q/~*k/*; note Laha: TU *kʼroŋ* "forest," Pu-peo and Laqua *riŋ*, an apparent loan from Vn. *riŋ*, id.; also Laha: TU *kəta* "eye," Laha: NL *ta*, Pu-peo *tɛ*, Laqua *te*, from *[ma]pḷa*. The apparent correspondences in the following roots must therefore be regarded as fortuitous (note Laha: TU *-ha* "ear"<*(N)qra[ḷiŋa]*):

	AT	Laqua	Pu-peo	Laha: TU	Laha: BB	Laha: NL
ear	*(N)qraḷiŋ[a]*	*rə*	*kərə*	*kəha*	—	—
rain	*qu(n)dzal*	*ðəu*	—	*kzen*	*zal*	—
alive/ raw	*(N)quzip*	—	—	*ktʼop*	—	*dəp*
bird	*[ma]mlok*	*nuk*	—	*manək*	*nok*	—

The two Laha pronominal forms included in the sketch (Laha: TU *in* "I" and *ay* "thou") are distinctive and appear to be isolated in Kadai. The Laha numerals, available only for "one" through "ten," are of considerable interest; cf. the following table, in which only the Laha: TU forms are cited, since the Laha: BB and Laha: NL numerals, essentially the same for "one" through "four," are loans from Thai for "five" through "ten":

	AT	Laqua	Pu-peo	Laha: TU
1	⎰ *atsa ⎱ *itsa	tiə	ćya	ćam
2	*drəwsa	ðe	sɛ	sa
3	*tuḷu	təu	taw	tu
4	*śu(m)pat	pe	pɛ	pa
5	*lima	mə	mə	ma
6	*ənəm	nam	mɨhnam	dram
7	*pitu	mətəu	mitiəw	t'o
8	*(m/)x[ə]waḷu	mədɨ	mɨrɨ	mahu
9	⎰ *ts[i][qə]wa ⎱ *ts[i]ya(m)	— məðiə	— mɨsya	sawa —
10	*p[o]ḷoq	pət	pət	pət

The above table serves to clarify several matters. Pu-peo shows the prefixed *m*/ for "six" (recorded as *mɨn ham*), as well as for the higher numerals, suggesting a possible origin from *[*li*]*ma* "five"; note also that Laha has the prefix only for "eight," precisely the numeral for which there is evidence for the prefix elsewhere (Formosa). Laha *ćam*, "one," shows an unexpected correspondence with Lati *tiam~ćam*, perhaps related to the alternative AT form for "nine" (= "10 minus 1"). Both Pu-peo and Laha—which maintain *s-* (<AT *ts-, *s-*)—strikingly confirm the cognation of the forms for "two" (<*[*drəw*]*sa*) and "nine," the latter showing an alternation between /*sya* and *sawa* (<*siwa* through assimilation) exactly paralleling that found in East Formosan (**ts iya~*tsiwa*). For "eight," the Laqua-Laha root must be reconstructed *m/hru<*m/x[wa]rú* (for Laha -*hu*, cf. Laha -*ha* "ear"<*qra[liŋa]* via Laqua-Laha *hra*). The Laha form for "six" is enigmatic; note that Pu-peo /*hnam* suggests an earlier consonant element, possibly */ʔ[ə]nam* (with ʔ nonphonemic here).

As can be seen from several forms cited above ("eye," "two," "four," "five," "nine"), the most conspicuous feature of Laha phonology is the maintenance of AT *a* (but Laha: TU -*en*<AT *-al* in "rain"). Of far more significance, however, is the unexpected retention of AT final *-l* in Laha: BB and Laha: NL (>-*n* in Laha: TU, -*u*=-*w* in Laqua), as shown conclusively by the forms for "rain" (in table above); note also "mouth" (in second table above), with *-n* in Laqua: Bon. and *-ø* in Laqua: Laj., perhaps from AT **-r* (but AT **-l\>-n* in **[bə]ŋəl* "deaf," below); in a third root the reconstruction is ambiguous (**-r/l*), because the Lq. cognate is lacking: T **xaw saan* "husked (uncooked) rice (**xaw*)" (Si. has *sa:r* as script form), Sek *gaw sa:l*, Mak *həw sa:n*, Laha: TU *sa:n*, Laha BB/NL *sa:l*, Pu-peo *kaða:n*, id. It also appears that AT final **-s* is represented by Laha *-t* in "weep": Laha: TU and Laha: NL *ńit*, Laha: BB *ńiet\<*[pra]ŋis* (**ŋ* palatalized before **i*), since the Kadai reflexes elsewhere all point to a root in **-s* rather than the AT doublet in **-ts;* in any event, this Laha material is the only solid evidence available from the mainland for reconstructing the final **-(t)s* in this basic root. Finally, Laha apparently has maintained AT **b* in Laha: TU *bɔt* "extinguish" *\<*(q/)obots,* contrasting with T **hmot\<*q/mbots* et al. (see ENDED), but Laha: TU also has *ba* "dog," apparently with secondary stop development paralleling that found in N. Li.

Laha supplies valuable cognates in a number of AT roots, notably "branch" (TU BB NL *ka*, Pu-peo *kɔ*); "betel" (TU *hla:ŋ*; the initial *hl-* speaks against a Thai loan); "deer" (TU *wa:ŋ*); "bone" (TU *t'ak*, BB NL *dak*, Pu-peo *da:k*, from **dlaak\< *ntlaak*); "liver" (TU *ta:p*, a likely Thai loan); "chin" (TU *ka:ŋ\<*ga:ŋ* or **Ga:ŋ*; Laha lacks *g*); "beard" (two roots: TU NL *nut;* BB *mom*, Pu-peo *mum*, Lq. *mun\<*mum;* both possible Thai or KS loans); "tongue" (TU *t'lin*, BB NL *let ma*, supplying valuable confirmation for a reconstruction of the type: **bli(n)-d[a/][sa]ma;* also Pu-peo *mia*, as if from **[bl]i[d]ma*); "blind" (TU *bɔt*, a possible Thai loan, since Laqua has *te lak* [see DEAF]); "high" (TU *wa:ŋ*, NL *kwa:ŋ\<*k/wa:ŋ*); "bury" (TU *tam;* see PLANT); "father" (TU *a:w*, from **abu/abu\<*ampu/ampu;* cf. T **aaw* "fa's y. bro" [see GRANDPARENT/]); "nephew/grandchild" (Vn. *cháu*) (BB *mli*, NL *mləy*, from **m/li;* see GREAT-GRANDCHILD). In one restricted Kadai root, not represented in Laqua (*hut* "earth"), Laha and Pu-peo supply a possible link with AN; cf. IN **butaʔ*, Proto-Philippine **bu( )taʔ* "earth, mud" (Charles cit.); Laha: TU *matuk*, Laha: NL *tuk*,

Laha: BB and Pu-peo *tuok* "earth," N. Kl. *tu,* S. Kl. *bu to,* Lt: MP *ti,* BP (Bon., Rob.) *mti,* id., all suggesting a KD reconstruction such as *[bu]tu[q],* perhaps from an earlier *butaq* through vocalic assimilation. Additional comparisons are afforded by Laha: TU *si* "comb"; IN **t'it'i[l]=*t'it'i[r] "comb, harrow," indicating AT *tsitsi[r,γ];* Laha: TU ŋan, Laha: BB *kaŋan* "deaf"; IN *bəŋəl,* id. (AT *ə>a,* as in "six"). In the following pair, both lacking known cognates outside Kadai, the Laha/Pu-peo material supplies valuable "normalizing" material, viz. "blood": TU *pa:t,* NL *pla:t;* cf. T *liat,* Sui Mak *phya:t,* Kam *pha:t,* Lk. *liet,* OB *bɔʔ* (<*pla:t),* S. Li *dat,* N. Li *tlat,* WS Li *hluat,* Kl. *plə,* Lt. *pio,* all from KD *p[u]lat,* but Lq. *kʻə<*"red" (q.v.); "salt": TU BB *ńɔ,* NL *nɔ,* Pu-peo *kańu,* S. Li *ńau,* Kl. *ńu,* Lt. *a/ńu,* but Lq. *ńuŋ,* apparently with secondary nasalization. Pu-peo itself supplies important connecting links for two AT roots: Pu-peo *riek,* Lq. *dek* "weep"; AT *γiyak* "cry out" (note *d~ð~r* inconsistently recorded in Bonifacy 1905 and 1908); Pu-peo *tʻro kəw* "knee" (cf. Laha: NL *pom kəw);* AT *t[o]ro[(t)s]* "post/knee." It is clear, from the limited forms available, that when scholars gain access to the full range of recently recorded Laha/Pu-peo material, a significant advance in our knowledge of Austro-Thai will be at hand.

[3] The writer has now (1973-74) made a beginning in this area, having contributed a paper ("The Problem of Tone Assignment in Austro-Thai") to the First International Conference on Comparative Austronesian Linguistics (Honolulu, January 1974). As anticipated, the problem is baffling in its complexity, and no general solution or set of solutions is at hand. A comparable problem is posed by Vietnamese, affected by the same three-tone system (text), but involving the basically monosyllabic/disyllabic roots of AA (Eastern or Mon-Khmer division), rather than the disyllabic/trisyllabic roots of AT. Maspero (*BEFEO 12,* 1912), taking the predominant tone A of Vn. (tones marked as in Chang 1972, Benedict 1972bis) as the "unmarked" tone (no special features), pointed out an apparent correspondence of tone B with final spirant (*-s,* *-h*) of Mon-Khmer. More recently, Haudricourt (*JA 242,* 1954) has attempt-

ed to show a similar correspondence of Vn. tone C with final glottal in Mon-Khmer. The material cited in these attempts is rather meager, at best, and much doubt has been cast on the whole matter by Proto-Mon-Khmer as provisionally reconstructed by the writer (Appendix II), especially as regards any close association of Vn. tone C with glottalization. To return to the AT stock, the PMY tones have been reconstructed in some detail by Chang (1947, 1953, 1966, 1972) and Purnell (1970), while F. K. Li (1965) has contributed a classical paper tying together the Thai and KS tonal systems. It is probable that a three-tone system of Thai/KS type will eventually be reconstructed for Kadai, although adequate comparative material is still lacking for the other, lesser-known KD languages. Significantly, however, the single reliable recording of Li (Wang 1952) exhibits in its limited material some evidence of relationship to the Thai/KS system, with the numerically predominant mid-level tone corresponding reasonably well with Thai/KS tone A, and the high-level and low-falling tones showing some correlation with Thai/KS tones B and C, respectively (a fourth, high-falling tone appears to be marginal). Despite this, we must content ourselves for the moment with citing the reconstructed Thai tones, with notes on variations in N. Thai or KS.

The obvious first step is an examination of the distribution of Thai/KS and MY tones in terms of initials and finals (rimes), employing the reconstructed AT roots. This study yields one immediate finding of some interest, viz. that the numerical predominance of tone A over tones B and C (approx. $2:1:1$ ratio), which obtains generally in both Thai/KS and MY (reflecting the basic Chinese pattern), also holds for the AT roots, indicating that any rules developed for tone assignment will have to be fitted into an over-all configuration. In general, an inspection of the tabulated material (see the Honolulu paper) reveals an absence of any fundamental correlation of tones with either initials or rimes, either in Thai/KS or in MY. This rules out, for example, voicing vs. unvoicing as a basic determinant here. Even on detailed inspection, the MY material, much more limited than that of Thai/KS, shows little if any evidence of significant skews away from the anticipated 2 : 1 : 1 tonal distribution, although the 5 : 5 : 6 distribution after initial *(n)t- may eventually prove to be of some importance. A similar detailed inspection of the Thai material, however, yields several interesting findings:

1. Correlation with vocalic length: before nasal finals, single vowels are significantly *more often* associated with tone A than with tone B or C (54 : 38 ratio [adding B and C], as contrasted with the anticipated 1 : 1 ratio), geminates/diphthongs somewhat less often (52 : 60 ratio); before glide (*-w, *-y) finals, on the other hand, single vowels are *less often* associated with tone A (16 : 27 ratio), geminates/diphthongs, more often (31 : 20 ratio). These skews appear to lie well outside the chance range, being particularly marked before final *-n and *-w (tone B shows an especially marked association with the single-vowel rime *-aw), but no simple explanation is at hand; it should be noted, perhaps, that geminate vowels and diphthongs are usually of secondary origin in Thai/KS, developed either through loss of intervocalic consonant or through VT (text).

2. Correlation with dental vs. labial stops: tone A, as contrasted with tones B and C, shows a *positive* correlation with initial *t-/*ʔd- (21 : 10 ratio [adding B and C]) and a *negative* correlation with initial *p-/*ʔb- (13 : 30 ratio). This markedly skewed distribution (the anticipated ratio is 1 : 1) is entirely enigmatic at this time.

3. Apparent correlation of tone A with Thai initial *thr- (of whatever AT origin) and *thl- (one example), also with initial *v- and *w- (but not *hw-), with tones B or C excessively rare or lacking after these initials. The numbers involved are rather small, however, hence the possibility of a chance unevenness of distribution can scarcely be ruled out at this time.

It seems clear, from the above analysis, that initials and rimes played, at best, only secondary roles in tone assignment in KD and MY. Since both these mainland stocks had already reduced to a monosyllabic, three-tone state at the earlier (proto-) reconstructed stages, we can posit an exceedingly complex process of tonal assignment taking place along with the syllabic reduction. The third tone (C) was of *sandhi* origin in the Chinese prototype and it is possible that *sandhi* rules were operative also at an early period in KD and/or MY, but it seems more likely that the three-tone system was taken over in both stocks, independently and at the same general period, without reference to *sandhi*. The most obvious variable would have been the number of syllables (1, 2, 3), with due attention to whatever other selective factors were involved in the choice of syllable(s) to be represented in the eventual monosyllabic KD and MY forms. AT roots were rarely (except for reduplicated types) monosyllabic, hence the question of tone assignment for such unreduplicated, monosyllabic morphemes is largely academic; cf. AT *(m)pu* "grandparent/grandchild, parent, uncle, male, husband," T *phu*ᴮ~*bu*ᴮ "male; clf. for human beings," KS *bu*ᴮ "father"; also PMY *ph[ou]*ᶜ "male of certain large animals" (MPT form). This lone example suggests different tone assignments in KD (tone B) and MY (tone C), with support for the latter from PMY *day*ᶜ "die"<AT *(ma/)play* (but note also PMY *tay*ᶜ "kill"<AT *[pa/]play*, without apparent tonal effect from the prefix; Thai/KS has tone A for this root, from prefixed form). In the reduplicated form, however, these AT roots almost always show tone A in Thai/KS; cf. the following:

	AT	Thai	KS
carry on back	*ba/ba*	*ba*ᴬ	—
lip	*bi[R]/bi[R]*	*bi*ᴬ~*phi*ᴬ	—
father/grandfather	*ta/ta*	*ta*ᴬ	*ta*ᴬ
foot	*til/til*	*tiin*ᴬ	*ti:n*ᴬ
wash/rinse	*ntsaw/ntsaw*	*dzaaw*ᴬ	—
plait	*zan/zan*	*saan*ᴬ	*sa:n*ᴬ
immerse	*ćəm/cəm*	*ćom*ᴬ	—
hold in hand	*kam/kam*	*kam*ᴬ	—
hold in mouth/ mouthful	*kam/gam*	*gam*ᴬ *(h)ŋam*ᴬ	— *[]ŋam*ᴬ

An identical pattern is found in a basic Thai root which appears to have been borrowed at an early period from AA (see Appendix II), viz. T *γo*ᴬ<*Go*ᴬ "neck," from AA *qo/Nqo*.

There are, however, two clearly exceptional forms: T *zoon*[B] "superpose; double"<AT *tson/tson* (via *dzoon*<*ntsoon*); PT *tay*[c] "pass lengthwise," KS *tay*[c] "flow"<AT *tay/tay*. In addition, two roots with irregular unvoicing of the initial (but reduplicated origin indicated by the geminate vowel) show tone C: T *paan*[c] "hemp"<AT *ban/ban;* T *faay*[c] "side"<AT *bay/bay* (via *phay/phay*). A third root of this type suggests the possible influence of prefixed *q/ (found in the KS cognate): T *baaŋ*[c] "surface," *paaŋ*[c] "open (plain, space)," KS *ʔba*[c] (ʔ*baŋ*[c]) "wide/broad"<AT *(q/)baŋ/(q/)baŋ*. With a non-labial initial, prefixed *q/ has perhaps produced the tonal variation found in T *hlin*[A]~*hlin*[B] "great/grandchild"<*(q/)li/l[i],* but note T *hlaan*[A], KS *qhlaan*[A] "grandchild/nephew," from a doublet *(q/)la/l[a]* of the same AT etymon; note also the same tonal variation in T *ʔdlay*[A] (<*q/dlal*<*q/ntal/tal*), KS *kle*[B] (<*tlal*<*tal/tal*) "ladder/stairs"<AT *(q/)(n)tal/tal*. For Miao-Yao, the comparable material is very limited, the best example showing tonal variation: PM *ntsaaw*[B], PY *ntsaaw*[c] "wash/bathe"<AT *ntsaw/ntsaw* (see table above).

The above analysis of tone assignment, limited to monosyllabic (usually reduplicated) AT roots, suggests that the problem as a whole might yield to a fairly straightforward solution, but this initial impression is quickly dispelled with the consideration of disyllabic roots, which constitute the vast bulk of AT etyma. Consider the following three-way contrast in Thai:

Tone A	Tone B	Tone C
AT *[w]a(ŋ)ku* "I"	AT *[b]antu* "support"	AT *a(m)pu* "gr. pare
[w]aku>T *kaw*[A]	*[b]antu*>T *daw*[B]	*apu*>T *paw*[c]
[w]əku>T *ku*[A]	*[b]əntu*>T *du*[B]	*əpu*>T *pu*[c]

There is no evident basis for tone assignment in contrasts of this type, which are found in MY as well as in KD. The vocalism hardly appears to be a factor (note the doublets above, with no tonal change), and the secondary voicing (*nt*>*d*) under tone B (above) also can be shown to be of no apparent significance, e.g. there is no correlation of tone with initial

voicing (see discussion above), and one encounters forms such
as T *buŋ^A "belly"<*[kə]mpuŋ on other than tone B. Contrasts
of the same type are found in roots showing the development
of secondary clusters, e.g. T *klaaŋ^A "middle"<*( )kaḷaŋ; T
kliŋ^B "roll"<[]k[u]ḷiŋ; T *klaaw^C~*(h)law^C "say/speak"<
*[]k[a]ḷu. There does, however, appear to be a partial correlation
of tone A with fore-stress forms (as opposed to the more typical end-stress forms in the above table) of Thai, whether the
Thai form is the result of loss of final syllable, e.g. T *phra^A
"rock"<*b[a]ḷa[saq], T *glam^A "feel for/touch"<*glam[aq], or
the product of loss of intervocalic consonant, e.g. T *nay^A "body
dirt" (Nung form)<*nda[k]i; T *fuuŋ^A "crowd"<*pu[ḷ]uŋ; T
*daaŋ^A "road"<*dza[ḷ]aŋ (via *dzraaŋ); NT *luaŋ^A "copper"
<*lu[y]aŋ; T *looy^A "swim/float"<*la[ŋ]oy (via *lo[ŋ]oy); for
the last, cf. T *ŋa^A "sesame"<*[lə]ŋa (end-stress) but NT (Dioi)
*ra^A<*la[ŋ]a (level stress with vocalic assimilation), without
tonal differentiation. There are a number of exceptional forms
on tone B or C, however, e.g. T *hooy^B "hang"<*xu[r]ay (via
*huay); T *braw^C "ashes"<*brab[uk], the latter contrasting
with T *maw^A "drunk"<*ma/buśuk; note especially T *lia^A "lick"
<*(m)bli[d]a/ but T *lin^B "tongue"<*(m)blin[da]/, from the
same AT etymon; note also the tonal contrast in the following
pair, each with initial cluster and "Procrustean" loss of final nasal: T *khriu^A "stink"<*kri[y]u[m]; T *khlui^C "flute"<*klu[ḷ]i[ŋ].
For Miao-Yao, which typically reflects fore-stress rather than
end-stress, the material is less extensive than for Thai/KS, and
the analysis to date has uncovered little evidence of tonal cor-
relations. As in Thai, however, fore-stress forms appear to show
a partial correlation with tone A, e.g. PMY *daay^A "come/arrive"
<*da(n)təŋ (T *thiŋ^A~*thəŋ^A, NT *daŋ^A); PMY *(n)to^A "deep"
<*(n)tu[biɣ]. Again as in Thai, however, exceptions occur
both on tone B and tone C; cf. PMY *ḷo^B "vomit"<*ḷu(w)aq;
PMY *pḷei^B "stone"<*b[a]ḷas[aq] (T *phra^A from this root,
above); PMY *maay^C "eye" (PM form)<*mapḷa (via *maat);
note also PMY *w[aŋ]^B and *k[ou]^B "I" (both PM forms)<
*[w]a(ŋ)ku, showing tonal identity in both the (typical) fore-

stress and the (atypical) end-stress forms (Thai has the anticipated end-stress forms *kaw*ᴬ and *ku*ᴬ, above).

A number of reduplicated disyllabic roots have been set up
for AT on the basis of Thai (rarely MY) forms; like the reduplicated monosyllabic roots (above) they tend to show tone A;
cf. T *pli*ᴬ "banana bud"<*p[u]li/p[u]li;* T *xaaw*ᴬ, NT *qhaaw*ᴬ
"white"<*q/abu/q/abu* (see ASHES/); T *k(h)laaw*ᴬ, KS
*klwaaw*ᴬ "spider"<*k/law[a]/law[a];* T *xaw*ᴬ, KS *qwa:w*ᴬ
"horn"<*[wa]qa/w[aqa],* but tone B appears in T *taw*ᴮ "gourd"
<*ta[b]u/ta[b]u* (see DIP/), as well as in T *kaaw*ᴮ "male of
animals" (Lao form)<*k/ampu/k/ampu* (via *k/abu/k/abu*),
the latter exhibiting a tonal contrast with T *aaw*ᴬ (SW)~*aaw*ᶜ
(Tho-Nung) "fa's y. bro."<*ampu/ampu* (via *abu/abu*) from
the same AT etymon (GRANDPARENT/), which yielded (as
monosyllabic doublet) T *phu*ᴮ~*bu*ᴮ "male," KS *bu*ᴮ "father"
and PMY *ph[ou]*ᶜ "male of large animals" (see above).

Trisyllabic roots, much fewer in number but perhaps more
likely to reveal significant patterning for tone assignment, appear to yield no clues in this area, e.g. the following trio of
roots, each showing preservation of a different syllable in KD,
all have the same tone (A): KS *qha*ᴬ "ear"<*(N)qraliŋ[a]*
(via *qhra*); T *ram*ᴬ "bran/chaff"<*[ndza]ɣam[i];* T *gaaŋ*ᴬ,
NT *Gaaŋ*ᴬ, KS *[]Gaaŋ*ᴬ "jaw/chin"<*[baR]a(N)qaŋ.* It would
appear from this evidence, as well as from all the foregoing,
that syllable structure per se has not played a predominant role
in tone assignment either in KD or in MY.

An analysis of those KD and MY forms showing incorporation
of AT affixes (see *Introduction*) has shed little light on the
general problem of tone assignment. KD forms incorporating
AT prefixed *q/* or *k/* display the same range of tones as forms
without this element. It is possible that prefixed *q/* has played
some role in tone assignment, as indicated above (see discussion of "surface/open/broad" and "grandchild"); cf. also the
following pair of AT etyma, each with KD doublets in which
the unstressed form (*ə+a>ia*) has either tone A or B while
the stressed form (*u+a>oo=ɔ:*) has tone C:

	Tone A	Tone B	Tone C
WHITE>MOON	*q/bəḻal		*q/buḻal
	>T *ʔbḻian^A		>T *ʔdoon^C
	*mbəḻal		
	>KS *nɨan^A		
FLESH/MEAT		*q/bəla	*bula[/bula]
		>*ʔblia^B (Si.)	>T *bla^C (Si.)
		*mbəla	*mbula
		>*nia^B	>Sek mlɔ^C
			>Dioi nɔ^C

As indicated above, AT prefixed *p/ appears to have had no tonal effect in the basic root represented by PMY *day^C "die" <*(ma/)play (PMY here reflects the unprefixed root), PMY *tay^C "kill"<*[pa/]play. A similar situation obtains in the following: PMY *wian^C "change" (tr., intr.)<*liɨan; T *plian^C ~*phrian^C "change" (usu. tr.)<*p/liyan, yet the unprefixed root also appears in Thai on another tone: *rian^A "buy" (="change/exchange") (Lao form). The Thai form incorporating the complete AT prefix *ma/ shows the anticipated tone A: T *maw^A "drunk"<*ma/busuk (above). In the following pair, from the same AT etymon (*iɣaŋ "red"), the Thai forms incorporating either prefixed *b/ or *m/, each with preceding *q/, show distinct tones: T *ʔdeeŋ^A "red"<*q/b/iɣaŋ (via *ʔdiaŋ <*ʔbriaŋ); T *hmliaŋ^B "rust"<*q/m/iɣaŋ.

Very little evidence is available on tones in relation to AT infixes, which are rarely incorporated in KD or MY forms. PMY has tone B for infixed */m/ in PMY *ńem^B "weep"<*[pra]ŋ/m-[/its] and PMY *hno(m)^B "hear/smell"<*s/m/[o]rom (but note PMY [PWA form] *[mr]om^C "listen"<*m/[o]rom), but perhaps a syllabic pattern is involved; cf. PMY *kḻəw^B "dog"<*[wa]kḻəw-[ma] (contrast the KD end-stress form: Thai/KS *hma^A). Another root shows evidence of tonal shifts connected with AT infixed */l/: PMY *ntoŋ^C "middle/center"<*[]ntəŋ, but PMY *ntroŋ^A, id. (PM form)<*[]nt/l/əŋ; also T *thooŋ^C "half"< *t/l/əŋ (via *tho[r]oŋ) but T *ʔdooŋ^A "parents of son/daughter-

in-law"(="the middlemen")<*nt/l̩/əŋ (via *q/ntrooŋ; Sek has
trɔɔŋ). In another root, represented only in KD, the same infix
(*/l̩/) did not affect the tone: T *suanᴬ "thrust into anus" (Si.
form)<*tsu(w)an; also T *suanᴬ "garden" (="the planted
place")<*tsu/l̩/an, NT *srianᴬ, id.<*tsə/l̩/an (unstressed form),
KS *swianᴬ<*tsu/l̩/an (via *suyan). One Thai form, on tone
A, incorporates both AT infixed */l/ and suffixed */a: T *kluaᴬ
"fear"<*[]k/l/u/a. The */a suffix perhaps played a role here,
since Thai forms incorporating this suffix appear consistently to
show this tone (A); cf. T *phuaᴬ "husband"<*pu/a (see
GRANDPARENT/); T *ʔbuaᴬ "flour"<*q/bu/a (see ASHES/);
T *muaᴬ "cattle" (Tho-Nung form)<*[l,l̩][ə]mbu/a (but KS *boᴮ
<*bu/a); T *tuaᴬ~*duaᴬ "body/self/clf./ for animals and spir-
its," KS *doᴬ "clf. for animals"<*[q/a](n)tu/a (see SPIRIT/);
T *hruaᴬ, NT *xriaᴬ "head"<*q/lu[b/]a; also PMY *puaᴬ "three"
<*tulu/a. For AT suffixed */(a)n, however, the relevant KD
forms show tones B and C as well as A; cf. T *fanᴬ, KS *finᴬ
"dream"<*[ś]u(m)pi/an (the unsuffixed root is represented by
PMY *mpeiᶜ); T *ʔbianᴬ "large winnowing basket" (Lao form)
<*[ta](m)pi/an; T *thranᴬ~threnᴬ "see"<*[ki]tra/n; also PMY
tɔnᴬ "son/offspring"<[na]to/n; but T *sianᴮ, NT *uanᴮ "thorn"
<*(n)dzuRi/an (via the assimilated forms *siri/an and *suru/-
an); T *raanᴮ "storey"<*pantar/an (or possibly *p/ar/antar);
T *nanᴮ "that," *hnanᴮ "there"<*(q/)na/n; T *buunᴮ~*uunᴮ
"yonder (other place)"<*uba/(a)n (with vocalic assimilation)
(see OTHER); T *khuanᶜ "scratch" (Si. form)<*kur/an. Thai
also has *niᴮ~*nayᴮ "this," *hniᴮ~*hnayᴮ "here"<*(q/)nəy,
on the same tone (B) as "that/there" and "other/yonder" (above),
indicating that these deictics constitute a form class in Thai,
comparable with that found with stress in Tagalic (see Note 4).
Finally, all three tones are associated with the following AT
root:

AT *(ma/)ka "hard"; T *kaᴮ, id.

AT *(pa/)ka/(a)n; T *kheenᶜ "reforge" (="harden") (via
*khaan, with secondary aspiration).

AT *(ma/)ka/(a)n; T *keenᶜ "hard" (via *kaan), with
stative prefix *(ma/).

T *[/]*ka*/(*a*)*n*: T **keen*ᴬ "hard part" (via *kaan), with nominalizing prefix.

Although the comparative data as a whole indicate that the two mainland stocks, KD and MY, split off from the ancestral AT superstock before any complete reduction to monosyllables had occurred, suggesting that the tonal systems had been taken over from the Chinese prototype in a parallel (and contemporary) but essentially independent fashion, the tonal material shows evidence of a partial correlation between the two (KD, MY) systems; cf. T **tooŋ*ᴬ, MY *m(*b*)*lɔm*ᴬ "leaf"<*(*m*)*boloŋ*; T **yɨaŋ*ᴬ "goat antelope/wild goat," PMY **yuaŋ*ᴬ "goat/sheep" <*[*b*]*iyaŋ* (the PMY form via *yiaŋ by dissimilation); T **hlɨaŋ*ᴬ, PMY **Gļiaŋ*ᴬ "yellow"<*(*N*)*quliaŋ* ~ *G[*u*]*liaŋ*; T **Gruay*ᴬ (but KS *[]*lay*ᴮ), PMY **qlay*ᴬ "penis"<*u(*N*)*q*[*a*]*lay*, contrasting with T **khi*ᴮ, NT **Gay*ᴮ, PMY *(*N*)*qay*ᴮ "excrement"<*(*m*)*pla*-(*N*)*qi*. This tendency for the tones to agree in KD and MY is also seen in roots handled somewhat differently, e.g. T **γa*ᴬ, NT **Ga*ᴬ, PMY **Nqaan*ᴬ "thatch grass"<*(*a*)(*N*)*qa*(*n*)[*təp*], as well as in roots which are essentially (on basis of present data) limited to the two mainland stocks, e.g. T **liŋ*ᴬ, PMY *ʔ*bliŋ*ᴬ "monkey"<*bliŋ. This partial correlation of tones suggests that an areal configuration not only determined the takeover of the Chinese tonal system in the two stocks but also shaped, at least in part, the manner in which this was realized.

This note would remain incomplete without at least mention of the possibility of reconstructing an accentual system, tonal or other, for the parent AT protolanguage. One might, for example, set up a LOW vs. HIGH distinction in forms of more than one syllable (phonemic on only two of the syllables), with LOW + LOW and HIGH + HIGH yielding tone A in Thai/KS, LOW + HIGH yielding tone B, and HIGH + LOW yielding tone C. Although the numerical preponderance of tone A (A : B : C ratio = 2 : 1 : 1) in KD and MY appears to reflect the situation in the Chinese prototype, as noted above, the development suggested above might well have yielded the same 2 : 1 : 1 ratio (assuming a random distribution of LOWs and HIGHs in proto-AT). One would anticipate that an accentual system of this type

would tie in with any pattern of phonemic stress that might
eventually be reconstructed for AN (see Note 4).

⁴ Phonemic stress has been reconstructed for Proto-Philippine
(PPh.) on the basis of evidence from Iloko (or another Cordil-
leran language with phonemic accent), Kapampangan, and Tagalog (or Bikol or Cebuano), and the consensus of scholars in
the field seems to be that it represents the retention of a proto-
AN feature rather than an innovation (Charles). Zorc has recently contributed an excellent study (1972) of stress in Tagalic,
providing detailed information on two languages in this group,
viz. Tagalog (Tg.) and Aklanon (Ak.). Using a modified Swa-
desh 200-word list, he points out that although penultimate
stress is considered the canonical stress in these languages (hence
it is left unmarked in Tagalog), about half the words on the
list (120 in Tg. and 94 in Ak.) have stress on the ultima. He
offers explanations of various types for about half these cases
of ultima stress, e.g. derivation from Proto-Tagalic roots with
*ə in the penult, as in Malay (Tg. *litáw* "float"$<$*lətáw*), or
with medial *-Cʔ- (Tg. *bigát* "heavy"$<$*bəgʔat*), or through
syncope (Tg. *kamáy* "hand"$<$*kama + i*), as well as member-
ship in any of several "form classes," including numerals (Tg.
limá "five," *pitó* "seven," *waló* "eight," etc.), vocatives (Tg. ʻ*amá*
"father," ʻ*iná* "mother") and deictics (Tg. ʻ*irí* "near speaker," ʻ*itó*
"near both," ʻ*iyán* "near listener," ʻ*iyón* "far away"); for the
last of these, cf. the similar form classes for deictics on tone B
in Thai (see Note 3). For the remaining half of ultima-stress
words, however, including 28 with cognates in both languages
(Tg. and Ak. ʻ*abó* "ashes," *likód* "back," *tiyán* "belly," *kagát*
"bite"), Zorc was unable to find any ready explanation.

This Philippine evidence appears to run counter to the view
generally held, by Dempwolff and most other workers in the
field, that all disyllabic AN roots were accented on the penult.
It would seem, in any event, that "morphemic stress" (Zorc)
can be set up at the proto-IN (if not proto-AN) level, since
Toba-Batak (TB.) shows precisely the same feature; cf. Tg.
tápus "to finish," *tapús* "finished"; TB. *tánom* "to dig," *tanóm*
"dug" (cit. in Zorc, personal communication, 1974), although

one might posit a lost final morpheme */- for the ultima-stress forms. Of potentially far greater significance, however, is the recent reconstruction by Shigeru Tsuchida of stress for proto-Tsouic, with indications of at least partial correlation with Philippine stress, e.g. Tsouic *matsá "eye" vs. *mátaq "unripe/raw"; Ibanag (Northern Philippine) *matá* "eye" vs. *máta* "unripe" (cit. from Tsuchida apr. Zorc 1974). Correspondences of this kind, if confirmed by future studies, would of course establish phonemic stress at the proto-AN level, but the problem promises to be a difficult one, e.g. from the above root for "eye," Palau has *mad*<*máta, since this language drops all but stressed vowels (Zorc 1972).

In view of the above, it is perhaps premature to speculate as to whether phonemic stress at the proto-AN level, if established, might not tie in with rules governing syllabic reduction or tone assignment in the AT languages of the mainland. As for syllabic reduction, the general rules already noted, with end-stress in KD but fore-stress in MY except under special circumstances, seem to apply, regardless of the PPh. stress, at any rate—e.g. AT *mapḷa "eye" yielded proto-KD *pla>*ta as if from an ultima-stress form (*mapḷá) reflected also in PPh. *matá, Tsouic *matsá, yet the same AT etymon also yielded PMY *maay (PM form)<*maat as if from a penult-stress form (*mápḷa) reflected also in Palau *mad*<*máta. There is inadequate material at hand even to make a start on comparing proto-AN stress with KD or MY tones; one of the minimal pairs in Tagalog presents a correspondence with tonal contrast in MY, but this, of course, might well be coincidental; cf. Tg. *'áso* "dog," PMY *kḷəw[B]<AT *[*wa*]*kḷəwm*[*a*]; Tg. *'asó* "smoke," PMY *ntshyo[c]–*(*n*)*tshyou*[c] <AT (*q/*)(*n*)*tsu*[*b/an*]. As suggested above (Note 3), it is possible that stress in AN as well as tone in KD and MY will eventually be shown to reflect, at least in part, an accentual system of the AT protolanguage, which has been greatly modified over the centuries by various areal and other shaping influences, including on the mainland the powerful three-tone system of Chinese.

[5] There appears to be a striking parallel to the AT *l vs. *ḷ

distinction in the Chibchan linguistic stock of Colombia, South America. Proto-Chibchan has recently been reconstructed by D. R. Christian and E. Matheson ("Proto-Chibchan," in *Janua Linguarum, Series Practica, no. 127* [1972]: 150-59). Like Dyen, the authors set up a contrast between $*n$ (all n reflexes) and $*N$ (both n and l reflexes) as opposed to $*l$ (both l and r reflexes) and $*r$ (all r reflexes), but the situation is very similar to that in IN/Formosa:

Proto-Chibchan	Guahibo	Cuiva	Guayabero
$*r$	*r*	*r*	*r*
$*l \ (=*l)$	*l,r*	*r*	*l,r,?*
$*N \ (=*l)$	*n*	*n*	*l*
$*n$	*n*	*n*	*n*

AUSTRO-THAI PRONOUNS

AFFIXED ELEMENTS

IN:

$*k/$: all 1st and 2d person pronouns except "I" (poss. dissim: $*aku < *k/aku$); separable in NgD. *ita* "we (incl.)," from $*k/ita$.

$*t'/$: 3d person pronoun: $*t'ida$ "they"; also $*[t']a[y]i$ "who."

$*/n$: cf. $*iya$ "he/she"; $*iya/n$ "that (one)"; also Old Ja. $kow/ən < *kaw$ "thou."

Yami:

$*k/$: *kamu* "you," but *imu* "thou" (unprefixed).

$*t'/$: 3d person pronouns: $siya < *t'iya$ "he/she"; $sira/ < *t'ida/$ "they."

$*y/$ with suffixed $*/n$: 1st person pronouns, e.g. *yakən* "I" (Ferr.), from $*y/aku/n$, but *aku* "I" (Og.-As.).

Formosa:

$*k/$: Ami: all 1st and 2d person pronouns; Bunun: only $*k/amu$ "you."

$*k(u)$: Rukai: all 1st and 2d person pronouns, with unusual and irregular forms, some with $*/n/$ infix, e.g. Tara-

makau dial. *ku/aku~*ku/n/aku "I," Maga and Tona
dials. *k/in/ami "we (excl.)."

*ik/ (from *i/k/): Kanakanabu: all 1st and 2d person pro-
nouns except "I" (iku, for *i/aku=*y/aku); also with
suffixed */n in iikimin "we (excl.)" (Ferr.).

*tsi/ with suffixed */n: Paiwan: all 1st and 2d person pro-
nouns; also */n in 3d person pronoun.

*ts/: Atayalic: 3d person pronouns.

*s/: Saisiat and Pazeh: 3d person pronoun.

*ts/ (from original cluster): Atayal: some 1st and 2d per-
son pronouns.

*il/ (prob. from *i/l/): Saaroa: 1st, 2d, and 3d person
pronouns.

*y/: Saisiat, Pazeh, Thao (perhaps also Bunun δ/) and
Sedik: 1st person pronouns, but ?ita "we (incl.)," for
*y/ita; contra Dyen (1962), where this element is in-
terpreted as a reflex of x₃.

*i(n): Puyuma: 1st, 2d, and 3d person pronouns, but note
?iŋku<*?inku "I."

"I"

IN **aku=*Waku: Niala (West Ceram) wau, Aloene (West
Ceram) au, Chomorro gwahu (Dyen 1962); cf. Miao (below).

For both Shan and Si., the regular pronoun is *kaw/ku, with
tu (basically a plural form) used mainly in the phrase *tu kha
"I" (*kha "slave") (obsolete in Si.).

WT distinguishes between ku "I" (superior to inferior, or
equal to equal) and ha<*ra (basically a dual form) "I" (friendly term used between intimate comrades of same sex, not related).

LT ku (subj.) and kui (poss.). S. Kl. i also (obj.).

S. Li həu and du are both glossed simply as "I" in our source
(Savina).

Miao (PW) **ku(ŋ), also MKC ko (Chang 1966, note 16),
from PM *kou; both from PMY *kou~*ko. PM **weŋ is represented in PE (MCF vai), MHY (we) as well as in Hunan:
Fenghuang and Layi P'ing we (Chang 1966), from PMY *w[aŋ],
for *w[uŋ] (dissim.); cf. IN **Waku (above).

The following roots are in evidence:

1. *wa(ŋ)ku~*waqu: generally in AN and Kadai, perhaps

Austro-Thai

Austro-Thai Personal Pronouns

	I	We	We Two (Tg.) *kita*	We (excl.)	We (incl.)
IN	*aku*			*kami*	*k/ita*
Yami	*/ake/n*			*/amee/n*	*/ate/n*
Oceanic	*aku*			*kami*	*(ŋ)ki(n)ta*
SEP	*aku*			*kami*	*kita*
SEP suffix	*-ŋku*			*-ma(m)i*	*-nta*
Formosa:					
East	*/aku*			*/ami*	*ita*
Tsou	*/aqu*			*a/q[]mi*	*[q]ata*
Kan./Saa.	*aku*			*/kimi*	*/kita*
Atayalic	*/aku*			*/ami*	*ita*
Thai:					
Khamti	*kaw*	*raw*	*ra*	*tu*	*raw*
Ahom/Shan	*kaw (~tu)*	*raw~ra*	*ra*	*tu* (obs.)	
Si./Lao/BT	*ku (~ra)*			*(mai-)phu*	*(mai-)raw*
White Tai	*ku~ra*	*raw*			
Tho-Nung	*kaw*	*tu*			
Dioi	*ku*				
Mak	*ʔe* / *ʔi~ʔyu*			*di*	*da*
Sui				*ta* (l.t.)	*tau*
Lakkia	*hao*	*hao-lu*			
Ong-Be (J.)	*zea* (h.t.)				
Ong-Be (Sav.)	*hou~du*				
S. Li	*ho* (WS Li)	*ho* (WS Li)			
N. Li	*kheu*	*dau*			
Laqua	*ya*				
N. Kelao	*i* (possessive)				
S. Kelao	*ki*				
Lati: BP	*ku~kui*		*cɔ* (WS Li)		
Lati: MP					

IN	kaw (~iyu)	kamu~iñu	iya	t'ida	iyan (~itu)
Yami	imu	kamu	siya	sira (/itu)	/itu~siya
Oceanic	kaw	kamu	iya	sida	(na)
{SEP	kaw	kamiw	iya		
{SEP suffix	-mu	-miw	-na	-nda	
Formosa:					
East	isu	amu~imu	(t)siya	(t)siya	/zu(~itu-) si/
{Tsou	su	mu	si	si	
{Kan./Saa.	/kasu	/kamu	/isa	/isa	/sa~/na
Atayalic	isu	/amu~/imu	hiya	hiya	q/asa
Thai:					
Khamti	mai	su	man	khraw	nan (~thran)
Ahom/Shan	mai	su~sɨ	man	khraw	nan (~thran)
Si./Lao/BT	miŋ (~hlaw)	su	man~khraw	khraw	nan (~thran)
White Tai	miŋ~su	mai-su /mai	man	mai~khraw	nan
Tho-Nung	miŋ~mai	/mai	man~khraw	/man	yen
Dioi	miŋ (N.T. qhɹia)	su			(nan)
Mak	ʔŋ	si	man (h.t.)		
Sui	ʔña~ña~ñie	sau			
Lakkia	ma	liu (h.t.)	kɛ	tu (l.t.) kɛ-lu	nan
{Ong-Be (J.)	eu		ncɔ(WS)~na (Loi)		
{Ong-Be (Sav.)	cm		ki		
{S. Li	mi	mo (Bas.)	uo	nɔ (WS Li)	na (WS Li)
{N. Li	mi (WS)~lu (Bup.)			to	
Laqua	mi	tɐt			a/to
{N. Kelao	mu	mu			lă/biɔ
{S. Kelao	ta (imperative)				
{Lati: BP	ve				
{Lati: MP	be (~ni[poss.])				
Miao	kɔ(ŋ)	ʔ[mn]e	ne(n)		di~i
Yao	mwei	ñ[a]n	n[a]n		ʔw(u)a~hwa

also in Miao. The Thai doublet reflects a stress distinction: *[w]aku>*kaw (stressed), *[w]əku>*ku (unstressed); cf. also Lq. *khəu,* from *[w]əqu. The doublet form with medial *q- apparently must be recognized for AT itself, since it appears in Tsou (but not Kan. or Saa.) and is the most likely initial reconstruction for several Kadai languages: OB (Jer.), Li, Lq., and Lt. Mulao, a language in the Kelao group, also appears to have a cognate: *sou* "I"; cf. Mulao *su,* S. Kl. *ku* "nine."

2. *[ʔ]ya: restricted occurrence: OB *zea* (h.t.), from *[]ya; N. Kl. *ya.* The latter is seemingly related to the S. Kl. form *i* (see above), with a further affinity with Mak *ʔe* and Sui *ʔi,* perhaps from a basic form *[ʔ]yia, as represented by Yao **yia.

"We"

The evidence here indicates that for AN and Kadai, at any rate, the basic terms were for "we (excl.)" and "we (incl.)," the latter with a significant root linkage (see below—No. 1) between AN and Mak. The distinction has been maintained in KS and in Khamti and WT (the latter with substitution of new form), but has been lost at a relatively late period in Thai generally, including N. Thai (Dioi). A shift in meaning from "we (excl.)" or "we (incl.)" to "we" or even "I" can be seen both in Thai and in other Kadai languages (see below—Nos. 2 and 3). The dual forms are clearly of late origin; Tg. has *kita* "we two" from IN *k/ita "we (incl.)"; Thai *ra "we two" (with later shifts to "we" or "I") appears to be directly cognate with KS *[]γa "two," from AT *[]γa[kit] "pair" (see GLOSSARY). MY shows no trace of this excl. vs. incl. distinction, hence it is not certain whether this feature was present at the AT level. The Miao forms for "we" are virtually identical with those for "three" (PM *pe, PY *pua), but YCR has *bua* (h.t.) "we," from *mpua, indicating PMY *(m)pua; cf. Form.: Fav. *turu* "we (incl.)," from the same AT root (*tuḷu "three").

The following roots are in evidence:

1. *[i](n)ta "we (incl.)": generally in AN (often with *k/ prefixed element), also Mak *da* (<*nta), perhaps also Lk. *ta* (l.t.) <*da "we (excl.)," from *nta.

2. *(n)taw: restricted occurrence: Lk. *tau* "we (incl.)," Lq.

dau ($<°ntau$) "we" (but perh. $<rau;$ cf. T $°raw$, id.).

3. $°(n)tu$: restricted occurrence: T $°tu$ "we (excl.)," probably the earlier meaning, also "we" (Dioi) and "I" (Shan Si.); S. Li *du* ($<°ntu$) "I"; cf. also Mak *di* ($<°nti$) "we (excl.)."

"Thou/You"

IN generally $°°kaw$ "thou," from $°kaśu<°k/aśu;$ cf. also AN $°ka$ "thou" (Blust 1972bis), suggesting the analysis $°ka/śu$ "thou" and $°ka/mu$ "you" for the earliest AN level. Dyen (1965) cites Tg. *ʔiyu* "thy/thee," from $°i(y)u<°iśu$ (contra Dyen, the "innovation" in meaning found here is in Tg. rather than in Form.).

Yami (Og.-As.) *kamu* "you," as in IN generally, but Ferrell cites *ińu*, id., an apparently isolated form within AN.

The normal Thai root for "thou" is $°mai/miŋ$, with a basic cleavage between Ahom/Kh./Shan and Tho-Nung on the one hand, and Si./Lao/BT/WT and Dioi on the other, closely paralleling the line of cleavage in the forms for "I" (see above). This line of cleavage, which is most unusual for the Thai languages, remains without explanation. WT has both forms, with $°mai$ shifting to the third person pronoun, also used in the plural form for "you." WT also shows a parallel development to that noted in the first person pronouns, with the basically plural form used for the singular in a special sense: *su* "thou" (friendly term used among intimates of same sex, not related). Lao *lau* (h.t.) $<°hlaw$ "thou" appears to be isolated in Thai. N. Thai $°qhria$ (Haud.), Yai *ria* (h.t.), perhaps better glossed as "thou/you," is perhaps from $°q/ra$ "you two" (cf. above under "We").

The curious KS series for "thou" also includes Then *ŋya* and Kam *na*. The KS forms for "you" appear to reflect the doublet represented in AN: Sui $sau<°(a)su$, but Mak $si<°(i)su$ (vocalic assim.).

Lk. *liu* (h.t.) "you," from $°[]l(y)u$, perhaps palatalized by an earlier prefixed element.

Miao $°°kou$ "thou," of limited occurrence (PE only), from PM $°kɔ(ŋ)$, yields PMY $°k$-, but with many possible finals (of low or back vowel + nasal type), hence $°kam$ ($<°kamu$) is a possibility at the PMY level. Miao also has a dual form (but defined in MCF as "thou"), again of restricted occurrence (PE)

and irregular even here: MTK *mo*<PM **mu,* but MLS *muŋ,*
MCF *məŋ*<PM **moŋ~*mɔŋ.*

The Yao root for "thou" (***mwei*) is well attested, but the
root for "you" is irregular and of limited occurrence: YHN *ńau,*
YLC *nyeu,* from **ń[e]w.*

The following roots are in evidence:

1. **[i](ń)śu* "thou; you": AN, Thai, and Yao. It appears that
both Yami and Yao have forms representing the nasalized root:
Yami *ińu*<**ińśu;* Yao **ń[e]w*<**eńu* (VT) <**ińśu.* These languages agree with Thai in assigning a plural number ("you")
to the root (the WT shift to "thou" is definitely of late origin
in Thai; see above), indicating that the AN meaning "thou" is
of secondary origin. In view of the material below (under 2.)
relative to the "thou">"you" shift in AN, it must be posited that
AN actually performed a "flipflop" in its development of the
AT second person pronouns. There is only the MY evidence
from the continent bearing on the initial vowel **[i]* of this root,
but on the basis of the AN material alone the alternative **a*
vocalism (in IN and Tsouic) appears to be the result of influence exerted by the root for "thou" (**k/amu* or **ka/mu);* note
the appearance of **[i]* in several AT pronouns (see Table below), including all those in the plural column.

2. **məy[u]* "thou; you": AN, Kadai, and Yao. Dyen (1974)
has suggested **məyu* as a reconstruction for the AN enclitic
pronoun (to explain the **-miw* forms, among others). An AT
reconstruction of this type also serves to explain Thai **mai̵*
(<**mayə*<**məy[u];* note Thai **-ay*<AT **-əy),* Ong-Be *mə~*
mɔ, Li **mi̵,* Lq. *mi,* N. Kl. *mu,* as well as Yao *mwei* (<**mwəy*
<**məy[u]).* The alternative Thai root **miŋ* appears to represent
a secondarily nasalized variety of this root. As pointed out above,
the AN meaning "you" appears to be the result of a "flipflop,"
as indicated also by the scattered AN evidence of the (earlier)
meaning "thou," at least for the **-mu* variety of the root; cf. SEP
-mu "thou" (**kamiw~*-miw* "you," but Mekeo and Pokau
"thou"); Yami *imu* "thou" (note the **i-* vocalism); Ml. *kamu*

"thou" (Winstedt 1927); also AN *mu* "thy": Ml. *mu*, Trukese *-b*<*-mu* (Dyen 1949).

3. *[ʔ]ŋ[ya]* "thou": Kadai only: KŚ and Kl. The Kl. form (ŋta) cannot be analyzed, but the agreement is possibly significant in view of the apparent KS-Kl. linkage in the first person pronoun ("I"—No. 2).

4. *[]ləw* "thou": Kadai only: Lao, Lk., and Li (Bup.). Lq. *təu* "you" is a possible cognate, from *t[]ləu;* cf. Lq. *təu* "three," from *təḷu*.

"He/She/They/That"

IN **iya* "he/she"; cf. also AN *ńa* "his/hers/theirs": Ml. *ńa*, Trukese *-n*<*-ń(a)* (Dyen 1949), apparently from *na+[i]ya* (see below); cf. also Cebuano Bisayan *naa*<*(n,ń)aa* "there (near addressee)" (Blust 1970).

IN **iyan* "that." IN *i[t]u* "this (Tg. Ho.), that (Ml.)"; Yami *-itu* "he"; "that (near)"; for the semantics, cf. Sa. *ie* "this," from *iya(n).* Form.: Thao *itu-* "there"; cf. also Pai. *-itsu* "this."

Oceanic: PPN **n[a,aa]* "there (near addressee)"; cf. Saaroa (below).

Atayalic *hiya* "he/she" is from AN *tsiya*, agreeing with Yami *siya*<IN *t'iya* and Pai. Thao *tsi[y]a*, distinct from the doublet represented by Sai. Paz. **siya*<AN *siya*. In some first and second person pronouns, Atayal has a distinct *ts*/ element, from an original AN cluster (see above). IN has the unprefixed form **iya* "he/she," but the prefix appears in the plural form **t'iḍa* "they."

Kan. *iisa* "that" (Ferr.), *isa~sana* "that (remote)" (Og.-As.). Saa. *kanaʔa* "that" (Ferr.) (cf. *kaniʔi* "this"), but *kanau* "that (near)," *ka:yu* "that (remote)" (Og.-As.). Saaroa also has *na:na* "there"; cf. *na:ni* "near."

Thai *nan* "that" and *hnan* (s.t., high series) "there" are the general terms; Dioi *nan* is used only in the comparative. T *thran* "that (Kh.), that (one, place)" (Shan Lao) (Kh. *than* rather than the anticipated *han*), also *[d]ran* (Lao doublet); Thai *yen* "that one" (Tho), from an original *yan*.

Sui *man* (h.t.) "he/she," from *[]man,* indicating an earlier prefixed element, but Thai has simply *man* (*men~min* forms in Tho-Nung).

Li: Ha Ki SC Loi *na* "he"; Bup. *no*<*na* "he/they"; WS Li *nɔ* is irreg.

PM **ne(n); PY **n[]=*n[a]n "he/she": YHN *nan*, YHA *nen*, YCR *nin*; from PMY *na(n)*.

PM **di~**i "that/there," but MCF *ai* is irregular.

Yao: YCR *ua* (h.t.) "that, there (at some distance)," from **ʔua*; *ua hwa* "over yonder"; YTP *vua* "that"; YHN *va* "that (one)."

The following roots are in evidence:

1. *na(/n): Kadai (Thai, Lakkia, and Li) and MY (Miao and Yao); also reconstructed for AN (see above): *na+[i]ya >*ńa.

2. *[i]ya(/n) "he/she/that": AN (generally) and Thai (Tho).

3. *ts[i]dra(/n): AN and Thai (note Thai *thran<*s[i]dra/n). but not Form.) and Thai.

4. *[i](n)tu "they/that": IN, Form. (Thao), and Kadai (Lakkia, Laqua, and Lati).

5. *[]wa "he/that": Kelao and Yao; possibly coincidental.

All five roots show a range of meaning from "he/she" and/or "they" to "that," indicating that the basic development in AT was along these lines via "that one." On the basis of range of occurrence, the root *na(/n) must be considered the most archaic, with evidence for both suffixed and nonsuffixed forms at the AT level.

The AT pronominal system as a whole can be reconstructed as follows, with evidence largely from the AN and Kadai groups:

Austro-Thai Pronouns

"I"	*wa(ŋ)ku	"we (exclu.)"	*[ ]
"thou"	*məy[u]	"we (incl.)"	*[i](n)ta
"he/she/that"	{*na(/n) / *[i]ya(/n)}	"you"	*[i](ń)śu
		"they/that"	{*ts[i]dra(/n) / *[i]tu}

Austro-Thai Numerals

	1	2	3	4	5
N	**ət'a **it'a	**duwa =**dəwha	**təlu	**ə(m)pat	**lima
ami	*at'a	*ḍuwa	*a/t[]lu	*apat	*lima
ormosa:					
East	*atsa *itsa(/i) *ndə(ŋ)ga	*(n)ḍusa	*tulu *təḷu	*supat *[s-]/l/pat	*lima *γasub
Tsouic	*tsa/ni	*[dr]usa	*təḷu	*supat	*ḷima
Atayalic	*qutux *kiŋal	*dusa *dasa	*təḷu	*səpat *səp/ḷ/at	*ḷima
hai	*(h)niŋ	*sooŋ			
am-Sui	*ʔdiaw	*[]γa			
akkia	in	hou			
ng-Be	au	vən~buən			
i:					
S. Li	ki	dau	śu	śa:u	ma
Seao	ki	dow	su	sao	ma
Bupäli	go=ko	liau	dəu=təu	deu=teu	bo=po
WS Li	čhə=śə	hləu	fu	čho=śo	pa
N. Li	i	trau	śu	śɔ	pa
Basadung	θsio	sao	vu	ću	ba=pa
Dogang	tsou	dau=tau	fo	tsau	ba=pa
FF Li	ə	tau	su	sət	ba=pa
Recon. Li	*kə	*draw	*tru	*śaw(ə)t	*ma
aqua	tiə	δe	təu	pe	mə
. Kelao	si	so	ta	pu	bu
. Kelao	tsi~tsɨ	δɨ	tɔ	pu	mlen~mu
ati:					
MP	tiam	su	ti	pu	m
BP (Rob.)	tiam	fu	te	pu	m
BP (Bon.)	ćam	fu	si~sie	pu	ŋ
M	*i	*(ə)war	*pe	*plou	*pr[]i
Y	*a	*(w)əy	*pua	*plei	*pla
MY		*(a)war	*pua	*pḷei	*pra

	6	7	8	9	10
IN	**eneme	**pitu	**walu = *ʔwalu	**t'iwa = *t'iʔwa	**pulu? [**belat]
Yami	*eneu	*pitu	*walu	*t'i[y]am	*pulu[?]
Formosa: East	*eneu(e)	*pitu	*(m/)walu; ma/wal(-pat); ma/spat; ka/spat	*t'i[y]am	*puluq; *ma/tsal; *k[e]/[tiaŋ]; *isit; *təʌey
Tsouic	*(m/)eneu	*pitu	*(m/)walu	*tsiya; *tsiʋa	*tsiya; *ma/tsal
Atayalic	*ma/talu; *ma/təlu	*(ma/)pitu	*(ma/)sapat; ɬapat(/pu)	*ma/i[d]u; *qa/i[d]u	*ma/pu[l]u; *ma/tsal; *[ ]ro[k]
Thai					
Li:					
S. Li	nom	thu	du	ed	(la)phuot
Seao	nom	situ	du	nof	pit
Bupäili	nom	dau=tau	gou=kou	vou	bŏd=pŏt
WS Li	tom	thou	xou	fa:l	fut
N. Li	tom	thau	au	ef	fuot
Basadung	dom=tom	tu=thu	kxu	fan	fudᵈ=fut
Dogang	dom=tom	tou=thou	ou	fal	fŭd=fŭt
FF Li	tet	thou	hou	fag=fai	fut
Recon. Li	*nem	ʌneʌ(is)(thu)	*ʋerx	*pʋal	*phʋuot
Laqua	nam	neŋ/em	emɒ/ɗi	eiɣ/em	ted
N. Kelao	naŋ	ši	nɒlɒu	ss	ned
S. Kelao	ča	ɣiˀ[2]	šiɣ	ku	tsɨ~ɣ[1]
Lati:					
MP	nam	ti	mui	lu	ted
BP (Rob.)	na	te	bə	lu	ed
BP (Bon.)	nə	ti	be	lu	ɒa~əa

	10	20	100	1,000	10,000
IN	*pulu? [*belat] [*ʔlat *pulu[?]]	[**likur]	*ɣatut'	*ribu	*umribu
Yami					
Formosa: East	puluɣ	*ma/pusal	*at'a [d]anaw	*kuɖaw	
	ma/tsal	*/kabutaqan	*iday		*ubal(/ən)
	k[e]iŋ	sam/i[ɣ]ah	*ma/baŋat	*kuzul	*tsaquɣ
	isit		*ka/butsul	*patək(/ən)	
	iɣketʃ		*naməl	*buquɣ	
			*tubui	*lubut	
			*ueue		
Tsouic	ʔas/an	*ʔasud/an	*ka/batsul	*pasɪŋbu	*pasi/
	ʔas/tsal	pusal			ma/ts[al]
Atayalic	ma/pu[ʃ]u	*(ma/)pusal	i[ɣ]ŋyeq/eq / i		*hmiin [*seen]
	ma/tsal				
Thai	[[]ro]k	*draaw	*(d)rooy	*[t]hriaŋ *ban	
Li:					
S. Li	(la) phuot		da:n	ŋuon	
WS Li	fut		va:ŋ	ŋen	
Pasadung	fud=fut		wan	nin	
FF Li	fut		van	ŋiŋ	
Recon. Li	*phwɔot		*rwaan	*tʃuan	
Laqua	pət		dəŋ	tʃeŋ	
N. Kelao	peu		jin	tu	
S. Kelao	tsi~ɗi[1]		tsin	gɛ	
Lati:					
MP	pət		ta/khre	ta/thuŋ	
BP (Rob.)	ed		la/khre	la/thuŋ	
BP (Bon.)	pa~əd		la/khɛ	la/tiŋ	la/tuŋ

NOTES

Reconstructed forms by Dempwolff (**) and the writer (*). Prefixed elements, often variable (shown within parentheses), appear in many of the Formosan numeral forms. Saaroa also has prefixed *u/* in special forms (used in counting) of the numerals "1" through "9" (exception: ənəmə "6"), contrasting with prefixed *ku/* for the regular numerals "5" through "10" (but note kənəmə "6"). Puy: Rikavong also has special forms used in counting, but only for the numerals "1," "2," and "3," in two instances formed through partial reduplication: *sa/saya* "1" (basic numeral is *sa*); *to/tolowa* "3" (basic numeral is *tili*, with irreg. vocalism). Siraya also has some partially reduplicated forms: *sa/sat* "1," *tou/touro* "3," *ni/nam* "6," and *pi/pito* "7," paralleling similar IN (Philippine) forms: Tg. *dalawa*<*da/ dəwha* "2," *tatlo*<*ta/təlu* "3" (Dyen [1962] also analyzes Tg. numerals "4" and "5" along similar lines), but this process (reduplication) has not been encountered in the Kadai numerals.

Prefixed (or anteposed) elements also occasionally appear in Kadai, with one apparent correspondence with Formosa; cf. Lq. prefixed *mə/* in "7," "8," and "9," Formosa: East and Tsouic *m(a)/* in "8," "10," and "20"; Atayalic *ma/* in "6" through "10" and "20." A correspondence with IN is indicated for the following: S. Li *la/* in *la/phuot kɨ* "11," *la/phuot dau* "12" (but *phuot* "10"), Lakia (N. Li type) *la/pum* "10," DC Loi *la/ŋin* "1,000"; also Lati: BP *la/* in "100," "1,000," and "10,000" (the form is a weakly stressed prefix, hence vocalism is uncertain); cf. IN **bəlat' "number between 10 and 20," e.g. Ml. *sa-bĕlas* "11," *dua-bĕlas* "12."

ONE

IN **ət'a (Ja. Ml.)~**it'a (Tg.). PO: Sa. *esa*<*atsa* "1," *asa*<*atsa* "oneness," also *ise*<*itsay* "one," from *itsa/i* (cf. Form.). Form: East *atsa* (Sai.); *t/atsa* (Bun. Thao); *tsa/ tsa/i* (Ami); *tsa/tsa/ya* (Puy: Rikavong: in counting); *tsa/t ~*tsa/tsa/t* (Sir.); *atsa* (E. Ruk.); *atsa~*itsa* (Puy.); *itsa* (Pai.); *itsa~*itsa/i* (Kuv.); also W. Ruk: Maga *dəga*, Tona *nəga*,

Mantauran *nəka;* also (Thomson 1873) *deŋa,* from **ndə(ŋ)ga.* Atayalic **qutux* (Ata.), **kiŋal* (Sed.).

TWO

Form. (East: generally) **ḍusa,* but W. Ruk: Mantauran *nusa,* app. from an original **(n)ḍusa.* Atayalic **ḍusa* (Ata.), **ḍasa* (Sed.), by assim.

THREE

Form: East **tuḷu* (Ami Ruk. Sai), **tuḷu~*təḷu* (Pai.), *təḷu* (Puy.), also **ma/taḷu* (Bun.), by assim. Lt. *si* "3," *sie pe* "30."

FOUR

Form: East **supat,* with vocalism reflected in E. Ruk: Tainan *so²at<*supat,* Kuv. *uspat~spat~supat* (Taintor 1874), Lailang (extinct) *suva;* also **[s-]/l/pat,* on basis of Taokas (extinct) *lepat,* with the prefix in the first syllable rather than the second, as in Atayal; Tsouic **supat,* on basis of Kan. *so:pata,* Tsou *supat* (Thomson 1873); Atayalic **səpat* (Sed.), **səp/ḷ/at* (Ata.).

FIVE

Form. (East: generally) **ḷima;* (Sai. Paz. Taokas) **γasub.* S. Kl. *mlen* "5" (Laj. *nlee*), *tsɨ mu* "15."

EIGHT

IN ***walu=²walu*: Aloene (Piru: West Ceram) and Lau (Solomons) *kwalu* (Dyen [1962] cit., from **q[]walu*). Form. (East: generally) **Walu* but (Ruk: Thomson 1873) **mə/Walu;* cf. also Hoanya (extinct) *(mi)aḷu,* Papora (extinct) *mahal;* also Taokas (extinct) *ma-hal-pat,* app. from "two fours" (see below); also (Fav.) **ma/spat* and (Sai. Thao) **(may-)ka/spat,* perhaps influenced by Atayalic.

NINE

IN ***t'iwa=*t'i²wa*: Aloene (Piru: West Ceram) and Lau (Solomons) *sikwa* (Dyen [1962] cit.); also (Tg.) **t'iyam.* Form. (East: generally) ***tsiwa;* also (Hoanya) **m/tsiya* and (Papora) *a/tsiya; also (Ruk.) *baŋat; Tsouic *tsiwa (Tsou Saa: Thomson 1873); *tsiya (Kan. Saa: Tsuchida).

TEN

IN **bəlat? "number between 10 and 20" (see above). Form. (Pai. Puy. Ruk. Ami) *puḷuq; (Bun. *ma/tsal; (Thao Sir.) *k[ə/]ṭiaŋ; (Paz. Taokas Papora Hoanya Fav.) *isit; (Kuv.) *təγay. T *[][ro]k, represented only by Tho *yuk* "dizaine." S. Kl. tsɨ "10," təδi¹ "30" (tonally distinct from δi² "7").

TWENTY

IN **liku[ḷ]=*liku[r] "number between 20 and 30." Form. (Ruk. Bun. Thao) *ma/pusal; (Puy.) *ma/kabutaqan; (Sai.) *sam/i[γ]ah.

HUNDRED

IN **γatut "hundred" (TB. Ja. Ml. NgD. Ho.), "million" (Tg.). PO: Sa. *lau* "hundred." Form: East *iday (Pai. E. Ruk.); *ma/baŋat (W. Ruk.); *ka/butsul (Sai.), apparently a loan (with assim.) from Atayalic; *ḷəman (Puy.); *ḷubut (Ami: Tauran and Kibi); Atayalic *ka/batsul (Ata.), *kə/baku[γ]i (Sed.).

THOUSAND

Form. (Pai. Puy. Ruk.) *kuzul; (Ami) *patək(/ən); (Bun.) *buquγ; (Ami: Baran) *ḷubut. T *[t]hriaŋ "thousand" (Ahom Kh. Shan) (Tho-Nung cognate lacking); D rɛŋ (h.t.) "million," from *[th]rɛŋ<*[th]r[ia]ŋ; also *ban "thousand" (Si. Lao BT WT); "four fifths of a viss, eighty rupees" (Shan).

TEN THOUSAND

Form. (Pai. Ruk.) *kuḍaw; (Ami: Kibi Taparon) *ubal(/ən); (Ami: Baran) *tsaquγ. T *hmɨin "ten thousand" (SW only); also *seen "hundred thousand (Ahom Kh. Shan Si. Lao), ten thousand (BT), million (WT)."

The numerals from "two" through "eight" show a substantial agreement in AN and Kadai, apart from the Thai, Kam-Sui, and Ong-Be groups of languages, which have replaced the original AT numerals (above "two") by early loans from Chinese (*AT* 1967bis). The Thai, Kam-Sui, and Ong-Be forms for "two" have all been derived from AT roots for PAIR and/or TWIN, respectively (see GLOSSARY). Thai *rooy (Si. Lao BT WT) ~ *drooy (Shan). The indicated AT reconstructions are *drəwsa "two," *tulu "three," *śu(m)pat "four," *lima "five"="hand" (see GLOSSARY), *ənəm "six," *pitu "seven," *(m/)x[ə]walu "eight." There is more variation in the forms for "one," but there is some evidence for an AT doublet root *atsa~*itsa, with PMY *a~*i as fore-stress forms; possibly also AT *( )ndaŋg[a] (Ruk. and Thai). The several PMY forms for "two" all appear to have been derived from AT *(N)qa(m)bar "twin, double(d)" (see GLOSSARY), paralleling the situation in Kadai (above). The higher PMY numerals at first inspection appear to be unrelated (above "five," PMY has borrowed from TB or ST; see *AT* 1967bis), but **pua "three" can be derived from *pu/a<*twu/<*t(u)lu, while *pley "four" exhibits an infix (*pley<*p/l/at) in the same position as in Atayal (*səp/l/at). PMY *pra "five," however, appears to have been derived from a distinct root for PALM/ SOLE/HAND (see GLOSSARY). There is much variation everywhere in the forms for "nine," although perhaps AT *tsiq[ə]wa can be inferred on the basis of the IN and Kl. forms; cf. also the Tg./Yami root *tsiyam "nine" and Lt. *[ts]iam "one," suggesting "9"="10 minus 1" (cf. the discussion in *AT* 1966). For "10," however, we again find evidence for a common AT root, the various Kadai forms pointing to an original *p[o]lok<AT *p[o]loq, whence IN *puluq; the final is confirmed by Tho yuk<*[][ro]k<*(ph)r[o]k, indicating a derivation of the basic *p(w)ot form (Li Lq. Lt.) from *p(o)(l)ok<*p(o)loq by dissim. The higher numeral forms show many shifts in meaning from one language or from even one dialect to another, one of the indicated derivations being quite baffling, viz. Ruk. *baŋat "nine," *ma/baŋat "hundred." Given this semantic interchange, several likely correspondences between Kadai and Formosan higher numerals can be pointed out, as shown in the following tabulation, the phonology offering little difficulty; note Form. *kudaw<*kudraw "twenty," */ṭiaŋ<*/triaŋ "ten"; also Thai *(d)rooy "hundred," from *d(o)roy<*d(ə)ray (vocalic assim.)<*nt(ə)ray; ban<*bal "thousand," also *hmɨɨn "ten thousand," from *hmyən<*[]mbyən<*[](ə)mbəl (unstressed form with vocalic assim.) (note Ch. *miwăn* "ten thousand," an apparent loan from an original AT *umbal); *seen<*saan< *(a)sal<*[p]usal (vocalic assim.) "ten thousand."

Thai/Dioi	Formosa
*draaw "20"	*kuḍaw "10,000"
*rooy "100" (SW: gen.)	
*drooy "100" (Shan)	*təɣai "10"
*ban "1,000"	*ubal "10,000"
*hmɨɨn "10,000"	
*[t]hriaŋ "1,000 (Thai)	*k[ə/]ţiaŋ "10"
"1,000,000" (Dioi)	
*seen "10,000" (BT)	*pusal "20"
"100,000" (SW: gen.)	
"1,000,000" (WT)	

Glossary

A

ABOVE/UP   See CLIMB.

ACCOMPANY   See CARRY (BY SEVERAL PERSONS).

AIM   See SHOOT.

ALKALI   See SALTY.

ANT   *(tsə)mot (68, 69)
   IN *t'əmut: Ml. Ja. Karo sĕmut (Brandstetter 1908).
   T *mot. Dioi mɔt. Yay met. Sek mɛk (Ged.), from *mɛt<*[]mot
(palatalized). KS *mot: Sui Mak Kam mət, Then met. OB mu
(Jer.), mɔˀ (Sav.), from *mo[t]. Li *[m][o]t: WS Li pot, SC
Loi but. Lt. mku me (n.a.) (for first element, cf. Kl. mi gə).

ANGLE, ELBOW   *[tsu]ruk; tsu[ra]k
(I)   IN **t'əḷuk=*t'əruk (Ml. NgD.)~*t'uruk (Tg.) "angle"
(stress distinction), perh. from an original *t'urak (vocalic assim.).
   OB khak-dok "elbow" (Jer.) (n.a.), from *[]rok; for the semantics, cf. IN **t'iku "elbow, angle."

(II)   T *sook~*sok (Shan) "elbow, forearm, cubit," from *suak
<*su(r)ak. Dioi suə "elbow," from *suak<*suwak. Yay Sek
suak, id. (Ged.).

ANIMAL   See FLESH (two entries).

APPEAR, ARRIVE, COME, BE BORN, LAY (EGGS)
   *[b][a]tu; *[b][a]t/l/u; *[b][a]ndu
(I)   IN **bətu "appear," from *batu (stressed form). PPN
**fotu "appear." SEP *potu "come": Mukawa Kwagila botu,
Paiwa votu; Capell: "SES [Southeast Solomons] have forms of it
meaning 'be born.'"
   T *taw "come" (Shan Lao), from *(a)tu. Dioi tau "to be
born, go out" (cf. Thai). KS *thaw "arrive/reach": Sui Mak
Kam thau, from *[p](h)(a)tu (second aspir.) (cf. Thai).

---

* Numbers in parentheses refer to text pages.

PY **thaw* "arrive" (YHN also "come"), perh. a loan from KS.

(II) Li *tlou:* S. Li *tou* "to be born/give birth; lay (eggs); living (=born); green (=living) [firewood]," N. Li *tlou,* Bup. *tθau* "give birth," from *(ə)t/l/u* (unstressed form; cf. IN PPN SEP under I).

(III) PMY **ndaw* "lay eggs" (YHN "create"="give birth"), from *(a)ndu.*

ARCHED   See BEND/BENT (two entries).

ARECA   *pilaŋ;* *(q/)(m)bilaŋ;* *pul[a]ŋ;* *[b]ulaŋ* (42, 43, 73, 74, 99)

(I)   IN **pinaŋ* "areca palm." Form: Ata. *pinaŋ* is loan from IN (prob. from Ml. *pinaŋ*).

(II) T *hmliaŋ* "tea/fermented tea (Kh. Shan Lao), betel (Si.)": Si. *miaŋ ma:k* (both h.t.) "betel and areca *(ma:k),*" from *hmbliaŋ<*q/mb(i)laŋ.*

(III) Form: Sai. *punəŋ,* app. distinct from Ata. *pinaŋ* (under I), but perh. from another (unknown) loan source in IN.

(IV) T *laaŋ* (BT WT Tho-Nung), usu.cw. *hmaak* "fruit," from *[b](a)laŋ,* prob. from *[b](u)laŋ* by vocalic assim. Li *[b]luaŋ:* S. Li *luoŋ~lɔŋ,* from *b(u)laŋ.* Laha: TU *hla:ŋ.*

ARM, HAND, SHOULDER, WING   *ta(m)paŋ[a]*

IN **ləŋən* "forearm" (Ml. also "sleeve"), app. from *[m]p/l/-aŋa/l/aŋa/n,* with *a>ə* through stress reduction in the final segments (cf. Form: Pai.). Form. *tabalaŋa(n)* "shoulder (Ruk: Og.-As.), armpit (Ruk: Ferr.)," from *tamp/al/aŋa(/n);* also (Paz.) *bilaŋan* "arm" (Bullock 1874), from *mp/l/aŋa/n;* (Pai.) *balaŋa* "wing," (Ami) *balaŋa-* "upper arm," from *mp/al/aŋa;* also *balaŋalaŋan* "arm (Pai: Mak.), armpit (Pai: Ferr.)," from *mp/al/aŋa/l/aŋa/n.*

N. Thai *viaŋ* "hand," from *pwiaŋ<*[tə]paŋ* (unstressed form). Lq. *paŋ* "arm." Lt. *ta pə* (Bon.), *peŋ* (Laj.) "shoulder," from *(ta)p[a]ŋ.*

Miao: PWA **mpaŋ* "hand/arm" (MPT MCh. "arm"), from PMY *mp[aa]ŋ,* from an earlier *[t]ampaŋ.*

ARMPIT   See TICKLE.

ARM-SPAN   See SPREAD OUT (ARMS).

ARRIVE   See APPEAR; COME.

ARROW   See BAMBOO; BOW.

ARROW, SHOOT   *pan[aq]; *pa/pan[aq] (57, 58)

(I)   IN **pana? "shoot, weapon" (Tg. Ja. "arrow"). PPN **fana "shoot with bow" (Maori "bow"). Form. *panaq "arrow (Ami), shoot arrow (Thao; Tsou); also (Ruk.; Saa.) *wa/pana[q] "shoot arrow"; *m/panaq "shoot arrow (Ami), fight with spears (Thao)"; also (Bun. Sai.) *[p/]m/naq "shoot arrow"; (Pai. Puy.) *p/n/anaq, id.

(II)   Form. (Puy. Sai.) *pa/panaq "arrow."

T *piin "arrow" (Si. Lao also "gun"), from *pyəən< *(pə)pən<*(pə)pan[aq] (unstressed form).

ARUM, TARO, YAM, SWEET POTATO   *biɣaq (8, 52, 74, 106)

IN **biɣa? "plant name" (Tg. "Homalomena," TB. Ml. NgD. "name of tuberous plant"). PO *piɣa: Fi. *via* "generic name of the giant arums of the genera Alocassia and Cyrtosperma," Motu *hira* "large sp. of edible arum" (cit. by Blust 1972); for Proto-MN, Chowning cites *vila* "elephant-ear taro (Colocassia macrorhiza)." PPN **pia "arrowroot, starch," from *mpi(ɣ)a. Form. (East) *biɣaq "leaf" (app. the distinctive feature of the plant).

T *phiak "yam (Si. Lao), sweet potato (Tho), kind of potato (Nung), kind of edible root (Ahom), kind of tuber (Shan)," from *phyaak<*ph(i)(ɣ)ak. N. Thai: Dioi pə "taro (tubercle)," Wu-Ming pliak "yam," from *p[h]riak (cf. Thai). KS *?ɣaak "taro": Sui ?ɣak~ɣak, Then zya:k, Kam ya:k (all h.t.), from *[p][]ɣaak<*[p](a)ɣak (vocalic assim.), but Mak has pə:k, a probable loan from N. Thai. Lk. ya:k (h.t.) "taro," from *[]ɣa:k (cf. KS). OB sak, id., from *phrak. Lq. rɔ "sweet potato," from *ra[q].

ASCEND   See CLIMB.

ASHES, DUST, FLOUR, GRAY, WHITE   *q/a[b]u; *q/bu(/a); *[q/]l/bu; *m/a[b]u; (m/)l/a[b]u; *k/l/a[b]u.

(I)   IN **abu=*ʔabu "ashes" (NgD. k/awo). Form. (East; Tsouic; Ata: Ciʼuli) *qabu, id. (Pai. Ruk. Puy. also "lime").

T *xaaw "white," from *qa/a[b]u. Dioi *hau,* id., from *qha[a]w (cf. Thai). Sek *haaw,* id. (Ged.) from *qhaaw (cf. Dioi). Li *khaaw,* id.: S. Li *kha:u,* WS Li *khau.*

(II)   Form. (Ata: Squliq Sed.) *qəbu- "ashes" (Ata. also "dust"). T **ʔbua "flour" (BT Tho), from *q/bu/a.

(III)   IN **ləbu "dust," prob. from *q/l/bu.

(IV)   IN *m/abu "gray" (Ho.); cf. also Tg. *abu/hin,* id.

(V)   Form: Ata. *mʼlavu* (Taintor 1874), Ciʼuli *malavu* "white," from *m/l/abu.

T *law "white" (Si.), from *la(b)u.

(VI)   IN **kul/abu "ash-colored" (TB. "gray," Ja. Ml. "ash-gray"), perh. from *k/l̥/abu.

N. Kl. *ru* "white," perh. from *(k-)ra(bu).

PM **klai "white," from PMY *kl̥ou, from *k[]l̥u(bu) <*k[]labu (vocalic assim.).

ASHES, DUST, FLOUR, POWDER, SAND, GRAY *q/[a]buk-
(/buk); *[a]puk(/puk); *[γa]buk; *(m)brab[uk]

(I)   IN **abuk=*ʔabuk "dust"; also (Blust 1973) the doublet (Cebuan Visayan, Iban) *(ʔ)abug "dust, sawdust" (app. with secondary voicing of final). PO: Sa. *ehu-ora* "be dusty." PPN **efu [cited under *(r)efu]=*efu(/efu) "dust" (Marquesan "become powder, obscure").

T **ʔbuk "soft, friable (=powdery)" (Lao).

(II)   IN *apuk "dust, sawdust" (Kelabit "fine ashes or dust in the air, sawdust"; Sentah, Beta "ashes") (Blust 1973). PO *apu: Arosi *sahu* "dust, sawdust" (Blust 1973).

KS *p(w)uuk "ashes": Mak *vuk* (h.t.), Kam *phu:k,* from *(pu)puk<*puk/puk.

(III)   IN **γabuk "dust, powder." Form. *[γ]abuk "sand (Kan. Saa.), lime (=ashes) (Ruk.)."

(IV)   IN **ḍabuk "ashes, dust, gray." PO *ndapu(/ndapu): Fi. *ndravu-ndravu/a* "ash-gray," *dravu-kasi* "dust." PPN *lafu/lafu "ash-gray (To. Fu.), dust-covered (Sm.)," from *ndapu/ndapu;

also **refu* "ashes" (Raratongan "dust"), from *d[a]pu.* Form. (Ami) *[d]abuk* "sand" (cf. Form. under III).

 T *daw* (SW Tho)∼*b[r]aw* (Nung) "ashes." Dioi *tau* (l.t.) "ashes, light blue," from *daw.* Sek *thau* [l.t.] "ashes," from *[d]aw* (cf. Thai Dioi). Lk. *plɛu* (l.t.), id., from *bl[a]w.* PB *deu,* id., from *r[a]w.* Li *praw*: S. Li *pau* "ashes (of tobacco), flour (of rice)," WS Li *ćhəu=śəu* "ashes."

ASSEMBLE, CONFINE, SHUT UP, COOP UP *k[a]raŋ
 IN **ka[l]aŋ=*ka[r]aŋ* "assemble."

 T *kh[r]aŋ* "confine (=\"assemble in one place\") (persons), shut up (animals)." N. Thai *k[r]aŋ, id.: Dioi *kyaŋ,* Wu-ming *klaŋ,* Po-ai *ćaŋ.* KS: Mak *ćaŋ* "imprison, shut up," from *[kr]aŋ.*

 Yao: YHN *khlaŋ* "coop up [fowl]," from PY *khla[a]ŋ, from *kh(a)laŋ.*

AUNT See MOTHER (two entries).

AXᴵ *bal[iyuŋ]; *[qa/]bal[iyuŋ]; *[k/]bal[iyuŋ]* (58, 97, 110)

(I) IN **bali[y]uŋ* "finishing ax (*Schlichtbeil*)" (Ml. "the large Malay ax").

(II) T *xwaan,* from *q(a/)ban.* Dioi *wan* (h.t.), from *(x)w[a,aa]n.* Sek *va:n* (h.t.) (cf. Dioi).

(III) KS *kwan*: Sui *kwan∼kuən,* Mak *ku:n,* Kam *kwen,* Then *wan.* Lk. *kuon<*kwan* (irreg. l.t.). Lt. *khu la* (n.a.).

AXᴵᴵ *[ma/]t[a]w[u]
 PPN **matau* (only Sm. and Fi.), from *ma/ta[w]u.*
 PM **tɔu,* from PMY *t[]w.*

B

BACK *[ku]lul
 Form. (Ami) *kulul.*

 T *lun* "after, next; past time," from *[k-]lun<*[k-]lul.* KS *lun*: Sui *lən* "the back"; Mak *lun* "the back; behind; after."

BACK, BEHIND *(qa/,ka/)li[kuz]
 IN **likud* "the back": Tg. *likod* "the back," *ta/likod* "from behind." PO: Fi. *ta/likur/a* "warm oneself at the fire" (=\"turn the back to\"). Form. *likuz* "the back (Thao); the back; back/

behind (Sai. Sir.; Saa.); tail (Kuv.)"; also (Puy.) *likuz/an "the back; back/behind"; (Ruk.) *li/likuz "back/behind."

T *hlay "back part of the shoulder (scapula)" (Si. WT), from *qlay<*q(a/)li(kuz). KS *[]lay "back": Sui lai (h.t.) (cf. Thai). OB lei (h.t.) "behind," from *hl[a]y; also da-lei (h.t., l.t.) "behind, posterior; the back," from *ta/l[a]y (cf. Tg. Fi.).

PMY **klaay=*klaay "kidney, lower back": MPT ʔdua "region of the lower back or waist," mploŋ ʔdua "shoulder-blade" ="leaf (mploŋ) of the back (ʔdua)," from *k(a/)li(kuz) (cf. Thai).

BAG, SACK, BASKET *(ka/)d[l]ay (115)

IN: Yami kaḻai "woven bag," from *ka[ḍ]ay. Form: East (Ruk.) *kaḍay "woven bag (W. Ruk. specified as for women's use)"; Atayalic: Ata. kare~kari id., from *kad[ay].

T *day "bag" (Si. Lao also "wallet"); also *kăday "sort of small basket" (Si.). Dioi tai (l.t.) "sack," from *day; also dai (h.t.) "basket," from *ʔday<*q/day (cf. Si.).

BAMBOO *plək[əs]

Form. (Pai: Kachirai; E. Ruk: Dainan; Ami: Kibi) *ṭəkəs (indeterm. s) "small bamboo."

Yao: YCR tok (l.t.) "a type of bamboo," from PMY *dok, from *tok(os) (initial voicing); cognates also apparently are present in Miao; cf. Kun Chang (1966, note 25 to p. 307): "Some Miao dialects (Kaopʼo, Kecheng, and Lushan) have a Chinese loanword [for "bamboo"] with a voiced initial [Anc. Ch. *dʼiuk] contrary to the [Anc. Ch.] *tʼiuk suggested by Chʼieh-yün [early Chinese rhyme-book]. . . ." (rather, the Arch. Ch. form: tiôk "bamboo" points to a loan from pre-PMY, with typical palatalization before the vowel ô, at a very early period antedating the initial *t->*d- voicing in PMY).

BAMBOO See RICE/SUGARCANE.

BAMBOO, WITHE, SPEAR *(m)boḻoq (20, 21, 48)

IN **buluʔ "sp. of bamboo." PPN *polo: Sm. polo "bamboo knife," from *mpolo. Form. *bulu[q] (Dyen: Q₁₂) "small bamboo (Sai Ruk: Tainan), arrow-bamboo (Kan.), spear (Pai.)."

T *took (SW)~*phrook (Nung) "bamboo strip (withe),"

from *p(h)(o)rok; also *hrok~*hrook (Nung) "sp. of bamboo" (BT "large bamboo," WT "male bamboo," Nung "kind of non-spinous bamboo"), from *(p)h(o)rok; also *hrook~*ćook (Tai To=Tho: Dodd 1923) "spear," from *(p)h(o)rok~*p(o)rok; for the semantics, cf. Paiwan. N. Thai: Wu-ming *ruk*, Yay *tuk* "bamboo strip," from *pruk. Sek *pruk*, id. (Ged.). KS *[]dyuk, id.: Sui *dyuk*, Mak *duk* (both h.t.).

BANANA   *b[u]li/b[u]li; *p[u]li(/p[u]li)   (18, 19, 47)

(I) IN: Yami *bənəbə* (Og.-As.), *vinəvə* (Ferr.), from *b[i]n[i]/b[i][ni] (cf. Formosa). Form. (Paz. Sed.) *bulibul; (Kuv.) *b[u]li-; (Pai. Puy. Ruk. Bun.) *bulbul; (Kan. Saa.) *ta/bulbul; (Sir.) *bulbil; (Thao) *bilbil; (Fav.) *bilpil; all from an original *buli/buli, with partial or complete assim. to *bili/bili.

(II) IN **pun[t]i, from *puniti<*pulipli<*puli/puli.

T *pli "banana flower/bud," from *(p[u]li)p[u]li. Dioi *pi kyɔi* "large bud of red bracteates on the end of bananas (*kyɔi*)," from *p[l]i. Sek *mak-pli* "banana flower" (*mak* is clf. for fruit).

BANK See NEAR; SIDE.

BARB See STING.

BARK, n.   *()p[u]lak   (15, 18)
Form. (Saa.) *pulak.
T *pliak "bark, rind, peel, shell, husk," from *plyak<*[]p(ə)lak (unstressed form). Sek *pla:k* "bark," from *p(a)lak (vocalic assim.).

BARK, RIND, SKIN, POD, HUSK   *(q/)u(m)pak   (15, 18)
IN *u(m)pak "bark" (Tg. "rind, skin, peel, bark").
T *fak "pod, scabbard" (Lao "scabbard, sheath, envelop, husk"), from *phwak<*(u)phak, prob. from *(q/u)pak (second. aspir. after *q/). Dioi *hɔk* "scabbard, sheath, case, pod," from *fwak<*phwak. KS *fwak "bean pod": Sui *wak~fak*, Mak *vak* (all h.t.) (Mak also "sheath/scabbard"), from *phwak (cf. Dioi). Li *fuak=*fwak: S. Li *faʔ* "carcass, empty container [shell of egg, empty box]"; WS Li *fuk* "snake skin," from *phwak (cf. Thai KS).

BARK, v. See CRY (OF ANIMAL).

BARTER, BUY, SELL *[t]u(N)qa[r,γ]* (85)

IN **tuka[l]=*tuka[r]* "barter" (TB. "price, buy"), from *tuNqa[r].

T *xaay* "sell." Dioi *kay*, id., from *qa[a]y.* Sek *kwaay*, id. (Ged.), from *qwaay<*(u)qaay.* KS *qwe*, id.: Sui *qe~pe*, Mak *će*, Kam Then *pe*, from *qw[aay]* (cf. Dioi Sek.).

BASIS, TRUNK (OF TREE, BODY), BUTTOCKS, HEEL
  [(m)po]sol

IN **puhun* "trunk (of tree), basis, origin." PO *(m)puu:* Fi. *vu-* "basis; (ic.) horizon (=basis of the heavens), alveoli (=basis of teeth)," also *mu-* "trunk (of body)"; Sa. *huu* "trunk (of tree)." PPN *fuu:* To. *fuu* "trunk (of tree)." Form. (Sir.) *pusul* "buttocks" (s₃).

T *son* "heel" (=basis of foot) (Shan also "the blunt end of anything, as a spear"; Lao also "extremity"; Tho "crest"). S. Li *śun* "the back" (=the trunk of body).

BASKET, SACK *k[a]roŋ*

IN **kaluŋ=*karuŋ* "sack" (Ho. "basket").

T *kh[r]ooŋ* "kind of basket (Ahom); large-mouthed basket (Shan); oblong basket to put fish in (Si.); small round basket with a strap, finely woven, for the use of women (WT); small basket for vegetables (Nung)," from *kh(o)roŋ<*k(ə)roŋ* (unstressed form). N. Thai *k[r]ooŋ*; Wu-ming *kloŋ*, Po-ai *ćooŋ* "kind of basket," Dioi *kyɔŋ* "kind of square basket with handles (for rice)," also *kyɔŋ* (d.t.) "suspended basket with cover (for meat)" (both tones irreg.).

BAST (FIBRE), HEMP *ban/ban*

IN **banban* "name of plant that supplies bast" (Tg. "bast; Marantha dichotoma").

T *paan* "hemp (the plant and the fibre)," from *(pan)pan.* Kl. *piə* "hemp," from *pa[n].*

BAT See RAT.

BAT, FOX (FLYING-), SQUIRREL *ka/luaŋ; *(ka/)luak*

(I) IN **ka/luaŋ* "bat" (Ja. *kalong* also glossed as "flying fox" =Pteropus).

(II) T *rook* (Ahom Lao)~*kărook* (Si.) "squirrel," from

*(ka/)ruak. Li *rwiak "bat": N. Li dri?, WS Li vik, from *[]rwak (palatalized)<*[]ruak.

BATHE See SPRINKLE; WASH.

BAY See OPEN (HINGED JOINT).

BEAN, PEA *(n)tub[a]

T *thua, from *thuwa<*tu[b]a. Dioi tuə (l.t.) "bean," from *dua<*ntua. Sek thua (l.t.), id. (Ged.) (cf. Dioi). KS *d[ow], id.: Sui Kam to, Mak thau, Then tau (all l.t.), from *d[ua] (cf. Dioi Sek). Lk. tou (l.t.), id., from *dow (cf. KS).

PMY **dop, from *top (initial voicing); cf. the early loans: Arch. Ch. dʲu "bean," from *du(ba) and təp~dʲəp "pulse," from *tup(a)~*dup(a), pointing to a late pre-PMY *t>d shift (Benedict 1972, n. 494 to p. 194).

BEAR, n. *kru(m)bay (8)

Form: East *ţumay; Tsouic *tsumay; Atayalic *k[r]umay: Sed. kumay~sumay; all from *krumbay.

T *hmi "bear," from *qmay (vocalic influ. by *q)<*qmbay, for *kr(u)mbay; also the doublet *hmiay "bear, large sp." (Lao), from *qmyay<*qəmay (unstressed form). Chuang *mui (h.t.), from *hmuy<*qmuay (vocalic influ. as in Thai)<*qumay. Dioi mɔi (irreg. l.t.). Yay miay (h.t.) (cf. Lao). Sek mi (h.t.) (Ged.) (cf. Thai). KS *?muy: Sui ?mi, Mak mui (h.t.); also *?myay: Kam me (h.t.); from *qumay~*qəmay (cf. the Thai doublet). Lk. kui, from *q(u)m(a)y (cf. KS). WS Loi moi.

PMY **krəp=*krop, from *krob<*krob[ay].

BEARD See HAIR; HAIR (BODY); FIBRE (two entries).

BEAT, DRIVE IN, FLUTTER, WING *[ka](m)pak(/[ka](m)-pak; *pak/pak; *pik/pik; *(m)puk/(m)puk

(I) IN **kapak "wings; flutter (=beat wings)," perh. from *(pa)k/pak, as in II. PPN **kapakapa "flap wings," from *kampak/kampak.

T *pak "drive in/into, stick in/into, plant, prick" (Tho "drive in with hammer blows"). KS: Mak pak "stick in [post]."

(II) IN **pakpak "beat, beat wings" (NgD. "drive in a nail"). Form. (Puy.) *pakpak "wing/wing feather"; (Ruk.) *(sa/)pak-pak "wing/wing muscle."

(III) Form. (Ami) *sa/pikpik "wing."

    T *piik "wing," from *(pik)pik. Li *phiik: S. Li fiʔ "wing; (ic.) slap," from *pik(pik).

(IV) IN **pukpuk "'beat with a tool" (Tg. "hammer blow"). Form. (Sir.) *bukbuk "hit (with fist)," from *mpuk/mpuk.

BEAT, DRIVE IN, POUND, STRIKE *[kə](n)təg; *[kə](n)tək; *[kə]tug; *[pa](n)tuk; *[m/a]tuk

(I)   IN **kətəg "pulse beat."

    T *toy "beat, strike, knock" (Si. also "attack with fists"); also *doy "to box, strike with fist" (Si.), from *ntoy.

(II) T *took "beat or drive in (by pounding, as in nailing, stamping)," from *(-o)tok. Dioi to<*took "penetrate (as a thorn or splinter)." KS: Mak to:k "to pound (as in nailing)." S. Li toʔ~dok "to pick (teeth)," from *took~*ntok.

(III) IN **kətug "beat" (Tg. "beat, pulsate," Ja. "beat out"). KS: Mak tui "beat (strike)."

(IV) IN **pa(n)tuk "to peck" (Ho. "nail/to nail"). PPN **patu "strike."

    T *tik~*tuk (BT) "beat, strike (fight), catch (fish, game)." Dioi tək "strike (general sense), catch (fish)."

(V)   Form: Ata. ʔatuk~m/atuk "to hammer."

BEAT, HIT, STRIKE, HAMMER *[p]o(N)qoḷ

IN **pu(ŋ)kul "throw, beat" (Ml. "strike, hit, beat, knock"). Form: Kuv. puqun "hit (with fist)" (Ferr.), from *puqu[l].

    T *ɣoon "beat, strike" (SW); also (d.t.) "stick (for beating), mallet, hammer (SW); to beat, strike, hammer (Tho-Nung)," from *Goon<*Nqoon<(o)Nqon. D hon (l.t.) "to strike"; also (d.t.) "mallet," from *Go[o]n (cf. Thai). Sek gɔ:l-mɔk "mallet" (n.a.), from *Gool<*(o)Gol (cf. Thai).

BEAT, STRIKE, POUND, WING *()(n)tab; *nt/r/ab; *(n)tab/tab; *(n)ta/tab; *t/r/a/tab; *[tə/]təb; *[(n)tu/]tub

(I)   T *dap "beat, strike, fight," from *ntap. Lk. tap "strike."

(II) KS *dyap "beat": Sui Then tyap, Mak tap (all l.t.) (Mak also "thresh rice"), from *ntyap<*nt/r/ap (cf. V).

(III) IN **tabtab* "beat (*klopfen*)" (Tg. "washed").

T *thaap* "to fly, move (=beat) the wing" (Si: ic.), from *(tap)tap* (irreg. initial aspir.). Lk. *ta:p* (l.t.) "pound (*piler*)," from *da:p<*nta:p<*n(tap)tap* (or poss. loan from Yao).

PY *ta:p* "pound (*piler*)" (Haud.), from PMY *daap*, from *tap/tap* (initial voicing).

(IV) IN *tatab*: Ja. *tatab* "bat (*Schlagholz*)" (="the beater"). Form: Ata. *təgətap* "wing, fan," *tətəgətap* "fan" (both = "the beater"), from an original *təta[b]<*tata[b]* (stressed form).

PMY *(n)taat* "wing" (="the beater"), from *(n)ta/t(ab)*, with second. vowel length, perh. from an original *(n)ta(b)/tab*.

(V) IN *t/r/atab*: Ja. *t/r/tab* "heart-beat" (cf. II).

(VI) T *top* "beat or strike (with hands), slap, clap, flap (wings)," from *[]təp; also *tɨp* "palpitation" (Si.), from *tyəp <*[tə]təp* (palatalized).

(VII) T *tup* "low beating, palpitation" (Si.); also *dup* "strike, beat, pound, hammer, smash" (Ahom "wash clothes"), from *ntup*. Dioi *tup* "strike, beat," from *[d]up* (cf. Thai).

Yao: YHN *top* "strike (with fist)," from PY/PMY *top*.

BEE   *( )(m)praŋ

T *phriŋ~*phrəŋ~*phriaŋ (SW)~*thɨaŋ (Tho-Nung) "bee; (usu. ic.) honey, wax" (Nung *thə:ŋ* "sugar," *me:ŋ thə:ŋ* "bee" [cw. "insect"]); both from (-ə)phraŋ (unstressed form, with second. aspir.). Dioi *tə:ŋ ka rien* "wild honey" (*rien* "wild bees," ic.), from *tiaŋ*. Sek *sɨŋ* "bee," from *[br]iŋ<*mpriŋ*. OB *saŋ* (Jer.), *səŋ* (Sav.), id., from *phraŋ*.

Miao: MPT *ntaŋ~nta* "sp. of bee," MCh. *ntaŋ* "large wild honey-bee," from PMY *ntaaŋ<*(-a)ntaŋ*.

BEE   See FLY: SWEET (two entries).

BEE, SUGAR, SWEET   *q/walu; *k/wal[u] (100)

(I)   Form: East *walu (w₂) "honey-bee (Bun. Paz. Kuv.), honey-bee/sugar (Puy. Ruk. Sai.), sugar (Pai.)"; *[hu]walu "honey-bee" (Sir. *houwalou*); *[w]alu "sugar"~*qalu "sugar-cane" (Pai: Tachaban); app. all from *q/walu; Tsouic *walu (w₁) "honey-bee" (Kan. Saa.); Atayalic *walu (w₂), id. (Sed.).

T *hwaan "sweet," from *q(a)/wan. Sek vaan (h.t.), id.
(Ged.), from *hwaan (cf. Thai). KS *qhwa(a)n, id.: Sui qhan
~fan, Mak khan, Kam khwa:n, Then khan~xwa:n (cf. Thai);
also Kam la:u (h.t.) "bee," from *hlaaw; app. from *q(a)/lau
<*q(a)/(w)alu.

Miao: MCF va (h.t.) "bee," from PM *ʔwua/ʔwuɛ, from
PMY *ʔw[a,aa]y, from *q/way or *q(a)/way.

(II) Li *kuay: WS Li kuai "wild bee," SH DC Loi kai "bee,"
from *k/way.

BEG PARDON   See BESEECH.

BEHIND   SEE BACK.

BEHIND, BACK, BUTTOCKS   *[(m)po(ŋ)]kor (12)
   IN **puŋku[l]=*puŋku[r] "hind-part" (Ja. "behind"). PO
*mpuku: Fi. mbuku "pointed hind-end, tail." Form. (Paz.;
Atayalic) *bukur "the back; back/behind," from *mpukur (cf.
PO).
   T *kon "buttocks."

BELCH   See YAWN.

BELLYᴵ   *[b]ə(n)təŋ (8)
   IN **bə(n)təŋ. PO *mpoto: Fi. mboto-.
   T *dooŋ "belly," from *ntooŋ<*(o)ntoŋ; also *nooŋ "calf"=
"belly (of leg)," from a secondary *ndooŋ; for the semantics,
cf. BELLYᴵᴵ. N. Thai *dɔŋ: Dioi tɔŋ: (l.t.) "belly"; Chung-chia
toŋ ka "calf"="belly (toŋ) of the leg (ka)" (Clark 1884). Sek
thuŋ [l.t.] "belly," from *[d]uŋ. OB hoŋ (l.t.) "belly, intestines,"
from *doŋ.

BELLYᴵᴵ   *b[a]raŋ; *[b][a]laŋ
   (I)   Form. (Ruk.) *baraŋ.

   (II) Miao: PW **plaŋ=*plaŋ "stomach." MPT plaŋ~pla, MCh.
plaŋ "belly, abdomen, stomach (seat of intelligence)"; MPT also
pla hlau "calf (=belly) of leg (hlau)"; for the semantics, cf.
BELLYᴵ; from PMY *plaaŋ, from *[b](a)laŋ.

BELLYᴵᴵᴵ   *[kə]mpuŋ
   IN **kəmpuŋ (Ml. also "bladder"); cf. also **kə(m)buŋ

"swell up"; see SWELL UP. PO: Fi. *kopu* "fish stomach."

T *buŋ* "belly, entrails, loins"; also *buŋ* (d.t.) "convexity of the belly" (Si: ic.), from *mpuŋ*. S. Li *buŋ* "blister (= a swelling)" (ic.) (cf. Thai).

BELLY, INTESTINES, MIND, SOUL *( )(*m/*)*ń[a]w[a]*

IN **ńawa "soul (*Hauchseele*)." Yami *uminawa* "breath," *umininawa* "breathe," from **umi/ńawa* and **um/in/i/ńawa*. PPN **manawa "belly" (Rarotongan "heart, courage") and **manawa-nui "heart, courage"; also **m[a,aa]nawa* "breath." SEP *manawa "belly (Wedau), conceive (Mukawa)."

PMY **hńou "intestines, mind, seat of emotions"; YCR "heart, mind; center of the personality; (physiologically conceived) the canal running from the mouth through the throat and intestines to the anus"; from *hńəu<*[](ə)*ńaw* (unstressed form, with vocalic assim.).

BELLY, STOMACH *[*k*][*a*]*tu*[ʔ]

Form: Ata. *kətuʔ* "stomach," from *katuʔ (stressed form).

T *tu "breast" (Lao) (?). Lk. *nam-tu* "stomach" (cf. *nam-tsen* "fruit"). OB *dau dɔn* (h.t., l.t.) "the pit (*dɔn*) of the stomach," from *tau<*(-*a*)*tu*.

BELOW See DEEP.

BEND/BENT, ARCHED, BOW, n. *[(*n*)*d*]ə(*n*)*koŋ*

IN **dəkuŋ "bend (be bent)." PPN **noku "bend," also **loku "bent, bowed, stooped"; both from *ndoku.

T *koŋ~*khoŋ (Lao doublet Nung) "bend; bent, curve" (Shan also "warp"; Si. also "stretch, as a bow"); also *goŋ "bend" (Si. also "bend a bow" and "arched"), from *nkoŋ; also (partly d.t.) *koŋ "bow," n.; also *kooŋ "bend; bent" (Shan also "curve" and "warp"), from *(*o*)*koŋ*. Dioi *kɔŋ* "ring, circle"; also (d.t.) "curve, curved, vaulted; circle, hoop"; also (d.t.) "vault, curve of an arch," from **k[o,oo]ŋ*. KS: Mak *koŋ ćwai* "bow of plow (*ćwai*)."

BEND/BENT, ARCHED, CROOKED *[*i*](ŋ)*kuŋ;* *(*m*)*b/*[*i*]-(ŋ)*kuŋ;* *[*i*]ŋ*kuk;* *(*m*)*b/*[*i*]ŋ*kuk;* **b/uŋkuk;* *uguk

(I) T *guŋ "circuit of a river, winding of a stream" (Si.), from *ŋkuŋ. KS: Mak *kuŋ* "bay"="curved/winding (place)."

(II) IN **bə(ŋ)kuŋ=*(m)bə(ŋ)kuŋ "to be arched" (NgD. "crooked," Ho. "curvature," TB. "hump"), from *(m)bi(ŋ)kuŋ (stressed form; cf. IV). PPN **poku "pimple," from *mpoku.

(III) IN **iŋkuk "crooked" (Ho. "curvature, hook").

T *guk "to be bent or crooked (Shan); to fold (= bend) (Si. Lao)"; Si. also *guk khau "kneel"="bend (*guk) the knee (khau)," from *ŋkuk. KS *gok "kneel": Sui ćok, Then kok (both l.t.) (cf. Thai).

Miao: PWA **ŋkhauʔ "bent" (MCh. "crooked"), from PMY *ŋkh[o]ʔ.

(IV) IN **biŋkuk=*(m)biŋkuk "crooked" (Ml. "crooked, bent"); also (Blust 1973) *biŋkug "crooked," prob. from *biŋkuk(kuk) (second. voicing). PPN **piko "bent" (Tuamotuan "bend, curve"), from *mpiko.

(V) IN **buŋkuk "crooked" (Ml. "humpbacked"), from *biŋkuk by vocalic assim.

(VI) Yao: YCR kuʔ (l.t.) "to bend over, to stoop" (kuʔ kuʔ "all stooped over"), from PMY *guʔ, from an earlier *guuk< *(u)guk, from *iguk by vocalic assim.

BESEECH, BEG PARDON *[p]o[h]on

IN **puhun "beg pardon" (Ml. "request, ask for, beg, beseech").

T *oon "beseech, flatter, coax" (WT "flatter, court; beg pardon"), from *(-o)(h)on; also *woon (d.t.) "beseech, persuade," from *(-o)won (secondary w between rounded vowels).

BETWEEN (PART), MIDDLE, NECK *( )kaḷaŋ; *[g]aḷaŋ; *kaḷ[i]ŋ

(I) IN **kalaŋ "support (*Unterlage*), part between (*Zwischenteil*)" (Ml. "prop up"; TB. Ja. [cw. "head"] "neck-support"). PO: Fi. kola "wedge."

T *klaaŋ "middle," from *k(a)laŋ. Sek *tlaːŋ, id., from *klaaŋ (cf. Thai).

PMY **klaaŋ=*kḷaaŋ "neck, throat"="the part between (the head and shoulders)," from *k(a)laŋ; for the semantics, cf. IN **γuʔaŋ "space between (*Zwischenraum*)," PPN **uʔa "neck, nape of neck"; Demp: "(space between head and shoulders=) throat, neck."

(II) IN **galaŋ "support" (Ml. "to prop up, shore up," Ho. "pillow").

(III) IN **kaliŋ "part between" (Tg. "rudder-pin," Ja. "pipe-ring"). PPN **kali "wooden pillow"="neck-support."

BIG *(q/)lab[a]
   PO *lapa: Sa. laha "big," Nggela lava "great (only in a few compounds)" (cit. by Blust 1972).
   T *hlaaw "very big (gros)" (WT), from *q(a/)lab(a). KS *laaw: Sui lau, Mak Kam la:u.
   PMY **hl[]=*hlo (PM; YCR YLC)~*hlua (YHN YTP), from *hlaw(a) (cf. Thai).

BIG, LONG *(q/)ɣay[a]
   IN **ɣaya "big." Form. (Kuv.) *ɣaya "big"; (Ami: Taparon Tauran) *[ɣ]a/[ɣ]aya "long (object)," with irreg. reflex (perh. influ. by earlier *q/; cf. Thai).
   T *ri "long," from *ray (influ. by earlier *q/; cf. KS). Dioi rai, id. Sek rai, id. KS *ʔɣaay, id.: Sui ʔɣai~ɣai, Mak Kam ya:i, Then za:i (all h.t.), from *q(a)/ɣay. Lk. ʔai, id. from **ʔɣay (cf. KS).

BILE See BITTER.

BIND *[t]a(m)bat
   IN **[t]a(m)bat "bind fast" (Ho. "bind together").
   T *mat "bind/tie together; bundle, sheaf," from *maat< *mbaat<*(a)mbat. Dioi mat "tie into a bundle" (cf. Thai).

BIND, TIE, KNOT, SQUEEZE *(ts)[i]rat
   IN **t'i[l]at=*t'i[r]at "tie (knot) on" (NgD. "bind fast").
   T *rat "bind or fasten tight, squeeze (strangle)" (Tho. "to knot"), app. from *raat<*(a)rat<*(i)rat (vocalic assim.). Li *[r]at: S. Li dat "press, compress, squeeze (strangle)" (cf. Thai).

BIRD *[ma]mlok (9, 10, 38, 80, 84)
   IN **manuk "fowl, bird." PPN **manu "animal, bird."
   T *nok. Dioi rɔk. Sek nok. KS *( )mlok: Sui Mak nok (l.t.), Then nɔk (h.t.), Kam mok. Lk. mlok. OB nok (Jer.), noak (Sav.).

Lq. *nuk.* Laha: TU *ma/nək,* BB *nok.* Kl. *ñie,* from *ml[ak]<
[ma]mlok (vocalic assim.).

PMY **nɔʔ=*(h)mlɔʔ: PM **noŋ (final assim. to initial),
but PT *hmu;* PY **nɔʔ.

BIRD See CALL (OF BIRDS/ANIMALS); FLESH.

BIRD, BIRD OF PREY *[bu]ruŋ
  IN **buluŋ=*buruŋ "bird."
  T *ruŋ "bird of prey (eagle, kite, hawk)" (SW).

BITE See GNAW; SEIZE (two entries).

BITE, GNAW, CUT OFF *( )kaɣap(/ɣap); *qaɣap(/ɣap);
  *( )kəɣəp(/ɣəp)
(I) IN **kaɣat "gnaw, bite," app. from *kaɣap/ɣ(ap), with
partial reduplication (cf. Form.; also the full reduplication in
PPN). PO *kaɣat "bite": Fi. *kat/ia,* Sa. ʔala. PPN *kati=*kati-
(/kati) "bite, nip," from *ka[ɣ]at/i. Form: East *kaɣa[t] (Bun.),
*wa/kaɣat (Ruk.), *m/kaɣa[t] (Ami Fav.), *k/m/aɣat (Pai.
Puy. Sai. Kuv.); Ata. *ka[ɣ]at~*k/m/a[ɣ]at "bite," app. from
*kaɣapr[]<*kaɣap(/ɣap) (cf. IN).

      T *kat "to bite (Si.); incise with the teeth (WT); to bite,
bite off; grind the teeth together (Shan); to gnaw (Lao); to
bite (one's nails), cut (grass), hew (trees) (Nung: Sav.); to
bite, chew (Nung: F. K. Li); to cut (Tho)," from *kaat<
*ka(ɣ)at. Dioi *kat* "to break, cut off, gnaw" (cf. Thai). OB *ka*
"bite," from *kaa(t) (cf. Thai).

(II) Form: Tsouic *[q/]m/aɣats (Saa.) "bite," from *q/m/aɣap-
(/ɣap) (cf. I).

      KS *qat: Sui *qat* "cut," Mak *kat* "cut with scissors," from
*qaat<*qa(ɣ)at (cf. Thai under I).

(III) IN **kəɣət "cut off," app. from *kəɣəp/ɣ(əp) (cf. IN
under I). PO *koɣo[t]: Sa. ʔolo "cut the ends off," also (Blust
1973) Arosi ʔoro "cut up, as for planting; cut off the top of a
tree or flower."

      PY *ky[]p=*kyəp "cut with scissors": YCR *ćap* "cut (with
scissors), harvest (with small blade)"; YHN *kyɔp* "cut (hair),
cut up (garment), gnaw," from PMY *krəp<*k[]ɣəp.

BITTER   See PUNGENT; SALTY.

BITTER, BILE   *(q/)(m)pali*

IN *a(m)pəni=*[ʔ]a(m)pəni* "bile": Ja. *ampəni,* Ho. *afeni* (Cap.), from *[ʔ]a(m)pani* (stressed form). Form. (Ruk.) *ma/pali(li)* "bitter, salty"; (Puy.) *qapəlil* "bitter," from *qa/-p[a]li/l[i]* (partial redupl.).

T *ʔbli* "bile," from *q/mpli.* Dioi *bi* (h.t.) "human bile," *di* (h.t.) "animal bile," from *ʔbli* (cf. Thai). Sek *ʔbli* "bile" (Haud.), *bli* (h.t.) "gall bladder" (Ged.). KS *ʔbi,* id.: Mak *ʔbəi,* from *ʔbli.* Lk. *ʔblai,* id., from *q/b(a)li<*q/mp(a)li.*

BLACK   See DARK (three entries).

BLAZE   See BURN.

BLIND   *(q/)(m)bop[r,l][a]*

IN **buta;* Yami *ma/buta.* Form. (Pai.) *ma/buṭa,* id.; also (Bun.) *bu[ṭ]a/an.*

T *ʔboot,* from *q(o)/bot<*q(a)/bot* (vocalic assim.). KS *ʔmbut:* Sui *ʔmut,* Then *met* (h.t.), Mak *ʔbət.* Laha: TU *bɔt.*

BLOOD   *( )ntsa[a]mu[ʔ]*

Form. (East) *dzamu[ʔ];* (Atayal) *ramoʔ* (Eg.) ~ *ramo* (Og.), from *dzamu[ʔ];* both from *ntsamu[ʔ].*

PMY **nćyaam,* from *[]ntsaam* (palatalized).

BLOW, WHISTLE, WIND   *iyup;* *[iyu]p/iyup;* *(n)s/iyup; *t/iyup*

(I)   IN **iyup* "blow." Form. (Ata.) *[i]yup~*[i]y/m/up;* (Ami Puy. Bun. Thao Sir.) *m/iyup* "blow (with breath)."

(II)   IN *piyup:* Ho. *fiukă* "whistle," from *iyup/iyup.* Form. (Fav.) *piyup* "blow (with breath)" (cf. IN).

T *phiw* "whistle" (Kh. Shan Si.), from *(iyu)p/iyu[p],* with second. aspir. (cf. IN). Li *viu:* S. Li *viu* "wind," also "flute" (both="the blower"), from *pwiu<*(u)piu* (labialized by the *u*)<*(iyu)p/iyu[p]* (cf. Thai); for the semantics, cf. BLOW/ WIND.

PY **pyom* "blow": YCR "to blow (animate beings)"; YHN "to blow, tr. (bugle, lamp); intr. (the wind)," from *pyom/pyop<*(iyo)p/iyop* (cf. IN Thai).

(III) IN: Bisayan *hu:yop* "blow" (Dyen), from *hiyup* (vocalic assim.). Form. (Sai. Kuv.) *s/m/iyup* "blow (with breath)" (Dyen:s₅).

KS *[]zup* "blow": Sui *fup~hup*, Mak *zəp*, Then *thep* (all h.t.), from *[](n)su(y)up<*[](n)si(y)up* (cf. Bisayan).

(IV) IN **tiyup* "blow" (Ho. *tsiuf/ina* "what is used for blowing," *tsiukă* "breeze"), from *t/iyup*. PPN **tiu* "wind" (but Tuamotuan *tiuu/a* "blown off course").

T *thiw* "whistle" (Kh. Lao). Sek *hit thiw*, id. (Ged.). Li *t[e]w*: S. Li *teu vat*, id.

BLOW, WIND   *[ts]ə(m)put(/(m)put)*; *[s]ə(m)buts(/(m)-buts)*

(I) IN *[t']ə(m)put*: Tombatu *seput* "blow," Uma *hopu*, Uma Juman *heput, hemput* "blowpipe" (Blust 1973).

T *phut~*but* "sprinkled with (= blown upon)" (Si.) (cf. Nung under II), from *(s)put~*[]mput* (second. aspir.).

(II) IN **puput~*put* (Capell) "blow," from *(tsə)put(/put)*, with partial reduplication. PPN *(pu)put-* "blow up (inflate)": Sm. *faʔa/puput/a* "inflate," To. *faka/put/a* "inflate," *puput/o* "inflated," from *(mpu/)mput-<*(tsə)mput(/mput)*; also *mapu* "whistle, breathe hard" (Fu. [Demp.] "blow"), from *ma/pu* or *ma/put* (second. formation).

T *phu* "blow, as with the mouth (Shan); exhale (Lao); to water (= blow water on) [vegetables] with the mouth (Nung)," from *pu(put)*; also *paw~*baw* (Nung: F. K. Li)~*bu* (Nung: Sav. doublet) "blow (mouth, wind)," from *(a)(m)pu<*[m]a/-(m)pu* (second. formation; cf. PPN). Dioi *pɔ*, id., from *p[əw]* <*(ə)pu* (unstressed form). Lq. *pəu* "wind," from *(ə)pu* (cf. Dioi).

(III) IN **həmbut'* "blow." PO: Fi. *uvuts/a* "blow (musical instrument)." PPN **pusi* "blow" (Maori "wind"), from *pus/i*; also *pusi/pusi*: Fu. *pusi/pus/i* "smoke a pipe" (Demp.).

T *wut* "blow" (Si.), from *(ə)but*; also *vut* "to blow, as in lighting tinder" (Si.), from *bwut<*(bu/)but*; also *vu* "blow" (Shan Si.), from *(bu)bu* (second. formation). Li *vuu[ts]* "wind": WS Li *vuʔ*, Bas. *vŏ*, WS Loi *vo*, SH DC SC Loi *vot,* Bup. *voad=voːt,* from *bwuu[ts]<*(*bu*)*bu*[ts]; also *ow "blow": S. Li WS Li *ou,* from *ə(*w*)*u*<*(*ə*)*bu*(*buts*).

BLOW NOSE   See SNEEZE.

BLUE, GREEN   *(*m*)*b*[*i*]*ru;* *mp[*i*]*ru*
(I)   IN **bi[*l*]*u*=*bi[*r*]*u* "blue."
    Miao: PE **nɔ "green"; PT *byo* "green," *byɔ* "blue"; both from PM *mbrɔ (Purn. cites **ńjrɔ), from PMY **mbrou.*

(II)   Miao: PC   PW   **nćru[]=*mpru[ɔ]   "green,   blue,"   from PMY **mpro.*

BOARD   See Flat.

BOAT[I]   *[*p*][*u*]*ra*[ʔ]*u*   (15, 59, 60, 111)
    IN **palahu=*para[ʔ]*u,* app. from *p[*u*]*ra*[ʔ]*u* by dissim. PPN **folau "canoe shed, fleet of vessels, sea travel, navigation," from *pərau (unstressed form). Form: Kuv. *broa* (Taintor 1874), from *[*p*][]*rua*<*p[*u*]*ra*[*u*] (cf. Thai).

    T **ria,* from *rya<*(*ə*)*ra* (unstressed form). N. Thai **rua:* Dioi *ruə,* Yay *rua,* from *(*u*)*ra.* Sek *rua;* cf. N. Thai. KS **ʔ*rwa:* Mak ʔ*dwa~zwa* (h.t.) "raft," Then *zya* (h.t.) "boat" (cf. N. Thai); also Kam *lo* (h.t.), from **hlo,* app. from *[]*lau*<*(*p-*)*rau.* Li **hrwa:* S. Li *da,* WS Li *fa* (cf. N. Thai KS).

BOAT[II]   *(*qa/*)(*m*)*baŋ*[*kaq*]; *[*w*]*aŋkaŋ*
(I)   IN **baŋka[ʔ]: Tg. *baŋka*ʔ; also **ʔ*abaŋ:* Tiruray ʔ*awaŋ,* Moken *kabâːŋ* "boat," Bukidnon Manobo *avaŋ* "small boat, dugout canoe" (Blust 1973); also Yami *avaŋ* (Og.-As.), *havavaŋ* (Ferr.). PO *(*m*)*paŋka:* Fi. *mbaka/nawa* "dugout canoe," Sa. *haka* "boat, stranger." Form: Kuv. *baŋka* "canoe" (Taintor 1874); also (W. Ruk. Sir.; Tsouic) **qabaŋ;* also (Fav.) *[*q*]*abak,* app. by assim. from *[*q*]*abakaq*<*[*q*]*abaŋkaq.*

    T **ʔ*baaŋ* "clf. for boats, canoes, rafts, also for certain objects of concave shape, e.g. bowls, dishes" (Tho also "tube"), from *q(*a*)*baŋ;* cf. also Nung *boːŋ l*ɨ "boat" (*l*ɨ<**ria;* see BOAT[I]), from **ʔ*booŋ*<*q(*o*)*boŋ,* app. from an unstressed form *q(*ə*)*baŋ* with vocalic assimilation: *q(*ə*)*bəŋ.*

(II)   IN **waŋkaŋ "boat, canoe," perhaps from an earlier *[]*baŋ-*

kaŋ (*b>*w* in unstressed position)<*[]*baŋkaq* (assim.). PO
**waŋka(ŋ) "canoe." PPN **waka "canoe" (Nukuoro "ship").

    PM **[]ɔ(ŋ)=*[ŋg]ɔ(ŋ); PY *dzhaaŋ (h.t.)<*ntshaaŋ;
both from an earlier **ŋgaaŋ~**ŋkaaŋ, from *(*a*)ŋ*kaŋ*, with
app. secondary voicing in PM.

BODY   See CHEST; FLESH (two entries); SPIRIT.

BODY, CORPSE   *[*b*]*a*(*n*)*traŋ*
   IN **bataŋ "corpse."
   T *ʔ*daaŋ* "body" (Nung); also *raaŋ "form, shape, appearance, figure, image" (SW); Si. also "(ic.) body"; Ahom "image,
form," also "body of a man, dead body (of man or animal),
skeleton"; both app. from an original *ʔ*draaŋ*<*ʔ*ntraaŋ*<
*ʔ(*a*)*ntraŋ*. N. Thai *ʔ*daaŋ* "body" (Dioi Po-ai) (cf. Nung).

BODY, FLESH   *[*da*]*Giŋ*
   IN **dagiŋ "flesh" (TB. "body").
   T *γ*iŋ* "body."

BONE   *(*q*/)(*n*)*tulaŋ* (5, 6, 62, 116)
   IN **[*t*]*ulaŋ*=*tuʔ[]*laŋ*, by metathesis from *q/*tulaŋ* (cf.
Thai): Proto-Philippine *tuʔlaŋ (Charles), but note Abaknon
Samal (Capul Island) *taʔulaŋ* (Charles cit.), by metathesis from
*tuʔalaŋ; also the doublet *tuʔ[]*lan* (Charles) and Old Ja. *tahulan*
(Charles cit.), Ho. *tolană*<*taulană (by metathesis from *tuʔ-
alan), from *tuʔ[]*l/an/aŋ*<*tuʔ[]*l/al/aŋ* (cf. Form.). PPN *tula:
Sm. *tula/* "coccyx." Form. (Sir.) *tu[*q*]*lal*; (Pai.) *təqlal (un-
stressed form), from *tuq[]*l/al/aŋ*.

   T *ʔ*duuk~***ka/ʔduuk* (Si.), from *ʔ*ntuuk*<*ʔ*ntwak*<*q/*ntu-*
(*r*)*ák*, app. by assimilation to the initial (prefix) from an earlier
*q/*ntu*(*r*)*aŋ*. Dioi *dɔ* (h.t.), from *ʔ*dook*<*ʔ*duak*<*q/*ntú*(*r*)*ak*
(note contrast in stress with Thai). Sek *rɔɔk* (Ged.), from
ruak<(*u*)*rak*. KS *ʔ*dlaak*: Sui *ʔdak~lak*, Then *za:k*, Kam
la:k (all h.t.), from *ʔ*d*(*a*)*lak*<*ʔ*dulak* (vocalic assim.)<
*q/*ntulak* (cf. Thai), but Mak *ʔdo:k*, from *ʔ*duak* (with stress
as in Dioi). OB *zək* (h.t.), from *ʔ*dək* (cf. Thai) or *hrək (cf.
Sek). Li *hrwiak: S. Li *driʔ*, N. Li *fi:k*, WS Li *fik*, from
*(*u*)*r*(*y*)*ak*. Laha: TU *t'ak*, BB NL *dak*; Pu-peo *da:k*, from
*dlaak<*ntlaak.

PMY °°*tshuŋ*=°*tshuŋ* (Miao: PE PWA MLL MKC)~°*suŋ* (Miao: MHY MKS; Yao: YHN), from °*th[]luŋ*<°*tuḷáŋ*; also °*mpuŋ* (Yao: YCR YTP), from °*ntwuŋ*<°*ntúḷaŋ* (note the contrast in stress).

BONE   See THIGH.

BORDER   See NEAR.

BORE, PIERCE, HOLE, TUBE, QUIVER   °*[t][a](m)buk*; °*[ta]buŋ/buŋ;* °*[tə]bək;* °*[tə]bəŋ(/bəŋ)*

(I) IN °°*tə(m)buk* "perforate," from °*ta(m)buk* (stressed form); also °°*tumbuk* (assim. form) "thrust through" (Ho. "perforate"). PO: Fi. *tombu* "hole in river bed" from °*təmbu[k]*; Form. (Sai.) °*tumbuk* "kill" [by thrusting through] (assim. form).

    T °*ʔbuak* "tube, pipe (water), quiver, container for chopsticks" (Tho-Nung); also °*hmook* "quiver (Kh.), tube, gun (Lao)," from °*hmuak;* both from an earlier °°*ʔ(m)buak*<°*[t](a)-(m)buk.*

(II) IN °°*buŋbuŋ*=°*(m)buŋ(m)buŋ* "hollow, tube," perhaps from an original °*[ta]buŋ/buŋ*<°*[ta]buŋ/buk* (second. voicing). PPN °*pupu:* Sm. *pupu* "quiver, scabbard," from °*mpumpu.*

(III) IN °°*təbək* "pierce, bore through," perhaps from an original °*təbuk* by vocalic assim. PPN °°*tefe* "circumcise."

    T °*ʔbok* "tube closed at one end, quiver, barrel of gun (Shan Si.); tube of bamboo containing four coconuts [measure] (Lao); hole, hollow, concavity, mortise, small vessel (WT)"; WT *ta bok* "eyes (*ta*) sunken in orbits," *bok ta* "orbit."

(IV) IN °*təbəŋ:* Proto-Igorot °*tɨbiŋ* "pierce" (Reid), perhaps from an original °*təbəŋ/bək* (second. voicing).

    T °*ʔboŋ*~°*ʔbooŋ* (s.t.) "pierce, perforate" (Shan also "the hole or opening into anything"), from °*ʔ(boŋ/)boŋ;* also (d.t.) °*ʔbooŋ* "hole, socket (Shan Si. WT); tube (Lao)" (Si. also "insert a handle"), from °*ʔboŋ/boŋ.* Dioi *bɔŋ* (h.t.) "pierce," from °*ʔb[o,oo]ŋ.*

BORN, BE   See APPEAR.

BORROW, LOAN   °*si(n)dzam*

IN ****hi(n)dam~*hińd'am=*hi(n)ẓam** "loan." Form: Pai.
səd'am "borrow" (Dahh cit.), from **sədzam* (unstressed form).

T ***[h]yɨɨm** "borrow"; (ic.) "lend," from **s(ə)yəm<*s(ə)yam*
(vocalic assim.). KS ***ćhiam** "borrow/lend": Mak *ćhi:m*, from
*h(i)jam<*s(i)dzam (palatalized).

BOTTLE   See DIP.

BOW, n. See BEND.

BOW, SPEAR, ARROW   ***[bo](n)tsoR** (12, 60)
    IN ****but'uɣ=*but'uR** "bow." PO ***punsu:** Fi. *vutsu* "end of
a bow"; also (Blust 1972) Mota *us*, Southeast Ambryn *his* "bow."
Form. ***butsuɣ** "bow (East: gen.; Tsouic; Atayalic), spear (Fav.)."

    T ***son~*sun** "bow" (Si.); also Si. *sor* (written form: Laj.),
as if a poss. l.w., but app. a doublet of Si. *kăsun* "bow to shoot
earthen balls" (Laj.).

    PMY ***shɔ(ŋ)=*tsɔ(ŋ)** "arrow"; for the semantics, cf. AR-
ROW/SHOOT.

BOWL   See CUP.

BRAIN   ***( )lu[]us**
    Form. (Ruk.) **lu[]us*
    PM ****hlɨ=*hlwɨ** (MCF *hlwe*); PY ****lei;** both from PMY
*(h)l(w)ei, from an earlier **(h)loi*.

BRAN   See STRAW.

BRANCH   ***[da]Nqa; *[(n)da](N)qa/n; *[da](ŋ)ka; *[d]aka/n**
(I)   T ***ɣa** "branch, branching (of tree, antlers, road)," from
*Nqa. Li ***Ga:** S. Li *a* "branch," WS Li *kha* "branch (of tree),"
from **Nqa* (cf. Thai).

(II)   IN ****[dd]aʔan**, from **[d]aqa/n*. PO ****daqa(n)** "branch,
twig." PPN ****laqa/laqa** "small branch," from **ndaqa/ndaqa*.
SEP: Capell: "[this root] means flower as often as branch, and
shows a strong tendency to develop the medial *h* [=ʔ] into *g*":
Suau Tavara *raga* "branch," Sariba Keherara *raga/raga* "branch/
bough," from **daga<*daNqa[n]*.

(III) Miao: MPT *ŋkhi* "crotch (legs, branches, fingers)," from
PM **ŋkh[-i]*; PY **tsha:* YCR *tsha* "to branch out; to fork,"

diaŋ-tsha "crotch of tree (*diaŋ*)"; YHN *(ka/)tsa* "vulva" (= "crotch"), *kiau tsa* "bifurcation"="branching (*tsa*) of roads (*kiau*)," *lau fan tsa* "fork" (n.a.); both from PMY *ŋkha~*tsha, from an earlier *(ŋ)kha.

(IV) T *kaan* "branch, bough," from *(a)ka/n.

BRANCH See FORK.

BRANCH, BROW *[]kiŋ; *( )k/l/iŋ

(I) T *kiŋ~*ŋiŋ (Nung doublet) "branch" (with assim. in Nung). OB ŋeŋ "branch" (cf. Nung); also *kiŋ* "finger"="branch of the hand" (Haud.).

(II) IN **kəniŋ "eyebrow"="branching of face"; for the semantics, cf. BRANCH/FOREHEAD

　　T *kliŋ "protuberance caused by an outgrowth of a branch, 'eye' of a tree" (Ahom).

BRANCH, FOREHEAD *p[i]lak[a]

　　Form. (Ruk.) *pilaka~*palaka (assim. form) "branch."

　　T *phraak "forehead," from *p(a)rak<*p(i)rak (vocalic assim., as in Ruk.); almost exclusively in the compound: *hna phraak = "branching (*phraak) of the face (*hna)"; for the semantics, cf. BRANCH/BROW. Dioi *na pya* "forehead," from *hna p(h)raak (cf. Thai). Sek *phraak*, id. (Ged.) (Haud. cites *na-prak*). KS **ʔna pyaak "forehead": Sui *ʔna pyak~na pyak*, Mak *na pya:k*, but Then has irreg. *pa:k<*pa(r)ak.

BREAD-FRUIT, JACK-FRUIT *[-a]laŋ[ka] (42, 43)

　　IN **naŋka "bread-fruit" (Tg. Ml. "Artocarpus integrifolia" = "jack-fruit" as cited by Shell.), app. from *[]laŋka (with *l>n as medial).

　　T *laaŋ "jack-fruit" (Ahom Kh. Shan), perh. also in thirteenth-century Si. (Rama Khamheng inscrip.) but meaning uncertain (Coedès 1923), from *(a)laŋ.

BREAK, SMASH, SPLIT *trak; *[(m)bə]trak

(I) T *thrak "break crosswise (stick, leg, string), smash, shatter (SW); broken (string) (Nung); explode (Tho)." Dioi *rak* "smash, break," from *[th]rak. Sek *rak* (h.t.) "break" (Ged.), from *[th]rak. Li *sak: S. Li *śak* "smash, break [stick]."

(II) IN ****bə*ṭak*=*(*m*)*bə*ṭ*ak* "split" (Ja. *bĕṭak* "firewood").
PO *mpotak: Fi. *mbetek/a* "smash into pieces"; also (Blust 1972) *pota: Sa. *hoa* "make an incision in," Mota *wota* "knock, break by knocking (as firewood)."

    T *tak "to break/be broken (stick, arms, legs, neck)," from *t[*r*]*ak*. KS *tyak "broken (a stick)": Sui *tyak~tak*, Mak Kam *tak*.

BREAK DOWN/OFF See CUT DOWN/OFF.

BREAST[I] *nu[*h*](/*nu*[*h*])

  IN *nunu: Ho. *nunu* "nipple" (Dyen 1964). SEP *nunu: Kiriwina Gawa Arifama *nunu*, Rakwa *nuni*, Oyan *nun* "breast," Tokunu *uno* "milk." Form. (Paz.; Tsouic; Sed.) *nunuh.

  T *hnu (Lao WT), perh. from *(*nu*)*h/nu*(*h*). OB *nu* "breast, milk" (Jer.), *nɔ*ʔ "breast" (Sav.), from *nu[*h*] (with vocalic influ. by *-*h*).

  Yao: YHN *nu* "breast, milk," YCR *ńɔ* (h.t.), id., app. from an original *ʔ*nu*<*(*nu*)*hnu*(*h*) with vocalic influ. (cf. Thai OB).

BREAST[II] *(*m*)*bu/*(*m*)*bu*

  Form. (Ata.) *bubu "breast; (cw. 'cow') milk"; also (Kan.) *mumu*, from **mbu/mbu*.

  Dioi *u* "breasts, milk, suckle," from *[*w*]*u*.

  Miao: MCF *və* (h.t.) "milk, breast," from PMY *ʔ*w*(*u*)*o*.

BREATH, HAVE See HAVE (POSSESSION)

BREATHE, SPIRIT, GHOST *tsumbaŋ(/*t*)

  IN ***t'umaŋət* "spirit (*Geist*)" (TB. "ghost of decreased relative," Ml. "soul, life, the spirit of life, consciousness"), app. from **tsumbaŋ/ət*. Form. (Bun.) *tsumbaŋ "breathe."

  T *[*h*]*ma*[*a*]*ŋ* "an imaginary evil spirit supposed to live on fish" (Ahom); also *hmaaŋ "to make imprecations, curse (=to call the evil spirits against)," from *s(*a*)*m*[*b*]*aŋ* (vocalic assim.). N. Thai *mwaaŋ "genie": Dioi Yay *fa:ŋ* (l.t.), Cao-lan *ma:ŋ*, from *(*u*)*m*[*b*]*aŋ*. Sek *maaŋ* "spirit, ghost" (Ged.) (cf. Thai). KS *hmaaŋ: Mak *ma:ŋ* (h.t.) "ghost/spirit/demon [glossed by Ch. *kuei*]" (cf. Thai).

BRIDGE See LADDER (two entries).

BRIGHT   See SHINE.

BROAD (SURFACE)   See WIDE.

BROKEN (OFF)   See NOTCHED.

BROOM   See SWEEP.

BROTH, SOUP   *( )ku[w][aq]
IN **ku[w]a? "broth" (Ml. "sauce").
Miao (PW) **kua "juice, soup," from PM *k[uo], from PMY
*k[o].

BROTHER (OLDER)   See SIBLING (OLDER).

BROTHER-IN-LAW   See IN-LAW.

BROW   See BRANCH.

BUBBLE, SPRING   *bu[k]al̤; *(q/)(m)bu[q]al̤
(I)   IN **bukal "to bubble" (Tg. "spring").

(II) IN *bual=*(m)bual "spring, well" (Blust 1970): Ml. bual
"bubbling up, like aerated water," TB mual "water, spring,
well," Maranao boal "bubble," boal-an "spring water," app. for
*(m)bu(?)al.
        T **bo=/?boo/ "spring, well, mine," from **bu(?)a(l̤).
Dioi bɔ (h.t.) "spring," from **bo (cf. Thai). KS **b[ə]n~**bo
"well, spring": Sui ?bən~bən, Mak ?bən, but Then mo (h.t.),
from **bo[l̤]<**bu(?)a[l̤].

BUFFALO   *k[a]R[]baw; *k[a]R[]b/l/aw   (45, 46, 58, 59, 101,
    111, 128)
(I)   IN **kəbaw=*kəɣbaw   (Charles)=*kəRbaw (unstressed
form): Ja. kĕbo, Ml. kĕrbao, TB. horbo; note also Tg. kalabao=
*k/al/abao (Demp.), who considers the Ja. cognate as the origi-
nal, unprefixed form; the root is considered a loan in the Philippines (Charles) and also appears to be late in Formosa: Kuv.
kavau (Ferr.), qa:bau (Tsuchida), but earlier k'ravao (Taintor
1874); note also Fi. karavau "cattle," perhaps with an infix in
the first syllable.

(II) T *grwaay, from *g[]rbaay<*k[]Rbaay (second. voicing
through assim.)<*k(a)Rbay<*k(a)Rb/al[/aw]; note also T

plaw "cattle" (calendar term), originally (prob. via Chinese b.l.) from *b/l/aw* (regular unvoicing of the initial)<*(k/)-b/l/aw*, with the first syllable unstressed and reinterpreted as the *k/* prefix. Dioi *wai*, from *[gr]wa[a]y*. Sek *vaay* (Ged.), from *waay* (cf. Dioi). KS *gwi*: Sui *kwi~kui*, Mak *həi*, Then *wei* (all l.t.), from *g[r]w[a]y* (cf. Thai). OB *tai* (Jer.), from *[krw]ay*. Li *tsoy* "buffalo/cattle": S. Li *tui*, WS Li *ćhoi=śoi*, N. Li dial. *toi~ćoi*, from *[kr]oy<*[kr]way* (cf. Thai). Lq. *həi* (Bon.), *khɛ* (Laj.), from *kh[rw]ay*. Lt: MP *ko;* BP *ko* (Rob.), *kua* (Bon.), from *kuay<*k[rw]ay*.

BUFFALO See CATTLE; DEER.

BURN, BLAZE *g[a]l[a]k*

 IN **galak* "to blaze."

 T *glook* "to burn (set fire to)," from *g(ə)lək* (assim.)< *gəlak* (unstressed form).

BURN, LIGHT, SHINE, MOON *[(n)da]maR*

 IN **damaγ=*(n)damaγ* "resin, light, torch." PPN **marama* "light," **malama* "moon, month" (To. "shine"); both from *ma/(n)dama[γ]*; To. also *ama* "torch," *lama* "to light" (Demp.), from *(n)dama[γ]*. SEP: Kiriwina *luma/lama* "light, shine (of sun)." Form. *(n)damaγ* "burning (Sir.), burnt field (Fav.), fire (Kuv: ic. Ami), moon (Ruk.)."

 T *hmay* "burn."

BURN, ROAST, HEAT, HOT, WARM *pla[l]u[h]; *plu[l]u[h]*

(I) T *ph[r]aw* "burn, set on fire, roast" (SW)~*thaw* "to heat (water); hot (wine), warm, tepid (water)" (Nung), from *pra(l)u(h)*. N. Thai *ph[r]aw* "burn" (Wu-ming). Sek *phraw*, id. (Ged.) (cf. Thai). KS *[]daw*: Mak *dau* (h.t.) "warm/hot [sun]," from *(ma/)praw* (cf. Form. under II). Li *saw*: S. Li *śau* "hot," from *(ma/)praw* (cf. Mak).

 PM *tho*: MKS MJC *thau*, MTK *thɔ* "reheat," MCF *tho* "heat (water), reheat (cold rice)," from PMY *thaw* (cf. Nung).

(II) IN **tunu* "burn, roast." PO: Fi. *tunu* "reheat food," *tunu/tunu* "warm." PPN **tunu* "cook on open fire." Form. (Sai.) *tuluh;* (Saa.) *-tsulu[h]* "burn (intr.)"; also (Pai. Ruk.) *ma/tulu[h]* "hot"; perh. from *taluh* by vocalic assim.

BURY See PLANT, v.; SUBMERGE.

BURY, GRAVE *[pə](n)dəm (5, 6)

IN *pəndəm: Ja. *pěndem* "bury," TB. *pondom* "grave" (Dyen, apr. Demp.), for *pəndəm (no Tg. cognate).

T *dɨm "place for depositing a corpse" (Si:ic.), from *dyəm < *(ə)dəm. OB dɔm "bury." Li *d[ə]m, id.: S. Li dom.

BUTTERFLY, CATERPILLAR *(q/)(m)bəŋ(m)ba[ŋ]

IN *mbəŋmbəŋ "butterfly" (Cap.), from *mbəŋmbaŋ (vocalic assim. forward); also (Blust 1973) *b[a,ə]lə(m)baŋ, id., from *b/l/əŋbaŋ; also (Blust 1973) *kalibaŋbaŋ, app. from *kali- (not identified) + *bəŋbaŋ (vocalic assim. backward; contrast Cap. cit.). SEP (Kiriwina Nada Paiwa Boniki) *(beba/)beba, id., from *mbəŋmbaŋ; also (gen.) *bebe*, id., from *mbəŋmbəŋ (assim. form; cf. IN); also (Pem Mukawa Kwagila) */bembem, id., from *mbəŋmbəŋ (both vocalic and consonantal assim.). Form. (Ami) *qali[b]aŋ[b]aŋ; (E. Ruk.) *qaliba[w]baŋ "butterfly," app. from *qali- (not identified) + *[baŋ]baŋ (cf. IN); cf. also Bun. *babaŋo* "worm," app. from *ba[ŋ]baŋ[u].

T **?boŋ~*?buŋ (Si: ic.) "caterpillar (Si. Lao WT), worm (Shan), silkworm (Ahom)," from *q/bəŋ(baŋ); also *?bɨa~*vɨa (Nung doublet) "butterfly," from **?b(w)ya<*?(bə)ba<*q/- bə(ŋ)ba(ŋ) (abbreviated form). Dioi bɔŋ ba (both h.t.), id., from *q/bəŋba(ŋ). KS: Mak ?bum ba, id., from *q/bəŋba(ŋ), with assim. of vowel and final (cf. SEP). Li *mɨiŋ, id.: S. Li mɨːŋ, from *mbɨiŋ<*(ə)mbəŋ(baŋ).

BUTTOCKS See BEHIND; HIND-PART; TAIL.

BUY See BARTER; CHANGE; EXCHANGE; SELL.

C

CACKLE See CALL (OF BIRDS/ANIMALS).

CAGE See ENCLOSURE.

CALF (OF LEG) See MUSCLE.

CALL See CRY OUT.

CALL (OF BIRDS/ANIMALS), CACKLE, CROW, v/n.,

FOWL, BIRD *guk(/guk); *ku[k]/kuk; *ku[q]/kuq;
*(ŋ)ga[k]/(ŋ)gak; *ka[k]/kak (85)

(I) IN **gukguk "animal cry" (Tg. "grunt [pig]," TB. "cry
of hawk," Ja. "bleat").

   T *guk "cackle" (Tho-Nung: ic.).

(II) IN **kukuk "cackle" (Ml. "to crow").

   T *kuk~*kok "cackle (Lao BT); to call, as barking deer
(Shan)"; Si. kuk "cackle"~kok "clucking of the hen." N. Kl. ko
"bird" (De B.), from *k[uk]. Lt. a/kŭ, id.

   Yao: YCR khok "sound of hen clucking to her chick."

(III) IN *ku(ʔ)kuʔ=*kukuʔ "cackle": Singhi bi-kukoh, Maranao kukoʔ (Blust 1970). Form. (Ami Fav.) *kukuq "fowl"; cf.
also (Kuv.) *-quq; (Puy. Bun.) *-kuk; (Pai. Ruk.; Kan. Saa.)
*kuka, id.

(IV) IN **gagak=*(ŋ)ga(ŋ)gak "bird call" (TB. "laugh
loudly, NgD. "cackle," Ja. Ho. "crow," n.). PPN **k[a,aa]kaa
"parrot sp." (Tuamotuan "chatter loudly, screech [like a bird],"
Uvean "song of bird after laying," Hawaiian ʔaaʔaa "male ʔooʔoo
bird").

   T *gak "noisily, with noise" (Si.); also *gaak/gaak "with
a loud, harsh, sudden sound" (Shan), from *gak/gak; also *ŋaak
"to call roughly" (Shan), from *ŋgaak<*(a)ŋgak.

(V) IN *kakak: Bukidnon Monobo kakak "cackle" (cited by
Blust 1970; n. 78).

CARESS See RUB.

CARRY (BY SEVERAL PERSONS), ACCOMPANY *[o]tsoŋ
   IN **ut'uŋ "carry (by several persons)" (Ho. "accompany").

   T *soŋ "escort, convey, accompany," a poss. b.l. from Ch. suŋ
"escort."

CARRY (ON BACK) *(m)ba/ba
   IN **baba=*(m)baba "carry on oneself" (Ho. "carry on
back"). PPN **fafa "carry on back."

   T *ba "carry on oneself (BT), suspend from shoulder (Shan),
carry on back (Kh.), carry on back in basket (WT), conical
basket used for carrying burdens on back (Ahom), carry on

hip, as children (Tho)"; also *ba (s.t.) "lead, conduct" (Si. Lao); from *(ba/)ba.

CARRY (ON SHOULDER), SHOULDER LOAD
   *(q/)(m)pekol; *[pe](ŋ)gol

(I) IN **pikul "shoulder load [*picul*]" (Ja. Ml. NgD. also "carry on shoulder").

   T *ʔbeek~*peek (Nung doublet) "carry on shoulder" (Tho also "load [of wood], sheaf [of rice]"); Nung be:k (h.t.) "carry on the shoulder something fastened on one end of a pole," pe:k (s.t.) "carry on the back"; from *(ʔ)(m)peek<*(q/)(e)(m)- pek<*(qa/)(m)pek[ol] (vocalic assim.). Li *pwi(i)k: S. Li piʔ "load (of firewood)," WS Li fit<*fik "load (of rice); carrying pole," from *[]pik (labialized), perh. from *pi/pik[ol].

   PM **ki=*kwi (MCF kwe) "carry on shoulder," from PMY *kw[ei]<*k[ol] (cf. MCF under II).

(II) T *goon "carry (something suspended on stick) over shoulder," from *(o)gon. KS *ŋ[o]n: Mak ŋun "carry on shoulder," from *ŋgon.

   Miao: MCF kwen (l.t.) from PM *gwin, from PMY *g[o]n <*g[ol] (cf. MCF under I; kwen is archaic doublet).

CASTOR OIL (PLANT)   *[dza]rak(/[dza]rak)
   IN **d'a[l]ak=*d'a[r]ak.
   T *[h]ra[a]ŋ (Ahom), from *[sa]raŋ/[sa]rak.

CASTRATE   See CUT.

CAT   See TIGER.

CAT, TIGER   *[p]u(n)tsa[q] (15, 16)
   IN **put'a[ʔ] "cat" (Ho. "catlike beast of prey").
   T *sia "tiger" (WT "generic name of large carnivorous animals"), from *sya<*(pə)sa[q] (unstressed form). OB zoa (h.t.), from *[]nsua<*[](u)nsa. Kl. dzie, id., from *dza<*ntsa[q].

CATERPILLAR   See BUTTERFLY.

CATTLE[I]   *[l,l][ə](m)bu(/a) (46, 77, 101)
   IN **ləmbu.
   T *mua (Tho-Nung), from *mbua<*mbu/a. KS *bo: Mak pho (l.t.), from *b[ua].

CATTLE[II] *Nu/a; *Nu/N[u]

(I) T *Nua: Lao BT ŋua, Si. ŋua~wua, Kh. WT ŋo, Shan
ŋo~wo, Ahom hu.

(II) PMY **ŋo(ŋ), from *Nu/Nu.

CATTLE See DEER.

CATTLE, BUFFALO *[(m)ba]ntriŋ; *(ka/)(n)triŋ (46)

(I) IN **bantiŋ=*(m)bantiŋ "wild cattle."

(II) Form. (Thao; Atayalic) *katiŋ "cattle" (Ata. also "buffalo,"
usu. ic.).

        T *[t]h[r]iŋ "buffalo" (Lao); *kădiŋ (s.t., low series) "wild
ox, bison" (Si.); both from *(kă/)(n)triŋ; cf. also Ahom liŋ
"cattle" (for regular *riŋ).

CAVE See PIERCED.

CENTER See MIDDLE.

CENTIPEDE *(q/)s[a]lep(/an) (38)

    IN **lipan (Demp.)=*halipan (Cap.): Ml. lipan~halipan,
NgD. ha/la/lipan. PO *h[a]li[p]a: Sa. hɛluhe, U. hɛliha.

    T *x[r]ep~*th[r]ep (Tho) (Lao "millepede"), from *q/hrep;
cf. also *hrep "tick" (Si. "crab-louse, wood-louse"). Dioi sip
"large venomous centipede; lice of cattle or buffaloes," from
*s[r]ip (for semantics, cf. Si.). OB zɔp "centipede, millepede,"
from *rɔp. Li *rip: S. Li drip~rip, WS Li rip.

    PY **sap, from PMY *s[r]ap.

CHAFF See HUSK; STRAW.

CHANGE See EXCHANGE.

CHANGE, EXCHANGE, BUY *liyan; *p/liyan

(I) IN **liyan "to be changed." PO *lia, id.: Fi. lia, Sa. lie.

    T *rian "to buy (a field)" (Lao), from ríyan. Cf. also
*lian "to change from place to place, leave a place, mobile"
(Si.), from *lyaan<*l(i)yán.

    PMY **wyen=*wian "change"; MCF YCR also "exchange";

YHN "change [clothes, money], modify [price], move/change [home]."

(II) T *plian~*phrian (Lao WT) "change, exchange, transform," a poss. b.l. (at a very early level) from Ch. *pien*, Anc. *piän*, Arch. *plian* "change." KS *p[ia]n "change": Mak *pi:n*, also a poss. b.l. from Ch.

CHASE See RUN (AFTER).

CHEST, BODY *[a](w)ak

IN **awak "body"; TB. irreg. *ak* "sacrum," app. from *(aw)ak.
T *ək~*ɨk (Lao doublet, Shan) "chest"; also *ok~*uk (BT WT) "chest, breast, heart," app. all from *(ə)(w)ak (unstressed form)~*(a)wak. Dioi *ak* "chest," from *ak or *ɨk (cf. Thai). OB *bak-ok* (Jer.), *bak-oak* (Sav.) "chest" (n.a.), from *-(w)ak.

CHEW See GNAW.

CHEW (SOFT/PREPARED FOODS) *[ma/]maq; *(q/)ma/m[aq]; *(q/)mə/m[aq] (44)

(I) IN **mama? "chew." PO *mama "chew (Fi.), betel quid (Sa.)." PPN **mama (To. Sm. also *ma) "chew" (Raratongan "prepare by chewing").
T *m[a,aa]k "chew the cud" (Ahom).

(II) T *(h)ma(a)m "chew soft foods (as infants, or to feed infants)" (Ahom "boiled rice," Shan also "chewed rice, such as is fed to an infant"). Dioi *kɛn mam mam* (h.t.) "to eat (*kɛn*) rice (like a child)," from *hmam hmam.
Yao: YCR *mam~am* (h.t.) "eat" (children's lang.), from *(?)ma/m(a).

(III) Yao: YCR *mom* "chew with the gums (as of person who has no teeth)"; Miao: MPT *moŋ* (h.t.) "chew with the gums, eat without teeth"; both from PMY *(?)mom.

CHEW, TASTE, FLAVOR *ńa[?]am(/ńa[?]am)

IN **[n]am[n]am=*ńa[?]amńa[?]am: Tg. *namnam* "taste/flavor," TB. *namnam* "taste with the lips"; also (Blust 1970, 1973) Ja. *ńam ńam-en* "the taste of something in the mouth," *ńam-en*, Ml. *ńam-an*, id., Iban *ńam ńam* "tasteless, insipid" (with semantic

polarization), Bukidnon Manobo *nanam* "taste, flavor," *naʔam*
naʔam "taste food to see if it is good." PO *ńami* (doublet form
cited by Blust 1973): Arosi *name, nami* "taste, lick," Bugotu
ńami "nibble, bite, taste," from *ńam/i;* also *ńamu:* Fi. *namu*
"chew and swallow," Gedaged *nam* "eat (when speaking of small
children)" (Blust 1973), from *ńam/u<*ńam/i* app. by assim.;
also Sa. *nana* "eat (children's word)," from *ńa[mu]/ńa[mu].*
PPN **namu=*namu(/namu)* "odor, flavor"; **namu/namu*
"chew, taste (Easter Island); nibble, chew with closed lips (Hawaiian)" (with suffixed -/u, as above).

   T *ńam~*hńam* (Lao) "chew (as children and edentulous
persons)" (Ahom also "eat with the lips from a bamboo joint";
Si. Lao "chew areca/betel"), app. from *(?)ńam<*ńa(?)am*
(with vocalic shortening). Dioi *ńam* "to swallow down rapidly."
KS: Mak *ńam* (h.t.) "chew food to feed infants," from **?ńam*
<*ńaʔam* (cf. Thai). WS Li *ńim* "to taste," from *ń[aʔa]m*
(with vocalic shortening and shift).

CHIEF, MASTER, RULE(R)   *[a]ćaw* (120)

   Cham *aćauv* "overseer, chief, master, patron." PPN *sau* "rule,
ruler" (Fi. "chief").

   T *ćaw* "master, lord" (Ahom "god, deity; master, owner;
king; great man"). KS: Mak *sau* "host, master."

CHILD   *[Na]wak; *[Na]w/al/ak* (20, 42, 64)

(I) Form: Tsou *oko* "child; small," from *[W]ak;* also Ami
wawa, app. from *Wa(k)/Wa(k).*

   Yao **-ŋwa* (PIM)~**ŋaw* (PKM), from PY *ŋ(a)w(a);*
Miao (PWA) **ńua=*ŋuaʔ:* MPT *ńwa~ńa* "child," *me/ńwa*
"children, the young of animals" (Sav.), *ńuaʔ* "small, little,"
me/ńuaʔ "child" (Heim.); MCh. *ŋwa~ŋa~ńa* "young child";
MCF *ŋaʔ* "the young of human beings and animals; foetus"; both
from PMY *ŋaw(a)(?)<*Naw(a)(k).*

(II) IN **anak=*Wanak* (Dyen, 1962): Niala (West Ceram)
wana. Form. (Pai. Puy. Ruk. Sir.) *Walak* "child"; also *[W]al/-
[W]alak* "child (Thao), young person (Paz.)."

   T *luuk,* from *lwak<*w[]lak.* Dioi *lǝk.* Yay Sek *lik*
(Ged.). KS *laak:* Sui *lak,* Mak Kam Then *la:k,* from *(a)lak.* Kl.

lə ye "child" (cf. *lə ɣe* "boy," *lə ɣo* "girl"), from **la[k]*. Lt: MP *li ńe*, BP *li i* (Rob.), *le e* (Bon.) (cf. Kl.).

CHILD See FATHER; SMALL.

CHILD (OFFSPRING) **[na]to; *[na]to/n*

(I) IN **natu "offspring" (Capell, who notes that this root does not occur west of Brandes' line). PO **natu "child, offspring."

(II) PMY **tɔn "son" (basic meaning is "offspring, both human and animal").

CHIN See JAW.

CHOP See HEW.

CHOP OFF See CUT.

CHOOSE **[p]iḷiaq*
IN ***pili?*. PPN **fili "select, choose."

T **liak*, from **lyaak<*(i)liák*. Dioi *le*, from **liak* (cf. Thai). Chuang **liek~*le:k*, from **liak*. KS **hl[yay]*: Mak *le*, Kam *lyai* (both h.t.), app. from **hlia[q]*.

CITRUS **m[i]law*
IN **limaw (Ml. "generic name for oranges, limes, and similar fruits"), app. by early consonantal metathesis from **milaw* (before the occurrence of the medial **l>n* shift). PPN **moli (Sm. "wild orange"), app. by vocalic metathesis from **mil[aw]* (contrast the IN metathesis).

T **naaw*: Si. Lao *na:u* "citrus, lemon," from **[ml]aaw< *m(a)law<*m[i]law* (vocalic assim.).

CLAM (GIANT) See SHELLFISH.

CLAW See SCRATCH (two entries).

CLIMB, ASCEND, MOUNT, RIDE, LIFT, ABOVE/UP
    *[tsa]ka; *[(n)tsa]ka/i; *[tsa]Nqa/i; *[a]ŋka/t; *[a]qa/t;
    *[a](N)qa/n; *[t]u(ŋ)ka/i; *[t]uka/t (58, 87, 88, 117, 118)

(I) KS **ćha* "climb": Sui Mak *sa*, Kam Then *ćha*, from **kha*, prob. from an original **s(a)ka* with second. aspiration.

(II) IN ***t'akay* "climb, mount" (Tg. "mount a vehicle or riding animal"). PPN **hake "up, upward," from **nsake<*nsakay;*

also *ha/hake "east" (To. Sm.); also *kake "climb," from the partially reduplicated form *(sa)ka/kay (contrasting with *ha/hake). SEP (gen.) *sake "up" (Dobu "rise [of sun]"); also (groups VI through VIII) *ka[k]e "ascend, go up" and (Mukawa only) *s[ə]ka[k]e: Mukawa *gae* "go up," *sugae* "embark."

(III) T *ɣay "lift, raise" (SW), from *Gay<*[tsa]Nqa/i.

(IV) IN **aŋkat "lift" (NgD. "to be elevated," Ho. "ascent"); also **paŋkat "elevation, rank," from *p/aŋkat.

(V) T *[q]it~*[q]iat (Lao doublet) "reach, attain (=rise to a height)," from *qya(a)t<*(ə)qa/t (unstressed form).

(VI) T *xin "climb, mount" (Kh. also "go upstream"), from *qyan<*(ə)qa/n (unstressed form; cf. Thai under V). N. Thai *qhin "climb, ascend," *Gin "on/above; north (=upstream)": Dioi *hɛn* and *kɛn* (l.t.), Sek *hin* and *khin* (l.t.) (Ged.), a doublet derived from *(N)qin (cf. Thai). OB *kən* "climb," from *(ə)[q]a/n. Li *khaan: N. Li *kha:n* "ascend," from *(a)[q]a/n (stressed form).

(VII) T *khwi "ride (horse)," from *khw[a]y<*[t]ukhay (cf. IN under VIII). Dioi *kwɔi~kɔi~kəi* (l.t.), id., from *gwoy~ *gəy<*(u)gay~*(ə)gay (unstressed form), from an earlier *(u)ŋkay~*(ə)ŋkay. Yay *kiay* (l.t.), id., from *giay<*(ə)gay (cf. Dioi). Sek *khooy* (l.t.), id. (Ged.), from *gooy (cf. Dioi). KS *i[ay]~*ć[ay], id.: Sui *ći*, Mak *se* (both l.t.), Then *kyi=ći*, from *(ń)ćay<*(ŋ)kay.

Miao: PWA *ćay (l.t.)=*tsyay "ride (horse)," from PM *dzya; also MCF *ki* (l.t.), id., from PM *ga; Yao: YCR *ke* (l.t.), YHN *ćei* (l.t.), id., from PY *ge~*je, possibly from an earlier *g[ay] or *g[əy], but more likely a b.l. from Chinese: Anc. *gʻyie*, Arch. *gʻia<*gʻyâ, originally from an AT root of the type *(a)ŋka (>*əga>*gya) (cf. I for the final, IV for the initial); the related TB loan for "ride (horse, vehicle)" is */gyân (Tibetan *zon-pa*, Kachin *jon*, Nung *zun*), with suffixed */n of either AT (cf. VI) or TB/ST origin, with the development of a secondary causative form in Tibetan following a TB canonical pattern: *s/kyân (Tibetan *skyon-pa* "to put astride upon a thing"); the related Burmese-Lolo form (*gi>*dzi "ride") retains voicing but reflects the secondary Chinese vocalism.

(VIII) IN **tukat* "climb/mount (*besteigen*)."

CLOSE   See NARROW.

CLOSE (FIST)   See SEIZE.

CLOSE (MOUTH)   See SEIZE.

CLOSE EYES, SLEEP   *iləp; *[q/]ilap; *m/i[l]əp; *m/ilap

(I)   IN **inəp* "lie down, sleep, dream."

(II)   T *hlap* "close eyes, sleep," from *q/lap. Dioi *lap ta* "close the eyes (*ta*)," *ta lap* "slumber." KS *qhlap "close eyes": Sui *khap*, Mak *lap* (h.t.); Mak also "sleep." Lk. *hep* "lie down," app. from *qhlep<*q(i)lap* (vowel influ. by *i). OB *lab* "lay down" (sic), *lab soaŋ* "sleep" (Jer.), *ləp~lap*, also (rarely) *nəp~nap* "lie down/sleep" (ic.), usu. *ləp soan~lap soan* (*soan* "sleep") (Sav.) (for the *n-* forms, cf. Li under IV).

(III)   Form. (Kuv.) *ma/i[l]əp* "sleep"; cf. also Taokas *mu-ləp*, id.

(IV)   Li *ńiap* "close the eyes": S. Li *ńiap*, from *mliap* (initial palatalized by *i)<*milap<*m/ilap.

CLOTHES   *[(N)q]ul̥uts; *[]ul̥us

(I)   IN **ulət'*, from *[q]ulut'* (stressed form). PO: Sa. *ulo* "wrap up." Form: East (Bun. Thao Kuv.) *(N)qul̥uts~*Nqul̥əts (Kuv: unstressed variant); Tsouic *ti-Nqul̥uts (Kan. Saa.)~ *[q]il̥uts (Tsou).

(II)   PM **ai̵=*ai̵ (PE: gen. MHY)~*ei̵ (MCF), from PMY *ou<*(w)u<*l̥u; PY **rui̵=l̥ui (h.t.) "shirt, clothes"; both from *[]l̥uu(y)<*[](u)l̥us.

CLOTHES, SKIRT   *[ta](m)pia[q]; *[k]u(m)piaŋ (11)

(I)   IN **tapi?* "apron (Tg.), skirt (Ml.), petticoat (NgD.), to clothe oneself (Ho.)." SEP *tapi (Aroma)~*tipi (gen.) "girdle/men's clothing" (Western Group: Kuni Kabadi "cloth"), the latter through assim. (*tapi>*tipi).

Dioi *pə* (l.t.) "clothes," from *bə<*bya<*mpya. Yay *pia* (l.t.) "skirt," from *bia (cf. Dioi). Sek *phia* (l.t.), id. (Ged.), from *bia (cf. Dioi Yay). Lq. *pie* "apron," from *pia[q].

(II) Form. (Ruk. Puy: Hinan) *kupiŋ~*kipiŋ "clothes," the latter through assim. (cf. SEP under I).

Li *viaŋ "clothes": S. Li vɛŋ, WS Li viaŋ, Loi dial. viaŋ ~vɛŋ, Bas. viaŋ, from *bwiaŋ<*(u)biaŋ<*(u)mpiaŋ. Lq. yɔŋ "skirt," from *yaŋ<*[]iaŋ. Lt. pu ve "clothes" (cf. pu he "trousers"), from *ve[ŋ]<*v[iaŋ] (cf. Li).

CLOUD^I *əm(/əm)
   Form. (Ruk. Sai.) *əm/əm (Ruk. [Ferr.] also "sky").
   PMY **ɔm "cloud" (YHN "dark, humid [weather]").

CLOUD^II *[a]wan
   IN *awan: Ml. awan.
   Li *vin: S. Li vin, N. Li vɔn.

CLOUDS See RAIN.

CLOUDY See MIST.

COAGULATE, FREEZE, THICK (LIQUIDS), CRUST
   *[(m)ba](ŋ)k[o]; *[ba]k[u]/n; *[ba](N)q[u/o]/n
(I) IN **bəku "coagulate, crust"=*bəku (Ml. bĕku "congealed, coagulated, frozen")~*baku (NgD. baku "congealed," also [Blust 1972] Minangkabau baku "coagulation"). PPN **paku "scab, congealed, dried up" (Sm. "crust, scab," To. "crust"), from *mpaku.

   Miao: PC **ŋka, PE **ńćo=*ntsyo "rice crust," from PM *ŋkuo~*ntsyuo, from PMY *ŋko~*ntsyo.

(II) Miao: MPT kho "congeal, congealed; thick (of liquids with viscosity," from PM *kh[ɔ(ŋ)], from PMY *kh[on].

(III) T *xon~*[γ]on (Si.)~*xun (Lao doublet) "coagulate, freeze; hardened, thick (liquids)," from *(N)qon. Dioi hun "hardened, rigid," from *qh[o]n. KS: Mak hun "scar (of knife wound), print (of foot)," from *[q]h[o]n (cf. Dioi).

COCONUT *[ni]yuγ (47, 48, 102)
   IN **niyuγ. PPN **niu.

   T *un (Shan), from *[ni](y)un. Li *(y)uun: S. Li u:n, N. Li dun, WS Li źoŋ<*yon, Loi dial. jun<*yun, prob. from *(u)(y)un (vocalic assim.).

COLD *[g][a]naw

IN *gənaw: Proto-Manobo (Southern Philippines) *gənaw "cold" (Bukidnon Manobo "to have chills and fever," Cagayano "chilled" (Elkins), prob. from *ganaw (stressed form).

T *hnaaw "cold, chilly (of person)," from *[g]anaw. KS *hno "cold, winter": Sui hno, Then no (h.t.), from *hn[aaw].

COLD, COOL (q/)ź[eŋ]en (14)
IN **diŋin "cool, cold."

T *ʔyen "cold, cool (weather, food)," from *q/ye(ŋ)en (with second. vowel shortening). N. Kl. ka yin "cold" (cf. Thai).

COLOR(ED), STRIPED, VARIEGATED, MARK *[ku]ray
IN **kuḷay=*kuray "color (Tg.), marbled (Ml.)."

T *laay "colored, variegated, striped, speckled, spotted" (Si. also "sign, mark"), from *(ka)lay (assim.). Dioi rai<*ra[a]y "striped (cat), motley-colored (dog), checkered (turban)." KS *[l/r]e "writing, mark": Sui Mak le, Then ze, from *[l,r][aay] (cf. Thai).

COME^I *( )ma[γi] (128)
IN **maγi. PPN **mai "motion toward speaker." Form. (Fav.) *ma[γ]i.

T *ma. Dioi ma (h.t., same series), from *hma. CT *hma. Sek ma (h.t.) <*hma. KS *hma: Sui hma, Mak Kam ma (h.t.). OB mia (Jer.), nea (h.t.) (Sav.) (palatalized). N. Kl. mo, S. Kl. xm, from Kl. *xm[u] (cf. Thai KS).

COME^II *[(N)q]alu
Form: Pai: Mak. kəlu<*kalu (stressed form); Paz. ʔalu< *qalu; both app. from *(N)qalu.

PMY **laaw=*laaw~*law (YLC), from *(-a)lu, with second. vowel lengthening.

COME See APPEAR.

COME, ARRIVE *da(n)təŋ
IN **datəŋ "come."

T *thiŋ~*thəŋ "reach, arrive (to, until)," from *thyəŋ< *(ə)təŋ (unstressed form, with second aspir.). Dioi taŋ (l.t.) "reach, arrive," from *daŋ<*ntaŋ<*(da)ntaŋ (vocalic assim.). Sek thaŋ (l.t.) "arrive" (Ged.), from *daŋ (cf. Dioi). KS: Mak taŋ "come, arrive" (cf. Dioi). Lk. taŋ (l.t.) "come," from *daŋ (cf. Dioi). OB *dɔŋ* (h.t.) "reach, arrive, until," from **tɔŋ<*taŋ* (cf. Mak). Lt: MP *thi;* BP *thi* (Rob.), *ti* (Bon.) "come," from **t(h)[əŋ].*

PMY ***daay* "come" (MPT YHN also "arrive").

COMPLETE   See JOIN.

CONFINE   See ASSEMBLE.

CONTROL   See HOLD (IN HAND, MOUTH).

COOK (IN BAMBOO CONTAINER)   **[]lam[aŋ]* (52)
   IN ***ləməŋ*, prob. from **lamaŋ* (stressed and assim. form).
T **hlaam*, from **( )(a)lam(aŋ).*
   Yao: YCR *hlam* "clf. for [internodal] sections of bamboo"< "cooking vessels."

COOK (WITH STEAM), ROAST, SINGE   **(q/)(n)draŋ-
   (/(n)draŋ); *( )tr[u]ŋ* (52, 53, 92, 106)
(I) IN ***da(n)daŋ* "to heat" (Tg. "to expose to fire or live embers to dry," TB. "singed," Ja. Ml. "steam pot"), from **daŋ-daŋ* (cf. Form.). PPN ***rara* "to heat" (Tikopian "singe," Nukuoro Sm. "roast," Rarotongan "cook food by turning over a fire"). Form. (Ami Paz.) **daŋdaŋ* "cook/ boil food."
   T **hniŋ* "cook with steam," from **q/ndiŋ<*q/ndyaŋ< *q(ə)ndaŋ*. Dioi *naŋ* (h.t.) "to stew, cook with steam," from **hnaŋ* or **hniŋ* (cf. Thai). Li **raŋ*: S. Li *daŋ* "cook (rice)," *draŋ* (d.t.) "roast (meat)"; N. Li *lɔŋ<*laŋ* "cook (rice)."
(II) T **[t]hruŋ* "cook (Kh. Si.); cook, prepare by means of fire (Shan), cook, as rice (Nung), distill, cook by steam (Lao); boil (Ahom)" (Tho form lacking). Dioi *rɔŋ* (h.t.) "cook in water," from **[th]r[u]ŋ.* Sek *ruŋ* "cook rice" (cf. Dioi), CT **thoŋ* "cook rice." KS **tuŋ* "cook (boil) rice": Sui Mak Kam *tuŋ*. OB *hoŋ* (l.t.) "cook (rice), distill (liquor)," from **[th]roŋ.*

COOL   See COLD.

COOP   See HUT.

COOP UP   See ASSEMBLE.

COPPER, BRASS   **lu[y]aŋ* (92, 93, 113, 127)
   IN ***luyaŋ* "brass" (NgD. "armlet"). Form. (Ata.) **m/laʔuŋ* "brass; armlet, bracelet," app. by metath. from **m/lu[]aŋ.*

T *dooŋ "copper (Lao BT Tho-Nung), copper/bronze (WT), brass (Ahom Kh.), gold (Si.)" (not used alone in Shan); also (Si.) *dooŋ γam "gold" (*γam "gold"<"dark/red"); (Shan Si.) *dooŋ ʔdeeŋ "copper" (*ʔdeeŋ "red"); (Shan Si.) *dooŋ hlɨaŋ "brass" (*hlɨaŋ "yellow"), an early b.l. from Ch. dʻuŋ, originally from *do(o)ŋ<*duaŋ (cf. Li)<*s/luaŋ (Ch. reg. has d-<*s/l-). Dioi luaŋ "copper," from *lu(y)aŋ. Sek luoŋ, id., from *luaŋ (cf. Dioi). KS *luaŋ, id.: Mak lu:ŋ (cf. Dioi Sek). OB hoŋ (l.t.), id., from *doŋ, a b.l. from Ch. (cf. Thai). Li *duaŋ: S. Li duoŋ, SH Loi doŋ "copper," DC Loi -doaŋ "gold" (cf. Si.), a very early b.l. via Ch. (cf. Thai).

CORD, STRING, ROPE   *(m)p[r,l]aḷi[s]
   IN **tali. PO *(n)tali: Fi. tali/a "to plait cord," ndali "string, cord, rope." PPN **ta[r,l]i "plait" (Maori tari "mode of plaiting; four-plait cord"). Form: East *ṭaḷis; Tsouic *taḷis (s₁/s₃) "rope/cord."

   T *saay "cord, string, thread, rope" (Nung also "sash, belt"), from *t[]ray<*t(a)ri[y] (with second. vowel lengthening). Dioi sai "rope," from *sa[a]y (cf. Thai). KS *[]zaay: Mak za:i (h.t.) "(ic.) cord (umbilical)," also ze (h.t.) "belt," from *[](n)saay (cf. Thai). Li *duaay: S. Li da:i "string, cord; (ic.) sash," WS Li tuai "belt/sash," SC Loi te<*ta:i "(ic.) umbilical cord," from *ntuay<*ntway<*nt[]lay<*nt(a)li[y].

CORN (MAIZE)   See RICE.

CORPSE   See SPIRIT.

COUGH, SPIT   *ka[a]k; *[(ŋ)ku]kak
   (I) T *khaak "spit, clear the throat, raise phlegm," perh. from *ka/kak.
      Yao: YHN khak "to spit (ic.)," also "phlegm (ic.)," from PY *kha[a]k.
   (II) IN **kukak=(ŋ)kukak "cough" (TB. "mucous expectoration").

COUNTRY   See VILLAGE.

COVER   See WEAR (ON HEAD).

COVER, ROOF   *(m)bu(m)buŋ

IN **bubuŋ "ridgepole": Ml. *buboŋ* "ridgepole," *bumboŋ*<
**buŋ/buŋ* "roof" (Dyen); cf. also ***t'alu(m)buŋ* "covering."
PPN **/*fufu* "ridge-pole."

T *muŋ~*vuŋ (Nung) "to cover, especially with roof" (Ahom
Nung "to thatch a house"), from *mbwuŋ<**mbu/mbuŋ*. N.
Thai *mwoŋ: Dioi *moŋ* "to cover (pot with sheets of paper),"
Yai *foŋ* (l.t.) "to roof a house" (cf. Thai).

PM **mbo "lid, roof," from PMY *mbo.

COVER, TURN UPSIDE DOWN, LID, HAT **kub/kub;*
**k/l/ub/kub;* **[(n)ta](ŋ)kub;* **[ta](ŋ)kup;* **[ta]k/l/up;*
**kəb(/kəb);* **k/l/əb(/kəb);* **[ta]kəp;* **[ta](ŋ)k/l/əp*

(I) IN **kubkub "to cover" (Ho. "turned upside down"),
perhaps from an original *kupkup via second. voicing.

Yao: PIM **kom=*kom~*kum "roof": YCR *kom*~*kum*
"to roof over; a roof," from PY *kom~**kum,* from an original
ku(u)m*<kum/kub.*

(II) IN **k/l/ubkub*: NgD. *k/ăl/ukup* "lid"; cf. also Ja.
k/r/ukub "a cover."

(III) IN ***ta(ŋ)kub* "to cover over with" (Tg. Ho. "lid");
also (Blust 1973) **[t]əkub* "cover, shut" (unstressed form). PO
**(n)taku(/(n)taku)*: Fi. *taku* "turtle shell"; also *ndaku/ndaku*
"(eye-)lid." PPN *taku: Fu. *taku* "turtle shell."

(IV) IN ***tu(ŋ)kup* "to cover" (TB. "lid"), app. from
**t[a](ŋ)kup* through vocalic assim.; cf. also (Blust 1973) **[t]ikup*
"shut, close" (Cebuano Visayan *tikup* "door or window shutter,"
tíkup "closed tight," *tik?up* [-?- unexpl.] "cover over an opening").
PO: Fi. *tuku* "to cover head with ashes."

T *kup "to patch or mend (=cover over) a hole (Shan);
large bamboo or leaf hat (= inverted lid or cover for head) (gen.
SW)." KS: Mak *kup* (l.t.) "to close (mouth, door), cover; (ic.)
a cover (of pan)," from *gup<**ŋkup.*

Miao: PW ***kau?* "hat," from PMY **kop;* Yao: YHN
plan gop (h.t.) "capsize" (*plan* "return"); YCR *gop* (h.t.) "semi-
spherical bamboo covering for chicks; to cover with same," also
"to turn over" (*bien gop* "turn upside down"), from **ŋkop;*
both from PMY **(ŋ)kop.*

(V)   T *klup* "large bamboo or leaf hat" (Tho-Nung), from *[]k/l/up* (cf. IX).

(VI)   IN **kəbkəb* "to cover" (Ja. "lid"), perhaps from an original *kəpkəp* via second. voicing (cf. I), with *u*>*ə* vowel shift through assimilation via the unstressed form: *kəkup* (note also the unstressed forms under III and VIII).

OB *khɔp kei* "to put on a lid (*kei*)."

(VII)   IN *k/l/əbkəb*: Tg. *k/al/ibkib* "crust."

(VIII)   IN *[t]əkəp* "cover, covering": Maranao *tekep* "cover with," Bikol *takóp* "lid," Ml. *tĕkap* "covering with a flat surface" (Blust 1973), app. from an original stressed form: *t[a]kəp* (cf. III).

(IX)   T *klop* "to cover (as with earth), conceal" (Si.), from *[]k/l/op;* for the semantics, cf. Fiji under IV. Dioi *kyɔp~ćɔp* "large bamboo hat," from *klɔp* (cf. V). Sek *tlo:p* "to cover the roof," from *klo:p*. KS *kl[o]p*: Mak *ćup* "bamboo hat."

PY *l̥(y)əp* "bamboo hat": YCR *lap*, YHN *gyɔp*, an early b.l. from Ch. *li*, Anc. *liəp*, Arch. *gliəp*, id., originally from the prenasalized form of the AT root: *[ta]ŋk/l/əp*.

COVER, WEAR (ON HEAD, BODY), HAT   *(qa/)[u]muk*
Form: Ata. *umuk=ʔumuk* "to cover (Eg. 1965bis); to cover the head, wear on the head (Eg. 1969)," *a/ʔumuk* "lid, cover" (Og.).

T *hmuak* "hat, cap"; also "to attire, clothe (=cover the body)" (Ahom), from *qmu[u]ak* (Thai lacks *-uua-)<*qa/-(u)muk*. Sek *muak* (h.t.) "hat" (Ged.), from *hmuak* (cf. Thai).

COVER (OVER)   See RIPEN FRUITS.

COVERING (OF HEAD)   See MANE.

CRACKED   See NOTCHED.

CROCODILE *[(m)b]uqay(/a)*
IN **buʔaya=*(m)buʔaya*. SEP *mpu[ʔ/]aya*: Wagawaga *m-ugaia*, Keherara *m-ogaia*.

T *(tă)[x]e* (SW) (Si. *tăkhe*), from *[x]ay* (vocalism influ.

by original *°q*); also *°[x]uay* "crocodile, shark" (Ahom *khroiń* =*khoi*), from *°(-u)[x]ay.*

CROOKED   See BEND/BENT.

CROW, n.   *°ak(/ak)*
   Cham *ak.*
   OB *ak* "crow," *ak/ak* "(ic.) to croak." Li *°aak*: S. Li *aˀ*, WS Li *eˀ*, WS Loi *ɛ-ɛ* (cf. OB), DC Loi *ɛk*, SH SC Loi *ɛt*, from *°(ak)ak.* Laha: TU *ə:k* (cf. Li).

CROW, v.   See SPEAK.

CROW, v/n.   See CALL (OF BIRDS/ANIMALS).

CROWD   See GATHER(ED).

CRUST   See COAGULATE.

CRUSTACEAN, SHRIMP   *°qu(n)zaŋ*
   IN *°°huɗaŋ~°°u(n)ɗaŋ=°ˀu(n)ɗaŋ* "crustacean" (Tg. "lobster," TB. "shrimp," Ja. Ml. NgD. Ho. "crab and other crustaceans"). PPN *°ˀura* "crustaceans."
   OB *zoaŋ* "shrimp; (ic.) lobster" (irreg. l.t.), from *°[ˀ]duaŋ*< *°[q/](u)ɗaŋ.* WS Li *fiaŋ* "shrimp," app. from *°fuaŋ* (dissim.) <*°hrwaŋ*<*°h(u)raŋ.*

CRY (OF ANIMALS), BARK, THUNDER   *°lo[l]oŋ*; *°lo[l]oŋ(/a)*
   (I)   IN *°°luluŋ* "to bark," perh. from *°lunuŋ* by assim. (cf. II).
   T *°rooŋ* "to cry (esp. of animals), call," from *°ro(r)oŋ*; also *°va rooŋ* "thunder" (Si.)="the cry (*°rooŋ*) of the heavens" (*°va*). KS: Mak *zuŋ pya* "thunder" (*°pya* "thunder, lightning"), from *°ruŋ.*

   (II)   Form. (Atayalic) *°luluŋ* "cloud," app. for "thunderstorm cloud"="the crier (thunderer)"; also Paz. *ruluŋ* "cloud," app. a loan from Atayalic (Sed. *ruluŋ*); also (Tsouic) *°luluŋa* "cloud" (Saa.), *°[s]u-luluŋa* "thunder" (Kan. Saa.) (n.a.), app. from *°luluŋ/a* by assim.
   Li *°l[oo]ŋ*: Bas. *niam loaŋ* "thunder" (cf. WS Li *ńa:m*, id.), app. from an original *°lo(l)oŋ* (assim.; cf. Tsouic).

CRY OUT, CALL   *°γiyak*
   IN *°°iyak=°γiyak* "cry out" (Tg. *iyak* is irregular; cf. Blust 1970: n. 50, who adds Kadazan *gizak* "cry, scream, yell").

T *riak "to call, name" (Shan also "say"); alsơ *briak "to cry, vociferate" (Si.), from *b/riak. Lq. dek<*rek, Pu-peo riek "weep."

CULTIVATE (FIELD), FIELD, WORK *[(m)bu]hat (38, 39, 95)

IN **buhat=*(m)buhat "to produce, perform" (Ml. "produce, cultivate"); also (Prentice) Kadazan -buvat "till the soil." PO **puat/a "harvest." Form. (Thao) *buhat "field (wet, rice)," *m/buhat "to work"<"to work the fields."

T *het "to do, make, work," *het na "to cultivate ricefields (*na)."

PMY **ay "to do, make" (YHN also "to cultivate fields"), from *[bu](h)ay.

CULTIVATE (FIELD), FIELD, WORK, YAM, SWEET POTATO *[(N)q]um[ah]; *[(N)q]um/al[/ah] (11, 105)

(I) IN **huma=*[?]uma "cultivated field" (Ml. huma "cultivated land, dry rice fields," bĕr/huma "to cultivate such fields"). PO **?uma "garden; to work, to plant, to clear ground." Form: East (Pai. Puy. Ami Bun. Sir. Fav.) *qumah (Dyen: H) and (Sai.) *qum/qumah "field (swidden, dry)"; Puy. also ic. "field (wet, rice)"; also (Paz.) *quma/mah, (Ruk.) *qumu/umah (vocalic assim.) id.; also (Ami Sir.) *m/qumah "to work"="to work the fields"; Tsouic (Kan.) *[q]uma[h] and (Saa.) *[q]um/-[q]uma[h] "field (swidden, dry)"; Atayalic (Ata: Squliq) *qumah "to work the field," *m/qumah, id.; also (Sed.) *kumu- "work" (kumpah~kəmpah, but komopach in Bullock 1874) and "field (swidden, dry)" kəmpahan from *Nqumu[h]<*Nquma[h] (vocalic assim.; cf. Ruk.).

(II) PPN **kumala "sweet potato"="the cultivated crop," from *kum/al/a<*Nqum/al/a[h]; for the semantics, cf. Ml. huma "cultivated land" (under I), pĕr/huma/n "cultivated land, the crops raised"; also IN **kali "dig"; SEP *kali, id. (Panyati "dig yams"); Form. *kali~*k/m/ali "dig," E. Ruk. kali "yam"; also PPN **hamo "to plant, set in soil" (Tuamotuan); sweet potato variety (Hawaiian Maori). Form. (Ata: Squliq) *qum/al/ah "field (swidden, dry)"="the cultivated land"; also (Ata: Ci'uli) *[qu]m/[q]um/al/ah "field (swidden, dry)."

T *man "potato, sweet potato, yam" (generic term). Dioi *man* "yams, potatoes." Sek *man* "yam." Li *mwal* "sweet potato": S. Li *va:i*, N. Li *muon*, Bup. *mɔn*, SH Loi *mon*, WS Loi *maŋ* <*man*, SC Loi *man*, DC Loi *man-mai* (<*mal/mal;* cf. the reduplicated forms under I), from *(u)mal*.

CUP, BOWL *[ma](ŋ)kok

IN **maŋkuk "cup" (Tg. "bowl," Ml. "cup, bowl, basin").

T *kook "cup for drinking (Kh.); cup, bowl, small vessel; concavity (Shan); pipe (Lao BT)," but Ahom "water pot, pitcher," also "horn" (perh. the earlier meaning); Si. "to draw out humors (from the body, as in cupping), suck out (as blood, milk)"; WT "piece of bamboo used for cupping," prob. from *(-o)kok (vocalic assim.); Dioi *kɔ lau* "mug (*godet*) for drawing up wine (*lau*)," *baŋ kɔ* "end of the horn of a young bull used as a cupping-glass (*pour se ventouser*)" (*baŋ* "tube"), from *kɔk;* cf. Ahom for the semantics. Lq. *kəuk* "horn" (cf. Ahom), a poss. loan from Ch. *kɔk*<*kuk*.

Yao: YHN *kok* "glass (for drinking)," an app. loan from Thai.

CURRENT See STREAM.

CUT *[kə]tats

IN *kə[t]at' "cut": Tiruray *ketas* "cut something with a knife," Iban *ketas* "cut (a knot, something taut)" (Blust 1973).

T *tat "to cut (wood, bamboo, grass, paper, string), cut off (head, leg, paper), hew." Dioi *tat* "cut, cut off."

CUT, CHOP *tak(/tak); *t[ə]k/t[ə]k

(I) Form: Paz. *ta:tatak* "to cut (grass, weeds)," from *ta/ta[k]-tak;* also Sed. *təmatak*, id., from *t/m/atak*.

Li *thak:* WS Li *thak* "cut asunder (something suspended)," WS Loi *thak* "cut."

(II) IN **təktək "chop off" (Ml. "chop, hack, give a cutting blow with a knife or sword"), probably an old derivative of the root under (I) through reduplication and unstressing: *tə/tək/tak<*tə/tak/tak (cf. Pazeh under I). Form: Ruk. *wa/təktək* "to cut person)"; also Puy: Rikavong *ətək*, id. (app. abbreviated form).

CUT, SLICE *x[i]lis; *x[i]lits; *x[i]ris; *x[i]rits

(I)   Form. (Ata.) *qilis* "a cut, wound."

(II) T *lit∼*liit* (Lao) "to cut off/away, trim, dismantle, un-sew," from *(-i)lit*. Dioi *lit*<*liit* "dismantle, unsew, take apart (house)," *lit* (d.t.)<*lit* "to thin out (woods)," from *(-i)lit* (cf. Thai).

PM **hl[a]ʔ* "to cut [grass, rice, throat]" (MPT "to cut, slice, cut with slicing motion"), from PMY *hl[et]*.

(III) Form. *q/m/əris* "to cut (grass, weeds) (Pai.); to cut (person) (Sai.)," from *q/m/iris* (stressed form).

(IV) IN **hiḷit'=*hirit'* "to cut up fine" (Ml. "to slice, cut fine, hash").

CUT DOWN/OFF, FALL DOWN/OFF, BREAK DOWN/OFF, COLLAPSE   *(N)qa(m)pak; *qa(m)paŋ; *[ta](m)bak; *[ta]baŋ

(I)   IN **ka(m)pak=*(ŋ)ka(m)pak* "strike with a crash, ax" (Ho. *kapa* "to fell").

T **ʔbak∼**ʔbaak* (Si. Nung) "to cut" (Kh. "to cut with downward blow," Nung "to cut, fell"), from *q(a)mpak*.

(II) T **ʔbaaŋ* "to be broken off; a (broken off) part," from *q(a)mpaŋ*. KS *paŋ* "collapse": Sui Mak *paŋ*.

PMY **(m)paaŋ* "fall in" (YCR "collapse, fall over [house, tree]"), from *(a)mpaŋ*.

(III) IN **təbak* "chopping knife [bolo] (Tg.); to clear forest (=chop down trees) (TB)," from *tabak* (stressed form). Form. (Paz.) *m/tamak* "cut (person)," from */tambak*.

T *vak* "to cut, chop, mince," from *bwak*<*[]bak (labi-alized), perh. from *[ta]ba/bak*.

(IV) IN **təbaŋ* "to cut down/off, fell," from *tabaŋ* (stressed form). PPN **tafa* "cut."

T *baŋ* "break down, fall into ruins." S. Li *baŋ* "broken (*cassé, brisé*), torn."

Miao: PE **pai* (l.t.) "fall in" (MCF "fall"), from PMY *b[uŋ]*.

CUT OFF, BREAK OFF, CASTRATE, SHORT   *[(m)p]o(n)doḷ; *[(m)p]otoḷ

(I) IN **pu(n)dul=*(m)pu(n)dul* "cut off." PPN **mutu* "cut off, ended," app. from **mbundul* (second. voicing of initial).

(II) IN **pu\ṭul* "break off, cut off," app. for **pu\ṭul* (Ja. *pu\ṭul* "broken off"). Form. (Bun.) **ma/pu\ṭul* "short"; (Sed.) **bu\ṭul*, id., from **mpu\ṭul*.

    T **toon* "castrate" (Shan also "break off the head of a plant"), from **(-o)ton*. Dioi *tɔn* "castrate, amputate." KS: Mak *ton* "castrate [fowl]," a prob. loan from Thai. OB *dun kɔi* "castrate [fowl=kɔi], kɔi dɔn* "capon" (both h.t.), from **tɔn*.

CUT OFF/UP **[t]a(m)pats*

    IN **[t]a(m)pat'* "cut, lop off": Tg. *tapás* "dehusking of coconuts," Cebuano Visayan *tapas* "cut sugarcane and clean it of its leaves," Ml. *tampas* "lop off," Iban *tampas* "piece of yam, etc. cut for planting" (Blust 1973).

    T **paat* "cut (the body), cut off (as in reaping), cut up (food; into slices), cut open (as the stomach)," from **[](a)pat*. Li **p(h)[a]t* "cut grass": S. Li *fɔt*, WS Li *pat*.

CYCLE (TIME) See WHEEL.

D

DAMP See WET.

DAMPEN See DIP.

DARK See RAIN.

DARK, BLACK, SHADE **q[o](n)zəm(/(n)zəm); *q[o](n)zam*
(I) IN **dədəm* "dark" (Tg. "shade"), an abbreviated form from an original **(ʔu)də[m]/(ʔu)dəm* (cf. Form.); cf. also **tidəm* "dark" (NgD. "black"). PO **ndo/ndo*: Fi. *ndrondro* "place of refuge (=dark place)." PPN *lolo*: To. *lolo* "shade, darkness," from **ndondo*. Form. **ma/qu[z]əm* "black (Thao Sir.), darkness (Fav.)"; (Puy.) **quzə/quzəm* "black"; (Pai.) **qəzəməzəmət* "evening," from **qəzəm/[q]əzəm/at* (unstressed form); also Saa. *səəsəma* "darkness," from **[qə]zə/[q]əzəm/a*.

(II) T **ʔdam* "black, dark." Sek *ram* (h.t.) "black" (Ged.), from **ʔram*. KS **ʔnam* "black": Sui *ʔnam*, Mak Kam Then *nam* (all h.t.), from **ʔnzam;* Mak also *ʔdam* "shade; dark (=cloudy)."

Lk *lam* (h.t.) "black," from *°ʔlam.* OB *lam* (Jer.), *zɔm* (h.t.)
(Sav.), id., from *°ʔdam* or *°ʔzam.* Li *°d[oo]m,* id.: S. Li *dɔm,* WS
Loi and N. Li dials. *dam,* WS Li *tam,* perhaps from *°[qo]dam*
(assim.). Lq./Lh. *°[][z]am,* id.: Lq. *dɔm,* Pu-peo *dam,* Lh: TU
lam. Kl. *°la[m],* id.: N. Kl. *laŋ,* S. Kl. *the luo.* Lt. *°(n)[z]am,* id.:
MP *lam,* BP *lam le* (Rob.), *ńă* (Bon.).

DARK, FOG/MIST, GLOOMY, SHADE/SHADY, BLACK,
 NIGHT *°(ma/)[i]ləm(/ləm)*
 IN *°(ʔ)iləm(/ləm):* Ml. *ilamlam* "hazy, vague," Palawan
Batak *ma/ʔiləm,* Mukah *b-ilem,* Kapuas, Baʼamang, Katingan
ba-bilɛm "black" (forms cited by Blust 1973 under No. 255);
also *°°ləmləm* "gloomy" (Tg. "mist"), an abbreviated form; also
°°maləm (*~°aləm* through metanalysis) "night," app. from
°ma/[i]ləm (cf. Palawan Batak). PO: Motu *malo* "middle of
the night" (cit. by Blust 1973), from *°malə[m].* Form: Kan.
°ta/əl̥əm "black," from *°/iləm* (vocalic assim.); also Saa. *°məl̥əm-*
"fog/mist," from *°m[a]/il̥əm* (cf. Palawan Batak).
 T *°rom* "shade" (WT also "shady"). Dioi *ram* "to shade" (s.t.),
app. through assim. from *°(ma/)[i]rəm* (cf. Palawan Batak).

DARK, NIGHT, EVENING, BLACK, RED, PURPLE *°[]kam;*
 °[]k/l̥/am; °()(ŋ)kəm; °()(ŋ)k/l̥/əm
(I) T *°kam* "dark in color, between blue and black, purple
(Kh. Shan); black, dark (Lao); black (blackened accidentally),
dirty (WT); violet (Nung: cw. ʻredʼ); color of blood, red (Si.)";
cf. also T *°[x]am* "dark, shady, cloudy (Tho-Nung); secret,
hidden (Si.)," KS *°qam* "dark (red)"; also T *°ɣam<°Gam*
"evening, night," Dioi *ham* (l.t.) "evening," KS *°ʔńam<°ʔŋam<*
°ʔNGam, id., OB *da-kom~da-kəm,* id. (Jer.), *kiem* (l.t.) "night"
(Sav.); note also the app. infixed forms (Si. only): *°[g,ɣ]lam*
"rather dark, darkly" and *°[g,ɣ]ram* (d.t.) "blackening, dark,
deteriorated."
 Yao: YHN *siʔ kam* "violet" (*siʔ* "red"), perhaps a loan/b.l.
from Ch. *kâm* "deep purple, violet."
(II) T *°klam* "bright cherry red" (Si.). Dioi *kyam~ćam* "violet," from *°klam.*
 Yao: YHN *klam tou* "soot"="the black (*klam*) of fire
(*tou*)."

(III) T *k[i]m* "gold" (Nung *kem*)="the dark/red (metal)," a b.l. from Ch. *kiə̂m*, from an original AT *kəm;* cf. also T *γam* (d.t. from root under I) "gold," from *Gam*, a doublet of *qam* (under I), Sek *gam*, Lq. *gəm*, perhaps also Lt. *kha*, id., but most KD languages show b.l. forms for "gold": Dioi *kim*, Mak *ćim*, Kam *tyəm=ćəm*, OB *kɔm* (Jer.), *kim* (Sav.), S. Li *khim*, WS Li *kɛm;* for the semantics, cf. NgD. *bulao* "gold"<IN **bulaw* "red."

PY *dzyəm* (h.t.): YCR *dziem* (h.t.) "twilight, dark," YHN *jɔm* "dark [sky, house]; night, evening," from PMY *ntsyəm*, from an earlier *ŋkəm*.

(IV) IN **kələm* "dark" (NgD. "waning of moon"). Cham *klam* "evening," from *k[]l[ə]m*.

PM **klu(ŋ)* "black, blue" (regularly "black"; MPT [Sav.] also "dirty"), from PMY *kl[əm]*; Yao: YHN *glɔm* (h.t.) "dark (weather)," from PMY *ŋklɔm*.

DARK-COLORED See RED.

DAWN See LIGHT.

DAY, SUN, SKY *( )(ŋ)waRi*

IN **waγi=*waRi* "day" (**mata waRi* "sun"="eye of the day"). Form. (Ruk. Bun. Sir.) *waγi* "sun" (indeterm. *w*).

T *wan~*ŋwan* (Li 1956) "day" (*ta wan* "sun"="eye of the day"), with *ŋ*- perh. a secondary development (cf. Dioi). Dioi *ŋon* "day," *kyaŋ-ŋon* "sun" (cf. *kyaŋ-laŋ* "sky"), from *ŋwan*. Sek *ńan* "day," app. from *ŋwan* (cf. Dioi). KS *(?)wan* "day": Sui *wan*, Mak *van*, Kam *man* (all h.t.), Then *wan* (l.t.). Lk. *wan* "day," *wan-~ŋan-* (s.t.) (ic.), perh. from an original *ŋwan* (cf. Dioi Sek); also *tau wan* "sun" (*tau*<"sky"; see SUN). OB *won* "sun," *da-wən* "day-time" (Jer.), *bɔn* "day," *da-bɔn* "sun"= "eye (*da*) of the day," from *wan*. Li *ven* "day" (*sa ven* "day" ="eye (*sa*) of the day"): S. Li *ven*, WS Li *vaŋ*<*van*, N. Li *van*. Lq. *vuon* "sun," *pə/vuon* "day" (cf. *nen* "moon," *pə/nen* "night") (Bon.), *mo ven* "sun" (Laj.) (*mo*<"sky"). N. Kl. *vlei* "sky," from *v[]Ri*, but S. Kl. *du vuə* "sun" (cf. *du die* "moon," *du dɛ* "star"). Lt: MP *lam va* "sun"; BP *wua* (Rob.), *na ma* (Bon.), id. (n.a.); BP also *ŋua* "day" (cf. Dioi Sek).

DEAF *(n)tul[i]ak(/tul[i]ak)*

IN **tuli* "ear-ache, deaf" (Tg. *tu/tuli* "ear-ache, ear-wax," from **tuli/tuli*), app. from an original **tuli[ak]*. PO: Fi. *tule=ndule* "ear-ache." PPN **tuli* (Sm. *tuli/tuli*).

T **hnuak*, from **q/nduak*, app. through secondary nasalization from an earlier **q/duuak<*q/ntu(r)úak<*q/ntu(r)iak* (vocalic assim.). N. Thai **[h]nuuk*: Dioi Yay *nuk*, Sek *nuuk* [h.t.] (Ged.) (cf. Thai). KS **ʔdak*: Sui *ʔdak~dak*, Mak *ʔdak*, Then Kam *lak* (all h.t.), from **ʔdwak<*q/ntu(r)uák* (contrasting stress). Lk. *yak* (h.t.), from **hrak<*[]rwak<*[]ruák*. OB *lak* (Jer.), *lɔk* (h.t.) "blind" (cw. "eye") (Sav.), from **hlak* (cf. Lk.); for the semantics, cf. IN **budu* "dumb (mute)," Form. (Sed.) **m/budu* "blind." Li **[t]hluak*: S. Li *dak*, WS Li *thoŋ hluʔ* (n.a.), from **t[]luak*. Lq. *lak* "blind" (cw. "eye") (cf. OB).

PM **(h)lɔŋ*: MCF *hlɔŋ* (irreg. l.t.), MCh. *laŋ*, MPT *laŋ* (Sav.), *la* (Heim.), from PMY **(h)luaŋ*; Yao **duaŋ* (h.t.), from PMY **ntuaŋ*; both from an earlier **(n)tluaŋ*, from an earlier reduplicated form: **(n)tluaŋ/tluak<*(n)tluak/tluak*, with **u* for **i* through vocalic assim., as in KD.

DECANT See POUR.

DECAY(ED) (WORMEATEN) See MOULD(Y).

DEEP   **(q/)(n)za[l][ə]m*
IN **daləm=*(n)daləm~*dalam* (NgD. doublet, through vocalic assim.) "inner, deep/depth." PO **lalom* "inner": Fi. *lom/a-*, Sa. *lalo-*, from **[nd]alom* through assim. PPN **lalo* "below, under" (Demp. also "deep"), from **ndalo[m]*. Form: Fav. *lallum* "in/inside," from **lal[ə]m* (cf. PO).

T **ʔdam* "deep (as a hole)" (Si. "to be drawn toward the bottom"), from **ʔd(ar)am<*ʔd(ar)əm* through vocalic assim. (cf. NgD.).

DEEP, DEPTH (WATER)   **(n)tu[biɣ]*
IN **[t]ubiɣ* "water depth" (cf. English *the deep*).
MY **(n)to=*(n)to* (PM PIM)~**(n)tu* (YHN) "deep."

DEER See FLESH/MEAT (four entries).

DEER, CATTLE, BUFFALO   **(q/)lu(w)aŋ; *[k/]lu(w)aŋ*
(I) IN **(ʔ/)nuaŋ*; Proto-Philippine **(ʔə)nuáŋ* "carabao" (Zorc

1974). Form. (Pai: Tokubun Shimopaiwan Kapiyan; E. Ruk: Taramakau; W. Ruk. Paz. Sir. Fav.) *luaŋ "cattle" (Ferr. also "buffalo"); (Bun.) *qa/luaŋ "deer (Cervus [Rusa] unicolor Swinhoii), cattle," whence Thao qnu:waŋ "deer, buffalo" as a loan (Bunun *l>n).

(II) T *kwaaŋ "kind of deer" (Shan "sambhur," Si. "hog-deer: Cervus porcinus"), from *klwaaŋ<*k(a)lawaŋ<*ka/luwáŋ (vocalic assim., with stress as in Proto-Philippine); also *klook "deer" [generic term] (Nung), from *kluak<*k/lúaŋ (consonantal assim., with different stress). Sek vuaŋ "hog-deer," from *(u)waŋ. OB toaŋ=twaŋ "goat/sheep," from *kwaŋ, app. with semantic contamination from the AT root for GOAT, q.v. Laha: TU wa:ŋ "deer," from *(a)waŋ (vocalic assim.). Lt:MP ui, BP ue (Rob.), kue (Bon.), id., from *(k/)w[aŋ].

DEMON See SPIRIT.

DEN, LAIR *[γu]mu[n]
    IN *γumun.
    T *muŋ, app. from *(γ-)mun through assim. to initial *γ-.
Dioi məŋ.

DENSE See THICK.

DEPTH See DEEP/DEPTH (WATER).

DESCEND See RECEDE.

DESIRE *k[ə]l[a]ŋ
    IN **kələŋ, app. from *kəlaŋ (through assim.). PPN **kolo "desire, intend."
    T *khraŋ "according to the desire" (Si.).

DESIRE, HUNGRY *[p]iya[ak] (13)
    IN **pi[y]a "desire." PPN **fia "desire, want"; also Fi. via/kana, Sm. fia/ʔai "to be hungry"="desire to eat."
    T *ʔyaak "to wish, desire; to be hungry (also thirsty)." N. Thai *ʔyiak "hungry," from *(-i)yaak. KS *ʔyiak, id.: Sui *ʔyak ~yak~ʔyi:k, Mak ʔi:k, from *(-i)yaak, as in N. Thai; also *ʔyaak, id.: Kam Then ya:k (h.t.), as in Thai. OB zɔk (h.t.) "hunger," from *ʔyɔk<*ʔya[a]k (cf. Thai).

DEW, FROST, SNOW *hamuγ; *[h/]l/amuγ; *ham/l/uγ

(I) IN *hamuɣ: Tg. *hamog* "dew" (cited by Demp. under **lamuɣ); also (Zorc 1972) *hamʔuɣ, id., from *ʔ/hamuɣ.

T *hmuay "snow (Kh.); frost, hoar-frost, snow (Shan); frost, fog, snow (Ahom)," from *h(a)muy; also *hmiay "fog, dew (BT); dew, very fine crachin rain, snow (WT)," from *hmyay<*h(ə)muɣ (unstressed form).

(II) IN **lamuɣ "dew, atmospheric precipitate" (Ja. *lamur* "dew"), from *[h/]l/amuɣ.

(III) Chuang *nai (h.t.) "snow," from *hnay<*hmlay< *h(a)ml[u]y<*h(a)m/l/uy (cf. KS). KS *hnuy "snow": Mak Kam *nui,* Then *nuei* (all h.t.), from *hmlui (cf. Chuang). Lk. *kyɋi,* id., from *hnai (cf. Chuang). Li *hmluaŋ: S. Li *muŋ* "snow, hail, frost," WS Li *hluaŋ* "snow," from *h(a)mluŋ<*h(a)m/l/uŋ.

DIE, KILL   *(ma/)play; *[pa/]play (21, 22, 36, 72, 119)

(I) IN **matay=*matəy "to die, be dead." PPN **mate "die." Form: East *matay (Pai. Bun. Sai. Thao Fav.); *m/n/atay (Puy.); Tsouic *matsay~*ma/matsay "die."

T *taay (SW)~*traay (Tho-Nung) "die," from *[m](a)pray. Dioi *tai,* id., from *ta[a]y (cf. Thai). Sek *praːi,* id. KS *tay, id.: Sui Mak Then *tai,* Kam *tei* (cf. Thai Dioi). Lk. *plei,* id., from *play. OB *dai* (h.t.), id., from *tay (cf. KS). Li: Bup. *laːd~ loːd,* id., app. from *laay<*[p]laay, from *[m](a)play (cf. Thai). Lq. *tie,* id., from *tyay. Kl. *ple u,* id. (n.a.), from *płay[]. Lt: Bp *pe* (Rob.), *phi* (Bon.), id., from *p[r]ay (with *r>h); also MP *pien,* id., perh. with secondary nasalization from an original nasal prefix: *m/pray>*mpye>*pien.

PMY **day "die," from *tay (initial voicing).

(II) IN **patay=*patəy "to die, be dead" (semantic merging with *matəy; cf. the partial merging in Formosa). Form: East *patay "kill (Fav.), die (Kuv.)"; *pa/patay "kill" (Pai.); *p/n/atay "kill" (Puy.); *ma/patay "die" (Sir.); *ma/patay "die," but *mi/patay "kill" (Ami); *wa/patay "die" [Ferr.]~ "kill" [Og.-As.] (E. Ruk.); Tsouic *[q]a/patsay "kill" (Tsou); *pi/[q]a/patsay "die," but *mi/[q]a/patsay "kill" (Kan.); *pa/- patsay~*pa/pa/patsay "kill" (Saa.).

PMY *tay "kill," from *(p/)tay.

DIFFICULT   *pa(n)yaq(/pa(n)yaq) (17)

IN **payaʔ "difficult" (Ml. "difficult, heavy, severe [as work or sickness]").

T *yaak "difficult, laborious, hard, poor, miserable," from *(-a)yak; also *hńaap "difficult (Kh.); hard, difficult, arduous (Shan); distress (Ahom); coarse, rough (Nung); fibrous, hard to chew (food), hard to open, turn or manipulate (WT); thick, concrete (Si.); rude, uncivil (Si. Lao)," from *(pa)nya/p(anyaq). Dioi dya~dyak "difficult, laborious; bad, wicked," from *ya(a)k; also ńat~ńɛt "laborious, difficult; ill-tempered and avaricious," from *(pa)nyaq/p[anyaq] (cf. Thai). KS: *[h]yak: Mak yak (h.t.) "diligent/laborious"; also *hńak: Sui hńak-hńan "rough, coarse"; both from an original *h(n)yak. Li *yaak: S. Li yaʔ "bad, wicked, cruel, difficult"; also *[n]eek: S. Li tek, WS Li teʔ, SH Loi dɛ:k, SC Loi dɛk, Ki dyĕ "bad" (vocalic influ. by original *-q), from *(n)yak.

DIG   See HOLE (two entries); SCRATCH (three entries).

DIG INTO, THRUST INTO, PLANT, GARDEN   *tsu(w)an; *tsu/l/an (11, 37, 38, 94)

(I) IN **t'uwan "digging stick" (TB. "to plant"). PO **sua(ŋ) =*sua(n) "clear a field, dig roots, hoe, pestle." PPN **sua "to clear a field, hoe (To.); to dig up the soil (Sm.)" (Walsh/Biggs include under **sua certain forms cognate rather with IN **t'ual "lever"; cf. Milner, who regards these two IN roots as a doublet pair; see LEVER).

T *suan "to thrust into the anus" (Si.).

(II) T *suan "garden (=the planted/dug up place)," from *su(r)an<*su[/r/]an. N. Thai *[sr]ian, id.: Dioi sə:n, Giay sian, Yay θian, but Cao-lan lun, Ts'un lin~yin, from *sryan<*s(ə)ran (unstressed form). KS *swian=*swyan, id.: Sui fyan~hyan~fiən, Mak fi:n, Then wyaan, from *suyan<*suran<*su/r/an.

DIP, DAMPEN, SOAK   *ćəm/ćəm; *ćam/ćam; *ć[u]m/ć[u]m

(I) IN **k'əmk'əm "dampen."

T *ćom "to immerse, be submerged, sink" (Shan also "to dip in water"), from *(ćom/)ćom. Li *ć[ə]m: S. Li ćom cɔŋ "plunge a cloth into indigo dye" (n.a.).

(II) T *ćam* "sponge up, sop up" (WT), from *(ćam/)ćam*. KS *ćam*: Mak *sam* "dip into."

Yao: YHN *ćam* "soak, macerate, ret (hemp)."

(III) T *ćum* "dip (in liquid)," "soak"; cf. also *ćup* "soak" (Lao) but *jup* (general Thai) "soak, dampen." N. Thai *ćum~*jum* "dip, soak, soaked," from *(cu)mcum*.

DIP, DIPPER, GOURD, BOTTLE *(n)ta(m)[b]u(/(n)ta(m)-[b]u)

IN **tabu=*ta(m)bu* "dipper": Tg. *tabo* "dipper made from coconut shell," TB *tabu/tabu* "bottle-gourd," Ja. *tawu<*tabu* "to dip water," *tabon<*tambu/an* "coconut shell," Ho. *tavu* "bottle-gourd," *tavu-ara* "water bottle." Form: Ata. *taqo* "gourd dipper," from *ta[b]u*.

T *taw* "gourd" (Shan also "bottle"), from *(tabu/)tabu*.

Yao: YCR *dam* (h.t.) "to ladle out; to dip out [water; fish with net; vegetables]," from PMY *ntam*, from *(ntambu/)ntambu* (note the preservation of the earlier meaning, as in Ja.). Miao: MPT *tau* "gourd, pumpkin" is a loan from Thai.

DIP UP, DRAW (WATER), EXTRACT *()taqak[i] (54)

PO and PPN **taʔaki* "extract (general PN); take out (food from fire, eel-trap from water) (Maori); draw water (Fi. Rotuman)."

T *tak~*tek* (Shan doublet)~*tet* (Ahom) "to draw, dip up (water, rice)," from *ta(q)ak* (vowel and final influ. by *q*). Dioi *tak* "draw up (water from a well, rice from a pot)." KS *taq* "draw water": Sui *te*, Mak *tak* (cf. vocalism in Thai).

DIRT *(N)q[a]lay (25)

PO **ŋkele* "dirt, dirty, black" (Fi. *qele* "earth"), from *ŋkəlay* (unstressed form).

T *γlay* "body dirt (SW), dandruff (Nung)," from *Glay <*Nq[]lay*. Dioi *hi~i* (l.t.) "body dirt," from *G[l]ay* (vocalic influ. by *G*) (cf. Thai). Sek *γi* "dirt" (cf. Dioi). KS *[]zaay* "dirt": Sui *zai*, Mak *za:i* (both h.t.), from *[][Gl]aay<*[]G(a)lay* (cf. Thai). OB *kɔi* (l.t.), from *gɔi<*[Gl]ɔi* (cf. Thai).

Yao: YHN *kla:i* "body dirt, scurf, dandruff," from PMY *[q]laay*, from an earlier *q(a)lay*.

DIRT (OF BODY/SKIN) *(n)da[k]i (25)

   IN **[dḍ]ak[i]. PO *ndaki: Fi. ndraki "bad (=dirty) weather."
T *nay (Nung), from *nday=*ndai<*nda(k)i.

DIRTY, FILTH(Y) *s[ə]lup; *[q/]s[i]lap

(I)   Form. (Ata.) *səlup "filth, refuse" (indeterm. s).

   Yao: PIM **hlop "dirty" (Haud. cites *hlup) (YCR also
"filthy"), from PY *hlop (PKM cognate lacking).

(II)   Form. (Kuv.) *pa/q[]silap "dirty."

DISH See TROUGH.

DISGUST, NAUSEA *[q/]iba; *[q/]iba/i; *[q/]ipa/i (15, 16)

(I)   T **ʔbia, from **ʔbya<*q/(i)ba. KS **ʔbia=**ʔbya: Sui
ʔbya~bya~ʔbiə, Mak ʔbi (cf. Thai).

(II)   IN **ibay=*[ʔ]ibay, from **ʔiba/i.

(III)   T *phiay "disgust" (Si.), from *phyay<*[q](i)pay (second. aspir. by the *q/), from *q/ipa/i.

DISTRIBUTE See DIVIDE.

DIVIDE, DISTRIBUTE *(q/)biyak; *(q/)bi[y]aŋ; *piyak

(I)   IN **biyak "to be divided, separated."

   T **ʔbiak "distribute" (Si.).

(II)   T **ʔbeeŋ "divide, share, distribute," from **ʔbiaŋ<
*q/bi[y]aŋ.

(III)   IN **piyak "to be divided, separated," a doublet of
**biyak (under I).

DOG *[wa]kləwm[a] (128)

   IN **at'u=*Wat'u: Niala (West Ceram: Piru) wasu (Dyen
1962), app. from *Watsu(ma). Form: East *[W]atsu; also (Puy.)
tsu/an; Tsouic *[W]a[ts]u (Tsou); Atayalic *hu-, from *tsu-.

   T *hma, from *[khr]ma. Dioi ma (h.t.), from *hma. Sek ma
(h.t.) (Ged.) (cf. Dioi). KS *hma: Sui hma, Mak Then ma,
Kam ŋwa (all h.t.) (cf. Thai). Lk. khwq, from *khma. OB ma
(h.t.), from *hma. Li *ma: S. Li ma, WS and N. Li pa. Lq.
mə (Bon.), ma (Laj.). N. Kl. mu, S. Kl. xmə (Bon.), hem (Laj.),
from Kl. *x[]mə<*khma (cf. Thai). Lt: MP mg=m; BP lim
(Rob.), mu (Bon.), from Lt. *l[]mu<*(k)l[]ma (cf. MYT).

PMY ****klu=*kḷəw** (YCR *klu*, YHN *klo*); also **kḷ[um]*; MYT *lyq<*lyǫ* (cf. PT *yaŋ*); from an original **[]kḷəw(ma)~*[]-kḷəwm(a)*.

DONE (PAST TENSE) See PASS.

DOOR **ta[b][a]; *[pi](n)ta[b]u; *[pi](n)tə[b]u*

(I) Form. W. Ruk. *briŋi-tawa, baleŋe-tabanu*, from **-taba(nu)*; for the first element, cf. Pai. *baliŋ* "door," Ata. *bəliŋ* "hole, cave"; cf. also Sir. *ŋataf* (Gravius 1661), *natap* (Bullock 1874) "door."

(II) Form. Thao *pitaw*, from **pitab[u]*.
OB *dau*, from **[]ntaw<*[]nta[b]u*.

(III) IN ****pin[t]u**, from **pintəu<*pintəb[u]*. Form. Puy. *apitoun=*qapitun* (Bullock 1874), from **qapitəb[u]n;* for the final -*n*, cf. W. Ruk. under I.

T **tu;* often used in the compound **paak tu* (**paak* "mouth/opening"), from **[]tub(u)<*[]təb(u)* (assim.); Si. has *prătu* (cf. W. Ruk. under I). Dioi *tu;* Chuang *tu~to* (cf. KS). Sek *tu*. KS **to:* Sui Mak Kam Then *to*, from **tə[b]u*. Li: Ha *teu<*tə[b]u*. Lq. *tu*. Lh. **tu:* TU *tu*, NL *təw*.

DOOR See HOLE.

DOUBLE See PILE UP.

DOUBLE(D) See TWIN.

DOVE, PIGEON[I] **(m)pəw[nay]*

IN ****punay** "dove." PO **mpune:* Fi. *mbune*, id. SEP *bune-(/bune)~pune~vune* "pigeon," from **(m)pune;* cf. also Mota *kpwona*, id. (Cap.).

T **baw* "yellow-breasted green pigeon" (Shan), from **mpaw*. Yao: YHN *bo ko~bo ku* "wild pigeon, turtle-dove, dove" (cw. "bird"), from **mp[əw]*.

DOVE, PIGEON[II] **(ŋ)kəw(/kəw); *k/ḷ/əw; *(N)qəw(/N)qew* (79)

(I) PN ****ku(u)ku(u)** "pigeon" (Marquesan "turtle-dove").
Miao: MCF *ko qi* "pigeon," MCh. *ŋkwa ku* "turtle-dove, wild pigeon," from PM **ŋkuo*, from PMY **ŋk[əw]* (first element of each).

(II) T **khraw* "dove (turtle-dove)." Dioi *rau* (h.t.), id., from **[kh]raw*.

(III) KS **Gwaw* "dove": Sui *qau~pau*, Mak *kau*, Then *peu* (all l.t.), from **Nqwaw<*(Nqa)w/Nqaw* (labialized).

Miao: MPT *Nqua* "dove, pigeon," from PM **Nq[uɔ]*; MKS *Nqau* "dove," from PM **Nq[ou]*; Yao: YCR *go* (h.t.) "dove," YHN *ko~ku* "wild pigeon, turtle-dove, dove (ic.)" (cf. DOVE, PIGEON[1]); all from PMY **(N)q[əw]*.

DRAGON, RAINBOW **ruŋ*

T **ruŋ* "rainbow" (Kh. *huŋ kin nam* "dragon drink water")= "(sky) dragon." Dioi *śɔŋ* (s.t., low series) "rainbow," from **[br][u]ŋ*, app. from **b/ruŋ*.

PMY ***roŋ* "dragon"; YCR irreg. *ćuŋ* (s.t., high series) "dragon; rainbow" (*ćuŋ-huŋ* "The dragon king [*huŋ*<Ch.]. Originally a gate-keeper in heaven, he was banished to the earth . . . for prophesying that there would be no rain, whereas a destructive flood soon came. The rainbow is evidence of his determination to return to heaven"), from **kluŋ* (Haud. cites **kluŋ* "rainbow"), from **k/ruŋ*; cf. Vietnamese *rôŋ*, Müöng *roŋ~hoŋ* (Cambodian calendar *roŋ*) "dragon"; also the Chinese loan *liuŋ*, id. (Benedict 1967bis); cf. also Anc. Ch. *γuŋ~kŭŋ*, Arch. *g̒[r]uŋ~k[r]ŭŋ* "rainbow" (cf. Yao).

DRAW (WATER) See DIP UP.

DREAM **[ś]u(m)pi(/an)*

IN ***i(m)pi* "to dream," from **[ś]u(m)pi* (vocalic assim.); cf. Maanjan *upi* (Dahl cit.); also ***nupi* "a dream," from **[ś]/n/upi*. SEP **ni(m)pi*, from **[ś]/n/i(m)pi* (cf. IN). Form. (Pai. W. Ruk.; Atayalic) **s(i)pi* (Dyen: X); (E. Ruk.) **wa/sipi*; (Sai.) **ka/sipi* (cf. IN).

T **fan*, from **phw(y)an<*[su]pi/an* (second. aspiration). KS: **fin*: Mak *fin* (ic.), from **phwin<*[su]pi/n* (cf. Thai). OB *bien* (h.t.), from **pien<*[]pi/an*.

PMY ***mpei*.

DRINK See SIP; SUCK.

DRINK, SIP, SUCK IN **(ə)(n)təm[i]*

IN *təmi: Old Bugis *təmmi* "drink" (Cap.). PO *ntomi: Fi. *ndomi-* "sip" (Cap.).

T *toom "suck in (flies, insects sucking flowers)" (Si. Lao), from *(-o)tom.

DRIZZLE (FINE RAIN) See RAIN.

DRIVE IN See BEAT (two entries).

DRUM See SOUND.

DRUNK *ma/buśuk (40, 99, 126)

IN **mabuk "psychic abnormality" (TB. "stupefied," Ml. "drunk," NgD. *mabok* "violent," *mauk* "drunk"), from *mabuśuk. Form: Ata. *məbusuk*.

T *maw "drunk, dizzy." Chuang *vi, from *mwi<*m(a)wuy <*m(a)wuś(uk). Sek *mau.* KS: Then *me* (cw. "liquor"), from *mwe(i) (cf. Chuang). OB *möe* (cw. "wine") (Jer.), *mei* (Sav.) (cf. Chuang). Li *mui: S. Li *mui,* N. Li *pui,* dial. *bui* (cf. Chuang and OB). Lt. *a/sŭ,* from *(ma)busuk.

DRY *(N)qaɣiaŋ

IN **kəɣiŋ, from *kəɣiaŋ<*kaɣiaŋ (stressed form)<*Nqaɣiaŋ; also **kaɣaŋ=*(ŋ)kaɣaŋ (assim. form) and **kəɣaŋ (unstressed doublet).

T *xai, from *qayə<*qa(ɣ)ia(ŋ); also *heeŋ "dry, dried up (esp. of water=shallow)," from *hiaŋ<*(q)h(ɣ)iaŋ; also *leeŋ "dry (weather/season=drought)," from *liaŋ<*[]riaŋ. Dioi *hə,* from *qhai (cf. Thai); also *reeŋ "calm, without clouds or simply without rain; dry; (ic.) dry season," from *riaŋ. KS *[ɣ][ia]ŋ: Mak *zi:ŋ.* OB *ziaŋ~zeaŋ* (h.t.) "dry (soil, well); dessicate, dry (in sun, near fire)," from *hriaŋ<*[]riaŋ (cf. Thai). S. Li *khə* (cf. Thai Dioi).

PMY *Nqhaay, from *Nqaɣ(iaŋ) (secondary length).

DRY (BY HEAT) See HEAT.

DRY (MEAT) See SMOKE, v.

DRY, HOARSE *[p]aɣaw

IN **paɣaw~**pəɣaw (unstressed form) "hoarse" (="dry throat").

T *hraaw "dry," from *(ph)(a)raw. Dioi *ho ruao* "dry throat (*ho*)," from *γa[a]w. KS *[γ]o "dry": Mak *zo*, from *γ[aaw] (cf. Thai). Lk. *hyau*, id., from *[]γaw.

DUCK *bets; *be[ts]/be[ts]; *b/l/e[ts]/bets (84, 127)

(I) T *pet, from *[b]et. Sek *pit* (Ged.). KS: Kam *pət*, from *p[e]t. OB *bit* (Jer.), *bət* (h.t.) (Sav.), from *p[e]t* (cf. Thai). Li *pet: WS Li *pet*, Loi dial. *bet∼bit*=*pet∼pit*, Bas *biĕ*=*piĕ*. N. Kl. *bə* (wr. *mber*), from *b[e][t].

(II) IN **bibi, a secondary formation from *bi/bit'<*bit'/bit' (cf. III).

(III) IN **baliwit' "wild duck," from *b/al/iwit'<*b/al/ibit' (cf. II).

KS: Mak *ɛp*, from *(p/l/)ɛp<*(p/l/)ɛpɛt (cf. IN). Li *eep: S. Li *ɛp*, from *(p/ĕl/)ep (vocalic assim.).

PMY *aap, app. from *eep (cf. KS Li), perh. a loan/b.l. from Ch. *ap*.

DUSK See RAIN.

DUST See ASHES (two entries); MOULD.

DUST, POWDER, FLOUR *[t]a(m)puŋ; *[ta]p[o]ŋ

(I) IN **təpuŋ "flour," from *tapuŋ (stressed form). Cham *tapuŋ∼puŋ*, id. Form. (Ata.) *tapuŋ "mildew, mold (=the crumbly growth)."

PY **buaŋ (h.t.) "dust": YCR *buŋ* "to be dusty, crumbly; to be fine or soft (in texture)," *nia buŋ* "dust" (*nia* "earth"); YHN *ni buoŋ* "dust," from PMY *mpuaŋ, from an original *(a)mpuŋ.

(II) T *phoŋ "dust" (Si. Lao) (Si. also "powder, pulverized matter") from *t[]poŋ (second. aspiration).

DUST, POWDER, MANURE[1] *pu(m)pun[u] (44, 97, 99)

Form. (Bun.) *pupunu "dust."

T *fun "dust, powder, manure," from *phwun<*(pu)pun; also *pun "reduce to a powder by pestle," *khaw pun "rice (*khaw) flour" (WT), from *(pə)pun (unstressed form). KS *[]voon: Mak *vən* (h.t.) "dust, manure," from *phwoon<*phwuun (dissim.)<*(pu)pun. OB *phɔn* (l.t.) "manure," from *bɔn<*mpɔn.

DUST, POWDER, MANURE[II] *(qa/)m(u/o)r

IN *(ʔ)amur "dirt, dust" (Blust 1970): Iban amur "mud, dust," Tg. amol "dirt, filth."

T *(h)mun (Shan Tho)∼*mon (Nung) "dust" (Shan mun "to be fine, minute in particles; dust, any powder," mun muk [mun on d.t.] "to be fine, dusty; dust"; Nung mon muk "dust"), from *(q/)m[u/o]n. Dioi mɔn (h.t.) "dust, dusty," from *hmon. KS: *mu "manure": Mak məu, from *mu[r].

DWARF See SMALL.

E

EAR *(N)qraḷiŋ[a] (17, 39, 40)

IN **taliŋa. PO *(n)taliŋa: Fi. ndaliŋa-, Sa. 'iliŋe-. PPN **taliŋa. Form. (East) *(n)ṭaḷiŋa; also (metath.) *ṭaŋiḷa; (Saa.) *tsaḷiŋa.

T *xru, app. from *xr(ɨ)a through contamination with *xru "hole">"(ear-)hole" (see HOLE/DIG); Si. also has the doublet (i.c.) *[xr]ɨaŋ, app. from the metathesized form *xraŋ(iḷa) (cf. Form.). Dioi rə, from *ria<*[q]ra(ḷiŋa), with vocalism affected by the original initial cluster. Sek rua (cf. Dioi). KS *qhya: Sui qha, Mak ćha, Kam Then kha, from *qh[r]a. Lk. (kan) ya, from *[]ra (cf. Dioi). OB sa, from *[qhr]a. Li *thyay: S. Li yai, WS Li zai, N. Li thai, WS SC Loi jai, DC Loi tsai, SH Loi thai, from *thya(r)i(ŋa). Lq. rə, from *[]ra (cf. Dioi Lk.). Laha: TU kə/ha, from [q]hra (cf. KS). N. Kl. rau, from *[]ra[ḷ] (cf. Thai). Lt. lu, from *[][r]a (cf. Thai Lq.).

EARTH, FIELD, MUD *(q)(m)pḷalaq (15)

IN **tanaʔ∼**tanəʔ "earth, land" (NgD. tana "field," tanah "earth, land"). Form. (Atayalic) *tsalaq "field (wet, rice)" (Ata: Squliq also "mud").

T *ʔdin "earth," from *q/dan (vowel influ. by *q/)<*q/ntan <*q/mpral(aq); cf. also *plak "mire" (Si.), from *p(ra)láq; also *pɨak "mud, bog" (Si.) and *dɨak "mud" (Kh. Si.), from *(m)pryaak<*(m)prə(l)áq (unstressed>palatalized). Dioi dən (h.t.) from **ʔdən (cf. Thai). Sek ʔbal, id., from *q/mp[r]al(aq). KS *[]daay, id.: Mak daːi (h.t.). Lk. nai, id., from *nday (cf.

Mak). OB *da phe* (both h.t.) "fallow (*phe*) land (*da*)," from *ta. Li *hrwan* "earth": S. Li *dan~den*, WS Li *faŋ*<*fan*, N. Li *fan*, Mef. *baŋ*(<*[]wan*), from *[p]hran*<*phral(aq)*.

PY **nd[]=*(n)taw* "earth": YCR *dau* (h.t.) "ground, earth, soil; area," YLC *tau* "earth," YTP *dau* (irreg. l.t.), id.; PM *nde(n)=*nte(n)* "earth": MCF *ta*, MCh (ic.) *nta*, MPT *ntia* (irreg. l.t.), from PMY *ntaa(n)*; both from an earlier *(n)ta[l] <*(n)tal(aq)*.

EARTH, FIELD, GARDEN *[d][a]γaq* (37)

Form: East (Bun.) *daγaq;* (Ami) *dəγaq* (unstressed form); (Ruk. Puy. Paz.) *daγəq* (app. by metath.); Tsouic (Tsou) *tsaγaq;* (Saa.) *tsaγəq* (cf. East), from *[d]aγaq* "earth."

T *riak*, only in comp. *suan riak* (Shan), *riak suan* (Si.) "garden" (*suan*, id.), from *ryaak*<*(ə)rak* (unstressed form). KS *ʔγa* "rice-field": Sui *ʔγa~γa*, Mak Kam *ya*, Then *za* (all h.t.). Lk. *ya*, id., from *ra.

EAT *(ma/)kaʔən; *[pa/] ka[ʔə]n

(I) IN *(ma/)kaʔən: Tg. *ka:ʔin*, Ml. *makan* "eat," TB. *mahan* "devour"; also (Blust 1972bis) Uma Juman *makan* "feed"; cf. also NgD. *k/um/an*, Ho. *h/um/ană* "eat"; analyzed by Dempwolff as *ka/ən* "das was zu essen ist, Speise," but perhaps part of the root (indicated especially by the evidence from KD and MY); yet suffixed */ən* does occur with this root: Tg. *kan-in*, Uma Juman *kan-en* "cooked rice," Mukah *uaʔ kan-en* "any special food," from *kaʔən/ən* (Blust 1972bis). PO **ka* "food," perhaps a secondary formation from *ka(ʔən)*; note also Fi. *kan/a* "eat," *kan/i* "eat something." PPN **kai* "eat," analyzed by Dempwolff as *ka/i* "etwas essen," but perhaps a secondary formation (cf. PO); also *(ŋ)kano=*kano* "meat, flesh," from *kaʔən/ən* (Blust 1972bis) and *k/in/a* "meat course (To.), eat two courses (Fu.), gullet (Sm.)." Form. (Ruk.) *wa/ka[ʔ]n;* (Puy. Thao Paz.) *ma/ka[ʔ]ən;* (Sed.) *mə/kan;* (Pai. Ami Sir.) *k/m/aʔən;* (Bun.) *maʔən*<*(k/)m/aʔən;* (Kan.) *k/m/[aʔ]ən, *k/m/a/ka[ʔ]ən.

T *kin~*in (Shan *ʔin*, as doublet) "eat, drink," from *[]kaʔən (vocalism influenced by *ʔ). Dioi *kən*, from *[]k(aʔ)ən. Chuang *kin* (cf. Dioi). Sek *kin* (cf. Thai). KS *tsaan: Sui *tsyan*,

tsye~*ćen*, *će*~*tsiə*, Mak *si:n*, Then *tsin*, Kam *tya:n*=*ća:n*, from
[]kaan<*[]ka[ʔ]ən* (vocalic assim.). OB *kon* (Jer.), *kɔn* (Sav.),
from *[]k[ə]n* (cf. Dioi). N. Li *kha:n*, SH Loi Lakia *khan*, from
khaan<*ka[ʔ]ən* (vocalic assim., with unprefixed root). Lq.
kə:n, from *[]kəən*<*[]ka[ʔ]ən* (vocalic assim., contrasting with
Li). N. Kl. *ka*, S. Kl. *ką* (wr. *kam*) (Laj.), *kə* (cw. "cooked rice")
(Bon.), from Kl. *k[a,ə]n*<*[]k[aʔə]n*. Lt. *kho* "eat, drink" (for
semantics, cf. Thai), from *k[a,ə][n]* (unprefixed root, as in Li).

(II) IN **pakan* "fodder" (TB. "feed"="give fodder to"). PO
pakan: Fi. *vakan/ia* "feed." Form: Ata. *pəkanyeq* "feed (an
animal)," from *pa/kan-* (stressed form).

EAT, FOOD *[pa]ŋal*
   IN **paŋan* "eat, food." PO *paŋa*: Fi. *vaŋa-rau* "fed (animals)," Sa. *haŋa* "eat." PPN *faŋa*: To. *faŋa*, Sm. *fa/faŋa* "feed";
also **f[a,aa]ŋaʔi*, id. (secondary formation; cf. PPN under I).
Form: Pai. *paŋał* "share of game flesh" (Dahl cit.), from *paŋal*.
   PY **ńen*=*ńan* (YCF)~*ń(y)en* (YHA YLC)~*ńin* (YHN)
"eat."

EEL See WORM.

EGG *[qi]qłəl[uɣ]* (86)
   IN **[t]əluɣ*=*(ʔi)[t]əluɣ* (Tg. *ʔitlog*). PO **qatoluɣ*~
**tolu[ɣ]*. Form: East (Pai. Sai. Kuv.) *(qə)țiļuɣ*, unstressed
form of *(qi)țiluɣ*, from *(qi)təluɣ* by assim. backward; Tsouic
(Kan.) *[q]itsu[ļ]uɣ*, from *[q]itsə[ļ]uɣ* by assim. forward.
   T *khray* "egg; lay an egg," from *khrəy*<*(q-)krəļ(uɣ)* (sec-
ond. aspir. after *q*). Dioi *kyai* "egg," from *k[h]ray*. KS *kay*:
Sui Then *kai*, Mak *ćai*, from *[kr]ay*.
   PMY **qyaw*=*qļaw* (Haud. cites Yao *klaw*), from *qłəļ(uɣ)*.

EIGHT See INTRODUCTION.

ELBOW See ANGLE.

ELDER See OLD.

ELEPHANT See TOOTH.

EMBROIDER See PIERCE.

EMPTY, BLIND¹ *()(m)puRaw* (18, 19)
   Form. (Ami Sai.) *ma/puRaw* "blind (=empty/vacant sight)."

T *plaw "empty, vacant." Yay pyu (l.t.) "empty," from *byu (cf. Sek). Sek plu (l.t.), id., from *blu<*mplu<*mp(u)lu< *mp(u)law (vocalic assim.); also lo "blind," from *(pu)law. KS *γo "empty" (Sui)~*go "blind" (Kam), from an original *[R]o <*[R]aw (cf. Sek). Li *plaaw "blind": S. Li la:u, N. Li pla:u, WS Li plau, from *p(a)law (vocalic assim.).

Yao: YHN blou "blind": Miao: MCE hlu, id., from PM *[mpl]ei; both from PMY *mplou, from an earlier *mplu (cf. Yay Sek).

EMPTY, BLIND" *(m)puqaŋ; *[p]ukaŋ

(I) IN **puʔaŋ "empty." PO *pua: Fi. vua "vacant."

T *puaŋ "idiot, without intelligence"="empty(-headed)" (Lao), from *[]pu(q)aŋ; also *vaaŋ "night-blind (Ahom); to be unsubstantial, empty, void, good for nothing; unable to see (Shan); dark, cloudy, darkened (=blind) (Si.); albino (=with poor vision) (Lao); blind (with the eyes of normal appearance) (WT), blind (Nung)" (WT Nung cw. "eye"), from *bwaaŋ <*mpwaaŋ<*mpu(q)aŋ; also *baaŋ "night blindness" (Lao), from *mpa(q)aŋ (vocalic assim.). Lk. pla phaŋ "blind" (Mao and Chou cit.), analyzed as "blue (phaŋ) eyes (pla)," but perhaps a cognate form (*pəqəŋ>phaaŋ).

Miao: MKL qhoŋ "empty, free," from PM *qhoŋ, from PMY qh[ua]ŋ (cf. PMY under II).

(II) Lt. mću kho "blind" (mću "eye"), from *kho[ŋ]<*kh[uaŋ].

PMY **khuaŋ "empty, free" (MCF MPT also "hollow"), from *(u)kaŋ.

ENCLOSE(D) *lə(m)b[o]

IN **lə(m)bu "enclosed" (Tg. "courtyard," TB. "ramparts enclosure," NgD. "village").

T *loom "enclose (as with fence, hedge, palisade, fortification)," from *lom(b)(o), with second. vowel lengthening; app. also *loop "sheepfold, goat-pen" (WT), from *lob, with similar lengthening.

ENCLOSURE, ROOM, TRAP, CAGE *( )k[u/o]r[u/o]ŋ (102)

IN **kuḷuŋ=*kuruŋ "enclosure" (Tg. kuloŋ "enclosure," baŋ/ kuloŋ "trap"). PPN **kolo "enclosed fortress."

T *kroŋ "cage (esp. for birds, fowl)" (Si. Lao BT); cf.
*khr[u,o]ŋ "room" (Ahom); *t(h)ruŋ~*t(h)roŋ<*k(h)ruŋ~
*k(h)roŋ "trap, cage or basket (for birds, fowl)" (Tho-Nung).
N. Thai *kroŋ "cage." KS: Mak zuŋ (h.t.) "pen (cattle)," from
*(k-)ruŋ.

Yao: YCR čhoŋ "clf. for rooms, narrow fields, small spaces;
a room"="enclosures," from PY *[khl]oŋ, from PMY *[khl̥]oŋ.

ENDED   *(q/)obots; *(q/)(o)(m)bots; *[u]mbuts

(I)   IN **ubut'=*[ʔ]ubut'.

   T *woot "stop, cease (Shan), die (Si.)," from *(o)wot.

(II) T *hmot "finished, complete" (Shan "to come to an end,
be finished"), from *q/mot<*q/mbot; also *moot~*hmoot
(Shan) "to extinguish/be extinguished" (Shan "to stop, put a
stop to, as a fire, to extinguish; to go out, come to an end, as a
light, fire or life"), from *(q/)ombot. Lh: TU bɔt "extinguish."

(III) T *mut "finished (Nung: ic.); to be destroyed, die" (Lao),
from *mbut.

ENEMY, WAR   *[m][u](ŋ-)tsak

   IN **mət'aʔ "enemy" (Ja. mĕsah), from *mut'aʔ (stressed
form); also *mu(ń)t'uʔ=*mu(ŋ)t'uʔ (Ja. muŋsuh), id., through
assimilation, app. from an original *muŋ[]tsaq. PO *mensa, id.:
Fi. metsa (cf. IN).

   T *sək "enemy" (Lao BT WT Tho)~*sɨk "enemy" (Lao),
"battle/war" (Ahom Kh. Shan), from *sək~*syak<*(ə)sak (unstressed form); also *sia "war" (Shan; used cw. *sɨk), from
sya<(ə)sa[q]. Dioi śak "rebellion, sedition." Yak sak (l.t.)
"enemy," from *zak<*nsak.

   PY **tsaʔ (l.t.) "rob"="steal," from PMY *dzaʔ, an app.
b.l. from Ch. tsei, Anc./Arch. dzʿək "robber, rebel, bandit," ultimately from an AT form *ntsəq<*[m]əntsaq (vocalic assim.).

ENLACE   See TIE.

ENTRAILS   See LIVER.

EVEN   See SMOOTH(E).

EVEN (-NUMBERED)   See JOIN.

EVENING   See DARK.

EXCHANGE, BUY, SELL   *ts[a]liw*

   IN *tsaliw*: Proto-Philippine *saliw* "exchange" (Charles cit.).
Li *hriw*: S. Li *diu*, WS Li *hiu*, SH DC Loi *jiu* "sell"; Bas.
kiu=ćiu "buy," *kiu-tu* "sell," from *s[]riw*.

EXCHANGE, CHANGE, BUY, SELL   *(m)bali; *pali; *pali/t*
   (122, 127)

(I)   IN **bɔli=*bɔli* (TB. Ml.)~*bali* (NgD.) "buy" (NgD.
"blood-price"), from *bali* (stressed form); also *bili* "buy" (Tg.
NgD. Ho.) (Ho. "cost") (assim. form). Cham *blei<*b[]li* "buy,"
pa/blei "sell." PO *poli*: Fi. *voli/a* "buy something," *i/voli*
"price"; Sa. *holi* "buy." Form. (Pai.) *b/n/əli* "buy," *pa/bəli*
"sell" (unstressed form; cf. IN); (Atayalic) *(m/)bali* "buy,"
bali- "sell."

   T*mlay* "exchange" (Tho), from *mblay<*mb(a)li*. KS
[]dyay "buy": Sui *dyai*, Mak *dai*, Then *zei* (all h.t.). Li: WS
Loi *dəi* "buy" (cf. KS).

(II)   T *thay* "change, exchange" (Si. "redeem," Lao "buy
back, exchange"; Ahom WT "change [=exchange] clothes"),
from *phlay<*p(a)li*. Lk. *plɛ* "sell," from *play* (cf. Thai).

(III)   IN **palit* "exchange gift" (TB. "take in payment [girl
as daughter-in-law for debts]," Tg. "substitute"); cf. also Tg.
palit/an "barter; to exchange."

   Miao: PW **phli=*phli?~*phle?* (MSY) "change": MPT
"change form (of insect emerging from chrysalis stage)," from
PMY *phl[et]*.

EXCREMENT, INTESTINES   *[(m)pl]a(N)qi; *[pl/n/]a[q]i;*
   (m)pl/l/a[q]i (17, 18)

(I)   IN **ta?i=*(n)ta(ŋ)?i* "excrement": generally *(n)ta?i*,
but Kalagan *takki*, Singhi *toki* (cit. by Blust 1973), from *taŋ?i*
=*taŋqi*. PO *(n)ta?e*, id.: Fi. *nde*, Sa. *ae* (with *i>e* after
q). PPN **ta?e*, id. (Nukuoro "rump"). Form. (East) *ta(ŋ)qi*:
generally *taqi*, but Ruk. *tsaki~tsake*, Bun. *take<*taŋqi* (*i*
>e* after the original *q*; cf. PO and PPN); also Sir. *taiŋ<*
[t]aŋ[q]i; (Tsouic) *taqi*, id.

T *khi* "excrement; defecate" (the general root, with irreg. *kh-* for *x-*). N. Thai *γay* "excrement," from *Nqay<
(-a)Nqi. Sek *γay*, id. (Ged.) (cf. N. Thai). KS *()qe*, id.:
Sui *qe~će*, Then Kam *ʔe* (all l.t.), Mak *će* (h.t.), from *(da)qi*
(<*ntaqi*)~*(ta)qi* (cf. Thai). Lt. *kwei* (l.t.), id., from
[G]ei<[Nq]ei<*(-a)Nqi* (cf. N. Thai Sek). OB *kai* (l.t.), id.,
from *gay<*[G]ay* (cf. Lk.). Li *[q]ay*, id.: S. Li *hai*, WS Li
qaːi (mef. form lacking), from *(-a)qi*.

PMY *(N)qay* "excrement" (MCF also "intestines"), from
(-a)(N)qi.

(II) IN **t/in/aʔi* "intestines." PPN **tinaʔe* "intestines, stomach." Form. (Puy. Ami) *t/in/aqi* "guts."

T *e=/ee/* "defecate (of children) (Shan); discharge
(urine, feces) (Nung); copulate (=discharge semen) (Tho),"
from *a(q)i* (effect of *q*), from an earlier *(t/n/)a(q)i*.

(III) Form. (Kuv.) *t/l/a[qi]* "excrement," *(t/)n/l/[t/]n/aq[i]*
"guts" (double infixation, partially redupl.).

T *say* "intestines," from *t/r/ay<*t/r/a(q)i*. Dioi *sai*,
id. KS *[]zaay*, id.: Sui *hai*, Mak *zaːi*, Then *thaːi* (all h.t.), from
[]nsaay []nt/r/a(q)i, with second. vowel length. Lk. *kyaːi=*
ćaːi, id. from *saːi*. Li *ray*, id.: S. Li *dai*, WS Li *raːi*, N. Li
dial. *rai~lai*, from *(t/)r/ay<*(t/)ra(q)i*.

EXTRACT See DIP UP.

EYE *mapḷa* (21, 22, 36, 69, 72, 73)

IN **mata*. Form: East *maṭa*; Tsouic *m[a]tsa* "eye"; Atayalic
mə/matsa "(eye-)ball" (Ata.).

T *ta* (SW)~*thra* (Tho-Nung), from *pra~*phra*. N. Thai
tra/pra: Dioi *ta*, Wu-ming *ra*. Chuang *rem pya* (Ting), perh.
from *re/mpya<*/mpra*. Sek *pra*. KS *[]da*: Sui Mak *da*, Then
ʔda, Kam *ta* (all h.t.). Lk. *pla*. OB *da* (h.t.), from *ta*. Li *sa*:
S. Li *sa~śa*, WS Li *ćha=śa*, N. Li *sa*, Loi dial. all *sa*, Dakili
tsa, Bas. *dza=tsa*, Mef. *txia*, Ki *xa*. Lq. *te* (Bon.), *lun da* (Laj.),
perh. from an original *lu/nda* (cf. Chuang). Laha: TU *kə/ta*.
N. Kl. *tau*; S. Kl. *bu mo kho=bu mokho* (cf. *bu tɨ* "face," *bu ləði*
"ear"), from *mothyo*; Lt. *mću*.

PM (PE PWA MLL) *maay*, from *maat<*mapḷ(a)*; also

(MKC MKS) **mu(ŋ), from *mu(*t*) (nasalized)<**mat;* PY
mut-* (YTP *mut-tsiŋ*)~mwəi (YCR YHN), from *mui<*mut
(cf. MKC MKS).

EYEBROW   See HAIR (BODY).

F

FACE, FOREHEAD[I]   *(*q*/)(*n*)*dza*[*q*]*ai*[*s*]   (14)

IN   **[*dḍ*]*a*ʔ*ay*=*[*dḍ*]*a*ʔ*əy* "forehead" (Ja. "face"), from
*[*ndz*]*a*ʔ*ay.* PPN ***la*ʔ*e* "forehead," from **nda*ʔ*e.* Form. East
*dzaqais "face (Bun. Kuv. Thao Paz.), forehead (Pai. Fav.),
face/forehead (Sai.)"; Atayalic *daq[*ai*]*s* "face."

T *hna "face; before/in front of," from **q/nda*<**q/ndza.*
KS *(ʔ)*na* "face": Sui ʔ*na*~*na*, Mak Kam *na* (all h.t.), Then
na (l.t.), from *(*q*/)*nda.* Lk. *kyɛ* "before/in front of," from
*[*q*]*ne*<**q/nay* (vowel influ. by original *q)<**q/nda*(*q*)*ay.*
OB *na* (h.t.) "face, surface, before," from *hna (cf. Thai).

FACE, FOREHEAD[II]   *b[]*loŋ*
   Form. (Sir.) *b[]*luŋ* "face."

Li *doŋ "face": S. Li *doŋ*, N. Li *dɔŋ*, Ki *dɔŋ*=*tɔŋ*, WS Li *taŋ*,
Loi dial. *daŋ*=*taŋ*, Bas. Ha *daŋ*=*taŋ*, from **bloŋ.* Lt: MP *lu*,
BP *pyom lu* "face" (Rob.), perh. from **pyo/mlu*<*/*mblu*[ŋ].
   PMY *blɔ(ŋ) "forehead."

FALL[I]   *dz[*a*]*toq*
   IN   ***d*ʹ*a*[*t*]*u*ʔ.

T **tok.* Sek *tok.* KS *tok "fall/drop down": Sui Mak Then
Kam *tok.* OB *dok* (h.t.), from **tok.* S. Li *thok*, from *(*s-*)*tok.*

FALL[II]   *da(*m*)*b*[*oq*]
   IN   ***ḍabu*ʔ "fall," for **dabu*ʔ (no Tg. cognate); also ***labu*ʔ=
*la(*m*)*bu*ʔ "fall, cast anchor," from *(*d*/)*l/a*(*m*)*bu*ʔ.

T *[*d*]*aaw* (Shan doublet). Li *daw: S. Li *dau*, WS Li *to* (l.t.).
Yao: PIM **dop "fall down," from *dob(*oq*) by vocalic assim.

FALL[III]   *[*t*]*uduy*
   Form: Ata. *mətoroi*, from **m/tu*[*d*]*uy.*

PY **tui (l.t.) "fall (rain)," from PMY *dui (YHN "fall [from
horse]"), from *duuy<*(*u*)*duy.*

FALL, LET FALL *°h[o]loγ*

    IN **°°*huluγ*** "slowly let fall, slacken (a line)" (Tg. "fall").
T °*hlon* "fall out or off (teeth, leaves)."

FALL DOWN/OVER See CUT DOWN/OFF.

FAN See MOVE BACK AND FORTH; WINNOW.

FAR, LONG °*a(n)daw[il]*; °*antaw[il]*

(I)   Form. (Puy. Ruk.; Tsouic) °*(m/)a[d]awil;* (Kuv.) °*m/ə-*
[d]a[wi]l (unstressed form) "far."

    T °*ńaw*~°*naw* (Lao doublet)~°*yeew* (WT) "long (in
space)" (Ahom also "distant, far"; WT "stretch [arm, neck],
raise oneself"), from °*(a)ndaw(il)*~°*(ə)ndaw(il)* (palatalized
in latter). Dioi *nɛu* "elongate, prolong" (cf. Thai). Li °*naaw*
"long": S. Li *na:u,* N. Li *ta:u,* WS Li *tau* (cf. Thai).

(II)   PMY °°*ntaaw* "long (in space)," from °*(a)ntaw(il)*; for
the semantics, cf. IN °°*d'auˀ*~°°*daəˀ* "far," PO °°*sau(ˀ)* "outside, far off," but SEP °*sau*~°*sau/sau* "far (Group I and II
languages), long (Group IV and VI languages)."

FART °*(k/)(ə)(n)tot;* °*()t/l̩/ot* (9, 10)

(I)   IN °°*kə(n)tut*~°°*ə(n)tut*~°°*u(n)tut* (assim. form).

    T °*tot.* KS °*tot:* Sui Kam *tət,* Mak *tut,* Then *tet.* OB *dut*
(h.t.), from °*tut.* Li °*th[u]t:* S. Li *thuot,* WS Li *thut.*

(II)   N. Thai: Po-ai *lɔt,* from °*[th]rot*<°*t/əl̩/ət* (vowel assim.);
Dioi *rat,* from °*[th]rat*<°*t/al̩/at* (vowel assim.). Sek *ret,* from
°*rat* (cf. Dioi). Lk. *kyot*=*ćot,* from °*tlot.*

    PMY °°*pwot,* from °*twot*<°*t/l̩/ot.*

FAT °*(ma/)tab[aq]*

    IN °°*[t]abə[ˀ]* (Tg. *tab'aˀ,* n., *ma/tab'aˀ,* adj.). Yami *matava*
"fat/obese (human)," from °*ma/taba[ˀ].* Form. Sed. *mətəbənau,*
id. from °*m/təbə-* (unstressed form).

    T °*taw:* Shan *tau-hɛ* "the [sebaceous] secretions which collect
on the hair at armpits (*hɛ*)" (=armpit-fat).

FAT, GREASE, OIL¹ °*(s)(i)maγ*

    Form. (East; Saa.) °*simaγ* "fat/grease (of animal)."
T *man.* Sek *mal.*

Miao (Hunan): Fenghuang *śiɛ*, Layi P'ing *śɛ* "oil," from PM **hm[]ŋ* (Kun Chang 1966, note 16); PT *ka/hmi be* "fat (*graisse*)" ="fat (*ka/hmi*) of pig (*be*)." Yao ***hmei* "fat, lard" (YHN also "odor; to smell"); all from PMY **hm[ei]*, from **s(e)m(e)(γ)* by vocalic assimilation (second. nasalization in Miao).

FAT, GREASE, OIL" **law/law* (8)
   Form. (Puy. Pai: Mak.) **lawlaw.*

   T **laaw* "fat, lard" (Nung), from **(law)law*. Dioi *lao* "fat (of man and some animals)," from **la[a]w* (cf. Nung).

FAT, OIL   **m[i]ńa[k]*
   IN ***mińak* "oil"~***məńak* (unstressed) "fat" (Ho. "oil"). PPN ***momona* "fat," from **mo(na/)mona;* cf. Easter Island *monamona* "sweet food."

   Kl. *nuɔ* "oil," *nu xmɨɔ* "fat"="oil (*nu*) of pig (*xmie*)," from **na[k]*. Lt. *mnɔ* "oil," *mnɔ me* "fat"="oil (*mnɔ*) of pig (*me*)," from **m[]na[k]*.

FATHER   **a/ba; *(m)ba(/mba); *(m)bapa* (64)

(I)   Form. (Paz. Sai.; Ata.) **(y/)aba.*

(II)   IN **mbamba*: Ho. *baba*. PO **papa*: Fi. (Vuda Lautoka) *vava* "father, fa's older brother, fa's si's husband," from **baba.*

   Li **[b]a*: WS Li *pa*, N. Li *ba*, Loi dial. *ba*. Kl. *bə*, only in *bə ve* "male," *po bə* "man (male)," from **ba.*

(III)   IN ***bapa=*(m)bapa.*

   T **pa* "parent's older sister," perh. from **(ba)pa* via "parent's older sibling"<"uncle." KS **pa*: Sui *pa* "parent's older sister," Then *pa* "aunt" (cf. Thai). Lk. *pa* "mother" (cf. Thai KS). OB (*nə-*)*ba* [h.t.] (Jer.), from **pa*. Li **pha*: S. Li *fa* "father, husband, male," WS Li *pha* "clf. for man (male)," WS Loi *pha* "older brother," app. from **pa[pa]* (with assimilation to final syllable). Lq. *pe*<**(ba)pa*. Lt. *pu*<**(ba)pa.*

   Miao: MCF *paʔ* (l.t.), from PM **baiʔ*, from PMY **ba[]*, app. from an earlier **bap(a);* also MCF *pa* "male (animals)," PT *pha* "father," MFPL *a/pha* "fa's father," from PM **p(h)aay;* Yao: YHN *fa* "father; (ic.) grandfather, ancestor," from PY **p(h)a;* both from PMY **p(h)a*, from **(pa)pa* (cf. Li).

FATHER, GRANDFATHER   **ta/ta* (65)

PO *tata*: Fi. (Talaulia Tavuki Kudavu) *tata* "father [address]";
Ngun (New Hebrides) *tata* "mo's brother [address]" (Cap. and
Lester). Form: cf. Ata. *y/ata* "aunt."

T *ta* "mo's father; wife's father," from *(ta)ta*. KS *ta* "mo's
father": Sui Mak Kam *ta* (Mak also "wife's father"). Lq. *te*
"grandfather," also "male (animal)."

PY *ta* "mo's father; wife's father" (usu. ic.), a loan from Thai.

FATHER/CHILD *[(t/)a]ma* (64)

IN **ama* "father." PO *t/ama*, id. PPN **tama* "child," but
Sm. both *tama* "child" and *tamaa* "father." Form. (East; Tsouic;
Sed.) *(t/)ama* "father"; cf. also Ata. *y/ama* "son-in-law," perh.
from "child."

Miao: MFPL *a/ma* "father."

FATHOM See SPREAD OUT (ARMS).

FEAR *(ma/)(ŋ)ku; *ku/at; *[]k/l/u/a; *m/l/ku/t; *m/taku;
*(n)t/l/a[ku]; *(m/)ta(ŋ)ku/t; *m/ki; *[]ŋki/a*

(I) PO **ma/ku*: Sa. mɛʔu "afraid," *ma/maʔu* "arouse fear";
also *ma/ŋkuŋku*: Arosi *ma-gugu* "to fear, start, shiver at sudden sound" (cit. by Blust 1972bis).

T *khu* "threaten, frighten with threats" (Si.). OB *maŋ*,
from *maŋ(ku)* < *ma/ŋku*.

(II) T *khoot* "frighten" (Ahom), from *khu/at*.

(III) T *klua* (SW), from *[]k/l/ua*. KS *[kh]lua* (cf. Thai).

(IV) Form: Pai. *markut* "fear/be afraid," from *ma/l/ku/t*.

(V) Form: Ata. *matəkumu* "paralyzed with fear," from *ma/-
taku-* (stressed form).

(VI) KS: Mak *thə* "frighten," from *thya*, app. from *thla* <
t/l/a(ku). Li *dla*: S. Li *da*, N. Li *tla*, WS Li *ta*, Loi dial. all
da=ta, from *ntla* < *nt/l/a(ku)*, perh. from *m/t/l/a(ku)* (cf.
Tumleo under VII).

(VII) IN **[t]akut*; also *ma/takut*: Manam (N. Papua)
matakur(a), Buru *əmtaku*, Tumleo (N. Papua) *mata* (Cap. cit.).
PO *ma/taŋku*: Sa. *ma/mataku* "fearful"; also PO **mataku(t)*
"afraid" (Grace). Form. (Sir.) *ma/takut* "fear/be afraid"; also
Sai. *imatiktikut*, id., from *ma/tikut* (app. assim. form).

(VIII) Form. (Fav.) *m/ki "fear/be afraid."

(IX) PMY **nćhia=*ntshyia "afraid," from *ŋkhia<*ŋkhi/a, perh. from *m/khi/a (cf. Li under VI).

FEATHER See HAIR (BODY).

FEEL (FOR), TOUCH *glam[aq]
 IN **d'ama².
 T *glam.

FEMALE, WOMAN, WIFE, MOTHER, GRANDMOTHER, SISTER *(q/)(m)ba[x]i; *(q/)(m)ba/ba[x]i; *(ma/)b/n/a[x]i; *(m)paxi (67)

(I) IN **bayi=*(m)ba[²]i "mother"; Dyen cites Tg. ba:²i "mother, grandmother"; also (Brust 1972bis) Bimanese va²i "grandmother," Palawan Batak ba²i² (final -² unexplained) "grandmothers and their sisters." Form. (Kuv.; Tsou) *(m)ba[h]i "grandmother"; also (W. Ruk: Tona) *[q]a/ba[h]i- "woman."

 T *me=/mee/ "mother, woman, female," from *mbee< *mba[x]i (vocalic influ. by *x). Dioi mɛ "mother; female of animals" (cf. Thai); also mai "prefix for young girls or young woman," from *mba(x)i (without influ. by *x). OB mai "female," ne mai "mother-in-law" (for first element, see III), from *mbai (cf. Dioi). Li *may~*mey: Bup mai, Mef. Ha bai=pai "mother"; WS Li pa:i "(ic.) woman; wife"; Loi dial. bai=pai "older sister (WS), (ic.) younger sister (WS), (ic.) daughter (WS SH), (ic.) hen (SH DC SC)," but S. Li mei "female," DC Loi bɛi=pɛi "older sister"; all from *mba[x]i (vowel influ. by *x). Lq. mei "mother, woman, female," nəi məi "younger sister" (nəi kəpə "younger brother"; see III).

(II) IN **babi=*(m)babi "female" (Ho. ana/bavi "sister of a man"="child/female"), from *(m)ba/ba²i, with vocalism influ. by original *q, as shown by Tg. baba:²i "woman" (Dyen), also Palawan Batak baba²i "woman, female" (cit. by Blust 1972bis). Form. (Ami) *ba/bahi; (Ruk.) *[q]a/ba/ba[h]i; (Pai. Puy.) *ba/bahi/an "woman" (Dyen: H).

(III) IN **binay=*binəy "woman" (Ml. bini "wife," NgD. ha/binɛi "female"). PPN **fine=*fine~*ma/fine (Sm.) "female." Form. (Fav.) *nay "mother," from *(b/)n/a[h]i.

T *naay "mo's mother, wife's mother," from *(b/a)n/a(x)i.
KS *ni "mother": Sui ni, Mak nəi, Then nei, from *(b/)n/i<
*(b/)na[x]i (vowel influ. by *x). OB ne "ancestress, grand-
mother, old woman," ne mai "mother-in-law," from *nay (cf.
KS) (for second element, see I). Lq. nəi "younger sibling" (with
sex modifiers; see I), from "younger sister" by extension.
　　Miao: MFPL a/nai "mother."

(IV) Form. (Sed.) *pa[h]i "grandmother."
　　OB bəi [h.t.] "older sister" (Jer.), from *pai. Lq. pəi, id.
　　PM (PE PC MHY) **mphai=*mpha?~*mphi? (MTK)
"younger sister," from PMY *mphai?~*mphi?, from *mph(a)?i.

FENCE, WALL　*(m)pa[r]a(/(m)pa[r]a);
　*(m)pa[γ]a(/(m)pa[γ]a)
(I) IN **pala=*para(/para) "scaffold" (Capell: "fence").
PO *(m)para: Fi. vara "scaffold," Sa. para "fence." Form. (Ata.)
*pa[r]a "stand for heads brought back from headhunting."

(II) IN *paγa "storage loft": Tg. paga "storage loft made of
bamboo attached to ceiling," Maranao paga "attic," NgD. pahe
"storage shelf above the hearth" (Blust 1970). PO *mpaγa: Fi.
baa "fish fence, enclosure"; also (Blust 1973) Arosi bara-na
"fence," Roviana bara "fence, wall," Eddystone bara "fort, forti-
fied place"; also *mpaa "fence, barrier," *mpa(i), *mpampa
"wall, boundary" (cit. by Blust 1973). PPN **paa "enclosure,
fence," from *mpa[γ]a.
　　T *fa=/faa/ "wall, fence, partition," from *phwa<
*p(a/)/pa[r]a. Sek va=/vaa/ "wall," from *[]pwa<*(pa/)pa[r]a.

FIBRE, BEARD　*(qa/)(m)b[u]lut (111)
IN **bulut "fibre." PPN **pulu "coconut husk" (Uvean "coconut fibre"), from *mpulu<*mbulu[t].
　　T **hnuat "beard" (WT also "tactile hair of animals; [ic.]
mustache"), from *q/nduat<*q/mbruat<*q(a)/mbrut. Dioi
yuat~yat "side-whiskers" (cw. "temples"), from *(mb)yuat
(cf. Thai). KS *( )n(y)uat "beard": Sui nyut, Mak nut (both
h.t.), Then nuet (l.t.) (cf. Thai Dioi). Lk. plut (l.t.), id., from
*blut. Laha: TU nut, id. (cf. Thai).

FIBRE, BEARD, CURLY (HAIR)　*(ma/)k[a]wad; *( )k[a]wat
(I) IN **kawad "wire, fibre." PPN **makawe "hair (of head),

thread, strand" (Marquesan "curly, of hair"), from *ma/kaway
< *ma/kawad.

    Lt. ma/khɛ "beard," from *ma/khay (cf. PPN).

(II) PPN **kawa "beard," from *kawat; for the semantics, cf.
FIBRE/BEARD.

    T *kuut "frizzled" (Lao), from *k(a)wat.

FIELD   See CULTIVATE (FIELD) (two entries); EARTH
(two entries).

FIELD (WET, RICE)   *[(m)b]əna (37, 94)

    IN **bəna=*(m)bəna "low-lying (flooded) land." Form:
Fav. bonna=bəna "fields (all kinds)."

    T *na. Sek na (Ged.). OB nea, from *(-ə)na (palatalized).
Li *na: S. Li na, WS and N. Li ta. Lq. ne. Lt. nu.

    Miao: MFPL na "mountain field."

FILTH(Y)   See DIRTY.

FINGER   See POINT (two entries).

FIRE *[ś]apuy

    IN **apuy=*Wapuy: Niala (Piru: West Ceram) wai, Cha-
morro (Marianas) gwafe (Dyen 1962). PPN **afi. Form. (East;
Tsouic; Atayalic) *sapuy (Dyen: x_1); Ata. hapuniq "fire," but
hapui~pə/hapui "to cook," pə/hapuy/an "fireplace"; for the
semantics, cf. HEARTH/FIRE.

    T *vay~*vi (Shan doublet in "fireplace"), from *pway<
*(a)puy. Dioi fi (l.t.), from *vi<*pw(u)y (cf. Shan). Sek vi
(cf. Dioi). KS *pwi: Kam pwi, Sui wi~vi~vui, Mak vəi, Then
wi (all h.t.). OB vəi (Jer.), bei (Sav.), from v[ə]y<*pw[ə]y.
Li *pwey: S. Li pei, WS Li N. Li fei, from *pw(a)y (cf. Thai).
Lq. pəi. N. Kl. pai, S. Kl. phi, from Kl. *p(h)əy, perh. through
second. aspir. from an original *ś[]pəy. Lt: MP pu; BP pe
(Rob.), pie (Bon.), from Lt. *puey (cf. Li).

FIRE   See HEARTH.

FIREWOOD   See HEARTH.

FISH   *b[u]law; *mb[]raw

(I) Form. (Puy: Chipon) *bulaw.

(II) PMY **njraw=*mbraw.

FISH-HOOK   See HOOK.

FIST   See HOLD (IN HAND, MOUTH).

FIVE   See HAND; PALM/SOLE; INTRODUCTION.

FLAT, FLAT SURFACE, PLATEAU, FLOOR, PALM/SOLE
    *[(n)dra](m)paγ

IN **da(m)paγ "flat" (Tg. "floor"). PPN **lafalafa~*lafa
(To.) "flat" (Sm. "level mountain top"); also **lapa "flat and/or
broad"; both from *nda(m)pa. Form. (Ata.) *(də)dapa[γ] "palm
(of hand)."

T *piin "blade (Si.), thigh of an animal (Ahom)" (both="flat
surface"), from *pyəən<*(ə)pan (unstressed form); also *biin
"floor, base surface" (WT also "sole [of shoe], plateau [elevated
plain]"), from *byəən<*(ə)mpan. KS *byaan: Then pya:n (l.t.)
"(inscribed) board," from *(ə)mpan (cf. Thai). OB phean
"flat," from *(ə)pan, with second. aspir. (cf. Thai KS).

FLAT, FLAT SURFACE, SOLE, FOOT, THIGH   *[d]apal

IN *[d]apan: Ilocano dapan "sole" (Dyen 1964). Form. *dapal
"foot (East: gen.; Tsouic; Atayalic); thigh (Pai.)," the former
by semantic extension from "sole."

T *paan~*phaan (Nung doublet); Kh. pa:n "flat part of an
object or instrument, as the blade of a knife"; BT pa:n "blade";
WT pa:n xa~xa pa:n "thigh" (xa "leg"); Tho pa:n "blade,"
kɛp pa:n "plank" (kɛp<"clf. for flat things"); Nung mai pa:n
~pha:n "wooden (mai) club for beating clothes in washing";
from *(a)pan. KS *paan: Mak pa:n "flat."

FLAT, BOARD, PLANK   *(m)pa(m)pan (59, 110)

IN **papan "board" (Ho. "writing slate"). PO *(m)pa(m)pa:
Fi. vava "board," bava "wash-strake of canoe," baba "side (esp.
side planks of canoe)," Sa. hapa "canoe seat." Trukese paap
"board, plank," from *mpa/mpa (Dyen). PPN **papa "flat
hard surface [board, plank, slab]," from *mpampa.

T *peen "flat (and thin); board, plank, plate (metal)," from
*(pa)pan; also *pheen "clf. for flat, thin objects (planks, cloth,
mats, fish-nets)" (Kh. "large plank," WT "side plank [of canoe]"),
from *(pə)pan (unstressed form); also *ʔbeen "flat, smooth"
(Si.), from *[]mpeen<*[](mpa)mpan. Dioi pɛn (l.t.) "clf. for
flat things," from *bɛn<*mpeen; also bɛn "clf. for planks, flat

stones, fields," from *[]mpeen. OB *bien* (h.t.) "plank," from
pien<(pa)pan. Li *pen: S. Li *pen* "clf. for paper, clothes,"
SC Loi *ben-khok=pen-khok* "foot"="flat part (sole) of foot
(*khok*)," Bup. *ben=pen* "table," from *(pa)pan; also *ben:
S. Li *ben* "plank," N. Li *ben* "table," from *mpen<*(mpa)mpan.

  PY **pen "board": YCR "board, plank; clf. for planks and
long flat objects," *tsau pen* "arch of foot (*tsau*)"; YHN "plank,
plate (metal)," *pu pen* "palm of hand (*pu*)"; from an original
*(pa)pan (cf. Thai).

FLEA   See LOUSE (two entries).

FLEA, LOUSE   *[ti]mula; *[ti]m[u]la/l[a] (9)

(I) IN: cf. Ilocano (Philippines) *timel* "flea" (R. Ferrell: pers.
comm.). Form. (Puy. Ami Kuv.; Tsouic) *qa/timula "flea";
(Ami: Ferr. "body louse"); also (Sai.) *ka/tim (abbreviated
form) and (Pai.) *qa/tim/tim (abbreviated and reduplicated
form) "flea."

  M(PW) **?mu(ŋ) "flea": MPT MTT *mu*, MSY *mo* (all
h.t.); YHN *muŋ* (h.t.), id.; from PMY **?mu(ŋ); also PM
*hmɔ(ŋ): MCF *hmaŋ* "flea," MPT *hmo* "chicken flea" (both
s.t. as above), from PMY *hmun; both from *[]mul[a]; also
Yao: YCR *mua* (h.t.), id., from **?mua<*[]mu(l)a.

(II) T *mlen~*hmlin (WT) "body/clothes louse" (WT "fowl
lice," BT "flea"). Dioi *nan* "body louse," from *mlan; also *mɛn*
"the newly hatched young of lice or fleas." Sek *mlel* "body louse."
KS: Mak *nan*, id. (cf. Dioi). OB *dien* "clothes louse," from *rien.

FLEE   See HIDE.

FLESH   See BODY.

FLESH, MEAT, ANIMAL, DEER   *(m)bula(/bula);
     *bula/bula/i (55, 56, 108, 109)

(I) T *bla "seasoned raw meat" (Si.), from *(bla)bla; also
nia~?bia (Si. doublet) "flesh, meat (esp. deer meat)" (Si.
also "deer"), from *(q/)(m)blia<*(q/)(m)b(ə)la (unstressed
form). Dioi *nɔ=/noo/* "flesh, meat," from *mloo<*mbloo<
*mblua<*mb(u)la. CT *no~mo*, id., from *mlo<*mblo (cf.
Dioi). Sek *mlɔ* (Ged.), id. (cf. Dioi CT). Laha: TU *nɔ*, id.

(II) Form. *bulabulai* "flesh/meat (Ruk: Tainan), animal (Ruk: Budai)," from *bulabula/i.*

FLESH, MEAT, ANIMAL, DEER, BIRD, PULP *()(N)Gayam; *Gaya(m)/Gayam* (55, 56, 108)

(I) IN **ayam* "dog (Tg.), fowl (Ja. Ml.)." Form. East *qayam* "bird (gen.), animal (Sai.)"; Tsouic *[q]ayam* "bird (Tsou Saa.), flesh/meat (Kan.)."

T *hñia* "flesh, meat (BT); flesh, pulp (WT), bait, prey, food (Kh. Shan Si. Lao)," from *[]NGa(yam)* (palatalized); also *hñam* "meat" (WT) and *hñam* (d.t.) "bait" (WT), from *[]NG(a)(y)am.* Northern Li *xaam* "flesh/meat": N. Li *a:m*, WS Li *xa:m*, WS Loi *kham*, SH Loi *ham*, SC Loi *gom*, DC Loi *əm*, from *xa(y)am.* Lq. *yəu*, id., from *[G]a(yam)* (palatalized). N. Kl. *a*, S. Kl. *hə*, id., from *[G]a* (cf. Lq.). Lt: MP *o*; BP *o* (Rob.), *ho* (Bon.), id., from *[G]a* (cf. Lq. Kl.).

PM **NGa* "flesh, meat," from PMY **NGay*; also PM *NGe*(ŋ), id.: MTT MSY *Nqa* (l.t.), from PMY *NGem*; both from an earlier *NGayam* (vowel palatalized); MPT "flesh (of animals, birds, humans, nuts and fruits); used in referring to wild game" (Heim.). PY *ɔ=*ɔ (YCR YHA YTP)~*a* (YHN) "flesh, meat," from *[G]a*, from *Ga(yam)*; also PPY *gui* "meat," from PMY *NGay*; app. also PY **jay=*gyay* "deer" (PPY *kɛ*), from a doublet form *ŋgay* (s.t.) (palatalized); YHN also *pyou jay* "pulp"="flesh (*jay*) of fruit (*pyou*)," *kyau jay* (*pe*) "white of egg"="(white) flesh (*jay*) of egg (*kyau*)."

(II) Form. *qaya/(qa)yam* "bird (Pai. Sir.), fowl (Fav.), animal (Puy: Rikavong)."

Lk. *mom* "flesh," from *məm<*(ə)m/əm<*[G]ə[y]əm/-[G]ə[y]əm (unstressed form; cf. S. Li). S. Li *ma:m* "flesh, meat," from *(a:)m/a:m<*aam/aam<*[G]a(y)am/[G]a(y)am.*

FLESH, MEAT, DEER, BODY[1] *[ba]nan
    Form. (Pai. Fav. Sir.) *bənan* "deer," prob. from *banan* (stressed form).
    T *naan* "deer" (Tho), from *(a)nan.* KS *naan* "flesh/meat": Sui *nan*, Mak Then *na:n* (Mak also "body") (cf. Tho). OB *nan* "flesh/meat," *nan hau* "body" (*hau*, id.).

FLESH, MEAT, DEER, BODY[II] *[bo](n)tol

 Form. *butul "flesh/meat (Pai. Ruk.); deer (Kan. Saa.)."

 T *ton "body, self." KS *[]don "body": Sui dən, Mak dun, Then zen (all h.t.), from *[]nton.

FLING See THROW.

FLOAT See SWIM.

FLOAT, LIGHT (WEIGHT) *h[ə](m)baw; *ma/paw(/paw) (I) Form. (Ata.) *(la/)həbaw "light"; (Ami) *(k)ahmaw~ *dahmaw, id., from */h[ə]mbaw; also (Pai.) *si-tabaw; (Puy.) *t/m/baw "float," from */[hə]baw; also (Kuv.) *məḷinamaw, id., app. from */[hə]mbaw.

 T *ʔbaw~*[h]maw (Ahom) "light," from an original *h(m)baw. Dioi bau (h.t.), id., from *ʔbaw. Sek vaːu, id., from *waaw<*(a)baw. KS: Mak ʔbau, id. (cf. Thai). OB bau (h.t.) "float," from *ʔbaw (cf. Thai Mak). S. Li bau nom "that which floats in water (nom)."

 (II) IN: Yami mapau "light." Form. (Fav.) *m/l/paw, id.; also (Ami) *ma/paw/paw "float."

FLOOD See OVERFLOW.

FLOOR See FLAT.

FLOUR See ASHES (two entries); DUST (two entries).

FLOWER See FRUIT.

FLOWER, SWEET POTATO, TARO *(q/)(m)buŋ[ah]; *buŋ[ah]/buŋ[ah] (51, 105)

(I) IN **buŋa "flower" (Tg. "fruit"). PO *puŋa: Fi. vuŋa "name of a tree with red blossoms (Erythrina)," also "coral rock (=red blossoms)." PPN *fuŋa "flower" (Sm.); also **puŋa "coral"; both from *(m)puŋa. Form: East *buŋah "flower (Sai.), sweet potato (=the flowering top) (Puy. Thao Ami: Og.-As.), taro (Ami: Ferr.)"; Atayalic *buŋah/i "sweet potato": Sed. buŋa, Ata. ŋahiʔ.

 T *ʔbuŋ: Tho man buŋ (h.t.) "potato" (cw. *man "generic term for potato/sweet potato/yam; see CULTIVATE); Nung man buŋ (h.t.) "sweet potato (Sav.), phiak buŋ bu "kind of vegetable (phiak)," phiak buŋ man "sweet potato" (F. K. Li).

KS *muŋ: Mak *muŋ "a kind of potato (taro) with edible leaves," from *mbuŋ. Lq. Pu-peo puŋ "flower."

(II) Form. (Kan.) *buŋa[h]buŋa[h] "flower."
    Kl. *bibi* (Bon.), *la bibi* (Laj.) "flower," from *b[uŋ]b[uŋ].

FLUTE *k[l,l]u[l]i[ŋ]
    IN **t'uliŋ.

T *khluy (Si. Lao), from *khlu(r)i(ŋ). OB *sui* "clarinet" (cf. Thai). N. Li: Bas. *tsui-lau* "nose-flute" (n.a.).

FLUTTER See BEAT.

FLY, v. See MOVE BACK AND FORTH; SPREAD (OUT).

FLY, BEE *(k/)u(m)baŋ; *(q/)[]mbaŋ
(I) IN *kumbaŋ: Ml. *kumbaŋ* "bumble-bee, beetle."
    OB *meŋ-vaŋ* (Jer.), *miŋ-maŋ* (Sav.) "fly" (*meŋ* ~ *miŋ* "insect"), from *(m)baŋ. Li *vaŋ: S. Li *vaŋ* "fly" (*vaŋ-vuoŋ* "mosquito"), DC Loi *veŋ* "fly," from *bwaŋ < *(u)baŋ.

(II) PY **[]uŋ = *[mb]uŋ "fly": YCR YHA *muŋ*,YHN *buŋ* (YCR also *muŋ-ńai* "mosquito"); also YCR *mwei-muŋ* (s.t., high series) "bee" (*mwei*, id.), from *ʔmuŋ < *q[mb]uŋ.

FLY, MOTH *[k]uman
    IN **kuman "maggot" (Ml.). PO: Fi. *kuma* "moth."

T *mleeŋ muan "the common fly; any flying insect" (Kh. Shan) (*mleeŋ "insect"); *mleeŋ ŋuan "fly" (BT) (with assim. of initial); *mleeŋ moon "gnat" (Nung); *mleeŋ wan "fly" (Si. Lao); *mleeŋ von, id. (Tho-Nung); all from *muan ~ *moon ~ *(m)wan < *(-u)man. Dioi *wan* "tinea moth" (cf. Si. Lao). Lk. *mun* "fly," from *mwan (cf. Thai).

FOG/MIST *[b]o/r/(m)bok
    Form. (Thao) *burbuk "fog/mist," prob. from *bu/r/buk.

T *hmook "fog, mist, cloud," from *(o)mbok (app. aspirated by the original *r). Dioi *lap mɔ* "fog" (*lap* "obscure, dark"), from *[h]mook. KS *hmook: Mak *mo:k* (h.t.) "fog/mist," *lap mo:k* "to mist" (cf. Dioi).

FOG/MIST See DARK.

FOOD See EAT.

FOOT *til/til

Form: Sir. (Utrecht MS., 1650) *tiltil* (Bullock 1874) *tintin,*
from **[t]il[t]il.*

T **tiin,* from **(tin)tin.* Sek *ti:n.* KS **tiin:* Sui Mak Kam *tin,*
Then *tien* (cf. Thai).

FOOT   See FLAT.

FOOT/LEG   ***[ko]koq; *[qo]qoq*
(I)   Form. (W. Ruk. Ami: Tauran) **kukuq;* cf. also Kan. *kəkə.*
   T **kok* "foot (of tree, hill), base, origin"; also "stem, trunk"
(cw. **may* "tree"); also **ko* "trunk, stem; clf. for trees and
plants." Dioi *kɔk* "origin, basis," *kɔk ka* "thigh" (*ka,* id.), *kɔk
mai* "foot of a tree (*mai*)"; also *kɔ* "stem of plants; clf. for trees."
KS: Mak *ko* "clf. for trees." OB *kok.* S. Li *khok,* WS Li *khɔk.* Lt.
ton kho "knee" (Laj.) (n.a.).

(II)   Form. (Ami: Baran Kibi) **ququq* (assimilated form).
   N. Kl. *qau* "foot," from **q[o][q].*

FORCE APART   See GAPE OPEN.

FOREHEAD   See FACE; SPLIT.

FOREST¹   **[q]u(n)tal* (15)
   IN ***hu[t]an=*[ʔ]u[t]an.* PPN ***ʔuta* "inland (=forested)."
   T **thian* "forest, wilderness; wild, savage," from **thyan<
(qə)tan (unstressed form; aspir. by **q/*); also **wan* "forest,
woods, desert" (Lao), app. from **(t)wan<*(u)tan.* Dioi *tə:n*
(l.t.) "uncivilized, savage," from **də:n<*ntə:n<*(ə)ntan.* Sek
thual (Ged.), from **(q)utal* (cf. Thai). OB *dan* "partridge," for
kai dan "fowl (*kai*) of the wild (*dan*)," from **tan;* cf. T **kay
thian* "wild fowl, pheasant." Li **(khay) thaan* "partridge": S.
Li *tha:n,* WS Loi *khai thaŋ<*than* (cf. Thai). Kl. *pu tiə* (n.a.),
from **[]ta[n]* (for *pu,* see WILDERNESS).

FOREST¹¹   **[a]lats*
   IN ***alat'.* Form. (Puy: Rikavong) **al/alats* "grove."
   S. Li *kɨ:n lat* "boar"="pig (*kɨ:n*) of the forest (*lat*)," WS Li
lat, id.; Loi dial. all *lat* "wild pig." Lt. *pu lu* (n.a.) "boar." For
the semantics, cf. the identical constructions elsewhere for
"boar": Ml. *babi hutan,* Kh. *mu thin* (both with root under
FOREST¹) and Si. *mu pa* (with root under WILDERNESS).

FORK, BRANCH, GROIN *ts[a]ŋa* (89, 90, 117)

IN ***t'aŋa* "to stand apart, be forked, branch out" (Tg. "branch"). PO *saŋa "fork, crotch." SEP *saŋa: Mukawa *saga* "space between thighs."

T *hŋa "branch (Lao), groin (Nung)." Sek *ŋa* "branch."

FOUR See INTRODUCTION.

FOWL See CALL (OF BIRDS, ANIMALS).

FOX (-FLYING) See BAT.

FRAGRANT **[a](m)pḷaŋ*

N. Thai: Chuang *pyaŋ~raŋ* (h.t.). KS *[]*daŋ*: Sui Mak *daŋ* (h.t.), Kam *taŋ*. Lk. *plaŋ*.

PY **daaŋ (h.t.) "scented" (YTP YHN); also YCR *taaŋ* (s.t.) from PMY **(n)taaŋ*, from an earlier **(a)(n)taŋ*.

FRAGRANT See SMELL.

FREEZE See COAGULATE.

FROG, TOADᴵ **[ta]b[i]la/b[i]la* (15)

IN **labi "toad," from **(tabi)la/bi(la)*. Form: Puy: Hinan *tabilaʔlaʔ* "frog," from **tabila/[bi]la*.

Kl. *mi ðu plo plo* "frog" (n.a.), from **b[]la/b[]la* (unvoicing of initial).

FROG, TOADᴵᴵ **op(/op)*; **qob/qob*; **(ŋ)kop*; **ap/ap*; *kap

(I) Form. (Puy.) **up/up* "bull-frog."

T *op: Shan *op* "bull-frog" (doublet of *kop*, under III), *a:ŋ-op* "frog," *khet-op* "toad" (*khet* "frog"); cf. also T *oop "croaking of frogs."

(II) Form. (Pai: Kachirai) **qub/qub* "frog," perh. from **q/ub*.

(III) T *kop "frog" (Shan "bull-frog"), perh. from **k/op*. KS: Mak *kwap* "long-legged frog," app. from *kop. OB *kɔp nea* (both l.t.) "frog" (*nea* "field"), from *gɔp<*ŋkɔp (cf. Shan *a:ŋ-op* under I).

Miao: PWA *kaiʔ "toad," from PMY **k[ɔp]*.

(IV) Form. (Ami) **ap/ap* "frog."

(V) Cham *kap* "very small frog (Rana gracilis) with piercing cry," perh. from **k/ap*.

FROG, TOAD, TADPOLE   *[t]akur[a]; *[ta](ŋ)kura/k[ura];
  *[t]akura/q[ura]; *(ta)kar[a](/qura); *(ta)qura(/qura)
(I)   IN *ka[t]ak: Ml. *kata*? "frog," app. from *ka/tak(ura).
Form. (Ruk.) *takura-; (Ami) *ta/takura~*ba/takura "frog."
  Lq. *kuan* "frog," from *(a)kun.

(II)   Cham *krak* "Rana tigrina (?); small frog with piercing
cry," also *kiak* "frog," from *k(u)rak<*k(u)ra/k(ura).

  T *khuak* (Ahom Lao)~*guak (WT) "tadpole," from
*(ŋ)k(h)uak, from an earlier *(ŋ)ku(r)ak(ura); also *ruak
"tadpole (Shan), toad (Nung)," from *(u)rak. Dioi *ruk* "tadpole," from *ruak (cf. Shan Nung). L *[r]aak: S. Li *da*? *mau*
"toad" (n.a.), from *(ku)ra/k(ura) (cf. Thai).

(III) Form. (E. Ruk.) *takura[q]ur "frog," from *takura/qur[a].

(IV) Form: Kan. *takaru:ra* "frog," from *takar[a]/[q]ura by
vocalic assim.
  WS Li *kha:l* "frog," from *kha[r]. Lt. *a/khe,* id., from
*/kha[r].

(V)   Form. (Pai.) *(ta)qura(/qur) "frog," from *(ta)qura-
(/qura); also (Bun.) *qu[r]u/qu[r]u, id. (assim. form).

FROST   See DEW.

FRUIT, ARECA, FLOWER   *(m)bu(w)aq(/i); *mbu[/mbuaq];
  *(q/)(m)b/l/u(w)aq; *(q/)(m)b/l/u[/b/l/uaq]   (20, 41, 42)
(I)   IN **bua*?=*(m)bua*? "fruit." Yami (a)buwa*? "areca,"
from *[qa/]bu(w)a*?. PPN **fua "fruit" (Easter Island "testicle"), from *pua; also **pua "flower," from *mpua. SEP *(fua)-
fua "fruit": Motu *huahua,* Kiriwina *uwa;* also *pua "areca": Motu
bua-, Kiriwina *bua;* from *pua~*mpua (cf. the PPN doublet).
Form. *buaq "fruit (Puy. Fav. Sir.), flower (Bun.)"; also (Ata.)
*bu(w)ay "flower," from *bu(w)a(q)i<*bu(w)aq/i; cf. also
Sai. *boway* "flower," from *buway, a prob. loan from Ata.

(II)   T *mu "areca" (Ahom Shan), from *mbu, prob. from an
original *mbu/mbuaq (cf. SEP).

(III) T **?blook "flower," from **?bluak<*q/b/l/uak. Dioi *dɔ*
"clf. for flowers," from **?dook<**?blook (cf. Thai). Sek *?blɔ:k*
(Haud.), *blɔɔk* (h.t.) (Ged.) "flower" (cf. Thai). KS *(?)nuak,

id.: Sui *nuk* (l.t.), Then *nuek* (h.t.), from *(q/)nduak<*(q/)-mbluwak* (cf. Thai). Laha: TU *ba:l*, id., from *b/al(/uaq)*. Lt. *miɔ*, id., from *mbyɔ<*mblɔ[q]<*mblua[q]* (cf. KS).

(IV) T *blu* "betel" (SW); also *(ʔ)(m)blaw*, id. (Tho-Nung), from *(q/)(m)b(a)lu;* both from *(q/)(m)b/al/u*, prob. from an original *(q/)(m)blu/bluaq* (cf. II). Sek *plu*, id., app. a loan from Thai (Haud. 1963bis).

    PY **pyou;* PM *tsri=*pli;* both from PMY *tsr[]=*plou* "fruit," from *b/l/ou* (cf. Thai).

FRUIT, TESTICLE, OYSTER *(n)t[i]ɣəm; *t[]ɣam* (62)

(I) IN **tiɣəm* "oyster." PO *(n)tiɣo*, id.: Fi. *ndio*, Sa. *i/ilo*. For the semantics, cf. Western U.S.A. "mountain oysters"="sheep testicles."

    Li *thrəəm* "fruit": S. Li *sa:m~ɕa:m*, WS Li *hom*, SH Loi *səm-*, DC Loi *thəm-*, from *t(ə)rəm* (vocalic assim.). Lq. *dəm*, id., probably for *rəm<*[tə]rəm* (cf. Li).

(II) T *thram~*kǎ/thram* (Si. Lao) "testicles"; for the semantics, cf. Easter Island *hua* "testicle"<PPN **fua* "fruit" (under FRUIT/ARECA/FLOWER). Sek *ram* "testicle."

G

GAPE/STAND OPEN See OPEN.

GARDEN See DIG INTO; EARTH.

GASP See OPEN (MOUTH).

GATHER, GROUP *[t][i](m)pun; *[ti]mbu[n]*

(I) IN **i(m)pun=*ʔi(m)pun;* also **[t]i(m)pun* and **ḷi-(m)pun=*ri(m)pun* "gather"; prob. all from *ti(m)pun~*t/r/i(m)pun*.

    Li *vun:* S. Li *vun* "gather, find, arrange (objects, luggage)," from *bwun<*mpwun<*(u)mpun<*(i)mpun* (vocalic assim.).

(II) PMY **mbom* "group, herd," from *[]mbo[n]* (assim.).

GATHER TOGETHER *[raŋ]kum*

IN *raŋkum: Maranao raŋkom, Ml. raŋkum "gather together," Bolaang Mongondow laŋkum "handful" (Blust 1973).

T *kum "gather, assemble, collect" (Ahom Kh. Shan).

GATHER(ED), CROWD *puluŋ

IN **puluŋ "gather" (Tg. "gathered; meeting, session"; TB. "gathered").

T *phru[u]ŋ "a swarm" (Ahom), from *ph(u)ruŋ; also *fuuŋ "crowd, herd, flock" (Shan "mass, large body, collection"), from *phwuuŋ < *phu(r)uŋ.

GEM See STONE.

GHOST See BREATHE; SPIRIT.

GINGER See PUNGENT; SHARP (TASTING).

GIRL See FEMALE.

GIRL, MAIDEN *(n)da[y]aŋ

IN **dayaŋ.

T *naaŋ, from *ndaaŋ < *nda(y)aŋ.

GIVE *(m)[ba]γa[ka]y

IN **bəγay, from *bəγa(k)ay (cf. PPN Kuv.). PPN **foaki= *foake (Maori Tuamotuan Rarotongan)~*foaki (To. Sm. Fu.), from *poakay < *bə[γ]akay. Form. (Kuv.) *bəγakay (complete form but with unstressed V₁); (Ruk.) *wa/baγay < *baγa(k)ay; (Paz.) *ba/baγa (partially redupl.); (Puy. Fav.; Sed.) *bəγay (unstressed form; cf. IN); (Pai. Ami) *pa/bəγay; (Thao) *γay < *[bə]γay.

T *hai, from *hγayə < *[]γa[]y (cf. Thao). Dioi hai (cf. Thai). Li *[r]ə: S. Li də, from *rai < *[]γayə (cf. Thai). Lq. muəi, from *mb[γ]ai. Lt: MP, BP yi (Rob.), from *yay < *[][γ]ay.

GLITTER See LIGHT (GIVE LIGHT); SHINE.

GLOOMY See DARK.

GLOW See LIGHT (GIVE LIGHT).

GLUTINOUS, STICKY *[da](m)p[u]lut; *mbulut

(I) IN **pulut "sticky substance (*Klebstoff*)" (NgD. "glutinous kind of rice"); also **dampul~**dəmpul (unstressed form), id., app. from *d[a]mpulut; also the doublet form: *pili[t] "sticky, adhesive" (Bukidnon Manobo "glutinous variety of rice") (Blust 1973). PPN **pulu* "gum, resin" (Rarotongan "sticky"); also *puluti* "to glue" (To. Fu. Sm.) and *pulu/puluti* "sticky" (Fi.); all from **mpulu[t]*.

    T *[br]ut* "sticky, viscous" (Nung), from **mprut*. Dioi *śut* "glutinous (rice)," from **vrut<*[br]ut* (cf. Nung).

(II) PMY ***mbḷut* "glutinous, sticky" (also applied to glutinous rice), from an earlier **mbḷuut<*mb(u)ḷut*.

GNAT   See INSECT (WINGED).

GNAW   See BITE.

GNAW, CHEW, BITE, GRIND TEETH **ŋat/ŋat; *(ŋ)kat(/kat);*
    **[ŋət/]ŋ[ə]t; *[kət/]k[ə]t; *[kit/]kit*

(I) IN ***ŋatŋat* "gnaw." PO: Sa. ŋaŋa "(gnawed away=) ulcerous." Form: Paz. ŋaŋadzip "bite," app. from **ŋa/ŋa(t)-dzip* (partially redupl. form), but possibly reflecting an archaic (un-suffixed) root: **ŋa/ŋa*.

    T *hŋeen* (SW)~*ŋeen* (Nung) "gnaw" (Lao "gnaw, nibble, graze, pasture"; WT "take object by seizing it in jaws"), from **(h)ŋaan<*(ŋan)ŋan<*ŋan/ŋat*. Dioi hɛn (irreg. l.t.) "tear with teeth, gnaw," from **hŋeen* (cf. Thai). KS: Mak ńaːi (h.t.) "chew (food)," from **hŋaay*, app. from **(ŋad)ŋat* (second. voicing; contrast the second. nasalization in Thai), but possibly reflecting an archaic suffixed root: **(ŋa/i)ŋa/i* (cf. Pazeh). OB ŋean "gnaw [bone]; (ic.) ruminate," ŋian ŋean "grind [teeth]," from **(ŋən)ŋan* (unstressed form). S. Li ŋaːi "ruminate [buffalo]," app. from **(ŋad)ŋat* (cf. Mak); also ŋaːn "carry in the jaws [as a dog]," from **(ŋan)ŋat* (cf. Thai).

    Yao: YCR ŋaat "bite," from **(ŋat)ŋat*.

(II) T *geet~*ket* (Shan) "gnaw (Lao); separate by pressing between two sharp edges, cut off with scissors, bite (Shan); cut, cut off, lop [branches], cut up [meat, bread] (Nung)," from **(ŋ)kat(kat)*. Dioi kiat (short vowel tone) "crunch, munch (as seeds, nuts)," from **[k]et* (cf. Shan).

(III) IN ***ŋətŋət* "grind teeth" (Tg. "rage," TB. "pain"); also Yami ŋətŋət/ən "bite," perhaps from an earlier **ŋatŋat* (vocalic assim.)<*ŋatŋat* (unstressing). PO: Fi. ŋoŋo "to be helpless."

(IV) IN *kə[t]kə[t] "bite, gnaw": Bukidnon Manobo *ketket* "of any sharp-toothed animal to gnaw away; gnaw a hole in something," Lawangan *kikit*, Tabojan ŋi*kit* "bite" (Blust 1973); also **kəkət "hold fast" (Ho. "grip, bite," n.), from *kətkət (partial redupl.), perhaps from an earlier *kətkat<*katkat (cf. IV).

(V) IN *ki[t]ki[t] "bite": Cebuano Visayan *kitkit* "wear something down bit by bit with the front teeth taking tiny bites; nibble," Paku *i-kikit*, Samihim ŋi*kit* "bite" (Blust 1973).

T *kit "shortened, cut off, to break" (Lao), from *(kit/)- kit; for the semantic development, cf. Tho-Nung and Dioi under BITE/GNAW.

GO See MOVE BACK AND FORTH.

GOAT *(k/)(m)biaŋ; *[b]iyaŋ; *(q/)(m)bia(q) (46, 101)

(I) IN **kambiŋ.

T *[b]eeŋ (Ahom doublet).

(II) Form. (Sai.) *biyaŋ "buck (male deer)."

T *yiaŋ "goat antelope (Shan), wild goat (Lao WT)," from *(i)yaŋ. S. Li *yaŋ* "sheep/goat," an app. b.l. from Ch. *iaŋ*, id., but note WS Li *ziaŋ*, SH Loi *jiaŋ~jɛŋ*, DC SC Loi *jɛŋ*, from *yiaŋ<*(i)yaŋ.

PMY **yuaŋ "sheep, goat," app. by dissim. from *yiaŋ <*(i)yaŋ (cf. Li) but poss. Ch. b.l./influ.

(III) T *be=/bee/ (Ahom Kh. Shan)~**beʔ (Si.)~*ʔbe (Lao BT WT Tho-Nung) "goat" (Nung also "sheep"), from *(ʔ)be(ʔ) <*(q/)bia(q). Dioi *bɛ* "sheep," from *ʔbɛ (with irreg. l.t.). Sek *bɛ* (h.t.) (Ged.), from *ʔbɛ (cf. Thai). KS *bia: Sui *pya* (l.t.). Lk. *ywie*, from *ywia<*[]bia. OB *mɛ* "goat, sheep," from *mbɛ<*mbia. N. Kl. *miɛ*, S. Kl. *mə mɛ*, from Kl. *miɛ<*mia< *mbia. Lt: MP *miɔ*; BP *mbe* (Rob.), *mio* (Bon.), from Lt. *mbio<*mbia.

GOD See SPIRIT.

GOURD *s[ə]k[u]ay (53)

Form. (Ata.) *səkuay~*səquay.

Li *xay: WS Loi *khai*, FF Loi *hai*, SC Loi *gai* "gourd," DC Loi *ai* "gourd," *hai* "dipper," SH Loi *hai* "pumpkin," from *skh(w)ay<*s[]k[u]ay.

GOURD   See DIP.

GRAIN   See HARD.

GRANARY   See HUT.

GRANDCHILD   See GRANDPARENT (two entries).

GRANDCHILD (GREAT-), GRANDPARENT (GREAT-)
   *(q/)li/l[i]; *(q/)li/a; *(q/)la/l[a] (26, 65, 69, 70, 73)
(I)   IN **nin[i] "great-grandchild (TB.), grandmother (Ja.),
grandparents (Ml.)," from *lini (assim. to medial n)<*lili.

   T *hlin~*hlen "great-grandchild; great-nephew/niece"
(Ahom "great-grandfather"), from *q/lin<*q/lil(i). Laha: BB
mli, NL mlay "nephew/grandchild" (glossed by Vn. cháu),
from *m/li(li).

(II)   T *[h]lia "great-great-grandchild" (Nung Dioi); also *hlia
"great-great-great-grandchild" (Si.) (Benedict 1943); both from
*q/lí/a~*q/li/á.

(III) T *hlaan "grandchild, nephew/niece," from *q/laan<
*q(a/)lal(a). Dioi lan (h.t.) "grandson, nephew," from *hla[a]n.
Sek la:n (h.t.) "grandson" (cf. Thai). KS *qhlaan "grandchild":
Sui qhan~khan~han, Mak Then la:n, Kam khwa:n (all h.t.)
(Mak also "sister's child" and "cousin"="fa's si's daughter").
Lk. khya:n "grandson," from *khla:n. OB lan [h.t.], from *hlan
(cf. Thai). Li *[ql]aal: S. Li han "nephew/niece," Bup lad
"child; young," WS Li la:l "child (general term) [cw. 'child']"
(cf. Thai KS).

GRANDMOTHER   See MOTHER.

GRANDPARENT, GRANDCHILD   *[(t/)a]mu; *[(t/a)]mu/a;
   *[(t/)a]mu/an
(I)   PO: Fi. (Nadrau) kamu "father [address]" (Cap. and
Lester), from */amu. Form. */amu "grandchild (Kan. Saa.)";
*t/amu "grandparents (Kan. Saa.), grandfather (Ruk.)"; also
*mumu "grandfather (W. Ruk: Maga)," app. from *[a]mu/[a]mu.

(II)   T *hmua "mother's father" (Lao), from *[]mu/a.
      PMY **mua "younger sister" (via "[grand]child").

(III) Form. (Puy.) *təmuan "grandparents, ancestors (Ferr.),

Austro-Thai

grandchild (Og.-As.)," from **t/amu/an* (stressed form).

T **hmoon* "great-grandfather" (Kh. Shan), from **[]muan* < **[]mu/an.*

GRANDPARENT, GRANDCHILD, PARENT, UNCLE, MALE, HUSBAND **(m)pu(/(m)pu); *(m)pu/a; *a(m)pu(/a(m)pu); *k/ampu*

(I) IN **pu "sir" [term of respect for older males]. PO **mpu:* Fi. *bu* "fa's parents (Bau), mo's mother (Nausori)." SEP **mpu/mpu:* Motu *bubu* "term of address to elders" (Capell: "this is the normal term for grandparent in Malekula and other parts of the New Hebrides, and they always are vocatives"). Form. **bubu* "grandparents (Pai. Fav. Ami), mother [through teknonymy] (Sed.)," from **mpu/mpu.*

T **phu~*bu* (Si. Lao) "male (human, animals, birds); clf. for human beings," from **(m)pu.* N. Thai **bu:* Dioi *pu* (l.t.) "clf. for men, spirits; male of birds," Yay *pu* (l.t.) "person," Sek *phu* (l.t.) "person" (Ged.), "male of birds" (Haud.), from **mpu.* KS **bu* "father": Sui Then *pu,* Mak *pəu* (all l.t.), from **mpu.*

Miao: MPT *phaɨ* "male of certain large animals," from PMY **ph[ou];* cf. also MCF *vu* (h.t.) "old woman, grandmother," from PMY **ʔw[ou],* perhaps from **(bu)bu.*

(II) PO **pua:* Fi: Macuata and Bua *vua-* "grandchild" (Bua also "si's child").

T **phua* "husband" (SW), from **phu/a;* cf. also **bo= /boo/* "father," app. from **bua<*mpua* (without morpheme boundary-marker). N. Thai **bɔ:* Dioi *pɔ,* Sek *phɔ* (Ged.) (both l.t.) "father" (cf. Thai). Lt. **p[ua]:* MP *pu,* BP *pɔ* "male (of animals)," also MP *li pu,* BP *li po* (Rob.), *ni po* (Bon.) "man (male)," also *pu so* "husband" (Bon.).

PY ***pua=*pua~*bua* "father-in-law" (<"uncle" through cross-cousin marriage), from PMY **(m)pua,* prob. from an earlier **(pu/)(m)pu/a.*

(III) IN ***ə(m)pu* "grandparent/grandchild"=**apu* (Tg. *apó* "grandchild," *apo* "grandfather, old man respected in the community")~**ə(m)pu* (unstressed form) (Tg. *impó* "grandparent," NgD. *ĕmpo* "parents-in-law"<"grandparents" through teknonymy); also **tumpu: Ho. *tumpu* "sir," from *t/əmpo (vocalic assim.; cf. NgD. *těmpo* "owner/proprietor"); also Yami *inapu* "ancestor," app. from *[t/]in/apu. PO **tumpu "grandparent, grandchild," from *t/əmpu (cf. IN): Fi. "ancestor" (Bau); fa's father (Nausori); grandmother and all female ancestors (Lau); grandmother (Talaulia Tavuki); grandparent, mo's bro's wife (Macuata); grandparent, mo's brother, mo's bro's wife (Bua) (CL). SEP *a(m)pu "mo's brother": Paiwa *yavu*, Mukawa *abu*, Ubir Wedau *avu*, Wagawaga *au*. PPN *tupu "king" (Sm.); *tupu- "forefather" (To. Fu. Sm.), from *tumpu< *t/əmpu (cf. IN PO); also **tupuʔa "ancient, venerable, having supernatural powers" [supernatural being/spirit/demon/goblin/idol], from *tumpu/qa. Form. (Thao) *apu "grandparents"; (Paz.) *apu/apu "ancestor."

T *pu "fa's father"; also *paw "great-grandfather" (Lao BT), from *(a)pu; also *aaw "fa's younger brother," from *(ábu)ábu<*(ámpu)ámpu (diminutive formation="little grandfather"). Dioi *pau um* "fa's father" (n.a.); also *pɔ au* "fa's (pɔ) younger brother" (cf. Thai). KS: Then *ʔo* "uncle," from *[aaw] (cf. Thai). Li *phau~p(h)əw (second. aspiration): S. Li *phau ~fau* "sir, old man; (ic.) genie, spirit of the hearth," from *(a)pu; WS Li *pəu* "grandchild (grandfather sp.)," *phəu* "grandfather," from *(ə)pu (basically a self-reciprocal term, as in IN). Laha: TU *a:w* "father" (cf. Thai Then).

Miao: PT *apu* "grandfather"; MFPL *awu* "fa's mother," app. from PMY *a(m)p[ou] (poss. secondary formation).

(IV) IN **makumpu: Bare'e (Central Celebes) *makumpu* "grandchild" (Cap. cit.), from *ma/k/əmpu (vocalic assim.) <*ma/k/ampu (stressed form). PO *makumpu~*makəmpu (cf. IN): Fi. *makumbu* "grandson," Sa. *maopu* "egg." PPN **mokopuna "grandchild," from *mə/k/əmpu/na (all unstressed form; cf. IN PO).

T *kaaw "male of animals" (Lao), from *(k/ábu)k/ábu <*(k/ámpu)k/ámpu (cf. the development of Thai *aaw, above).

GRANDPARENT (GREAT-) See GRANDCHILD (GREAT-).

GRASS *[ro](m)pot; *[ri]mbot[ol]

(I) IN **lumput=*rumput, perh. by vocalic assim. from

rimput (cf. II). PO: Fi. *rumbu* "a kind of basket" (<"woven grass").

OB *bət* (Jer.), *bɔt* (h.t.) (Sav.), from *pot*.

(II) Form. (Sai.) *[r]imbutul*.

GRASS   See THATCH (-GRASS).

GRASSHOPPER   *(m)balaŋ; *b[a]lak (20, 21)

(I)   IN **balaŋ; also (Ml. and Maranao) *bilalaŋ (Blust 1973).
T *[ń]aaŋ (Nung), from *mbraaŋ<*mb(a)raŋ.

(II) T *tak (SW)∼*thrak (Tho), from *prak∼*phrak. N.
Thai *trak/prak: Dioi *tak*, Wu-ming *rak*. KS *[]dyak: Sui *dyak*,
Mak *dak*, Then *zyak* (all h.t.).

GRAVE   See BURY.

GRAY   See Ashes (two entries).

GREASE   See FAT (two entries).

GREEN   *(q/)hi [dz]aw
    IN **hid'aw.
    T *xiaw (Shan also "black"; Ahom "deep-dark, dark in color"),
from *q[h]i[z]aw. Dioi *hɛu*, from *qhɛu<*qhiaw (cf. Thai).
Sek *heu* "light green," from *qheu<*qhiaw (cf. Dioi). KS *syiu:
Sui *su∼hyu*, Mak *yəu*, Then *yiu*, from *qhyiu<*qh(i)y(a)w
(cf. Thai); cf. also the Mak doublet: *yəu ywa:u*. Lk. *yau* (cf.
KS). Li *khiaw: S. Li *kheo∼khio*, WS Li *khiu*, N. Li dial.
khiau∼khiu∼kheu (FF Loi "blue"), Ha *khiau* "green," *khio*
"blue," Ki *khio* "blue."

GREEN   See BLUE.

GRIND TEETH   See GNAW.

GROIN   See FORK.

GROWL   See RUMBLE.

H

HAIL   See LIGHTNING.

HAIR, BEARD   *(n)dza[a](m)[bot]
    IN **d'[a,ə](m)but "hair" (TB *d'abut* "plant hair, chest hair,"
d'ambut "plant hair, animal hair," Ja. *d'ĕmbut* "pubic hair").

Li *nom "head hair": S. Li *nom*, N. Li SH Loi *tom*, Bas. Ki Ha *dam=tam*, from *ndzom(bot)* (vocalic assim.). Lq. ðam, id., from *sam(bot)*. Kl. *sa[m]*, id.: N. Kl. *ma* saŋ (n.a.), S. Kl. lə so (cf. *bu* lə ði "ear," *do* lə *pu* "breast"). Lt. *a/so*, id., from */sa[m]*.

PMY **śyaam=*syaam "beard" (YCR also "mustache").

HAIR, HAIRY^I   *[p][]ra(m)[b]o[t]
   IN **[l]a(m)but=*[r]a(m)bot "hairy" (Ja. Ml. "head hair"); cf. **d'[a,ə](m)but "hair" (see under HAIR/BEARD) and *lumput=*rumput "grass" (but Sai. *[r]imbutul) (see under GRASS).
   T *phrom "head hair," from *p[]rom(bot) (with vocalic assim.). Dioi *pyɔm* "fallen hair," from *p[hr]om (cf. Thai). Sek *phram* "head hair" (Ged.), from *p[]ram(bot) (without vocalic assim.). KS *pyam*, id.: Sui Mak Kam *pyam*, Then *pem*, from *p[r]am(bot) (cf. Sek). Lk. *kyom=ćom* (irreg. l.t.), id., from *[pr]om(bot) (with vocalic assim., as in Thai Dioi).

HAIR, TOPKNOT   *(q/)u(m)bal
   IN **bulu=*(m)bulu "down, hair, feather." PO *(m)pulu: Fi. *vulu/a* "pubic hair," *mbulu-kovu* "hair-knot," Sa. *hulu* "hairy." PPN **fulu "hair, feather."
   T *pru "hairy, covered with hair" (Si.: ic.).

HAIR, TOPKNOT   *(q/)u(m)bal
   IN **ʔuban "gray hair/gray-haired." PO *ʔupa "gray hair" (Blust 1972): Nggela *uva-na*, Bogotu *ufa* (irreg. loss of initial), Gilbertese *ia*. Form. *qubal "hair (head, body, pubic), feather/down (Sed.), head hair (Pai.), body hair (Ruk: Budai)."
   T *muay "topknot" (SW only) (Lao also "head"), from *mbuay<*(u)mbay.

HAIR (BODY), BEARD   *(n)qo(m)bi(t)s(/(N)qo(m)bi(t)s)
   IN **kumit' "beard," from *Nqumbits (cf. Form.); also **gumi, id., from the partially reduplicated form *kumi/kumit'<*Nqumbi/Nqumbits, with secondary voicing. PO: Fi. *kumi*, id. PPN **kumikumi "beard, chin," also (through vocalic assim.) *kumukumu "chin (To. Uvean), pendulous lichen" (To. add. gloss). Form. *(N)qu(m)bis "pubic hair (East; Ata: Squliq, ic.) (Pai: Mak. also "axillary hair"); beard, body hair, feather/

down (Ata: Ci'uli); also *misa/misi "beard" (W. Ruk: Maga
Tona), from *(Nqu)mbis/(Nqu)mbis; also *[G]um[b]is, id.
(Sai: rumis~romis), through secondary voicing (cf. IN **gumi);
also (through vocalic assim., as in PPN) *[q]ubus "pubic hair"
(W. Ruk: Maga); *[qu]b/l/us "body hair" (Kuv.); *q[u]m[b]us/
q[u]m[b]us "beard (Kuv. mu:mus); body hair, beard (Tsou
muʔmuu~mʔumʔu)."

   T *hmooy "pubic/axillary hair" (Shan also "beard"), from
*q(o)moy<*q(o)mboy<*q(o)mbiy (vocalic assim.; cf. PPN
Form.); also *m[o]m "beard" (Tho-Nung), from *mo/m(oy)
<*(qo)mbo/(qo)mbos (partial redupl.; cf. Kuv. Tsou). Dioi
mi (h.t.) "pubic hair," from *hmi<*q(o)mi<*q(o)mbiy (without vocalic assim.; contrast Thai); also mɔm~mum "beard,
body hair" (cf. Tho-Nung). Li *mɨɨm "beard/whiskers": S. Li
mə:m, WS Li pum, Loi dial. bəm~bə:m=pəm~pə:m, from
myəm<(qə)mo/(qə)mos (unstressed form; contrast Tho-
Nung Dioi). Lq. mun<*mum, Pu-peo mum; Laha: BB mom
"beard" (cf. Tho-Nung Dioi).

HAIR (BODY), EYEBROW   *[gu]mul

   Form. *gumul "body hair, feather/down (Puy.), pubic hair
(Sai)."
   OB mui (Jer.), mei (Sav.) "eyebrow" (cw. "eye"), the latter
form suggesting a poss. loan from Ch. mei, id.

HAIR (BODY), FEATHER   *k[u](m)pur; *(N)q[u](m)pur (28)

(I) Form. (Thao) *kupur "body hair, feather/down."
   Dioi pɛn "body hair or feathers, hairy," Wu-ming pun
"body hair." CT phun~phon, id. (initial app. influ. by earlier
*kh-<*k-). Sek pul "body hair; (ic.) eyebrow." KS *tsun "body
hair": Sui tsən, Mak zun, Then sun (all h.t.) (Mak also "feather"),
from *k(h)un<*kwun<*k(u)bun<*k(u)mpun (cf. Thai and
Li under II). Kam pyən "body hair." Lk. kyɛŋ=ćɛŋ, id., from
*pyɛŋ (cf. Kam). OB vun "hair" (Jer.), bɔn<*wɔn "body hair,
feathers; (ic.) eyelash, eyebrow" (Sav.), from *(k)wun.

(II) T *xon "body hair, feather, down, wool; (ic.) eyelash,
eyebrow," from *xwun (dissim.)<*x[]mpun (cf. KS under I).
Li *hŋu[u]n: S. Li hu:n "body hair, feather, mane; (ic.) eye-

lash, eyebrow," WS Li ŋoŋ<*ŋon "body hair; (ic.) head hair, eyelash, eyebrow," N. Li dial. *hun~hin* "eyelash," from *[Nq]uun.

HAIR (HEAD) See HEAD.

HALF See MIDDLE.

HAMMER See BEAT.

HAND See PALM.

HAND, FIVE *(ka/)[l]ima; *(ka/)lima (15)

(I) IN **lima "five"; also *ka/lima "hand" (Philippines: Cala-miano), cited by Mohring, who interprets it as an infixed form from **kima "giant clam"<"scraper" (see SHELLFISH/CLAM). PO *lima "five": Fi. *lima,* Sa. *lime.* SEP: Ubir Oyan *ima*<*[l]ima "hand." PPN (gen.) **lima "hand, five." Form: East (gen.) *ḷima "hand, five," but Ruk. *ḷima "five," *(qa/)ḷima "hand"; Tsouic, Atayalic *ḷima "five."

(II) PO *nima "hand": Sa. *nime-.* SEP: Ubir Oyan *nim*<*nim[a] "five." PPN (To. Uvean) *nima "hand, five," from *(ka)lima (medial *l>n).

T *mɨ "hand," from *mya<*(-i)ma. Sek mɨ, id. KS *( )mia, id.: Sui *mya~miə,* Mak *mi* (all h.t.), Then Kam *mya* (both l.t.) (cf. Thai). Lk. *mie,* id., from *mia (cf. Thai and KS). OB *mə* (Jer.), *me* (Sav.), id., from *mya (cf. Thai). Li *ma "five": S. Li *ma,* WS Li *pa,* Loi dial. *ba=pa;* also *[]mə "hand": S. Li WS Li *mə,* Loi dial. *məg=mə,* from *mya (cf. Thai and KS). Lq. *mə* "five," also *kha mi* "hand" (Laj.) (cf. *kha pa* "arm" et al.), from *mya (cf. Li). N. Kl. *mbu* "five," from *ma; also *mau* (Clarke), (*bi*) *mou* (De B.) "hand," from *[l-]ma; S. Kl. *mu* "five" (ic. "15"), from *ma; also *mlen* "five" (Laj. *nlle*), *mle* "hand" (ic. "finger"), from *mla(n)<*lma(n), by metath. (with second. nasal.). Lt: BP *mg=m* "hand; five" (Rob.), ŋ "five" (Bon.); MP *mg=m* "five," *cha mg=śa m* "hand," all from *m(u)<*ma.

HANDFUL See SEIZE.

HANDFULS (TWO) See HOLD TOGETHER.

HANDLE See STICK.

HANDLE, STICK, STEM   *[ts]a(ŋ)kaḷ; *[tsa]ŋgaḷ (12)

(I)   IN **t'aŋkal "handle of tool."

    T *gan~*kan (Nung doublet)~*khan (Lao doublet) "handle, stick, rod, petiole [leaf stem]," from *( )(ŋ)kan; also *kaan~*keen (Shan doublet) "handle (Lao Tho); stem, stalk, as of a leaf (Shan); fibre of leaves (Si.)," from *(a)kan. Dioi *kan* "button (of cap), peduncle [stem] (of fruit), handle (of pot cover)." KS *gan: Mak *kan* (l.t.) "handle," from *ŋkan; also *kaan: Then *ka:n tien* "leg"="stalk of foot (*tien*)," from *(a)kan.

(II)   KS: Mak *ŋan* "peduncle," from *ŋgan.

HANG   *xu[r]ay(/xu[r]ay)

    IN **u[ḷ]ay=*u[r]ay "hang loose," with app. loss of initial *ʔ through earlier reduplication: *uray/uray<*(ʔ)uray/(ʔ)uray; cf. also **layḷay=*rayray "hang," from *(ʔu)ray/(ʔu)ray, with complete loss of initial syllable. Form: Ata. *qǝmuziʔ* "hang (intr.)," *sǝquziʔ* "hang (tr.)," from *q/m/u[r]ay~*s/qu[r]ay.

    T *hooy "hang, suspend" (Kh. "hang, suspend, dangle; fasten in a manner which will allow free motion upon the point of suspension"), from *huay<*hu[r]ay.

HARD, HEART (HARD PART), GRAIN, STONE   *[ma/]ka;
   *[ma/]ka/ts; *(ma/)(ŋ)ka/n

(I)   IN *maka: Tg. *pa/maka* "to sling" (Cap.) (for semantics, see PPN). SEP *maka "tooth (= the hard part)." PPN **maka "stone (= the hard part), sling-stone; to sling, throw."

    T *ka "hard, firm, robust," also "to temper (=harden) steel" (Lao). KS: Sui *ka* "hard."

(II)   IN **makat' "hard."

    OB *kiet* "coagulate (= harden)."

    Miao: MCF *koʔ* "hard, stiff," from PM *k[u]ʔ; Yao: YHN *kat* "congeal, freeze" (for semantics, cf. OB); both from PMY *kat.

(III)   T *keen "hard, solid, firm," also (mostly on d.t.) "hard part of anything (grain, heart of tree or fruit, pupil of eye)," also *kheen "to reforge (=harden) (metal)" (Si.); cf. also *khan~*xan "robust, strong" (Lao also "firm, hard"); app. all

from *(a)ka/n. Dioi *kien* "heart, hard center, hard," also *kien~
kɛn* (l.t., same series)<*gien~*gɛn* "hard (as rice)," from
*(ŋ)keen. Lk. *nam tsen*<*ken* "fruit" (cf. *nam tu* "stomach").

HAT   See COVER (two entries).

HAVE (POSSESSION), ACQUIRE (POWER), MANA, HAVE
    BREATH   *[m]a/naŋ; [b]a/naŋ

(I)   IN **mənaŋ* "acquire," from *manaŋ* (stressed form). PPN
**mana* "supernatural force" (To. Fu. "thunder," ic.). SEP *mana*
"wind" (usu.) but Dobu also has *bo-mana* "supernatural power"
(Capell, in "The word *mana*, a linguistic study," *Oceania 9: 1*
considers this to be a PN l.w. in this meaning).

(II) IN   **bənaŋ*: Ja. *wĕnaŋ* "have power," from *banaŋ*
(stressed form).

    KS **naŋ* "have" (Mak *naŋ ziŋ* "have strength"="strong").
    Yao: HY *naaŋ* "to have breath, be alive," from *(a)naŋ*.

HEAD, HAIR (HEAD), TOPKNOT   *q[a]lu[b](u); *q[a]lu-
    [b/]an; *q[]lu[b/]a; *k[]lu[b/]a; *k[a]la[b](u) (25)

(I)   IN **hulu~**ulu=**ʔulu* "head," from *qulub*<*qalub*
(vocalic assim.). Cham *haluv~halau*, id. (latter form through
assim.). SEP *qulu* "head (most languages), crown of head
(Kiriwina), hair (Sariba Nada Gumasi). PPN **ʔulu* "head, hair."
Form. *qalub(u)* "head hair (Puy.), eyebrow (Sai.)"; *quḷubu*
"head hair (Bun.), eyebrow (Kan.)," from *qaḷubu* (vocalic
assim.; cf. IN); also (Pai. Kuv. Sir.) *quḷu*; (Ruk.) *qa/quḷu*
"head" (cf. IN).

    Lq. *ru* "head" (Laj.).

    PM **heu=*qhleu* "head": MCF *haŋ*, MKS MPT *hau*,
MHC *hou*, MLL *xu*, but MKL *fhu*, MWN *fau* (Purn. cites last
pair as "irreg."), from PMY *qhḷ[up], from an earlier *q[]ḷuup
<*q(u)ḷup* (vocalic assim., as in IN and Form.).

(II) IN **haluwan=**ʔaluwan* "prow (=head of boat)," from
**ʔalub/an.

(III) T *hrua (SW)~*thrua* (Tho-Nung) "head" (Si. also
"chief" and "hair," Nung also "chief"), from *qhrua*<*q[]ru(w)a
<*q[]rub/a. N. Thai *xria* "head," from *q[]rə(w)a* (unstressed
form).

(IV) T *khrua "chief, superior (=head)" (Si.), from *k[]ru(w)a (cf. III).

(V) Form. (Ami) *ka[ḷ]a[b]u "eyebrow," from *kaḷubu by vocalic assim. (cf. doublet in Cham under I).

    T *klaw "topknot" (Si. Lao also "head"). Dioi kyau "head; end, extremity; chief." Sek thraw (Ged.), tra:w (Haud.) "head," from *k(h)ra(a)w (cf. Tho under III). KS *kaw "head; end": Sui ku, Mak ćau, Then kəu, from *klaw (cf. Thai). Lk. kyəu =ćəu "head," from *kləw<*k(ə)ləw (unstressed form). OB hau "head; (ic.) chief; end," from *hrau. Li *(h)rwaw "head": S. Li dau, WS Li vo, N. Li fo~o, N. Li dial. wou~vo~vau~ wau, also (ic.) -ho, from *(h)(u)raw (app. a metath. form).

HEAP   *[ta](m)bon; *[ti](m)bun

(I) IN **ta(m)bun (Ja. "grass heap").

    T *voon (Shan "heap or mound made in an upland field"), from *bwoon *(o)bon<[a]bon (vocalic assim.).

(II) IN **timbun (TB. Ja. Ml. "heaped up").

    T *muun "to heap, a heap" (Si.), from *mbuun<*(u)mbun <*[i]mbun (vocalic assim.).

HEAR   *[də]ŋaɣ; *[də]ŋiɣ (12, 13)

(I) IN **dəŋəɣ (Dyen cites ḍənəɣ), from *dəŋaɣ by vocalic assim. (cf. Paiwan). PPN **roŋo. Form. (Pai.) *-dəŋa[ɣ].

    Dioi ńɛ (h.t.) "hear, listen," from *hńɛ<*[]ŋay. KS *hŋay: Sui hŋai, Mak hai.

    PMY *hay: YCR hai "hear, sense, perceive, feel," from *hŋay.

(II) Form. (Ami) *m/[ḍ]əŋiɣ.

    T *ŋin~*ńin; Si. has yin<*ńin as a bound form in dayyin (Egerod 1959bis compares with IN *dəŋəɣ). Dioi ńin "hear; (ic.) wake up."

HEART   See LIVER.

HEART, LUNGS   *( )pots[oq] (12, 85)

  IN **put'uʔ "heart, bud (*Herzblatt*)" (Ja. "lungs").

    T *poot~*pot (Nung: F. K. Li) "lungs," from *[]pots(oq).

Dioi *pot*∼*pət*, id. KS *puut*, id.: Sui Then *put*, Mak *pət* (cf. Thai).

HEART (HARD PART)   See HARD.

HEARTH, FIRE, FIREWOOD, LIGHT (FIRE)   *(n)d[a]puɣ; *( )(n)ta(m)p[uɣ] (53, 54, 106, 119, 126)

(I)   IN **dapuɣ "hearth." PO *(n)dapu: Fi. *mata/dravu* "hearth," but Sa. *rɛhu* "leaves for cooking." PPN **lafu: To. *lafu* "kitchen for banqueting," *ta/lafu* "hearth on boat," Sm. *ta/lafu*, id., from *ndapu.

T *viin "firewood," from *(ə)vun (vocalic assim.)< *(u)vun (stressed form)<*pwun<*(du)puɣ (vocalic assim.). Dioi *fɛn* (l.t.), id., from *v[i]n (cf. Thai). Sek *vil*, id. (cf. Thai). OB *biːn*, id., from *viːn (cf. Thai).

PMY **dou "fire" (MPT MCF also "firewood"), from *du(puɣ) (vocalic assim.).

(II)   PPN **tafu "make, light, tend (fire), cook," from *tapu[ɣ]. T *taw "hearth, kiln," from *tab[uɣ]<*[]tamp[uɣ]. Li: *thaw: N. Li *thau* "light [fire]," from *tamp[uɣ].

PM *taiʔ: MPT *taiʔ* "to light [lamp] (Sav.); to burn [oil], use a fuel (Heim)," MCF *teu*ʔ "to light (*allumer*)," from PMY *t[op]; from *[]tup[uɣ] (vocalic assim.); also Yao: YHN *ka do* (h.t.) "hearth," from PMY *nt[o]; from *ntu(puɣ) (cf. MPT MCF).

HEAT   See BURN.

HEAT, DRY (BY HEAT)   *( )kolob

IN **kulub "to heat" (Ja. "to cook vegetables"). Yami *mi/-k[u]l[u]b* "burn (mountain)."

T *kroop "dried by fire or heat" (Si.), from *[]k(o)rop.

HEAVY   *(m)b[ə]Raqət (14, 52)

IN **bəɣat=*bəɣʔat (Dyen)=*mbəRʔat (Ja. *a/bot*), from *mbəR(a)qat<*mbəRaqət (vocalic assim.). PPN **mamafa, from *ma/b(əR)a[t]. Form: Ami (Taparon Tauran) *vaʔkət*, app. from *b[əR]aqət.

T *hnak(ot), from *q/ndak(ot)<*q/mbrak(ot); generally *hnak, but Nung *nak/kət*=*nakət (both h.t.). Sek *nak* (h.t.)

(Ged.), from *hnak (cf. Thai). KS *hṅaat: K̇am ṅa:t (h.t.), from *q/mbra(q)at (vocalic assim., as in IN); also *[]dak: Mak dak (h.t.) "pregnant" (="heavy with child"), from *[]brak(ət) (cf. Thai). Lk. tsa:k, from *[](a)nak (cf. Thai).

HEEL See BASIS.

HEMP. See BAST (FIBRE).

HERE See THIS.

HEW, CHOP, PLANE *( )ta[γ]aq (13)
  IN **taγaʔ "hew, plane." PO *taγa "to adze" (Blust 1972). PPN **taa "strike" (Fi. "chop with knife"). Form. *t/m/aγaq "cut wood (Thao), hew (Fav.)."
  T *thaak "hew, smooth or square (as wood)" (Ahom also "chop with a *dao*"), from *t(h)a(r)ak. KS *te "chop (wood)": Then te, from *ta[q] (vowel influ. by original final *-q).

HIBISCUS *(m)b[a][γ]o
  IN **baγu=*(m)baγu. PPN **fau. Form: Ata. bao-lyeq∼ mao-lyeq (Og.), from *(m)ba[γ]u-.
  T *po=/poo/, from *po(r)o<*pa(r)o (vocalic assim.)< *[b]a(r)o (unvoicing of initial).

HIDE, FLEE *[bu]ni
  IN **buni "hide (oneself)."
  T *hni "flee, escape, go away."

HIGH, TALL *s[u][l]aŋ
  T *suuŋ "high, tall," from *swaŋ<*su[l]aŋ. N. Thai *saaŋ "high": Po-ai laaŋ, Yay θaaŋ, from *swaaŋ. Sek saaŋ, id. (Ged.) (cf. N. Thai). KS *hwuaŋ "high, tall": Sui waŋ∼wuəŋ, Mak vuuŋ, Then waaŋ (all h.t.), from *s(w)uaŋ (cf. Thai). Lk. khya:ŋ=ćha:ŋ "high," from *sa:ŋ (aspir. not explained). OB haŋ, id., from *hwaŋ (cf. Sui Then). Laha: TU wa:ŋ, NL kwa:ŋ (<*k/wa:ŋ), id. (cf. Then).
  PM **xhe(ŋ)=*hre(ŋ) "high"; also PWA *hlaŋ "high, grow tall"; PY *hr[a,aa]ŋ=*hl[a,aa]ŋ "high"; all from PMY *hraaŋ∼ *hlaaŋ<*h(a)raŋ∼*h(a)laŋ<*h(u)raŋ∼*h(u)laŋ (vocalic assim.).

HINDER, WARD OFF *[ta](ŋ)ki(y)ats

IN *******ta*(ŋ)*kit′* "ward off" (NgD. *taŋkis* "parry," *takis* "push away"). Form: East *ta(ŋ)*kits* "knife/sword (for headhunting)": Pai: Kulalao *t′akit* (Dahl cit.), Mak. *t′agit*.

T *kiit (Si.)~*kɨat (Lao) "hinder, prevent," from *[]*ki*(*y*)*at*; also *geet (Shan) "head off, thwart, hinder, obstruct," from *ŋ*keet*<*ŋ*kiat*. Dioi *kit* "hamper, impede," from *k[*ii*]*t*.

HIT See BEAT.

HIT (TARGET) See SHOOT.

HOARSE *[*q*][*e*]*lep*

T *h[*r*]*eep* (Ahom irreg. *hip*), from *qhreep, prob. from *q(*e*)*rep*.

Yao: YHN *khlep*, from PMY *[*qhḷ*]*ep*<*qhḷeep (cf. Thai).

HOARSE See Dry.

HOLD See SEIZE (two entries).

HOLD (IN HAND, MOUTH), SQUEEZE, HANDFUL, FIST,
    MOUTHFUL, CONTROL   **kam/kam*; **kam/gam*;
    **kəm/kəm*; **gəm/gəm*; *k[*u*]*m/k*[*u*]*m*

(I) IN *******kamkam* "take hold of (*zufassen*)." PPN *kakam: Sm. *ʔaʔam/i* "fetch," from *kamkam.

T *kam~*kham (WT doublet Lao BT) "hold in the hand, take hold of; fist, handful; control, govern." Lk. *ka:m* "take hold of," from *(*kam/*)*kam*.

(II) IN *kamgam: NgD. *k/ăr/aŋgam* "handful" (Demp. cites under *kəmkəm).

T *gam~*kham (BT) "mouthful; hold in the mouth"; also *ŋ*am* (s.t.) "to bite, bite hard, as a dog" (Shan); also *hŋam (s.t., high series) "lay hold of, grasp, clinch as some part of the body" (Shan); app. all from an original *kamgam. KS *[]ŋ*am* "mouthful": Sui Mak ŋ*am* (h.t.); also *ńam "compel": Sui *ńam*<*[]ŋ*am*; also **ʔ*ńam*: Sui ʔ*ńam* "to hold," Mak *ńam* "to clench the fist; to take hold of," from *ʔŋ*am*; all from *( )ŋ*gam* <*(*kam/*)*gam* (cf. Thai).

Yao: YHN *gam* "to crush with hand, squeeze with hand," also "copulate (animals)," from PMY *ŋ*gam*<*(*kam/*)*gam* (cf. KS).

(III) IN ****kəmkəm "close/clench (*zuhalten*)" (Tg. "handful," TB. "close the mouth").

Li *k[ə]m: S. Li *kom luoi* "press [with the hand], squeeze" ="squeeze (*kom*) down (*luoi*) on," from *(*kəm*/)*kəm*.

(IV) IN ****gəmgəm "to make a fist" (Ml. "fist," NgD. "both hands full," TB. "to rule"). PO *ŋom: Fi. ŋom/a "hand-hold, grip," from *ŋgəm<*(gəm/)gəm. SEP: Motu *gomu<*gəm "mouthful." Form. (Ruk.) *wa/gəmgəm "squeeze (in hand)."

(V) T *kum "hold with the hand, retain" (Si. Lao), from *(kum/)kum.

HOLD TOGETHER, HANDFULS (TWO) *[a](ŋ)kop

IN ****a(ŋ)kup "hold together" (NgD. "take with both hands").

T *koop "draw up with both hands; two handfuls," from *(o)kop (vocalic assim.).

HOLE See PIERCED.

HOLE, DIG *ru(w)aŋ

IN ****ḷuwaŋ=*ruwaŋ "hole, opening" (Ho. "chasm"). SEP *lu(w)a "hole (Bwaidoga), dig (Keapura)." PPN ****lu[a,o] "hole."

T *ru~*xru (Ahom Kh. Shan doublet) "hole" (*xru ʔdaŋ "nose/nostril"="nose-hole"), from *(q/)ru(waŋ); also *ruaŋ "dig" (Si.), from *ruwaŋ; also *rooŋ "ditch, canal, gully, ravine," from *ruaŋ; for the semantics, cf. Hova.

HOLE, DOOR *lu[b](/a,/an)

IN: Yami -nəban "door," from *-ləban<*-lub/an (cf. Form.). Form.: East *q/lub~*q/ləb (unstressed form)~*ləb/an, id.; also (Pai.) *lub/a "hole"; (E. Ruk.) *-lələb/a "door"; Tsouic (Saa.) *-lub/a~*-ləb/a "door"; Atayalic *(q/q/)lu[b], id.

Dioi *lu* "round hole dug in the ground," from *lu[b/-].

HOLE, PIT, DIG lu[b]aŋ

IN ****lubaŋ "pit" (NgD. "hole, cave," Ml. also "hole"). Form. *lu[b]aŋ: Pai. ḷuwaŋ "grave" (Dahl cit.), Puy: Rikavong loaŋ "hole."

T *luaŋ "dig out, penetrate into (a hole) (Si. Lao); have a hole made into or through (Shan)," from *luwaŋ; also *looŋ "a hole, as a hole in the floor" (Kh. Shan), from *luaŋ; also *looŋ (d.t.) "valley" (Lao), from *luaŋ; for the semantics, cf. HOLE/DIG. Li *l[ua]ŋ: WS Li luŋ "to shovel (=dig)" (cf. Thai).

HOLLOW   See PIERCED.

HOOK, FISHHOOK   *k[a](m)bet; *k[a]wet

(I) IN *kabit "hang on, cling to"="hook on to" (Blust 1970): Iban kabit "hook something (on something), hang from, cling to," Tg. kabit "fastened, attached, connected," Maranao kabit "hang on to a vehicle."

T *ʔbet "fishhook" (Lao "fishing line").

PY *bat (l.t.) "fish with line" (Haud.): YCR bat "to hook, catch (fish) with hook," from PMY *mbat.

(II) IN **kawit "hook" (Ml. "a hook; to hook"), with *b>w in the final unstressed syllable.

KS *[ts]eet "fishhook: Mak se:t, from *keet<*kweet< *k(e)wet (vocalic assim.).

HORNᴵ   *waqa; *waqa/w[aqa]

(I) Form. waqa "horn (Ami Bun. Thao), deer (Sai.)"; (Atayalic) *waqa/nux "deer."

(II) Form. (Bun: Katoguran) *waqawaqa.

T *xaw, from *(wa)qaw(aqa). Dioi kau, from *qaw. Sek kaw (Ged.), from *qaw. KS *qwaaw: Sui qau~pau, Mak ka:u, Then Kam pa:u, from *(w)aqaw (labialized). Lk. kou (l.t.), from *gow<*[qw]aw (cf. KS). OB bau, from *waw<*[qw]aw (cf. KS). Li *[qw]aw: S. Li hau "horn, corner, angle," WS Li həu "horn," Bas. hau "buffalo horn (as war signal)," N. Li vo "horn."

HORNᴵᴵ   *kloŋ[o]
   IN **t'uŋu. Form. (Tsouic) *tsuŋu.
   PMY **kyɔ(ŋ)=*klɔ(ŋ), from *kloŋ(o)~*klo(ŋo).

HORN, HUMP (OF CATTLE)   *[ta](n)dok; [ta]ndo[q] (5)

(I) IN **tanduk "horn."
   T *hnook "hump (of cattle)" (Ahom "rhinoceros horn"), from *(-o)ndok (vowel assim.).

(II) T *no=/noo/ "horn, protuberance" (WT "rhinoceros horn"),
from *ndoo<*(-o)ndo[q] (vowel assim.).

HORNET See SWEET.

HOT See BURN.

HOUSE See HUT (two entries); VILLAGE.

HOUSE, HUT¹ *b[a]roŋ (24)
   IN **baḷuŋ=*baruŋ "hut."
   Li *[b]lo[o]ŋ "house": N. Li ploŋ, WS Li plɔŋ, Loi dial. all
blóŋ=ploŋ, Ha Bas. Dakung bloŋ=ploŋ, from *[b](o)loŋ (vocalic assim.).

HOUSE, HUT¹¹ *[ba]lay
   IN **balay "house, hut, hall"; Yami *balay "house." PPN
**fale "house" (Tikopian "hut").
   Kl. hle "house," from *[]lay.

HUMP (OF CATTLE) See HORN.

HUNGRY See DESIRE.

HUNT See RUN (AFTER).

HUSBAND See GRANDPARENT.

HUSK See BARK, n.

HUSK, CHAFF *xə(m)[pa]
   IN **həmpa~**əpa=*ʔə(m)pa "husks of grain, chaff."
   Li *x[ə]m "husks, chaff": WS Li xom, from *xəm(pa).

HUSK, SCALE *( )k[]lab/l[ab]; *k[ə]lab(/i) (19, 28)
(I) T *klet "scale (of fish, pangolin), scab," from *klat<
*klap/l(ap). N. Thai *klat "(fish) scales": Dioi kyat, Po-ai ćet
(cf. Thai). Chuang *klap, id. (Haud.). Sek tlɛk, id., from *klɛt
(cf. Thai). KS *kyat, id.: Mak ćat.

(II) Form. (Ata.) *kəlabi "empty husk of grain."
      T *kleep "husk (of grain)" (Nung also "scab"), from
*( )k(ə)lap(i) (vowel influ. in both directions). Dioi rɛp "husks
of rice, coarse bran," from *(kh)rɛp; Wu-ming rip "husk of
grain" (cf. Thai).

HUT See HOUSE (two entries).

HUT, HOUSE, GRANARY, COOP *[tsa]paw; *[ts/]l̥[/a]paw;
 *[tsap/]l/aw; *[tsa]p/r/aw

(I) IN *t'apaw "roof" (<"house"): NgD. *sapau,* Ho. *t-afu,*
Maanjan (Siong) *hapau,* Siang, Lawangan *sapo* "roof," Parigi
sapo "house" (Dahl). Form. (Pai.) *tsapaw "rest hut in fields."

(II) Form. (Kuv.) *ləpaw "house," from *[ts/]l̥[/əpaw] (unstressed form).

(III) T *law~*laaw (Si. doublet) "coop (hen-house), granary"
(often cw. "fowl" or "rice"; Si.: ic. also "pig-sty" and "prison"),
from *[tsap/]l/aw.

(IV) PMY **ćraw=*praw "house," from *[tsa]p/r/aw.

HUT, HOUSE, SHELTER, WALL *(n)diaŋ(/(n)diaŋ); *tiaŋ

(I) IN **diŋdiŋ "wall." PO *ri(-ri): Fi. *ri/ri* "wind shelter,"
Rotuman *ri* "house"; also *ndindi "wall of a house" (Blust 1972).
  Lq. *neŋ* (Bon.), *niŋ* (Laj.) "house," from *nd[ia]ŋ.

(II) T *thiaŋ "temporary abode, booth (Shan); hut (as in rice-
fields)" (BT Tho); (ic.) latrine (BT)."

I

IN, INSIDE, INLAND *(q/)(n)zaya
  IN **ḍaya=*ḍaya (Tg.)~*ḍaya (Ja.) "inland."
  T *naɨ (SW)~*ʔdaɨ (Tho-Nung) "in, inside," from *(ʔ)(n)dayə.
Chuang *ʔdaɨ "in." Sek ʔdə (Haud.), rə (h.t.) (Ged.), id., from
**ʔr[aɨ] (cf. Thai). OB *ze* (h.t.), id., from **ʔdaɨ (cf. Thai).

INDIGO *[t][a]ɣom (16, 112, 113)
  IN **taɣum.
  T *hroom (SW only), from *[t]hroom<*[to]rom (vowel assim.). Dioi *rɔm* (h.t.) "indigo (polygonum tinctorium); the dye
that it furnishes," from *[th]ro[o]m; cf. also *rim* "Indigofera
tinctoria." KS *[ʔ][ɣ]om: Mak *yom* (h.t.) "large-leafed indigo
tree."

IN-LAW (BROTHER-, SISTER-) *baya[w] (67)
  IN **bayaw "related by marriage" (Tg. "brother-in-law").
  T *baɨ~*săbaɨ (Si.) "female affinal kin (wife of younger uncle, brother, son, nephew, grandson)" (să-<*saaw "young woman"), from *(să)bayə; cf. also *baɨ (s.t.) "watch, take care of, protect."

INTESTINES See BELLY; EXCREMENT.

IRON *(m)baxliaq (60, 61, 93, 113, 126)
  IN **bat'i=*(m)bat'i (Ho. basi "gun"); also **bət'i (Ho. vi "iron") (unstressed form); from *(m)bakli<*(m)ba[x]li(aq); cf. also the apparent loan words: Palawan Batak baribari "iron, metal," Iban bari "steel" (Blust 1972bis). PO *pesi: Fi. vesi "name of a spear." Form. (Thao Kuv. Sir.; Ata.) *(m)baliq (with assim. of final in Thao Kuv.) "iron/metal" (Ata. also [Og.] "copper"), from *(m)ba[x]liaq; also (Pai.) *balituq "silver," from *(m)bali(q)-(pu)tuq="the white [putuq] metal [(m)baliq]," with early loans by Siraya (*mbalituk) and Kan. Saa. (*balituk) (see WHITE/SILVER").
  T *hlek, from *hleek (vocalic shortening through influ. of *q)<*hliaq; also the variant *h[r]iak "tin ore" (Kh. Shan), from *hliyak<*xliyaq, through influ. of *x (cf. Dioi). Dioi riɛ hau "tin"="white (hau) iron/metal (riɛ)," riɛ fɔn "lead"="black (fɔn) iron/metal (riɛ)," from *[h]riek<*[h]riak (cf. Kh. Shan). N. Thai *mwa: Dioi Yay fa (l.t.), CT ma, from *mb(w)a (labialized)<*mba(xliaq). Sek ma (cf. N. Thai); also riek "tin (cf. Dioi). KS *qhlet: Sui khət~hyət~set, Mak lit, Then let, Kam khwət (all h.t.), from *qhle[q], with assim. of final (also vocalic shortening, as in Thai). Lk. khyạk (nasalized), from *m[]khyak<*mb[a][q]liak. Li *xluaay: S. Li da:i, WS Li xuay, WS Loi khoi~hlɛi, Bas. hwai, SH Loi gai~hai, DC Loi hai, from *(b-)xlaay (labialized)<*(ba)xli<*(ba)xli(aq). Lq. ði, from *(l)ya[q]. Kl. yɔ, from *ya[q]<*(baxl)iaq. Lt. khɛ, from *kh[l]ay (cf. Li).
  PMY **hlia?=*hḷia?, from *xḷiaq<*xliaq, through influ. of *x (cf. Kh. Shan Dioi).

IVORY See TOOTH.

J

JACK-FRUIT See BREAD-FRUIT.

JAR *[kə](n)de
  IN **kənd[i] "water jar," for *kəndi (no Tg. cognate).
  T **de "jar for measuring arrack" (Si. de:).

JAW *qabay
  Form. (Ata.) *qabay "jaw," also [Og.] "chin."
  T *hwaay "jawbone" (Lao), from *qaway; also *waay "molar
  (=jaw) teeth" (cw. "tooth") (Nung).

JAW, CHIN, TOOTH (MOLAR) *[ba][R]a(N)qaŋ (17, 18)
  IN **baɣaŋ=**baɣʔaŋ (Dyen)=*baRaŋ~*(ba)Raʔaŋ: Tg.
  bagaŋ, Ho. vazană "molar tooth," Ja. waŋ "jaw" (*R>ø); also
  (omitted by Demp.) Ml. rahaŋ, id.; also (Blust 1972bis) Kelabit
  beraʔaŋ (unstressed form). PO *paɣa "molar tooth": Arosi hara-
  (na) (Blust 1972bis), from *baRa(ʔaŋ). PPN **aʔa "jawbone,"
  from *[R]aʔaŋ. Form: Ami wahaŋ "molar tooth," app. from
  *waRa(q)aŋ, for *baRa(q)aŋ.
  T *gaaŋ "chin, lower jaw," from *[G]aaŋ<*Nqaaŋ<*[R](a)-
  Nqaŋ (irreg. *g through dissim. from the original initial *R).
  Dioi haŋ (l.t.) "jaw," from *G[aa]ŋ (cf. Thai). Sek ka:ŋ [l.t.]
  "chin," from *[G]aaŋ (cf. Thai). KS *[]Gaaŋ, id.: Sui Raŋ, Mak
  ga:ŋ, Then ʔa:ŋ (all h.t.), from *[h](a)Gaŋ<*[R](a)Nqaŋ
  (*R>h). OB ŋaŋ, id., from *NGaŋ<*Nqaŋ. Li *h(y)aŋ: S. Li
  haŋ "jaw; (ic.) chin," Loi dial. hiaŋ~hɛŋ "chin," from *G(y)aŋ
  <*[R-]Gaŋ (palatalized by original initial *R>y). Laha: TU
  ka:ŋ, id., from *[G]a:ŋ.

JOIN, UNITE, COMPLETE, PAIR, EVEN(-NUMBERED)
  *[r]a(n)kap; *[ra]ŋgap; *[za]kəp; *[la]ŋkəp; *gəp; *g/l/əp;
  *g/l/əp

(I) IN **laŋkap=*raŋkap "unite" (Ja. "doubled," Ml. "pair,"
TB. sa/rakkap "united threads in weaving").
  T *kap~*kaap (Tho) "join, unite, together with" (Tho
also "flow together"), from *(-a)kap. KS *kaap: Mak ka:p
"bifurcation (of road)," from *(-a)kap (cf. Thai). OB kɔp
"collect [money]," kɔp lei "flow (lei) together." Li *khaap: S. Li

kha:p "knot" (cf. Toba-Batak), from *(-a)kap* (app. aspirated by the original *r-).

PY *kap* "join together, bring together, assemble, spin (thread)"; YCR also "collect [money]" (cf. OB); YHN also "bifurcation, confluence" (cf. Tho OB) and "lined (=doubled) [garment]."

(II)   PM (PC PW) **ŋgaiʔ=*ŋgeiʔ "pair"; PE *ńuʔ, id., from PM *ńeiʔ; both from PMY *ŋg[ap].

(III)   IN **ḍakəp "fit together" (Tg. "joined," Ja. "laid against one another"). PO *rako: Fi. *rako* "catch crabs," Sa. *raʔo* "stick fast," *raʔoh/-* "join with something."

T *kop* "put together, unite together as in one, join (metals) (Shan); full (=complete) (Si.)"; also *koop* "mix together, be in accord" (Si. Lao), from *(-o)kop* (vowel assim.). OB *kop* "unite."

(IV)   **laŋkəp∼*lə(ŋ)kəp (assim. form, cited by Blust 1970) "complete" (Tg. "incorporated, joined with").

(V)   T *gop* "pair (Kh.); to be even-numbered, form pairs; to be complete (Shan); join with, associate with (Si. Lao); top of house (=joining of rafters) (Si.); fork [in road] (Lao); confluent [water] (BT)."

(VI)   IN **gənəp "complete" (Ml. also "even [-numbered]").

(VII)   T *grop* "complete" (Si. Lao).

K

KICK   *(b/)i(n)ti(y)aq (13)

IN **bintiʔ "kick with the lower leg," from *b/intiaʔ (note Ja. irreg. *binte*).

T *tiak∼*tia (Lao), from an earlier *[]tiyaq. OB *hiek*, from *diak<*ntiyak (cf. Lao). Li *thiik: S. Li *thiʔ, from *(i)thiak (vocalic assim.).

PY **dhiʔ, from PMY *nthiʔ, from *(i)nthiaʔ (cf. Li).

KILL   See DIE.

KISS See SUCK.

KNEE See POST.

KNIFE, SWORD^I *[t]a/(n)tab(/a) (119)

Form. (Fav.) *ta/taba "knife/sword (for headhunting)."

T *ʔdaap "sword," from *(-a)ntap; cf. also *taaw "knife, sword" (Shan) and Sek tau "knife," both b.l.'s from Ch. tâu, id., whence also Cham tauw, id. (*ta/tab>*taw~*taaw).

KNIFE, SWORD^{II} *[t]azaw

Form: East *tazaw "knife/sword (for headhunting" (Puy. Paz. Sir.); also *[z]a[z]aw(s) "small knife" (Bun.), app. an assimilated form; Atayalic *[z]a[z]aw "knife/sword (for headhunting)" (cf. Bunun).

Sek raaw (h.t.) (Ged.), from *hraaw<*ʔ(a)raw. Li *[d]aw "knife": S. Li dau. Kl. mi du, id. (n.a.) (see KNIFE/SWORD^{III}).

KNIFE, SWORD^{III} *maḷat

IN **malat "parang, sword": Uma Juman malat "parang," Iban malat "short sword" (cit. by Blust 1973). Form. (Sai.) *ma[l,ḷ]at "knife/sword (for headhunting)."

T *miit "knife," from *me(y)et<*ma(r)at. Dioi mit, id. KS *miit, id.: Sui Mak mit, Then miet, Kam mi:t. Lk mɛ, id., from *may(at). OB miet, id. (cf. Then). Kl. mi du, id. (n.a.).

KNOT See BIND.

KNOT, TIE *[iś][ə](N)qop[r,l][o]

IN **ikət "twist, knot (together)" (the Malay ikat weaving technique), from *i[sə]kət<*i[sə]kut (vocalic assim.; cf. Form.), from *i[sə]Nqut. Yami ikut "bind," from *i[sə]kut (without assim.). Form. (Puy: Rikavong) *i[sə]qi[t]u "tie," from *i[sə]qu[t]u (vocalic assim.; contrast IN); (Pai.) *is[ə]quṭ, id., from *is[ə]-qut[u] (without assim.); (Thao) *q/m/uṭ/quṭ, id., from *[isə]qut[u]/qut[u].

T *xoot "knot, tie in a knot" (WT also "embroider, type of embroidery made with small rings in relief"), from *(o)qot. Dioi hɔt "knot; to make a knot," from *qhoot<*[s]əqot. Sek hɔ:t "a knot," from *qhɔ:t (cf. Dioi). OB hut "a knot; crooked (=knotty) [fingers]," hut hut "frizzy [hair]" (cf. Dioi Sek).

L

LADDER, BRIDGE   *( )[a](n)dra; *[sa]dra/n (61)

(I) IN **anḍa "upward" (Ja. "ladder"), from *anẓa (cf. IN under II). Form: Sir. *kada* "ladder," app. from */a[d]a.*

T *[dr]a: Ahom *śa* "ladder," Shan *sʿa* (l.t.) "ladder formed of a single bamboo with pieces inserted horizontally for the feet."

(II) IN **həd'an "ladder," from *haẓa/n (stressed form; cf. IN under I). Form. (Kuv.) *sa[d]an "bridge"; for the semantics, cf. Fav. *kittas* "bridge, ladder."

LADDER, STAIRS, BRIDGE   *(q/)(n)tal(/tal) (61, 111)

Form. *taltal "stair, ladder (Pai: Mak.), bridge (Sir.)"; also (Kan.) *tətal "ladder," prob. from *taltal.

T *ʔday~*kă/ʔday (Si.)~*ʔduay (Tho), from *ʔdlay<*ʔdlal <*ʔdaldal<*q/ntal/ntal. Dioi *lai* (h.t.) "stone steps in front of a house," from *ʔdlay. Sek *ray* (h.t.) "stairs, ladder" (Ged.) (cf. Dioi). KS *kle "stairs/ladder": Sui *kle, Mak *će*, Kam *kwe,* from *tle<*tlay<*tlal<*taltal (cf. Thai). Lk *puŋ-kyę*=-*ćę,* id. (secondary nasalization following *puŋ-),* from *-kle (cf. KS). OB *lei,* id. (cf. Dioi). S. Li *ta~tha,* id., from *(tal/)tal~ *tal(/tal).

Miao: PWA **ntai "ladder, stairs," from PM *nta<PMY *nt[et], from an earlier *ntai/t[ai]; also MCF *tye,* id., from PM *ti<PMY *tei, perhaps from *(tal/)tal, but PY *thei, id., must be considered a b.l. from Ch. *tʿi,* Anc. *tʿiei,* id.

LADY   See GIRL.

LAIR   See DEN.

LAND (MAINLAND)   See VILLAGE.

LANGUAGE   See SPEAK.

LAO   See under MAN (THE PEOPLE).

LAO (KELAO)   See under MAN (THE PEOPLE).

LARVA   See WORM.

LAUGH[1]   *(n)tlaw[a]; *tla/tlaw[a]; *tla/tla; *(ka/)tla

(I) IN **[t]awa: Tg. *tawa.* Form. (Sai. Ami Kuv. Sir.) *(ma/)ṭawa.

Li *[ty]aaw: S. Li ya:u, N. Li ta:u, WS Li ćau. Lq. ðəu
<*səw, Pu-peo ðaw<*saw, from *tsaw<*tlaw. Laha: TU so,
BB du so, NL ay so, from ts[aw] (cf. Lq.). Kl. kha (duə), from
*thy[aw]. Lt. a/su, from */ts[aw].

(II) IN *tatawa: NgD. tatawɛ, also Ml. tĕrtawa. Form. (Ruk.
Thao) *ma/ṭaṭawa.

Miao (PW) **lua, from PMY *l[aaw], from *(tlat)laaw
(cf. III).

(III) IN *tata: TB. tata. Form. (Kan. Saa.) *ma/tsatsa.

MY **tlat, from *tla/t(la); also PM (PC doublet) **tɔ?,
from PMY *t[ɔt], app. from an earlier *twat<*tlat.

(IV) PPN **kata.

LAUGH¹¹ *(N)qiḷaw
Cham Jarai klau, from *k[]law<*Nq[]law.

T *xrua, from *xruaw (cf. Sek; final *-uaw lacking in Thai),
from *q(u)raw<*q(i)raw (vocalic assim.). Dioi riao~rɛao~
riu (all h.t.), from *hriaw<*qh(i)raw. Sek ruaw (h.t.) (Ged.),
from *hruaw<*qhuraw. KS *kua: Sui Then ku, Mak ću, Kam
ko, from *[qr]ua (cf. Thai). OB zeao~ziao (h.t.), from *hriaw
(cf. Dioi).

LAY (EGGS) See APPEAR.

LEAF¹ *(m)boḷoŋ (39, 47)
IN **buluŋ (Ho. "young [=large] leaves"); Yami bu(w)uŋ,
from *buluŋ.

T *tooŋ "large leaf (as used for wrapping, etc.), esp. of the
banana," from *p(o)roŋ. Dioi rɔŋ (h.t.) "large leaves of certain
plants (banana, taro), used in wrapping," from *hrooŋ<
*(pho)roŋ. Yai roŋ (h.t.) "banana leaf" (cf. Dioi). Sek rɔ:ŋ
"dried leaf of banana tree" (cf. Dioi).

PMY **mblɔŋ=*mbḷoŋ; PY **nɔm (s.t.); both from PMY
*m(b)ḷɔm<*m(b)ḷɔŋ (assim.).

LEAF¹¹ *pa[x]/pa[x]; *(q/)(m)p/aḷ/a[x](/pa[x]) (8)
(I) IN **papa?: Ja. papah "midrib of a palm frond," Ml. papah
"coconut frond," Maranao papa? "shoots of vegetables" (Blust

1972bis), from *pa[ˀ]paˀ. PO *papa: Arosi *haha-(na)* "frond of a palm" (Blust 1972bis). Form. *pahpah: Ata. *pahpah* "flower" (Og.), *həpah* "flower," *pəhəpah* "to flower" (Eg.); Sed. *paˀeppah* ~*pappah*~*papah* "flower" (<the flower leaf); Ami *papah* "leaf" (Dyen: Q_1); app. also Sir. *hapa,* id. (cf. Ata.).

KS *pwa: Kam *pa,* Sui *wa*~*va,* Mak *va,* Then *wa* (all h.t.), from *(pa/)pa (labialized).

(II) IN **p/al/apaˀ (also **p/al/apuˀ) "plant material" (Tg. "pulpy leaf of plants like the banana," Ml. "coconut frond," Maranao "midrib of a leaf" [Blust 1972bis], NgD. "palm leaf," Ho. "leaf-vein"). Form.: Ata: Takonan *zapazap* "flower," from *(p/)l̥/apa[h]/l/ap[ah].

T *ˀbai, from *ˀbayə<*q/mpaya<*q/mp/al̥/a[]. Dioi *bai* (h.t.), from *ˀbai (cf. Thai). Sek *bə* (h.t.) (Ged.), ˀbə (Haud.), from ˀb[ai]. Li *bə: S. Li *bə,* WS Li *pə* (cf. Thai).

LEAK(Y) *lu[ŋg]a[r]

IN **luŋga[l̥]=*luŋga[r] "leaky."

T *rua "to leak: leaky," from *ru(ŋ)a<*ru(ŋg)a(r). Dioi *ruao* (h.t.)=*ruau* "to leak; receptacle with a leak in it," from *hruaw<*q/ru(ŋ)ar *(-r>-w through dissim.).

LEAN ON See SUPPORT.

LEARN See SPEAK.

LEECH¹ *[lim]a(n)taq (18, 23, 24, 119)

IN **lima(n)[t]ək "small leech," app. from an earlier *lima(n)taˀ through reduced stress on the final syllable; also **lintaˀ "leech," an abbreviated form preserving the final syllable. Form: Pai. *limat'ək* (Dahl cit.), from *limatək (cf. IN).

T *daak~*dak (Nung) "leech (esp. land leech)" (Ahom "snail"), from *(a)dak<*(a)ntaq, as indicated by the Shan doublet: *ta:k* (l.t.)<*daaq "small leech, water leech," *tɛk* (l.t.) <*de(e)q "land leech" (vowel influenced by the final *-q). Dioi *ta* "large leech of the ricefields," from *[d]a[ak]. Sek *tha:k* [l.t.] "land leech," from *daak. Li *theek: WS Loi *thɛ,* SH Loi *thɛak,* DC Loi *thɛk,* SC Loi *thɛt,* from an original *thaaq (with vocalic influence as in Shan, above).

LEECH^II *( )(m)b[]liŋ

T *pliŋ* "leech (esp. water leech)," from *bliŋ*. Sek *pliŋ*. KS *p[l]iŋ*: Mak *piŋ*; also *m[l]iŋ*: Kam *mi:ŋ*, from *mbliŋ*.

PM *mbr[]*=*(?)mbli(ŋ)* (MCF MPT: Heim. both irreg.) (MPT [Heim.] "water leech," [Sav.] "land leech" and "water leech," both ic.), from PMY *(?)mbliŋ*.

LEFT (HAND)¹ *(k/)weR[i]*

IN **wiγi*=*k(a)/wi[R]i*: Ml. *k/iri*. Yami (*ka/*)*uri*, from *(ka/)wiRi*. PO: Fi. *ma/wi*, from *(k/)m/a/wi[R]i*. PPN **kaui(i)*, from *ka/wi[R]i*; also **mauii*, from *(k/)m/a/wi[R]i*. Form. (East; Tsouic) *(ka/)wiRi*; (Kuv.) *k/m/a/wi[R]i*; (Puy. Sir.) *(k/)m/a/wiRi* (all Dyen *w₁*); also (Atayalic) *wi[R]il* (Dyen *w₁*), app. from *wi[R]i/l*.

Sek *vel.* Li *viiŋ*: S. Li *vieŋ*, WS Li *viŋ*, from *wiR(i)*<*weR(i)* (vocalic assim.).

Yao: YHN *kwɛŋ*; Miao: MCF *khi*, from PM *khi(ŋ)*; both from PMY *kwɛŋ*~*kh[w]iŋ*, from an earlier *k(h)weR(i)*, the latter showing vocalic assim. (cf. Li).

LEFT (HAND)¹¹ *[ki]wa*

IN **kiwa*.

Lk. *wa*.

LEG See FOOT/LEG.

LEVER, LIFT (NET), UPROOT *(n)tsu(w)al̥*

IN **t'ual*: Tg. *sual* "lever," Ja. *sol* "uproot," also (Blust 1972bis) Bukidnon Manobo *suwal* "of a pig, to root up the ground." PO *nsua*: Fi. *tsua* "stick for lifting net." PPN **sua* "turn over [soil], raise up"; To. "root in earth (of pigs), turn over, lift"; Sm. "grub up (soil), plough," also (Milner) "to lever or prize something up"; Maori "lever, raise with lever"; semantic merging with root under DIG INTO, q.v.

T *soon* "to fish with (=lift) a landing net" (WT), from *suan;* also *joon* "to dig out, clear away, as weeds and bushes (Kh. Shan); spoon, net in form of a large spoon (Si.); draw up (=lift), take (with a glass, basket) (Lao)," from *nćoon*< *ntsuan* (palatalized by high vowel *u*). Dioi *sɔn* (l.t.)~*suan* (s.t., high series) "scrape, clean [road, border of ricefield]," from *zuan*~*suwan*, from *(n)su(w)an*. KS *s[ua]n*: Mak *son* "to weed (dry field)," from *suwan*.

LICK, TONGUE   *[b]li[d]aq;   *(m)bli[d]a[/blidaq];
     *(m)bli(n)d[a/][sa]ma

(I) IN **dilaʔ "tongue," with very irreg. forms: Tg. *dilaʔ*, TB.
dila "tongue," Ja. *dilah* "flame, lamp," *liḍah* "tongue," Ml. *lidah*,
NgD. *d'ela*, Ho. *lela* "tongue"; all app. from an earlier *blidaʔ
~ *blilaʔ (assim.). Form. (Pai: Tamari) *lidaq, id. (cf. IN).
     OB *lek (h.t.) "lick," from *hliak<*[b]li(d)aq.

(II) IN **dilap=*ẓilap (NgD. *d'elap*, Ho. *lelakǎ) ~ **dilat=
*ẓilat (Dyen) (TB. Ja. *dilat*, Ml. *d'ilat*) "lick," both from
*blila/bl[ilaq]. Form. (Pai: Kunanao) *lida/lid[aq]; (Sir.)
*dadila[q]<*d[il]a/dila[q] "tongue"; both from an original
*blida/blidaq~*blila/blilaq (cf. IN under I).
     T *lia "lick," from *[b]li[d]a. Dioi *riɛ*, id., from *ria (cf.
Thai).
     PY: PIM **bia=*blia "lick" (Haud. cites PY *blie, with
discrepant h.t.), from PMY *mblia, from *mbli(d)a (cf. Thai).

(III) Form. (Paz. Thao) *dasama "tongue" (s₂), from *lida/-
sama (an old compounded form); cf. (Pai: most dialects Puy:
Hinan Ami; Tsou; Atayalic) *sama~səma (unstressed form),
id. (s₂); (Bun.) *[sə]ma/[sə]ma, id.; also (E. Ruk. Puy: Chipon
Kuv.) *lidam; (Pai: Tokubun W. Ruk.) *ḷidam, id., app. abbreviated from an original *[b]lida[sə]m[a] (*s₂>⌀ is a common
Formosan shift).
     T *lin~*lit (Nung doublet) "tongue," from *[b]lind(a-).
Sek *lin*, id. KS *ma, id.: Sui Mak Then Kam *ma*, from *[]ma
(cf. Form.). Lk. *wą̄~ŋwa*, id., from *[]ma (cf. KS). OB *lim~
liem (Jer.), *lien* (Sav.), from *li(i)n (cf. Thai). Li *hliin, id.:
S. Li *dien*, N. Li *tlien*, WS Li *hliŋ<*hlin, Loi dial. *hlien*, from
[]lin<[b]lin(da-) (cf. Thai). Pu-peo *mia*, id., from *mbli[d]a
(cf. PMY *mblia "lick"). Laha: TU *t'lin*(<*hlin), BB NL *let
ma*, id., from *[b]li(n)d[]ma, indicating partial retention of an
earlier complex form.
     PMY **mbret=*mblet "tongue," from *mblid(a-).

LIFT   See CLIMB.

LIFT (NET)   See LEVER.

LIGHT (WEIGHT)   *()(n)sap[r,l][a]qal

Form. (Pai. Puy.) *sataqal ($s_{1/2/3}$).

KS *( )za~*sa: Sui *za* (h.t.), Then ?za (l.t.), but Kam *khya* =*ćha*, from *( )(n)sa(taqal). Lk. *kyie*=*ćie*, from *kyia= ćia*, from *s(y)a*. OB *kho* (Jer.), *khei* (Sav.), both app. from an earlier *kh[al]>*kh[aw]>kho, contrasting with *kh[al]>*kh[ai] >*khei*, with initial *kh*<*[q]. Li *khal*: S. Li *khə*, WS Li *kha:l*, from *[q]al. N. Kl. *kau* (cf. OB).

Miao: PE **fha=*sha, app. also MSY *śue* and MCh. *śə*, from PM **θhuε=*suε, from PMY *saay<*sat(aqal); also Miao: PWA *śi, from PM *sai, from PMY *sa<*sa(taqal); YHN *sou~ syou*, from an earlier *su, app. from an original *su(taqal)< *sut(aqal)<*sat(aqal).

LIGHT (WEIGHT) See FLOAT.

LIGHT See BURN.

LIGHT (GIVE LIGHT), GLOW, GLITTER, SHINE
*[ga](n)ts[a]ŋ (81)

IN **ga(n)t'aŋ "easily kindled (=at glowing point) (TB. Ml.), burned up (Ja.)." PPN **[ka]kaha=*[ka]kaha~*[ka]kasa (Sm.) "burn, burning" (Sm. "glowing hot," To. "red hot," Tua-motuan "very hot," Raratongan "shine"), from *ka(n)sa.

T *sooŋ "to light (give light), glitter," from *(o)soŋ<*(ə)səŋ (assim.)<*(ə)saŋ (unstressed form).

LIGHT, SHINE, MOON, SUN   *(n)ts[i]laγ; *ts[u]laγ

(I) IN **t'inaγ "light (*Licht*)." PO: Fi. *tsina* "torch," *tsinawa* "light/shine"; Sa. *sine* "torch," *sinel/i* "shine upon," from *(n)sinaγ. SEP *sina: Motu *dina* "sun." PPN **sina=*sina~*hina (Fu. doublet) "grey-haired, white-haired" (Fu. *sina* "white," *hina* [Demp.] "to light"), from *(n)sina; also **maasina "moon," from *ma/sina. Form. (Ami Thao; Tsou) *tsilaγ; (Sai.) *tsa/- tsilaγ "sun."

T *hlian "to dazzle (Lao); shiny, scintillating (WT); pol-ished, smooth (Tho-Nung)"; also *hliam "shine, shiny, glossy, smooth"; both from *hlyaan<*h(i)lan<*s(i)lan.

(II) Dioi *luam~luom* (both h.t.) "shiny, glistening," from *hluam<*h(u)lan<*s(u)lan (cf. Thai under I). KS *hl[u,uu]n: Mak *lun* (h.t.) "(ic.) bright" (cf. Dioi).

LIGHT, SHINE, MOON, SUN, DAWN, MORNİNG *ts[i]ŋa[a]γ

IN **t'iŋaγ: NgD. *siŋah* "torch." PO: Fi. *siŋa* "sun"; Sa. *siŋe/-siŋe* "shine (stars)," *ćiŋe* "day." PPN **[seŋ(a,i)]seŋ(a,i) "day-break" (Easter Island *heŋa* "brightness"; Sm. *seŋaseŋa* "yellowish," *seŋiseŋi* "twilight"; Tikopian *faka/seŋi* "glare"; To. *heŋiheŋi* "early morning").

T *hŋaay "light, moonlight; shining (Ahom); moonlight (Si. BT: cw. "moon")"; moon (Tho-Nung)"; also *ŋaay (s.t., low series) "morning; breakfast." Dioi *ŋay* "breakfast" (for semantics, cf. Thai). KS *ŋa(a)y "early meal": Sui Then *ŋe*, Mak *ŋa:i* (cf. Thai Dioi).

LIGHTNING *l̦i[dz]ap; *m/l̦i[dz]ap; *l̦a[dz]ap; *m/l̦a[dz]ap; *b/l̦a[dz]ap

(I) Form. (Kuv.) *l̦idzap.

Dioi *diap piah*~*piah diap* (*piah* "thunder"), from *yap< *(ri)yap. Lk. *toŋ yap* (cf. *toŋ pla* "thunder") (cf. Dioi). KS: cf. Mak *yap* "to wink, blink [eye]." Li *y[i,ii]p: WS Li *zip zau*, from *(-i)yap (cf. Dioi).

PM **l[]=*lyaʔ (PW; MJC)~*liʔ (PE; MTT) "lightning": MCF "reverberation, refraction of light; (cw. "sky") lightning"; MPT "twitch, flutter; (cw. "sky") lightning," from PMY *lya[p], from *li(y)ap.

(II) T *mleep (Ahom *mlep*, Kh. Shan Lao Nung *mɛp*~*mɛ:p*, Si. *lɛ:p*), also *(m)weep (Si. *lɛ:p wɛ:p*) "glitter, shine; lightning" (latter often cw. *va "the heavens"), from an original *ml̦iap< *m/l̦i[z]ap.

(III) Form. (Pai.) *l̦adzap, perh. by assim. from *l̦idzap.

(IV) Form.: cf. Paz. *malapend* (Bullock 1874) (n.a.).

T *mlaap (Shan Lao *ma:p*, Tho *mya:p*), also *(m)waap (Shan Si. *wa:p*) "to glitter; lightning" (latter often cw. *va), from an original *m/l̦a[z]ap.

(V) T *plaap "glitter; lightning," from *blaap (initial unvoicing) *b/l̦a[z]ap. Laha: TU *p'le* "lightning," from *p'lay[ap].

LIGHTNING, HAIL *k[i]l̦ap(/l̦ap); *g[i]l̦ap

(I) IN **kilap "glitter" (TB. "lightning"); also **kilat "lightning," from *$kilap/l[ap]$ (cf. Form.); Yami *tsitsilat*, id., from *$ki/kilat$. Form: Pai: Tokubun *kiats*, Shimopaiwan *kaliats*, id., from *$kiat \sim {}^*k/l/iat$, app. through metanalysis (as infixation) of an original *$kilat < {}^*kilap/l[ap]$, but perhaps pointing to an original *$kiap$, whence *$ki/l/ap$; note Puy. *kipkip* (Og.-As.), *kəmaklip* (Ferr.), id., the latter app. from *$k/m/ak/l/ip$; also (Ruk. Sir.) *$likat$, id., app. from *$kilat$ by metathesis, from an earlier *$kilap/l[ap]$.

T *$khrep \sim {}^*khret$ (Ahom Nung: Sav.) $\sim {}^*khrat$ (Nung: F. K. Li) "hail" (often cw. *$maak$ "fruit"="hailstones"="lightning stones"), from *$k[i]rap(/rap)$ (cf. IN). Dioi *rit* "hail," from *$[kh]rit$ (cf. Thai). OB *ma-hiet*, id. (Jer.) (*ma-* "fruit"), from *$h[r]et$ (cf. Thai Dioi).

(II) IN **$gilap$ "glitter," also (unstressed form) **$gəlap$ "darkness (TB. Ml.), lightning (Ja.)."

LIME *$[(N)q]apuR$ (44, 97, 99)

IN **$kapu\gamma = {}^*kapu[R] \sim {}^{**}apu\gamma = {}^*[\mathfrak{?}]apuR$, from *$(N)qapuR$. Form. (Ami Bun.; Tsouic) *$qapu\gamma$.

T *$puun$ (Si. Lao), from *$(u)pun$ (vocalic assim.); also *$foon$ (Tho), from *$phwoon < {}^*phwuan < {}^*(a)phun < {}^*(q)(a)pun$ (secondary aspiration after the original *q-).

LIPS *$(m)biR/(m)biR$

IN **$bibi\gamma = {}^*(m)bibiR$, from *$(m)biRbiR$ (cf. Form.). PO **$mpimpi(\gamma)$. PO: Fi. *mbe/mbe* "vulva." SEP *$(m)bi(m)bi$. Form. (East: gen.) *$bi\gamma bi\gamma$; also (Kuv. Ami: Baran) *$k(a)tu/bi\gamma$.

T *bi (Nung: F.K. Li) (cw. *$paak$ "mouth"), from *$(bi/)bi$; Nung (Sav.) has the irreg. *phi*, perhaps from *$(bi)Rbi(R)$ via *hbi.

LIPS See MOUTH.

LIQUOR/WINE *$q[u]law$ (40, 73, 98)

Form. (Puy. Fav.; Ata.) *$qulaw$.

T *$hlaw$. Dioi *lau* (h.t.), from *$hlaw$. Sek *law* (h.t.), from *$hlaw$. KS *$qhlaaw$: Sui *qhau ~ khau ~ hau*, Mak Then *la:u* (h.t.), prob. from *$q(a)law$ (assim.). Lk. *khyau = ćhau*, from *$khlaw$. Lt. *khu* (cw. "drink"), from *$kh[l][aw]$.

LIVE, LIVING, RAW *$(N)quzip$; *$qu(n)zip/qu(n)zip$ (5)

(I) IN **hu*ḍip*=*[ʔ]u*ḍip* "live." PPN **ma*ʔuri* "life, life principle, alive, soul," from *ma/qudi(p). Form: East (Ami) *ma/-qu[z]ip; Tsouic (Saa.) *ma/Nqutsip "alive/to live."

T **dip "unripe, raw" (Shan also "to live, be alive"; Ahom dip "alive"~lip "unripe"). Dioi dip (h.t.) "raw," from **ʔdip. Sek rip (h.t.) "raw, unripe" (Ged.), from **ʔrip. KS **ʔdyip "raw, not ripe": Sui ʔdyup~dyup, Mak ʔdip, Then lip (all h.t.). OB zɔp (h.t.) "green (not dry), raw meat," from **ʔd[i]p. Li *hrwiip "raw": S. Li diep, N. Li fiep, WS Li fip, from *h(u)rip. Laha: TU ktʻop "alive," NL dəp "unripe," from *(k/)d[o]p (cf. OB).

(II) Form. (Pai: Ferr.) *q/m/uzi/quzip; (Pai: Mak.) *(q/)-m/uzi/(q/)m/uzip "animal" (="living thing"), from *quzi[p]/-quzip.

PY **yem [h.t.]=**ʔyem "located, dwell" (also "live"), from PMY **ʔyem, from *q[]yem/[q]yep; PM ***ʔñɔ(ŋ) (s.t.), id., from PMY **ʔnom, from *q(o)ñem (assim.)<*q(o)nyem; also PY **ñem "raw," from PMY *ñem<*nyem; PM *(ʔ)ñuŋ: MCF ñu (h.t.) "raw," MPT ñuŋ~ñu~ño (l.t.) "fresh/green (timber, vegetables, water), raw (meat)," from PMY *(ʔ)ñu[m], from *(q)nyuum<*(q)(u)nyim (assim.).

LIVER, ENTRAILS, HEART (EMOTIONS), MIND *[q]aplay; *[qa]play/a; *[qa]pla/p[lay]

(I) IN **hatay~**atay=**ʔatay "liver, heart/emotions (Gemüt)." PPN **ʔate "liver" (Tikopian "entrails, intestines," Tuamotuan "heart"). Form. (East: gen.) *qatay "liver"; (Sai.) *ma/-qaṭay "guts."

T *thaay "mind" (Shan: lit.), from *(qa)tay (second. aspir. by *q-).

(II) T *tai̥ "heart (Ahom), entrails, bowels (Si.), gizzard (WT Nung)," from *tayə<*[]tay/a. Dioi tai "cloaca of birds" (cf. Thai). KS: Mak ta "viscera of birds," from *tai̥ (cf. Thai).

(III) T *tap "liver," from *[]plap<*[]pla/p(lay). Dioi tap, id. Li *[p]lap: WS Li plap "fowl stomach" (cf. Thai). Laha: TU ta:p "liver" (app. Thai loan).

LIZARD *[b]i(n)ya[wak]

IN **yawak=*bi(n)yawak "name of a large lizard, the varanus": Ml. biyawaʔ; also (Blust 1974) Kadazan biavak "very big lizard"; but Tg. bayawak (vowel assim.), NgD. băd'awak (prob. from *bănyawak) and Ja. mĕńawaʔ<*[b]ănyawak.

T *[ń,y]e=/[ń,y]ee/ "kind of lizard which burrows in the ground, sand lizard (Shan); Draco Toeniopterus (large lizard of the woods) (Si.)," from *yia<*(-i)ya(wak); cf. also *[a,aa]y "tree lizard" (Kh.), perh. from the assim. form (cf. Tg.).

LOAN   See BORROW.

LONG   See BIG; FAR.

LONG (SPACE)   *(qə)law
   Form. (Ami; Ata.) *q[ə]law; cf. also Puy: Chipon tatəlau, app. from *ta-qəlaw, paralleling Ami (Ferr.) *ti-q[ə]law.
   T *law "long and straight" (Shan).

LONG (TIME) *law[ats]
   IN **lawat'.
   PMY **law.

LOOK AT   *[ti]l̲iak
   IN **tilik. PO: Fi. tele "direct the eyes toward something."
   T *liak "look at curiously" (Lao).

LOOK AT, SEE   *[ti](n)dz[a]w; *[ti]dz[ə]w
   (I) IN **tin[d̲]aw~**tind'aw "look at closely," from *ti(n)z̲aw. PPN **tiro "look at" (Hawaiian "watch closely").
   (II) T *ʔdu "look at" (WT "look at attentively from nearby"; Ahom Shan also "see"). KS *[]do "see": Mak do (h.t.), Then ʔdo.

LOUSE   *(ŋ)kat[l̲u]; *qatl̲u (4, 22, 73)
   (I) IN **kutu "louse, head louse," from *katu by assim. PPN **kutu. Form. (East: gen.) *kuṭu; (Tsouic) *kutsu "head louse."
   Yao: YCR ćho "body louse"; Miao: MPT ńćhau "head louse"; both from PMY *(ń)ćho(u)<*(ŋ)khou<*(ŋ)ku(tl̲u); also Yao: YHN sei "head louse," from PMY *tshei<*tshat<*khat <*kat(l̲u) (without vocalic assim.).
   (II) Form. (Fav.) *[q]aṭu~*[q]uṭu "head louse."
   T *thraw "head louse," from *[q](a)tru (second. aspir. by

the original **q*). Dioi *rau* (h.t.), id., from **[th]raw.* Yay Sek *raw* (h.t.), id. (Ged.) (cf. Dioi). KS **t(y)u,* id.: Sui *tu,* Mak *təu,* Then *tiu.* OB *kat* "lice" (Jer.), *kɔt* "head louse" (Sav.), from **[q]at.* Li **[]traw:* S. Li *śau* "louse," SH Loi *sou,* DC SC Loi *fou* "lice," from **[q](a)tru.*

LOUSE, FLEA[I] **pru(m)baś*

IN ***tuma* "louse, clothes louse." PPN ***tuma* "louse." Form: East **tum[b]as* "head louse" (Sai.); **[t]umbus∼*[t]umbəs* "body/clothes louse" (Bun.), from **[t]umbas* (vocalic assim. forward), whence Thao *tumbus,* id., as loan; **[t]um[b]us∼ *[t]um[b]əs* "body/clothes louse (Ami: Og.-As.; Kuv: Tsuchida), flea (Ami: Ferr.), gnat (Kuv: Ferr.)" (cf. Bunun) (Dyen: *s₂*).

T **hmat* "flea (Kh. Shan Lao WT Tho Nung), body louse (BT), plant louse (Si.), kind of ant (Ahom)"; also **ʔbat* "kind of louse found on the body of a dog" (Ahom doublet), both from an original **ʔ(m)bat<*[tə](m)bat.* Dioi Sek *mat* (h.t.) "flea," from **hmat* (cf. Thai). KS **hmat,* id.: Sui *hmat,* Mak Then *mat,* Kam *ŋwat* (all h.t.) (cf. Thai Dioi). Lk. *khwot,* id., from **khwat<*hmat* (cf. KS). OB *mat* (Jer.), *mɔt* (h.t.) (Sav.), id., from **hmat* (cf. Thai KS). Li **m[ua]t,* id.: S. Li *mat,* N. Li *pɔt,* Loi dial. *but∼bot,* Bas. *bŭ* (usu. cw. "dog"), from **(u)mat <*(tu)mbat.*

PMY ***ta(m)* "louse" (YCR "fleas, body lice," YHN "clothes louse"; MPT [cw. "red"] "body louse"; [cw. "black"] "bedbug"), from **[pr]am(baś)∼*[pr]a[baś]<*[pr]u(m)baś* (vocalic assim. backward; contrast Form.).

LOUSE, FLEA[II] **[ba](m)bulay* (9)

Form. (Paz.) **babulay* "head louse; (ic.) body louse."

T **ray* "louse/flea (Si.), kind of louse or mite (Ahom), minute lice of animals and fowls (Shan), bird lice (Lao), chicken louse (Nung)." Dioi *rwi* "lice of fowls," from **rway<*(u)ray< *(u)lay* (**l>*l̥* through influ. of back vowel **u*) (cf. Thai). Sek *ri* "chicken louse" (Ged.) (cf. Dioi). KS **[]mbyay* "chicken flea": Sui *myai∼byai,* Mak *byai,* Then *ʔbai* (all h.t.), from **[]mb[]lay.*

PY ***ʔlaay;* YCR *laai* (h.t.) "itching due to lice or mites on the skin"; *put laai* "to have (*put*) lice," app. from *[](a)lay* (vocalic assim.).

LUNGS   See HEART.

M

MALE   See PENIS.

MALE   *la(N)q[i](/la(N)q[i])* (20)

IN **laki* "man (male), married man" (TB. *lahi/lahi*, Tg. *la/laki*), from *laNqi* (cf. Form.). Cham *lakei<*laki* "boy, man, male." SEP *laki/laki~*la/laki* "great": Capell: in SEP [this root] has first come to mean "adult man," then "adult," "full grown," "large." Form. (Paz.; Ata.) *laqi* "child" (Ata. also *laqi na laqi* "grandchild").

T*laaŋ* "grandchild (Ahom), child (Shan), young man (Nung)," from *(laŋ)laŋ<*laN(qi)/laN(qi)*. Dioi *laŋ* "male," from *l[a,aa]ŋ* (cf. Thai). Lk. *lak* "man (male)" (cf. *lak-kya=Lakkia*); also *la:ŋ* "son-in-law," a loan from Yao (below).

PY **laaŋ* "son-in-law, young man" (YCR also "sire, progenitor": *tuŋ-laaŋ* "boar [*tuŋ*] used for breeding purposes"), from *(laŋ)laŋ<*laN(qi)/laN(qi)*, paralleling the Thai development.

MAN (HUMAN BEING)   *()(N)[G][o][l]on* (27, 68, 69)
   In **ulun*.

T *gon* (irreg. initial g- for *γ-*), from *[G]o(r)on*, with second. vowel shortening. Chuang *won*, from *[G]won<*Goon*. Dioi *hun* (l.t.), from *Gun*. Sek *hun* (l.t.) (Ged.) (cf. Dioi). KS *()[N]en*: Sui *zən~zen*, Mak *jin*, Then *ʔyin* (all h.t.), Kam *ńen*, from *()NGen<()NGon*. Lk. *ŋyun*, from *[N]un<*NGun* (cf. KS). OB *bon*, from *won<*[G]wɔn<*Goon* (cf. Chuang). Lt. *a/khu*, from *[G]o[n]*.

MAN, PEOPLE[1]   *(m)plaw[u](/plaw[u])*; *pl/l/aw[u]*

(I) IN **[t]awu* "man (*Mensch*)." PO **tau* "man, person." PPN *tau*: Fu. *tau* "person"; To. *tou/tai*, Sm. *tau/tai* "seaman"= "man of the sea (*tai*)." Form. (East) *taw(/taw)*; (Tsouic) *tsaw(/tsaw)* "man/human being."

T *taw* "child" (Lao), app. by semantic extension from

"person," from *(taw/)taw. Lq. kə/dəu "man (human being),"
from */ntəu<*nt(y)aw.

PY *taw (l.t.) "clf. for people, animals (and certain objects: door, ax, key)," app. by extension from "animal beings"
(and certain objects so conceived), from PMY *daw, from an
earlier *taw (initial voicing).

(II) Form. (Bun.) tamlau "man/human being," from *[t̯]/m/law,
from an original re-infixed form: *t̯/m/l/aw.

T *laaw "the Lao" (Si. Lao), from *(a)law<*(/a)l/aw.
Kl: cf. the Chinese name for this group: Lao (see also under
MAN/PEOPLEᴵᴵ).

MAN, PEOPLEᴵᴵ   *(ta/)məl̯ayu; *b[]l̯ayu
(I) IN *məlayu "the Malay" (Ml.). PO **tamole "man," from
*ta/məlay(u).

PM **hmuŋ "the Miao," from PMY *hm[ə]n; PY **m[]n=
*m[yə]n "person"="the Yao": YCR myen, YTP myɛn, YHN mun;
both from PMY *(h)m(y)ən, from *( )məl̯(ayu) (cf. the Chinese term: Man=Yao); also MPT mlau "the Miao" (Sav.),
MCF qa/nau "the Kanao" (qa is clf.), from PM *ml̯aw<PMY
*ml̯[an], app. from an infixed form: *m[]la/l/u (cf. MAN, PEO-
PLEᴵ); cf. also the Chinese name: Miao, prob. from Arch. Ch.
*ml̯iau, by metath. from *m[]l̯ayu; also the Chinese name: Yao,
from *(a)yu.

(II) T *day "the Thai," from *bray<*b[]l̯ay(u). Dioi ʔyai~yai
(=yay), also ʔyui~yui (F.K. Li 1957bis) and *yoi (=Dioi), "the
Dioi," from *( )yay<*[b]l̯ay(u) and *( )(o)yay<*[b](ə)l̯ay(u).
Li *hray "the Li": S. Li dai, N. Li haːi, but *hlay indicated by
Bup. θlai "man," from an original *[p]h[]ray<*[p]h[]l̯ay(u);
cf. the variant forms cited for this ethnic name: B'lai, B'li, Dli,
Lai, Loi, Le (Benedict 1942: note 3). Lq. ka beu "the Laqua"
(=Ka Beo), from *biau<*b[l]iau, app. by metath. from
*b[l]ayu (cf. Kelao, below; also Miao, above). Kl: cf. the
Chinese name for this group: Lao (see under MAN/PEOPLEᴵ),
written with a character normally read liao, app. by metath.
from *[]l̯ayu (cf. Laqua), suggesting an early semantic merging
of the two roots (MAN/PEOPLEᴵˑ ᴵᴵ).

MANA See HAVE (POSSESSION).

MANE, COVERING (OF HEAD) *(n)tsuŋkuk
 IN **t'uŋkuk "head covering" (Ho. "place on the head with long hair").
 T *guk~*guuk (Shan doublet) "mane," from *(-u)ŋkuk.
 PMY **(n)tsoŋ "mane," perh. a loan/b.l. from Ch. tsuŋ, id., from Anc. Ch. tsuŋ (character not found in pre-Han texts).

MANURE See DUST (two entries).

MANY *liaw
 Form. (Pai.) *liaw.
 OB liao (Jer.), leao (Sav.).

MARK See COLOR(ED).

MAT See SPREAD (OUT).

MEAT See FLESH (three entries).

MIAO See MAN (THE PEOPLE).

MIDDLE See BETWEEN (PART).

MIDDLE, CENTER, HALF *[]ntəŋ; *( )(n)t/l/əŋ (19)
 (I) PMY **ntoŋ "middle, center."
 (II) IN **tələŋ "middle" (Ja. tĕlĕŋ). PO: Fi. tolo "trunk of the body; middle part of a thing" (Blust 1972).
 T *troŋ "straight, accurate" (Si. troŋ~kroŋ) (="in the center/centered"), from *[]t[]roŋ; also *thooŋ "half" (Lao BT), from *tho(r)oŋ; also *ʔdooŋ "parents of son/daughter-in-law" (="the middlemen") (SW), from *[]ntrooŋ<*[]nt(o)roŋ. Dioi dɔŋ (h.t.), id., from *ʔdɔŋ (cf. Thai). Sek trɔɔŋ, id., from *ʔdrɔɔŋ.
 PM **ntrɔŋ "middle, center," from PMY *ntroŋ.

MILLET, RICE *[b]a(N)qu[Ru]
 Form. (W. Ruk: Mantauran) *baquRu "cooked rice"; (Pai.) *baqu or *baqu[R] "millet," from *baqu(Ru) or *baquR(u); (Saa.) *[q]uRu "cooked rice," from *(ba)quRu.
 T *xaw "rice": Ahom "paddy, boiled rice"; Shan "the rice plant, boiled rice"; WT "cereal; rice (general term)," from *(a)qu(ru) or *(a)qu(r)u. Dioi hau "rice, cereals," from *qhaw (cf. Thai). Chuang *Gaw "rice," from *Nqaw. Sek *γaw, id.

(Ged.), from *Nqaw (cf. Chuang). KS *Gəw~*qəw, id.: Sui
ʔau, Then xau, Kam ʔou (all l.t.), Mak həu (h.t.), from *(N)qəw
<*(ə)(N)qu (unstressed form): Mak həu is fully defined as
"rice, paddy (used before the names of the five cereals)." Lk.
kou "rice," from *[q][ə]w (cf. KS). OB ŋa:u, id., from *NGa:u
<*Nqaaw (cf. KS).

MIND   See BELLY; LIVER.

MIST   See FOG/MIST; RAIN.

MIST, CLOUDY   *[ka](m)bot
   IN **kabut "mist." PO: Fi. kambu, id., from *kambu(t).
   T *ʔbot "cloudy."

MONKEY¹   *(m)b[ə]γuk (78, 79)
   IN **bə[l]uk=*bəγuk (Prentice): Ml. běruʔ, NgD. beruk
"kind of monkey"; also (Prentice) Old Ja. wruk, Busang bəruk
and (by metath.) Kadazan gobuk, Timugon gabuk. Form. (W.
Ruk: Mantauran) movoroko<*mubu[γ]uk, app. from *mbuγuk
<*mbəγuk (vocalic assim.).
   OB ma-lu (Jer.) (n.a.). Li *nuk: S. Li nuk, WS Li nɔk, Loi
dial. nok~noh, from *nduk<*mbruk. Lq. tɔk, from *prɔk<*brɔk
(initial unvoicing)<*bruk.

MONKEY¹¹   *bliŋ
   Form. (Pai: Shimopaiwan Mak.) *labiŋan, app. by metath.
from an original *bliŋ/an.
   T *liŋ. Dioi liŋ. KS: Mak liŋ. Lk. liŋ.
   PM **ʔle(ŋ); PY **biŋ (h.t.)=*bliŋ (Haud.); both from
PMY *ʔbliŋ.

MOON   See BURN; LIGHT (two entries); WHITE (two
   entries).

MORNING   See LIGHT.

MORTAR, POUND (IN MORTAR), PESTLE   *[l]o(ŋ)k[l,l]oŋ;
   *(la)(ŋ)k[l,l]ok (38, 95, 118, 126)

(I) IN **lət′uŋ "mortar" (unstressed form); Tg. (also Yami)
*lut′uŋ, id. Form. (East; Saa.) *lutsuŋ (Atayalic) *luhuŋ<
*lutsuŋ, id.

T *klooŋ "to husk (=pound in mortar) paddy" (Ahom); also Si. *khau klɔ:ŋ* (~*glɔ:ŋ*) "rice (*khau*) partly shelled (=pounded in mortar)," from *(o)(ŋ)kloŋ*. KS: Sui *tyuŋ* "to hull (rice)," Then *tyuŋ* "to pound," from *[kl]uŋ*.

(II) Form. (Puy.) *ləsok~lasok* "pestle" (Og.-As.), *rəsok* "stone pestle" (Ferr.); all from *l[a]tsuk;* cf. also Puy. *karsukan* "wood pestle" (Ferr.), app. from *ka/l[ə]tsuk/an*.

T *khlok* "pound in a mortar" (Si. *khlo:k,* with second. length); also *grok* "mortar," from *ŋkrok* (for *ŋklok*). KS: Mak *sok* "pound in a mortar; (ic.) pestle for pounding pepper," from *kh[l]ok*.

MOTHER See FEMALE.

MOTHER, AUNT, FEMALE   *[(t/)i]na(/na)
IN **ina* "mother"; also *t/ina*: Bulu (Celebes) *tina* "female of birds" (Cap. cit.), Ml. *bĕ/tina* "female of animals." PO *t/ina*: Fi. *tina* "mother; mo's sister" (Macuata also "fa's sister"), *tina/-tina* "female of animals" (CL); also *nana*: Fi. (Vuda Lautoka) *nana* "mother; (ic.) mo's sister" (CL), from *(ti)na/na* (cf. PPN). PPN **tina[na]* "mother" (Tikopian *tinana*). Form. (East; Tsouic) *(t/)ina,* id.; also (Sir.) *(in/)ina,* (Saa.) *-ina* "woman."
T *na* "mo's younger sibling (<"mo's younger sister," by extension) (SW); younger sister/ (ic.) mo's younger sister (Tho-Nung)." Dioi *na* "uncle; (ic.) mo's younger bro., mo's younger si." KS: Mak *na* "mo's bro's wife" (<"mo's younger sister"). Lk. *na* "mo's younger bro." (cf. the semantic extension in Thai).

MOTHER, AUNT, GRANDMOTHER, SISTER (OLDER)
   *[a]ya[ʔ]; *ya[h] (64)
(I) Form: Ata. *yayaʔ* "mother," from */ayaʔ.*
(II) Form. (Paz.) *yah* "older sister."
T *ya* "fa's mother." Sek *ya,* id. (Ged.). KS *ya* "grandmother": Sui Mak *ya,* Then *zya;* Sui also "old woman," Mak "fa's mother (also ic. "mo's mother"), old woman." Li *ya*: S. Li *ya,* WS Li *za* "old/aged," SC Loi *ja* "mother." Lq. *yə* "grandmother."
PY *ya* "fa's sister" (Haud.).

MOULD(Y), DECAY(ED) (WORMEATEN), DUST
   *(q/)(m)buk(/buk); *(q/)(m)bək(/bək)

(I) IN **bukbuk=*(m)buk(m)buk "decay (Mulm)" (Tg. Ml. "weevil," Ja. "powder," Ho. "decay, dust"). PO *puk(puk): Fi. *vuk/a* "mouldy," Sa. *huhu* "run out as powder"; also (Blust 1972) Gilbertese *bubu* "dust, sawdust, powder."

T *hmuk* "mould, mouldy" (Lao); also *muk* "dust" (Shan Nung: ic.) (Shan *mun-muk* "to be fine; dusty; dust"); both from *(q/)mbuk.

(II) IN *bəkbək=*(m)bək(m)bək "decay (Mulm)": Ja. *běběk* "crushed, trampled," Bukidnon Manobo *bekbek* "pulverize by pounding or stepping on" (cit. by Blust 1972). PPN **popo "decay" (Easter Island "deteriorate; smell of dampness"; Marquesan "woodworm," Nukuoro "rotten," Fi. "wormeaten"), from *mpompo.

T *hmok* "mouldy, mould" (Lao doublet WT), from *q/mbok.

MOUNT See CLIMB.

MOUTH *[ŋ]u(n)dzuj

Form. *ŋudzuj "mouth (E. Ruk.; W. Ruk: Tona), nose (Pai.)"; for the semantics, cf. IN **ŋu[t']u "lips," Fi. ŋusu "mouth"; Form. (E./W. Ruk.) *ŋu/ŋutsu "nose"; (Tsouic) *(ta)ŋutsu "nose (Tsou Kan.), mouth (Saa.)"; (Ata.) ŋuhuu<*ŋutsu "nose," all from a distinct but perhaps distantly cognate AN root.

PM **ndyeu=*ndzyeu, from PMY *ndz[oi] (palatalized), from an earlier *ndzuy; PY **dzui, from PMY *ndzui, from an earlier *ndzuuy<*(u)ndzuy.

MOUTH, LIPS *[m]/l/ut; *[m]ut/[m]ut; [m]ut/[m]it; *(m/)l/u[t]/(m/)l/it

(I) IN **mulut "mouth" (Ho. "lips"), from *m/l/ut. Form. (Sir.) *muḷut "mouth," from *m/l/ut.

PM ***ʔlo "mouthful" (MCF MPT: Sav. "mouth"), from PMY *ʔ[l][ui], from an earlier *[-/]l/u[t].

(II) Form. *mut/mut "mouth (W. Ruk: Maga); mouth, lips (W. Ruk: Mantauran)."

(III) Form. (Ruk: Thomson 1873) *mut/mit "mouth"; cf. also (W. Ruk: Maga Tona) *-mit "lips."

(IV) Form. (Thao) *ɭuɭit* "mouth"; (Paz: Bullock 1874) *ɭuɭi[t]* "lips"; also (Pai.) *ɭəɭət,* id. (unstressed form), all from an original *(m/)ɭ/u[t]/(m/)ɭ/it.*

MOUTH, OPENING, SPEAK *pabaq;* *papaq;* *(m)ba(m)baq;* *wawaq* (13)

(I) Cham *pabaḥ* "mouth, orifice."

(II) T *paak* "mouth, opening; to speak," from *(pa)pak<* *pabak* (assim. forward). Sek *pa:k* "mouth." KS *paak,* id.: Sui *pak,* Kam *pa:k.* OB *bak* (h.t.) "mouth, beak, mouthful," from *pa[a]k.* Li *paak*: S. Li *paʔ* "morsel, mouthful, swallow" (cf. Thai).

(III) IN **babaʔ*=*(m)ba(m)baʔ* "mouth, opening" (NgD. *bawa* "to call," Ja. *b/r/abah* "to speak loudly"), from *pabaʔ* (assim. backward). PPN **fafa* "mouth" (Easter Island *haha*), from *papa;* also *pafa*: Easter Island *baha* "aperture, opening," from *mpapa.*

   T *baak* "space" (=opening) (Shan; used with *na* "before"); also *baak* "word" (Lao), from *(ba)bak.*

(IV) IN **wawaʔ* "opening" (Tg. "river mouth," Ho. "mouth"). PO: Sa. *wawa-* "mouth." PPN */wawa*: To. *ta/vava* "space between the teeth," Sm. *ta/vava* "opening, cleft," *pu/vava* "open the mouth."

   T *wa* "say, speak"; also *waw,* id. (Lao), from *wa/w(a).* Lt. *vui pio* "speak" (n.a.), from *waw[]* (cf. Lao).

MOVE BACK AND FORTH, SWING (ARMS), WAG (TAIL), WALK, RUN, GO, SWIM, FLY, ROW, PADDLE, FAN
   [q]a(m)bay; *k[ə]bay;* *[k/]ɭ/ə(m)bay;* *k[a](m)pay;*
   [k/]ɭ/apay; *[k]ap/l/ay;* *k[i]pay;* *(ki)pay(/pay)*

(I)   IN **a(m)bay*=*[ʔ]a(m)bay* "move back and forth" (TB "swing the arms," Ja. "beckon").

   T *hwaay* "swim" (WT Nung "to paddle"), from *q(a)way<*q(a)bay.* KS *waay* "fan": Kam *wa:i* (cf. Thai).

(II)   T *kway* "swing, throw with swinging motion of the arm (Shan); turn, agitate, stir up (=move back and forth) (Si.

Lao WT)" (Si. also "shake, rock, as a baby"), from *k[]way<
*k[]bay (unstressed form). KS: Mak *kui mi* "scold with the
finger"="shake (*kui*) the finger (*mi*) at," from *kw[ay] (cf.
Thai). Li *woy: S. Li *uoi~ui* "shake [head], wag [tail], swing
[arms in walking]," from *(o)way<*(ə)way (unstressed form).

(III)   IN *ləmbay "to fly" (Cap. cit.), app. from *(k/)l/əmbay
(unstressed form). SEP *ləbe "to fly (gen.), to swing (Motu),
to run (Tavara Keherara)," from *ləbay.

(IV)   IN **kapay "move back and forth" (Ml. "move the hand
back and forth"). PO *kampe: Fi. *kambe/a* "to get the spear
ready to throw [by moving it back and forth]."

   T *baay "to row/paddle; oar/paddle" (Shan "to move
by making a motion like that of wings or oars") (SW), from
*(a)mpay; also *vaay "to row/paddle; oar" (Nung), from
*bwaay, prob. from *baay/baay (cf. VIII). Dioi *fay* (l.t.) "oar,"
from *va[a]y (cf. Nung). Sek *pha:i* [l.t.] "oar," from *baay. KS
*paay "go": Sui *pai*, Mak Then Kam *pa:i*, from *(a)pay (for
the semantics, see VI and VII).

(V)   IN *k/l/apay: Tg. *k/al/apai* "fin."

(VI)   T *phraay "walk, go," from *(a)pray<*(a)p/r/ay.

(VII)   IN **kipay "move back and forth" (Ml. *kipai* "wag the
tail," NgD. *kipai* "beckon," *bă/kipai* "to have fins").

   T *pay "go" (Ahom "go, march"; Shan "put forth the
foot, step, march"), from "walk (=swing the arms and legs
back and forth)." Sek *pai* "go." OB *boe* "walk, go" (Jer.), *bəi*
(h.t.) "go" (Sav.), from *pai. Li *pay "walk": Bup. *bai=pai.
N. Kl. *pai*, id.

(VIII) IN *paypay: Tg. *mag/paipai*, also *paipai/an* "to fan,"
p/am/apai "fan."
   OB *phəi* "fan."

MUD   See EARTH.

MUSHROOM   *(a)(ŋ)kulat (15, 17, 18)
   IN **kulat.
   T *h[r]et (SW: Ahom cognate lacking) ~*wet (Nung), from

an original *hrwet<*(k)huret. Dioi *rat,* from *(ku)rat. Li
*[r]it: S. Li *dit.*

PM **ńće=*ŋke, with the unpalatalized velar initial maintained in MHY ŋki̵ (form lacking in Purnell), also in T'ung-
t'ou-chai ŋgu (h.t.), Hsiao-chang gəi̵ (h.t.) (these forms all
from Northern Miao dialects spoken in Hunan, cited by Y. S. Li
et al. 1959), from PMY *ŋkaw, from an earlier *(a)ŋku; PY
*ćou, from an earlier *tsou<*[]ku (palatalized by the high
vowel); both from *(a)(ŋ)ku[l̤at].

MUSSEL *( )k[a][γ]aŋ
  IN *kə[l̤]aŋ=*kə[γ]aŋ, prob. from *ka[γ]aŋ (stressed form).
  Yao: YHN kya[a]ŋ, from PMY *kraaŋ<*[]k(a)raŋ.

N

NAIL (FINGER/TOE-) See SCRATCH.

NAME *( )a(ń)ja; *( )a(ń)ja/n (7)
(I) Form. (Tsou Saa.) *ŋ/aja; cf. also Kan. ŋanai, app. from
*ŋandai <*ŋ/anja/i (cf. PO under II).

  T *ji̵ "name"; also *ji̵a "lineage"; both from *jya<*(ə)ja
(unstressed form). Dioi śɔ (l.t.)<*jɔ, app. from *(ə)jə (vocalic
assim.). Sek sɔ [l.t.], from *jɔ (cf. Dioi).

(II) IN **ag'an=*(ŋ/)ag'an (Tg. ŋ/alan). PO *a(n)sa: Fi.
yatsa-, Sa. s/ata-. Form. (East; Sed.) *ŋ/ajan.

  KS *ʔdaan: Sui ʔdan~dan, Mak ʔda:n, Then la:n (h.t.),
from *ʔjaan<*q/(a)jan. Lk. ya:n (h.t.), from *ʔyaan<*ʔjaan
(cf. KS).

NARROW *(e)(N)Gep
  T *γeep, from *Geep<*(e)Gep. Sek γeep (Ged.). Lk. yep,
from *[G]ep. OB sɔŋ kεp (l.t.) "defile in the mountains (sɔŋ),"
koŋ kεp "strait" (koŋ "sea"), from *gεp<*[G]eep.
  PMY *NGep, from an earlier *NGeep<*(e)NGep.

NARROW, CLOSE, BAG, BASKET *[tsu](m)pit
  IN **t'umpit "narrow; blowgun (=something narrowed)"
(Ho. "to close [=to narrow] a bag," Ml. "blowgun," also "small

bag [=something narrowed] of plaited leaves"); also ***t'ǝ*(m)*pit* "narrow" (unstressed form); also (Blust 1973) *tsipit "squeeze, pinch, narrow" (assim. form).

T *pit "to close, stop up (=to narrow)" (Si.); also *bit "basket braided like a mat" (Shan), from *mpit (cf. Ml. semantic development). KS *bit: Mak *pit* (l.t.) "large basket (as for manure)," from *mpit (cf. Shan).

NAUSEA See DISGUST.

NEAR, BORDER, SHORE, BANK **[tǝ](m)biŋ*; **[tǝ](m)b/l̩/iŋ* (I) IN ***tǝ(m)biŋ* "border, shore" (Ml. "high bank of a river"). PO *tembe: Fi. *tembe* "border," *tembe/ni/ŋusu* "lips"= "border (*tembe*) of mouth (*ŋusu*)."

(II) T *briŋ: Ahom *phriŋ* "near," *phriŋ-śup* "lips"="border (*phriŋ*) of mouth (*śup*)"; Kh. *piŋ-sop* "lips," *piŋ-hu* "ear"= "border (*piŋ*) of ear (*hu*)"; Nung *pik-khyu~pik-śu* "ear," from **piŋ-* (assim.). OB *niŋ* "dike (of rice-field)," *nɛŋ* "bank (of river)," *neŋ* "shore (of sea)," *neŋ-bak* "lips"="border (*neŋ*) of mouth (*bak*)," from *mbriŋ.

NECK See BETWEEN (PART).

NEEDLE See STING, n.

NEST **(tsa)raŋ* (7)
   IN ***t'a[l̩]aŋ*=**t'a[r]aŋ*.
   T *raŋ.

NEW **(q/)(m)ba(qa)Ro*
   IN **baɣu=**(m)baRu*; also **baʔaɣu=*baʔaRu. PO: Sa. *haʔalu*, from *paʔaRu; also Fi. *vou*<**po[R]u* and U. *haolu*< **pa[ʔ]oRu* (unstressed forms). PPN **foʔou, from **poʔo[R]u* (unstressed form). Form. (Ruk. Fav.; Saa.) *baɣu; (East: gen.) *baqaɣu.

   T *hmai, from *hmayǝ<**hmá(R)o*<**q/mbá(R)o*. Dioi Sek (Ged.) *mo*=/*moo*/ (h.t.), from *hmoo<**hma(R)ó* (vocalic assim.). KS *hmay: Sui *hmay~hwǫi*, Mak Then *mai*, Kam *mei* (all h.t.) (cf. Thai). Lk. *wai* (cf. Sui). OB *na:u*, from **mra:u* <*mbáRu through metathesis. S. Li *ma:n* "new, fresh," from **mba:n*<**mbáR(o)*; N. Li *nɔ*, Bas. WS Li *no*, from *mro< **mb(a)Ró*.

NIGHT   See DARK (two entries).

NOSE   *[i](ń)juŋ; *(q/)(ń)jaŋ (6)

(I)   IN **ig'uŋ; also (by vocalic assim. forward) **ug'uŋ (no forms cited by Demp.). PO **isu(ŋ); also *untsu(ŋ): Fi. *utsu-* (cf. IN). PPN **isu. Form. (Kuv.) *ujuŋ (cf. IN and Fiji); also (Thao Paz.; Sed.) *mujiŋ, app. from */jiŋ<*[i]juŋ by vocalic assim. backward (contrast Kuv.); also (Pai.) *mujiŋ/an "face."

OB ləŋ (Jer.), zoŋ (h.t.) (Sav.), from *ʔdoŋ<*ʔd[u]ŋ.

(II)   T *ʔdaŋ. Sek daŋ (h.t.), from *ʔdaŋ. KS *ʔnaŋ: Sui ʔnaŋ ~naŋ, Mak Then Kam naŋ (all h.t.), from *ʔńjaŋ<*q[]ńjaŋ. Lk. naŋ (h.t.), from *ʔnaŋ (cf. KS). Lq. taŋ, from *[q/]daŋ. Lk. ńă<*ńa(ŋ), from *ńjaŋ (cf. KS Lakkia).

NOTCHED, CRACKED, BROKEN (OFF)   *ts[u](m)biŋ; *tsu(m)beŋ (12)

(I)   IN **t'u(m)biŋ "notched" (Ho. "fragment"="broken off piece").

T *(h)win "cloven, torn (Si.); to splinter, be broken (Lao)" (Lao *sop win* "harelip," cw. *sop* "mouth"), from *(s)[u]bin; also *ʔbin "notched" (Shan "broken off, as a very small piece from a larger piece of earthenware"), from *[]bin. KS *[]biŋ: Mak biŋ (h.t.) "notched," from *s[ə]biŋ (unstressed form).

(II)   T *hweeŋ "torn, broken" (WT "lateral slit, of a jacket or shirt"), from *s[]weeŋ<*s(e)beŋ (vocalic assim.). Li *veŋ: S. Li veŋ "notched [bowl], harelipped [person]," from *bweŋ< *(u)beŋ.

PY *bhɛŋ (h.t.)=*mbhɛŋ (YTP mbhɛŋ) "cracked," from PMY *mphɛŋ, from *ts[]mbɛŋ.

O

OAR, STERN   *da[a]y[uŋ]

IN **dayuŋ "oar."

T *daay "stern" (SW only) (=rudder; cf. Germ. *ruder* "oar"). Dioi tay (l.t., s.t.) "buttocks," from *da[a]y.

ODOR *kə(ŋ)kriŋ (16)

IN **kə(ŋ)k'iŋ "odor of urine."

T *klin "odor (good or bad)" (Si. Lao). Dioi kiɛn~kian "odeur de sauvage" [of urine of wildcat], from *kl[i]n.

ODOR, SMOKE *[s,h]atsap

IN **hat'ap "smoke" (TB. "smoked"); for the semantics, cf. SEP: Pem bau "smoke," IN **bahu "odor"; also Thao *s[]ma-rum/n "smoke"<*s/m/arum "smell" (see SMELL/FRAGRANT).

T *saap "odor (usu. unpleasant: sweaty, rancid)," from *(a)sap.

OFFSPRING See CHILD (OFFSPRING).

OIL See FAT.

OLD, ELDER, RIPE *[(n)tu]qas; *(n)ta[q]u[/tuqas] (25)

(I) IN **tuʔa "old" (NgD. "ripe"), also the doublet **tuwa "old" (with medial *-w- replacing the original *-q-) and *ma/-tuwa "old (TB), older children (Ho.)"; *ma/ntuwa: Ml. mentua (~mertua) "parents-in-law" (cit. by Blust 1970). PO **tua "grandfather" (Fi.), also *ma/tua "ripe" (Fi. Sa.) (cf. IN). PPN **ma/tuʔa "parents" (Tikopian "mature, elder," Tuamotuan "mature, ripe"). Form. (Thao Kuv.) */tuqas (s₁/s₃/s₄) "older (brother, sibling)," also (Thao: Dyen cit.) *tuqa/tuqas "old (person)" (="adult").

T *ke=/kee/ "old, ripe, mature," from *qay<*qas, with irreg. initial *k- for *x- (<*q-), but with vocalism reflecting the original *q-. Dioi kiɛ "old; spoiled" (="overripe"). KS: Mak će "old" (koŋ će "old man"), from *ke=/kee/ (cf. Thai).

(II) Form. (Thao: Ferr.) *taqu/tuqas "old (person)" (="adult"), app. by metathesis from *tuqa/tuqas (cf. Dyen cit. under I).

T *thaw "old, aged," from *ta(q)u: Nung thau "word added to kinship terms to denote a man's senior relatives," e.g. po thau "father (po) of a man," me thau "mother (me) of a man"; Ahom a thau "grandmother." Dioi tau (l.t., same series) "to last a long time," from *daw<*ntaw.

OPEN, GAPE/STAND OPEN, FORCE OPEN/APART, OPPOSE, SEPARATE, BAY, RIVER *[(m)b]aŋaq;

*[b/]n/aŋ[aq];   *[(m)ba]ŋa[q/]ŋa[q];   *[(m)b]akaq;
*[ba]ga[q/]gaq;   *[ba]gaŋ(/gaŋ);   *[ba]kaŋ(/kaŋ)

(I)   IN **baŋa=*baŋaʔ (NgD. baŋah; cf. Blust 1973) "stand open," perhaps from an original *baŋga. PO *paŋa "wide open" (Blust 1973): Mota waŋa "open the mouth, gape" (cit. by Blust 1972). PPN **faŋa "bay (=opening)," from *paŋa<*baŋa; cf. also maŋa (Fi.) and maŋamaŋa (Sm.) "vulva," app. from *mbaŋa(/mbaŋa).

T *ŋaak "to rend asunder; go aside (Ahom); to open, gape; to be open, separated; to pull trigger of gun (Shan)," from *(ŋak)ŋak, perhaps from an earlier *(ŋgak)ŋgak.

(II)   IN **b/in/aŋa=*b/in/aŋa[ʔ] "river" (Ho. "river mouth" ="opening").

T *aŋ "lie open, stretch out" (Si.), from *(b/n/)aŋ(aq); cf. also *aaŋ "very deep water, gulf, abyss" (Lao).

Yao: YCR nuŋ (h.t.) "to open (the eyes)," from PMY **ʔnuŋ, from *[]nuŋ[aq]<*[b/]n/aŋ[aq].

(III)   IN **ŋaŋa=*(bə)ŋa(ŋa) "stand open": Ja. wĕŋa "stand open" (Demp. cites under **baŋa=*baŋaʔ), from *bəŋa(ŋa); Tg. ŋaŋa "open the mouth," TB. ŋaŋa/n, Ml. ŋaŋa, NgD. kă/ŋaŋa "stand open (mouth)," from an original *(ba)ŋa/ŋa (stressed form)<*(ba)ŋa/ŋaq (assim.)<*(ba)ŋaq/ŋaq (partial redupl.).

OB ŋa (h.t.) "river," from *hŋa<*[p]h[]ŋa<*[b][]ŋa-(/ŋaq). S. Li ŋa "open [mouth, door, eyes, umbrella]," from *[ba]ŋa[ŋaq].

(IV)   IN **bə(ŋ)kaʔ=*bakaʔ (Tg.)~*(m)bə(ŋ)kaʔ (Tb. Ja.) (unstressed form; cf. I) "discord" (Tg. "war," Ja. "discord, conflict"), also Maranao (Blust 1972) bekaʔ "widen an opening." PO *poka: Sa. hoka "burst open, come apart," Nggela voka "divide, separate, divorce" (cit. by Blust 1972).

T *kaak "lees, refuse, bran, that which remains of fruit from which the juice has been extracted (=the separated part)" (Si.), from *[](a)kak.

(V)   IN **gagaʔ "to use force" (TB. NgD. "to resist, oppose"), app. from *(ba)ga[q/]gaq (abbrev. and partially redupl. form).

(VI) IN **$gaŋ$~**$gaŋgaŋ$ "to gape" (Ja. "fissure"), app. from *$(ba)gaŋ(/gaŋ)$ (cf. IV).

T *$ŋaaŋ$ "to open, break open (fruit); to pull apart, pull (trigger)" (Si. Lao also "to separate, disunite, oppose"), from *$(ŋaŋ)ŋaŋ$, prob. from *$(a)ŋgaŋ<$*$[g]aŋ/gaŋ$ (second. nasalization), but possibly from a distinct doublet *$(ba)ŋaŋ/ŋaŋ$ (cf. Thai under I); also *$hŋaaŋ$ "to separate from (a person)" (Shan), from *$[](a)ŋgaŋ$.

(VII) T *$kaaŋ$ "to put away a wife without divorcing her" (Shan), from *$(kaŋ)kaŋ$; also *$khaaŋ$ (s.t.) "to live apart without being divorced" (Shan), from *$kaŋ(kaŋ)$, app. from an earlier *$(ba)kaŋ/kaŋ$.

OPPOSE See GAPE OPEN.

OTHER *$iba[q]$; *$iba[q]/an$; *$uba[q]$; *$uba[q]/an$

(I) IN **iba? "to be other, change," perhaps from *$iba/$ (cf. II).

(II) IN **$iba[$?$]/an$: TB. *leban* "the others," from *$la/iba/an$ (Demp.).

T *$bian$ "other (person), friend, companion" (Kh. "others, people in general"; Lao also "with"), from *$byaan<$*$(i)bá/an$; also *iin "other, another (person, place, time)," from *$(i)yaan$ $<$*$i(b)a/an$.

(III) IN **uba? "to be other, change," perhaps from *$uba/$ (cf. II and IV).

T *$buun$ "yonder (other place)" (SW), from *$bwan<$ *$(u)bá/(a)n$; also *uan "friend, companion" (Lao), from *$uwan$ $<$*$ú(b)a/(a)n$; also *uun "yonder" (Shan); "other, distant (Lao)," from *$uwun<$*$u(b)un<$*$ú(b)a/(a)n$ (vocalic assim.). KS **?$b[oo]n$: Mak ?$bən$ "together (=with)" (cf. Lao under II), from **?$buan<$**?$uban=uban<$*$ubá/(a)n$.

OTTER *$[s][a]naq[u,o][y]$

Form: Ata. *sənaqoi*, from *$[s]ənaquy$, prob. from *$[s]anaquy$ (stressed form).

T *$naak$, prob. from *$(a)nak$. Li *$naak$: S. Li *na*?, SH Loi *teak*, DC SC Loi *tɛk* (cf. Thai).

OUTSIDE *$(q/)(m/)lu(w)aG$

IN **luwar (Tg. *luwal*, TB. NgD. *ruar*, Ja. *luwar*, Ml. *luar*) ~*lu²a² (Iban ŋe-*luah* "be outside," Tg. *luwa²* "sticking, bulging or protruding out") (doublet cited by Blust 1970), app. from an original **lu(w)aG*.

T *nook, from *mlook<**m/look*<**m/luak*. N. Thai *rook: Dioi *rɔ*, Wu-ming *rok*, Po-ai *look*, from *[*ml*]*ook*<*[*ml*]*uak*. KS **²*nuak*: Sui *²nuk*~*nuk*, Mak *nuk*, Then ŋuek (<*nuek by assim. to final) (all h.t.), from **q/mluak*<**q/m/luwak*.

OVERFLOW, FLOOD *ba[*saq*]; *(*q/*)*ba/ba*[*saq*]

(I) IN **baha²=*basa² "flooding": Tg. *baha²*, Ml. *bah;* also (Blust 1969) Lemiting (Borneo) *sia*, Long Kiput (Borneo) *se* "water." PO *paa: U. *haa* "spring flood."

(II) IN **ba/ba*[*ha*]²/*an*: Ja. *wa/wah/an* "flooded."
    T *²*ba* "overflow, spill."

OYSTER   See FRUIT.

P

PAIR, TWIN, TWO   *[*pa*]*ts*[*a*]ŋ

IN ***pat'aŋ* "pair." PO *pasa: Sa. *hata* "accompany each other." PPN **maasaŋa "twin," app. from *mbasanga (second. voicing of initial and unexplained vocalic length, with suffixed /*a*/).

T *sooŋ "two," from *(*-o*)*soŋ*<*(*-ə*)*səŋ* (assim.)<*(*-ə*)*saŋ* (unstressed form), phonetically *sɔ:ŋ*, perh. an early (Anc. Ch. period) loan/b.l. from Ch. *śuaŋ* "pair," Anc. *ṣɔŋ*, Arch. *sŭŋ*, from an earlier *saaŋ (Ch. *u*<*aa). Sek *so:ŋ* "two" (cf. Thai). Lk. *θuoŋ* "double," app. a recent loan from Ch. *śuaŋ*. OB *toaŋ* "pair," from *suaŋ (cf. Lk.).

PAIR, TWO   *( )ɣ*a*[*kit*]

IN **ɣ*akit* "pair, couple">"raft (laid parallel)" (Dyen): Ml. *rakit* "raft," also "fit together in an orderly arrangement"; cf. Ml. *pasaŋ* "pair," also "fit together," from ***pat'aŋ* (see PAIR/ TWIN/TWO).

T *ra "we two." KS *[]ɣ*a* "two": Sui ɣ*a*, Mak Then *za* (all h.t.), Kam *ya*.

PALM/SOLE, SLAP, HAND, FIVE   *(ta)(m)pag;
 *[ta](m)pa/p[ag]; *p/l/ag/l[/ag]; *mp/l/a/mp/l/a[g];
 *[]p/r/a[/p/r/ag]; *[ta](m)pak; *[ta]pa/pak

(I)   Form: E. Ruk. *sətapai* "palm," from *-tapa[g]; Ata. *təməpag*
"hit (with palm of hand)," from *t/m/apag* (stressed form,
with infix).

    Miao: MCF *pha* "palm/sole," from PM *[m]ph[uɛ]; Yao:
YCR *ba:i* (h.t.) "to slap; to strike with the open hand; (ic.)
clap"; both from PMY *mphaay*, from an earlier *(a)mpha[g];
cf. also PM **mbuɛ* "clap," from PMY *mbaay*.

(II)   IN **[t]ə(m)pap* "hand-breadth," from *ta(m)pap*
(stressed form), from an original *ta(m)pa/p[ag].

    T *fa* "palm, sole," from *phwa*, prob. from *pa/pa[g].
Sek *pa*, id. KS *p(h)wa* "palm": Sui *wa* (h.t.), Mak *fa*, Then
wa (l.t.) (cf. Thai). Li *fa*: S. Li *fa mə* "hand" (cw. Li *mi*
"hand"), from "palm (of the hand)."

(III) IN **palag'* "palm" (Ho. "sole"), from *palag/l[ag]<
*p/l/ag/l/ag.

(IV) SEP: Motu *palapala* "palm," from *mpala/mpala[g].

(V)   PMY **ćra=*pra* "five" (="hand"<"palm"), from
*[]p/r/a[p/r/ag]; cf. the semantic extension in Li (under II).

(VI) IN **tapak* "palm/sole"; also **təpak* "strike with the
flat of the hand" (Ja. also "palm") (unstressed form). PO
tampak: Fi. *tambak/a* "to lay the hands on something." PN
tapa: Sm. *tapa* "beckon with turned palm," from *tampa[k].

(VII) T *faak* "slap" (WT), from *phwaak*, prob. from
(ta)pa/pak. Dioi *fa* "a slap," from *fa[ak]* (cf. WT).

PALM/SOLE See FLAT.

PAN See VESSEL.

PARDON, BEG See BESEECH.

PARENT See GRANDPARENT.

PASS, PAST, DONE (PAST TENSE) *( )k[u]wa
    IN *kuwa* "done" (Capell). PO *kua*: Fi. *kua* "have done

with" (Cap.). PPN *kua* "past tense sign (Cap.)"; verb aspect marker (Walsh and Biggs).

T *kwa* "pass, surpass, more (than)," poss. an early b.l. from Ch. *kuo* "pass; mark of comparative, of preterite," Anc. *kuâ,* Arch. *kwâ;* T *kwa* (s.t.) "go" (Ahom Kh. Shan) appears to preserve an earlier meaning (past=gone); cf. Nung *pi kwa* "last year (*pi*)." OB *koa*=*kwa* "pass; mark of comparative" (cf. Thai). Li *kwa*: S. Li *kwa* "by (pass by); mark of comparative, of superlative" (cf. Thai OB).

PASS LENGTHWISE *tay/tay*
IN **taytay*=*təytəy* "to stride; footbridge; row": Ml. *titi* "to walk along a narrow path or the trunk of a tree," *titi/an* "footbridge formed of the trunk of a tree"; Ho. *teti* "traverse," *tetez/anǎ* "bridge").

T *tay* "pass over or lengthwise; walk; creep, crawl (the 'lengthwise' passing of worms, etc.)" (Shan "pass lengthwise, move along," BT "pass over [a bridge]"), from *(tay/)tay*. KS *tay*: Mak *tai* "to flow (sweat, blood, etc.)" (cf. Thai).

PASS NEAR/THROUGH/ACROSS *l[i]wət*
IN *liwə[t]* "pass near": Tiruray *liwet* "go around but close by something or someone," Long Semado *liwet* "to and fro," Ml. *liwat~lewat* "via, through, by way of; step over (as a sleeping person)" (Blust 1973).

T *loot* "to pass through hole/tunnel (Shan Lao); to pass across (WT)," from *l(i)wət*.

PEA See BEAN.

PEARL See STONE.

PENIS[I] *tu[l]ak*
Form. (Paz.) *tulak*.
T *thook* (Si.), from *thuak*<*tu(l)ak*.

PENIS[II] *[bu]tu[q]*
IN **[b]utu[q]*.
T *tu* "private parts of a male child (vulgar)" (Shan), from *tuuq*<*(-u)tuq*.

PENIS See SQUIRT; WORM.

PENIS, MALE *(u)(N)q[a]lay*

IN *m/u(ʔ)an[ay]*: Balinese *m-uani* "male" (form cited by Blust 1970), with irregular final *-i* for *-e*. PO **ŋmane* "male, husband, spouse, male cross-sibling," from *m/wane<*m/uʔanay*. PPN **taʔane* "male," from *ta/ʔanay*. Form. (Pai.) *uqalay*; (Kuv.) *u[q/]l/alay*; (Ruk.) *sa-u[q]alay* "man/male."

T *ɣruay* "penis" (Ahom *khroi~ćoi* "male genitals," also *ćoi* "child's penis; borer/awl"), from *Gruay<*(u)Gray<*(u)Nq[]lay*. Dioi *wai* "penis," from *[Gr]uay*. KS *[qh]lay* "penis": Mak *lai* (h.t.). Lt. *i hle* "urine"="water (*i*) of the penis (*hle*)," from *hlay<*q[]lay*.

PY **kyay* "penis"; Miao: MPT *qau*, id., from PM *q[ɔu]*; both from PMY *qlay*.

PEPPER See PUNGENT.

PERSON (SELF) See STAND.

PESTLE, MORTAR *(q/)[s]alu* (38)

IN **halu* "pestle." Form. (Bun. Kuv.; Ata.) *(qa/)salu*; (East: gen.; Sed.) *(qa/)sulu~*(qə/)sulu*, id. (by assim.).

Li *raw*: S. Li *drau* "mortar," Bas. *ro* "rice mortar," from *(a)ru*.

PETTICOAT See SKIRT.

PICK See PIERCE.

PICKLE *(q/)(m)pələŋ* (54)

IN *pələŋ*: Batak *poloŋ* "sour preparation from palm wine or gherkins and lemons, fermented with yeast from rice and fish" (Wulff cit.).

T **ʔblooŋ* "to pickle, let become sour (various vegetables, also often with some maceration)" (WT "preserves [of fruit, meat, etc.]"), from *q/mp(o)loŋ*.

PIEBALD See SPOTTED.

PIERCE, PICK, POKE (WITH STICK), EMBROIDER, SEW *(n)tsu(ŋ)kit* (63)

IN **t'uŋkit* "to pick" (Ho. "to work with sharp instrument," NgD. "embroidery"). PO *nsukit*: Fi. *tsukit/a* "dig up with a stick"; also (Blust 1973) Arosi *su-suki* "poke fruit off a tree with a pole" (cf. Tg. *suŋkit* "hook for picking fruit," cited by Blust 1973). PPN **suki* "pierce, spit (in cooking), stabbing pain": Sm. *suʔi* "pierce; [Demp.] to thread needle, embroider."

T *khwit~*kwit* (Lao doublet) "to pierce, thrust": BT *tam huʔ khwit* "to sew, in making designs" (*tam huʔ* "weave"), from **suk(h)it* (aspir. by initial **s-*, labial. by **u*). Dioi *kwit* "poke with the end of stick," also *kwit~kwi* "pierce, extract with a point" (cf. Thai).

PIERCED, HOLLOW, HOLE, CAVE   **[]p[ə]loŋ*; **b[ə]loŋ*

(I) T *ploоŋ* "to pierce, be pierced, penetrate; to go through, have a hole made into (Shan); hole (Lao); hole, tube, funnel, hollow, natural cave (Si.); without partitions [=hollow from end to end] (WT)"; also **ploŋ* "open, when nothing hinders the view" (Si.); also **proŋ* "pierced, open-worked, transparent" (Si.); all from **p(o)loŋ~*p( )roŋ*. Dioi *pyɔŋ* "to open (stomach of an animal)," from **p[l]ooŋ* (cf. Thai).

Yao: YHN *plɔŋ khɔt* "pierced (by hole [*khɔt*])," from PMY **plɔŋ*.

(II) Form. **bəluŋ* "hole, cave (Tsou), hole (Pai.), cave (Pai: Mak), den (Sir.)."

T *brooŋ* "what is not full, almost empty, empty; (ic.) hole," from **b(o)roŋ*. Dioi *śɔŋ* (l.t.) "hole, cavity, cavern, opening," from **jɔŋ<*brooŋ* (cf. Si.). Sek *sɔːŋ* "hole" (cf. Dioi). OB *zoŋ* "hole (eye of needle)," from **roŋ*. Li **s[uu]ŋ*: S. Li *śuoŋ* "to be pierced, have a hole made into; hole"; WS Li *ćhuŋ* =*śuŋ* "hole"; SH Loi *soŋ-hai*, DC Loi *soaŋ-hai* "posteriors"= "anus"="excrement (*hai*) hole"; from **[br]uuŋ* (cf. Dioi).

PIG   **( )(m)ba(m)buy* (89, 90, 128)

IN **babuy*=**(m)ba(m)buy*. Form. (East; Tsouic; Sed.) **babuy*.

T *hmu*, from **hmbu<*( )mbubuy<*( )mbabuy* through as-sim. N. Thai: Wu-ming *mau* (h.t.), from **hmaw<*( )mbab(uy)*, without assim. Sek *mu* (h.t.) (Ged.), from **hmu* (cf. Thai). KS *hmu*: Sui *hmu*, Mak Then *məu*, Kam *ŋu* (all h.t.), from **( )mbu* (cf. Thai). Lk. *khu*, from **h/mu* (cf. Thai KS). OB *mo* (Jer.), *mau* (h.t.) (Sav.), from **hmaw* (cf. N. Thai). Li

*maw: S. Li mau, N. Li pau, Mef. Ha SH Loi bau=pau, DC SC Loi bou=pou; also *[m]uy: Bup. boi=poi; both from *mbab[uy]~*(mba)mbúy. Lq. mu (cf. Thai). N. Kl. ma, S. Kl. xmiə, from Kl. xm[ui]<*( )mbuy. Lt: MP mɨ, BP mmbi (Rob.), me (Bon.), mi (Laj.), from Lt. *mb[ui] (cf. Kl.).

PM **mpuɛ=*mpuɛ~*buɛ (MCF), from PMY *mpaaw~*baaw app. from an earlier *(a)mbaw (cf. N. Thai Li).

PILE UP, SUPERPOSE, DOUBLE   *tson/tson (16)

IN **t'ut'un "pile up" (TB. Ja. Ml. "piled up," Tg. "doubled," Ho. "doubling"), from *t'un/t'un.

T *zoon "place one upon another, superpose; double," from *dzoon<*ntsoon<*(tso)ntson<*tson/tson.

PINCH, PINCERS   *(N)q[u](n)tip; *q[u]ndip

(I) IN **kə[t]ip "pinch off" (Ml. kĕtip "pinch with finger-nails," NgD. katip "pincers"), from *Nqətip; also *kutip: NgD. kutip "pinch off" (stressed form). PO *kotif: Fiv. kotiv/a "cut off," i/koti "scissors." PPN **[ko]koti "cut, clip." Form: Puy. ləqtip "narrow," from */q[ə]tip<"pinched."

OB tip (l.t.) "to carry, put under the arm," from *dip<*ntip (for the semantics, cf. Lao under II). Li *thiip: S. Li thiep "take with pincers, with chopsticks; (ic.) fire-tongs"; WS Li thip, Loi dial. thiab~thieb~thəb, Mef. tib=thip "chopsticks," from *(qi)tip (second. aspir. by *q-, with vocalic assim.).

(II) T *hniip "pinch; pincers" (Lao "take with pincers, pinch; press, squeeze, carry while pressing, as something under the arm"; Nung "to pinch, take with chopsticks"), from *(qi)ndip (cf. Li under I).

PIQUANT   See PUNGENT.

PIT   See HOLE.

PLAIN   See WIDE.

PLAIN(S)   *[pa](n)d[a]ŋ

IN **pa(n)daŋ "grassy plains" (Tg. "meadow," Ml. "a plain, open country, as distinguished from jungle").

T *doŋ~*duŋ (Lao doublet Si.) "plain (esp. paddy plain)," app. from *(ə)dəŋ (vocalic assim.)<*(ə)daŋ (unstressed form).

PLAIT See SEW.

PLAIT, WEAVE **zan/zan* (8, 62)

IN **ḍanḍan "plait cables."

T **saan* "weave (baskets, mats), plait," from **(san)san.* KS **saan* "plait, weave (baskets)": Sui *han,* Mak *sa:n,* Then *tha:n* (cf. Thai). Lt. *so* "weave," from **sa[n].*

PLANE See HEW.

PLANK See FLAT.

PLANT, BURY **(q/)(n)t[a]ləm* (5, 6, 36, 37)

IN **tanəm "to lay in the earth, bury, plant." PPN **tanu "bury." Form: Ami *taləm* "bury, grave" (Dahl cit.), from **taləm.*

T **ʔdam* "to plant, transplant (rice)," from **ʔd[l]am<* **q/nt[]lam<*q/nt[a]ləm* by vocalic assim. Dioi *dam* (h.t.) "to plant, till," from **ʔdam* (cf. Thai). Sek *tam* (Haud.), *tram* (Ged.) "transplant," from **tlam.* KS **ʔdlam* "to plant young rice plants": Sui *ʔdam~lam,* Mak *ʔdam,* Then *zam,* Kam *lam* (all h.t.). OB *zom* (h.t.) "transplant," from **ʔdom<*ʔdlom,* from **q/nt[]ləm* (without vocalic assim.). Laha: TU *tam* "bury."

PLANT, v. See DIG INTO.

PLATEAU See FLAT.

PLATFORM, STOREY **[p](/r/)an[t]ar(/an)*

IN ***pan[t]al=*pan[t]ar* "elevation (*Erhöhung*)"; Wolff cites TB. *pattar* "raised platform," from **pan[t]ar;* Ml. *pantaran* "veranda," Tg. *pantalan* "wharf," from **pan[t]ar/an;* also NgD. *parantaran* "veranda facing river and area in front of it," from **p/ar/an[t]ar/an.*

T **raan* "storey" (**rian raan* "house [**rian*] on piles"), from **[p]/ar/an[tar]* or **[pant]ar/an.*

PLATFORM See TRUNK.

PLUCK **(q/)(m)bit(/bit)*

IN **bitbit "hold with the fingers" (Ho. "lift with fingers").

T **ʔbit* "twist off (as in plucking), pluck." KS **ʔbit* "pick (flowers)": Sui *ʔbit~byət~ʔbyet,* Mak *ʔbit,* Then *mit* (h.t.). Li **miit:* S. Li *miet* "pinch with the fingers," WS Li *mit* "pluck (flowers)," from **mbiit<*(mbit)mbit.*

POD   See BARK, n.

POINT, FINGER[1]   *[tu](n)di(y)aŋ; *[t/l/u]diaŋ;
  *[tu](n)d/l/iyaŋ

(I)   IN **tudiŋ "point" (Ml. "point to with finger"). Form.
(Ata.) *pin/tudiŋ "point."

  Dioi niaŋ "finger [=the pointer]," from *ndiaŋ<*ndiyaŋ.
Yay ńiaŋ (h.t.), id., from *hńiaŋ<*q/ndiaŋ (palatalized). Sek
nieŋ (Haud.), ŋiaŋ (h.t.) (Ged.), id., from *hniaŋ (with assim.
of initial to the final).

(II)   Form. (Ata.) *t/l/udiŋ "finger."

(III) Li *dliaŋ "finger": S. Li yeŋ, WS Li ziŋ, N. Li tleaŋ~theŋ,
FF Loi -theŋ, SH DC Loi ćiaŋ, SC Loi jiaŋ, from *d/l/iyaŋ.
Lq. nie, id., from *ndlye<*ndliya[ŋ]. Lt. le (Laj.), id., from
(d)le<(d)liya[ŋ].

POINT, FINGER[II]   *tu(ń)źuk; *t/l/uńźuk; *(n)tu(ń)źuq;
  *tu[ź]i[k]; *[tu](ń)źi[q]; *ti[ź]u[q]; *n[d]i[ź]u[q];
  *(m)p[r,l]a[ludzuq]

(I)   IN **[t]und'uk "point." PO *[t]usu: Sa. usu "point,
forefinger." PPN *tu[s]u: To. tuhu "forefinger," tuhu/i "point."
Form. (Pai: Mak.) */tuźuk "finger"; (Pai: gen.) *t/m/uźuk
"point"; cf. also (Tsou) *źu/źuk "finger."

(II)   IN *t/l/und'uk "forefinger" (Ml.).

(III) IN **tu(n)duʔ=*(n)tu(n)duʔ "indicate (=point out)"
(Ho. turu "indication," tundru "finger," fa/nundru "forefinger").
Form. (Puy. Sai.) *t/m/uźuq; (Ami) *mi/tuźuq "point"; also
(Sai.) *ta/tuźuq "finger."

  PM *ntai̵ "point with finger": MPT ntai̵, MCh. ntai~
ntɛ, MCF teu, from PMY *ntou, from *ntu(zuq); PY **doʔ (h.t.)
"finger," from PMY *ntoʔ, from *ntu(ź)uq.

(IV)   PO *ntusi: Fi. ndusi/a "point with finger," i/ndusi "forefinger," from *ntusi[k] (cf. PPN under I). PPN **tusi "point
(to), indicate, delineate."

(V)   T *ji~*ći (Tho-Nung) "point out, show," from *źi[q].
Sek ńi (Ged.) "point," from *ńźi[q].

(VI)　Form. (Sed.) *tiźu[q]~*t/m/iźu[q] "point."

(VII)　T *niu~*liu (Kh.) "finger," from *ndiu<*ndi(ź)u[q].

(VIII)　IN: Yami *tanulu* "finger," from *tanud'u[q]. Form. (Pai. Bun; also Ami by metath.) *taludzuq(/an), id.

　　PM **nt[]i=*nt[a]i "finger," from PMY *nt[a].

POISON (FOR FISH)　*(n)tu(m)ba (15, 16, 57)

　　IN **tuba=*tu(m)ba "name of plant used for stupefying fish, fish poison." PO *(n)tufa: Fi. *tuva=nduva,* Sa. *uhe* "fish poison"; Chowning cites *tuva=*tufa "derris." Form. (Sai; Atayalic) *(ta/)tuba "fish rattan" (lit. transl. of Jap. gloss).

　　T **ʔbɨa "poison" (Nung "to catch fish by using a kind of poison"), from **ʔbya<*[t]əba (unstressed form). Dioi *bə* (h.t.) "to poison (fish)," from **ʔbɨa (cf. Thai). Sek *via* "to poison" (Ged.), from *via<*bwia<*[t]uba (stressed form).

　　Miao: MPT *tau* (l.t.), MCh. *təu* "poison," from PM *d[ou]; PY *tom* (l.t.) "to fish with poison" (Haud.); both from PMY *do~*dom<*to~*tom (initial voicing), from an earlier *to(ba) ~*tom(ba).

POKE (WITH STICK)　See PIERCE.

POST　See STAKE; STICK.

POST, KNEE　*(n)t[o]ro[(t)s]

　　IN **tulut'=*turut' "post, stick." PO *nturu: Fi. *nduru* "short housepost," Maori *turu~tuu* "kneel," Rotuman *fu* "knee" (Biggs). SEP: Mailu *turu(-na),* id. Form. (Ami Puy: Rikavong) *turus "knee" ($s_1/s_2/s_3$).

　　Li *rou "knee": S. Li *dou,* WS Li *rou,* N. Li dial. *ro(u)~lo(u),* from *(to)ro (cf. Pu-peo). Pu-peo *tʰro kəw* "knee" (cf. Laha: NL *pom kəw,* id.), prob. from a partially redupl. form: *t[o]ro/t[o]ro[(t)s].

POST, RAFTER, SPAR　*[k]a(n)tsaw

　　IN **kat'aw "rafter." PPN **kaso "rafter" (Fi. "cross-spar on outrigger").

　　T *saw "post, pillar." Dioi *sau* "column, pillar." KS *[]zaaw "pillar": Sui *lau,* Mak Then *za:u* (all h.t.), from *(k)azaw<*(k)ansaw.

358 Austro-Thai

POTATO (SWEET) See CULTIVATE (FIELD); FLOWER;
 TUBER; TUBER (EDIBLE).

POUND See BEAT (two entries).

POUR, DECANT *[i]liŋ
  IN **iliŋ "pour" (Ja. "decant"). PPN **[li]liŋi "pour," from
*[i]liŋ/i[liŋ].
  T *rin "pour" (Si. "decant"); also *ʔdiŋ "pour out/away" (Tho-
Nung), from *ʔriŋ<*q/[i]riŋ. Sek riŋ "pour, pour out (shed)."

POUR OUT *( )tu(m)paq
  IN **[t]umpaʔ.
  T *thook "pour out" (SW), from *thuak<*tubaq<*tumpaq;
also *thaw "pour in large quantity" (Tho), app. from *thab(aq)
<*tabaq<*tubaq (vocalic assim.). Dioi pɔk (tone for long
vowel) "pour (water, rice)," from *pook<*puak<*(u)paq. Li
*thook "pour": S. Li thɔʔ (cf. Thai).
  PY *to: YCR to "pour out (liquids)," YTP tu "pour (water),"
from *[]tu(paq).

POWDER See ASHES.

PRICK, STICK, PIERCE *tsak(/tsak)
  IN **t'akt'ak "stick" (Ja. "pierce").
  T *sak "prick, stick (tattoo), pierce, peck."

PULL LENGTHWISE, STRIP [s]urut
  IN **uḷut=*urut "stroke, pull lengthwise" (Ho. "pull through
the hands"). Form. (Ami) *mi/[s]urut (s is indeterm.) "pull."
  T *ruut~*root (Nung) "pull or strip off (leaves, rice)" (Si.
also "to milk, squeeze out"), from *(u)rut. Dioi rut~rɔt "pull
off [coins from a string, grains of rice]."
  Yao: YHN gut "defoliate" (cw. "leaves") (Haud. cites gut
"traire"), from PY *[ḷ]ut<PMY *[r]ut, from an earlier *ruut<
*(u)rut.

PULP See FLESH/MEAT.

PUNGENT, PIQUANT, BITTER, SALTY *p[a]xet; *[pa]x/ḷ/et
 (14, 43, 44, 107)
(I) IN **paʔit "bitter"; Yami *ma/pa[ʔ]it "salty." Form.

ma/pa[x]its (Dyen: Q_1) "bitter (Paz.); bitter (ic.), salty (Bun.); sour (Kan.)," app. from *°/pa[x]it* through influence by *°x*.

T *°phet* "pungent" (Ahom also "salty," Tho "piquant"), from *°p[]het*.

(II) Li *°xrit*: S. Li *drit* "piquant (pimento)," WS Li *xet* "pungent," from *°x/r/it<°(pa)x/r/it*.

PUNGENT, PEPPER, GINGER   *°l[][ʔ]iya(/n)*

   IN **°liya=°ləyʔa* (Dyen 1947a)*=°ləʔia* (Blust 1974)*=°laʔiya* ~*°luʔiya* (Dyen 1974bis) "ginger." PO: Sa. *lie*, U. *lia*, id.; for proto-MN, Chowning cites *lahia=°laʔia*, id. (cf. Ml. *halia*, perhaps from *°lahia* by metath.). SEP *°liya* "ginger" (Nada "chili pepper").

   KS *°lian*: Sui *lyan* "hot, as pepper," Mak *li:n* "pungent, pepper," from *°liyan<°liya/n*.

PURPLE   See DARK.

PUSH INTO   See STICK (INTO).

Q

QUAKE   See SWING.

QUIET   See SAD.

QUIVER, n.   See BORE.

R

RABBIT   *°( )lotok(/a)*; *°m/loto[k/a]* (46, 101, 121)

(I) Form. (Pai. Ruk. Bun: Ibaho; Ata: Takonan) *°lutuk*; (Tsou) *°lutuka*; (Kan.) *°lituka* (app. by dissim.).

   T *°thoʔ* (Si. Lao)~*°tho* (Nung), from *°thoʔ[a]<°thok[a]*, from *°(r-)tok[a]* (initial aspir. by *°r->h*).

   Miao: PWA *°lua* (h.t.), also MCF *loʔ* (h.t.), from PM *ʔluɔ(ʔ)*, from PMY *°ʔ[l]ɔ(t)*, from an earlier *°[]lo(toka)*~*°[]lot(oka)*. Yao: YCR *thou*, HYN *thu* are b.l.'s from Ch. *t'u*, Anc. *t'uo*, Arch. *t'o*.

(II) Dioi *ńut tɔ*, from **my[o]to<*m/r[o]to(ka)*; cf. Ch. *mao* "rabbit (calendar term)," from Anc. *mau*, Arch. *mlô(g)*.

RAIN   **(q/)[u](n)dzal*
    IN ***hud'an~**udan=*ʔuzan* (Dyen), from **ʔu[ndz]an*. PPN ***ʔuha*, from **ʔunsa*. Form. (East) **qudzal;* (Tsouic) **[q]utsal;* also Ata. *qoal/ax* "rain," *m/qoal/ax~q/m/oal/ax* "to rain," from **qu[dz]al*.

    Lq. *ðəu*, from **zəw<*(u)zal;* Laha **(k/)zal:* TU *kzen*, BB *zal*. Kl. *mən diə* (*mən* "sky"), from **zyə<*(u)za[l]*. Lt. *a/ńa*, from **/ńza<*(u)nza[l]*.

RAIN   See SKY.

RAIN, DRIZZLE (FINE RAIN), MIST, SNOW, CLOUDS,
    DUSK, DARK, SKY   **γ[a](m)bon; *[γa](m)pon.*
(I) IN ***γa(m)bun* "atmospheric precipitation" (TB "dusk," Ml. "hail," Ho. "mist," NgD. "sky"); also (unstressed/abbreviated form) **ə(m)bun* "atmospheric precipitation" (Tg. "fine rain," TB. "clouds," Ja. "clouds, dew," Ml. "dew," NgD. "dew, mist"). PO **γapu* "haze, mist, fog" (Blust 1972). PPN ***afu/afu* "drizzle," from **[γ]apu[n]/[γ]apu[n]*.

    T **hmon~*hmun* (Lao doublet) "dark, dull" (BT "blue," WT "gray"), from **hmbon<*r[]mbon* (**r>h*); cf. also **ʔbon* (Si. Lao)~**ʔbun* (Shan) "on, on top of; the space above"<"sky," from **(r)[]bon*. Yay *bun* (h.t.) "sky," from **ʔbun* (cf. Shan). Sek *ʔbin* (Haud.), *bin* (h.t.) (Ged.), id., from **ʔbin<*(r)(ə)bon* (cf. Thai). KS **ʔb[o]n*, id.: Mak *ʔbən* (cf. Thai Sek). Lq. *mən*, id., from **mb[o]n*. Kl. *mən*, id. (ic. "rain") (cf. Lq.). Lt: MP *vo*, BP *mbo* (Rob., Bon.), *bə:n* (Laj.), from **(m)b[o]n*.

(II) T **fon* "rain (esp. fine rain)" (Shan also "rain cloud"), from **phwon*. Dioi *hun* "rain," from **fwun<*phwun*. Sek *vin* (Haud.), *vin* (h.t.), id. (Ged.), from **pw[o]n* (cf. Thai). KS **p(h)w[ə]n*, id.: Sui *fən~wən*, Mak *vin*, Then *xwen*, Kam *pyən* (all h.t.) (cf. Thai). Lk. *fen*, id. (cf. KS). OB *phun* (Jer.), *phɔn* (Sav.), id. Li **pwun*, id.: S. Li *pun*, WS Li *foŋ<*fon*, SH DC SC Loi *fun* (cf. Thai).

PMY *(m)pwon "snow; cloud" (Purnell cites as distinct roots) (YHN also [cw. "sky"] "overcast" and "drizzle").

RAINBOW See DRAGON.

RANCID See SMELL.

RAT See SQUIRREL.

RAT, BAT *labaw (26)
IN **labaw "rat" (NgD. bă/lawao). PO *ka/lapo: Fi. kalavo. Form. (Pai.) *ku/labaw; (Kuv.) *m/labaw.
Dioi wao "rat," from *wa[a]w<*(-a)baw; also (d.t.) "bat." KS: Mak təkau waːu "bat" (təkau "horned owl"), from *(-a)baw. OB ze lau "bat" (ze "rat"), from *lab(aw).

RATTAN *q/[u]way (62)
IN **uway=*[ʔ]uw[a,ə]y. PO: Sa. ue. Form. (East: Tsouic; Atayalic) *quway.
T *hwaay, from *q(a)way (vocalic assim.). Sek vai [h.t.], from *[h]way. OB bɔi (h.t.), from *hwɔi<*hwaay (cf. Thai).

RECEDE, DESCEND *t[o]γon
IN **tuγun "descend." PO *[t]uγu: Sa. ulu "(descend into the water=) wade."
T *thron "recede (BT WT Tho-Nung); walk or go backward, recede (Shan); go backward, draw back (Si.)."

RED, DARK-COLORED, REDDEN, SHAME(D) *iγaŋ;
*(q/)b/iγaŋ; *(q/)m/iγaŋ; *iγa(?); *m(a)/iγa(?);
*[i]γa(?)/i; *m(a)/iγa(?)/i
(I) IN **iγaŋ "deep red" (Ja. "to be in disgrace"="shamed" ="red-faced"); also (unstressed form) **iγəŋ "dark-colored" (Ml. "black"). Form. (Ami Bun.) *(qa/)iγaŋ "blood"="the red (substance)."
CT *rəŋ "red," from *ryaŋ<*(i)raŋ. Sek riːŋ=riiŋ (Haud., Ged.), id., from *(i)riŋ (vocalic assim.). KS: Mak laŋ (h.t.), id., from *[ʔ]laŋ<*q/[i]γaŋ (*γ>l under influence of *q/). OB ziŋ (h.t.), id., from *hriŋ<*q/r[ia]ŋ<q/(i)raŋ. Li *hleeŋ, id.: S. Li deŋ, N. Li thlɛŋ, from *hliaŋ<*q/riaŋ<*q/(i)γaŋ (cf. Mak).
PM *ʔl[](ŋ)=*ʔli(ŋ) "red" (MCF "violet"), from PMY

*ʔl[*aa*]ŋ, from *q/(*a*)*laŋ*<*q/(*i*)*laŋ* (vocalic assim.)<*q/(*i*)*γaŋ* (cf. Mak Li).

(II)   IN **biγaŋ=*b/*iγaŋ* "redden" (TB *beraŋ* "anger," Ja. *wiraŋ* "shame," Ml. *beraŋ* "rage"; cf. Ja. under I). Form. (Sir.) *meipgang*~*mipgang* "red," from *ma/*b*[*i*]*γaŋ*.

T *ʔdeeŋ "red," from *ʔbreeŋ<*ʔbriaŋ<*q/*b*/(*i*)*γaŋ*. Dioi *diŋ* (h.t.), id., from *ʔdiŋ (cf. Thai). Kl. *plaŋ tai*, id. (n.a.), from *blaŋ (initial unvoicing)<*braŋ<*b/[*i*]*γaŋ*.

(III) IN *m/*iγaŋ*: Ml. *merah*/*meraŋ* "deep red."

T *hmliaŋ "rust"="the red (substance)," from *q/*mriyaŋ* <*q/*m*/(*i*)*γaŋ*. Lq. *neŋ* "red," from *mreŋ<*mr[*ia*]ŋ<*m/(*i*)*γaŋ*.

(IV) IN **iγaʔ "red," from the partially reduplicated form: *iγa/*iγaŋ*, with epenthetic **ʔ (*iγa/*ʔiγaŋ*); cf. NgD. *ira*/*iraŋ* "bright red," Ml. *merah*/*meraŋ* "deep red." Form. (Kuv.) *tə/*baγeiq* "red," from *ba/[*i*]*γaq* (vocalism influenced by final -*q*).

KS *hγa "red": Sui *xa*, Then *hya*, from *q/[*i*]*γa*; also *γak: Sui *γak* "rust" (cf. Thai under III), from **(i)γaʔ*. Lk. *khə* "blood" (cf. Ami Bun. under I), from *q[*r*]*a*<*q/[*i*]*γa*.

(V)   IN *m(*a*)/*iγaʔ*: TB *m*/*ira* "red hen," Ja. *m*/*irah* "ruby," Ml. *merah* "red." PO *meγa: Sa. *mela* "to glow, make red-hot," from *ma/*iγa*. SEP *maγa: Kuni *maya* "red ochre," from *ma/(*i*)*γa*. PPN **me(*ʔ*)*a* "reddish," from *ma/*ʔi*(*γ*)*a*; also **maa "ashamed," from *ma/(*iγ*)*a*.

(VI) Form. (Ruk.) *əγai "blood" (cf. Ami Bun. under I and Lq. under IV), from *iγai (stressed form)<*iγa/*i*.

T *aay~*raay (Lao doublet BT) "shame/ashamed," sometimes with *hna "face" (="face-reddened"), from *aray <*iray (vocalic assim.), whence *a(*r*)*ay* and *(*a*)*ray*>*raay, from **[i]γa*/*i*. Li **[r]ey*: S. Li *dei* "(ic.) to have shame, blush" (="redden face"), from *raʔi (vocalism influenced by earlier *ʔ)<**(i)raʔ*/*i*.

(VII) SEP *maγai "ashamed": Motu *hɛ-marai*, Paiwa *vini-mayɛi*, Ubir *ma*/*mai*, from *ma/(*i*)*γa*/*i*.

T *(*h*)*ńay* "ridicule" (="put to shame"), from *(*h*)*mryay*

<*(q/)m/(i)ray<*(q/)m/iɣa/i. N. Thai *mlay "rust" (cf. Thai under III and Sui under IV), from *mray<*m/[i]ɣa/i. KS: Mak myai, id. (cf. N. Thai).

PY *ʔ́nay "ashamed": YCR ́nai (h.t.), from *q/mryay (cf. the development of T *(h)́nay "ridicule").

RETURN   See TURN.

RETURN HOME   *(m)[p][u]laŋ
IN **pulaŋ=*(m)pulaŋ (NgD. tă/mpulaŋ "start back"). PPN */pula: Sm. a/pula, from */mpula.
KS: Mak laŋ, from *(p-)laŋ. OB liŋ~lə:ŋ (both h.t.) "return [to village, to home]," from *( )lyaŋ<*( )(ə)laŋ (unstressed form). Li *[b]liaŋ: S. Li lə:ŋ, from *blyaŋ<*b(ə)laŋ<*mp(ə)laŋ (cf. OB).

RIB   See SIDE (OF BODY).

RICE¹   *boR[a]ts (50, 104)
IN **bəɣat'=*bəRat' "hulled rice," from *buRats (stressed form; cf. Form.). Form. (East; Tsouic; Atayalic) *buRats~ *bəRats (unstressed variant) "rice (uncooked grain)."
T *bo:t "rice (Lao), maize (Si: ic.)," from *bo(Ra)t (with compensatory vowel lengthening). Li *b[o]i: S. Li bui "cooked rice," Bup. böe "rice (unhusked)," from *boR(ats).

RICE¹¹   *(k/)(m)b[]law
T *(k/)(m)braw: Si. kă/brau "unbroken (=unhulled) rice"; also mau (s.t.) "(ic.) new rice, bruised and flattened in a mortar," the latter from *mraw<*mbraw.
PMY **mblaw=*mbḷaw "rice (plant)."

RICE¹¹¹   *(q/)(m)ba[r,ɣ]i (51)
IN **ba[l]i=*ba[ɣ]i: NgD. bari "a meal of rice," Ho. vari "rice."
T *ʔb[a]n: Ahom ban "a kind of paddy." Li *[mw]an: S. Li muon "growing rice," from *mban<*mba[r]. Kl. mo~mɔn (ic. "eat") "rice (cooked)," from *ma(n)<*mba(n).

RICE   See MILLET.

RICE (PLANT)   *[a]gra; *[p/a]gra/i; *[a]kra; *[p/a]kra/i (50, 51)

(I) Form. *aja* "cooked rice (E. Ruk.), rice plant (Fav.)."

(II) IN **pag'ay=*pag'əy* "rice plant, rice in the straw [*paddy* <Ml. *padi*]" (Ho. *fari* "sugarcane," *tsimpari/fari* "wild rice"). Form. (East; Tsouic; Atayalic) *pajay* "rice plant" (Sai. also "cooked rice").

(III) T *kla* "rice seedling" (BT "rice plant"). Sek *tla*, id., from *kla*. KS *kya* "young rice plant": Sui *ka~dya~ʔdiə*, Mak *ći*, Then *kya*. OB *la* "rice plant, rice seedling," from *kla*.

(IV) Li *[ky]ay*: SC Loi *kei* "rice (row) (=growing rice)," from *[kl]ay*.

RICE, SUGARCANE, BAMBOO, TREE *[q/]imay; *[ć]umay (49, 103, 128)

(I) IN **imay=*[ʔ]imay* "rice in husk (TB.), cooked rice (Ml.)." Form. (Ami Kuv.) *q[ə]may* "cooked rice," from *q[i]may* (stressed form).

PY **m[]ey=*hmey~*hmɛ (YLC) "rice (milled)" (YCR *hmei* "uncooked hulled rice"), from *hmyay<*(qi)may.

(II) Form. *ćumay* "rice plant (Puy.), cooked rice (Paz.)."

T *may* "tree/wood" (Ahom Shan also "bamboo"). N. Thai *mway* "tree," from *(-u)may. KS *may* "tree": Sui Mak Kam *mai* (Mak also ic. "bamboo"). OB *moi* "sugarcane"; for the semantics, cf. Hova under RICE (PLANT). Li *may* "sugarcane": S. Li *mai*, WS Li *ma:i* (cf. OB).

RIDE See CLIMB.

RIGHT (HAND) *(N)q/(wa)nal
IN **wanan=*ʔwanan (Aloene -kwana-, cit. by Dyen 1962), from *q/wanan; also *ka/wanan (Ho.)~*ka/nan (Tg. Ja. Ml.); Yami *ka/wanan*; all from *Nqa/(wa)nan. Form: East (Ami Ruk. Kuv.; also by metath: Pai. Puy.) *(N)qa/wanal~*wanal (only Ruk.); also (Sai. Paz.) *(N)qa/nal, from *(N)qa/(wa)nal (cf. IN); Tsouic *walan, from *wanal by metath. (cf. Pai. Puy.); Atayalic (Ata: Ci'uli) *qa/nal/i, from *qa/(wa)nal/ (cf. Sai. Paz. and IN).

T *xwa, from *q/wa(nal). N. Thai *Gwa: Dioi *kua*, Po-ai *kwa* (both l.t.), from *Nq/wa(nal) (cf. Thai). Sek *khwa* (l.t.)

(Ged.), from *Gwa* (cf. N. Thai). KS *xwa: Sui *fa,* Mak *pha,* Then *wa* (all h.t.) (cf. Thai). Lk. *kyei=ćei,* from *kyai<*knai <*k/nal, from *q/(wa)nal* (cf. IN Form.). Li *nin: S. Li *nin,* WS Li *ten,* from *[q/]nan* (vowel influ. by original *q/)< *[q/]nal* (cf. Lk.).

RIND   See BARK, n.

RING   See WHEEL.

RINSE   See WASH.

RIPE   See OLD.

RIPEN FRUIT, WARM (UP), COVER (OVER)   *(q/)(m)pəm; *[p/r/]əm; *()p/l/əm; *(q/)mpum; *[p/r/]um; *[]p/l/um (54)

(I)   T *pom* "warm" (Tho); also **?bom* "ripen fruit" (Shan "cover over, as when plantains are ripened in the ground," Si. "shut up fruit, in order to ripen it"), from *q/mpom.* Li *phəm: WS Li *phom* "cover the mouth with the hand."

(II)   IN **pə[l]əm=*pə[r]əm* "ripen fruit artificially."
    T *oom* "to bask [warm] a little in the sun (Ahom); to warm oneself by the fire (Shan); action of putting children to bed and to sleep (=to warm up children by covering them) (WT); macerate, make ripe in water, make simmer (Lao); kind of ragout (Si: ic.)," from *(por)om.* Dioi ɔm "heavy heat (of weather); to ripen (*blettir*), as fruit," from *oom* (cf. Thai).

(III)   T *thom~*thəm* (Kh. Central Shan) "to cover, cover over (esp. with earth, as in filling in)" (WT "to cover over (cover entirely)"), from *th(y)əm<*p/l/əm.* Li *pləm: S. Li *tom* "to cover oneself (with a covering)," WS Li *plom* "to cover (with a cover/lid)."

(IV)   T **?bum* "ripen fruit" (Lao doublet), a doublet of **?bom* (see I).

(V)   T *um* "cook slowly, let simmer (Lao); shut up (bananas) to make them ripe (Nung)," from *(p-r)um.* Dioi *um* "to warm up gently something covered or enveloped": *um kyɔi=ɔm kyɔi* "to ripen bananas (*kyɔi*)." KS: Mak *?um* "spoiled, over-ripe." OB *um da* "to cover the eyes (*da*)." S. Li i:m "to warm oneself by the fire," from *[]u:m* (app. palatalized by the original */r/).

(VI) T *tuum* "to cover, envelop" (Lao), from *pluum*<
[]p(u)lum (cf. III).

RIVER *ts[u](N)Gay*
   IN **t'uŋay* (TB. "brook"), from *t'uNGay*.

   T *γe*=/γee/ "river (Ahom), body of flowing water (Kh. Shan),
arm of river (Si.)," from *γay* (vowel influ. by original *G-*).
Dioi ńɛ (h.t.), from *hńɛ*<*hNɛ*<*s[]NGay* (cf. Thai). Li
khay: Loi (all dial.), cw. *nom* "water," from *(s-)[G]ay*.

RIVER See OPEN (HINGED JOINT).

ROAD *(n)dza[l]an; *dza[l]aŋ* (8)
   (I) IN **dalan*~**d'alan*=*zalan* (Dyen)=*(n)zalan*, app.
from *[ndz]alaŋ* by assim. Yami *d'a/d'alan*. PPN **hala*, from
nsala. Form. (East; Tsouic) *dzalan* (cf. IN); also (W. Ruk.
Puy: Ferr.) *dza/dzalan;* (E. Ruk: Dainan) *ka/dzalan/an*.

   (II) Form. (Pai: Mak doublet Sir.) *dzalaŋ*.
     T *daaŋ*, from *dz(a)raŋ*. Lt. tsa:ŋ, from *dza(r)aŋ*.

ROAR, THUNDER *Nom*
   Li *Nɔm* "thunder": S. Li *pa daŋ ɔm*="heaven sound roar"
(see SOUND/), WS Li ńa:m, Bas. niam loaŋ="roar cry" (see
CRY/), SH DC Loi ŋiam, SC Loi om.
   Yao: YCR ŋom "to roar, snarl [tiger]."

ROAST See BURN; COOK.

ROCK See STONE.

ROLL *(ŋ)g[u]liŋ; **g[a]liŋ; *[k][]liŋ* (19, 20)
   (I) IN **guliŋ* "roll" (Ml. "to roll, usually to roll along as a
wheel, to roll oneself on the ground"); also (assim. backward)
**guluŋ* "a roll/roller"; also (assim. forward) **giling* "to roll
(tr.), grind [between rollers]." PO: Fi. ŋgili "to rub (=roll)
between the hands."
   Yao: YHN kliŋ niŋ (both l.t.) "to roll (intr.) [stones]"
(niŋ "go/walk"), from PY/PMY *gliŋ*.
   (II) IN **galiŋ* "roll" (TB. "turned"). PO *kali*: Sa. ʔɛli "to
lie rolled up."

(III) T *klíŋ "to roll, roll over and roll over, roll oneself (on the ground)," from *[]k[]líŋ.

ROOF See COVER.

ROOM See ENCLOSURE.

ROOM (OF HOUSE), WING (OF HOUSE)   *(n)tsu[r]am[bi]
   IN **t'uḷambi=*t'urambi "wing of house" (Ja. "outer court of mosque"); also **ambi "addition" (Tg. "overhanging roof"), from *(t'ur)ambi.
   T *suam "room, compartment" (Si. "latrine of pagoda"), from *su(r)am(bi). KS *zuam: Sui fum~hum (l.t.), from *nsuam. Li *[ua]m: WS Li om "room (of house)," from *(-u)(r)am(bi).

ROOT   *[pa](ŋ)kaḷ (52)
   IN **paŋkal "trunk, root, origin" (usually "root").
   Lk. kan.

ROPE See CORD.

ROTTEN, SPOILED   *(q/)boɣok
   IN **buɣuk "spoiled" (Tg. bugok "spoiled," bulok "rotten"). Form. (Pai. Sai.; Ata: Ci'uli) *(ma/)buɣuk "rotten (as log)."
   T *ʔdook~*ʔdok (Ahom) "rotten (Lao); rotten (of hard things) (Tho); to become putrid (of dead animals) (Ahom); decay (Kh.); dead, dry (wood) (WT); dried, withered (as wood) (Shan)," from *ʔbro(o)k<*q/b(o)rok. Dioi duk "rotten, wormeaten, spoiled," from *ʔd[o]k (cf. Ahom). KS *ʔd[o]k: Mak ʔduk "decayed, spoiled" (cf. Dioi).

ROUND   *(q/)b[a]ḷuR (20, 21, 43)
   IN **bəluɣ, from *baluɣ (stressed form).
   T *ʔduaŋ, from *ʔbruaŋ<*q/baruŋ. Dioi dɛn (h.t.), from *ʔdeen <*ʔbreen<*ʔbraan<*q/baran (vocalic assim.). KS *ʔduan: Mak ʔdu:n (cf. Thai). Lk. kyon=ćon, from *[pr]on<*[br]on (initial unvoicing). Li *bluan: S. Li luon, N. Li pluon, from *balun (cf. Thai Mak).

ROW, v. See MOVE BACK AND FORTH.

RUB See SCRAPE.

RUB, CARESS   *ulup

T *luup* "rub, caress" (Si. also "touch"), from *(u)lup. Dioi *rup* "touch, caress, smooth (repasser)," from *ru[u]p<*(u)rup <*(u)l̥up (*l̥>*l̥ through influ. of back vowel *u); also *rum* "to graze, caress with the hand," from *rum(/rup).

Yao: YHN *lup* "caress," from PY/PMY *lup, from an earlier *luup<*(u)lup.

RULE(R) See CHIEF.

RUMBLE, GROWL, THUNDER, SNORE *(ŋ)guruq; *gərəq; *ŋguruŋ; *gərəŋ

(I) IN **gul̥uʔ=*(ŋ)guruʔ "rumble" (Ml. "thunder"). PO *(ŋ)kuru: Fi. *kuru* "thunder," Sa. *a/kuru* "rumble." PPN **[ŋulu]ŋulu "grunt, rumble" (To. "grunt, grumble, growl," Sm. "sleep"="snore"), from an original *ŋgulu; also (To. Sm.) *ta/ŋulu; (Fu.) *tu/ŋulu "snore."

(II) T *grook "snoring" (Si.), from *g(o)rok.

(III) PY *gluŋ: YCR *juŋ (irreg. h.t.) "growl [dog]," YHN *gluŋ* *gluŋ* "rumbling (of thunder)," from PMY *ŋgl̥uŋ, from an earlier *ŋgl̥uuŋ<*ŋg(u)ruŋ, prob. from an original *(ŋ)guru[q]/(ŋ)-guruq.

(IV) Form. (Pai. Ami) *gərəŋ "thunder," prob. from an original *(ŋ)gərə[q]/(ŋ)gərəq.

RUN See MOVE BACK AND FORTH.

RUN (AFTER), CHASE, HUNT *buɣa(a)w (8, 9, 57, 109)
IN **buɣaw "put to flight"=*buɣəw "put to flight, chase, hunt" (Dyen).

T *phraw (Nung)~*thaw (Tho): Nung *tik phyau* "hunt," by analogy with *tik pya* "to fish"="to catch (*tik*) fish (*pya*)." N. Thai: Po-ai *tau* "hunt," from *praw. KS *p(u)ɣaaw "run": Sui *pyau*, Mak *ywa:u* (<*uɣa:u). Li *[r]aw "run": S. Li *dau*.

PY **pl̥[]=*pla(a)w "flee, escape"; Haud. cites PY *plaw "run"; Miao: MPT *plau* "depart, run away (Heim.); (ic.) roam (Sav.)," from PM *pl̥[ou]; from PMY *pl̥[a,aa]w~*pl̥[o], the latter perh. through assim. *p(u)l̥aw>*p(u)l̥u>*p(o)l̥o (cf. KS).

S

SACK   See BASKET.

SACK, BAG, POCKET, BASKET   *[ka](n)tl[u/o]ŋ (62, 63)

IN **kanṭuŋ "basket, pocket." PPN **kato "basket" (Marquesan "pouch, pocket," To. [Demp.] "pocket, sack, basket").

T *thoŋ~*thuŋ (Si.) "sack, bag, pocket," from *thloŋ~*thluŋ, from *(k-)tloŋ~*(k-)tluŋ (second. aspir. by *k-). Dioi śɔŋ "sack," from *thloŋ (cf. Thai). N. Thai *thluŋ, id. (F. K. Li).

SAD, STUNNED, QUIET   *l[i]ŋaw

IN **liŋaw "quiet" (Tg. liŋao "stunned," NgD. lă/liŋao "sad"). PPN **liŋo=*(liŋo/)liŋo "quiet."

T *hŋaw "sad" (Si. also "stunned, silent"), prob. from *(r-)ŋaw (second. aspir. by *r->h).

SALT   *(qa/)k[l,l̩]i[r]a[h]; *[]k[l,l̩]u[r]a[h] (17)

(I) IN **t'ila[ʔ]=*t'ira[ʔ]. Form. (Pai. Ami Bun. Thao) *(qa/)tsirah.

T *klia, from *klya<*[]kli(r)a. Lk. kyie=ćie, from kyia <*kli(r)a (cf. Thai).

(II) Dioi kuə, from *k[l]ua<*[]klu(r)a. Sek tlua (Ged.), from *klua (cf. Dioi). KS *klua: Sui kwa~ʔduo, Mak ćwa, Kam ko (cf. Dioi Sek).

SALTY   See PUNGENT.

SALTY, ALKALI   *q/[pə](ń)jaŋ; *q/[]ńźaŋ (6)

(I) Form. (Pai. *qa/pə[j]aŋ "salty."

T *ʔdaŋ~*ʔdaaŋ (Si.) "potash"; *nam ʔdaŋ "lye" (*nam "water"). KS *(n)daŋ "alkali": Sui ʔnaŋ~naŋ, Kam naŋ, Mak ʔdaŋ, Then laŋ (all h.t.). Lk. yaŋ (h.t.) "salty," from *ʔyaŋ. OB zɔŋ (h.t.) "salted [vegetables]," from *ʔdɔŋ.

(II) Miao: MCF ńaŋ xi "bitterness, sadness" (xi "heart"), from PM *ń[aŋ]; PY *[ʔ]ńuŋ "astringent (tea)" (YHN)~*ʔńaaŋ "bitter (intensifier)" (YCR), from an earlier *ʔńaŋ~*ʔńaaŋ, from *q(a)/ńaŋ<*q(a)/ńźaŋ.

SAND   *bəw(n)draj

Form. (Pai. Sai. Paz. Thao Fav.) *bu(n)daj.

T *draay.* Dioi *nam sɔi* (l.t.) "sand, gravel," from *zooy<
(u)[dr]a[a]y. Sek *ʔyo:i* (cf. Dioi). KS *de:* Mak *de*, from
[dr][aay]. Li *phəw:* S. Li *phəu*, N. Li *pho* (irreg. aspir.), from
[b]əw(draj). Lt. *ňǎ*, from *[bəw]ndra[j].*

SAY *( )k[a]lu*

IN *kanu* (Ilocano *kano* "it is said"); *kənu* (Iban *kenu* "word
used to mark a quotation") (unstressed form) (both cit. by
Blust 1970); **kunu* "one says, it is said (*dicitur*)" (Tg. *kuno*,
Ja. *kono*, Ml. *kunu/n*, Ho. *hunu*) (assim. form). PO *kunu*: Sa.
ʔunu "say, think."

T *klaaw* "say, relate, make a complaint," from *[]k(a)lu*
(second. lengthening); also *law~*hlaw* (Lao) "speak, address,
relate, recite," from *[k]h(a)lu.* Sek *pak-tla:u* "speak" (*pak* for
pa:k "mouth"), from *klaaw* (cf. Thai).

SCAB See SKIN.

SCALE See HUSK; SKIN.

SCALE OFF, SCALES (FISH) *qulap*

IN **hunap=*[ʔ]unap* "fish scales." PO: Sa. *uneh/aʔa* "fish
scales," *uneh/i* "scale off." SEP: Motu *una(hi)* "fish scale"; cf.
Capell: "in some [SEP] languages [this root] takes the transitive
suffix with a thematic consonant and becomes verbal, to scale
fish." PPN **ʔuna(fi)* "fish scale(s)" (Sm. *unafi* "fish scales,"
also [Cap.] *unafi/a* "peeled off").

T *hliip* "to scale or peel off," from *hlyəəp<*q(ə)ləp* (unstressed and assimilated). Li *luap* "fish scales": S. Li *la:p*,
WS Li *luap*, from *(-u)lap.*

SCATTER See SPRAY.

SCRAPE See SCRATCH (three entries).

SCRATCH *( )(ŋ)k[u][ɣ]aw*

Form. (Thao) *k/m/uɣaw* "scratch (with fingernails)"; also
(East) */kaɣaw*, id., app. by vocalic assim.

T *kaw~*gaw* (Nung doublet) "scratch (oneself)," from
(ŋ)kaw<(ŋ)kwaw<*[](ŋ)ku[r]aw.* Dioi *kaw* "scratch, scratch
oneself."

SCRATCH, SCRAPE, DIG, CLAW *kar(/kar); *kar/kar/an; *kur(/kur); *ku[r/]an

(I)   IN **kaḷkaḷ=*karkar "scratch." Form. (Bun. Kuv.) *(m/)karkar "dig."

   T *khaan "to scratch, make a scratch (as thorn or nails of animal)" (Kh. Shan), from *kan(kan). Lq. kɔn "claw," from *(kan/)kan.

(II) IN: Yami *karkar/ən "scratch (with fingernails)" (unstressed form).

(III) IN **kuḷkuḷ=*kurkur "scratch" (Tg. "scraped"). Form. (Ami) *mi/kurkur "dig."

(IV) T *khuan "scratch" (Si.), from *khu(r)an<*kur/an.

SCRATCH, SCRAPE, DIG, CLAW/NAIL *(ŋ)kus(/kus); *kuts/kuts; *(ŋ)kut(/kut); *(N)qu[t,ts](/qu[t,ts]); *kəs(/kəs); *(kus/)qəs; *(ŋ)kə[t,ts](/kə[t,ts]); *kits(/kits); *[kas/]ka[s]; *kats(/kats)

(I)   IN **kuku "claw, nail." PO *(ŋ)ku(ŋ)ku: Fi. kuku- "claw, nail," ŋguŋgu "hoof." PPN **mai/kuku "nail, claw, hoof." Form. (Paz.) */kus (kali:kux, poss. from *k/l/is/kus; cf. VIII); (Bun. Thao; Tsou; Sed.) *kuskus; (Sai. Kuv. Sir.; Saa. Kan.) *k/l/uskus; (Pai. Ruk.) *k/l/uskus/a(n) "claw/nail" (Dyen: s₂).

   T *guy "to turn up (=scratch or dig up) dirt (Ahom): to scratch, as a hen (Si.)," from *ŋkuy.

(II)   IN *kut'kut' "scrape, scratch": Cebuano Visayan k/al/-uskus, kuskus "scrape or scratch to remove something from a surface," Iban kukus "scrape out" (Blust 1973); also Tg. kuskós "rub, scrub, scrape," i/kuskós, kuskus/in "rub."

(III) IN *ku[t]ku[t] "claw, scratch": Ml. kukot "clawing, to claw," Iban kukut "nail (of finger, toe)," Tg. kutkót "pry out (something) with the paws or the fingers," Maranao kokot "scratch, esp. with the fingernails," Cebuano Visayan kútkot "scratch, as head" (Blust 1970). Form. (Kuv.) *k/m/utkut "dig."

   T *khut "dig" (SW); also *gut, id. (Nung), from *ŋkut (cf. the nasal/oral under VII), but perhaps to be recognized (as by F. K. Li) as an early loan/b.l. from Ch. chü, Anc. gʼiuət "dig." Dioi *kut*, id., from **[g]ut* (cf. Nung). Sek *khut* (l.t.), id. (Ged.), from **gut* (cf. Nung Dioi). KS **gut*, id.: Sui *tsət*, Mak *kut* (both l.t.) (cf. Nung Dioi Sek).

Yao: YHN *khut* "to claw," from an earlier **khuut* < **kut(kut)*.

(IV)   T **xuut* "to scrape, as with a knife; to scratch with the nails; to tear or mar the skin (Shan); to tear (Ahom); to scrape, rake, trim by scraping (Si.); to scrape, shave (Lao); to trim [pencil, piece of wood]" (WT), from **(xut)xut*. Dioi *hɔt* "to grate (as salt), scrape (as a table)," from **qh[uu]t*; also *hut* "dig," from **[G]ut* < **Nqut*, as shown by Yai *hut* (l.t.), id.

PMY **qhwot* "hole" (YHN also "sunken eyes"); for the semantics, cf. HOLE/DIG.

(V)   Form. (Fav.) **ma/kəs;* (Ami) **mi/kəskəs* "to scratch (with fingernails)."

(VI)   Form: Ami *kinoʔəs* "claw/fingernail," from **k/n/u[s]/qəs;* also Kuv. (Ferr.) *noqəs* "claw," from **(k/)n/u[s]/qəs* or **(k/)l/u[s]/qəs*, contrasting with *knuskus* "fingernail," from **k/l/uskus* (Tsuchida has *qa:məs* "claw," from **q/m/əs*).

(VII)   T **khot* "to take up or out, as food from a dish, to scoop out with the hand, to dig out" (Shan); also **khoot* "to scrape, bone, take off" (Si.), from **kot(kot)*; also **goot* "to shave" (BT), from **ŋkoot* < **ŋkot(kot)*.

(VIII) IN ***kit'kit'* "scrape" (Tg. "rubbed").

T **[kh]iit* "strike with sliding motion, as match on its box; draw a ruling line (Shan); draw, mark with lines, rub against something (Si.); scratch out, cross out (Lao)," from **kit(kit)*; perhaps also **[kh]it* "rub, wipe" (Si. Lao) (cf. Tagalog), from the unreduplicated root.

(IX)   PM **k[ai]:* MCF *ka* "scrape, scratch"; MCh. *kei~ki* "scratch"; MPT *ke* "scrape off (something from surface) (Heim.); scratch [the head], scrape [as horse the ground] (Sav.)," from PMY **k[a]*, from an earlier **[kas/]ka[s]*.

(X)   IN ***kat'kat'* "scratch." PPN **(ka/)kas/i:* To. *kakah/i* "scratch," Fu. *kas/i* "name of a mussel used for scraping," Sm. *ʔaʔas/i* "scrape."

SCRATCH, SCRAPE, DIG, STRIKE (LINE)　*(ŋ)g[a]ru[t/ts]; *g[a]rits; *k[a]rits; *g[a]ru[d]; *k[a]rud

(I)　IN **galut~**galut'=*garut~*garut' "scratch." PO *(ŋ)-karu: Sa. karu "scratch with the fingernails," Nggela ŋgaru, Mota karu "scratch" (Blust 1970). Form: Pai. garuts "comb" (Dahl cit.), from *garut, app. from an earlier *garut/r[ut].

　　T *gruut "to rake (Shan); to scratch, tear, rub strongly (Si.)," from *g(u)rut<*g(a)rut (vocalic assim.). Dioi kɔt "to scratch (oneself, as from itching)," from *[gr][uu]t.

(II)　IN **galit'=*garit' "scratch" (Ml. garis=guris "scratch-line; a scratch, score"); cf. also **gulit'=*gurit' "scratch" (Ml. guris). PO *(ka/)kari: Fi. kari~ŋkari/a "scratch," Sa. ʔa/ʔari "tear off, split off." PPN **kai "points scored in a game" (cf. Malay).

(III)　IN *kərit' "scrape off": Iban keris "scrape off, shave off," Tg. kalis "scraped clean" (Blust 1970 but later [pers. comm. 1973] listed to be withdrawn), from *karit' (stressed form).

　　T *kriit "draw a line, e.g. with a knife" (Si.), from *k(i)rit <*k(a)rit (vocalic assim.).

(IV)　T *gru=/gruu/ "prepare unused ground for cultivation by scraping (Shan); rub, scratch (Si.)," from *g(u)ru[d], from an earlier *g(a)ru~*g(a)ru[d] (vocalic assim.)<*g(a)ru/g(a)rud (cf. V).

(V)　IN **kə[l]ud=*kə[r]ud "scrape," from *ka[r]ud (stressed form), probably (along with IV) showing secondary voicing from an original reduplicated root: *karut/karut>*karud(/karut). Form. (Puy.) *k/m/əru[d,t] "dig."

SEE　*[ki](n)tra; *[ki]tra/i; *[ki]tra/n; *[hi](n)tra/i (28)

(I)　IN **kita "see" (Ja. was/kita "foresee"). PO *kinta: Fi. kinda "have a premonition." Form. (Sai.) *kita; (Sir. Fav.; Atayalic) *(k/)m/ita; (Paz.; Saa.) *(k/)m/kita.

　　Lt. to, from *[ki]t[r]a.

(II)　PPN **kite "see, appear, know"; also (To. Sm.) *ki/kite "predict"; from *kitay<*kita/i.

　　Lq. thəi, from *[ki]t[r]ay (second. aspiration).

(III) T *[t]hran~*[t]hren (Si. Lao) "see" (Nung also "feel")
(Ahom has irreg. *han*), from *thra/n<*[ki]tra/n (second. aspiration). Dioi *ran* (h.t.), from *[th]ran. CT *then, from *th[r]en
(cf. Thai doublet). Sek *ren* (h.t.), from *[th]ren (cf. Dioi).

(IV) IN **hi(n)tay "look toward" (Ja. "cast a glance," Ml. "to
spy, peep at, watch for").

SEE   See LOOK AT.

SEED   *b[i]nsaq

IN **bini?=*binhi? (Tg. *binhi?*), from *binha? by assim.
backward; also **bǝni? (unstressed form). Form. (Bun.) *binsa?;
(Sai.) *binsi?, by assim. (cf. IN).

T *van~*ban (Si. Lao), from *b(w)an<*(ba/)ban (partial
redupl. and assim. forward). Dioi *hɔn* (s.t., high series), from
phwɔn<(pa/)pan (initial unvoicing and second. aspiration).
KS *?wan: Sui Then *wan*, Mak *van* (all h.t.), from *q/wan<
*qa/ban(saq). OB *zean* "seed, grain," app. from *(v)yan (cf.
Thai). S. Li *fen*, from *phw[a]n (cf. Dioi).

PY *sa? "sesame" (Haud.)<"sesame (seeds)."

SEIZE, HOLD, CLOSE (MOUTH), BITE   *[t]aNqap;
      *[t]a(N)Gap

(I) IN **taŋkap "seize, grasp, hold fast," from *taNqap.

PMY *(N)qaap "to close (mouth)": MPT "close (mouth,
door, umbrella)"; YCR *gaap* (h.t.) "to close (by bringing two
sides together) [mouth, door]"; YHN *gap* "close (mouth)," *gap niŋ*
~*jap niŋ* "carry (niŋ) under the armpit"; from *(a)(N)qap.

(II) IN **taŋgap "seize, grasp, hold fast," from *taNGap.

T *gaap "to seize or hold with jaws/pincers, bite," from
*(a)gap (irreg. initial *g for *γ). Yay *hap* (l.t.) "bite," from
*Gap. Sek *γap*, id. (Ged.). KS: Kam *Gap, id. (Haud.). OB
kɔp (l.t.) "bite; (ic.) grind [the teeth]," from *gɔp<*[G]ɔp.

Yao: YCR *kap* (l.t.) "close [mouth], clip together [papers],"
from PY/PMY *gap, from an earlier *[G]ap (shift to velar).

SEIZE, HOLD, CLOSE (FIST), HANDFUL, BITE   *kǝp(/kǝp);
      *[ta](ŋ)kǝp; *(ŋ)kup/(ŋ)kup; *(ŋ)gup[/(ŋ)gup]

(I) IN **kǝpkǝp "seize, hold" (Tg. "carry under the arm").
PPN **koko "squeeze, press."

T *khop "bite (=seize with teeth)." Li *kh(y)əp: S. Li khip "handful (of rice, etc.)," WS Li khop "grab a handful."

(II) IN *[t]a(ŋ)kəp "catch, trap" (Ja. "seize") (Blust 1973). Li *gəp: S. Li gop~hop "close the fist," WS Li vop "fist" (cw. "hand"), from *ŋkəp.

(III) IN **kupkup "seize, hold" (Ja. "snatch"). PO *(ŋ)ku(ŋ)-ku(p): Fi. kukuv/a "hold fast," also ququ/tsa "hold in hand, cling to," vaa/ququ "hold fingers like claws." PPN **kuku "draw together" (To. "grasp," Tikopian "clinch, close the hand," Sm. "take hold of, grasp").

(IV) T *ŋup "seize, carry away, take with avidity" (Si.), from *ŋgup; also *grup "seize with the claws (of animals)" (Si.), from *g/r/up; also *up "seize with the mouth" (Si.), app. from *(g/r/)up.

SELL   See BARTER; CHANGE; EXCHANGE (two entries).

SELL, BUY   *dzu(w)al̦ (85)
    IN **d'ual "sell."
    T *zɨ "buy," from *zya<*z(ə)a[l̦] (unstressed form). D sɛ (l.t.), id., from *z[ya] (cf. Thai). Sek sɨ [l.t.], id. (Ged.), from *zɨ (cf. Thai). Lk. wei, id., from *way<*(zu)wal̦. OB ven "sell" (Jer.), bean<*wean "buy" (Sav.), from *(ə)wan<*(ə)wal̦. Li *[z]uan "sell": SC Loi joaŋ<*joan. Lt. va, id., from *wa[l̦].

SEPARATE   See OPEN; SPLIT.

SEPARATE(D)   *tsa[r]ak
    IN **t'al̦ak=*t'arak "separated."
    T *ćaak "separate, separated," from *tsraak<*ts(a)rak.

SESAME   *l̦əŋa (51)
    IN **l̦əŋa. PPN (To. Sm.) *l̦əŋa "saffron."
    T *ŋa. Dioi ra, from *ra(ŋ)a. KS *ʔŋya: Sui ʔŋa~ŋa, Mak ŋa, Then ŋya=ná (all h.t.), from *[](ə)ŋa (palatalized). Li *ŋɨa: S. Li ŋə, from *ŋya (cf. KS).

SEW, PLAIT, WEAVE   *(m)plaqi[s]; *(m)pla/pl[aqis]; *pl/m/[aqis] (63)
    (I)   IN: Tg. tahiʔ "sew," app. by metath. from an original

*taqih (Dyen). Form. (Puy: Rikavong Ami Bun.) *(m/)taqis;
(Ruk.) *wa/taqis (Dyen: s₁) "sew."

Thai *thak~*dak (Nung) "plait (Si. Lao), plait (mats)
(Nung)," from *(n)tak, perh. from *m/tak (cf. Form.). OB
dɔ? "sew," from *ntɔ?. Lt. pe, id., from *play<*pla(q)i(s).

(II) Form. (Paz.) *ta/taqis "sew"; cf. also Tsouic form (infixed) under III.

Lq. tat "weave" is a loan from Yao (see below).

PMY (PWA and PY) *ntat "loom; to weave" (YHN also
"to plait mats"), from *ntat(aqis), from *mpla/pl(aqis) (cf.
Form. and Thai); also MCF tɔ? "weave," from PM *tɔu?<PMY
*t[ai?], apparently from an original *ta?i<*[pla/]plaqi[s], with
atypical stress on the second syllable.

(III) Form. (Pai. Puy. Thao Sai. Kuv. Sir.) *t/m/aqis; (Tsouic)
*t/m/aqis~*t/m/ta/taqis; (Atayalic) *ts/m/aqis (Dyen: s₁)
"sew."

Lq. thɛm "sew," app. from *t/m/(aqis). Kl. dɨ thɛ "weave"
(n.a.), perh. from []*thɛm (cf. Lq.).

SHADE See DARK.

SHADE/SHADY See DARK.

SHAKE See SWEEP; SWING.

SHAME(D) See RED.

SHARK, CROCODILE *[ma]ŋi[w]ak
IN *maŋiwak "shark" (Cap.), from *ma/ + nasal + *iwak
"fish" (Cap.); cf. SEP *pa/iwak "shark" (Cap.).

T *ŋiak "crocodile, dragon" (WT "sp. of fresh water shark"),
from *ŋwiak<*ŋ(i)(w)ak.

SHARP *r[a]dzay
Form. (Pai.) *[r]adzay "sharp (as blade)."
PMY **ray=*ray~*ryay (YHN), from *r(a)yay.

SHARP (TASTING), GINGER, PEPPER *[ts]iqaŋ (48, 103, 127)
IN **t'a?aŋ "sharp (tasting)" (Ml. "pepper," NgD. "Spanish
pepper"), app. from an earlier *t'i?aŋ through vocalic assimilation backward.

T *xiŋ "ginger," from *qiŋ<*[si]qaŋ (assim. forward, contrasting with IN, with *°q* influence as a probable additional factor). KS *°siŋ*, id.: Sui Mak Then *siŋ*, from *°[qh]iŋ* (cf. Thai). Lk. *ʔiŋ*, id., from *°[qh]iŋ*. OB *kiaŋ*, id., from Ch. *kiaŋ* as a b.l. (indicated by the initial). Li *°khiaŋ*, id.: S. Li *khəːŋ*, WS Li *khiŋ*, from *°[si]qaŋ* (probably distinct from the Ch. form, as shown by the initial).

PM *°qhe(ŋ)~°khe(ŋ)* (MCF) "ginger," from PMY *°qh[ia]ŋ ~°kh[ia]ŋ*. Yao: YCR *suŋ*, id., from *°kh(y)aŋ* (cf. MCF).

SHELL (OF TORTOISE)   *°( )k[a]raq*

IN *°°kalaʔ=°karaʔ* "shell" (Tg. "karett-tortoise," Ho. "mother-of-pearl").

T *°kraʔ* "shell of the hawkbill tortoise" (Si.); Laj. cites *tau kraʔ* "tortue [*tau*] à écailles." KS: cf. Mak *ća* "skin sloughed off by snake," from *°[kr]a*.

SHELLFISH, CLAM (GIANT), SNAIL   *°[ki]ma* (59)

IN *°°kima* "giant clam." Form: Ata. *kəmasuts* "shellfish, snail," app. from *°kəma-* (unstressed form).

Li *°ma*: S. Li *ma* "large shellfish (called *bénitier*)" (cw. "shellfish").

SHELLFISH, SNAIL[I]   *°(N)qohoḷ* (26, 79, 97, 98)

IN *°°kuhul* "snail" (Tg. *kuhol*), from *°Nquhul*.

T *°hooy* "shellfish" (WT Nung "snail"), from *°(o)hoy*. KS *°qhuy* "snail, shellfish": Sui *qhui~khui*, Mak *ćhui*, Then *khuei*, from *°q[]huy*.

PY *°kwei*: YCR *kwei* "snails; shellfish"; YHN *kwei* "snail, slug" ~*kwai* "shellfish"; PM *°[g]wɨ*: MCF *kui* (l.t.) "snail; (ic.) slug"; MPT *qɨ* (l.t.) "snail (Heim.); shellfish, shell; (ic.) snail, slug (Sav.)"; from PMY *°kwei~°[g]wei*, app. from an earlier *°[q]wei*, with secondary voicing in Miao, the MPT irreg. initial *°q* reflecting the original postvelar initial.

SHELLFISH, SNAIL[II]   *°tsi(tsik)*

IN *°°tʼitʼik* "shell, scale (fish)," prob. from *°tʼik/tʼik*. PPN *°°sisi* "shellfish sp."

Li *°sey*: S. Li *sei* "(ic.) shellfish"; WS Li *ćhei=śei* "snail"; WS Loi *sɛi*, SC Loi *sei-* "bivalve."

SHELTER   See HUT.

SHINE   See BURN; LIGHT (GIVE LIGHT); LIGHT (two entries).

SHINE, GLITTER, BRIGHT   *NGil̲aŋ; *Nqil̲aŋ

(I) IN **gilaŋ "glitter," from *NGil̲aŋ. PPN **kikila~**ŋiŋila "shine, glisten," from *(ŋ)gi(ŋ)gila<*(N)Gi[laŋ]/(N)Gila[ŋ].

(II) T **riaŋ "shine/shining" (Si. "shining, glittering"), from *ryaaŋ<*(i)raŋ; also *ria "shine, glitter" (Shan Lao), from *(i)ra/(i)raŋ. KS *qh[l̲][ia]ŋ "bright": Sui qhaŋ~khaŋ, from *q(i)l̲aŋ.

PY **gwyaaŋ (h.t.)=*gwiaŋ "bright, clear": YCR also "to be light; light"; YHN "to shine [moon, sun]; to light (*éclairer*); smooth (=shiny)"; from PMY *[Nq][l̲]iaŋ, from *Nq(i)l̲aŋ (cf. Sui).

SHIPWRECK(ED)   See SINK INTO.

SHOOT   See ARROW.

SHOOT, AIM, HIT (TARGET), TOUCH   *(n)tə(m)bak (58) IN **təmbak "shoot" (TB. "aim").

T *thuuk~*thïik (Lao BT doublet) "hit (target), touch," from *thwak<*t(ə)bak and **thəək<*tə(w)ək (vocalic assim.). Sek thik (l.t.) "to hit" (Ged.), from *dik<*ntik (cf. Thai).

SHORE   See NEAR; SIDE.

SHORT   See CUT OFF; SMALL.

SHOULDER, ARM   *(q/)(m)baɣa; *(q/)baɣa/n (13, 58, 97, 98)

(I) IN **baɣa=*(ʔa/)baɣa "shoulder" (TB. 'a/bara). PO **(qa/)paɣa, id. SEP: Capell: "the root occurs in SEP entirely with the k- prefix": Mukawa kabara, Paiwa kavara, Sawabwara kahara "shoulder." Form. (Sai. Ami: Kibi, Taparon, Tauran) *qa/baɣa, id.

T *ʔba=/ʔbaa/ "shoulder," from *q/ba(r)a. Sek va, id. (Ged.), from *wa<*(qa/)ba. KS: Mak ha, id., app. from *[qhw]a <*q/ba(ɣ)a. Lk. ywie (h.t.), id., from *ʔywia<*q(ə)bya (unstressed form)<*qa/b(a)ɣa. OB wia (Jer.), bea (h.t.)<*wea (Sav.), id., from *ʔwia (cf. Lk.). Li *va, id.: S. Li WS Li Loi va, from *wa (cf. Sek). Lq. muə, id., from *mb(ɣ)a.

(II) Form. (Pai. Paz. Ami: Baran) *qa/baɤa/(a)n* "shoulder."

T *xeen* "arm," from *qeen<*qween<*qwaan<*q(a)wan <*q(a)ba(r)a/n*. Dioi *kien* "arm, sleeve," from *q[ee]n* (cf. Thai). Sek *keen* "arm" (Ged.), from *qeen* (cf. Dioi). KS [q]hyin: Sui *ćhin~śin*, Mak *hin* "arm," Then *khyin* "sleeve," from *qhyen* (cf. Thai). Li *va(a)n*: S. Li *dri? dau van* "scapula" ="bone head arm," WS Li *va:n* "arm," Bas. *van* "upper arm," WS Loi *vaŋ<*van*, SH Loi *van*, DC Loi *-fan*, id. from *wa(a)n <*q(a)wan* (cf. Thai).

SHRIMP   See CRUSTACEAN.

SHRINK, CONTRACT   *[p][i]trot*
    IN **pitut* "to contract" (Ja. "shrunken").

    T *[t]hrot~*[t]hrut* (Shan doublet) (Tho form lacking) "shrink, contract, draw back" (Nung also "shrunken"), app. from *[p-]trot* (with second. aspiration after the original *p-*). Dioi *rɔt* "to shrink (*se retirer*) [of cloth shrinking, water in river getting low, man aging]," from *[th]rot*.

SHUT UP   See ASSEMBLE.

SIBLING (OLDER), BROTHER (OLDER) */ka; *k/l/a(/k/l/a);
    *(ŋ)ka/(ŋ)ka; *ma/ḷ/ka/ka* (122)

(I)   PPN *tua/ka* "older brother (Fi.), older sibling of the other sex (Sm.)." Form. (Ruk.) *ta/ka* (also *ta/taka, *taka/taka, *taka/tataka*); (Sir.) *sa/ka* "older sibling."

(II)   Form. (Tsouic) *k/al/a* (also *kala/kala*) "sibling" (ic. "older sibling" and "younger sibling").

    Lq. *kə:n* "older brother," from *ka:n<*ka:l<*(kal)kal< *k/l[/a]k/l[/a]*.

(III) IN **kaka=*(ŋ)ka(ŋ)ka* "older sibling." Form. *kaka* "sibling (Pai.), older sibling (Ami Kuv. W. Ruk: Maga)."

(IV)   Form: Pai. *markaka* "brothers," from *ma/ḷ/kaka*.

SIBLING (OLDER), MAN (YOUNG)   *(qa/)baw* (67)
    Form. (Puy.) *baw* "older sibling"; cf. also Pai. *mar/balaw* "wife," perh. from */b/al/aw*.

    T **?baaw* "young (unmarried) man": Nung *pi ba:u* "older

brother" (*pi*<*bi "older sibling"), from *q(*a*/)*baw*. Sek *ʔba:u*
"young man" (cf. Thai).

SIDE *[(*n*)*ts*][*i*](*m*)*paŋ*; *[*ts*][*a*]*mpaŋ*; *[*t*][*a*](*m*)*baŋ* (66, 122)
(I) IN ***t'i*(*m*)*paŋ* "side road, road fork" (NgD. "fork, fish
spear"). PO *nsimpa: Fi. *tsimba/tsimba* "the other side." PPN
**sipa "oblique, awry [=to one side]," also "fish spear," from
*nsimpa.

    Li *p[*ia*]*ŋ*: S. Li *pɛŋ* "side (of body); clf. for paired mem-
bers or organs," from *(*i*)*paŋ*.

    Miao: PW **phaŋ "side": MCh. *phaŋ* "side (left, right),"
phaŋ phlo one cheek (*phlo*)"; MPT *phaŋ plo* "cheek" (Sav.),
from PM *ph[*ɔ*]*ŋ*, from PMY *ph[*u*]*ŋ* (second. aspiration by the
initial *ts).

(II) IN ***t'ampaŋ* "side road, road fork," perh. by vocalic
assim. from ***t'impaŋ* (under I).

(III) IN **tambaŋ "side, opposite side." PO *tampa: Fi. *tamba*
"side, the other side," Sa. *apa* "side." PPN **tafa "side, edge"
~**tapa "edge," also "bark cloth"=*tapa* (decorated on one
side); from *ta(*m*)*pa*.

    T **biaŋ~*viaŋ (Lao doublet WT) "side (esp. one side
of things divided lengthwise)," from **biaŋ~*mwiaŋ<*(*ʔ*)-
(*m*)*biaŋ*, from *ʔ*(*ə*)(*m*)*baŋ* (unstressed form), for *[*t*](*ə*)(*m*)*baŋ*.
KS **ʔmb[*ɨ*]*aŋ* "side": Sui *ʔbyaŋ*~*ʔmyaŋ*, *waŋ*, *ʔwəŋ*~*ʔwuəŋ*, Mak
ʔbu:ŋ, Then *ma:ŋ* (all h.t.) (cf. Thai).

SIDE, SHORE, BANK **bay/bay*

    IN *baybay: Tg. *baybáy* "border, edge, shore," Pangasinan
baybáy "sea, seaside," Ilocano *baybáy* "open sea," Bukidnon
Manobo *beyvey* "bank of a stream" (forms cited by Blust 1970
under *baSay, later [pers. comm. 1973] listed to be withdrawn);
cf. also *(*ʔ*)*a*(*m*)*bay* "side-by-side" (Blust 1970).

    T *faay "side" (SW only), from *phwaay<*(*pay*)*pay*<
*(*bay*)*bay* (with irregular unvoicing and aspiration). Li *fay:
S. Li *fai* "side [right, left], bank of a river" (cf. Thai).

SIDE (OF BODY), RIB *[*ta*]*gəR*[*a*]*ŋ*; *[*ta*]*qaRaŋ*

(I) IN *[*t*]*agəRaŋ* "rib": Yami *tagəraŋ*; also (Blust 1972bis)

Ivatan *tagraŋ*, Ifugao *taglaŋ*, Kelabit *segeraŋ* (initial *s-* unexplained), Long Anap *tegaaŋ*, Miri *tagreŋ*.

    T **gro(o)ŋ* "rib": Si. *gro:ŋ* (second. lengthening), from **g(o)roŋ<*g(ə)rəŋ<*g(ə)raŋ* (vocalic assim.).

(II) Form. (Paz.) **taqaɣaŋ*; (Sed.) **təqəɣaŋ* (unstressed form) "rib."

    T **[x]raaŋ* "side of body," from **x(a)raŋ*; **ʔduuk xraaŋ* "rib"="bone" (**ʔduuk*) of the side of the body (**xraaŋ*)." Li **kh[a,aa]ŋ*: S. Li *drɨʔ khaŋ* "rib" (*drɨʔ* "bone"), from **kh[r]aaŋ* (cf. Thai).

SILVER See WHITE (three entries).

SING/SONG See SPEAK.

SINK INTO, SUNKEN, SHIPWRECK(ED), MUD **( )k[a]ɣəm; *q[]ɣəm*

(I) IN ***ka[l]əm=*kaɣəm* "sink into": TB. *harom*, Ja. *kĕrĕm*, Ml. *karam*, NgD. *kahem;* also (Blust 1972bis) Long Anap *kaam*, Maranao *kagem* "sink, capsize."

    T **k[l]om* "to be muddy; mud, mire" (Shan).

(II) T **hlom* "sink into (mud), fall through (floor)" (Si. Lao also "mud"); **hlom* (d.t.) "to be shipwrecked, sink." D *rəm* "sink into (as in mud, into a hole)," from **rom*. KS **qhlom* "mud": Sui *khum~hum*, Mak *lum*, Then *lem* (all h.t.).

    Yao: YHN *khlom* "sunken (eyes)," from PMY **[qhl̥]om*.

SIP See DRINK.

SIP, SUCK, DRINK **[tsi]ɣup; *[tsi]ɣ[ə]p; *[si]ɣup*

(I) IN ***t'iɣup* "sip." Form. (Kuv.) **tsiɣup* "drink"; also (Pai: Mak.) **ts/m/iɣup* "suck."

(II) Form. (Puy. Ami) **(m/)tsiɣəp* "suck (as fruit)."

(III) IN ***hiɣup* "sip" (NgD. *hirup* "sip," *ihop* "drink"). Yami **m/[h]iɣup* "drink." PO **iɣup*: U. *ilu* "sip," *iluh/i* "sip something."

    PMY ***hop* "drink" (YCR YTP YHN also "suck [infants at breast]"), from **(si)ɣop*.

SISTER (OLDER) See MOTHER.

SISTER-IN-LAW See IN-LAW.

SIT *(m/)z[u,o]k(/z[u,o]k

IN **ḍukḍuk "sit"; also **ḍuk "place of residence (*Wohnsitz*). Cham tɔq (Blood), from *d[u]k. Form. (Ami Fav.) *m/[z]uq, app. from */zuk(/zuk), but note Cham.

T *[s,z][u,o]k (Ahom).

SKIN See BARK, n.

SKIN, LEATHER *(q/)mbuḷaŋ; *(m)b/l/uḷaŋ

(I) T *hnaŋ "skin, leather, bark," from *q/ndaŋ<*q/mbraŋ. Sek naŋ (h.t.) "skin" (Ged.), from *hnaŋ (cf. Thai). KS *[]ra, id.: Sui Ra~ha, Mak ja (all h.t.), from *[]ra(ŋ). OB nɔŋ (h.t.) "skin, leather (untanned)," from *hnɔŋ (cf. Thai). Li *nuaŋ "skin, bark": S. Li naŋ, WS Li nuaŋ, from *nduaŋ<*mbruaŋ <*mb(u)raŋ (cf. Thai). Lt. i mle "sweat"="water (i) of the skin (mle)," from *mla[ŋ]<*mb[]la[ŋ].

(II) IN **baluḷaŋ "thick hide (leather)," from *b/l/uḷaŋ.

SKIN, SCALE, SCAB *[]kiḷip; *kiḷi[p/ḷip]; *k[u]ḷip/ḷ[ip] (19, 28)

(I) T *kliip "thick scale of any bulbous plant" (as the onion) (Shan); garlic (WT: ic.); leaf, petals of flowers (Si.); flower-petals (Nung: F. K. Li); skin (of onion), scale (of fish), scab (Nung: Sav.), from *[]k(i)lip. N. Thai *klip: Dioi kip "scale, scab," Wu-ming klip "fish scale."

(II) PPN **kili "skin" (Sm. ʔili/ola "healing membrane"= "scab"), from *kilit<*kilip/l(ip) (cf. III).

(III) **kulit "skin" (Ml. "skin, leather, bark, shell"); Yami kulit "skin, bark"; from *kulip/l(ip). Form. (Puy: Hinan) *kuḷit "skin (of fruit)," from *kuḷip/ḷ(ip) (cf. IN).

SKIRT See CLOTHES.

SKIRT, PETTICOAT *ts[a](m)pin (11)

IN **tʼapin "lining (Tg.), supplementary piece of clothing (Ho.)."

T *sin~*sɨn (Tho) "skirt, petticoat" (Lao "robe"), from *swin <*s[]bin<*s[]mpin. KS *[sw]in "skirt": Mak fin (cf. Thai). Lq. pien "small shawl (*fichu*)," from *[]pin.

SKY *[ndu]laŋ[it]

IN **laŋit. PO **laŋi(t) "sky"; also **laŋi "wind." SEP °laŋi "sky" (Wedau "rain"); cf. Capell: "in New Heb. the word mostly means 'wind.'" PPN **laŋi (Maori Tikopian "weather," Nukuoro "rain"). Form. (Puy: Hinan) °laŋit̠ (cf. also Puy. araŋit "cloud" in Bullock 1874); (Saa.) °l̠aŋits: both perh. from °l̠aŋit/l̠(aŋit).

Miao: PW/PM **ndu(ŋ), from PMY *ndua(ŋ); PE **vai, from PM *wu(ŋ)<PMY *[l̠]ua(ŋ); PY **ruŋ=*l̠uaŋ (PIM) ~*l̠uŋ (PKM); all from PMY *ndl̠ua[ŋ]~*ndl̠u[ŋ], from an earlier *nd(u)l̠aŋ.

SKY See DAY; RAIN; SUN.

SKY, RAIN, THUNDER *b[a]luŋ; *(m)b[u]luŋ

(I) Form. (Ata: Ci'uli) *baluŋ "thunder."

(II) Form. (E. Ruk.) *su-bul/buluŋ; (W. Ruk.) *ta-buluŋ/a(n) "sky"; also (Sir.) *bulum "sky, cloud," by assim. from *buluŋ; perh. from an earlier *baluŋ by vocalic assim.

PM **nɔŋ=*mlɔŋ (PT *mu); PY **bluŋ "rain"; both from PMY *mluŋ~*mbluŋ, from an earlier *m(b)luuŋ<*mb(u)luŋ; for the semantics, cf. SEP and PPN under SKY.

SLAP See PALM/SOLE.

SLEEP *ti(n)zoR

IN **tid̠uɣ=*tid̠u[R]; also (by vocalic assim.) **tud̠uɣ= *tud̠uR. PO *[t]uru: Sa. me/uru. Form: East (Bun. Fav.) *ma/tu[z]uɣ; Tsouic (Saa.) *ma/ta/tutsuɣ (vocalic assim., as in IN PO).

T *noon "lie down, sleep," from *nzoon<*(o)nzon<*(i)nzon through assim. forward (cf. IN PO Form.). Dioi *nin, id., from *ni[i]n<*nziin<*(i)nzin<*(i)nzon through assim. backward (contrast Thai). Sek *nuun (Ged.) (cf. Thai). KS *nun: Sui Mak Then *nun (cf. Thai). OB lab soaŋ "sleep" (lab "lay down") (Jer.), soan "sleep" (Sav.), from *soon<*(o)son through assim. (cf. Thai). Li *[ts]oo[l]: S. Li ćɔn, DC Loi -ćoan, SH Loi ćoan ~-ćun, Ha dzun=tsun, WS Loi ćoa<*ćoo[l], Bup. dou=tou <*tsow<*tsoo[l], from *t(o)so[l]<*t(i)so[l] through assim. (cf. Thai OB).

SLEEP   See CLOSE EYES.

SLICE   See CUT.

SLIP OFF/AWAY   *(q/)luts/luts*

IN *lut'lut'* "slip off, slip away": Cebuano Visayan *luslus* "for something that wraps something and is attached to it to slip off," Ml. *lolos* "slip off; bolt away" (Blust 1973).

T *hluut* (Lao)~*hlut* (Si.)~*luut* (Shan) "to slip, be untied, unloosed" (Lao "escape, as from the hand").

SMALL, SHORT, DWARF, CHILD   *(q/)(n)tlek; *[e]tlek; *[p/e]ndlek; *[p/a](n)dlak; *[pu](n)dluk*

(I)   IN **ə(n)tik* "small" (Ja. "dwarf").

T*ʔdek* "child" (Lao "small"), *lek~*hlek* (Lao) "small," both from an original **ʔdlek; cf. Si. *dek lek* "children," Lao *dek nɔi~lek nɔi* "small (nɔi)." OB *lək-* (Jer.), *lɛk* (Sav.) "child." Li *t(h)lek: S. Li *lek* "child," WS Li *hlək* "child; small," SH SC Loi *hlək*, SC Loi *tiək* "child."

(II)   IN **itik* "small." PPN **iti,* id. Form. (Puy.) *lik(ə)ti,* from *tlik/tli[k]; also (Saa.) *m/n/it[i]k* "short."

Li *tik* "small": S. Li *tik.*

(III)   IN **pindik* "short [stature]," prob. from *p/indik.

(IV)   IN **pandak* "short [stature]," prob. from *p/andak.

T *l[a]k* "small in stature; dwarf" (Ahom), from an original *dlak.

(V)   T *duk* "short, dwarfish in nature" (Shan), from an original *dluk. OB *nok* "small," *lək-nok* "child" (Jer.), *lek lɔk* (h.t.) "child" (Sav.), from *ʔ(n)dlok (for first element, see I). Li *t(h)l[u]k: N. Li *tok,* WS Li *tɔk* "small," Dogang *hlok* "child," from *[]dl[u]k.

SMASH   See BREAK.

SMELL   *kri[y]u[m]* (25)

IN **k'iyum* "to smell, sniff, 'nose-kiss.' "

T *khriw* "to stink (Nung); smell putrid, having the smell of raw fish or flesh (Ahom); acrid, too penetrating odor (Lao);

to exhale a strong odor, heady, like certain perfumed alcohols (WT)," from *khriu(m)*.

SMELL, FRAGRANT   *s[a][r]om; *s/m/[a]rom

(I) IN **ha[l]um=*ha[r]um "fragrant/fragrance, aroma," from *sa[r]um. Form: Pai. *salum* "perfume" (Dahl cit.), from *sa[r]um.

     T *hoom "smell good, fragrant" (Ahom "to smell"), from *sroom/hroom<*s(o)rom (vocalic assim.). Dioi *hɔm* "fragrant, perfumed" (cf. Thai).

     Miao: MCF *haŋ* "strong [odor: sweat, excrement, fire]," from PM *hoŋ; PY *hɔm "fragrant (YCR), to smell (flairer) [v.t.] (YHN)"; both from PMY *hɔm (cf. Thai).

(II) Form. (Pai: Mak.) *səmarum "to smell (perceive odor)," from *s/m/arum; also (Thao) *[s-]marum/n "smoke" (Bullock 1874; for the semantics, cf. ODOR/SMOKE.

     PMY **hno(m) "to hear; to smell [tr.]" (MPT "to hear; to sense, feel [pain]; to sense, be conscious of smell or odor, to smell"), from *hmrom<*s[]m[o]rom; also Miao: MPT *mloŋ*, MTT MSY *noŋ* "listen," from PWA **mloŋ (Purnell, text: 74), from PMY *[mr]om, a doublet formation from *[s]m[]rom.

SMELL, STINK, RANCID, FAT(TY)   *sañir (25)

     IN **hañil=*hañir "fatty" (Ja. "too fat, rancid," Ml. "fatty, rancid," NgD. "stink," Tg. *b/anil* "fat," Ho. *l/ani* "fish odor," *m/ani* "stink").

     T *aay=ʔaay~*ñaay (Nung) "to smell (good or bad), odor, exhalation, vapor, steam, smoke," from *-a(ń)i(r)~*(-a)ñi(r). Dioi *sɔi* (s.t.) "vapor, odor, breath," from *so(ń)i<*sɔñi(r) (unstressed form). Li *hñaay: S. Li *ha:i* "to stink, smell bad"; also (d.t.) "to smell, scent (flairer)"; WS Li *ñai* "to smell (intr.)"; also (d.t.) "to smell (tr.)," from *s(a)ñi(r) (cf. Thai). Lq. *nen* "fat (graisse)," from *nin<*ni[r].

SMILE   *(tsə)ńum(/ńum); *( )ńam(/ńam)

(I) IN *t'əñum: Ml. *sĕñum.* Cham *ńim<*ńum.
     T *ńum~*ńim (Si.).
     Miao: MPT *ńu ńa* (l.t., h.t.) (cw. "laugh"), from PM *ńu(ŋ) *ʔń[εŋ] (for second element, see II); Yao *ńum ńum*

(d.t.) (cw. "laugh"); both from PMY *ńum, from an earlier
ńuum<(ńum)ńum.

(II) T *[h]ńa[a]m "laugh" (Ahom), perh. from *s(a)ńam
(stressed form, with vocalic assim.).

    PM *ńu(ŋ) *ʔŋ[ɛŋ] (for first element, see I), from PMY
*ńum *ʔń[aam].

SMOKE, n. *(qa/)(n)tsu[b](/an)

    IN **a[tʼ]u=*[ʔ]a[tʼ]u, from *ʔatʼu(ban); cf. Yami aʔub, app.
from *[ʔ]a[h]ub(an)<*qa/sub(an). PO ***ʔasu "smoke, steam,
tobacco plant." PPN **ʔahu=*ʔahu~*ʔasu (Sm.), from *ʔa(n)su.
Form. (Sir.) *[q]atsu; (Puy.) *qatsuban, prob. from an original
*qa/tsub/an.

    PM **nćh[o]=*ntshy[o] "to smoke (food)": MCh. ntshyo
"smoke," n.; MPT ntshyo "to produce smoke, to smoke [fire],"
from PMY *ntshy[o]; MPT also ntshyau "smoky," from PMY
*ntshyou; PY **śyou "smoke," from PMY *tshyou; all from PMY
ntshyo~(n)tshyou, from *ntsho~*(n)tshou (palatalized by
the original *u).

SMOKE, n. See ODOR.

SMOKE, STEAM   *[G][u]wa[b]; *[G][u]wa[b/]an

(I) IN **uwab "steam" (Ml. also "vapor").

(II) T *ɣwan "smoke," from *ɣ(u)wa(w)an (second. vowel
shortening)<*G(u)wab/an; for the suffix, cf. SMOKE, n. Dioi
hɔn (l.t.)~ɔn (irreg. h.t.) "smoke," from *Gon<*[Gw]an. Sek
gon, id. (cf. Dioi). KS *[Gw]an, id.: Sui Kam kwan (l.t.), Then
wan, Mak kwan (irreg. h.t.). OB kuan (l.t.), id., from *[G]wan.
Li *[hw]an, id.: S. Li han, DC Loi hoan-, SC Loi hoon-, SH Loi
hon-, WS Loi goa-.

SMOKE, DRY (MEAT)   *(q/)źiaŋ(/źiaŋ) (14, 55, 87, 108)

    IN **diŋdiŋ "dried meat" (TB. "smoked meat"), from an
original *diaŋdiaŋ; cf. also *daʔiŋ "jerked fish" (Blust 1970),
a possible complex doublet via metathesis: *q/diaŋ>*ʔ/diaŋ>
*daʔiŋ (*d for *d after *ʔ/; cf. Thai).

    T **ʔyaaŋ (SW)~*ʔyaŋ (Lao) "to smoke, dry (meat, fish,
rice)"; also **ʔdiaŋ "boucanée [meat]" (Nung) and **ʔyeeŋ "fumé

[fish]" (Nung). Dioi *dyaŋ* (h.t.) "to dry over the fire, smoke (meat, rice)," from *ʔy[a,aa]ŋ* (cf. Thai). Sek *yuaŋ* (h.t.) "to roast" (Ged.), from *ʔyuaŋ<*ʔyiaŋ* through dissim. OB *teaŋ* "*boucanée*" [meat]," from *siaŋ*.

SMOOTH(E), EVEN *p[a]rats; *[]p[]ras

(I) IN **palat'=*parat'* "to smoothe" (NgD. "even").

(II) T *play* "to smooth, polish; even, polished, smooth" (Si.).

SNAIL See SHELLFISH (three entries).

SNAKEᴵ *(q/)(n)śulaR

IN **ulaɣ=*ulaR*, with irregular medial -*l*- rather than the anticipated -*n*-, perhaps through dissimilation from an original initial *ńś-. PPN **la* "snail-like," app. from *(u)la* (for the semantics, cf. PPN under SNAKEᴵᴵ). Form. (Ruk. Puy. Ami Thao) *[n][ś]ula[R]* "snake," with irreg. nasal shifts throughout, app. through assim. to the earlier *[n]*; also (Ata.) *sula[R]* "hemorrhoids" (="worms").

T *hliam~*hniam* (Nung) "boa, python," from *s[]lam* (with assim. in Nung). Dioi *nə:m* (h.t.), id., from *hniam* (cf. Nung). KS *ʔzuy: Sui *hui~fui*, Mak *zui*, Then *thuei* (all h.t.), Kam *sui* (l.t.), from *q/nsuy<*q/nsul(aɣ).

PMY *ʔnaaŋ, from *q/n[ś]a(l)aŋ<*q/n[ś]u(l)aŋ (vocalic assim.).

SNAKEᴵᴵ *(u)ŋata (27)

IN *ŋata* "snake, worm" (Haud.). PO **ŋmata=*ŋwata, from *(u)ŋata. SEP: Mota *mwata*, from *ŋwata. PPN **ŋata "snake, snail, slug, sea-slug."

T *ŋu* "snake," from *(u)ŋu<*(u)ŋa; also *ŋoot "lycodon [snake]" (Si.), from *ŋuat<*(u)ŋat. N. Thai: Dioi ŋə, Yai ŋiˀa, from ŋya<*(ə)ŋa (unstressed form). Sek ŋua (cf. Thai). Lk. ŋyie, from *ŋyia (cf. N. Thai). OB ŋia (Jer.), ŋea (Sav.) (cf. N. Thai Lk.). Li *thya: S. Li ya, WS Li za, Bas. ya, WS SC Loi ja, N. Li SH Loi tha, from *(ŋə)ta (second. aspir.). Lq. ŋi̵, from *ŋya (cf. N. Thai). Lt. kuŋ, app. from *kə/ŋ[a].

SNATCH See SEIZE.

SNEEZE, BLOW NOSE *[qa]sin; *q[a]siŋ; *q[a]s[ə]ŋ

(I) IN *bahin "sneeze": Tg. *bahin,* Ilocano *baen* (R. Ferr.: pers. comm.), app. for *ba?hin<*ba/q[]sin.

    Li *sin "sneeze": S. Li *śin en* (n.a.).

(II) Form. (Ami) *ba/q[]siŋ~*ma/q[]siŋ; (Pai.) *b/n/aq[]siŋ "sneeze" (s_3).

(III) IN **hat'əŋ=[?]at'əŋ "loud breathing" (Ho. "breath"); also **ət'əŋ "loud breathing" (Ml. "blow nose"); both from *q/tsəŋ<*q/səŋ. Form. (W. Ruk.) *wa/ba[q-]səŋ; (Puy.; Tsou) *pa/[q-]səŋ; (Kan. Saa.) *ma/qasəŋ "sneeze"(s_3).

    T *saŋ "come out with force (Shan), blow nose (Si.)," also *thaŋ (s.t.) "come out with force, cause to come out with force, as mucus of nose; (ic.) blow nose" (Shan); both from an original *[ts]aŋ<*q/saŋ (initial effect as in IN), from an earlier *q(a)səŋ through vocalic assim. N. Thai *saŋ "blow nose" (Po-ai). KS: Mak *saŋ,* id., app. from *qsaŋ; cf. the parallel KS series represented by Sui ?γaŋ~γaŋ~hŋaŋ, Then *zaŋ* (h.t.), id., from **?(ŋ)γaŋ<*q/(ŋ)γaŋ.

SNORE See RUMBLE.

SOAK See DIP.

SOLE See FLAT; PALM/SOLE.

SOUND, RESOUND, THUNDER, DRUM *[g]ə(n)daŋ

    IN **gəṇḍaŋ "kettle drum," for *gəndaŋ (no Tg. cognate).

    T **?daŋ "sound, resound" (Kh. "sound of drum or gun fired, rumble of thunder," BT "thunder"); *va ?daŋ "thunder"="sound of the heavens (*va)," for *g(ə)daŋ. Dioi *daŋ* (h.t.) "sound, noise; voice, song of birds," from **?daŋ. Lk. *toŋ pla* (both l.t.) "thunder" (*toŋ yap* "lightning"), from *doŋ<*(o)daŋ (vocalic assim.). Li *daŋ: S. Li *daŋ* "to cry, make noise [thunder, snore, water, horse]," *pa daŋ ɔm* "thunder"="sky sound roar" (see ROAR/). Lq. *mən dɔŋ* "thunder" (*mən* "sky"). Kl. *zɨ dɔŋ,* id. (cf. *zɨ fɛ* "wind," *zuə* "sky").

SOUR *(q/)atsəm

    IN **at'əm. PPN **masa "sour, bitter," from *m/asa[m]< *m/aso[m] (vocalic assim.). Form. (Ami: Baran Kibi Taparon) *q/atsəm/tsəm;* (Ami; Tauran) *ts/l̥/əm/n;* (Puy: Chipon) *q/a/r/tsəm,* whence Pai: Tamari *qarsəm* as loan.

T *som.* Dioi *sɔm.* Sek *saːm,* from *(a)sam<*(a)som* (vocalic assim., as in PPN). KS *som:* Sui *hum~fum,* Mak *sum,* Kam *sem,* Then *them.* Lk. *khyom=ćhom,* from *som* (irreg. aspir., app. from the earlier *q/*).

SOW, v. See SPRAY.

SPACE *(q/)[a]waŋ*

IN **awaŋ* "open space (*Luftraum*)." PPN **awa* "channel" (Tuamotuan "pass, channel in a reef, port, harbour").

T *hwaaŋ~*waŋ* (Lao doublet) "space, interval," from *(q/)(a)waŋ;* also *waŋ* "deep place in stream, precipitous cavern" (Shan); *waaŋ* "abyss (in river), gulf" (Tho).

SPACE See WIDE.

SPAN (ARM-) See SPREAD OUT (ARMS).

SPAR See POST.

SPEAK, LANGUAGE, SING/SONG, CROW *(N)qaɣi*

IN *kaɣi:* Proto-Manobo *kagi* "word or saying" (Elkins), Bukidnon Manobo *kagi* "say, speak, talk" (Blust 1970), from *Nqaɣi.* Form. (Pai. Sai.; Kan. Saa.; Atayalic) *kaɣi* "language" (Sai. also ic. "speak"), from *Nqaɣi* (cf. IN).

T *xaan~*xan* (Si. doublet) "speak, answer, reply," also *[x]a* "voice of someone calling or interrupting" (Si.), from *qar(i)* ~*qa(ri),* with second. vowel length; also *xan* (s.t.) "sing (birds), crow (cock)"; also *kay* (with unexplained *k-* for *q-)* "fowl"="the crower," from *[q]a(r)i.* Dioi *han* "respond, consent," also "crow of the cock, cry of the pheasant," from *qhar(i);* also *kai<*[q/k]ay* "fowl." Sek *hal* "to crow" (Ged.), from *qhar(i);* also *kai* "fowl," from *[q/k]ay.* KS *jan~*ćan* "to crow": Sui *ćan* (l.t.), Mak *ćan* (h.t.), Then *yan,* from *(N)[q]an;* also *qaay* "fowl": Sui *qai,* Mak Then *kaːi,* Kam *ʔaːi* (with second. length associated with *-ɣ->ø*). Lk. *kai,* id., from *[q/k]ay.* OB *kɔi,* id., from *[q/k]ay.* Li *khay,* id.: S. Li WS Li *khai,* from *qhay.* Lq. *khai,* id. N. Kl. *kai,* id. Lt. *ka,* id., from *ka[ay]* (cf. KS).

PMY *°qaay*=*°(N)qaay* "to crow": MCF "song of birds"; MCh. "make a cry, call (birds, animals, insects; (ic.) thunder"; MPT "to call; song of birds; (ic.) thunder" (Sav.), from *°(N)qa(γ)i*, with second. length (cf. KS and Lt.); also PM *°qε* "fowl," from PMY *°q[ay]*; PY *°ćay* (s.t.), id., from *°q(y)ay* (poss. influ. from the original final *°-i*), apparently independent of the early Ch. loan: *ki=ći*, Anc. *kiei*, Arch. *kieg* (with -g perhaps reflecting PAT *°-γ*).

SPEAK, TEACH, LEARN   *°sual̦*

Form. (Ami) *°sual̦* "language," *°p/sual̦* "speak/say"; (Kan.) *°-sua[l̦]*, id.; cf. also Sir. *°ma/susu* "speak."

T *°soon* "teach, learn," from *°suan*. Dioi *sɔn*, id. KS: Mak *son* "teach," a prob. loan from Thai.

SPEAR   See BAMBOO; BOW.

SPIDER   *°(k/)l̦aw[a](/l̦aw[a])*

(I)   IN **°lawa* "spider, web" (Tg. *lawa~lawa/lawa~la/lawa;* Ml. *lawa/lawa*); Yami *°ala/lawa* "spider." PO: Fi. *lawa* "net," *lawa/lawa* "web," *mbuta/lawa* "spider"; Sa. *lawa* "web." SEP *°lawa* "web"; also (in Group II languages in metath. forms) with prefixed *°ka/*: Sinaugoro *ka/vara/vara* Rubi *ka/waiaa* "spider." Form. (Sir.) *°l̦awa;* cf. also (Ata.) *°l̦auqay*, app. from *°l̦aw[a]/*.

T *°k(h)laaw*. Dioi *kwau*, Wu-ming *klwaaw* (cf. Mak). Mak *ćwa:u*, from *°klwaaw*<*°(kla)w/klaw* (labialized). Lk. *paŋ-khyo* =*-ćho*, from *°-khlo*<*°-khlwaw* (cf. Mak).

Miao: MPT *ka lau* "(types of) spider" (*ka* "insect"), from PM *°l̦[ou]*, from PMY *°[l̦][ɔ]*<*°l̦(a)wa*<*°lawá*.

SPIRIT   See BREATHE.

SPIRIT, DEMON   *°pi[l̦]i;* *°( )pu[l̦]i(/li)*

(I)   Form. (Saa.) *°pil̦i* "spirit," perh. from *°pul̦i* by assim. (cf. II).

T *°phi*=/*phii*/ "spirit, demon, ghost": BT *fi* "demon," *yet fi* "funeral ceremony"="do/make/work (*yet*) the spirits (*fi*)," from *°pi(r)i*.

(II)   Form. (W. Ruk.) *°pul̦ili* "spirit."

T *°puy* "ritual ceremony of the cult of the genies" (WT),

from *[]*pu*(*r*)*i*. Dioi *pɔi faŋ* "superstitious ceremony in which one offers to the devil [*faŋ*] a sacrifice in compensation for the soul of the sick person which he has and which one asks him to release."

SPIRIT, GHOST, CORPSE, BODY   *[*q/a*]*ntu;* *[*q/a*]*(*n*)*tu/a*
(I)   IN **hantu*=*[ʔ]*antu* "ghost" (Ja. "body, carcass").
      Lt. *tu* (l.t.) "clf. for animals," from *du*<*ntu;* for semantics, see II.

(II)   PPN **ʔatua* "deity (=spirit)," from *ʔa[t,nt]u/a*.
      T *tua~*dua* (Lao) "body; self; clf. for animals and spirits" (WT "body [of persons and animals]; clf. for all animated beings or those considered as such: persons, animals, spirits, characters of writing, playing cards"), from *(n)tu/a*. Dioi *tuə* (l.t.) "clf. for animals," from *dua*<*ntu/a*. KS *do*, id.: Mak *to* (l.t.), from *dua*<*ntu/a*.

SPIRIT, GOD   *s[u][y]aŋ*
      IN **hi[y]aŋ* "god (*Gottheit/gottlich*)," app. by assim. from *huyaŋ*.
      T *suaŋ* "powerful evil spirit, the devil (Shan); genii (Si.: ic.)," from *súwaŋ*, app. by assim. from *suyaŋ* (contrast IN); also *saaŋ* "god, demon" (SW), from *swaaŋ*<*suwáŋ*.

SPIT   See COUGH.

SPLEEN   *[l,ḷ][i](m)paa[k](/paak)*
      IN **limpa* "spleen" (Ml. *limpa* "liver," *limpa kĕt'il* "little liver" ="spleen").
      T *paaŋ* "spleen" (Si. "liver and spleen disease"), from *paaŋ/paak*<*paak/paak*.

SPLIT   *( )kr[i][ḷ]ak*
      Form: East */tǝḷak*: Pai. *mintsǝrak* "split (as, wood becomes split)," from */t[i]ḷak* (stressed form).
      T *kriak* "split (wood, firewood) (BT Tho); slice, cut into slices, cut wood into laths (Si.)."

SPLIT   See BREAK.

SPLIT, SEPARATE   *(m)b[a]ḷaq(/b[a]ḷaq)* (14, 20)
      IN **bǝlaʔ*=*(m)bǝlaʔ* "split" (Ml. "split, cleave, divide, cut

in two lengthwise"), from *(m)bala? (stressed form). PO *mpola:
Fi. *mbola* "split, break"; also (Blust 1973) Arosi *hora* "space
between two rocks, narrow fissure," Motu *pola-ia* "split a log
into two or four pieces." PPN **fe[r,l]a* "spread out, open"=
"separate"; also *fe[r,l]a/fe[r/l]a: Rarotongan *?era/?era* "wide
open (of eyes)."

T *braak* "to separate, be separated" (Tho also "branching
[of road]"), from *b(a)rak, app. from an original *barak/barak.
KS *pyaak* "separate": Sui *pyak*, Then *pya:k*, from *praak<
*b(a)rak, with regular unvoicing of the initial (not redupli-
cated; contrast Thai).

SPOILED See ROTTEN.

SPOTTED, PIEBALD *(q/)(m)b[a]laŋ (20)
IN **bəlaŋ=*(m)bəlaŋ "spotted" (Ml. "piebald, variegated;
spotted, striped"), from *(m)balaŋ (stressed form).

T **?blaaŋ "spotted, piebald" (Lao *ba:ŋ*), from *q/b(a)laŋ;
cf. also **?b[l]eeŋ "florid, flowery; white spots on the face" (Lao
bɛ:ŋ), from **?bliaŋ<*q/b(i)laŋ. Sek *?bla:ŋ* "spotted with white"
(cf. Thai). KS *naaŋ: Mak *na:ŋ* "smallpox="spotted (face)";
cf. also **?daaŋ: Mak *?da:ŋ* "flowery"; both from *(q/)(n)daaŋ
<*(q/)(m)b(a)raŋ.

SPOUSE See WOMAN.

SPRAY, SCATTER, SOW, SPRINKLE, SQUIRT, SPRING, n.

SPRAY, SCATTER, SOW, SPRINKLE, SQUIRT *[t]abuγ;
*[s]a(m)buγ; *tsa(m)buγ; *(n)tsa(m)baγ; *( )(m)b[u]γ/a
(12, 26, 39, 96, 97, 128)

(I) IN **tabuγ "scatter" (Ml. also "sow, as seed").
T *bon~*bun (Lao doublet)~**?buan (Shan and Si.
doublet) "eject from mouth, squirt, spit," from *(tə)bun~
**?(a)bun, for *[t](a)bun. Li *vun: WS Li *vun* "to spit (phlegm),
from *wu[l]<*(ta)bu[γ].

(II) IN **ha(m)buγ "scatter" (Ml. "scatter, as rice, pearls,
money, etc. at festivals," NgD. "sprinkle").

(III) IN **t'a(m)buγ "scatter" (Tg. "sowing of seeds by scattering").

(IV) IN **$t'əba[l]$=*$t'ə(m)ba[γ]$~*$t'aba[γ]$ "scatter about" (Ja. Ml. *sěbar* "scatter, sow," NgD. *sawar* "scatter seed"), perh. originally from *$t'a(m)buγ$ through vocalic assim. PO *$nsofa$: Fi. *tsova* "pour out."

T *$hwaan$ "to sow (scatter seed)," from *$s(a)wan$. Sek *va:l* [h.t.], id., from *$hwaal$<*$s(a)wal$ (cf. Thai). OB *bien*< *$wien$, id., from *wan<*[]*ban*. Li *$vaal$: S. Li *va:n* "far apart, scattered (*clairsemé*), not close [cloth, rice planting]," N. Li *va:i* "to water (=spray/sprinkle) vegetables," from *$[h]waal$ <*$[s](a)wal$ (cf. Sek).

(V) IN **$buγa$ "to spray" (Tg. also "spit out," TB. *gam/bura* "water spray"). PO *$fuγa$: Sa. *hula/a*, U. *hula/hula* "spring"= "the sprayer/squirter."

Miao: MCF *hńaŋ* "sow (seeds)," from PM *$h[mbl][ai]$ <PMY *$h[mbl][a]$, from *[]*$mb(u)γa$; PY/PMY *ha "sow seeds," from *$(bu)γa$ (note the role played by prefixation).

SPREAD (OUT) *$(m)bilaj$

IN **$bəlag'$=*$bilag'$ (Tg. *bilád* "exposed to the sun")~*$bəlag'$ (TB Ja. Ml. Ho.) (unstressed form); Blust (1972bis) also cites Ilocano *bilág* "to sun, dry in the sun." PO **$(m)pola$ "spread *out*" (Fi. "mat"), corresponding to the unstressed form; Blust (1972bis) cites *mpilas*: Roviana *bilasa* "scorched by sun or fire." PPN **$fola$ "spread/spread out."

T *phe=/phee/ "spread, spread out" (Ahom also "to sun paddy"), from *$phia$<*$bi(r)a(j)$ (initial unvoicing, with "Procrustean" loss of final) (Thai lacks *$-ey$ and *$-iay$); also *$plaay$ (WT Nung)~*$praay$ (Si.)~*$b[r,l]aay$ (Tho) "to spread, extend," from *$(m)p[a]lay$ (vocalic assim.).

SPREAD (OUT), FLY, MAT *$(q/)(m)paR(/(m)paR)$; *$(q/)(m)pəR(/(m)pəR)$

(I) IN **$hampa[l]$=*$[ʔ]ampa[γ]$, app. for *$[ʔ]ampa[R]$ "spread out, stretch out": Ml. *hampar* "spread out (as mats, carpets, grains, etc.)," *hampar/an* "carpet"; Ja. *hampar* "(spread the wings=) swoop (birds)"; also (Dahl cit.) Chamorro *gwafag* "mat." PO *$ampa$~*$empa$ (unstressed form): Fi. *yamba* "mat"; Sa. *epa* "lie, like a mat." PPN *$[ʔ]apa/[ʔ]apa$~**$ʔepa$ (unstressed form): Fu. *apa/apa/i* "stretch out the hands"; To. *ʔe/ʔepa* "spread out," Sm. *epa* "mat," from **ʔampa/ʔampa~*ʔempa*. Form. (Ami Fav.) **ma/q[]ba[R]* (Thao **ma/r/ba[R]*) "to fly," from **/q(a)mpa[R]*.

T **phiin* "clf. for mats, woven objects, clothing, nets, skins," from **phyəən<*(qə)pən* (unstressed form, with aspir. of initial by **q-*). Also **bian* "mat (of plaited bamboo)" (WT), from **byan<*(-ə)mpan*. Dioi *pɛn* (l.t.) "clf. for skins, mats, carpets," from **bɛn<*mpɛn* (cf. WT). OB *phan* "spread (mat); clf. for mats, hammocks (=nets)," from **(qa)pan* (stressed form). Li **phian* "spread (mat, covering)": S. Li *phian*, WS Li *phəŋ* (cf. Thai).

Miao: MCF *phaŋ* "clf. for clothing, coverings, mats"; MCh. *phau* "clf. for quilts, skins," MPT *pho* (Heim.) "clf. for sheets, skins of leather; (ic.) a wing," *phau~fau* (Sav.) "clf. for covering wing (=spread out surface)," from PM **phɔ(ŋ)*; Yao: YHN *fun* (*<*phun*) "clf. for coverings and mats"; both from an original **(q/)par;* also Yao: YCR *phaan* "clf. for mosquito nets," from **(q/)apar*.

(II) Form. (Pai.) **mi/pə[R]pəR]* "to fly," perhaps originally through vocalic assim. from **(qə/)pa[R]pa[R]* (unstressed form).

T **ʔbin* "to fly," from **ʔmpin<*q/mpən*. Dioi *bin* (h.t.), id., from **ʔbin;* perh. also Dioi Yay *bin* (h.t.), N. Thai **ʔbin* "mat" (but note Sek). Sek *bil* (h.t.) (Ged.), *ʔbil* (Haud.) "to fly," from **ʔb[i]l;* cf. also *biin* (h.t.) (Ged.), *ʔbi:n* (Haud.) "mat." KS *pwen~*[bw]en* "to fly": Kam *pen*, Sui *win~vyən~ vyen*, Mak *vin* (all h.t.), Then *wen* (l.t.), from **(m)pe/(m)pen;* also **ʔbiin* "mat": Mak *vin;* also **ʔbiin* "mat": Mak *ʔbin*, Then *mien* (h.t.) (cf. N. Thai). Lk. *pon* "to fly," from **[]pon*. OB *bɔn* (h.t.), id., from **pɔn* (cf. Lk.). Li **bin*, id.: S. Li *bin*, WS Li *pen*, from **mpin* (cf. Thai).

SPREAD OUT (ARMS), ARM-SPAN, FATHOM **[da](m)pa*

(I) IN ***dəpa=*dəpa* (Dyen)=**dəpa* (Tg. *dipa*)~**dəpa* (Ja. *ḍĕpa*) "fathom," from **dapa* (stressed form). PPN ***rofa* "span, fathom" (Maori "spread out," Fu. "measure by fathoms").

(II) T **wa* "fathom" (Shan "fathom, four cubits, measure equal

to the extended arms; Lao also "to extend [as wings]"), from
[]ba<[]mpa; cf. also *ᵔʔba (s.t., high series) "to measure (land)"
(WT), app. for *[də]ba<*[də]mpa (unstressed form).

SPRING, n.   See BUBBLE.

SPRINKLE, BATHE   *[di]γots
   IN **diγut' "sprinkle" (TB. *duris* through metath.; Ja. "bathe");
Yami *ma/diγut' "wash/bathe oneself." Form. (Ami) *m/diγuts;
(Puy. Sir.) *(d/)m/iγuts; (Kuv.) *m/duγits (through metath.;
cf. TB.), id.
   T *rot~*hrot (Shan) "sprinkle, throw water," from *rot~
*throt<*d[]γots.

SQUEEZE   See BIND; HOLD (IN HAND, MOUTH).

SQUIRREL   See BAT.

SQUIRREL, RAT   *(m)puk[]tu
   Form. (Bun.) *puk[]tu "squirrel."
   T *buk "large field-rat" (Si: ic.), from *mpuk.
   PMY *mp[o]k "squirrel": YHN *bɔk,* YCR *bop* (h.t.) (with
assim. of final).

SQUIRT   See SPRAY.

SQUIRT, PENIS, VULVA, URINE/URINATE   *pi[γ]/pi[γ];
   *p/l/i[γ]/pi[γ]; p/l/i[γ]; *m[b]i[γ]/m[b]i[γ]
(I)   IN **piγpiγ "squirt." PPN **fifi "vagina" (cf. Atayalic).
Form. (Atayalic) *pi[γ]pi[γ] "vulva (=the squirter)"; cf. also
Paz. *papi,* id., perh. from *pa/pi[γ].
   Li *pi: S. Li *pi* "to blow nose (=squirt snot)," WS Li
pi "penis (=the squirter)," from *(pi/)pi.
(II)   IN *p/l/iγpiγ: Tg. *p/al/gpig* "soiled (=squirted upon)."
(III)   IN **pəliγ "penis" (cf. WS Li).
(IV)   IN **miγmiγ "to water/squirt," from *mbiγ/mbiγ. PO
*(mi/)mi: Fi. *mimi* "run out in a jet/stream," *mi* "urinate"; Sa.
mimi, id. PPN **mimi "urine, urinate."

SQUIRT, URINE, SEMEN   *ćirit
   IN **k'iḷit=*k'irit "to empty by squirting" (Ho. "urine"). PO

***si[d,r]i(t)*=**siri(t)* "semen, masturbation, draw water"; cf. also Trukese *si/ir* "urine" (Dyen 1949).

T **ćhi(i)t*~*ćit (Shan doublet) "squirt, inject (by squirting)," from *ćhi(r)it*. Li **hli[i]t*: WS Li *nam hlit* "semen" (*nam* "water"), from **(ći)lit*.

STAIRS See LADDER.

STAKE, POLE, POST **[g][a]laq;* **[q][]laq*

(I) IN ***gala?* "pole for pushing boats (*"Staken"*)" (Ml. "long thin pole such as is used on native boats for poling or mooring them").

(II) T *hlak "stake" (Shan "a post erected for fastening anything"), from *qlak<*qlaq, perh. from *glaq through assim. Sek *lak* (h.t.) "stake" (Ged.), from *hlak (cf. Thai). KS **q(h)lak* "stake, post": Sui *qhak*~*hak*, Mak *kak* (cf. Thai).

STALK See THIGH.

STAND **( )dzəŋ(/dzəŋ)*

IN ***d'əŋ* "stand," ***d'əŋd'əŋ* "to stand." Form. (Ami) **-m/[dz]əŋ*.

Chuang *soŋ (l.t.) "to stand/standing," from *zoŋ. Sek *?yon*, id.

STAND, PERSON (SELF) **(q/)(n)ź[u]ɣ[i]*

IN **diɣi=**(n)diɣi*~**d'iɣi* (NgD. doublet) "stand, person, self" (Ml. *diri* "person," *sĕn/diri* "self," *bĕ/diri* "stand"; NgD. *bă/diri* "to be raised in rank," *d'ihi* "post"; Ho. *andri*=*ndri* "pillar"), app. from **(n)duɣi* through vocalic assim. PO: Sa. *lili* "door post," from **[d]ili* (assim.)<*ndiɣi. Form: East: Thao *mili:li* "stand," from **m/[z]iɣi* by assim. (cf. Sa.); Sai. *miriri?i*, id., from **m/[z]i/[z]i[ɣ]i*; Tsouic (Kan. Saa.) **m/tsiɣi*, id.

T **?yiin* "stand, standing," from **?y[ə]n*<**?y[u]n* (initial effect). Chuang **?din*=**?yin* "standing" (cf. Thai). KS **?yun* "stand/standing": Sui *?yon*~*yon*~*?yuən*, Mak Kam *yun*, Then *yin* (all h.t.). Lk. *yun* (h.t.) "standing," from **?yun* (cf. KS). OB *ćun* "stand up" (Jer.), *zuon*~*zun* (both h.t.) "(ic.) standing" (Sav.), from **?zun*. Li **ću(u)n*: S. Li *ćuon* "stand up; hold oneself erect, be upright, erect; individual (person)"; WS Li *ćuŋ*<*ćun "stand," DC Loi *ćoan*, SW Loi *tsuen*, WS Loi *tsən*, Bup. *tsun*, id.

STAR *[bi](n)tuqan

  IN **bi[t]u²ən, from *bitu²an (stressed form). PPN **fetu²u.
Form. (Pai. Puy.) *bituqan; (Bun. Sai.) *bintuqan.

  T *²di: Nung da:u di (both h.t.) "star"="sky (da:u) star (di)"
(see SUN/STAR/SKY), from *²nti, app. from *[]inti[qan]<
*[]intu[qan] through vocalic assim. KS *²di: Mak ²da:u ²dəi
"constellation" (cf. Nung). Kl. du dɛ (cf. du vuə "sun," du die
"moon"), from *d[an]<*d(w)an<*du(q)an<*ntu(q)an. Lt.
ćoa (Bon.), from *tua<*tu(q)a[n]; also khən (Laj.), from
*khan; both from an earlier *[]tuqan.

  PM *qu(ŋ), from PMY *q[an].

STAR See SUN.

STEAL, THIEF *m[a]li[ŋ]

  IN **maliŋ "thief."

  PM **ńe(ŋ); PY **nim "steal" (Purn. "rob") (MCF MPT
also "rob"); both from an earlier *mḷim<*mḷiŋ (assim.).

STEAM See SMOKE.

STEM See HANDLE.

STERN See OAR.

STICK, n. See HANDLE.

STICK, HANDLE, POST, TREE *(n)ti(y)aŋ

  IN **tiyaŋ "post" (NgD. "mast"). PO *ntia: Fi. ndia "handle,
stick." PPN **tia "stake, post" (Tuamotuan "penis").

  T *deeŋ~*theeŋ (Lao) "stick, bar, ingot" (Shan "a bar or
long piece of anything"), from *(n)teeŋ<*(n)tiaŋ.

  PMY **ntyaŋ=*ntiaŋ "tree, wood."

STICK, v. See PRICK.

STICK (INTO), PUSH INTO, THREAD *(n)tsuk(/(n)tsuk);
    *[tu]tsuk

(I) IN **t'ukt'uk "stick into" (NgD. "strung on"="threaded");
also **t'ut'uk "to stick" (doublet form). PO *(n)su(n)su(k):
Fi. tsotsok/a "to spear fish," Sa. susu/i "to stick something." PPN
*susuk: To. huhuk/i "penetrate," Fu. susuk/i "to stick," Sm.
susu²/i "bore through the stem hole of a coconut."

T *zuk "to push into (stick into ashes, stick a log into fire)" (WT "to thread"), from *nsuk.

(II) IN *[t]ut'uk "to stick."

STICKY See GLUTINOUS.

STING, BARB, NEEDLE *[(n)ts]əŋət
    IN **t'əŋət "sting [stinging part of insect]." PO *nsoŋo: Fi. tsoŋo "barb." PPN *soŋo: Sm. soŋo "penis of child (=the little stinger)."
    T *ŋoot "scorpion (=the stinger)" (Lao), from *(o)ŋot. OB ŋɔʔ~ŋaʔ "needle," from *ŋ[o]t. Li *ŋut, id.: S. Li ŋut, WS Li kot.

STINK See SMELL.

STONE *(qa/)(n)tril[ay]
    Form. (Pai.) *qaṭilay.
    T *thrin. Dioi rin (h.t.), from *[th]rin. Sek riil (h.t.) (Ged.), from *[th]riil (second. vowel length). KS *d[r]i[l]: Sui Then tin, Kam tyin=ćin, Mak tui (all l.t.), from *nt[r]i[l]. OB dien, from *rien<*riin (cf. Sek). Li *siin: S. Li śien, Bup. shin, WS Li ćhiŋ=śiŋ<*śin, Loi dial. sien, from *thrii[l] (cf. Sek).

STONE, GEM, PEARL *(m)ba[]at[u]
    IN **batu=*(m)batu "stone" (Ja. watu "stone," batu "stone-fruit") (Cap. cites *(m)batu). PPN **fatu "stone" (Rarotongan "crop stone," To. "gizzard"). Form. (East; Tsouic; Atayalic) *batu "stone."
    T *pat "gem (Ahom), grains of glass of divers colors (Si.), glass pearls (Lao), pearl (WT)," from *paat(u) (cf. Dioi). Dioi lɔk pat (tone for long vowel) "pupil of the eye" (lɔk is clf. for spherical objects), from *paat. Lq. pə "stone," from *paa[tu].

STONE, ROCK *b[a]las[aq]
    Form. *balasaq "stone (Puy.), intestinal parasite (=calcified mass) (Pai.)"; for the semantics, cf. PPN under STONE/GEM/PEARL.
    T *phra "rock, cliff, mountain" (Shan "flat stone"), from *[b][]ra(saq). Dioi pya "precipice," from *p[r]a. Sek phra "cliff,

rock" (Ged.). KS *pya* "rock, rocky hill": Sui Mak Kam *pya,*
Then *pa,* from *p[r]a.* Lk. *kya=ća* "mountain," from *[pr]a.*

PY *plei* "stone" (Haud.) (Purn. cites PIM **pyei*), from PMY
p[!]ei, from an earlier *p[]las(aq).*

STOP, STOP UP, STOPPER *qa(m)bat; *[tsu](m)bat;*[tu]mpat*
(I) IN **a(m)bat=*ʔa(m)bat* "hinder" (Tg. "stop").

T *hwat~*ʔbat* "to have the nose stopped up": Nung *bat*
"to suffocate," *daŋ wat~daŋ bat* "head cold" (*daŋ* "nose"),
from *hwaat~*ʔbaat<*q(a)bat~*q(ə)bat* (unstressed form).
Dioi *bat* "to cease," from **ʔbat* (cf. Thai).

(II) IN **t'umbat* "stop up/stopper."

(III) IN *tumpat*: Ml. *tumpat* "to stop up, plug."

STOREY See PLATFORM.

STRAW See THIGH.

STRAW, BRAN, CHAFF *[ndza]γam[i]* (51, 62)
IN **dayami=*dayami* (Tg. Ja.)~*d'əyami* (Ml.)=*z̧ayami*
(Dyen) "stalk, straw, stubble," from *[ndz]ayami.*

T *ram* "bran, chaff." Sek *ram* "rice bran."

STREAM, CURRENT *qaγuts; *qaγus*
(I) IN **hayut'~**ayut'=*ʔayut'* "stream." PPN **ʔau* "current."

(II) T *[x]ruay* "stream, torrent," from *q(a)ruy.* N. Thai *qhroi*
"current," from *q(ə)ruy* (unstressed form). Yay *vi* (h.t.) "mountain stream," from *qhrwi<*qhruy.* Sek *ri* (h.t.), id. (Ged.)
(cf. Yay). KS *kuy*: Sui *kui* "stream," Mak *ćui* "large irrigation
canal," from *[qr]uy.*

STRETCH(ED) *[γ][ə](n)təŋ* (16)
IN **γə(n)[t]əŋ* "stretch."

T *tiŋ* "stretched out, tightened" (Si.); also **ʔdiŋ* "pull out,
stretch out" (Si. Lao); both from *( )(n)tiŋ<*( )(n)tyəŋ<
( )(ə)(n)təŋ (palatalized). Li *di:ŋ*: S. Li *yet di:ŋ* "to stretch
(oneself) out" (n.a.), from *nti:ŋ* (cf. Thai).

STRETCH(ED), TIGHT *(kə)(ŋ)krəŋ* (16)
IN **kəŋk'əŋ* "stretched tight."

T *kh[r]ɨŋ "stretch, strain" (Si.). KS: Sui xaŋ "tight," from *[khr][ə]ŋ. Li *kiŋ: S. Li kiŋ "tight," from *k[r]ɨŋ.

PY *gyɔŋ "tight, taut [rope]": HYN gyɔŋ, YCR jɔŋ, from PMY *ŋg[r]ɔŋ (second. voicing).

STRIKE (LINE) See SCRATCH.

STRING See CORD.

STRIP, v. See PULL LENGTHWISE.

STRIPED See COLOR(ED).

SUBMERGE, BURY *ləb/ləb; *(q/)lub/lub

(I) IN **ləbləb "inundate, submerge." PPN **lolo "flood, overflow, "heavy rain." Form: Pai. ləʊləʊ "dip" (Dahl cit.), from *ləbləb; also (Puy: Rikavong) *lə[b]lə[b] "fog/mist."

T *l[i,ɨi]p "submerge" (BT: cw. "water"), from *(lip)lip. Sek lɨp "bury."

(II) T *luup "overwhelm, submerge, overspread" (Shan), from *(lup)lup; also *hlup "obscure, darkish (Si.); deep, profound, sunken (=submerged) (Lao)," from *q/lup.

PY *plup~*pyop (Haud.)=*plop (YCR pyop) "bury," from *[lo]p/lop; also PM *lɔ(ŋ), id.: MPT lo, MCh. lao, from PMY *lo[m], from *lom/lop.

SUCK *tsəp/tsəp; *ts[i]p/ts[i]p; *sup/sup

(I) IN **t'əpt'əp. PO: Sa. toto "suck on." Form. (Paz. Kuv: Ferr.) *tsəptsəp; (Kuv: Tsuchida) *ts/m/[əp]tsəp "suck (as fruit)."

T *soop "to hunt for anything by the sense of smell, to scent a track" (Shan) (for the semantics, cf. III), from *(sop)sop.

(II) Form. (Sir. Fav.) *ts/m/iptsip "suck (as fruit)."

(III) Form. (Bun. Kuv.) *s(/m/)upsup "suck (as fruit)."

T *suup "suck in with mouth, absorb, swallow up (Si.); inhale (Lao); to scent, smell (=inhale odors) (Tho-Nung)"; also "pump," v./n. (Si. Lao), from *(sup)sup.

SUCK See SIP.

SUCK, KISS *[k]ućup

IN ****kuk'up* "kiss" (Ml.). PO *kunsuf/: Fi. *kutsuv/a* "fornicate."

T *ćup~*ćuup (Si. doublet) "suck, kiss," from *(*u*)*ćup*. Dioi *sup,* id. KS: Mak *sup* "kiss."

SUCK, SMOKE, DRINK *(*q*/)*ud;* *q/*ud*/*ud* (13)

(I) Form. (Bun.) *qud "drink."
  T *ut "to smoke" (Lao).

(II) IN *****udud* "to smoke tobacco." Form. (Thao) *smi/*quḍquḍ;* (Sai.) *q/*m*/*uḍquḍ* "suck (as fruit)."

  T *ʔduut~*ʔdoot (Nung doublet) "to suck, inhale, smoke," from *q(*u*)*d*/*ud*.

  Yao: YHN *dut* "suck [breast/fruit], suck in [raw egg], snuff [tobacco]; (cw. "snot") snivel," also *duʔ* "suck blood," from PMY *n[*d*]*ut*, from an earlier *nduut<*(*u*)*ndut* (second. nasalization) (cf. Thai).

SUGARCANE *[(*n*)*t*]*o*[*b*]*os* (51, 104, 126)

IN ***təbu=*təbus(*u*): Tg. *tubo,* TB. Ja. Ml. *těbu,* NgD. *tewu;* also (Blust 1969) Lemiting (Borneo) *sau,* Long Kiput (Borneo) *těso,* from *tubus(*u*) (stressed form). PO *(*n*)*tofu*: Fi. *ndovu,* Sa. *e*/*ohu.* Form. (Ruk.) **tubus;* (Pai. Bun.) **təbus;* (Sai.) *ka/*təbus;* (Tsouic) *(*qə*/)*təbus* (s₁) (all except Rukai are unstressed forms; cf. IN).

T *ooy (Ahom also "sweet"), from *(*o*)*woy*<*(*o*)*boy*< *(*o*)*bos.* Dioi *ɔi* (l.t.), from *(*w*)*ooy* (cf. Thai). KS *oy: Sui *ʔoi*~*ʔui,* Mak *ʔoi* (cf. Thai). Li *ooy: S. Li *ɔi* "maize"; for the semantics, cf. Mak *həu pya* "corn" (*həu* "rice/cereal"), OB *phia* (Jer.), *tea* (Sav.) "cooked rice"; also Hova "sugarcane" under RICE (PLANT); also RICE/SUGARCANE.

SUN See DAY; LIGHT (two entries).

SUN, STAR, SKY *(*q*/)*a*(*n*)*draw;* *(*q*/)*a*[*t*]*raw*

(I) IN ***a(*n*)*daw*~***ha(*ŋ*)*g'aw*=*[*ʔ*]*a*(*n*)*z̧aw* (after Dyen) "day, sun"; cf. Bisayan *adlaw* "day" (Dyen analyzes as metathesized form with infixed *l*). PO ***qanso "daylight, day, sun." PPN ***ʔaho~***ʔaso (Fu. Sm. doublet; cited by Demp.) "day (as opposed to night)" (Tuamotuan "daylight"), from ***a(*n*)*so.*

Form. (Pai.) *qadaw "sun"; also (Puy.) *kadaw and (Sed.) *-daw, id.

T *ʔdaaw "star" (Nung da:u di="sky star"; see STAR), from *q(a)draw. Sek traaw "star" (Ged.), from *ʔdraaw (cf. Thai). KS *ʔdaaw: Mak ʔda:u ʔdəi "constellation (stars)" (cf. Nung). Li *raaw "star": S. Li dra:u, WS Li rau, N. Li dial. rau~lau, from *(a)raw (cf. Thai Sek).

(II) T *[t]hraaw "open air, sky" (SW), usu. in comp. *klaaŋ-[t]hraaw="the middle (*klaaŋ) of the sky ([t]hraaw)," from *(q/)(a)traw (with second. aspir. by the *q/). Lk. tau wan "sun," tau ʔbliet "star" (cf. Nung and Mak under I), with tau ="sky."

SUNKEN See SINK INTO.

SUPERPOSE See PILE UP.

SUPPORT, LEAN ON *[(m)b]antu
IN **bantu=*(m)bantu "support" (Ml. "help, aid, assist").

T *daw "support, lean on," from *ntaw<*(a)ntu; also *may daw~*(may) du (Lao) "(walking) stick, cane" (*may "wood"), from *(a)ntu~*(ə)ntu (unstressed form). Dioi tau (l.t.) "prop up," from *dau<*ntau (cf. Thai).

SURFACE See FLAT (two entries).

SWALLOW, v. *[]dun; *[d/]l/un; *[]tən; *( )t/l/ən
(I) T *dun "give a drink to (=make swallow) a sick or helpless person" (Shan). Dioi dun (irreg. l.t.) "swallow gluttonously," from *[]dun. KS *ʔdun: Mak ʔdun, from *[]dun.

(II) IN **lunlun "gulp down," a partially reduplicated form from an original *d/lun/lun<*d/l/un.
OB lun "swallow down" (cf. IN).

(III) T *ton "give a drink to (=make swallow)" (Shan), a doublet (s.t., high series) of form cited under I.

(IV) IN **tələn, from *t/l/ən. PO *tolo: Fi. vi/tolo, Sa. hi/olo "(desire to swallow)=be hungry" (cf. IN).

T *kliin (gen. SW), app. from an earlier *tliin<*tələn (dissim., or poss. vocalic effect); also in (Kh. Shan), from *(təl̟)ən; also *nɨn (Tho-Nung), from the reduplicated form: *(ɨ)n/ɨn. Sek *tlɨn* (for *tlɨ:n*), probably from *klɨɨn (Sek regularly has *tl-<*kl-*).

SWEEP See WINNOW.

SWEEP, DUST, SHAKE, BROOM *[ta]pə(t)s; [ta]paʦ(/pats)

(I) Form: East *tapəs: Pai. *t′apəs~t′/m/apəs* "winnow" (Dahl cit.), from "sweep" (see WINNOW/SWEEP for semantics).

PY *phwot: YCR *phwot* "sweep; clear away," YHN *phɔt* "to dust" (cw. "dust"), from *phə[ts], app. from a secondary *pəts/pəts (cf. IN under II).

(II) IN **pat′pat′ "to shake, clear" (Ho. "to sweep, clean," NgD. "broom; sweep"), probably from *(ta)pats/pats (cf. Paiwan), perhaps through vocalic assim. from an earlier *(ta)pəts/pəts.

T *pat "to sweep, brush (clothes), dust" (Si. also "shake"); *ńu pat "broom"="the sweeping (*pat) straw (*ńu)," from *(ta)pats. Dioi *pat* "broom; to sweep."

SWEET See BEE.

SWEET, BEE *m[a]mlets (24, 100)

IN **mamit′~*manit′ "sweet," from an original *mamlit′ (with -m- preserved in the former through assim. to the initial). PPN *mami: Fu. *mami* "sweet," Sm. *mami* "sugere in coitu." Form. (Saa.) *mami[ts] "sweet."

T *mim "hornet" (Si: ic.); "sp. of small bee" (Lao); also *min "kind of small bee of the woods which produces savory honey" (WT), app. from *mim(lit)~*min(it), from *mamlit (with vocalic assim.). Lk. *mlet* "bee."

SWEET, BEE, WASP, HORNET *( )(n)t[a]boq; *t[a]boq/an
(45, 100)

(I) Form. (Puy.) *tabuq "sweet"; also (Ata.) *buq "honey."

T *to "hornet" (Si. "kind of wasp"), from *[]tób(oq)< *[]táb(oq) (vocalic assim.). KS *ʔdu: Mak ʔdəu "kind of large bee," from *[]nt[o] (cf. Thai). Li *[bw]ok: WS Li fɔk "honeybee," from *(to)bóq (with vocalic assimilation, as in Thai, but with contrasting stress).

Miao: MPT *ntau* "sp. of wasp, of hornet" (Sav.), from PM **ntau*, from PMY **nt[o]* (cf. Mak).

(II) IN ****tabuʔan* "bumble-bee (Ja.), wasp (Ml.)," from **tabuʔ/an*="the sweet one"; also (Blust 1973: note to No. 79) **tabuʔuan*: Maranao *taboʔoan* "large bee," Bukidnon Manobo *tevuʔuan* "social wasp," app. a secondary formation (cf. Formosan forms). Form: Fav. *tappoesan*=**tapusan* "honey-bee," app. from **tapuqan*, for **tabuqan*.

SWELL UP   **[kə](m)boŋ; **[kə](m)poŋ; **[kə](m)baŋ*
(I)   IN ****kə(m)buŋ* (Ml. "to swell, swollen").

T **booŋ* "to swell, puff up," from **(o)boŋ*. Li **booŋ*: S. Li *bɔŋ* "belly (=a swelling)"; cf. BELLY^{III} (**[kə]mpuŋ*).

(II) T **poŋ* "to swell, become big (as the belly)" (Si.). Dioi *pɔŋ* "puffed up, distended." KS: Mak *poŋ* "to rise (water)."

Yao: YCR *boŋ* (h.t.) "to rise (as leavened dough)," from PMY **mpoŋ*.

(III) IN ****ka(m)baŋ*~****kəmbaŋ* "to swell up, come into bloom."

SWIM, FLOAT   **la[ŋ]oy*

IN ****laŋuy* "swim." Form. (Ruk.) **wa/laŋuy;* (Sai. Paz.) **la/laŋuy;* (Puy: Rikavong Ami Kuv.) **m/laŋuy;* (Pai. Sir.; Atayalic) **l/m/aŋuy;* (Tsouic) **(maka/)laŋuy* "swim."

T **looy*~**hlooy* (WT)~**luy* (Shan) "swim, float," from **(h)lo(ŋ)oy*<**(h)la(ŋ)oy* (vocalic assim.). KS: Mak *lui* "float" (cf. Thai). Li **ley*: S. Li *lei* "swim," from **lay*<**la(ŋo)y* (contrast Thai Mak).

SWING (ARMS)   See MOVE BACK AND FORTH.

SWING, SHAKE, QUAKE, TREMBLE   **[a]yon*

IN **ayun* "swing" (Ml. "swing, rock, oscillate"). PO **esu* (unstressed form): Sa. *esu* "to be unstable," *esu/esu* "earthquake."

T **yoon* "shake, vibrate, tremble (as floor when walking upon it) (Shan); oscillate, balance (Si.)," from **(o)yon*<**(ə)yon* (unstressed form).

SWORD   See KNIFE (three entries).

T

TABU **[ta](m)buŋ; *[ta]mbun* (71)

(I) Cham *tabuŋ* "tabou; interdiction religieuse; interdit, prohibé, défendu; funeste, fatal, néfaste; malheureux, désastreux; esprit des animaux morts." PPN ****tapu** "forbidden [=tabu]," from **tampu.*

Miao: MPT *mpo* (l.t.) "bad omen, pertaining to tabu," from PM **mb[ɔ(ŋ)]*, from PMY **mb[om]*, from an earlier **mboŋ* (assim.).

(II) T **hmun* "bad omen" (Lao), from **[]mbun.*

TADPOLE See FROG.

TAIL, BUTTOCKS, ANUS **[(m)b]u(n)tut; *[mbu]nt/l/ut; *[mbu](n)t/l/ut*

(I) IN ****buntut** "tail" (NgD. "sting of a bee"). Form: Paz. *mutut* "buttocks," from **mbutut.*

T **tuut* "anus" (Si.), from **(-u)tut.*

PMY **twei* "tail," *from *[]tui.*

(II) Form: Paz. *dulut* "tail," from **ntulut<*(mbu)nt/l/ut.*

(III) T **sut* "end," from **t/r/ut.* Dioi *śɔt,* id., from **ćɔt* (vocalism influ. by **/r/*). KS **[]zot* "tail": Sui *zət∼hət,* Mak *zut* *∼zət,* Then *thet* (all h.t.), from **[]nsot* (cf. Thai). OB *tuʔ,* id., from **su[t].* Li **sut,* id.: S. Li *śut,* WS Li *ćhut=śut* (cf. Thai).

TALL See HIGH.

TARO See FLOWER; TUBER (EDIBLE).

TEACH See SPEAK.

TEN See INTRODUCTION.

TESTICLES See FRUIT.

THAT (ONE) **[i]ya; *[i]ya/n* (28, 29)

(I) IN ****iya** "he/she." PPN ****ia,** id. Form. (Sai.) **siya,* id.; also (Sai. Paz.) **/siya* "they," from **s/iya* (see INTRODUCTION: PRONOUNS).

(II) IN ****iyan* "that." PO **ia* "this" (Blust 1972): Sa. *ie*, Mota *ia* (for the semantic reversal, cf. THIS/HERE).

T **yen* "that one" (Tho).

THATH (ONE), THERE[I]   **na; *(q/)na/n*

(I) IN **/ńa* "his/her" (enclitic genitive form): Ml. */ńa* (Dyen 1974); also (Blust 1970) Cebuano Bisayan *naa* "there (near addressee)," from **[ń]a;* app. from an earlier **na + iya* (see root under THAT (ONE)). PO **/ńa* "his/her" (enclitic genitive form): Bugotu */ńa* (Dyen 1974). PPN ***n[a,aa]* "there (near addressee)," also "possessive article," from **[ń]a.* Form. (Tsouic) **na*: Saa. *na:na* "there" (cf. *na:ni* "here"), *kanaʔa* "that" (cf. *kaniʔi* "this"), app. from an earlier **ńa* (cf. IN).

Li **na*: S. Li *na* "he/she," Ki Ha SC Loi *na* "he," Bup. *no*<**na* "he/they," WS Li *na* "that/there."

(II) T **nan* "that" (Si. Lao also "he/she"); also **hnan* (s.t., high series) "there," from **(q/)nan;* cf. THIS/HERE for prefixed element. Lk. *nan* "that."

PM ***ne(n);* PY **n[]*=**n[a]n* "he/she": YHN *nan*, YHA *nen*, YCR *nin*; both from PMY **na(n).*

THATH (ONE), THERE[II]   **ts[i]dra(/n)*

IN ***tʼida* "they"; Yami *sira-itu*, id. (for -*itu*, see THAT/ THEY).

T **thran* "that (one, place), there" (Shan Lao) (Kh. has irreg. *than* "there"), from **s[i]dra/n;* also **[d]ran* (s.t., low series) (Lao doublet), the abbreviated **(-dra/n)* form.

THATH, THEY   **[i](n)tu*

IN ***i[t]u* "this (Tg. Ho.), that (Ml.)" (Ml. also *s/itu* "there"). Yami -*itu* "he," also "that (near)" (Og.-As.); *sira-itu* "they," *u-itu* "that" (cf. *u-ya* "this") (Ferr.). Form. (Thao) **itu-* "there," but note Pai. -*itsu*<**-itu* "this."

Lk. *tu* (l.t.) "they," from **du*<**ntu.* Lq. *to*, id. Lt: BP *a/to* "that."

THATCH (-GRASS), GRASS   **(a)(N)qa(n)[təp]; *( )NGa(n)[təp]*

(I) IN ***hatəp~**atəp*=**ʔatəp* "thatch/roof covering" (Ml. "thatch, usu. of palm leaves; hence any roof covering"; NgD. "palm frond as building material"). PO ***ʔatop* "thatch; the sago palm [for thatching]"; cf. Chowning: "the [Melanesian] name *hato* for 'sago' means 'thatch' in some present-day languages and reflects a Proto-Austronesian *hatəp* for 'thatch.'" PPN **ʔato* "thatch" (Easter Island "to roof," Marquesan "build a house").

T *γa "thatch grass," from *Ga<*Nqa. Dioi *ha* (l.t.) "kind of couch-grass," *ran ha* "house (*ran*) covered with this grass," from *Ga (cf. Thai). KS *ʔGa "thatch grass": Sui Mak Kam Then *ya* (all h.t.), from *[]Nqa. Li *hña, id.: S. Li *ha*, WS Li *ña*, from *[]ŋya<*[]Nq]a.

PMY *Nqaan "thatch grass," from *(a)Nqan[təp].

(II) T *hña "grass," from *[]NGa. Dioi *ña* (h.t.), id., from *hña (cf. Thai). Yay *ñia*, Sek *ñua* (both h.t.) (Ged.), from *hñya (cf. Thai). Li *ŋen, id.: S. Li *ŋen*, N. Li *ka:n*, Loi dial. *kan*, from *ŋgan<*[NG]an.

THERE See THAT (ONE) (two entries).

THEY See THAT.

THICK (LIQUIDS) See COAGULATE.

THICK, DENSE *(n)təb[əl]

(I) IN **təbəl "thick [both senses: 'not thin,' also 'dense']."

(II) T *təp~*thɨp (Lao doublet) "thick, entangled" (SW); also *dɨp "thick, dense" (Si.), all from *( )(n)təp<*( )(n)təb(əl).

THIEF See STEAL.

THIGH See FLAT.

THIGH, BONE, STALK *(m)paqa; *( )paqa/i (17, 18)

(I) IN **paʔa "thigh, stalk." PPN **faʔa=**faʔa~*paʔa "stalk [esp. leaf-stalk, petiole]" (Fi. *baa* "stalk of taro leaves"); also (To. Fu.) *paʔapaʔa "stalk" (forms cited by Demp.); all from *(m)paqa. Form. *paqa "thigh (Puy.), leg (Sir.)."

T *xa "thigh/leg" (WT also "paw"). Dioi *ka* "thigh," from *qa. Sek *kwa* "leg" (Ged.), from *qwa<*(p-)qa (labialized). KS *qwa, id.: Sui *pa~qa*, Mak *ka*, Then Kam *pa* (Mak "thigh, leg; branch [of river]; side [of firetongs]"), from *(p-)qa (cf. Sek). Lk. *kwa* (l.t.) "bran (=stalks)," from *[qw]a (cf. KS).

OB *wa* "bone" (Jer.), *mai-wa* "thigh" (Jer.), from *qwa (cf. KS Lk.). Li *[q]a: S. Li *ha* "clf. for trousers (=trouser leg)," WS Li Bas. Loi dial. *ha*, Mef. *ka* "thigh."

(II) IN **paʔi "thigh, stalk" (NgD. "bone, thigh"), from *paqa/i (vocalism influ. by *q). Form. *paqi "buttocks (Thao: Ferr.), hips (Thao: Dyen cit.), bran (=stalks) (Ata.)," from *paqa/i (cf. IN).

Miao: MCF *pa*, MPT *pua* "thigh," from PM *pua/puɛ, from PMY *p[aa]y, from *[]pa(q)a/i.

THIS, HERE   *[i]nəy; *q/nəy

(I) IN **ini: Tg. *d/ini* "here," Ml. *ini* "this," Ho. *ini* "that." PO *ini: Sa. *ini* "a certain," U. *ini* "that" (cf. the semantic reversal in Ho.). PPN **nei "here, near speaker." Form. (Tsou; Sed.) *(i)ni; (Paz.) *m/ini; (Puy.) *ini/a "this"; also (Paz. Sai.) *d/ini "here" (cf. Tg.); cf. also Ami *uni* "this."

T *ni (Si. Lao BT WT)~*nay (Ahom Kh. Shan)~*ni/nay (Nung) "this." Dioi Sek *ni*, id. KS *naːy, id.: Sui *nai*, Mak Then Kam *naːi*. Lk. *ni* "this," but *wan nai* "today"="this (*nai*) day (*wan*)." Li *n[ey] "this/here": S. Li *nei*, WS Li *ne*. Lt: BP *nay*, MP *ni* "this (one)."

Yao: YCR *nai* (l.t.) "that, these (close to person addressed)," from PMY *nay; for semantic reversal, cf. THAT/THERE (Tg. Ho. "this").

(II) PO *[ʔ]a[n]i: Arosi *ani* "that one, referring to something already mentioned; that one, there, referring to something out of sight" (cit. by Blust 1972); for the semantic reversal, cf. Yao under (I). Form: Ata. *qani* "this/here"; cf. also Puy. *kaniʔaʔ* "here" (*ʔiniʔaʔ* "this"); Saa. *kaniʔi* "this (*naːni* "here").

T *hni~*hnay "here" (s.t., high series) (distribution parallel to doublet under I), from *(q/)ni~*(q/)nay; cf. THAT (ONE)/THERE for prefixed element, showing exact parallelism in Thai.

PMY *ʔn[]=*ʔnay~*ʔney (secondarily nasalized in Miao) "this/here": YCR *nai* (h.t.) "this (close to speaker)."

THORN   *(n)dzuRi; *dzuRi/a; *dzuRi/an (10)

(I)   IN **$[dd]u\gamma i =$*$[dd]uRi$, from *$[ndz]uRi$. PO **$su\gamma i$ "bone, needle." PPN **hui "bone," from *$nsui$. Form. (Pai. Bun.) *$dzu\gamma i$.

(II)   SEP *$suri/a$: cf. Capell: "the west and central [languages] have a suffixed -a that is presumably an article."

(III) T *$sian \sim$ *$yian$ (Ahom), from an earlier *$zian <$*$dzian$ <*$dzi(r)i/an$. N. Thai: Dioi ɔn, Yay ʔwan, from *$uan <$ *$(zur)u/an$. Sek ʔo:n (Haud.), ʔɔn (Ged.) (cf. N. Thai). KS: Mak dun, from *$[dz]un <$*$[dz]ur(i)$. Li *$hian$: S. Li $hi:n$, from *$hyaan <$*$syaan$ (cf. Thai).

THOU   See INTRODUCTION.

THREAD, n.   See YARN.

THREAD, v.   See STICK (INTO).

THREE   See INTRODUCTION.

THROW   *$(s/)b[u]li(y)a\eta$ (20, 60)
   Form. (Ata.) *$s/buli\eta \sim$ *$m/buli\eta$ (Eg.), *$m/b\partial li\eta$ (Og.) "throw"; also (Og.) $muli\eta$ "throw away," from *$b/m/uli\eta$.

   T *$phlee\eta$ "to muster all one's strength, throw (as in shooting an arrow" (Si.), from *$phlia\eta <$*$(s/)b[]lia\eta$ (second. unvoicing/ aspir.); also *$phr[ia]\eta$ "throw off" (Ahom), from *$phriya\eta$. KS *$pee\eta$: Sui $pe:\eta$ "shoot (arrow)," Mak $pe:\eta$ "throw, shoot (arrow)," from *$p[l]ia\eta$; also *$pia\eta$: Then $pya:\eta$ "shoot (gun)," from *$p[l]iya\eta$ (cf. Thai).

THROW, FLING   *$(m)b[a]la\eta$
   IN **$bala\eta =$*$(m)bala\eta$ "fling" (Ja. "throw").

   OB $ha\eta$ "throw," from *$[d]a\eta$. Li *$[d]a\eta$: S. Li $da\eta$ "fling, throw," from *$b(a)la\eta$.

THRUST INTO   See DIG INTO.

THRUST THROUGH/INTO   *$tso(n)zol$
   IN **$t'undul$ "thrust" (Tg. "to stick," Ml. "thrust with horns").

   T *son "thrust [bar] through [hole] (Shan), thread [needle] (Si.), plait [mat] (WT)"; also *zon (s.t., low series) "thrust forward or into (esp. fuel into fire)" (app. variable stress).

THUNDER   See CRY (OF ANIMAL); ROAR; RUMBLE.

TICKLE, ARMPIT *k[i]li(/k[i]li); *k[i]li(/k[i]li);
*kele(/kele); *qele/q(ele); *q[e]le(/q[e]le)

(I) IN **kili "shoulder"=*kili/: Tg. kili/ti "tickling" (not
cited by Demp.)~*kilikili: Tg. kilikili "armpit" (Demp: "shoulder"); also **kilik "armpit" (Ho.), shoulder (Ja.), carry under
the arm (Ml.), carry [=under the arm] an infant (Tg.)," from
*kili/k(ili). Cham kəlĕk "tickle" (Blood), from *k[i]l[i]k (cf. IN).
PO *ki(l,r)i: Fi. kili~kiri "armpit" [Hazlewood], kiri "tickle
under the armpits [Capell], Nggela kilikili "tickle a tired pig
under the belly to make it go" (cit. from Blust 1972).

T *kări: Kh. ćuŋ kări "tickle" (n.a.). Li *[r]i: S. Li di
"armpit."

(II) T *kăli: Kh. kap kăle (prn. kăli) "armpit"; also *kălit:
Shan sop kălit "armpit" (n.a.), app. by assim. (*k>t after i)
from *kălik<*kăli/k(ăli) (cf. IN).

(III) T *(ke)re "armpit" (Ahom ke-re, Shan hɛ>*rɛ, Si. rɛ,
both ic.); also *rek "tickle a person under the armpit" (Ahom),
from *(ke)re/k(ere).

(IV) IN *(ʔ)irək=*(ʔ)ilək (Kelabit)~*(ʔ)irək (Bukidnon
Manobo and Cebuano Bisayan) "armpit" (Blust 1970), app.
from *ʔili/ʔ(ili).

(V) PPN **maʔene "tickle" (*i>e after *q); also **nene "or-
gasm, sensory pleasure" (Marquesan "tickle, excite"), from
*(ʔe)ne/(ʔe)ne "(clitoral) tickling." Form: East (Fav.) *li[q]li[q]
"armpit," from *[qi]li/[qi]li; Tsouic (Tsou) *l[]qil[]qi, id., from
*qil[i]/qil[i]; Atayalic (Ata.) *liliq, id., from *q[i]li/q[i]li.

OB sɔp lek~sap lek (h.t.) "armpit" (n.a.; cf. Shan under II),
from *hlek<*qleq<*q(e)le/q(eleq).

TIE See BIND; KNOT.

TIE, ENLACE *[b]ə[ɣ][ə](ŋ)kots
IN **bəkət'=*bəɣkət' "bundle" (Tg. bigkis "bundle, waist-
band; bound, to tie"; Ml. bĕrkas, TB. borhos "bundle"); Proto-
Philippine *bəɣkəs~*bɑɣkəs "to tie around" (Teduray "tie in
a bundle") (Charles cit.); app. from an original *bəɣ[ə]kuts (assim. backward); also **buŋkut' "bundle," app. from *bə[ɣ]ŋkut'

(assim. forward). PO *po(ŋ)ko: Sa. ho²o "to bind magically," i/ho²o~hoko "bundle," from *bə[γ](n)kə[ts] (cf. IN). Form: Sir. vugot "bind," from *bugu[ts]<*buŋku[ts] (assim. forward, as in IN).

T *koot "embrace" (Si. Lao also "enlace"), from *(o)kot. OB kɔt (l.t.) "tie up [boat, buffalo, hands and feet], enlace," kɔt mɔk hut "make a knot (hut)," tuk pha kɔt hau "turban" (hau "head"), from *gɔt<*(o)ŋkot.

TIGER   See CAT.

TIGER, CAT   *s[a]rimaw
   IN **haḷimaw=*harimaw "beast of prey" (Ml. "tiger").
   T *me(e)w~*ml[e,ee]w (Ahom doublet) "cat," from *myaw <*(-i)maw and *mlyaw<*(ḷi)maw (by metathesis); also *hmeew (Nung: F. K. Li), id., from *hmyaw<*[sr]imaw. Dioi mɛu (h.t.), id. from *hmeew (cf. Nung). OB niu, id., from *mliu (cf. Ahom). Li *mliaw, id.: S. Li WS Li SH Loi Bas. Mef. miu, Ha miou, DC Loi miau, but Bup. niau, WS Loi niu (cf. OB). Kl. lə mɛ, id. (n.a.).
   PY *maaw "tiger (YTP), weasel (YHN: cw. "tiger")"~*maw "tiger (YCR)," perh. also Yao: PIM **lom "cat," from PY *[ḷ]om, from PMY *[r]om, from *[]rəm(aw) (unstressed form).

TIGHT   See STRETCH(ED).

TIMBER   See TRUNK.

TOAD   See FROG (three entries).

TONGUE   See LICK.

TOOTH¹   *ip[a]n
   IN **ipən=*(ŋ/)ipən (Tg. ŋipin, Ho. nifi), showing an old IN article *ŋ/ (Capell; cf. NAME), app. from an earlier *(ŋ/)ipan (stressed form); Yami *ŋəpən (both syllables unstressed). PO **nipon~**lipon, from */ipon (cf. IN). PPN **nifo, from */ifo (cf. PO). Form: East (Bun.) *nipən; (Sai.) *nəpən (unstressed form); (Thao) *nipin (assim. form), all from *n/ipən (cf. PO PPN); also Atayalic (Ata.) *γapən/; (Sed.) *γəpən (unstressed form), app. from an earlier compound: *[-i]pən.

T *van~*ven (Lao) "teeth (Si.); jaw/jawbone (Lao); teeth (of harrow) (Nung: Sav.), teeth (ic. "gums") (Nung: F. K. Li), from *[]pwan, app. from an earlier *(u)pan, for *(i)pan. Dioi *fan* (l.t.), only ic: *fan ruao* "teeth of harrow" (n.a.), *fan hεu* "denture (teeth and jaws)" (*hεu* "teeth"), from *van (cf. Thai). KS *pw(y)an: Kam *pyan*, Sui *wyan~vyan*, Then *wen* (all h.t.), from *(u)pan (cf. Thai). Lk. *wan* (cf. KS). OB *tiem*<*tien (Jer.), *tɔn*<*tan (Sav.), from *[]tyan<*[]pyan<*(i)pan, showing retention of the earlier *i vocalism. Li *phw(y)an: S. Li *phen~fen*, WS Li *fa:ŋ*<*fa:n, Bas Ki Ha Loi dial. *fan*, from *(u)pan with second. aspiration (cf. Thai KS); also *[sy]an: Bup. *saŋ*<*san, Mef. *xien=sien*, from *phyan<*(i)pan with second. aspiration (cf. OB), indicating a basic *(u)pan~*(i)pan doublet at the proto-Li level. N. Kl. *paŋ*, S. Kl. *du pio* (for *du*, cf. *dɔ bu ŋu* "neck"), from Kl. *p(y)a[n]<*(i)pan.

TOOTH[II] *(t]aGi(/Gi)

IN **gigi, from *(ta)gi(/gi). Cham *tagei*, from *tagi. Form: Sir. *gidauw* "front tooth," app. from *(ta)gi-.

Li *hay: S. Li *hai* "clf. for tooth," from *(a)hi.

TOOTH, IVORY, ELEPHANT *ga(n)diaŋ; *kadiaŋ (86, 87, 117, 119)

(I)   IN **gadiŋ "ivory."
      Sek *ne:ŋ* "tooth," from *ndeeŋ<*ndíaŋ.

(II)   T *jaaŋ "elephant," from *gyaaŋ<*ga(d)yaŋ<*ga(d)iáŋ; this is distinct from the very early Chinese loan from the same source: Ch. *siaŋ* "elephant"<"ivory" (the earlier meaning), Anc. *ẑiaŋ*, Arch. *dziaŋ*, from *yaŋ (normal shift)<*(gad)iáŋ. Dioi *saŋ* (l.t.) "elephant," from *ja[a]ŋ (cf. Thai). Sek *sa:ŋ* (l.t.), id., from *jaaŋ (cf. Thai Dioi). OB *seaŋ* (l.t.), id., from *ja[a]ŋ (cf. Thai). Kl. *kho*, id., from *thyo<*thy[aŋ], from *[d]yaŋ (cf. Thai). Lt. *mso*, id., from *mtyo<*mty[aŋ], from *[nd]yaŋ (cf. Sek under I).

   PMY *dzhaaŋ "elephant": Miao: MCF *shaŋ* (l.t.), from PM *dzhaŋ; Yao: YCR *tsaaŋ* (l.t.), from *dz[h]aaŋ, from an earlier *gyaaŋ (cf. Thai).

(III) Form. (Atayalic) *kadaŋ "molar tooth," from *kad[ia]ŋ (vocalic assim.).

PY *kyaŋ "elephant": YHN kyaŋ<PKM *kyaŋ; PIM *ćwaŋ ~ćaŋ (Haud.), from *k(ad)iáŋ (paralleling Thai, which has *jaaŋ<*gyaaŋ<*ga(d)iáŋ).

TOOTH (MOLAR)   See JAW.

TRAP   *ts[a]ru (57)
IN **t'əlu=**t'əru "trap" (TB "rat trap"), from *t'aru (stressed form).

T *haaw "trap for transfixing wild animals (Shan), trap (piège) (Lao)," from *sraaw/hraaw<*s(a)ru.

TRAP   See ENCLOSURE.

TREE   See STICK; TRUNK.

TREMBLE   See SHAKE.

TROUGH, DISH   *[d]ulaŋ
IN **dulaŋ (Ja. ḍulaŋ is irregular) "food vessel (*Essunterlage*)" (Ja. "food dish," Ml. "salver or tray, usu. of wood," NgD. "trough"); also (Blust 1970) Cebuano Bisayan "wooden basin for washing," Hanunoo "shallow wooden tub or basin."

T *raaŋ "trough" (Shan also "large wooden bowl cut out for holding water," WT also "oval iron dish"), from *rwaaŋ<*ruwáŋ <*(u)ráŋ. KS *duaŋ: Mak du:ŋ "trough; wooden trough for feeding pigs; box; (cw. "ink") inkstand," from *ruaŋ<*rúwaŋ <*(ú)raŋ (contrast Thai). OB doaŋ "trough," from *ruaŋ (cf. Mak).

TRUNK, TREE, TIMBER, PLATFORM   *(m)bataŋ
IN **bataŋ "trunk, pole, stage/platform." PO **pata(ŋ) "shelf, tree-trunk." PPN **fata "shelf" (Maori "elevated stage for food storage").

T **?daŋ "upright/supporting timber" (Si. "the middle timber which rises to the roof"), from *( )ntaŋ. Lk. ta:ŋ (l.t.) "trunk," from *daaŋ<*(a)ntaŋ (cf. Thai). Lt: MP mme, BP ma te (Rob.), mia te (Bon.) "tree," from *m[b]ata[ŋ].

TUBE   See BORE.

TUBER, SWEET POTATO *[ga](n)doŋ
  IN **gaduŋ "name of a tuber."
  OB nɔŋ kɔk "sweet potato" (n.a.), from *n[d]ɔŋ kɔk.

TUBER (EDIBLE), TARO, SWEET POTATO, YAM
  *(m)p[r,l]al̩[əts]; *(m)p[r,l]al̩i; *mb[r,l]al̩i

(I) IN **talət' "taro." PO **ntalo(s) "taro, Colocasia sp., taro variety." PPN **talo "taro (Colocasia)."

(II) Form: East *(n)tal̩i "taro" (Ami Ruk. Bun. Thao), sweet potato (Kuv: Taintor 1874); Tsouic (Tsou) *[ə]tsa[l̩]i; Atayalic (Ata.) *tsa[l̩]i- "taro."

(III) PMY **ndɔi "yam": MCF "yams and sweet potatoes"; MPT (ic.) "turnip" and "carrot"; YCR "edible tuber; (ic.) potato; turnip"; YHN "tuber; (ic.) yam; sweet potato," from *ndawi < *ndal̩i; YHN also di (doublet of dɔi), from *nd(a)wi, and don (di don "sweet potato," fan don "potato"), from *ndal̩(i).

TURN, RETURN *(m)b[a]l̩ik; *(m)b[a]l̩ik/(m)b[a]l̩ik (20)
(I) IN **balik=*(m)balik "reverse side; to turn upside down" (Ml. "to turn, return; on the contrary").

(II) PO: Fi. mbali/mbali "foolish" (="turned upside down").
    T *blik "turn, return" (Lao "turn, as from one side to the other; return"; WT "turn, make a half-turn, return"), from *(blik/)blik.

TURN, WIND *(q/)b[i]l̩it
  IN **bilit "to wrap (=wind around)"; also **bəlit (unstressed form) "to wind" (Ml. "a coil, turn; a necklace or a bandage; to encircle, as a snake"). PO *feli: Fi. veli "wound around, a curl." PPN **firi=*fili "plait, braid (=wind)" (Tikopian fi/firi "necklet, girdle of flowers"). Form: Sir. parit=[b]ărit "turn around," from *bəl̩it.
  Sek ʔbli:t "to spin (make turn) a top," from *ʔb(i)lit.

TWIN *[a]piaj; *p/[a]piaj
(I) IN *apij (Blust 1972bis): Palawan Batak ʔapid, Singhi anak ber-opid "twins," Kadazan maŋ-apid "marry two wives," Uma Juman apir "either of the halves of two things joined." PO *apis: Roviana avisi "twins, when of the same sex" (Blust, 1972bis).

(II) IN *p/apij*: Uma Juman *p-apir* "twins" (Blust 1972bis).

T *feet* (Si. Lao)~*fe*=/*fee*/ (Shan), from *feej* (>*feet* ~*fee* rather than *feey* or *fey*, forms excluded in the phonemic pattern of Thai), from *fiaj*<*phwiaj*<*(p/)phiaj*.

TWIN   See PAIR.

TWIN, DOUBLE(D), TWO   *(N)qa(m)bar*

IN **kə(m)bal*=*(ŋ)kə(m)bar* "twin" (Ja. *kĕbar* "doubled," *kĕmbar* "twin"), from *(ŋ)ka(m)bar* (stressed form), from *(N)qa(m)bar*. SEP *kampa*: Motu *hɛ-kapa* "twins," Roro *aka-bani* "eight"="pair of fours."

KS: Mak *wa* "twin" (cf. OB). OB *vən* (Jer.), *bə:n* (h.t.) (Sav.) "two," from *hwən*<*q[]wan*.

PMY *(a)war*~*(ə)wər* "two"; Purn. cites PM **ɔ[] and PY **i*, but forms are highly irregular: PW **ɔu(ŋ), from PM *ɔ(ŋ) <*on*<*(ə)(w)ər* (unstressed form, with vocalic assim.); PE **ɔ, from PM *ɔu*<*ɔi*<*(w)ər*; MKC MWN *a*, from PM *uɛ* <*aay*<*(a)(w)ar*; MHY *i*, from PM *ei*<*ɔi*<*way*; also PT MYT *va*, from PM *way*<*war*; PY *(w)i*: YCR YHN *i*, but YTP *vi*, from *(w)əy*<*(w)ər* (cf. PW).

TWO   See INTRODUCTION; PAIR (two entries); TWIN.

U

UNCLE   See GRANDPARENT.

UNITE   See JOIN.

UP (ABOVE/UP)   See CLIMB.

UPROOT   See LEVER.

URINE (/URINATE)   See SQUIRT (two entries).

V

VARIEGATED   See COLOR(ED).

VESSEL, JAR, PAN, BASIN   *baŋ[a]*; *b/l/aŋ[a]* (55, 108)

(I)   IN **baŋa*: Tg. *baŋa* "jar"; Yami *baŋa*~*vaŋa* "earthenware pot (for cooking rice)."

(II) IN **b/al/aŋa "shallow vessel (Tg. *balaŋa*), earthenware vessel (Ml.), iron pan (TB.), sacred pot (NgD.), cooking pot (Ho.)." Form. *balaŋa "mortar (=pounding vessel) (Pai.), pond (=water vessel) (Sir.)."

T *aaŋ "basin, pitcher, jug, jar, pan," from *(a)(r)aŋ(a); cf. also *ph[r]aaŋ "shallow basin" (Shan), from *b(a)raŋ(a).

VILLAGE *(q/)alaŋ
Form. (Atayalic) *qalaŋ.
PMY *raa(ŋ), from *(a)ra(ŋ).

VILLAGE, HOUSE, LAND (MAINLAND), COUNTRY
*(qa/)balu(/a) (23)
IN **banua "land" (Ml. "a large region or country, continent"). PO **panua "land, earth, village, people, house." SEP *panua "village" (Panayati also "earth"; Dobu and Bwaidoga "house"); cf. Capell: "Frederici . . . traces *banua*=people to Buru and Minahassa; *banua*=village, place, to Buru and the Moluccas." PPN **fanua "land." Form: Fav. *assaban=asaban* "village," from *[q]a/qabal; also Bun. *vau* (Bullock 1874), id., from *ba[l]u< *balu (assim. to the final *-u).

T **ʔbaan "village" (Nung also "country," Si. also "house"), from *q(a/)ban. Sek ʔbaːn "village" (cf. Thai). KS **ʔbaan, id.: Sui ʔban, Mak ʔbaːn, Then maːn (h.t.) (cf. Thai). Lk. ʔbaːn, id. OB *vo* (Jer.), *be* (h.t.) (Sav.), id., from **ʔba[]<*q/ba[]. Li *bwal(u), id.: S. Li *bau*, SC Loi *au*<*waw; WS Loi *fa*, SH DC Loi *fan*, Bup. *vun*<*bwan.

VOMIT[1] *lu(w)aq (27)
IN **luwaʔ=*luaʔ (Dyen) "spit out, vomit"; cf. also *γuaʔ =*γuwaʔ "spew, spill out" (Maranao "vomit") (Blust 1973), perhaps for *Ruwaʔ, a doublet formation for the original *luwaq through assimilation to the final.

T *raak, from *rwaak<*ruwák. Dioi *ruə*, from *ruak<*rúwak. Sek *ruak* (Ged.) (cf. Dioi). KS: Mak ʔoːk, from *[r]uwak. OB *doak*, from *roak<*rúwak. Li *eek: S. Li ɛʔ, from *aaq (vowel influ. by *-q)<*(raw)aq<*(ruw)aq (assim.).

PMY **o, but YCR has *lo*, both from an original *lo, generally yielding *wo>*o.

VOMIT^{II} *(m/)u(n)ta[q] (27)

IN **u(n)ta?=*(m/)u(n)ta? (Ja. m/utah~w/utah, Ml. m/untah). PO: Sa. mo/a. SEP *mu/muta, from *m/uta[q]. Form. (East; Ata.) *m(a)/utaq.

Miao: MPT ntua, MCh. ntɔ, from PM *nt[uo]<PMY *nt[o], from *nt[wa]<*(u)nt[a] (with irreg. loss of final *q).

VULVA^I *(m)pu(N)qi

IN **puki, from *puNqi. PO: Fi. mata/vuki "(eye/vulva=) ulcer on sole of foot." Form. (Ami: Tauran) *puki "vulva," from *puNqi; (Tsou) *buki "penis" (often associated with "vulva"), from *mpuNqi; also (Bun.) *puqu "vulva," from *puqi (vocalic assim.).

T *hi, from *hNi<*hNGi, from *hNqi (secondary voicing), from *(pu)Nqi (secondary aspiration). KS *hńi: Mak ńəi (h.t.), from *hNi (cf. Thai).

Miao: MPT pau? (l.t.), from PM *b[ou]?<PMY *b[o]?, from *buq[i] (secondary voicing with fore-stress; contrast the same feature in Thai with end-stress); also the doublet: MPT pi? (l.t.), from PM/PMY *bi?, from an earlier *biq[i]<*buq[i] (vocalic assimilation; contrast Bunun).

VULVA^{II} *[p]ati

Form. (E. Ruk.) *pati.

Li *thay: WS Li thaːy, from *[p](a)ti (second. aspiration).

VULVA See SQUIRT.

W

WAG (TAIL) See MOVE BACK AND FORTH.

WALK See MOVE BACK AND FORTH.

WALL See FENCE: HUT.

WAR See ENEMY.

WARD OFF See HINDER.

WARM See BURN.

WARM (UP) See RIPEN FRUITS.

WASH^I *(m)b[a](n)tsaq; *b[a]ts[ə]q; *b[a](n)tsuk

(I) IN **bat'aʔ=(m)bat'aʔ "wet" (Ja. "dissolve"); Protophilippine *basaʔ "wet, to wash" (Charles ċit.). Form. (Ami) *mi/batsaq; (Bun.) *ma/[b]atsaq; (Pai: Kapiyan Raisha) *b/n/atsaq "wash (clothes)."

  T *zak "wash (clothes)," from *nsak. KS *[]zak∼*sak, id.: Sui lak (h.t.), Kam sak, from *( )(n)sak (cf. Thai). Lk. wak "wash," app. from *zwak<*(b-)zak (cf. Lk. under III). OB dɔk "wash clothes," from *zɔk<*nsɔk (cf. Thai).

(II) IN *bat'ə ʔ: TB. baso "watery," NgD. bisa "wet" (metath.) (Dyen 1965). Form. (Sai.) *batsə[q] "wash (clothes, utensils)"; (Pai: most dialects; Puy: Hinan) *b/n/atsəq "wash (clothes)."

(III) IN **bat'uʔ "wash." Form: Atayalic *mahuq "wash (clothes)" (Ata.), from *[b/]m/atsuq.

  T *zuk "wash (Ahom), wash (as the face) (Shan)," from *nsuk. KS *[]zuk∼*suk "wash (clothes)": Mak zuk (h.t.), Kam syuk, from *( )(n)suk (cf. Thai). Lk uk "wash," app. from *zwuk<*(b-)zuk (cf. Lk. under I). OB tuk "wash [clothes, plates, the body, hands], clean (by washing), rinse (mouth), bathe"; tok "wash," tok-hu [body] "bathe" (Jer.), from suk.

  PMY **ntsho "wash (launder)": MCF "to agitate in the water to wash (clothes)"; MPT "scrub, wash by scrubbing (clothes)"; YCR also "scrub" and "rub against (as cat against hand)" (with second. aspir. and irreg. loss of final *q).

WASH" *suɣats; *(n)suɣas

(I) IN **huɣat' "wash" (Tg. "wash up"). Form. (Puy: Chipon) *m/[s]uɣats "wash (hands, feet)"; (Ata.) *q/m/[s]u[ɣ]ats "wash [utensils, dishes, food]" (s₂).

(II) T *suay "wash, wipe (Lao); wash (a part of the body or any object) (BT); wash (one's body or part of one's body, an animal's skin) (WT)"; also *zuay "to clean by washing (Si: ic.)," both from *(n)su(r)ay; also *[x]uay "wash [the head, the hair]" (Tho), from *syuay<*suɣay. Dioi sɔi "wash [the body, vegetables]," from *suay (cf. Thai). Sek so:y "wash" (cf. Dioi). Li *wua[s]: S. Li uot "wash [face, table, rice, clothes]," WS Li vuai "wash (face)," N. Li voa:i "wash"; WS Loi voai∼voe, SH Loi voe "wash" (the latter cw. "face"), from *ɣuas<*(s)uɣas.

WASH (FACE/BODY), BATHE *γa[q][u]p

Form. (Pai.) *m/n/[γ]aqup; (Puy.) *m/γ[]q/n/up; (Ami) *m/γuqup<*m/γaqup (assim. forward; contrast KS) "wash (face)."

T *aap "wash (body), bathe," from *[]a(q)ap (cf. KS). Dioi ap, id. KS *(γ)a(ʔ)ap "bathe": Sui ʔap, Mak za:p, Then ʔya:p, from *γaqap<*γaqup (assim. backward; contrast Ami). Li *a[a]p "bathe": WS SC Loi ab=a[a]p (SC Loi cw. "water") (cf. Thai).

WASH, RINSE *[lu]tsaw; *[li](n)saw; *saw/saw; *ntsaw/ntsaw (114, 119)

(I) IN **lu[tʼ]aw "rinse out" (Tg. lusao "make liquid," l/ag/usao "movement in water"; TB. luso "to clean by rinsing").

(II) Form. (Puy.) *-lisaw~*l/m/isaw; (Ruk.) *wa/linsaw "wash (utensils)."

(III) Form. (Ami) *mi/sawsaw "wash (utensils)."

(IV) T *dzaaw "wash for gold (Ahom: irreg. vocalism); wash or sift for gold or silver, using the hand to stir the sand and water in the vessel (Shan) (cf. Tg. under I); wash, clean (as rice) (Si.); wash (as rice before cooking) (Lao); wash in a sieve or basket (WT); wash (a part of the body or an object) (Tho); wash (one's body), clean (rice by washing) (Nung)," from *(dzaw)dzaw<*(ntsaw)ntsaw.

PMY **ntsaaw "wash (bathe)": MCF also "wash [bowl]"; MPT "wash [body], wash out [vessel], wash something off in water or other liquid"; from *(ntsaw)ntsaw (cf. Thai).

WASP See SWEET.

WASP, BEE *ŋgoboŋ

Form. (Ata.) *ŋəbuŋ "wasp," from *ŋubuŋ (stressed form) <*ŋgubuŋ.

Li *vooŋ: S. Li vɔŋ "clf. for bee" [vɔŋ un], from *bwooŋ< *(o)boŋ.

Miao: MCh. ŋkai~ŋke "wasp, kind of wild bee"; MPT ŋke ~ŋkhə "sp. of large wasp" (Sav.), ŋkaɨ (l.t.) "wasp" (Heim.), from PM *ŋg[aɨ]<PMY *ŋg[ou], from an earlier *ŋgow< *ŋgob[oŋ].

WATER¹ *( )(n)zalom* (9, 10)

IN **[dd]anum*. Yami *ḷanum* (Og.-As.), *ranum* (Ferr.), from
[z̧]anum. PPN **lanu* "liquid, fresh water," from *ndanu*. Form.
(n)zalum: Ami *nanom*<*nzalum* (assim.); also Puy. *zanum*
<*nzalum* (assim., followed by loss of initial nasal element).

T *nam*~*naam* (Si.), from *nza(l)(a)m*<*nza(l)(o)m*,
with vocalic assim. Dioi *ram*, from *(nz)ram*<*nza(a)lam*. Sek
nam (cf. Thai). KS *( )nam*: Sui Mak *nam* (h.t.), Then Kam
nam (l.t.) (cf. Thai). Lk. *num*, from *nz(al)um*. OB *nam* (Jer.),
nɔm (Sav.), from *n[o]m* (cf. Lk.). Li *nom*: S. Li DC SC Loi
nom, N. Li WS Li SH Loi Lakia Bas. Mef. Bup. Ki *nam* (cf.
Lk. OB).

WATER¹¹ *q/wah[a]R*

IN **wayəγ*=**ʔwahəR* "water": Ja. *we/*, Ml. *air*~*ayar*, NgD.
aer/ (but TB. *aek* is irregular); also (Blust 1972bis) Bukidnon
Manobo *wahig* "water, river, stream"; also (Dyen 1962) Aloene
(Piru: West Ceram) *kwel*, Lau (Solomons)*kwai* "water"; from
**ʔwahaR* (stressed form).

Li *ya* "river": S. Li *ya* (intervocalic *h*>*y*, as in IN). Lq.
hɔŋ (Bon.), *hoŋ* (Laj.), from *( )ha[R]*. N. Kl. *u* (*wu* in comp.),
S. Kl. *u* (comp. only), from *(w)a[R]*. Lt. *i*, from *yay*<
( )[h]a[R].

PM *oŋ*, from PMY *aaŋ*; PY **w[]m* (h.t.)=**ʔwam* (YHA
YHN)~**ʔwom* (YCR YTP) (latter with vocalic assim.); both
from an earlier **ʔwa(h)aR*, with final *-m* for *-ŋ* in PY through
assim. to the initial.

WE See INTRODUCTION.

WEAR (ON HEAD), COVER *(n)tu[ŋ](/duŋ)*

IN **tuduŋ* "head covering" (Ml. *tuduŋ* also "to cover with
a cloth, veil or other object," *tuduŋ/an* "a lid or cover"; NgD.
tă/tuduŋ "lid/cover"), prob. from *tuŋ/duŋ*.

PMY *ntoŋ* "wear (hat)" (MPT "wear on head; carry on head;
carry overhead as an umbrella").

WEAR (ON HEAD, BODY) See COVER.

WEAVE See PLAIT; SEW.

WEEP *()*praŋi*(t)*s*; **pr/m/aŋits*; **[pra]ŋ/m[/is]*; **[praŋ/]l/i[s]*;
**[pr/]m/aŋ/l/is*; **[pr/]l/m/[a]ŋis*

(I)   IN **taŋit'*. PPN **taŋi* "cry, weep." Form. (Bun.) **taŋits*
"weep"; (Sir.) **taŋi[ts]/taŋi[ts]* "tears."

T **hay*, from **hŋay<*(t)h[]ŋay<*t(a)ŋiy;* also **hŋe*
"weeping countenance" (Si.) and **ŋe* "cries, weeping of children" (Si.). Dioi Sek *tai*, from **ta(ŋ)i<*[]ta(ŋ)iy*. KS **?ŋe:*
Sui ?*ŋe*, Mak Kam *ŋe* (h.t.) (cf. Thai: Si. variants). Lk.
piẹ, from **py[](ŋ)e<*[]pr[](ŋ)ay*. OB *ŋai* (Jer.), *ŋɔi* (h.t.)
(Sav.), from **hŋay* (cf. Thai). Li **ŋey* (S. Li)~**ŋay* (WS Li),
from **(tə)ŋi* (unstressed)~**(ta)ŋi* (stressed). Laha *ńit~ńiet*,
from **ŋi[ts,s]*. Lt. *ćuŋ*, from **ćuŋ[]<*ćaŋ[is]*.

(II)   Form: East **(t/)m/aŋits* (Ami Sai. Thao Paz. Sir.);
**t/m/taŋits* (Puy.); Tsouic **(t/)m/aŋits* (Tsou Kan.); **t/m/-
taŋi[ts]* (Saa.).

(III)   PMY ***?ńe(m)*, *from **?ŋe(m)<*?ŋi(m)*, from an earlier
**(ta)ŋ/im(/is)<*(ta)ŋ/əm(/is)* by vocalic assim.

(IV)   Kl. *li*, from **(praŋ/)l/i(s)*.

(V)   Form. (Ata.) **m/aŋ/l/is*, from **(s/)m/aŋ/l/is*.

(VI)   Form. (Sed.) **l/m/iŋis*, from **(s/)l/m/aŋis*, with re-
infixation (in the first syllable) and vocalic assim.

WET, DAMP   **m/p[a]yak*; **(q/)(m)p[i](y)ak*

(I)   Form. (Paz.) **ma/payak* "wet," perh. from **/piyak* by
vocalic assim.

(II)   T **piak* "damp, wet, humid" (Lao also "moisten"); also
[?b]ik* "damp, moist, nearly dry" (Shan), from *?byak<*
**q/mp[i]yak*; also **[?]y[ia]k* "damp" (Kh.) and ***yik* ?*yak* "moist,
damp (as undried clothes)" (Shan).

WHEEL, CYCLE (TIME), RING   **()kurap(/a)*; **(N)qurap*

(I)   IN **ku[l]ap=*ku[r]ap* "skin disease" (TB. Ml. "ringworm"
=the disease with rings on skin); cf. also ***kulapu=*kurapu*
"name of a fish or marine animal" (Tg. "sp. of mussel"=the
ringed/circular animal). PPN ***lafa* "ringworm," from **(ku)raf/a;*

cf. also PPN *kulapo: Sm. ?ulapo "name of a sea-cucumber (Holothuria)"="circular animal" (cf. IN).

T *kroop "circuit, frame, border, side" (Si.), from *kruap; also *kraap "sides of boat (=circular rim around a boat)," from *krwaap; both from an original *kúrap~*kuráp. KS *khuap: Kam khuəp "wheel," from *khu(r)ap.

(II) T *xuap~γuap (Lao)~*xoop (WT) "periodic revolution; (ic.) week, month, year"; also *[x]a[a]p "wheel, anything round and flat" (Ahom), from *xwap; both from an original *(N)qúrap ~*quráp; cf. also *γoop "circle, ring; circuit, period of time; encircle," from *Nqoop<*Nquap (cf. Thai under I) and *roop "circuit, turn; encircle," from *ruap<*(u)rap. Dioi hɔp "periodic revolution; (ic.) month, year"; also "circle, circular; surround"; both from *qhuap/qhoop (cf. Thai). KS *h[wa]p: Sui hap "cycle," Mak hop "cycle (generally 30 days)," an app. loan from N. Thai (cf. Dioi).

WHISTLE See BLOW.

WHITE See ASHES.

WHITE, MOON *x[i]las
Form. (Pai. Puy: Chipon Sai. Paz.; Sed.; also Fav. as app. loan from Sed.) *qilas "moon"="the white (shining) object"; also Sai. *bulalas "white," app. through assim: *l̩>l from *bul̩al (see following root) + *[xi]las.

PMY *hla "moon, month" (MPT also "white [of egg]"); YHN la "moon," from *hla; also lai (s.t.) "(ic.) month," from *hlay; both from *hla[s].

WHITE, MOON, SILVER *(q/)(m)bul̩al (15, 20, 36)
IN **bulan=*(m)bulan "moon"; also **bulay "white," app. from an earlier *bul̩al/i; note also Yami bulawan "silver"="the white substance," a probable loan from Ami (below). PO **pula(n) "moon; to shine, twinkle": Fi. vula "moon," vula/vula "bright"="white." PPN **pu[l,r]a "shine, glow"="glowing white," from *mpula[n]. Form. (Puy: Hinan Ami Bun. Kuv. Sir. Thao; Tsouic) *bul̩al (Ata. *bula-tiŋ) "moon"; also (Puy: Hinan) *bul̩/n/al "white"; also (E. Ruk.) *bal̩ulan "silver," by metathesis from *bul̩alan<*bul̩al/an (with assim: *l>l̩), and (Ami: Kibi)

bulawan, id. (*ˈl>w*); note also Sai. *bulalas* "white," app. from *bulal* + *[xi]las* (see above root).

T*ˈʔblian* "moon," from *ˈʔblyan<ˈq/b(ə)lal* (unstressed form); also *ˈʔdoon* "white" (SW only), a doublet from the stressed form: *q/bulal>ˈq/blual>ˈq/duan>ˈʔdoon*. Dioi *də:n* (h.t.) "moon," from *ˈʔblə:n* (cf. Thai). Sek *ʔblian* "moon" (Haud.), *blian* (h.t.) "moon, month" (Ged.) (cf. Thai). KS *nian=ˈnyan* "moon": Sui *nyan~nyen~niən*, Mak *ni:n*, Then *nya:n*, Kam *ńa:n*, from *ndian=ndyan<ˈmblian<ˈmblyan* (cf. Thai). Lk. *ʔbien*, id. (cf. Thai Sek). OB *sa* (Jer.), *sɔi* (Sav.), id., from *phra[l]<ˈb[]la[l]* (initial unvoicing). Li *ńaan* "moon, month": S. Li *ńa:n*, WS Li *ńa:ŋ<ˈńa:n*, SH Loi *nian*, Bas. Mef. Ki *niaŋ* *<nian* (cf. KS). Lq. *nen* "moon" (cf. KS Li). Kl. *du die*, id. (cf. *du vuə* "sun," *du dɛ* "star"), from *dyai<ˈblai<ˈb[]la[l]*. Lt. *mćoa*, id., from *mblua<ˈmbula[l]*.

WHITE, SILVER[I]   *(m)pirak;* *(m)bu[r]ak* (91)

(I) IN **pilak=*pirak* "silver" (Ho. "tin, lead"). Form: Ata. *pila*, Paz. *pi:la* "silver" must be regarded as loans (cf. Yami *pila*), but note also Sai. *papila*, id., from *pa/pila<ˈp(il)a/pila*.

T *phiak* "white," from *phyak<ˈphi(r)ak*. Chuang *piak* (l.t.), id., from *biak<ˈmpiak* (cf. Thai). Lk. *piek* (l.t.), id., from *biek<ˈmpiek* (cf. Chuang). OB *pheak* (l.t.), id., from *beak<mpeak* (cf. Chuang Lk.). N. Kl. *ru*, id., from *(pi)ra[k]*.

(II) IN *burak* "white": Iban *burak* "white," Tg. *bulák* "cotton; white silk-cotton tree or kapok tree" (Blust 1970), perhaps from an earlier *mpurak* (with irreg. *mp>b*). PO *(m)purak* "white": Roti *fulak*, Bugotu Nggela *pura* (Blust 1970, 1972); also Fi. *vula* "white," with irregular *l* for the anticipated *r* (Blust 1972: note 29), app. through semantic merging with the above root (WHITE/MOON/SILVER).

KS *b[ua]k* "white": Mak Kam *phu:k* (l.t.), from *bu[r]ak*, perhaps from an earlier *mpu[r]ak* (cf. IN).

WHITE, SILVER[II]   *p[u]p[r,l]i[q];* *p[u]p[r,l]u[q]*

(I) IN **putiʔ* "white." PO *-fu[t]i*: Sa. *ɛ-hui* "egg white." Form. (Thao) *ma/puti* "white" (unexplained loss of final).

(II) Form. (Pai.) *balituq* "silver," from *(m)bali(q)-(pu)tuq-*

424 *Austro-Thai*

"the white [*puṭuq*] metal [(*m*)*baliq*]" (see IRON), prob. through assim. (**puṭiq>*puṭuq*); also (Kan. Saa.) **balituk* "silver" through early borrowing (with final **q>k*).

Lq. *ptɔ* "silver," from **p[]tu[q]*. Lt. *ćɨ i* "white" (n.a.), from **ć[u][q]*.

WIDE, TOO WIDE   **(q/)lu[q]aγ*

IN ***luʔaγ=*luʔaγ*: Tg. *luag* "wide"; also (Blust 1970) Iban *luar* "wide, open," Bukidnon Manobo *luʔag* "wide" (NgD. *să/ruah* "too wide" has irregular *r* for *l*).

T **hluam* "too wide, loose," from **q/lu(q)am*.

WIDE, BROAD (SURFACE), PLAIN, SPACE
    *(q/)baŋ/(q/)baŋ

IN ***baŋbaŋ* "wide, spread out" (TB. "spacious," Ml. "to be flat and broad," Ho. "limitless space").

T **baaŋ* "surface of the earth" (cw. "surface") (Si.), from **(baŋ)baŋ*; also **paaŋ* (s.t., high series) "level, as tract of land; clear, cloudless; extensive plain (Shan); open (unconfined) space (Kh.); high land, plain (Ahom)," from **(paŋ)paŋ<* **(baŋ)baŋ* (irreg. unvoicing of the initial). KS: Mak *ʔba ʔbaŋ* "wide/broad" (Sui Mak also *ʔba*), from **q/ba(ŋ)q/baŋ*. OB *baŋ* (h.t.) "clear, luminous," from **ʔbaŋ<*q/baŋ*; for the semantics, cf. Shan.

WIDOW(ED)   **(qa/)(m)baḷ[u]*
    IN ***balu*.

T **hmaay*, from **hmbaay<*q(a)/mbay<*q(a)/mbal(u)*. KS: **[h]maay*: Mak *maːi* (h.t.) (cf. Thai).

WIFE   See FEMALE; WOMAN.

WILDERNESS   **r[i](m)ba*
    IN ***[l]imba~**[l]a(m)ba=*[r]imba~*[r]a(m)ba* (assim.).

T **pa*, app. through secondary unvoicing: **[r]ba>*[h]ba>*pa*. Kl. *pu tiə*, from **[]pa* (for *tiə*, see FOREST¹).

WIND, n.¹   **(k/)( )baḷi*
    Form. (East; Atayalic) **baḷi*.

OB *van* (Jer.), *bɔn* (Sav.), from **van<*bwan<*[]ban* (labialized). N. Li *van* (cf. OB). Kl. *zɨ fɛ* (cf. *zɨ dɔŋ* "thunder"),

from *$pw\varepsilon$<*$pwai$<*$[]pai$<*$[b]a(r)i$. Lt. *kue,* from *$kwai$<
$k[]bai$<$k[]ba(r)i$.

WIND, n." *$(k/)lob/lob$

Form. (Bun.) *lub/lub "wind"; (Pai.) *$ka/lub/lub/an$ "sky";
for the semantics, cf. SKY (PO "sky"~"wind").

T *$lom,$ from *$(k-)lom$<*$(k-)lom/lob$. Dioi *rum.* Chuang
*$rom.$ Sek *lum.* KS *$()lom$: Sui Mak *lum* (h.t.), Kam *lem;* also
*rom: Then *zem;* both from *$(k-)lom$ (cf. Thai). Lk. *yom,*
from *rom.

WIND, v. See TURN.

WINE See LIQUOR/WINE.

WING See ARM; BEAT (two entries).

WING (OF HOUSE) See ROOM (OF HOUSE).

WINNOW, SWEEP, WIPE, FAN *$[ta](m)pi(/(m)pi)$;
　*$[ta]mpi/an$ (39)

(I) IN **$ta(m)pi$ "remove dust and chaff, winnow" (NgD.
"pound rice"). PPN **$tafi$=*$tafi$~*$tapi$ "sweep": Fu. *ta/tafi*
"sweep" (Demp. "cleanse"), *tapi* "wash" (Demp.); Sm. *tafi*
"sweep," *ma/tafi* "wiped away" (Demp.), *tapi* "wipe off" (Demp.),
from *$ta(m)pi$. Form. (Puy: Hinan) *$tabi$ "mortar" (=*"rice-
pounder"), from *$tampi;$ also (Ruk.) *$wa/bibi$ "wipe," from the
partially reduplicated form: *$(ta)mpi/mpi$.

T *wi "fan; to fan" (Shan also "shake, as dog his tail"),
from *$(bi)bi$<*$(ta)(mpi)mpi$ (cf. Ruk.). Dioi *pen pi*~*pin pi*
(h.t., l.t.) "hand-fan" (n.a.), from *bi<*$mpi;$ also *wi* (h.t.) "to
clean grain with a *dong wi* (winnowing basket)," from *hwi
<*$(phi)bi$ (initial unvoicing and second. aspiration). Sek *phi*
[l.t.] "fan," from *$[b]i$ (cf. Dioi). KS *bi: Mak *pəi* (l.t.) "fan,"
pəi pəi "winnow (rice)," from *$(ta)mpi$ and *$(ta)mpi/mpi$.

Yao: YCR *pei* "to skim off [rice water]," from PY/PMY
*$pei,$ from an earlier *$[ta]pi$.

(II) T **$?bian$ "large winnowing basket" (Lao), from **$?bi/an$
<*$(tə)mpi/an$.

WIPE See WINNOW.

WITHE See BAMBOO.

WOMAN See FEMALE.

WOMAN, WIFE, SPOUSE *(qa/)(n)saw[a]* (67)

IN **t'awa*=(?a)t'awa* "spouse" (Tg. *?a/sawa* "spouse," NgD. *sawɛ* "wife"). PO **(a)nsawa* "spouse." SEP *[q]a/sawa*, id.

T *saaw* "young (unmarried) woman," from *(a)saw(a)*. Sek *saaw*, id. (Ged.). Lk. *kyau*=*ćau* "female," from *sau*<*nsaw*.

WOMAN (YOUNG) *sia[q]*

T *se*=/see/ "young girls" (Si: ic.), from *sia[q]*. KS: Sui *śa* "wife," from *s[i]a[q]*.

PY *sie?*=*sia?* "young woman" (Haud.) (YCR *sia?* "woman, girl, daughter").

WORM, LARVA, PENIS *(q/)u(n)zay*

IN **uday* "worm" (Tg. "intestinal worm," Ja. "anal maggot"). PPN **ule* "penis," from *unday*.

T **?di* "glow-worm" (Lao), from *q/day* (vowel influ. by *q/*). Dioi *duai*~*dai* (both h.t.) "larva of the large bamboo weevil," from **?duay*~**?day*<*q(u)day*~*q(ə)day* (unstressed form); also *nai* (h.t.) "penis" (the "decent" term, perh. because basically nonsexual), from *q(ə)nday* (cf. PPN).

WORM, EEL *[tu]la[q]i; (n)tula(/la)*

(I) Form: Ata: Squliq *təlaqii*, Ci'uli *tala?e* "eel," from *t[u]laqi* (stressed form without vocalic assim.; cf. II).

T *pla hlay* (Si. Nung) "eel" (*pla* "fish"), from *[]la(q)i;* cf. also *pla hlaat* (WT), id.

(II) IN *[t]una* "eel," from *tula,* app. an abbreviated form of *tula?i*<*tulaqi* (cf. Atayal under I). PO *ntuna,* id.: Fi. *nduna.* Form: (East) *tula,* id.

T **?dian* "worm," from **?ntian*<*q/ntlian*<*q/ntəlan* (unstressed form; cf. Sek). Dioi *də:n* (h.t.), id., from **?də:n* (cf. Thai). Sek *tlual,* id. (Ged.), from *tulal*<*tula/la* (partial re-dupl.). KS: Mak *zan,* id., from *[l]an*<*(tu)lal* (cf. Sek). Li: SC Loi *voan*=*vuan,* id., app. from *[t]uwan*<*tulan*<*tulal* (cf. Sek).

WORM (INTESTINAL) *[pa](n)tiaq*

Form. (Ata.) *padiq* "tapeworm," from *pantiaq.

T *tɨak* "intestinal worm" (Kh. also ic: "earthworm"), from *tyaak<*[]tiáq. KS *t(y)a: Sui (all dial.) *ta* "worm," from *t(y)aq.

Y

YAM See CULTIVATE (FIELD); TUBER (EDIBLE).

YARN, THREAD *[q/]l/[a]bay; *(q/)(m)bay

(I) IN **labay* "yarn," prob. from *q/l/abay.

(II) T *hmay* "thread," from *q/mbay. Sek *mi*, id., from *(q/)may (vowel influ. by *q/). KS *[ʔ]may "thread/yarn": Mak *mai* (h.t.) (cf. Thai). Lk. *kui* "thread," from **ʔmay (cf. KS). OB *mɔi* (h.t.) "thread, line," from *hmɔi (cf. Thai). Li *v[o]y: WS Li *voi* "thread/yarn," from *woy<*way<*( )bay.

YAWN, BELCH *[tə]ɣa[ʔ]ab

IN **təɣab* "belch" (Tg. "yawn"); Proto-Philippine *təɣaʔab (Charles cit.).

T *hraaw* "yawn," from *[th]ra(ʔ)ab. Dioi *ruao* (h.t.), id., from *hra[a]w (cf. Thai). Lq. *yeu*, id., from *[]ɣaw. Kl. *ko rə*, id., from *ra<*[]ɣa[ʔab].

PM **hu* "yawn," from PMY *hou; PY **h[]=*hɔ (YCR) ∼ *ha(a)w (YHN, YLC), id.; all from an earlier *ha(a)b< *(tə)ɣa(ʔ)ab.

YELLOW *(N)q[u]liaŋ; G[u]liaŋ

(I) IN **kuniŋ*, from *Nquniŋ<*Nquniaŋ. PO: cf. Kusaian (Carolines) *raŋ-raŋ* (Izui), perh. from *(ku)lyaŋ/lyaŋ. Form. (Sir.) *ma/kuliaŋ.

T *hliaŋ, from *hlyaŋ<*q[]liáŋ. OB *laŋ* (h.t.), from *hlaŋ (cf. Thai). Li *hyiaŋ: S. Li *hieŋ*∼*yɛŋ*, WS Li *ziaŋ*, WS Loi *jiaŋ*, DC Loi *thiaŋ*, SH Loi *theŋ*, Ha *zəŋ*, from *(k)h[l]iaŋ (cf. Thai). Lq. *nin*, from *ni[ŋ] (cf. IN). N. Kl. *nyi*, S. Kl. *the ni*, from Kl. *ni, from *ni[ŋ] (cf. Lq.). Lt. *a/hni* (written *an hi*), from *hni[ŋ] (cf. IN).

(II) PM **Glɛŋ; PY **wy[a,aa]ŋ (s.t.); both from PMY *Gḷiaŋ <*Gḷiaŋ (assim. to the back vowel *u).

Combined References

Aymonier, Étienne, and Antoine Cabaton
    1906   *Dictionnaire Čam-Français,* Paris.
Beauclair, Inez de
    1946   "The Keh Lao of Kweichow and their History According to Chinese Records," *Studia Serica,* 5, 1-44.
Belo, Jane
    1936   "A Study of the Balinese Family," *American Anthropologist, n.s., 38,* 12-31.
Benedict, Paul K.
    1939   "Semantic Differentiation in Indo-Chinese," *Harvard Journal of Asiatic Studies, 4,* 213-29.
    1940   "Studies in Indo-Chinese Phonology," *Harvard Journal of Asiatic Studies, 5,* 101-27.
    1941   "A Cham Colony on the Island of Hainan," *Harvard Journal of Asiatic Studies, 6,* 129-34.
    1942   "Thai, Kadai, and Indonesian: a New Alignment in Southeastern Asia," *American Anthropologist, n.s., 44,* 576-601.
    1942   "Tibetan and Chinese Kinship Terms," *Harvard Journal of*
    bis   *Asiatic Studies, 6,* 313-37.
    1943   "Studies in Thai Kinship Terminology," *Journal of the American Oriental Society, 63,* 168-75.
    1943   "Secondary Infixation in Lepcha," *Studies in Linguistics, 1,*
    bis   xix.
    1945   "Chinese and Thai Kin Numeratives," *Journal of the American Oriental Society, 65,* 33-37.
    1947   "Languages and Literatures of Indochina," *Far Eastern Quarterly, 6,* 379-89.
    1947   "An Analysis of Annamese Kinship Terms," *Southwestern Jour-*
    bis   *nal of Anthropology, 3,* 371-92.
    1948   "Archaic Chinese °g and °d," *Harvard Journal of Asiatic Studies, 11,* 197-206.
    1948   "Tonal Systems in Southeast Asia," *Journal of the American*
    bis   *Oriental Society, 68,* 184-91.
    1966   "Austro-Thai," *Behavior Science Notes, 1,* 227-61.
    1967   "Austro-Thai Studies," *Behavior Science Notes, 2,* 203-44.
    1967   "Austro-Thai Studies: 3. Austro-Thai and Chinese," *Behavior*
    bis   *Science Notes, 2,* 275-336.
    1972   *Sino-Tibetan: A Conspectus,* Cambridge: University Press.
    1972   "The Sino-Tibetan Tonal System," in *Langues et Techniques,*
    bis   *Nature et Société,* eds. L. Burnet and J. M. C. Thomas, Paris: Klincksieck.
Biggs, Bruce
    1965   "Direct and Indirect Inheritance in Rotuman," *Lingua, 14,* 383-415.
Biggs, Bruce, D. S. Walsh, and Jocelyn Waqa
    1970   *Proto-Polynesian Reconstructions with English to Proto-Polynesian Finder List,* Auckland: University of Auckland, Anthropology Department (mimeographed).

Blood, Doris W.
  1962 "Reflexes of Proto-Malayo-Polynesian in Cham," *Anthropological Linguistics 4, no. 9*, 11-21.
Blust, Robert A.
  1969 "Some new Proto-Austronesian trisyllables," *Oceanic Linguistics 8, no. 2:* 85-104.
  1970 "Proto-Austronesian addenda," *Oceanic Linguistics 9, no. 2:* 104-62.
  1972 "Proto-Oceanic addenda with cognates in non-Oceanic Austronesian languages: a preliminary list," *Working Papers in Linguistics 4, no. 1:* 1-43.
  1972 "Additions to 'Proto-Austronesian addenda' and 'Proto-Oceanic
  bis addenda with cognates in non-Oceanic Austronesian languages,' " *Working Papers in Linguistics 4, no. 8:* 1-17.
  1973 "Additions to 'Proto-Austronesian addenda' and 'Proto-Oceanic addenda with cognates in non-Oceanic Austronesian languages,' II," *Working Papers in Linguistics 5, no 3:* 33-61.
  1974 *The Proto-Austronesian word for "two": a second look*, paper presented at the First International Conference on Comparative Austronesian Linguistics, Honolulu, January 1974.
Bonifacy, Auguste
  1905 "Étude sur les langues parlées par les populations de la haute Rivière Claire," *Bulletin de l'École Française d'Extrême-Orient, 5,* 306-23.
  1906 "Étude sur les coutumes et la langue des La-ti," *Bulletin de l'École Française d'Extrême-Orient, 6,* 271-78.
  1908 "Étude sur les coutumes et la langue des Lolo et des La-qua du Haut Tonkin," *Bulletin de l'École Française d'Extrême-Orient, 8,* 531-58.
Boodberg, Peter A.
  1937 "Some Proleptical Remarks on the Evolution of Archaic Chinese," *Harvard Journal of Asiatic Studies, 2,* 329-72.
Borua, Golap Chandra
  1920 *Ahom-Assamese-English Dictionary*, Calcutta: Baptist Mission Press.
Brandstetter, R.
  1908 *Malaio-polynesische Forschungen; IV: Mata-Hari, oder Wanderungen eines indonesischen Sprachforschers durch die drei Reiche der Natur*, Luzern.
Brown, N.
  1837 "Comparison of Indo-Chinese Languages," *Journal of the Asiatic Society of Bengal, 6,* 1023-38.
Bullock, T. L.
  1874 "Formosan Dialects and their Connection with the Malay," *China Review, 3,* 38-46 (cit. from Ferrell 1969).
Burling, Robbins, and P. C. Bhattacharya
  1956 "Lexico-Statistic Dating of Garo-Bodo Separation," *Journal of the University of Gauhati, 7,* 67-73.
Calder, J.
  1882 "Notes on Hainan and its Aborigines," *China Review, 11,* 42-50.

Capell, Arthur
   1943   *The Linguistic Position of South-Eastern Papua*, Sydney: Aus-
          tralasian Medical Publishing Co.
   1945   "The Origin of the Oceanic Languages," *Journal of the Poly-
          nesian Society, 54*, 62-65.
   1962   "Oceanic Linguistics Today," *Current Anthropology, 3*, 371-96.
Capell, Arthur, and R. H. Lester
   1945- "Kinship in Fiji," *Oceania, 15*, 171-200; *16*, 109-43, 234-53,
   46   297-318.
Chang, Kun
   1947   "On the Tone System of the Miao-Yao Languages," *Bulletin
          of the Institute of History and Philology, Academia Sinica, 16*,
          93-110 (in Chinese).
   1953   "On the Tone System of the Miao-Yao Languages," *Language,
          29*, 374-78 (abbreviated version of Chang 1947).
   1957   "The Phonemic System of the Yi Miao Dialect," *Bulletin of
          the Institute of History and Philology, Academia Sinica, 29*,
          11-19.
   1966   "A Comparative Study of the Yao Tone System," *Language,
          42*, 303-10.
   1972   "The Reconstruction of Proto-Miao-Yao Tones," *Bulletin of the
          Institute of History and Philology, Academia Sinica, 44*, 541-
          628.
Charles, Mathew
   1974   *Problems in the reconstruction of Protophilippine phonology
          and the subgrouping of the Philippine languages,* paper pre-
          sented at the First International Conference on Comparative
          Austronesian Linguistics, Honolulu, January 1974.
Ch'en, C. K. See Li, Y.C., K. C. Ch'en, and C. K. Ch'en.
Ch'en, K. C. See Li, Y. C., K. C. Ch'en, and C. K. Ch'en.
Chêng, Te-k'un, and Liang Ch'ao-t'ao
   1945   "An Introduction to the South-western Peoples of China," *Jour-
          nal of the West China Border Research Society, 16*, Series A,
          23-38.
Chowning, Ann
   1963   "Proto-Melanesian Plant Names," in *Plants and the Migrations
          of Pacific Peoples. A Symposium* (Tenth Pacific Science Con-
          gress, Honolulu, Hawaii, 1961), ed. Jacques Barrau, Honolulu:
          Bishop Museum Press.
Clark, G. W.
   1884   *Kweichow and Yün-nan Provinces*, Shanghai.
Clarke, Samuel R.
   1911   *Among the Tribes of Southwest China*, London, China Inland
          Mission.
Coedès, Georges
   1923   "Nouvelles notes critiques sur l'inscription de Rāma Khamheng,"
          Journal of the Siam Society, 17, part 3, 113-20.
   1935   "L'origine du cycle des douze animaux au cambodge," *T'oung
          Pao, 31*, 313-29.
   1949   "Les langues de l'Indochine," *Conferences de l'Institut de Lin-
          guistique de l'Université de Paris, 8*, 63-81.

Coedès, Georges, and J. Burnay
   1926 "Notes d'etymologie tai, no. 1: le nom de nombre 'cent,'"
         Journal of the Siam Society, 20, 49-52.
Couvreur, Séraphin
   1930 *Dictionnaire classique de la langue chinoise,* Sien-hsien: Im-
         primerie de la Mission Catholique.
Csoma de Kórös, Alexander
   1834 *Essay towards a Dictionary, Tibetan and English,* Calcutta:
         Printed at the Baptist Mission Press.
Cushing, Josiah N.
   1914 *A Shan and English Dictionary,* 2d ed., Rangoon, American
         Baptist Mission Press.
Dahl, Otto C.
   1973 "Proto-Austronesian," *Scandinavian Institute of Asian Studies,
         Monograph Series* 15.
Dempwolff, Otto
   1938 "Vergleichende Lautlehre des austronesischen Wortschatzes, Bd.
         3: Austronesisches Wörterverzeichnis," *Beihefte zur Zeitschrift
         für Eingeborenensprachen, Bd. 19.*
Diguet, Édouard
   1895 *Étude de la langue taï,* Hanoi.
   1910 *Étude de la langue tho,* Paris.
Dobson, William A. C. H.
   1962 *Early Archaic Chinese: a Descriptive Grammar,* Toronto: Uni-
         versity of Toronto Press.
Dodd, William C.
   1923 *The Tai Race,* Cedar Rapids, Iowa, Torch Press.
Dyen, Isidore
   1947a "The Malayo-Polynesian Word for 'two,'" *Language, 23,* 50-55.
   1947b "The Tagalog Reflexes of Malayo-Polynesian D," *Language, 23,*
         227-38.
   1949 "On the History of the Trukese Vowel," *Language, 25,* 420-36.
   1951 "Proto-Malayo-Polynesian °Z," *Language, 27,* 534-40.
   1953a *The Proto-Malayo-Polynesian Laryngeals,* Baltimore: Linguistic
         Society of America.
   1953b "Dempwolff's R," *Language, 29,* 359-66.
   1962 "Some New Proto-Malayopolynesian Initial Phonemes," *Journal
         of the American Oriental Society, 82,* 214-15.
   1964 "The Position of the Malayopolynesian Languages of Formosa,"
         Asian Perspectives, 7, 261-71.
   1965 "Formosan Evidence for Some New Proto-Austronesian Pho-
         nemes," *Lingua, 14,* 285-305.
   1974 *The Proto-Austronesian enclitic genitive pronouns,* paper pre-
         sented at the First International Conference on Comparative
         Austronesian Linguistics, Honolulu, January 1974.
   [1974 *A Reconstructional Confirmation: the Proto-Austronesian Word
   bis] for "Two"* [mimeographed].
Egerod, S.
   1959 "A Note on Some Chinese Numerals as Loan Words in Tai,"
         T'oung Pao, 47, 67-74.

1959 "The Etymology of Siamese /dâjjin/ 'to hear,'" *T'oung Pao,*
bis 47, 423-25.
1965 "An English-Atayal Vocabulary," *Acta Orientalia, 29,* 203-20.
1965 "Verbal Inflexion in Atayal," *Lingua, 15,* 251-82.
bis
1966 "Word Order and Word Classes in Atayal," *Language, 42,*
346-69.
1966 "A Statement on Atayal Phonology," in *Essays Offered to G. H.*
bis *Luce, vol. 1,* eds. Ba Shin et al., Ascona, Switzerland: Artibus
Asiae.
1969 "The Origin of Headhunting—An Atayal Text with Vocabulary,"
*Bulletin of the Institute of History and Philology, Academia
Sinica, 39,* 291-326.

Elkins, Richard E.
1974 *A Proto-Manobo Word List,* paper presented at the First International Conference on Comparative Austronesian Linguistics,
Honolulu, January 1974.

Esquirol, J.
1931 *Dictionnaire kanao-français et français-kanao,* Hongkong.

Esquirol, J., and G. Williatte
1908 *Essai de dictionnaire dioi₃-français,* Hongkong.

Ferrell, R.
1966 "The Formosan Tribes: A Preliminary Linguistic, Archaeologi-
cal and Cultural Synthesis," *Bulletin of the Institute of Ethnology, Academia Sinica, 21,* 97-130.
1966 *Paiwan Vocabulary (Makazayazaya Dialect)* (typescript).
bis
1967 *Atayal Vocabulary (Sqolyeq dialect): Selected and Translated
from Naoyoshi Ogawa's Atayaru Goshu (Japanese-Atayal Word
book,* Taihoku, 1932), Taipei.
1969 "Taiwan Aboriginal Groups: Problems in Cultural and Linguistic Classification," *Institute of Ethnology, Academia Sinica,
Monograph 17* (includes "Comparative Vocabulary").

Forrest, R. A. D.
1964 "A Reconsideration of the Initials of Karlgren's Archaic Chinese," *T'oung Pao, 51,* 229-46.

Gedney, William
1965 "Yay, a Northern Tai Language in North Vietnam," *Lingua,
14,* 180-93.
1970 "The Saek Language of Nakhon Phanom Province," *Journal of
the Siam Society, 58,* 67-87.
1971 "A Puzzle in Comparative Tai Phonology," paper read at the
4th Conference on Sino-Tibetan, Indiana University, October
1971 (mimeographed).

Goodenough, Ward
1962 Comment in Capell 1962.

Gordaliza, Fr. Th.
1908 "Estudio sobre el dialecte thô de la región de Lang-sön," *Anthropos, 3,* 512-32.

Grace, George W.
1969 "A Proto-Oceanic finder list," *Working Papers in Linguistics 1, no. 2:* 39-84.

Graham, David C.
1937 "The Customs of the Ch'uan Miao," *Journal of the West China Border Research Society, 9,* 13-70.

Gravius, Daniel
1661 *Het Heylige Evangelium Matthei en Johannis Overgeset inde Formosaansche tale, voor de Inwoonders van Soulang, Mattau, Sinckan, Bacloan, Tavokan, en Tevorang,* Amsterdam (cit. from Ferrell 1969).

Greenberg, Joseph
1953 "Historical Linguistics and Unwritten Languages," in *Anthropology Today,* ed. A. L. Kroeber, Chicago: University of Chicago Press.

Guignard, Théodore
1912 *Dictionnaire laotien-française,* Hongkong.

Haudricourt, André G.
1947- "Introduction à la phonologie historique des langues miao-yao,"
50   *Bulletin de l'École Française d'Extrême-Orient, 44,* 555-76.

1951 "Variations parallèles en Mélanésian," *Bulletin de la Société Linguistique de Paris, 47,* 140-53.

1952 "Les occlusives uvulaires en Thai," *Bulletin de la Société Linguistique de Paris, 52,* 86-89.

1953 "A propos de la restitution du karen commun," *Bulletin de la Société Linguistique de Paris, 49,* 129-32.

1954 "Les origines asiatiques des langues malayo-polynésiennes," *Journal de la Société des Océanistes, 10,* 180-83.

1956 "De la restitution des initiales dans les langues monosyllabiques: le problème du thai commun," *Bulletin de la Société Linguistique de Paris, 52,* 307-22.

1960 "Note sur les dialectes de la région de Moncay," *Bulletin de l'École Française d'Extrême-Orient, 50,* 161-77.

1962 Comment in Capell 1962.

1963 "La langue sek," in *Proceedings (Trudy) of the International Congress of Orientalists* (Moscow, 1960), Moscow.

1963 "Remarques sur les initiales complexes de la langue sek," *Bul-
bis   letin de la Société Linguistique de Paris, 58,* 156-63.

1965 "Problems of Austronesian Comparative Philology," *Lingua, 14,* 315-29.

1966 "The Limits and Connections of Austroasiatic in the Northeast," *Indo-Iranian Monographs, 5.*

1967 "La langue lakkia," *Bulletin de la Société Linguistique de Paris, 62,* 165-82.

Heimbach, Ernest E.
1966 *White Meo to English Dictionary,* Chiengmai, Thailand: Overseas Missionary Fellowship.

Hosie, Alexander
1897 *Three Years in Western China,* 2d ed., London, G. Philip and Son.

Houghton, Bernard
1896 "Outlines of Tibeto-Burman Linguistic, Palaeontology," *Journal of the Royal Asiatic Society (1896)*, 23-55.
Izui, H.
1965 "The Languages of Micronesia; Their Unity and Diversity," *Lingua, 14*, 349-59.
Jeremaissen, Carl C.
1892 "Loi Aborigines of Hainan and Their Speech," *China Review, 20*, 296-305.
Kähler, H.
1962 Comment in Capell 1962.
Karlgren, Bernhard
1923 *Analytic Dictionary of Chinese and Sino-Japanese*, Paris: P. Geuthner.
1957 "Grammata Serica Recensa," *Bulletin of the Museum of Far Eastern Antiquities, Stockholm, 29*.
Lajonquière, Étienne E. Lunet de
1904 *Dictionnaire français-siamois*, Paris: Imprimerie National, E. Leroux.
1906 *Ethnographie du Tonkin septentrional*, Paris, Leroux.
LeBar, Frank M., Gerald C. Hickey, and John K. Musgrave
1964 *Ethnic Groups of Mainland Southeast Asia*, New Haven: HRAF Press.
Li, Fang-kuei
1940 "The Tai Dialect of Lungchow," *Institute of History and Philology, Academia Sinica, Monograph Series A, No. 16*, Shanghai.
1943 "Notes on the Mak Languages," *Institute of History and Philology, Academia Sinica, Monograph Series A, No. 20*, Shanghai (in Chinese).
1945 "Some Old Chinese Loan Words in the Tai Languages," *Harvard Journal of Asiatic Studies, 8*, 333-42.
1948 "The Distribution of Tones and Initials in the Sui Language," *Language, 24*, 160-67.
1949 "Tones in the Riming System of the Sui Language," *Word, 5*, 262-67.
1954 "Consonant Clusters in Tai," *Language, 30*, 368-79.
1956 "Siamese *wan* and *waan*," *Language, 32*, 81-82.
1957 "The Jui Dialect of Poai: Phonology," *Bulletin of the Institute of History and Philology, Academia Sinica, 28*, 551-66.
1957 "The Jui Dialect of Po-ai and the Northern Tai," *Bulletin of bis the Institute of History and Philology, Academia Sinica, 29*, 315-21.
1965 "The Tai and Kam-Sui Languages," *Lingua, 14*, 148-79.
1966- "Notes on the T'en (Yanghuang) Language. Pt. I: Introduction 67 and Phonology," *Bulletin of the Institute of History and Philology, Academia Sinica, 36*, 419-26; 37, 1-45.
Li, Y. S., K. C. Ch'en, and C. K. Ch'en
1959 "Some Problems Concerning Initials and Tones in the Miao Language," *Yu yen yen chiu, 4*, 65-80 (translated by Y. H. Chang, in Herbert C. Purnell, Jr., ed., *Miao and Yao Linguistic*

Studies, Ithaca, Cornell University, Department of Asian Studies, 1972).

Lombard, Sylvia J.
1968 *Yao-English Dictionary,* ed. Herbert C. Purnell, Jr., Ithaca, N.Y.: Cornell University, Southeast Asia Program.

Mao, Tsung-wu, and Tsu-yao Chou
1962 "[A Brief Description of the Yao Languages]," *Chung kuo yü wen, 113,* 141-48 (in Chinese). (Translated by Y. H. Chang in Herbert C. Purnell, Jr., ed., *Miao and Yao Linguistic Studies,* Ithaca, Cornell University, Department of Asian Studies, 1972.)

Minot, G.
1940 "Dictionnaire tay blanc-français," *Bulletin de l'École Française d'Extrême-Orient, 40,* 1-237.

Mix, H. W., ed.
1920 *An English and Shan Dictionary,* Rangoon: American Baptist Mission Press.

Mohring, Hans
1964 "Tangan—Ein Beweis für Prä-austronesisches Substrat? Eine Bemerkung zur Etymologie von LIMA, RINGA und TANGAN," *Studia Linguistica,* 108-17.

Needham, J. F.
1894 *Outline Grammar of the Tai (Khâmti) Language,* Rangoon.

Ogawa, A., and Erin Asai
1935 *Myths and Traditions of the Native Tribes of Formosa,* Taihoku (Taipei): Taihoku Imperial University (in Japanese).

Pallegoix, D. Jean-Baptiste
1896 *Dictionnaire siamois-français-anglais,* revised by J. L. Vey, Bangkok.

Prentice, D. J.
1974 *Yet another PAN phoneme?* paper presented at the First International Conference on Comparative Austronesian Linguistics, Honolulu, January 1974.

Purnell, Herbert C., Jr.
1970 "Toward a Reconstruction of Proto-Miao-Yao," unpublished Ph.D. dissertation, Ithaca: Cornell University.

Reid, Lawrence A.
1974 *The Igorot Subgroup of Philippine languages,* paper presented at the First International Conference on Comparative Austronesian Linguistics, Honolulu, January 1974.

Rhodes, A.
1651 *Dictionarium annamiticum, lusitanum, et latinum,* Rome.

Robert, J.
1913 "Notice sur les Lati," *Revue d'Ethnographie et de Sociologie, 4,* 338-52.

Ruey, Yih-fu
1956 "The Ethnical Problem of the Kehlao Tribe," *Academia Sinica, Institute of History and Philology (1956),* 269-301 (in Chinese).

Savina, François M.
1916 "Dictionnaire miao-tseu-français," *Bulletin de l'École Française d'Extrême-Orient, 16,* i-xxii, 1-246.

1924   *Dictionnaire etymologique français-nung-chinois,* Hongkong.

1926   "Dictionnaire français-mán, precédé d'une note sur les Mán Kim-Di-Mun et leur langue," *Bulletin de l'École Française d'Extrême-Orient, 26,* 11-225.

1931   "Lexique dày-français, accompagné d'un petit lexique français-dày et d'un tableau des différences dialectales," *Bulletin de l'École Française d'Extrême-Orient, 31,* 103-99.

1965   "Le vocabulaire bê, présenté par A. G. Haudricourt," *Publications de l'École Française d'Extrême-Orient, 57.*

Schmidt, Wilhelm

1906   "Die Mon-Khmer-Völker, ein Bindeglied zwischen Völkern Zentralasiens und Austronesiens," *Archiv für Anthropologie, 33,* 59-109.

Shafer, Robert

1940-   "The Vocalism of Sino-Tibetan," *Journal of the American Ori-*
41   *ental Society, 60,* 302-37; *61,* 18-31.

1942   "Annamese and Tibeto-Burmic," *Harvard Journal of Asiatic Studies, 6,* 399-402.

1957   "Quelques équations phonétiques pour les langues li d'Haïnan," *Rocznik Orientalistyczny, 21,* 385-408.

Shellabear, William G.

1925   *Malay-English Vocabulary,* Singapore: Methodist Publishing House.

Simon, Walter

1929   "Tibetisch-chinesische Wortgleichungen, ein Versuch," *Berlin, Universität, Seminar für Orientalische Sprachen, Mitteilungen, 32,* 157-228.

Solheim, Wilhelm G.

1967   "Southeast Asia and the West," *Science, 157,* 896-902.

1969   "Reworking Southeast Asian Prehistory," *Paideuma: Mitteilungen zur Kulturkunde, 15,* 125-39.

Speiser, Felix

1934   "Versuch einer Kulturanalyse der zentralen Neuen Hebriden," *Zeitschrift für Ethnologie, 66,* 128-86.

Stübel, Hans

1937   *Die Li-Stämme der Insel Hainan: Ein Beitrag zur Volkskunde Südchinas, unter Mitwirkung von P. Meriggi,* Berlin: Klinkhart und Biermann.

Suggs, Robert

1960   *The Island Civilizations of Polynesia,* New York: New American Library of World Literature.

Swinhoe, Robert

1871   "The Aborigines of Hainan," *Journal of the North China Branch of the Royal Asiatic Society, 7,* 25-40.

Tablan, Andrea A., and Carmen B. Mallari

1961   *Pilipino-English/English-Pilipino Dictionary,* New York: Washington Square Press.

Taintor, E. C.

1874   "The Aborigines of Northern Formosa," *Journal of the North China Branch of the Royal Asiatic Society, 10,* 53-88 (cit. from Ferrell 1969).

Thomson, J.
1873 "Notes of a Journey in Southern Formosa," *Journal of the Royal Geographical Society, 43*, 97-107 (cit. from Ferrell 1969).
Ting, V. K.
1929 "Notes on the Language of the Chuang in N. Kuangsi," *Bulletin of the Museum of Far Eastern Antiquities, 1*, 61-64.
Tsuchida, Shigeru
1968 *Kavalan Word List and Saisiyat Vocabulary, both November, 1968* (cit. from Ferrell 1969).
Utrecht Manuscript
1650 (cited from Ferrell 1969).
Walsh, D. S., and Bruce Biggs
1966 *Proto-Polynesian Word List I*, Auckland: Linguistic Society of New Zealand.
Wang, Li
1952 "Preliminary Study of the Language of the White Sand Li of Hainan," *Lingnan Journal, 11*, 253-300 (in Chinese).
Winstedt, Richard O.
1927 *Malay Grammar*, 2d ed., revised, Oxford: Clarendon Press.
Wolff, John
1974 *Proto-Austronesian *r and *d*, paper presented at the First International Conference on Comparative Austronesian Linguistics, Honolulu, January 1974.
Wulff, Kurt
1942 "Über das Verhältnis des Malay-Polynesischen zum Indochinesischen," *Det Künglige Danske Videnskabernes Selskab, Historisk-filologiske Meddelelser, 27*, ii.
Zorc, R. David
1972 "Current and Proto-Tagalic stress," *Philippine Journal of Linguistics, 3, no. 1*, 43-57.
1974 *A tentative Philippine wordlist: the qualitative use of vocabulary in classifying languages*, paper presented at the First International Conference on Comparative Austronesian Linguistics, Honolulu, January 1974.

Appendix I*

IN THE present paper the writer presents a general solution to the complex problem of the affinities of the Indonesian languages. The two following premises are basic to the thesis developed here:

1. The true Indonesian substratum on the Asiatic mainland is represented by four scattered languages in southern China, northern Tonkin, and Hainan, all of which constitute a single linguistic stock (Kadai).

2. The recognition of the Kadai stock, which shows numerous points of contact with Thai, opens the way to a new interpretation of the latter as a more distant member of an archaic Thai-Ḳadai-Indonesian linguistic complex.

Although these suggestions are new and perhaps unexpected, it can be said that they accord with the general picture as reconstructed from historical and cultural data. It is generally agreed that the Indonesian migrations have proceeded from the Asiatic mainland, but the evidence brought forward has been of a generic rather than specific nature, and the area of departure has not been delimited. The linguistic speculation has been notable for range rather than relevancy,[1] and the cultural treatment has in some instances been equally unsound.[2] It is hoped that the argument developed below will provide a number of solid *points d'appui* from which further ramifications can be anticipated.

The newly recognized Kadai stock comprises the Li dialects of the island of Hainan, the Kelao language of southcentral China, and the Laqua and Lati languages of the China-Tonkin border region. The term "Kadai" has been compounded by the writer from "Dai," one of the forms of the Li term for themselves,[3] and the kă- prefix found in Laqua kădăŭ, Kelao kătsü "man (homo)." These languages, with the exception of Li, are not generally known to the scientific world, and our available sources are rather meager. The Li dialects have been described by a number of European observers, the most thorough of whom have been Savina and Stübel-Meriggi.[4] Bonifacy has pub-

---

[1] For some of the earlier speculation, see W. Churchill, *The Polynesian Wanderings* (Washington, 1911), largely devoted to a criticism of MacDonald's Semitic theory.

[2] An outstanding example is furnished by Handy's derivation of the Polynesian Tangaloa cult from southern China (*Polynesian Religion*, Bulletin of the Bernice P. Bishop Museum, no. 34, 1927, pp. 312–330).

[3] Other variants are: B'lai, K'lai, S'lai, S'ai, Hiai, Lai, Loi, Le, Dli, B'li. The Chinese character employed for this name is pronounced *li* in North China dialects, *lai* in Cantonese, and *loi* in Hoklo.

[4] R. Swinhoe, *The Aborigines of Hainan* (Journal of the North China Branch of the Royal Asiatic Society, Vol. 7, 1871), pp. 25–40; J. Calder, *Notes on Hainan and its Aborigines* (China Review, Vol. 11, 1882), pp. 42–50; E. H. Parker, *The Li Aborigines of K'iung Shan* (China Review, Vol. 19, 1890), pp. 383–387; C. C. Jeremaissen, *Loi Aborigines of Hainan and their Speech* (China Review, Vol. 20, 1892), pp. 296–305; F. M. Savina, *Lexique dày-français, accompagné d'un petit lexique français-dày et d'un tableau des différences dialectales* (Bulletin de l'École Fran-

° Reprinted from *American Anthropologist*, Vol. 44, No. 4, Part 1, pp. 576–601, October–December 1942.

lished word-lists of Kelao, Laqua, and Lati,[5] while additional material on all three languages has been supplied by his compatriot, Lunet de Lajonquière.[6] A third Kelao source has been furnished by Samuel R. Clarke, the author of a popular account of the little-known tribal groups in southern China.[7]

The Kedai languages have received scant attention from anthropologists and linguists. Li has evoked occasional comment, yet no real analysis has been attempted. The obvious Thai element in the language was noted by Parker over half a century ago,[8] and this theme was further developed by Strzoda.[9] The less apparent Indonesian affinities were first pointed out by Terrien de Lacouperie, who suggested a relationship with the Indonesian languages of Formosa.[10] In more recent times P. Mus[11] and H. Maspero[12] have further extended this line of thought and have supplied the first concrete bits of evidence. Maspero, a sound and generally conservative scholar, concludes that the Li numerals "certainly" belong to the Indonesian family (*op. cit.*, p. 230).

The three mainland languages (Kelao, Laqua, Lati) have attracted still less attention. Bonifacy, who recorded Laqua, noted the analogy between the Laqua and Cham numerals,[13] but this observation seems to have been over-

---

çaise d'Extrême-Orient, t. 31, 1931), pp. 103–199; H. Stübel, *Die Li-Stämme der Insel Hainan; Ein Beitrag zur Volkskunde Südchinas, unter Mitwirkung von P. Meriggi* (Berlin, 1937).

[5] A. Bonifacy, *Étude sur les langues parlées par les populations de la haute Rivière Claire* (Bulletin de l'École Française d'Extrême-Orient, t. 5, 1905), pp. 306–323; *Étude sur les coutumes et la langue des La-ti* (*Ibid.*, t. 6, 1906), pp. 271–278; *Étude sur les coutumes et la langue des Lolo et des La-qua du Haut Tonkin* (*Ibid.*, t. 8, 1908), pp. 531–558.

[6] E. Lunet de Lajonquière, *Ethnographie du Tonkin Septentrional* (Paris, 1906). Word-lists on pp. 357 (Kelao), 340 (Pen-ti-Lolo = Laqua), and 359 (Lati).

[7] *Among the Tribes in South-west China* (London, 1911).

[8] E. H. Parker, *Siamese Words in Hainan and China* (China Review, Vol. 18, 1889), p. 198.

[9] W. Strzoda, *Die Lie auf Hainan and ihre Beziehungen zum asiatischen Kontinent* (Zeitschrift für Ethnologie, Bd. 43, 1911), pp. 193–236. Strzoda concludes, however, that "Die meisten Li-Numeralia . . . sint Rätsel und lassen sich nirgends unterbringen" (pp. 219–220).

[10] *The Languages of China before the Chinese* (London, 1887). See especially his conclusions on p. 73: "In the numerals, for instance . . . similarities exist with those of some tribes of Formosa. But they are remote, and do not come from a direct relationship; they are apparently survivals of a former state of things, previous to their respective migrations, when their various ancestors had relations between themselves on the continent." An English traveller in Hainan, B. C. Henry, had somewhat earlier sought to connect the Li with the Malay on onomastic grounds (B'lai or B'lay = Malay), in his article, *The Close of a Journey through Hainan* (China Review, Vol. 12, 1883), pp. 109–124, esp. p. 115.

[11] Review of Savina, *Monographie de Hainan* (1929), in Bulletin de l'École Française d'Extrême-Orient, t. 30, 1930 (pp. 436–444). Of his own Cham and Malay comparisons, however, Mus remarks: "Ces rapprochements sporadiques restent jusqu'ici de simple curiosité."

[12] Review of Savina, *Lexique dày-français* (1931), in Bulletin de la Societé de Linguistique de Paris, t. 34, pt. 3, 1933, pp. 228–236.

[13] Cit. supra, 1908, p. 557. Bonifacy adds the following remark: "Là paraissent s'arrêter les ressemblances entre les deux langues [Laqua and Cham], à supposer même que celles que nous signalons ne soient pas purement fortuites."

THAI-KADAI-INDONESIAN

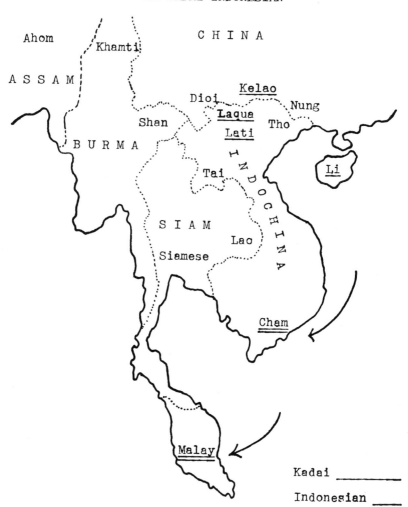

looked by Maspero and other scholars. Kelao and Lati have gone almost entirely unnoticed, although W. Schmidt has seen fit to classify the latter as an independent linguistic entity.[14] It was Bonifacy's observation on Laqua that led to the writer's discovery of the relationship between Laqua and Li, and thus ultimately to the concept of a single unified Kadai stock.

[14] *Die Sprachfamilien und Sprachkreise der Erde* (Heidelberg, 1914). Schmidt places Laqua in an artificial "Eastern Thai" group.

The Kadai-speaking groups are all of marginal type, as should be expected on the basis of our substratum theory. The Li, who inhabit the mountainous central and south-central parts of Hainan, are under economic pressure from their powerful Ong-Be (Thai-speaking) and Hoklo (Chinese-speaking) neighbors. The Kadai groups on the mainland rank even below the Miao and Lolo, and generally regard themselves as autochthonous. The Laqua, who call themselves Ka Beo, in the upper Rivière Claire valley of northern Tonkin, are described by Lunet de Lajonquière as follows:

> *Ils se considèrent comme aborigènes et il est certain qu'ils sont venus dans la contrée avant toutes les autres tribus montagnardes (cit. supra, p. 339).*
>
> *C'est une variété* [of economic life] *en complete décadence. La plus grande partie des terres qu'ils cultivaient ont été déjà cédées aux Meo, qui paraissent devoir les absorber (ibid., p. 341).*

Of the Lati, also in the upper Rivière Claire valley, the same writer states simply that *"Ils se prétendent aborigènes" (cit. supra, p. 358).* Bonifacy places his estimate of the number of Lati at only 450 (76 families).

The Kelao or Lao, who call themselves Thü, range over an extensive area in south-central China and northern Tonkin, but their true home appears to be Kueichou province, whence they have migrated into the northern Tonkin border region (cf. Lunet de Lajonquière, *cit. supra*, p. 356). Clarke, who has given us the fullest available account of the Kelao, stresses the aboriginal nature of the group:

> The Keh-lao, however, are now nearly extinct; many of them have married into Chung-chia [Thai] and Old Chinese families. Some writers have spoken of them as extinct. As far as we know, there are now only several hamlets of them in the Anshun prefecture [west-central Kueichou], which altogether do not number more than two or three hundred families. These people claim, and rightly, we believe, to be the real aborigines of that region. In some parts of the province the Miao claim to be the aborigines, but where the Miao and Keh-lao occupy the same district, the Miao allow that the Keh-lao were there before themselves (*cit. supra*, p. 13).

Another missionary writer, Aloys Schotter, also attributes a low rank to the Kelao:

> *Le plus bas dans l'échelle sociale c'est peut-être le groupe des Blancs* [White Miao]. *La tribu des Kë-lao est peut-être plus dégradée encore surtout quant aux moeurs.*[15]

The languages spoken by these primitive groups fall into two major divisions, viz. Li-Laqua and Lati-Kelao, which together constitute the Kadai stock. Dialectical differences can be established both for Li and Kelao, and are of such magnitude that they must fully be taken into account. The numer-

---

[15] *Notes ethnographiques sur les tribus du Kuey-tcheou* (Anthropos, Bd. 6, 1911), pp. 318–344; citation from p. 318.

ous Li dialects can be classified under the headings of "Southern Li" and "Northern Li" on the basis of their treatment of original nasal initials. In Northern Li these initials tend to be transformed into the homorganic stops, whereas in Southern Li they are uniformly retained; cf. N. Li *ba~pa*, S. Li *ma* "dog" (Thai **hma*); N. Li *dau~tau*, S. Li *nau* "long" (Thai **ñau*); N. Li *ka*, S. Li *nga* "horse" (Annamite *ngüa*). The "Central Dai" dialect recorded by Savina and most of the dialects recorded by Jeremiassen and Stübel belong in the Northern Li group, while the "Southern Dai" dialect of Savina, the Yulinkau dialect of Swinhoe and Calder, and the K'iung-Shan dialect of Parker belong in the Southern Li group. Kelao similarly shows a dialectical cleavage between "Northern Kelao" (dialect recorded by Clarke) and "Southern Kelao" (dialect recorded by Bonifacy and Lunet de Lajonquière). The distinctions here, both lexical and phonetic, are even more marked than those that obtain in Li, but conform to no easily recognizable pattern. It is apparent that a full treatment of the linguistic problems of Kadai would require detailed phonetic information on a wide range of dialects for at least four languages, and it is not unlikely that further exploration in the Tonkin-China border area will reveal still other members of this stock. Unfortunately, we lack the materials necessary to implement a complete study of the whole stock,[16] and must content ourselves with a survey of the more salient points.

All four Kadai languages are of monosyllabic, isolating type, with full tonal systems as in Thai. The Kadai word-order, like that of Thai and Indonesian, shows object following verb, and modifying elements (including genitive constructs) following modified elements; thus, Malay *mata hari*, Li *sa ven*, Thai **ta wǎn* "sun," lit. "eye (of the) day." Kadai, like Thai, lacks the affixation apparatus of Indonesian, yet prefixed forms abound in the Lati-Kelao branch of the stock, e.g. Lati prefixed *m-* in *m-tšua* "moon," *m-bo* "sky," *m-ti* "earth," *m-ni* "ox," *m-go* "cat," *m-so* "elephant," *m-si* "beak, mouth," *m-tšu* "eye," *m-ngǎ* "oil"; Lati prefixed *a-* in *a-ña* "rain," *a-lia* "rat," *a-k'o* "monkey," *a-ti* "tiger," *a-kǔ* "bird," *a-li* "fish," *a-k'e* "frog," *a-k'u* "man," *a-sa* "hair," *a-ñu* "salt." Kelao has prefixed *bu-* occasionally corresponding to Lati prefixed *m-*, as in Kelao *bu-to* "earth," *bu-tsüe* "beak" (*bu-tsü-lüa* "mouth"). Laqua has prefixed *kǎ-* in *kǎ-dǎǔ* "man," *kǎ-zio kǎ-pǎ* "boy," *kǎ-zio ka-mǎi* "girl," where *zio* stands for "child" and *pǎ* and *mǎi* are the sex modifiers.

On the phonetic side, the Kadai languages present a fairly uniform pattern of relatively simple type, though mixed (indeterminate) and front-rounded vowels are uncommonly abundant. Li exhibits the greatest range of initials

---

[16] None of our records of Kadai languages is satisfactory as regards transcription. Savina employs the cumbersome and inadequate *qu'ôc-ngû* system of Annamite, while Bonifacy makes use of a modified version of the same system. In the present study open vowels are written as short vowels (*ĕ*, *ŏ*), and the "bearded o" (*o'*) and "bearded u" (*u'*) as front rounded vowels (*ŏ*, *ü*).

and finals, with Laqua not far behind, while Lati and Kelao have undergone a process of extreme modification, in the course of which almost all final nasals and stops have been eliminated.[17] The phonetic attrition shown by Lati and Kelao has proved to be one of the chief stumbling blocks in our analysis of Kadai phonology. When it is realized that Li and Laqua, the better preserved pair of languages, stand in much the same relationship to Indonesian, some inkling of our difficulties can be gained. The investigation of the phonetic shifts exhibited by the Thai roots in Li, the best recorded of the Kadai languages, has brought to light a number of significant variations, especially as regards initials, which are useful in the study of Thai itself. Thus, the writer has reconstructed a separate phoneme *hr (surd r) for archaic Thai on the basis of the equation Ahom r- = Siamese h- = Tho t'-; in this series Li significantly has s-, suggesting an original *sr-:

	Ahom	Simese	Tho	Li
stone	*rin*	*hĭn*	*t'in*	*sien*
louse	*rau*	*hău*	*t'au*	*său*
break	*rak*	*hăk*	——	*săk*
carry	*rap*	*hap*	*t'ap*	*sap*

The variations in initials between S. Li and N. Li are often of unusual type, e.g. S. Li d- = N. Li f-, corresponding to Thai d- (Siamese d- = Shan l- = Khamti n-):[18]

	Siamese	Shan	Khamti	S. Li	N. Li
earth	*dĭn*	*lin*	*nin*	{ *dăn* { *den*	*fan*
bone	*kădŭk*	*luk*	*nuk*	*drŭ*	*füök*
raw	*dĭp*	*lip*	*nip*	*diep*	*fiep*

Aspiration of initial stops is characteristic of Li; cf. Li *hăn*, Thai *$guăn$ "smoke"; Li *ha*, Thai *ga "thatching grass"; Li *hang*, Thai *$gang$ "jaw"; Li *hăn*, Thai *$k'ăn$ "crow of a cock"; Li *hău*, Thai *$k'ău$ "horn," also "mountain"; and Li *k'ău*, Thai *$kău$ "old"; Li *k'ăi*, Thai *$kăi$ "fowl." Li often simplifies the complicated diphthongs and triphthongs of Thai, but note Li medial -*ie*- = Thai -*ĭ*-, -*ĕ*-, as in Li *dien*~*tlien*, Thai *$lĭn$ "tongue"; Li *diep*~*fiep*, Thai *$dĭp$ "raw"; Li *liep*, Thai *$lĕp$ "fingernail," and Li -*öü* = Thai -*aü*, as in Li *böü*, Thai *$baü$ "leaf"; Li *tšöü*, Thai *$tšaü$ "heart"; Li *t'öü*, Thai *$taü$ "low." S. Li retains final -*k* after short vowels but substitutes a glottal stop[19] after long vowels, while

---

[17] Lati has retained the final stop only in *a-liep* "claw" (Thai *$lĕp$ "fingernail") and the Annamite loan-word *but* "pen."

[18] Thai *d*- and *b*- are best reconstructed as lenis surd stop initials, since they belong in the high tonal series along with the regular surd stops (*t*- and *t'*-, *p*- and *p'*-). Li agrees with the majority of Thai languages proper in having *b*- for Thai *b*-, as in Li *böü*, Thai *$baü$ "leaf."

[19] Represented in Savina's transcription by the Annamite tone *nặng*.

N. Li uniformly retains the final velar stop; cf. Li *p'ŏk*, Thai **vŏk* "hatch"; Li *t'ŏk*, Thai **tŏk* "fall"; Li *fĭ'*, Thai **pik* "wing"; Li *t'o'*, Thai **t'ok* "pour"; Li *sa'*, Thai **sak* "pestle"; S. Li *drü'*, N. Li *füök*, Thai **ɖuk* "bone."

The morphological and phonological points developed above point to Thai rather than to Indonesian, yet the lexical elements of Kadai bear the unmistakable imprint of the latter stock, along with an equally deep imprint of the former. In brief, the numerals and a scattering of nouns, pronouns, and adjectives show Indonesian affinities, while many of the remaining elements show Thai affinities. On the basis of this distribution, the writer at first regarded Kadai as a composite of Indonesian and Thai, with the former as the more likely substratum. Further analysis of Thai, however, has led to the view presented below; to wit, that Thai, Kadai, and Indonesian together constitute a single linguistic complex. Kadai is the "transitional" member of this triune, though in the main it approaches Thai rather than Indonesian. Both Thai and Kadai have reduced a number of disyllabic roots to monosyllables, have developed complete tonal systems, and have discarded the original morphological apparatus of affixes.[20] Throughout this elaborate linguistic metamorphosis, however, a number of basic lexical landmarks have persisted and it is to these that we shall direct our attention.

The Kadai numerals are of fundamental importance in the present connection, since the Indonesian affinities of the stock are more apparent there than elsewhere. The following table of Kadai numerals, in which reconstructed Indonesian (IN) roots taken from O. Dempwolff's recent work[21] have been incorporated, serves to illustrate this point.

	IN	Laqua	S. Li	N. Li	S. Kelao	N. Kelao	Lati
one	**'it'a'*	tiă	kü	ü	tsi	si	tšăm
two	**ɖuwa'*	δe	dau	trau	δü	so	fu
three	**təlu'*	tău	su	su	tŏ	da	si
four	**'ə(m)pat*	pe	sau	so	pu	bu	pu
five	**lima'*	mö	ma	pa	mlĕn	mbu	ng
six	**'ənam*	nam	nom	tom	tšö	nang	nă
seven	**pitu'*	mö tău	t'u	t'au	δi	ši	ti
eight	**walu'*	mö dü	du	au	šiă	vleu	be
nine	**t'iwa'*	mö δiă	pöü	föü	ku	su	lu
ten	**puluh*	păt	p'uot	fuot	tsü	beu	pa

The following variants are worthy of comment: S. Kelao *mlĕn* "5" but

[20] For the general argument here, see the Thai discussion below.

[21] *Vergleichende Lautlehre des austronesischen Wortschatzes; Bd. III; Austronesisches Wörterverzeichnis* (Beihefte zur Zeitschrift für Eingeborenen Sprachen, Bd. 19, 1930). Forms as cited by Dempwolff, with the exception of *y* for *j*, *w* for *v*, and *r* for *γ*. "Facultative" nasal infixes are enclosed in parentheses.

tsü mu "15" (cf. N. Kelao *mbu* "5"); Lati *tšăm* "1" but *pa tšă* "11"; Lati *pa* "10" but *fu pe* "20", *sie pe* "30" (*si* "3").

Some of the leading features of Kadai phonology are illustrated in the above table of numerals. N. Li *pa*<*ma* "5," *tom*<*nom* "6", and *föü*<*pöü* "9," *fuot*<*p'uot* "10" are all regular developments (see the discussion above). Li *kü*∼*ü* "1" are probably independent of the IN root, and the analysis of Li *su* "3," *sau*∼*so* "4" is not certain. For the latter, Maspero suggests a development comparable with that found in Tarema (Formosa), which has *suatto* <*suat*<*səwat*<*səbat*<*s-pat* "4." Li *du*∼*au* "8" belong to a puzzling series in which S. Li initial *d-* corresponds to N. Li initial *h-* or vocalic anlaut, e.g. *dai*∼*hai* "iron," *dai*∼*hiai* "a Li," *duoi*∼*ui* "fat" (n.), *döü*∼*öü* "thin." These forms seem to have been derived from roots with labial+liquid initial cluster; cf. the variant form *b'lai* "a Li," and the frequent correspondences with Thai initial *r-*, as in S. Li *da*, Thai **rŭa* "boat"; S. Li *dăt*, Thai **răt* "squeeze"; S. Li *düön*, Thai **rüan* "house" (N. Li *plong*). We can infer a bifurcate development of the type **walu'*>**wlu'* or **blu'*>*du* (S. Li), and **walu'*>**wau'*>*au* (N. Li). Li *p'uot*∼*fuot* "10" attest to a pair of shifts, viz. final *-h*>*-t*, as in IN **darah*, Li *dat*∼*tlat* "blood," and medial *-u-*>*-uo-*, as in Thai **nŭng*, Li *ñuong* "mosquito." The development here has been of the type **puluh*>**p'luh*>*p'lut* >**p'ut*>*p'uot*.

Laqua parallels Li in the developments *mö du*>**walu'* "8" and *păt*>**puluh* "10." Laqua *tiă*<**it'a'* "1," *tău*<**təlu'* "3," and *mö δia*<**t'iwa'* "9" reveal IN affinities not apparent in Li. The Laqua vocalic shift *a*<*e*∼*ö* is found in the forms *δe* "2," *pe* "4," and *mö* "5"; cf. Laqua *pö*, IN **batu'* "stone"; Laqua *pe*, IN **bapa'* "father"; Laqua *te*, IN **mata'* "eye"; Laqua *ne* Li *na*∼*ta*, Thai **na* "rice-field"; and, medially, Laqua *dön*, Li *dan* "100"; Laqua *nen*, Li *ñan* "moon." The appearance of *mö* "5" in the Laqua numerals "6" to "8" is suggestive of a quinary system; cf. the S. Kelao numerals cited by Lunet de Lajonquière: *sü-u* "2," *to-u* "3," *pu-u* "4," *nlĕ-u* "5," but *tšĕ-ni* "6," *dž-ni* "7," *suo-ni* "8," *ku-ni* "9."[22] Laqua and Li have a common root for "100" (*dön* ∼*dan*), which is independent of the IN root (**ratut'*).

The Kelao and Lati numerals are, in general, further removed from the IN system as reflected in Laqua and Li. Notable, however, are S. Kelao *mlĕn* (Bonifacy)∼*nlĕ* (Lajonquière)<IN **lima'* "5," and N. Kelao *vleu*<IN **walu'* "8," which show retention of the liquid phoneme *l*. Kelao *pu*∼*bu*, Lati *pu* "4" reflect an *a*>*u* vocalic shift, which is especially characteristic of Lati; in the table below, the contrast with the Laqua *e*∼*ö* vocalism is made clear:

---

[22] The IN system is decimal rather than quinary, yet the Formosa languages show irregular features suggestive of the latter, e.g., Sek-hwan has 5+1=6, 5+2=7, etc., and Tsui-hwan and Bu-hwan have 3×2=6, 4×2=8; vide T. L. Bullock, *Formosa Dialects and their connection with the Malay* (China Review, Vol. 3, 1875, pp. 38–46).

	IN	Li	Laqua	Lati
four	*'ə(m)pat	—	pe	pu
five	*lima'	ma∼pa	mö	ng(u)
father	*bapa'	fa∼ba	pe	pu
eye	*mata'	sa	te	m–tšu

The variability reflected in the Kadai numerals appears also in other aspects of the vocabulary. Scarcely any roots prevail everywhere, and there are a number of confusing "partial equations," yet many significant features emerge. One of the most notable of these features is the regularity shown in the roots for "dog," "pig," and "horse," the first two with Thai affinities, the last with Annamite:

		Laqua	S. Li	N. Li	S. Kelao	N. Kelao	Lati
dog	*hma (Thai)	mǎ	ma	pa	χmǎ	mu	mu
pig	*hmu (Thai)	mu	mau	pau	χmüǎ	ma	me
horse	*ngüa (Ann.)	rre	nga	ka	ngüǎ	niau	ngo

Note the N. Kelao and Lati shift u<a in mu<*hma "dog," and N. Li p-<m-, k-<ng- (vide supra). These loan-words, if such they be, must be of some antiquity, in view of the selective nature of the distribution (there is no trace of the prominent Thai-Chinese root *ma "horse"), as well as the noteworthy equation S. Kelao χm-=Thai hm-, the latter a reconstructed phoneme (surd m) not found in any of the modern Thai languages. In the same general class belongs the correspondence between Laqua k'ǎi, Li and N. Lelao k'ai, Lati ka "fowl," and the Thai root *kǎi; contrast the earlier stratum reflected in the series IN *manuk "fowl, bird," Laqua nuk, S. Kelao ñie "bird," and Thai *nǒk "bird."

The following group of comparisons, arranged roughly according to natural lexical divisions, is intended to serve as an index of the Kadai-Indonesian relationship:

1. Laqua vuon (Lajonquière mo ven) "sun," Li ven "day," sa ven "sun" ("eye of the day"), S. Kelao du vuǎ "sun," IN *wari' "day, sun" (IN medial -r-<Laqua and Li -n). Cf. also N. Kelao vlei "sky," which shows a contrasting type of development (*wari'<*wli<vlei).

2. S. Li (pa) pǔn "rain," IN *ə(m)bun "atmospheric precipitate" (Tagalog 'ambon "fine rain").

3. Li nom∼nam, IN *danum "water."

4. Laqua pǎi, Li pei∼fei, S. Kelao p'i, N. Kelao bai, Lati pie, IN *'apuy "fire." For the Li development (*'apuy>*api>pei), cf. Li ngei, IN *tangit' "weep"; Li nei, IN *'ini' "this."

5. Laqua *pung*, IN **bunga'* "flower."
6. Laqua *kă-dăŭ*, Li *ău*, IN **tawu'* "man (homo)."
7. Laqua *pe*, Li *fa*~*ba*, S. Kelao *ă-ba*, Lati *pu*, IN **bapa'* "father." For the vocalism, see the analysis above.
8. Laqua *ru* (Lajonquière), S. Li *dau*, N. Li *fo*~*o*, IN **'ulu'* "head." The Li development has been **'ulu'* > **wlu* > *du*~*o*, exactly paralleling IN **walu'* > Li *du*~*au* "8."
9. Laqua *δam*, S. Kelao *lă so*, N. Kelao *ma sang*, Lati *a-sa*, IN **d'a(m)but* "hair." The original palatal initial has everywhere been assibilized: **d'a(m)but* > **d'am* > *δam* and *sang*~*sa*~*so*. For the Laqua initial δ-, cf. Laqua *δău*, IN **hud'an* "rain."
10. Laqua *te*, Li *sa*, N. Kelao *dau*, Lati *m-tšu*, IN **mata'* "eye." Li appears to have developed a sibilant initial through aspiration (**mata'* > **m-t'a* > *sa*); see the discussion below of the Thai root **ta*. S. Kelao perhaps retains the root in the compound *du vuă* "sun," paralleling Li *sa ven*, Malay *mata hari* ("eye of the day"), yet this dialect also has *du die* "moon," *du dě* "star." The picture is further complicated by the evidence from Lati, which has *m-tšu* "eye," *m-tšu* "month" (on different tones as recorded by Bonifacy), but *m-tšua* "moon" and simply *tšua* "star."
11. Laqua *rö*, Li *yăi*~*t'ăi*, N. Kelao *rau*, Latu *lu*, IN **talinga'* "ear." For Laqua *rö* < **talinga'*, cf. Laqua *rre*, Annamite *ngüa* "horse" (Laqua *-ö* < *-a*; see the analysis above). The Li forms point to an original **ñăi* or **niăi* with palatalized nasal initial, whence S. Li *yăi* (through further palatalization) and N. Li *t'ăi* (*n-* > *t-* is the regular N. Li shift). This reconstruction is supported by two outside comparisons, one with Thai (Dioi) and the other with IN, as shown in the table below (Central Li from Savina, Shaved Head Li and White Sand Li from Stübel):

		S. Li	C. Li	Shaved Head	White Sand
ear	**talinga'* (IN)	*yăi*	*t'ăi*	*t'ai*	*džai*
finger	**niang* (Dioi)	*yeng*	*tleăng*	*t'ěng*	*džing*
			t'eng		
snake	——	*ya*	*t'a*	*t'a*	*dža*
yellow	**kuning* (IN)	*yěng*	——	*t'ěng*	*džiang*
		hieng			

12. S. Li (*hai*) *p'en*, S. Kelao *du pio*, N. Kelao *bang*, IN **'ipən* "tooth."
13. Li *k'ok*, N. Kelao *k'au*, IN **kaki'* "foot."
14. Lati *tšu*, IN **t'ut'u* "breast."
15. Li *dat*~*tlat*, IN **darah* "blood." For the final, cf. Li *p'uot*~*fuot*, IN **puluh* "10."
16. Laqua *nen* "fat" (n.), S. Kelao *nuă*, Lati *m-ngă* "oil," S. Kelao *nu* χ*müă*, Lati *m-ngă me* "fat" ("oil of pig"), IN **miñak* "oil"~**mənak* "fat."

17. Laqua *küön*, N. Li *k'an*, S. Kelao *kă mǒn∼mǒn kă* (*mǒn* perhaps for *mo* "rice"), N. Kelao *ka*, Lati *k'o*, IN **ka'∼*ka'ən∼*ka'i* "eat." Note also Laqua *ngăm* "drink," IN **pangan* "eat" (cf. Lati *k'o* "eat," also "drink").

18. Li *sop∼sap*, Lati (*ngua*) *so*, IN **rabi* "night." Cf. also Javanese *sĕrap* "twilight,"[23] and the equation Li *s-* = Thai *hr-* analyzed above.

19. Li *ngei*, IN **tangit'* "weep."

20. Laqua *tie*, IN **matay∼*patay* "die." For the vocalism, cf. Laqua *te*, IN **mata'* "eye."

21. Li *diep∼fiep* "raw," IN **huḍip* "live." Note "raw" = "green" = "alive" a semantic association appearing also in the Thai root **ďĭp* (vide infra). For the medial diphthong in Li, see the analysis above.

22. Laqua *dăm*, Li *dŏm* "black," IN **'i(n)təm* "black," **ḍəḍəm∼tiḍəm* "dark."

23. Laqua *nin*, S. Li *yĕng∼hieng*, N. Li *t'ĕng*, S. Kelao *t'e ni*, N. Kelao *nyi*, Lati *a-hni* (recorded as *an hi*), IN **kuning* "yellow." Li **ñeng* or **nieng > yĕng ∼t'ĕng* (vide supra); **nieng < *kuning*, with medial diphthong as in No. 21.

24. Li *tik∼tok*, IN **ḍikih∼*'ə(n)ṭik∼*iṭik* "small."

25. Laqua *k'ău*, S. Li *hau*, Lati *ku∼kui*, IN **'aku'* "I." Li *hau < *k'au* (vide supra).

26. Li *nei*, IN **'ini'* "this."

In addition to the above, a number of significant correspondences exist within the Kadai stock itself, thus serving to tie the group together. The more important of these lexical agreements are listed below:

1. Laqua *nen*, Li *ñan* "moon." Possibly related to IN **bulan* "moon"; thus, **bulan > *wulan > *dan* (paralleling **walu' > du* "8," **'ulu' > du* "head") *> ñan* (through assimilation to the final nasal). Cf. Li *nuk*, IN **bəluk* "monkey."

2. Laqua *mǒn* "sky," *mön dǒng* "thunder," S. Kelao *mön düă* "rain," Lati *m-bo* "sky" (Lajonaquière *büön*).

3. Laqua *mön dǒng*, Li *pa dang om*, S. Kelao *zü dǒng* "thunder."

4. Laqua *hǒng*, S. Kelao *ngă-ye* "water" (but *zǒng ngŭă* "drink"); N. Kelao *u*, Lati *i* "water"; cf. N. Kelao *du*, Lati *m-ti* "earth." S. Kelao retains the element *u* in the compounds *u ngĕ uă* "tears" (Lati *i m-tšu*), *i lă-pu* "milk" (Lati *i tšu*). A possible comparison exists with IN **wayər* "water."

5. Laqua *dăm*, Li *sam* "fruit"; S. Kelao *mă*, Lati *mi* "fruit."

6. Laqua *pĕǒ < *plǒ*, Li *da∼tla* "fish"; S. Kelao *lü*, Lati *li* "fish." Cf. Thai **pla* "fish."

7. Laqua *kăuk*, Li *hău < *k'ău*, S. Kelao *pă-ku*, Lati *kui* "horn." Cf. Thai **k'ău* "horn."

8. Laqua *mă∼măi*, Li *mei*, S. Kelao *mu* (*vĕ*), Lati *mia* "female, mother." Cf. Thai **me* "mother."

---

[23] Cited in R. Brandstetter, *Malaio-polynesische Forschungen; IV: Mata-Hari, oder Wanderungen eines indonesischen Sprachforschers durch die drei Reiche der Natur* (Luzern, 1908), p. 6.

9. Laqua *mon*, S. Li *mom*, N. Li *păm~băm* "mouth." Cf. Annamite *mŏm* "muzzle, snout."

10. Laqua *mun*, Li *müöm~püöm* "beard" (cf. the treatment of nasal finals in the foregoing example). Cf. Thai **mŭm* "beard" (only in the northern Thai speeches: Dioi *mum*, Tho *kang mum*, Nung *mom*.

11. Li *p'a möü*, N. Kelao *mau* "hand." Cf. Thai **mü* "hand."

12. Laqua *nie*, S. Li *yeng*, N. Li *t'eng~tleăng* "finger" (Li **nieng*, vide supra). Cf. Dioi (Thai) *niang* "finger."

13. S. Kelao *plă*, Lati *pio* "blood"; cf. S. Kelao *ple u*, Lati *p'i* "die."

14. Laqua *ði*, S. Kelao *öü tu* "urine."

15. Laqua *ñung*, Li *ñau*, S. Kelao *ñu*, N. Kelao *nyö*, Lati *a-ñu* "salt." Cf. IN **'uyah* "salt."

16. Laqua *yeu*, S. Kelao *hă*, N. Kelao *a*, Lati *ho* "meat, flesh." Li has the puzzling forms *mam~am*.

17. Laqua *măi*, Li *mau~pau* "year."

18. N. and S. Kelao *vu*, Lati *vu* "go."

19. S. Li *müön*, N. Li *püön~pöü*, S. Kelao *χm*, N. Kelao *mu* "come." Cf. Malay *mari*, Cham *mörai~mai* "come," indicating the development IN medial *-r->*Li *-n*, as in **wari*>*ven* "day."

20. Laqua *neng*, Li *děng~t'lěng* "red." Cf. Thai *đeng* "red."

21. Laqua *mi*, Li *mü~măü* "thou." Cf. Thai **maü* "thou," Annamite *măi* "thou" (pejorative).

We have, finally, to consider the nature of the affinity of Kadai and Indonesian with the Thai group of languages, spoken over a wide area in southern China, Siam, French Indochina, Burma, and Assam. The Thai family includes Ahom, Khamti, and Shan, in the west; Siamese and Lao, in the south; White Tai and Black Tai, in the east; Nung and Tho, in the northeast; and Dioi, in the north. Despite the geographical extent of this group, the several languages are closely interrelated, and thus rather detailed reconstructions of the parent speech can be made. The earliest systematic investigation in this field was Maspero's study of the Thai tonal system.[24] This study was supplemented by several brief articles by G. Coedès and J. Burnay,[25] but no comprehensive review of the problem appeared until almost a quarter of a century later, when K. Wulff published his monumental work on Chinese and Thai.[26] The writer has further extended the analysis undertaken by Wulff and has filled in cer-

---

[24] *Contribution à l'étude du systeme phonétique des langues thai* (Bull. de l'École Française d'Extrême-Orient, t. 11, 1911), pp. 153–169.

[25] The most important of these are: *Note sur les tons et les initials du vieux siamois à l'époque de Sukhodaya* (Journal of the Siam Society, Vol. 21, 1927), pp. 103–117; [v] *et* [χ] *et leur origine* (*Ibid.*), pp. 119–126.

[26] *Chinesisch und Tai: Sprachvergleichende Untersuchungen* (Det Kgl. Danske Videnskabernes Selskab., Historisk-filologiske Meddelelser, Vol. 20, pt. 3, 1934).

tain lacunae in that scholar's work,[27] so that our present knowledge of Thai phonology may be regarded as reasonably complete.[28]

As regards the affiliations of Thai, the generally accepted view has been that Chinese and Thai constitute a single "Eastern" division of the Sino-Tibetan or Indo-Chinese stock, in opposition to the Tibeto-Burman or "Western" division. It is this view that has been developed by Maspero, Wulff, and, most recently, R. Shafer (largely on the basis of Wulff's work),[29] and that has given rise to attempts at direct Siamese-Tibetan comparisons, such as those of O. Schrader.[30] The writer must plead guilty on the same charge, though in modified form.[31] Almost alone among students of the Thai languages, Coedès and Burnay have evinced a healthy skepticism of the dogma of a Chinese-Thai relationship. Conrady, a pioneer in Far Eastern linguistics, sought to connect Indo-Chinese, including Thai, with the Austric stock (Mon-Khmer, Khasi, Munda, et al.) established by Schmidt, in terms of a "common substratum" (*gemeinsame Unterschicht*).[32] Wulff, apparently under the influence of Conrady, has attempted to demonstrate the existence of infixes in Siamese, which he compares with those characteristic of the Austric languages. Of Conrady's proposed Indo-Chinese-Austric grouping, Wulff makes the following assertion:

> The similarity of the formations [infixes] in both languages [Siamese, Javanese] rests not on chance, since the relationship of Malayo-Polynesian with Indo-Chinese, which Conrady sought to show with insufficient means, is certain [sicher]. (*cit. supra*, p. 17, note 1)

---

[27] Notably in Ahom, where Wulff failed to make use of the most important lexicon on that language (Borua, *Ahom-Assamese-English Dictionary*, Calcutta, 1920); Tho, completely neglected by Wulff but for which we have two utilizable sources, viz. E. Diguet, *Étude de la langue Thô* (Paris, 1910), and Fr. Th. Gordaliza, *Estudio sobre el dialecto Thô de la región de Lang-sön* (Anthropos, Bd. 3, 1908), pp. 512–532; White Tai, for which an excellent source has recently appeared, viz. G. Minot, *Dictionnaire tày blanc-français* (Bull. de l'École Française d'Extrême-Orient, t. 40, fasc. 1, 1940, pp. 1–237.)

[28] The writer has in preparation a comparative dictionary of the Thai languages, based in large part on materials collected by the Sino-Tibetan Philology Project of the Works Progress Administration, sponsored by Prof. A. L. Kroeber of the University of California during the years 1935–40. The writer here wishes to record his indebtedness to Prof. Kroeber for having made possible this investigation of Far Eastern languages, of which the present paper may be regarded as a by-product.

[29] R. Shafer, *The Vocalism of Sino-Tibetan* (Journal of the American Oriental Society, Vol. 60, 1940), pp. 302–337; (Vol. 61, 1941), pp. 18–31.

[30] *Transcription and Explanation of the Siamese Alphabet* (Asia Major, Bd. 1, 1924), pp. 45–66; *Siamese Mute H* (*Ibid.*, Bd. 3, 1926), pp. 33–48.

[31] Vide the occasional references to Thai problems in his articles, *Semantic Differentiation in Indo-Chinese* (Harvard Journal of Asiatic Studies, Vol. 4, 1939), pp. 213–229, and *Studies in Indo-Chinese Phonology* (*Ibid.*, Vol. 5, 1940), pp. 101–127.

[32] A. Conrady, *Eine merkwürdige Beziehung zwischen den austrischen und den indochinesischen Sprachen* (Kuhn Festschrift, München, 1916), pp. 475–504; *Neue austrisch-indochinesische Parallel* (Asia Major, Introductory Volume, 1922), pp. 23–66.

Maspero, in a review of Wulff's work,[33] has convincingly dismantled the thesis of Thai infixation, and with it much of the Conrady-Wulff hypothesis. A similar hypothesis has been brought forward by J. Przyluski in the well-known account in *Les Langues du Monde*.[34] Przyluski suggests that Thai is transitional between Sino-Tibetan (Chinese and Tibeto-Burman) and Austric, yet offers no support for this view, other than a few comparisons of demonstrative pronouns in Siamese, Annamite, Khasi, and Palaung.

The writer's conclusions differ significantly from any of the above. The thesis presented here holds that Thai has a truly genetic linkage with Kadai and Indonesian rather than with Chinese and Tibeto-Burman (Sino-Tibetan), but has undergone extensive modification under Chinese influence. A similar view was propounded many years ago by Gustav Schlegel, in a highly unsystematic and unscientific fashion.[35] Schlegel was unaware of the existence of the Kadai group, but pointed out many analogies with Malay, and in general seems have been on the right track. The writer has developed the present hypothesis entirely independently of Schlegel, and largely as a by-product of his own synthesis of the Kadai stock.

The writer has long been aware of the fact that the lexical resemblances between Chinese and Thai are of a restricted range which fails to support the generally held view of a genetic relationship between the two languages. A careful analysis of the material assembled by Wulff, in addition to his own supplementary material, has made this fact still clearer. The primary lexical agreements lie in the numerals, especially from "3" to "10" and "100," a few words for parts of the body, certain animal names, and a number of terms for cultural objects and the like. Let us examine these loosely defined categories in some detail.

The Thai numerals from "3" to "10" and "100" are in fairly close agreement with the Chinese: Thai *sam, Ch. *sâm "3"; Thai and Ch. *si "4"; Thai *ha, Ch. *nguo "5"; Thai *hrŏk, Ch. *liuk "6"; Thai *tšĕt, Ch. *ts'iĕt "7"; Thai *pet, Ch. *pwat "8"; Thai kău, Ch. kiəu "9"; Thai *sĭp, Ch. *žiəp "10"; Thai *pak, Ch. *p/\k "100." Thai ordinarily agrees with Chinese as opposed to Tibeto-Burman, yet shows interesting variations in the direction of the latter, e.g. Thai *ha, TB *l-nga "5," with h-<ng- as in Thai *han, Ch. *ngan, TB *ngan "goose"; Thai *hrŏk, TB *d-rug "6." The Chinese forms for "7," "9," and "10" illustrate the diphthongization characteristic of that language, the -ău=-iəu equation being particularly well attested: Thai *k'ău, Ch. *k'iəu "hill"; Thai *k'ău, Ch. *kiəu "pigeon"; Thai *kău, Ch. *g'iəu "old"; Thai *gău, Ch. *g'iəu "owl" (Tibeto-Burman has final -u in this series). On the basis of the above phonetic evidence, the borrowing of this numeral system must be

[33] *Bulletin de la Société de Linguistique de Paris*, t. 36, pt. 3, 1935, pp. 183–187.

[34] Edited by A. Meillet and M. Cohen (Paris, 1924), pp. 361–384 (*Le Sino Tibétain*).

[35] *Siamese Studies* (T'oung Pao, t. 2, n. s., 1902, Supplement).

assigned to an early period antedating the *r->l-*, *-a>-uo* shifts in Chinese. The Thai forms are still irregular, however, with **pet* "8" rather than **puăt*, and **sĭp* "10" rather than **zĭp*, and cannot be reconciled on any scheme of genetic relationship (for the latter, cf. Thai **suk*, Ch. **źiuk* "ripe."

The regular Thai numerals for "1" and "2" are **hnüng* and **song*, respectively, which appear to be remnants of the original Thai numeral system. The corresponding Chinese terms, significantly enough, appear only in the combinations **sĭp ĕt* "11" (Ch. **'iĕt* "1"), and **ńi sĭp* "20" (Ch. **ńźi<*ńi* "2"). In addition, a basic root **džau* "20" is preserved in Lao and the western Thai languages, and **roi* "100" is found in Siamese, Lao, and some of the eastern Thai languages.[36] The evidence from the numeral system, therefore, cannot be held to speak in favor of the theory of a genetic Thai-Chinese relationship.

The common roots for parts of the body are as follows: Thai **χen* "arm," Ch. **kien* "shoulder"; Thai **veng* "leg," Ch. **γieng* "shin, shank"; Thai **fa*, Ch. **pa* "palm of the hand"; Thai **eu*, Ch. **'iäu* "waist, loins." In this group belong also Thai **hnong*, Ch. **nuong* "pus"; Thai **ńiau*, Ch. **nieu* "urine, urinate." Thai **nga* "tusk, ivory," Ch. **nga* "molar tooth," must be considered in relation to the loan-word for "elephant" (infra), the regular Thai roots for "tooth" being **k'riau* and **văn*. Similarly, Thai **p'iu* "cuticle, epidermis" is connected with Ch. **piu* "skin, hide," but the regular Thai root, **hnăng*, "skin, hide," has no Chinese correspondence. Basic roots for parts of the body such as "eye," "nose," etc. are significantly lacking in this list.

The group of common roots for animal names is equally enlightening in its exclusiveness. Here we find Thai and Ch. **ma* "horse," and the associated roots: Thai **an*, Ch. **'ân* "saddle"; Thai **k'i*, Ch. **g'yie>k'i* "ride (a horse)." These correspondences strongly indicate that the Thai peoples borrowed the horse-complex directly from the Chinese. This group also includes Thai **džang*, Ch. **ziang* "elephant,"[37] Thai **nguă*, Ch. **ngiəu* "bull, ox, cow";[38] Thai **t'ŏ* (restricted distribution), Ch. **t'uo* "hare"; Thai **kăi*, Ch. **kiei* "fowl";[39] Thai **p'rüng*, Ch. **p'iwong* (equivalent to **p'üong* "bee";[40] and, from the above dis-

---

[36] Cf. the penetrating study by Coedès and Burnay, *Notes d'étymologie Taï, No. 1: Le nom de nombre "Cent"* (Journal of the Siam Society, Vol. 20, 1926), pp. 49–52. Coedès and Burnay identify **roi* "100" with the root **roi* "to string." They further conclude that **pak* "100" is common Thai because of the concordance of tones, yet admit the possibility of its having been borrowed from Chinese by the parent Thai speech.

[37] Cf. the associated correspondence between Thai **nga* "tusk, ivory" and Ch. **nga* "molar tooth." The root for "elephant" has a restricted extension in Tibeto-Burman (Burmese *ts'ang*).

[38] Ch. **ngiəu* should have produced Thai **ngău* rather than **nguă*. The latter corresponds rather to the root **ngua* "bull, ox, cow" of the Kachin-Nung-Burmese division of Tibeto-Burman.

[39] For the finals, cf. Thai **găi* "who, which," Ch. **viei* "why, how, what"; Thai **k'ăi*, Ch. **k'iei* "to open." The Thai root for "egg" (**k'răi*) is independent of the Chinese roots (**luân, *d'ân*).

[40] The interesting Chinese root **miĕt* "honey," an ancient loan-word from Indo-European (Sanskrit *madhu*; Old Slavic *med ŭ*; Tocharian *mit*, whence Ch. **miĕt* through diphthongization;

cussion, Thai *han, Ch. *ngan "goose (wild)";⁴¹ Thai *k'ău, Ch. *kiəu "pigeon";
Thai *gău, Ch. *g'iəu "owl"; perhaps also Thai *ngüăk "crocodile, dragon, si-
ren," Ch. *ngâk "crocodile." Significantly lacking are roots for "dog," "fish,"
"bird," "snake," and the like.

The fourth and last of the groups mentioned above includes Thai *ngön,
Ch. *ngiĕn "silver" (Tibetan *dngul*); Thai *gram (restricted distribution), Ch.
*lâm < *glâm "indigo" (Tibetan *rams*);⁴² Thai *tšiă, Ch. *t'śie "paper"; Thai
*hmük, Ch. *mək "ink"; Thai *băi, Ch. b'ăi "cards (for playing)." Here also
may be placed Thai gěm, Ch. *iäm < *giäm "salt," and Thai *guăn, Ch. χiuən
"smoke"; it should be noted that the regular Thai root for "salt" is *klüa rather
than *gěm. It is apparent that no great importance can be attached to this
group of roots.

The above lists of the principal Thai-Chinese correspondences have been
carefully drawn up, and should give an accurate picture of this aspect of the
problem. There are, to be sure, additional correspondences, some of which have
been cited above, but these hardly affect the picture as a whole. Below, by way
of contrast, are listed the basic Thai-Indonesian correspondences on which our
conclusions have been built. That these are truly basic correspondences as
compared with those between Thai and Chinese is sufficiently clear even after
a cursory inspection of the material.

1. Thai *wăn "day," ta wăn "sun" ("eye of the day"); IN *wari' "day,
sun"; Laqua vuon, Li ven "day, sun."

2. Thai *blüăn "moon"; IN *bulan; Laqua nen, Li ñan.

3. Thai *dau "star"; IN *'a(n)daw~*ha(ŋ)g'aw "sun"; Li tšěm drau "star."

4. Thai *fŏn "rain" ("fine rain," as opposed to *hra "heavy rain, shower");
IN *'ə(m)bun "atmospheric precipitate" (Tagalog 'ambon "fine rain"); Li (pa)
pŭn "rain."

5. Thai *năm "water"; IN *danum: Li nom~nam.

6. Thai *vai "fire"; In* 'apuy; Laqua păi, Li pei~fei.

7. Thai *na "rice-field"; IN *bəna' "low-lying land, flooded land"; Laqua
ne, Li na~ta "rice-field."

8. Thai *nŏk "bird"; IN *manuk "fowl, bird"; Laqua nuk "bird."

9. Thai *răng "nest"; IN *t'alang (Toba-Batak, Javanese, Malay, Dayak
sarang).

Greek μέθυ "wine"; English *mead*), is not found in Thai, which makes use of the periphrasis "bee-
water" (Siamese and Shan năm p'üng), or even equates "bee" with "honey" (Ahom, Tho) or
with "wax" (Lao).

⁴¹ In view of the correspondences for "fowl" and "goose," it is somewhat surprising to find
distinct roots for "duck" (Thai *pĕt, Ch. *ap).

⁴² The prototype must have been *ram-s rather than *gram-s, since the latter could have
yielded only *grams in Tibetan. On this line of reasoning, Chinese *lâm < *glâm includes a prefixed
g- element, and the Thai borrowing can thus be dated as posterior to this prefixation, but anterior
to the subsequent *grâm > *glâm > *lâm development in Chinese (completed ca. 500 B. C.).

10. Thai *rüă "boat"; IN *paḷahu (Malay *pərahu* "prau"); Li *da*.

11. Thai *tu "door" (often in composition with *pak "mouth, opening"); IN *pintuʻ; Laqua *tu*.

12. Thai *hruă "head"; IN *uluʻ∼*huluʻ; Laqua *ru*, Li *du*∼*o*.

13. Thai *ta "eye"; IN *mataʻ; Laqua *te*, Li *sa*.

14. Thai *dăng "nose"; IN *ugʻung∼*igʻung (Malay *hidong*, Cham *idung*); Laqua *tang*.

15. Thai *văn "tooth"; IN *ipən; Li (*hai*) *p'en*.

16. Thai *pot "lungs"; IN **put'uh* "heart" (Tagalog *puso'*, Toba-Batak *pusuʻ* "heart," Javanese *pusuh* "lungs").

17. Thai *gĭng or *grĭng "body"; IN *daging "body, flesh."

18. Thai *duk "bone"; IN **ta(n)duk* "horn"; Li *drü*∼*füök* "bone."

19. Thai *lüăt "blood"; IN *darah: Li *dat*∼*tlat*.

20. Thai *măn "fat, oil"; IN *miñak "oil"∼*mənak "fat"; Laqua *nen* "fat," Lati *m-ngă* "fat, oil."

21. Thai *pu, "grandfather"; IN **ə(m)puʻ* "grandfather, grandchild" (reciprocal term).

22. Thai *dăm "black"; IN **i(n)təm* "black," *dədəm∼*tidəm "dark"; Laqua *dăm*, Li *dŏm* "black."

23. Thai *sŏm "sour"; IN **at'əm*.

24. Thai *bot "blind"; IN *butaʻ.

25. Thai *tai "die"; IN *matay∼*patay; Laqua *tie*.

26. Thai *dĭp "raw, green, alive" (Ahom has the doublet forms *dip* "living, to be alive," *lip* "unripe"); IN *hudip "live"; Li *diep*∼*fiep* "raw."

27. Thai *kĭn "eat"; IN *kaʻ∼*kaʻən∼*kaʻi; Laqua *küön*, Li *k'an*.

28. Thai *tŏt "flatus ventris"; IN **ə(n)tut*∼**u(n)tut*∼**kə(n)tut*; Li *t'uot*.

29. Thai *ku "I" (pejorative); IN *akuʻ; Laqua *k'ău*, Li *hau*.

30. Thai *ni "this"; IN *iniʻ; Li *nei*.

In the above set of correspondences, the most obtrusive single feature is the development of monosyllabic roots in Thai from the disyllabic roots typical of Indonesian. It must not be assumed that all the roots involved were originally disyllabic, since in some instances monosyllabic roots can be postulated for proto-IN itself, e.g. *təm∼*dəm "black, dark" (No. 22), *tay "die" (No. 25), *kaʻ "eat" (No. 27), *tut "flatus ventris" (No. 28), and cf. *danum "water" with *inum "drink," apparently from a root *num.[43] The real criterion here lies in comparison with Thai and Kadai, as well as with the more remotely related Mon-Khmer languages, e.g. IN *mataʻ, Thai *ta<*m-ta (vide infra), Mon-Khmer *mat (Annamite *măt*) "eye," where *mata is the only feasible reconstruction for the parent stock. The material assembled in this paper lends itself

---

[43] Cf. the remarks in R. O. Windstedt, *Malay Grammar* (Oxford, 1927), p. 20, and S. H. Ray, *A Comparative Study of the Melanesian Island Languages* (Cambridge, 1926), pp. 38 and ff.

to the view that the majority of Thai-Kadai-Indonesian roots were disyllabic rather than monosyllabic, and that Thai and Kadai have undergone extensive phonetic reduction. The writer has elsewhere called attention to a parallel reduction in the aberrant Cham dialect spoken on the island of Hainan, and to similar phenomena in the standard Cham speech of the mainland, e.g. Cham *bulan*∼*lan* "moon," *apuči*∼*puči* "fire" (through aphaeresis).[44] This aspect of Thai-Kadai phonology, therefore, calls for no especial demonstration.

The varying types of phonetic development shown by the Thai roots under consideration are in part explicable in terms of stress variations. Kadai offers an excellent instance of this in the bifurcate development shown by S. Li *du*, N. Li *au* "8," from IN **walú‘*, where we must reconstruct as follows: **walú‘* > **wlu* > *du*, **wálu‘* > **wau* > *au*. Similarly, for Thai we must postulate shifts of the type: **danúm* > **năm* "water," **pintú‘* > **tu* "door," **matá‘* > **ta* "eye," but **pút'uh* > **pot*, "lungs," **məñak* > **măn* "fat, oil," **búta‘* > **bot* "blind," etc. The stress seems normally to have been on the last syllable, but certainly not always so.

The finals of this group of roots present fewer problems than the initials. Among the vocalic finals, we have Thai *-a* = IN *-a* (Nos. 7 and 13); Thai *-u* = IN *-u* (Nos. 11, 21, and 29); Thai *-i* = IN *-i* (No. 30); Thai *-au* = IN *-aw* (No. 3); Thai *-ai* = IN *-ay* (No. 25). Thai **vǎi*, IN **'apuy* "fire" suggest a simple *-ǎi* = *-uy* equation, perhaps via an intermediate form *-uei* (cf. Cham *apuči*), yet Thai has both *-ui* and *-uei* series, the latter of some importance. Two independent bits of evidence indicate that Thai **vǎi* was developed from a root **vi*, probably via an intermediate form **viei*, thus paralleling the development shown by Thai **kǎi*, Ch. *kiei* "fowl" (see note No. 39). Firstly, Dioi and a group of related dialects[45] have the form *fi* rather than the regular **fǎi* (contrast Dioi *kǎi* "fowl"); secondly, Li has *pei*∼*fei*, from **pi*∼*fi* (cf. the discussion above), rather than **pai*∼*fai* (contrast Li *k'ai*, Thai **kǎi* "fowl"; Li *lai*, Thai **klǎi* "far"). The lone possible analogy here is furnished by Thai **hǎi*, Li *ngei*, IN **tangit'* "weep," with Thai *h-* < *ng-* as discussed above.

Nos. 10 and 12 must be considered in relation to each other. These two comparisons are, admittedly, uncertain ones, but the parallelism between them, extending even into Kadai (Li), has led to their inclusion in our list of correspondences:

	Indonesian	Thai	Kadai (Li)
boat	**paḷahu*	**rüǎ*	*da*
head	**hulu*	**hruǎ*	*du*
	*'ulu		

---

[44] See the writer's article, *A Cham Colony on the Island of Hainan* (Harvard Journal of Asiatic Studies, Vol. 6, 1941), pp. 129–134.

[45] The form *fi* "fire" is cited for the Tai Yoi, Kon Yai, and To-jen dialects in W. C. Dodd, The Tai Race (Cedar Rapids, Iowa, 1923), word-lists on pp. xiv-xxi.

The aspiration in these roots seems to have played a role in the *l>r* shift. For the final of Thai **rüǎ* "boat," a possible parallel exists in IN **'at'u'* "dog," Thai **süǎ* "tiger."

The consonantal finals are regular for the most part. Final *-r*, which is lacking in Thai, is replaced by *-n* (**wari'>*wǎn* "sun, day"), as in loan-words from Khmer or Pali, e.g. Siamese *k'ǎnun*<Khmer *k'nur* "jack-fruit." In this connection, cf. Siamese and Lao *pun*, IN **apur~*kapur* "lime" (probably a loan-word in these southern Thai speeches). Final *-h*, also foreign to the phonemic system of Thai, is represented by *-t*, as in Kadai (**darah>*lüǎt* "blood"). Final stops and nasals are preserved in Thai, with the exception of *-t'>-t* (No. 16). The most likely instance of interchange of nasal finals is furnished by IN **rumah*, Li *düön*, Thai **rüǎn* "house," perhaps via the forms **ruam>*ruan*.

Short medial vowels are predominant in the Thai roots under consideration, and must be regarded as characteristic of these basic roots as a group. IN medial *-a-* is represented by *-ǎ-* (Nos. 1, 2, and 9); cf. also IN **balakang*, Thai **hlǎng* "back" (n.). Thai ordinarily has *-ǎ-* for IN medial *-ə-* (Nos. 15, 20, and 22), yet has *-ŏ-* in one instance (No. 23); for the latter, cf. IN **tirəm*, Siamese *hoi irŏm* "oyster," undoubtedly a loan-word in Siamese (in composition with the Thai root **hoi* "shellfish"). IN medial *-u-* is represented by *-ǎ-* (Nos. 5 and 14) and *-ŏ-* (Nos. 4, 8, and 28), as well as by *-u-* (No. 18).[46] After the labial stop initials *p-* and *b-*, Thai has *-o-* rather than *-ŏ-* for IN medial *-u-* (Nos. 16 and 24). An additional equation is furnished by Nos. 17 and 26, yielding IN medial *-i-*=Thai *-ǐ-*. The medial vowel of Thai **kǐn* "eat" (No. 27) cannot be satisfactorily explained on the basis of our present knowledge, though the contrast with the *-a-* vocalism of Li is matched by Thai **dǐn*, Li *dǎb~fan* "earth," perhaps related to IN **tanah~*tanəh* "earth, land."

The treatment of initial consonants in Thai presents a number of interesting features. The first of these to come to the writer's attention is the peculiar aspiration of the Thai roots for "eye" (No. 13) and "die" (No. 25) in the Tho-Nung group of dialects.[47]

	IN	Laqua	Siamese	Tho	Nung
eye	**mata'*	*te*	*ta*	*t'a*	*t'a~ha*
die	**matay*	*tie*	*tai*	*t'ai*	*t'ai~hai*

[46] Note Thai medial *-ǎ-*<*-u-* only before final nasals. Thai medial *-ŏ-*<*-u-* seems to be the normal development before final stops; cf. Thai **hrŏk*, Chinese **liuk* "6"; Thai **mŏt*, Malay, Javanese, Karo *sěmut* "ant" (cited in Brandstetter, cit. supra, p. 37). For Thai medial *-u-*<*-u-* before final velar stop, cf. Thai **luk* "anything round," IN **kəluk~*pəluk* "bend, curve."

[47] Our sources for Tho and Nung are in agreement on this point, and there can be no doubt as to the reality of the phenomenon in question. An additional check is furnished by the form *t'a* "eye" cited for a dialect of Tho-Nung type by Yu Wên, *A Vocabulary of a Non-Chinese Tribe inhabiting the Tapingfu Area of Kwangsi Province, with Chinese Transliterations and Notes* (Academia Sinica, Bulletin of the Institute of History and Philology, Vol. 6, pt. 4, 1936), pp. 505–552 (in Chinese).

With one partial exception, these are the only roots so treated in Tho and Nung,[48] hence this phenomenon cannot be explained in terms of Thai itself. On the basis of Indonesian, however, we can postulate a development of the type: $*mata' > *m\text{-}ta > *m\text{-}t'a > t'a \sim ha$; $*matay > *m\text{-}tay > *m\text{-}t'ay > t'ai \sim hai$, with secondary aspiration after the nasal prefix.[49] The Li form *sa* "eye" can be explained along the same lines. The remarkable parallelism shown in the treatment of these two roots constitutes perhaps our most significant single piece of evidence for a Thai-Indonesian linkage.

The reconstruction of initial *ɓl-* for Thai, as in the root $*ɓliǔn$, represents a new advance in Thai phonology. As ordinarily reconstructed, Thai has initial *ɓl-, pl-, p'l,* and *br-, pr-, p'r,* but neither *ɓl-* nor *ɓr-*. The typical Thai initial *d-* series shows the following equation: Siamese and Lao *d-* = Ahom, White Tai, Tho, Nung, Dioi *d-* = Shan and Black Tai *l-* = Khamti *n-* (vide supra). Three roots, however, diverge from this equation in the direction of the initial *ɓ-* series, and in one of these roots *ɓl-* is actually preserved in the archaic Ahom language, hence we can safely reconstruct all three roots with initial *ɓl-*:

a. Siamese and Lao *ɗok* "flower," but Ahom *blok*, Tho *biok*, Nung *beok* Black and White Tai *ɓɔ̌ < ɓok*, Shan *mok < ɓok*.

b. Siamese and Lao *ɗüǎn*, Ahom *dön*, Shan *lön* "moon," but Tho and Nung *büön* "month," Black Tai *büǎn*, White Tai *bön* "moon."

c. Siamese *ɗi*, Ahom, Tho, Nung *di*, Shan *li* "bile," but Lao and White Tai *bi*, Dioi *di* "animal bile"$\sim$*bi* "human bile."

Reconstructions: $*ɓlok$ "flower," $*ɓliǔn$ "moon," $*ɓli$ "bile."[50] Note that initial *ɓl-*, which is of labial type, is best preserved before the labial vowel *o*, and worst preserved before the front vowel *i*; also that Black and White Tai preserve *b-* in all three roots. Initial *br-* cannot be reconstructed for Thai, and may be represented simply by *ɓ-*; cf. Thai *ɓɔ̌m* "ripen fruits," IN $*pɔlɔm$ "ripen fruits artificially" (Toba-Batak *porom*, Malay *pɔram*), perhaps via a form $*pɔrɔm$.[51]

Some interesting equations appear among the stop consonants, especially

---

[48] Tho and Nung *t'en* "wasp" correspond to the general Thai root *ten*, but the doublet form in initial *h-* is lacking in Nung. The regular development with unaspirated initial *t-* is observed in a long series of Thai roots, including *tǎp* "liver," *tǎm* "low," *tǎng* "glue," *tǎu* "turtle," *tǎt* "cut," *tǔm* "full," *tin* "foot," *tǒk* "fall," *tǒm* "mud," *tǒn* "tree trunk," *tǒt* "flatus ventris," and *tuǎ* "animal."

[49] A good parallel here is furnished by Tibetan, which has aspirated all initial surd stop or affricate consonants after prefix *m-*, e.g., Tibetan *mt̆'in* "liver", corresponding to Tibeto-Burman *m-šin*.

[50] For Thai *ɓlok* "flower," cf. the subsidiary IN root represented by Bisaya *bolak*, Tagalog *bulaklak* "flower," which Brandstetter (cit. supra, p. 22) derives from a root *lak* "to unfold." No IN comparison has been uncovered for Thai *ɓli* "bile."

[51] This comparison is semantically too specific to be trusted, and we should expect Thai *pǒm* rather than *ɓǒm*. IN *l > r* as in $*pɔlahu > *rüǎ$ "boat," $*t'alang > *rǎng$ "nest"; IN *ɔ > ǒ* as in $*at'ɔm > *sǒm$ "sour."

in the labial series. Thai ordinarily has *t*<*t* (Nos. 11, 13, 25, and 28), and *ɖ*<*d*
(Nos. 3, 18, and 26), while the correspondence shown in Thai *dăng* IN *ʻug'ung*
∼*ʻig'ung* "nose" (No. 14) must be considered in connection with the IN
doublet forms *ʻa(n)daw*∼*ha(ŋ)g'aw* "sun" (No. 3). Thai *dăm* "black" must
therefore be equated directly with IN *dədəm*∼*tidəm* "dark" rather than with
ʻi(n)təm "black" (No. 22). The palatal stop (*t'*) of IN is represented in Thai
by *s*- as an initial (No. 23), but by -*t* as a final (No. 16).[52] The velar correspondences are regular: Thai *k*=IN *k* (Nos. 27 and 29); Thai *g*-=IN *g* (No.17). In
the labial series, however, we find two types of correspondences, viz. Thai *b*
=IN initial *b*- (Nos. 2 and 24), Thai *p*=IN initial *p*- (No. 16), but Thai *f*=IN
medial -*b*- (No. 4), and Thai *v*=IN medial -*p*- (Nos. 6 and 15). Thai *pu*, IN
ə(m)pu' "grandfather" (No. 21) would seem to run counter to this scheme,
but in this instance IN has the doublet roots *tumpu'* "forefather, sir" and *pu'*
"sir," the latter evidently the basic etymon from which Thai *pu* was derived.
This explanation of Thai *f* and *v* as secondary phonemes deirved from medial
labial stops clears up one of the most abstruse aspects of Thai phonology. Li
(southern dialect) and the Kadai languages in general have preserved the labial
stop in these roots:

	Indonesian	Li	Thai
rain	*ʻə(m)bun*	*pŭn*	*fŏn*
fire	*ʻapuy*	*pei*	*văi*
tooth	*ʻipən*	*p'en*	*văn*

It is a striking fact that, in the above set of comparisons, initial *b* and *ɖ* appear to the exclusion of the sonant stops *b* and *d*. An examination of the stock of
Thai roots assembled by the writer shows an overwhelming predominance of
basic roots with initial *b* and *ɖ*, some of the most important of which are listed
below:

Initial *b*-: *bon* "arum," *bli* "bile," *bau* "bridegroom," *bö* "butterfly,"
běk "carry (on shoulders)," *bŏt* "cloud" (v.), *biă* "cowrie shell," *bău* "cru-
cible," *bo* "pit, well, mine," *blok* "flower," *bĭn* "fly" (v.), *bĕt* "fish-hook,"
baü "leaf," *bău* "light (not heavy)", *buă* "lotus, water-lily," *ba* "mad," *ba*
"shoulder," *bok* "speak," *bok* "tube," *buei* "cocoanut spoon," *ban* "village," *bat* "wound," *bong* "hole," *bot* "blind," *blüăn* "moon."

Initial *ɖ*-: *ɖüăt*, "boil" (v.), *ɖěk* "child," *ɖĭn* "earth," *ɖăp* "extinguish,"
ɖüă "fig," *ɖŏng* "forest," *ɖi* "good," *ɖam* "handle" (n.), *ɖon* "high, hill,"
ɖong "kind" (n.), *ɖăi* "ladder," *ɖu* "l'ook," *ɖoi* "mountain," *ɖong* "parents
of in-laws," *ɖeng* "red," *ɖăng* "shield" (n.), *ɖŏm* "smell" (v.), *ɖut* "suck,"

---

[52] Dempwolff's reconstruction of *t'* rather than *s* for IN is open to criticism; cf. the review
by A. Capell, in Bull. of the School of Oriental Studies, Vol. 9, 1938, pp. 459–462. Thus, IN
ʻat'əm "sour" is represented by Tagalog *'asim*, Toba-Batak *'asom*, Javanese *'asěm*, Malay *'asam*,
Dayak *'asem*, all with initial *s*.

đet "sun, sunshine," *dap* "sword," *đăi* "thread," *đăng* "pillar," *duăng* "fish-trap," *đŏng* "winnowing instrument," *đüăn* "worms," *đăi* "obtain, be able."

In contrast to this impressive array, the sets of roots with initial *b* and *d* seem restricted indeed. With initial *ḃ-* we find *ḃĕ* "goat" (but *ḃĕ* in Lao and White Tai), *ḃe* "raft," *ḃu* "mountain" (but Siamese has *ḃ'u*, as in loan-words) *ḃăn* "seed, kind," *ḃrŭk* "tomorrow," *ḃra* "large knife," *ḃi* "fat, big," *ḃi* "elder sibling" (perhaps etymologically connected with the foregoing), *ḃo* "father," while with initial *d-* we find *dong* "belly," *drai* "sand, gravel," *dak* "leech," *diăng* "true, correct," *dang* "road," and *do* "weave." The contrast is so marked that one is tempted to conclude that roots with *ḃ-* and *d-* belong to the older Thai-Kadai-Indonesian stratum, and roots with *b-* and *d-* to one or more younger superimposed strata, including Chinese loan-words such as *ḃăi* < Ch. *ḃ'āi* "cards" (vide supra). The existence of the roots *ḃi* "elder sibling" and *ḃo* "father," with initial *ḃ-*, does not constitute a conclusive argument against this view, inasmuch as the Thai kinship nomenclature as a whole appears to have no intimate connection with the Indonesian. The presence of initial *ḃ-* or *d-* in a given root may even be used as supporting evidence for a proposed Indonesian comparison, e.g. Thai *ḃa*, IN *ḃara'* "shoulder" (*ḃara' > *ḃaa > *đā*, contrasting with the development shown in *wari' > *wăn* "day, sun"); Thai *đĕk* "child," IN *đikih ~ *'ə(n)ţik ~ *iţik* "small" Li *tik ~ tok* "small."

Still another problem is presented by Thai *liŭăt* < IN *darah* "blood" (No. 19), apparently via a form *dlat* (*dl-* is not retained in Thai). A possible analogy here is furnished by the Thai root for "tongue," which the Li dialects treat in a parallel manner:

	Indonesian	S. Li	N. Li	Shaved Head	Thai
blood	*darah*	dat	tlat	slat	*liŭăt*
tongue	*dilah*	dien	tlien	slien	*lĭn*

Yet Thai has *pla* "fish," corresponding to S. Li *da*, N. Li *tla*, Shaved Head Li *sla*, with initials as in the above series, hence no certain conclusions can be drawn.

The above discussion does not exhaust the possibilities of the complex Thai-Indonesian field, and it is possible that a more searching analysis of Indonesian material will yield further comparisons, yet it is believed that most of the important lexical correspondences have been uncovered. The writer has eliminated from the discussion certain obvious loan-words in Siamese, e.g. *muăng* "mango" < IN *maŋga*. Attention should be called, however, to the noteworthy agreement between Thai *nga* and IN *ləngaʻ* "sesame." The Thai root *nga* is widely extended in that stock (Siamese, Lao, Shan, Ahom, White Tai, Nung), hence cannot be regarded as a recent loan from Indonesian.

It is apparent that our judgment must be based almost entirely on lexical rather than morphological analogies, inasmuch as the rather elaborate affixation system of Indonesian is not represented in Thai. We must remember, however, that the reduction of disyllabic or trisyllabic roots to monosyllabic forms, as in Thai, necessarily involves the loss or incorporation of affixed elements. Thus, if a root *tay* "die" be reconstructed for proto-IN on the basis of the doublet roots *matay*~*patay*, and the elements *ma-* and *pa-* be regarded as prefixes, the purely phonetic development *matay* > *m-tay* > *tai*, paralleling *mata'* > *m-ta* > *ta* "eye" (vide supra), necessarily entails the loss of this prefixed element. In other instances, the affix may have been incorporated in the derived form; cf. IN *miñak* "oil"~*mañak* "fat," Lati *m-ngă*, Thai *măn* "fat, oil" (No. 20), and IN *ka'*~*ka'ən*~*ka'i*, Thai *kĭn* "eat" (No. 27).

Of some interest in this connection are the traces of prefixes preserved in Siamese. Siamese prefix *kă-*, by far the most prominent of the lot, is found with a few words for parts of the body (*kă-đuk*, *kă-điau* "bone," *kă-đo* "male genitals," *kă-bŏ*~*bŏ* "stomach"), and with some animal names (*kă-tai* "hare," *kă-tšok* "sparrow," *kă-te* "tupaya"), but is characteristically associated with curious derived forms, e.g. *bong* "stick"~*kă-bong* "cudgel," *đong* "oscillating" ~*kă-đong* "distorted, twisted," *tšŭn* "push"~*kă-tšŭn* "touch lightly," *tŭn* "mole"~*kă-tŭn* "kind of large rat." No great importance can be attached to this prefix, yet one possible IN correspondence has been uncovered, viz. Siamese *kă-đuk* "bone," IN *ta(n)duk* "horn"; cf. the *kă-*~*tă-* interchange in *kă-bŏng*~*tă-bŏng* "mussel."

The problem of the development of tones in Thai cannot satisfactorily be handled until good material on Kadai tones is made available. As reconstructed, the Thai tonal system includes two series of tones, one connected with roots having surd initials, the other connected with roots having sonant initials (a similar system is found in Annamite and Chinese). Each of these series, furthermore, includes three tonemes, the original values of which are uncertain. It is probably significant that almost all the Thai roots having IN correspondences are associated with a single toneme, represented in Siamese by the mid-level tone (with sonant and unaspirated surd stop initials) or the high-rising tone (with other surd initials). The only exceptional roots here are *năm* "water," *ni* "this," *pu* "grandfather," and *sŏm* "sour."

Aside from the rudimentary prefixes found in Siamese, the Thai stock closely conforms to the classical type of monosyllabic, isolating languages. Maspero has successfully refuted Wulff's thesis of infixation in Siamese (see note No. 33), hence no comparison with Indonesian infixes can be made. As pointed out above, Thai agrees with Indonesian and Kadai, and sharply diverges from Chinese, in placing modifying elements after rather than before modified elements. This significant agreement in syntax contributes no little support to our Thai-Kadai-Indonesian hypothesis. Attention must also be called to the traces of a distinction between inclusive and exclusive forms for the 1st pers. pl. pronoun in Thai, as represented by the exclusive form *tu* "we" in Khamti, Lao, and archaic Siamese.[53] This distinction is paralleled in Indonesian in the forms *$kita'$* "we" (inclusive), *$kami'$* "we" (exclusive).

The Thai-Kadai-Indonesian hypothesis, as outlined in the present paper, bears far-reaching implications for the history of the peoples of southeastern Asia and Oceania. If we accept the view that these three linguistic stocks are genetically related, we must place the center of their dispersion somewhere in the South China area, the present home of the Kadai tribes as well as the early home of the Thai peoples.[54] On the basis of this distribution we can conclude, with a high degree of probability, that the proto-IN-speaking peoples migrated from the South China coast, perhaps via the island of Hainan, to Formosa on the north, the Philippines on the east, and Annam, Borneo, Java, Sumatra, and the Malay Peninsula on the south. The Cham and Malay linguistic areas, in southern Annam and the Malay Peninsula, respectively, surely are to be regarded as Indonesian enclaves on the Asiatic mainland, not as possible points of departure for the Indonesian migrations.

In still broader perspective, Thai-Kadai-Indonesian appears in its true light as the northern division of Schmidt's Austric superstock.[55] The archaic cleavage between Thai-Kadai-Indonesian on the one hand, and Mon-Khmer on the other, must have come about in the South China-Indochina area, with subsequent localizations of these two divisions in the north and south, respectively. The anomalous position of Malay at the present day, south of the main body of Mon-Khmer speeches, can be explained only on the basis of a sea-borne migration from the islands of Indonesia. Thai and Kadai in the north, Cham in the east, and Malay in the south, show a peripheral distribution with respect to the Mon-Khmer languages. As suggested above, Cham and Malay fall into their place in this picture as intrusive Indonesian languages overlying a Mon-Khmer substratum.

Annamite, too, takes its proper place as the northeasternmost member of

---

[53] Cf. the discussion in G. Coedès, *Nouvelles notes critiques sur l'inscription de Rāma Khamheng* (Journal of the Siam Society, Vol. 17, 1923), pp. 113–120.

[54] The general Thai movement southward into Indochina appears to have begun on a large scale only toward the close of the first millennium A. D. The first group of Siamese inscriptions, the Sukhodaya, are from the 13th to 16th centuries, and the famous Rāma Khamheng inscription, the earliest monument of the Siamese language, is dated no earlier than 1292; cf. G. Coedès, *Notes critiques sur l'inscription de Rāma Khamheng* (Journal of the Siam Society, Vol. 12, 1918), pp. 1–27, and *Recueil des Inscriptions du Siam; Première Partie: Inscriptions de Sukhodaya* (Bangkok, 1924).

[55] The writer accepts Schmidt's postulation of an Austric superstock including Mon-Khmer and Austronesian, even though this relationship has not yet been thoroughly demonstrated. In the present instance, the Austric hypothesis is useful in interpreting certain roots which Thai and Mon-Khmer have in common, notably Thai *γo*, Mon-Khmer *go* (Annamite *ko*) "neck." Cf. the Thai-Khmer comparisons listed in Wulff, cit. supra, pp. 68–70, and the Dioi-Khmer and Dioi-Bahnar comparisons in D. Doutreligne, *Contributions à l'étude des populations Dioy du Lang Long* (Anthropos, Bd. 26, 1931), pp. 35–53.

the Mon-Khmer stock. Annamite stands in relation to Mon-Khmer somewhat as Thai stands in relation to Indonesian. Like Thai, it has suffered much phonetic attrition, has developed a complete tonal system, and has lost its morphological apparatus of affixes. These changes must be attributed to Thai influence, in view of the not inconsiderable body of Thai roots in the language. The overwhelming majority of basic roots, however, are of Mon-Khmer rather than Thai origin. On the analogy of our analysis of Thai, there can be no question as to the genetic nature of the Mon-Khmer-Annamite relationship.[56]

With Thai, Kadai, and Annamite in their proper settings, the linguistic picture of southeastern Asia assumes definitive shape for the first time. There remains only one linguistic problem of major importance, viz. the affinities of the Miao-Yao stocks of languages, spoken throughout much of central and southern China and northern Siam and Indochina. Our material on these languages is scanty and generally poor, and almost no comparative work has been done on the group.[57] Miao and Yao are well differentiated divisions of a single stock, and each appears in a number of dialectical varieties, with Miao showing the greater variation. Pateng, spoken in the Rivière Claire section of Tonkin, is a subsidiary member of the stock.[58] Miao-Yao resembles Thai-Kadai and Annamite in its monosyllabism and tonality, and further investigation may reveal a relationship with Proto-Austric or with one of its later divisions. A final judgment here must await the reconstruction of Mon-Khmer and the assembling of more material on the Kadai languages.

The proposed classification of Southeast Asiatic languages is as follows·

```
                    ⎧ Thai
                    ⎪ Kadai
                    ⎨ Indonesian              ⎧ Chinese
Proto-Austric       ⎪ ⎧ Mon-Khmer   Sino-Tibetan ⎨ Tibeto-Burman
                    ⎪ ⎩ Annamite                 ⎩ Karen
                    ⎩ ?Miao-Yao
```

[56] H. Maspero, *Études sur la phonétique historique de la langue annamite* (Bull. de l'École Française d'Extrême-Orient, t. 12, 1912), pp. 1–126, was so impressed by the monosyllables and tones of Annamite that he postulated a genetic kinship with Thai, even in the face of the dominant Mon-Khmer lexical element. Przyluski, in *Les Langues du Monde* (*cit. supra*), rightly breaks with Maspero on this point and classifies Annamite with Mon-Khmer.

[57] Limited comparative notes on two Miao dialects are found in Yu Wên, *The Influence of Liquids upon the Dissolution of Initial Consonant Groups in the Indo-Sinic Family* (Journal of the North China Branch of the Royal Asiatic Society, Vol. 69, 1938), pp. 83–91. A brief and somewhat confused study of two Miao and two Yao dialects has been made by Fang-kuei Li, *A Yao Dialect in Ling-Yün, Kwangsi Province* (Academia Sinica, Bulletin of the Institute of History and Philology, Vol. 1, 1930), pp. 419–426 (in Chinese).

[58] Vide A. Bonifacy, *Monographie des Pa-teng et des Na-ê* (Revue Indo-Chinoise, n. s., t. 10, 1908), pp. 696–706, 773–786.

On the ethnological side, the Kadai group offers the most promise for future investigation. At present, our material on this group is confined to the scraps of information gathered by Bonifacy and Lunet de Lajonquière, together with Stübel's fairly extensive study of the Li tribes (see sources cited above). Stübel points out a number of Indonesian and Micronesian parallels, e.g. in weaving (cit. supra, p. 293) and basketry (id., p. 294), and expresses his astonishment at the general cultural similarity to the tribes of Formosa (id., p. 296). It may be that the Li retain certain Indonesian culture traits that have been discarded by the Sinicized Kadai tribes of the mainland. It is fairly evident, however, that the general ethnological picture of Thai-Kadai-Indonesian has been destroyed beyond repair, and that our linguistic thesis must stand or fall on its own merits.[59]

WASHINGTON, D. C.

---

[59] The writer has not had access to the most recent comparative study on the Li, viz. Chung-see Liu, *Preliminary Study of the Origins of the Tribes of Hainan Island* (Meridio-Occidentale Sinense, Vol. 1, No. 1, 1940), pp. 1–23.

Appendix II

AUSTRO-THAI AND AUSTROASIATIC[1,2]

The reconstruction of Austro-Thai in its broad outlines, along with the establishment of a core Austro-Thai vocabulary, naturally leads to the question: Can a relationship be set up between this group of languages and Austroasiatic? Schmidt (1906) proposed that an "Austric" superstock be recognized—to include Austronesian along with Austroasiatic—and presented 215 comparisons between the two stocks. The problem has been much discussed since that time, but remarkably little of value has been added: Winstedt[3] offered some direct comparisons between Khasi and Malay, Cowan[4] emphasized the presence of some specific lexical tie-ups between Achinese and Cham and/or Mon-Khmer (this point still stands in need of clarification, but a Mon-Khmer substratum in Sumatra seems the least likely of several possible explanations), and Kuiper,[5] in a contribution of some importance (1948), compared the Munda languages with Austronesian. The writer (1942, note 55 to p. 599) provisionally accepted the "Austric" thesis but made no detailed study of the problem at that time. Now, with the availability of Austro-Thai reconstructions supposedly tapping an even deeper level, we are in a position to examine the relevant material.

As clearly demonstrated by Schmidt—and emphasized repeatedly by later writers—the Austroasiatic and Austronesian families exhibit a basic similarity in morphology, with striking correspondences in prefixes and infixes. Pinnow[6] has presented a strong case for including suffixes in the basic Austroasiatic pattern, which would bring it even closer into line with the Austronesian pattern. The mainland Austro-Thai languages (Kadai and Miao-Yao) provide no significant new information on this point, inasmuch as they tend to reduce all forms to monosyllables, with consequent disruption of the affixation features. In view of this we shall emphasize in this paper a comparison of phonological systems and of specific lexical forms. The basic question to be answered can be formulated as follows: In addition to the congruency in over-all configuration, which might be ascribed to areal factors, do Austro-Thai and Austroasiatic share a common corpus of roots from the core vocabulary, sufficient to justify a conclusion that these two superstocks are genetically related, or are the lexical agreements that exist of a lesser order, to be explained in terms of borrowing/substratum or the like?

Comparative Austroasiatic studies languished for many years after Schmidt's pioneering efforts in the early 1900s, but in 1952 Shafer[7] presented some provisional reconstructions for the Palaung-Wa languages, and in 1959 Pinnow[8] provided a powerful impetus for the field as a whole in his comprehensive analysis of the intricate Munda materials. Recently, protolanguage sound systems have been set up for several local groupings in the eastern Austroasiatic region, including Proto-Jeh-Halăng[9]—contributing to Proto-North-Bahnaric[10]—and Proto-Viet-Muong,[11] while Benjamin[12] has presented comparative material on the Aslian (Malay Peninsula) languages (the basis for our cited Aslian reconstructions). Shorto has contributed several important papers in the field, including an analysis of the Northern Mon-Khmer (Palaung-Wa) languages,[13] and has now achieved a provisional reconstruction of Proto-Mon-Khmer vocalism.[14] As a result of this surge of activity in the field, we are now in a position to make a preliminary survey of the Austroasiatic stock as a whole from the very special point of view of comparing the phonological framework with that of Austro-Thai and of uncovering any basic lexical agreements that might exist. This effort is perhaps premature, but we do have available the possibility of using reconstructed Austro-Thai forms to confirm, so to speak, suggested reconstructions for Austroasiatic, as can be seen in the analysis that follows.

Austroasiatic Consonants

Oral								Nasal/Oral		Nasal
p	b					w		mb		m
t	d	$[ts]$	$[dz]$	s	$[z]$	l				n
$ć$	j			$[ś]$		r	y		$[ńś]$	$ń$
k	g			$[\gamma]$	$[!]$					$ŋ$
q	G			$[R]$		Nq				
$ʔ$				h						

The above schema of reconstruction for AA consonants is similar to that for AT (see *Introduction*), and it is anticipated that the obvious lacunae, especially in the nasal/orals, will eventually be filled in as comparative AA studies continue. Shorto[15] has set up a series of prenasalized plosives for Old Mon: *(ŋk), *ńć, *nt, *mp; *ŋg, *ńj, *nd, *mb, to explain variant complex forms such as ʔba, mba, ʔmba "father" [<*ʔ(m)ba], while Kuiper (1948) has pointed out the existence of nasalized obstruents in Munda, with the development: nasal/stop>nasal, as commonly found in AT (see *Introduction*); cf. Sa. *umul*, Mu., Ho *umbul*, Sora *um-mul-ən* "shadow"<PM *umbul; Sre *mbur*, Theng *hmăl*, perhaps also (through metathesis) Khm. *mlup*, id., all from PAA *[u]mbul. There is an AT comparison for one root (Munda forms adapted from Kuiper): Ku. *ma*, Mu., Ho *maʔ* "cut, hew," Ku. *kuma*, Mu. *humaʔ* "beat, strike," Ku. *kua* (<*kuba), id., Sa. *hubaʔ* "hew, slash," all from PM *[](qu)(m)-bak; Mon *bak* "cut, cut down," PW: Da. *mɔk*, Ri. *mak~mɔk*, Wa (Tung Va) *muk*, id., from PMK *(u)(m)bak (see below for the vocalism); cf. AT *(N)qa(m)pak~*[ta](m)bak "cut down/off, chop," perhaps from an earlier *(N)qu(m)pak~ *(N)qu(m)bak by assimilation. There is also an AT comparison for *ńś (see "blood," below) and an apparent early loan by Thai confirms the reconstruction of *Nq in the following root for "neck": Kh. *kɔŋkɔ*<*kɔ/ŋkɔ (redupl.), Ju. *kuŋka*, Sa., Mu. *hɔtɔʔ* (Pinnow: prob. old compound) [cf. Mon *katak* "nape of neck"]<PM *qɔ(/Nqɔ); Mon *kɔ[kɔʔ]*, Khm. *kɔ*, Bahn. *ako*, St. *kou*, Vn. *ćô[kó]*, Srê *ŋko* (note the preservation of the nasal/oral here as in the root for "shadow"); PW: Ri. *kok*<*ko/k(o)*, Da. *kɔŋ*<*kɔ/ŋ(kɔ)*, Wa (Tung Va) *ŋɔʔ*<*ŋgɔʔ*<*ŋkɔʔ* (cf. Srê); Aslian *tə/ŋkɔk* (cf. PW)<PAA *qɔ(/Nqɔ), whence Thai *ɣoo[ɣɔ:]*<*Goo<*Nqoo[Nqɔ:], all by regular shifts.

The evidence for a distinct postvelar series for PAA comes largely from Munda, with *q especially well represented. There are two sets of reflexes here: Kh., Ku. *k*=Mu., Sa. *h*=Sora, Gu. ∅ (Pinnow: *q); Kh., Ku., Sora, Gu. *k*=Sa., Mu. *h* (Pinnow *q/k). The comparative evidence suggests that the former is for (original) initial *q, the latter for (original) medial *q; cf.

PM *qaso "pain, ill(ness)" (Kh. kɔsu, Mu. hasu, Sa. haso, Sora asu:, Gu. isi); PW: Da. katsu, Ri. s'uʔ, Pal. seu, Wa (Tung Va) saiʔ "to be in pain," contrasting with PM *[]qa:p: Sa. haʔb "take into the mouth, nip," Mu. haʔb "bite," Korwa haʔb "cut," Ku. kap, Sora ka:b "bite with the incisors"; Khm. kap "cut, cut off," Bahn., St., Srê, Jeh kap "bite," Aslian *kap, id., Por hap, id. (the eastern AA forms indicate short medial *a); AT *[t]aNqap ~*[ta](N)Gap "seize, hold, close (mouth), bite" (see below for vocalism). This analysis of PAA *q casts further doubt on the widely held view that PAA *qa "fish" (PM *qa, PMK *ka) is somehow cognate with IN *ikan, id., the latter considered a suffixed form: *ika/n. This is possible but unlikely in view of the above; also note that the AN root is to be reconstructed *iśikan, as shown by Bunun (Formosa), with *ś>ø in IN (see Tables) [no known cognates in MY or Thai and related languages].

Final *-q, as found in many AT roots, appears to be indicated for the following AA root for "leaf": Munda: Kh. ulaʔ, Sora o:la:-n, Gu. o:la:, Remo o:la:~ula:; Mon sla~hla [hlaʔ], Khmu hlaʔ, Ri. laʔ, Vn. lá (for tone, see below), Khm. slɔk "leaf," sla "betel" (<the betel leaf, chewed with areca nut), Khs. slak ~sla, Aslian *səlaʔ, all from PAA *ś[u:]laq (for initial, see below). Khasi, which regularly replaces PAA final *-k by *-ʔ and has final -k only marginally (Henderson[16]), also has final -k corresponding to Mon -ø in khwak "vampire bat," Mon kawa [kəwaʔ] "bat," suggesting PAA *k[a]waq, but Luce[17] gives an OM form kilwa "bat" and cites Malay kəlawar, id., the latter possibly from IN *kəlawaɣ<*k/l/waɣ. Final *-G is also a possibility for the PAA consonantal schema, perhaps in the root for "arm/hand," as suggested (for PM) by Pinnow: Sa., Ho, Ku. ti (ti:), Kh. tiʔ, Mu. tiʔ~ti:, So. (ə)sʔi:-n, Gu., Remo ti ~titi:; Mon tei~tai [toa], Khm. tai [dai], Khmu, Ri. tiʔ, Wa (Tung Va) taiʔ, Pal. dai~dei, Vn. tay [tai] [note ngang rather than sác tone], Aslian *ti[ŋ,k], Khs. kti<PAA *(k/)tiG (final *-g is also possible here; see below).

The evidence for glottal stop as a phoneme at an early level in AA is rather more substantial than in AT, where */ʔ/ is only marginally represented, notably in Atayal; cf. ramuʔ "blood" (below); *y/aya?* "mother" (cf. PNB **ya?* "grandmother"). Proto-North-Bahnaric (PNB), as reconstructed by Smith (see Note 10), shows a well-attested distinction between final **-?* and **-ø* (vocalic final), e.g. **ya?* "grandmother," **u?* "drink," **phi?* "full (after eating)," as distinct from **kla* "panther/tiger," **phe* "husked rice" and (from roots cited above) **hla* "leaf," **ti* "hand." It is possible that the final **-?* is secondary in some instances, as noted below for "one," but in general it would appear that this final must be recognized at the PMK level, and by inference at the PAA level. The distinction between final **-?* and **-ø* seems to be poorly or irregularly maintained in MK generally. Shorto (Note 13) has shown that in Northern MK only one of these finals is to be reconstructed (he opts for **-?*); note also Khmu (=*khmu?* "person"; see Smalley[18]), which has final -? for AA roots: *ka?* "fish," *blu?* "leg," *ti?* "arm/hand" (main except: certain pronominal forms: *bɔɔ* "you") but vocalic final in loans from Thai and elsewhere: *haa* "five," *?yuu* "stop," *pii* "year." Haudricourt[19] has sought to show that Vietnamese reflects final **-?* in its *săc* (high<surd initial) and *naŋ* (low< sonant initial) tones, but some basic problems remain here, e.g. PNB has **ka* (rather than **ka?*) "fish" corresponding to Vn. *cá* [ká], also **ćaw* "grandchild" corresponding to Vn. *cháu,* **pun* "four" corresponding to Vn. *b'ôn,* the last possibly to be explained in terms of an earlier prefixed **?/* (see below). The fact that the Vietnamese tones in question occur freely with finals (notably final **-w* and nasals) which are not glottalized in PNB or elsewhere in MK constitutes a major difficulty for the Haudricourt hypothesis, hence the basic question of just how tones were originally assigned to AA roots in Vietnamese remains to be answered.

Preglottalized consonants, which appear in Mon, Bahnar, and elsewhere, must be reconstructed at the PMK and probably also the PAA level, with the indicated analysis: **?+C*(onsonant). These elements are well represented in PNB, which lacks **?g* but has **?ŋ*: **?bom* "tuber" and **?me* "rain"; **?dok* "monkey" and **?naw* "new"; **?ju?* "sour" and **?ńaw* "wash hands"; **?ŋam* "sweet"; note also **?bok* "grandfather," *?ba?* "father" (cf. Mon forms cited above). It seems likely that these clusters originated from prefixed *ˀq/ or similar forms, as in Thai, which forms a Sprachbund with MK in its preglottalized consonant series (only *ˀb, *ˀd, *ˀy, and possibly *ˀj in Thai, but the closely allied Kam-Sui languages also show the preglottalized nasals, which must be reconstructed for the parent Kadai protolanguage). The Kadai clusters have typically been derived from *q/ forms, especially the ubiquitous AT *q/ prefix, e.g. Thai *ˀba=/ˀbaa/ "shoulder," from AT *q/baɣa via *ˀba(ɣ)a (regular loss of unstressed intervocalic *ɣ). Two excellent AT/AA correspondences bear on this point; cf. AT *(N)qa(m)bar "twin, double(d), two"; PM *a(m)ba:r; Mon ˀba (OM ˀbar), Bahn. ˀba:r, Pal. ar (<*ˀba:r), Ri. kə/ˀar (re-prefixed), Khs. ar, Wa (Kengtung) a:, Nic. q: (<*ˀam[ba:r]), Aslian *ˀmba:r "two," from PAA *ˀa(m)ba:r; also AT *qa/baŋ "boat" (Thai *ˀbaaŋ "clf. for boats"); Mon kˀbaŋ "boat" (re-prefixed; cf. Riang form for "two"). Kadai also tends to replace initial *t- and other consonants in initial unstressed syllables with *ˀ-, as in AT *(n)tu(m)ba "fish poison">Thai *ˀbia via *təba; cf. AT *(n)tobos "sugarcane"; Mon ˀbau (also written tˀbau), id., from an earlier *[to]bo[s] (see below for the final). The PNB root for "sugarcane" is *kataw, apparently from *ka/to[bos] (cf. Formosa: Saisiat ka/təbos "sugarcane"), reflecting AT prefixed *ka/~*qa/; Khmer has ɔbau=ɔmbau, as if from an earlier *[ˀt]o(m)bo[s], suggesting the possibility of loss of initial unvoiced stops when preglottalized. There is also evidence that prefixed *ˀ/ can yield secondarily aspirated surd stops, as in AT; cf. Munda: Kh. uˀphe~uˀfe "three"; Kh. iˀphɔn~iˀfɔn, Ku. uphunia "four"; also Ri. kə/pun~kə/phuon (cf. kə/ˀar "two"), Pal. pho:n, phun, Vn. b'ôn (perhaps from *ˀpôn; see above), id. These forms all suggest an extension of the prefixed *ˀ/ of "two" to the adjoining numerals: Kuy has ˀabia "two," ˀapay "three," ˀapoon "four"; PNB has *ˀmoyˀ "one" (with secondary glottalization through assim.) and *ˀba:r "two"; Kantu has muyˀ "one," from *ˀmuy; cf. also PNB *ˀbaˀ "father," with secondary glottalization.

The postvelar continuant *R can be reconstructed for eastern

AA, it appears, on the basis of the following root, which has an excellent AT comparison: AT *(k/)weR[i] "left (hand)"; cf. Mon *jwi* (<*j/wi*), Khm. *ćweŋ*<(*ć/weŋ*), Brou *avêr* (cf. *atoam* "right"), Pal. *i-ve* (cf. *i-təm* "right") (poss. loan from Burmese *lak-wai*>*-wɛ*), Aslian *(sa)w[e]l*, but Central Sakai [Semai] (Wilkinson[20]) *k'ŋwil* (<*k-n-wil;* cf. *kĕntok* "right"), id.<PMK *()w[e]R;* cf. the AT reflexes: Mal. *k/iri,* Fiji *ma/wi,* Paiwan (Formosa) *ka/viri,* Kuvalan (Formosa) *kumawi:li*< *k/m/a/wi:li,* Sediq (Formosa) *ʔiril;* Sek (Kadai) *vel,* Li (Kadai) *vieŋ~viŋ;* Yao *kwɛŋ*<*k/wɛŋ.* AT *R and *γ tend to fall together, and the distinction is made with difficulty (AT *R: Jav. *h~ø*=Yami *r*=Paiwan *r~R*=Kuvalan *l;* AT *γ: Jav. *r*= Yami *y*=Paiwan *ø*=Kuvalan *γ*). For final *-γ, there is one good comparison, indicating general replacement by *-i* in AA; cf. AT *ts[i]ŋa[a]γ "light, shine, moon, sun, dawn, morning" (Fiji *siŋa* "sun," Samoan *seŋi/seŋi* "twilight," Tongan *heŋi/heŋi* "early morning"; Thai *hŋaay*<*sŋaay* [*-γ>-i* after the long vowel] "light, moonlight; shine; moon," *ŋaay* "morning; breakfast"); PM *siŋgi* "sun/day"; Khm. *thŋai,* Mon *tŋai,* id. (both from *[ma]t-ŋai;* cf. Halăng *mat ŋai* "sun"="eye of the day"; also IN *mata-waγi,* Thai *ta-wan,* id.), Pal. *săŋai~săŋei,* Wa (Tung Va) *śiŋaiʔ,* Ri. *s'əŋiʔ,* Da. *ts'i* (<*ts'[ŋ]i*), id., Vn. *ŋày* "day" (*măt trði* "sun"="eye of the heavens"), Khs. *sŋi,* Nic. *heŋ* (<*seŋ[i]*) "sun," Sakai [Semai] *təŋiʔ* "day," *mat-təŋiʔ* "sun" (cf. the analysis above); also Bahn. *nar* "day," *mat-nar* "sun," St. and Chrau *nar* "sun," showing *ŋ>n* assimilation to *t,* viz. *[ma]t-ŋar>*t-nar>nar.* If this analysis is correct, we must infer an earlier PAA final *-γ, generally yielding final -i (as in Thai) but -r in Bahnar. Munda provides another possible example of final -r for an earlier *-γ; cf. Sa. *kur* "behind, after," AN *(w)ikuγ* "tail" (Paiwan *iku*), but this form might better be compared with AT *[(m)po](ŋ)kor* "behind/back/buttocks" (Thai *kon* "buttocks"). Munda does, however, offer an excellent comparison for medial *-γ-: Kh. *suruʔb* "to breathe, gargle," Sa. *siṛuʔb* "to sip, suck in audibly," Mu. *siʔb* (<*si[r]iʔb*) "to smoke," Sora *sərub* "to suck, sip," *sumrub* (<*su/m/rub*) "to suck with noise"<PM *si[γ]up* (Kharia and Sora *i>u* by assim. for V₁); AT *[si]γup "to sip, suck, drink"; Munda has a unique set of reflexes here: Kh., Sora r=Sa. r̥=Mu. ∅, suggesting a reconstruction such as *γ (not noted by Pinnow, who simply includes this root under Sa., Mu. r̥, r=Kh., Sora r); cf. also Khm. sro:p "absorb, suck up, swallow up, gulp in," Pal. hrup~hrip, Wa (Praok) rip "drink." The evidence from these roots suggests the provisional reconstruction of *R as well as *γ for PAA; neither phoneme can be reconstructed in initial position with any confidence.

The glottal (laryngeal) series in AA is represented by *h as well as *ʔ (above). Final *-h, which is uncommon in AT, is prominent in AA, but the only comparison with AT unfortunately is for Munda, which has lost this final: AT *nu[h]/nuh "breast" (Hova "nipple"); cf. PM *nunu "breast, nipple, suck, suckle" (*contra* Pinnow, distinct from PM *ńu "drink"; note Sa. nunu "breast," ńu "drink"). There is also one AT (only in AN) correspondence for medial *h, indicating loss of this element: AN *mbahu "smell (bad), stink, odor"; cf. Bahn. bou~mou, Mon mou~mau "smell(ing)," apparently from *mba(h)u (see above for the initial). Of particular importance here is the fact that AA final *-h does *not* correspond to Malay and Javanese final -h, the latter a reflex of IN/AN final *-q. On this basis, several promising AA and IN/AN or AT comparisons must be excluded, including the very comparison upon which Schmidt leaned so heavily, viz. PMK *pooh (Shorto): OM poh, SM /puh/ "to shoot with pellet-bow," Khm. /bɔh/ "to throw, to gin [cotton]"; also *p/n/ooh: SM /nuh/ "pellet-bow," Khm. /phnɔh/ "bow for beating cotton"; also Bahn. panah~pənah~prah "shoot (bow, crossbow)," Kontu ponoh "arrow"; cf. AT *pan[aq]~*pa/pan[aq] "arrow/shoot" (often "bow" in IN/PN) (Thai *piin "arrow"). Schmidt (*contra* Pinnow) certainly analyzed the AA forms correctly, but was mistaken in interpreting the *-an- of the AT root as infixed */n/ (the AN infix is vocalized as */ən/), and in equating AA with Malay/Javanese final -h (to make matters worse, the vocalism also appears to be divergent); Pinnow appears to confuse the AA root with eastern AA *pań "shoot (bow)" as well as with PM *panić "bowstring."

Apart from the palatals (see below), the remaining stops present a relatively clear picture. AT *p/b, *t/d, and *k/g occur in all positions, but the voiced members are uncommon as finals. At first glance, the AA languages appear to have only one reconstructable set of stop finals, including *-ć (see below) as well as *-p, *-t, and *-k (and now *-q, see above). The corresponding Munda finals are generally recorded as glottalized sonants and must be handled morphophonemically as sonants, but might be reconstructed at the PM level as surds. Kharia occasionally has final -ʔb for -ø elsewhere, and fortunately there is a good AT comparison available to indicate that PM final *-b must be reconstructed for this series; cf. Kh. ukuʔb, Sa. oko, Mu. uku "conceal, hide"<PM *okob; Kh. lɔʔb "to be burnt," lɔʔblɔʔb "warm, hot," Sa., Mu. lɔ "to burn, scald," lɔlɔ "to heat; hot, warm"<PM lɔb(/lɔb); cf. AT *( )kolob "heat, dry (by heat)." A third comparison indicates that this final *-b has been dropped in eastern AA; cf. Kh. rɔmkuʔb (<*rɔ/m/kuʔb or *rɔŋkuʔb by assim. to the final) "unboiled rice," Sora ruŋku:-n "husked paddy and millet of all kinds," Remo, Pareng (Gorum) ruŋku, Gu. ruku, Ju. runku:~ruku:, id.<PM *rɔ(ŋ)kub (*ɔ>u by assim. for V₁); Chong ruko, Por rokho "rice," Khmu rəkoʔ "rice in husk," Pal. răko~răkao, Da. ko, Ri. koʔ, Wa (Tung Va) ŋgauʔ (<*ŋkoʔ), Sakai [Semai] rəkuaʔ "husked rice"<PMK *ro(ŋ)ko<*ro(ŋ)ku[b] by assimilation. A fourth root shows the equation: Mu., Ho final -ʔb=Kh. final -m, with an excellent IN comparison with final *-b; Mu. uruʔb, Ho urub "burn," Kh. urum "warm," rum "burn"; cf. IN *urub "burn" (no known cognates in Kadai or Miao-Yao); the Kharia form is probably a derivative of an original reduplicated form: *urub/urub> *urum(b/urub), a development closely paralleled in several roots in AT (see *Introduction*). It is possible that other voiced final stops will eventually be reconstructed for AA roots, including *tiG or *tig "arm/hand" (see above).

As within Austro-Thai, the palatals and the dental affricates/ sibilants present problems. The palatal series is poorly developed in Austro-Thai, and the surd stop (*-ć) is entirely lacking in final position. The configuration in Austroasiatic on first examination would appear to be almost the reverse, without any evidence of dental affricates, but a closer analysis indicates that a pattern essentially identical with that of Austro-Thai must be reconstructed at the PAA level. Shafer (1952) noted that the Palaung-Wa languages show evidence of three sets of initials of *s type, but he did not suggest a reconstruction. The actual situation, including material from Danaw (Luce 1965), is even more complex, especially when considered together with reflexes elsewhere in Mon-Khmer, Khasi, and Munda. The reconstructed schema for Palaung-Wa is as follows; the Vu, Amok, and Angku forms are from Shafer, the remaining from Luce; Danaw and Riang tones are high unless marked low (ˋ):

The Riang forms (Luce) are for White Striped Riang; the Black Riang forms have the same initials except for *ts-=ty-* (*tsaŋ* "bitter," *kətsàn* "heavy," *tsɔŋ* "foot/leg").

As Shafer has shown, Palaung normally retains voicing (regularly lost elsewhere in PW), but the above table shows that it is lost after *dz* and *z*; similarly, Danaw and Riang regularly have low tone after original voiced initials, yet they show high tone after *z* (but low after *dz*).

The PW reconstructed schema appears faithfully to reflect the basic PAA pattern, as shown by the following table, with the exception of the initial *ts-* vs. *tsh-* distinction, which is undoubtedly a PW innovation, resembling a similar distinction often found in the neighboring TB languages.

Notes on Table:
"hair": Khasi (standard: Cherrapunji) *śñiuʔ*, Mnar dial. *suʔ*.
"snake": cf. the Cambodian calendar form *msañ*, which reflects an archaic (prefixed) Muong level; the PW correspondence here provides support for this view (Benedict 1967) and also indicates that these animal terms formerly had some extension in Austroasiatic.
"leaf": cf. Vn. *lá*; note that the Chamic form *sula* reflects the early vocalism for V₁ in this root, indicating that it was an early loan from AA.
"bathe": North Bahnaric (incl. Bahnar) *hum*, South Bahnaric

	PW	Danaw	Riang	Pal.	Wa:TV	Vu	Amok	Angku
hair	*s[o]k	ńok	huk	huʔ	haik	hak	suk	sʻuk
snake	*b/sań	păθen	heiń	hanʔ	-ʔuiń	—	—	—
leaf	*[ś]la	la	laʔ	hla	laʔ	—	la	la
bathe	*[ś]um	θɔn	hum	—	hɔm	—	—	—
blood	*ś/n/am	kănan	na:m	hnam	nam	nam	nam	sinam
eat	*zuam	sue	sʻuam	hɔm	sɔm	sa:m	—	—
bird	*tsim	tsen	sʻi:m	sim	śi:m	sʻim	—	—
pain	*(ka)tsu	katsu	sʻuʔ	seu	saiʔ	sʻa	—	—
louse	*tsi	tsi	sʻiʔ	sai	śiʔ	—	—	—
cooked	*(a)tsin	atsen	sʻi:n	si:n	śi:n	—	—	—
sun/day	*tśeʔiń	tsʻi	sʻumɛʔ	seuʔ	śińŋaiʔ	sʻańɛ	ĵi-	—
salt	*tśʰuak	tsʻa	kʻumɛʔ	sɛʔ	—	—	—	—
bitter	*ćaŋ	tsaŋ	tyaŋʔ	saŋ	so:ŋ	—	—	—
heavy	*(ka)dzan	kătsăn	kətyʻen	tyan	ĵi:n	—	—	—
foot/leg	*į[o]ŋ	—	tyɔ:ŋ	{dyan / dyen}	tyauŋ	ćɔŋ	ćuŋ	—

	PAA	PM	PW	Khasi	Mon	Khmer	Bahn.	St.
hair [AN *busuk]	*sok	*s[o]k	{ *s[o]k / *s/n/ok }	{ su? / śńiu? }	sok	sák	sok	sok
snake [Muong saň]	*b/sań	—	*b/sań	—	—	—	—	—
leaf [Chamic *sula]	*śu:laq	*ula[?]	*[ś]la	{ slak / sla }	{ sla / hla }	{ slǝk / sla }	hla	la
bathe	*śum[a]	*um[a]	*[ś]um	sum	hum	—	hum	um
blood [AT *( )ntsaam-]	*[i]ńśa:m	*m/ińa:m	{ — / *s/n/am }	{ — / sna:m }	ćhim	jha:m	{ maham / pham }	maham
eat	*ʑ[c]m	*ɔm	*ʑuam	—	gaćem	—	—	ćum
bird [Vn. chim]	*ts[e:]m	{ *si:m / *tsi:m }	*tsim	{ kasim / kasem }	ćim	—	śe:m	—
pain	*qatso	*qaso	*katsu	—	—	—	—	—
louse [Vn. cháy]	*s[t]ey	*tsɛs	*tsi	ksi	ćai	ćai	śi	si
cook(ed) [Vn. chín]	*[i]tsin	*isin	*atsin	—	ćin	—	śin	sin
sun/day [AT *ts[i]ŋaɣ]	*ᵧŋeʑt	*siŋgi	*iʑŋeʑt	iʑs	tŋai	thŋai	nar	nar
foot/leg [Vn. chân]	*ʈɛʑ	*ʈ[e]ʑ	*ʈ[o]ʑ	—	ʈeʑ	ʈeʑ	ʈeʑ	{ tʲeʑ / tʲeʑ }

(incl. Stieng) **um;* note that Stieng shows initial **ś->ø-* here and in "leaf," contrasting with medial **-ś->-h-* in "blood."

"blood": AT **( )ntsa[a]m[uʔ]:* Formosa (East, Atayalic) **dzamuʔ<*ntsamuʔ;* MY **nćyaam<*[]ntsaam* (palatalized); the AA root now supplies first-hand evidence for the initial palatalizing element (**i-*) of the root, which also palatalized the AA root, along with loss of the stop element (**nts>*ńć>*ńś*); note PAA **ś>ø* in Munda in this cluster, paralleling initial **ś->ø-;* note also the consistent vowel length shown in this root, with MY correspondence; Mon *ćhim<*(i)him<*(i)ham* by assimilation, supplying evidence for the **i* vocalism for V₁.

"eat": this root might also be reconstructed with initial **ź-,* especially in view of PM initial **j-,* but the PW series suggests a dental rather than a palatal.

"cook(ed)": Vn. *chín* "ripe"; cf. the PW series, where the gloss (Luce) is "ripe, cooked."

"sun/day": cf. also Vn. *ŋày* "day"; the AA root might also be reconstructed **ts[i]ŋ[g]aγ,* on the basis that V₂ shows the effect of assimilation to an original V₁, also that the PM nasal/oral **-ŋg-* represents an archaic doublet of the AT root (**ŋg>ŋ* is characteristic AT shift); see above for an analysis of the MK forms.

It now appears that AA, like AT, prefers **ts* to **ć,* at least in initial position. PM **ć* as an initial is distinctly peripheral, with one good comparison with MK, viz. **ćaćak* "tear/torn" (only Kherwari group cognates); cf. Mon *ćak* "torn," also Khm. *ćak* "prick, pierce, perforate." The AA cognates of PW **ćaŋ* "bitter" are uncertain; Khasi has both *ksaŋ* and *kəthaŋ,* the latter comparable with Mon *kataŋ,* Bahn. St. *taŋ,* but the PM root is to be reconstructed **(ə)səŋ:* Kh. *ɔsɔŋ* "bitter"; Sora *asaŋ* "of raw taste," *asaŋ-ən* "acerbity," *pisaŋ~pisiŋ* "astringent" (A. Zide[21] cites *pisaŋ~əsaŋ* "bitter"). Pinnow reconstructs PM **ś* for the series: Kh., Mu., Sa., Sora, Gu. *s*=Ku. *s~ś,* contrasting with PM **s* for the series: Kh., Mu., Sa., Ku. *s*=Gu. *s~ø*=Sora *ø,* but the comparative evidence (see Table) suggests that the former series derives from PM **s,* the latter from PM **ts,* showing retention of the stop element after prefixed *g/ or *k/ ("bird" and "louse") but not after *q- ("pain"). An additional comparison is available for AT *s, viz. Sora *sĕrum* "to smell" (Kuiper cit.), from PM *ser[o]m; cf. AT *s[a]rom "smell/fragrant" (IN *harum, Paiwan *s/m/arum, Thai *hoom<*sroom/ hoom, MY *hɔm).

It is not clear at this time whether the final palatal stop (usually -ć, but -ʔj in Munda) commonly found in AA roots is to be reconstructed as AA *-ts rather than *-ć, in keeping with the AT pattern, which lacks the final surd stop (*-ć). It is possible that AA has final *-s for an original *-ts, but in the most promising correspondence available the complex AT etymon shows interchange of final *-ts with *-s and even *-t; cf. AT *(ŋ)kus(/kus)~*kuts/kuts~*(ŋ)kut(/kut) . . . *kəs(/kəs) . . . (ŋ)kə[t,ts](/kə[t,ts])~*kits(/kits)~kats(/kats) "scratch, scrape, dig, claw/nail"; Khm. *kos* "scratch, scrape," Central Sakai [Semai] *kos* "scrape"; also Khm. *kakis* "scratch continually and light," probably from *ka[s]/kis. More surprisingly, final *-s is preserved in the Aslian group in one key cultural root, far from any possible late borrowing source (AN final *-s preserved only in Formosa and Borneo); cf. AT *(n)tobos "sugarcane" (Thai *ooy<*owoy<*obos); Aslian *b[u]s, id.: Bersisi [Mah Meri] *bois, buh;* Sakai [Semai] *busś, bus* (entry lacking in Benjamin); see above for other MK forms for this cultural root.

AA *y occurs both initial and as a final (*-ai=*-ay, etc.), as in AT, and is subject to intervocalic loss, again as in AT. Three AT comparisons are available here: Bahn. *hiup* "blow, whistle," from PAA *[ś]iup<*[s]iup through palatalization; cf. AT *iyup~*[iyu]p/iyup~*(n)s/iyup~*t/iyup "blow/whistle" (Thai *phiu~*thiu); Khm. *pek,* St. *bek* "to be separated," Bahn. *pek* "to separate," Khs. *piaʔ~phiaʔ* "to divide, split," from PAA *piak; cf. AT *(q/)biyak~*piyak "divide/distribute/separate" (Thai *ʔbiak "distribute"); PM *luaŋ "iron" (cit. by Bhatta-charya[22]); cf. AT *lu[y]aŋ "copper/brass" (Dioi *luaŋ,* Sek *luoŋ* "copper"); for the semantics, cf. Atayal (Form.) *baliq~balyeq* "iron, metal, copper"<AT *(m)baxliaq "iron" (Thai *hlek, N. Thai *mwa).

The characteristic AT distinction between *l and *ḷ, as maintained intact in some Formosan languages, is not in evidence in AA, and the question remains of whether it might be reconstructable for this stock. Both *r and *l commonly remain as such both in PM and PMK, the most promising possible exception being complicated by an apparent infixed */r/; cf. PM *jura[ʔ] "thorn"; Mon jala, Bahn. jəla, Theng jĕrla, Aslian *jə/r/laʔ: Tembi [Temiar] jərlaʔ~ja:lak, Sakai [Semai] jərlak< PAA *j[u]la[ʔ] or *j[u]/r/la[ʔ] (whence PM *jura[ʔ]). It should also be noted that PM appears to have medial *-l- corresponding to AT *-ḷ- in one root ("heat," above). Munda has both r and ṛ, the latter generally interpreted (as in Pinnow) as the result of areal influences (Indic, Dravidian). It possibly stands for an earlier PAA *ḷ in some roots; cf. PM *ramba[r,r]a "green gram [chickpea]," "leguminous plant [Phaseolus varieties]"; Mon ʔbai (also written tʔbai) "bean"; PW *rəbai, id.: Da. bai, Ri. rəbai~bai, Pal. rəbai, Wa (Tung Va) pɛ, apparently from *ra(m)ba[ḷ]a, with *ḷ>y (=i), a shift sometimes found in AT. Final *-ḷ is a possible reconstruction for the following root, which would otherwise be difficult to explain: PM *ba[q]a "flower"; Mon pako, Alak pakao, Srê bəkao, Aslian *bəkaw, but Kaseng pakai and Khm. phka, id., from PAA *ba[q]a[ḷ]. Initial *ḷ-, on the other hand, is a possibility for the following MK root for "sesame," probably to be considered a relatively late acquisition from AT: Rengao rəŋa, Mon laŋau~daŋau, PW: Da. lɔŋ ŋaʔ, Ri. lək ŋaʔ, ləŋaʔ, Pal. rəŋa, Wa (Tung Va) ŋaʔ, ŋyeʔ, ŋɛ<PW and PMK *[ḷ]əŋa (Palaung regularly has r, l for PW *r, *ḷ); cf. AT *ḷəŋa (IN *ləŋa, Thai *ŋa, Dioi ra<*ra(ŋ)a.

Austro-Thai has a rich set of consonant clusters (see Table), which have been reconstructed for the most part only with great difficulty because of the widespread tendency toward simplification of various kinds, notably to t, ṭ, ts, s, h, and the like. We must now ponder the question: Did Austroasiatic once have a similar set of clusters, or any clusters at all? The resemblance between the MY forms for "dog": *kḷəw~*kḷ[um] and Mon *kluiw=kləw* has long been noted, and in 1966 Haudricourt[23] suggested a connection also with Vn. *chó*, since *ch-* sometimes corresponds to an earlier **kl-* (Vn. *chúôi* "banana," Thai **kluay*, id.), Khmu *sɔʔ*, and even Kh. *sɔlɔʔ~śɔlɔʔ* (forms adapted). The PM root is probably **sɔ*, often with various accretions (perhaps *sɔlɔʔ<*klɔ/lɔʔ*), which, together with the evidence from eastern AA languages, point rather to an original PAA **ts-;* cf. PW: Da. *tso*, Ri. *s'oʔ*, Wa (Tung Va) *soʔ* (suggesting PW **tso*), St. *sõu*, Chrau *śo*, Alak, Halăng *ćo*, Aslian **ć[o]ʔ*, Khs. *kseu*. There are two completely "irregular" forms, however, viz. Pal. *ă/ʔoʔ* and Bahn. *ko*. The latter form, which is usually simply omitted when cognate lists are given (!), virtually compels us to reconstruct the cluster **kl-* or the like; Guilleminet[24] cites *ćo* only as a dialectical variant used by the Rengao subtribe of the Bahnar, and the language lacks any substantial parallel for this alternation. The original cluster might have been **kḷ-* rather than **kl-* on the basis of the AT correspondence, and, if we follow the Mon (and perhaps Khasi) evidence in reconstructing the final as **-əw*, we arrive at a perfect fit with the AT root: PAA **kḷəw;* AT **[wa]kḷəwm[a]* [AN **(w)atsu;* Kadai **khl[]ma*].

There is no firm evidence for other PAA consonant clusters, and it appears that simplification had generally taken place, although certain groupings of cognate forms at times suggest the possibility of an original cluster, e.g. those for "eight": PM **tham* (Kh.)~**tam* (Sora, Gu.); *pham* (St., Halăng, Chrau), *tham* (Brou, Boloven, Churu), *tam* (Suk), *ntəm* (Amok), *tsan* (*<*tsam*) (Da.), *daća:m* (Mon), *tam* (*<*sam*) (Vn.), *ham* (Alak, Kaseng), all as if from an earlier PAA **(m)pram>* **(m)phram*. One basic root comparison indicates that the labial cluster had already been simplified in medial position at the PAA level; cf. PM **mət*, PMK **mat<*PAA **mət* "eye"; AT **mapḷa*, id. (IN **mata*, Thai **pra>*ta*). This highly significant comparison indicates not only fore-stress with loss of final syllable, as is characteristic of Miao-Yao [MY **maay<*maat<* **mapḷ(a)*], but also simplification to **t* (as in Formosa: East; see Table), leading to centralization of the vowel (**a>ə*). Note that this does *not* mean that we are to reconstruct *°t* and the like for PAA, simply that the prototype for PAA *°mət* had been developed in that fashion, as discussed below.

The PMK vowel system has been reconstructed by Shorto (1973) as follows: /*i ii e ee a aa ə əə ɔ ɔɔ o oo u uu; iə uə ai*/. Shorto postulates three principal types of variation: (1) between short and long vowels (2) between simple vowel and diphthong: *ii~iə, uu~uə,* occasionally *aa~ai* (3) between diphthong and ə: *iə~ə, uə~ə.* Pinnow (1959) sets up a vowel schema of Thai type, which adds a high central (ɨ) and low front (ɛ) vowel to the above 7-vowel system, for the "younger" stage of Munda, developed from an "older" stage lacking *e* and *o.* Much remains to be done in the analysis of the correspondences between the Munda and MK systems, but it appears that neither *°ɨ* nor *°ɔ* will be required at the PAA level, leaving a six-vowel schema much like that of AT (/*i e a ə o u*/). AT has the diphthong *°ia,* but apparently lacks *°ua;* it is possible that both clusters (*°ia~°iə; °ua~°uə*) will eventually be reconstructed for PAA, but not *°ai* (Shorto), which seems dubious even at the PMK level (see "kite," below). As indicated by the variations noted by Shorto, there has been much "leveling off" of diphthongs; cf. (long vowels written as geminate clusters) PW *°(k/)liat* "lick," Khm. *liit,* id., Bahn., St. *ləpiet,* Jeh *lapiat* (*<°l/p/iat*) "tongue," Khs. *thəliet* (*<°t/liat*), id.<PAA (eastern) *°liat;* also PW *°kuan* "child," Khm. *kuun,* Mon *kon~kwen,* Bahn., St. *kon,* Vn. *con* [*kɔn*], Boloven *kuon, kuən,* Khs. *kuun,* Nic. *kooen, koon,* id.; also PM *qɔɔn,* id.<PAA *°quan.* Inasmuch as Khmer shows "leveling off" of both basic clusters (*°ia>ii; °ua>uu*), the vowel clusters that do appear in that language stand in need of an explanation. It appears that in AA, as in AT, we must postulate vocalic transfer (VT), or the moving of a vowel forward in syllabic reduction: $CV_1CV_2C > CCV_1V_2C$, etc.; cf. Chong *paliŋ* "above" ~*pliŋ* "(comp.) cloud," Jeh, Halăng *pliŋ,* Lemet *mpliŋ,* Aslian *°(m)baliŋ* "sky," from PAA (eastern) *°(m)baliŋ,* yielding Khm. *bhlieŋ* (*<°[]bliaŋ*) "rain/to rain." Many of the vocalic variations and/or "irregularities" in MK will eventually be explained, it seems, in terms of influences (esp. stress distinctions) exerted by the "missing" V_1 in the $C[V_1]CV_2(C)$ formula; cf. PAA (eastern) *kalaŋ "kite (bird)" (Pacoh kalaŋ; also Nic. kalâŋ "sea eagle"), whence the early loan to Chamic *kalāŋ (Headley[25]); also MK (generally) *klaaŋ, whence the early loan to MY *klaaŋ; also *kəlaŋ (unstressed)>*kələŋ (assimilated), whence the early loan to ST *k/ləŋ (Benedict 1972); also *kĕlaŋ (unstressed), whence Khm. khlaeŋ (Shorto reconstructs *k-laiŋ); also *kĭlaŋ (unstressed) >*kiliŋ (assimilated), whence Khs. kliiŋ; also cf. Mon bak, Ri. mak~mɔk, Da. mɔk, Wa (Tung Va) muk "cut/cut/down" (see above), from PMK *(u)(m)bak; PM *[](qu)(m)bak.

The question of whether to reconstruct vocalic length at the PAA level is of some concern inasmuch as Pinnow (with reservations) reconstructed this feature for PM on the basis of its presence in Southern Munda (Sora, Gutob, et al.). As can be seen from the above example (PM *qɔɔn "child"<AA *quan), this length might be secondary in many if not all cases. N. Zide[26] has attempted an interpretation of this length in terms of laryngealization, but this hardly seems feasible at the PAA level. A similar problem exists in AT, in which length can generally be analyzed as of secondary origin, often as the result of VT (see above), e.g. AT *ma/play "die">Sek praay. A similar process can be seen at work in AA, it appears, either in reduplicated forms or elsewhere; cf. AT *(q/)ud~*q/ud/ud "suck/smoke/drink" [Thai *ut "smoke"<*ud; *ʔduut "suck, inhale, smoke"<*q/(u)dud]; PM *uut "suck, drink, swallow"<*(ud/)ud (note final *-d>-t, as in Thai); AT *g[a]rut "scratch" [Thai *gruut "scratch, tear, rake"<*g(u)rut through assimilation and VT], a complex doublet of AT *k[a]rud "scrape"; Khs. khruut "scratch"<*k(u)rut; also (see above) PMK *kap "bite/cut"; PM *[]qaap, id., from *[]aqap; cf. AT *[t]aNqap. Perhaps the best evidence for vocalic length at the PAA level is furnished by PM/PMK *aa corresponding to MY *aa in "blood" (above); cf. also the following, with consistent vocalic length distinction shown, yet VT could be invoked in explanation; the AT roots are *(q/)(m)paR "spread out/fly" and *(N)qa(m)bar "twin, double(d), two":

	PM	Mon	Khmer	Bahnar	Jeh	Vietnamese
fly	[*apir]	pau>pɔ	par	par	pal	bay [bay]
two	*a(m)baar	ʔbar>ʔba	bir	ʔbaar	baal	vai [vaay]

Note that Khm. *bir* "two" shows vocalic effect from the initial *ʔb- (<*q/b-); cf. also Mon *ʔdak*, Khm. *dɨk* "water"<PAA *ʔdak (<*q/dak); cf. also Mon *sla~hla*, Khm. *slɔk~sla* "leaf/ betel (leaf)"<PAA *śu:laq; the postvelars have a similar vo- calic effect in AT, especially in Kadai. The PM form *apir "fly" probably represents an old AA doublet; AT also has *(q/)(m)- pəR(/pəR) "fly," apparently yielding Thai *ʔbin, Sek *bil~bɨl. The different reflexes for PAA final *-r in Mon apparently reflect the old length distinction.

We are now in a position to review the basic lexical agree- ments between AT and AA. Schmidt (1906) presented a large number (215) of such agreements, but the vast majority of them are of mediocre quality or even entirely unconvincing, e.g. IN *susu "breast," Sa. *susu* "to sniff, snort." Most of the significant lexical agreements that we have turned up have already been cited above; we review them here by categories:

NUMERALS: only "twin/two," with AA showing the derived meaning.

PRONOUNS: only a somewhat similar contrast in demonstra- tives: AA type *na (Pinnow 1965: 15.1) "this, 3rd perss. sing. prn., that" and type *ni/ne[27] (Pinnow: 15.2) "this"; cf. AT *na "that (one), there," and *[i]nəy "this, here" (IN *ini, Thai *ni~*nay).

KINSHIP TERMS: in general entirely distinct, but with iso- lated correspondences; cf. PNB (and PMK) *yaʔ "grandmother" (above) and Thai *ya, id. (but Atayal y/ayaʔ "mother"); also PMK *(m)bap "father" (Boloven *mbap*, Churu *ba:p*), AT *(m)bapa. The most interesting possible agreement in this category is supplied by PM *aji "older sister (Sa., Ho), older brother's wife (Kh.), sister-in-law (Ku.), grandmother (Mu.)"~*ajiŋ (unex- plained final; cf. the IN nasalization) "older sister (Ju.), younger sister (Sora)"; also Semang [Jehai] *ajoi* "younger sister" (Ben- jamin [personal communication] describes this as a vocative term), apparently by VT from *(o)ji (cf. the AT form); cf. IN *a(ń)g′i~*ha(ń)g′i "younger sibling"~"sibling of the other sex," Formosa (East; Atayalic) *(suw)aji "younger sibling," from AT *(s[o]w)a(n)ji; in view of the semantic shift in Munda one might also compare Thai *aay~*ɨay(<*ay/ay) "eldest in sibling series" (former used mainly for males, latter for females), from *a(j)i, a regular shift for Thai.

BODY PARTS: three basic roots ("hair," "eye," "blood"), also (Munda only) "breast." In addition, two MK roots of restricted occurrence have likely sources in AT or Miao-Yao; cf. AT *(u)(N)q[a]lay "penis/male"; PW *klɛ "penis": Da. *le* (high tone), Ri. klɛʔ, Wa (Tung Va) kliʔ; also Miao *hmi(ŋ) "tooth"; Khm. *thmeń,* Bahn. *samiŋ;* note also Khs. *dop* "bark"; MY *dop "skin/bark."

NATURAL PHENOMENA: "day/sun" presents the only significant agreement.

ANIMAL LIFE: "dog" presents the only significant agreement, since "fish" has been rejected as an "imposter." Three roots in this category have been exported, at an early period, to neighboring language families: *k[a]laŋ "kite" to Chamic, MY, and ST (see above); *k[u]la "tiger" to ST (Burmese-Lolo *k/la, Chinese hu<*xlo<*khla; see Benedict 1972); and *p[]ləm "leech" to Chamic (Headley 1973) and MY (Yao *p[l]om).

VERBS: include several of interest ("fly," "smell," "suck/drink," "cut/bite") but hardly a core vocabulary ensemble.

OTHER GENERAL: "left (hand)" is the outstanding example here.

CULTURAL ITEMS: present many historical problems, because of the different time levels involved and the possibility of early loans from AN through the Chamic languages, which have long been in close contact with Mon-Khmer languages, with many loans in both directions (see the discussion in Headley 1973). A number of forms found in MK only, with no known cognates in Munda, appear to be relatively late loans from IN/AN/AT; cf. Mon *pasai* "iron" (Schmidt [1906] also cites Sa. *pɛsi* "iron staple"), IN *bat′i~*bət′i, id. (Mal. *bĕsi*); Bahn. *təlei,* Khs. *təlai* "cord," IN *tali, id. (Mal. *tali*) (note the similar vowel treatment, suggesting borrowing via Chamic, which has *-i>*-əy); PMK *kmpor "lime" (Shorto): MM *gapuiw,* SM

/həpo/, Khm. /kɔmbao/, IN *kapuγ, id. (Mal. *kapur*) (note the nasalization in the Khmer form, as in "sugarcane"); PMK *kdiiŋ (Shorto): Khm. /khti:ŋ/ "wild ox"~*k-n-diiŋ: SM /kəloiŋ/ "gaur," AT *ka/(n)triŋ "cattle/buffalo"; Khm. *prāk* "silver," IN *pirak, id.; Khm. *mās*, St. *mahi*, Biat *maih* "gold," IN *əmat′, id. (Mal. *ĕmas*), but Shorto[28] suggests a derivation by infixation from PMK *iʔaas "shine/shining." Two other forms, although restricted only to MK, appear to be somewhat earlier loans from AT: "boat" and "sesame" (above). Of special importance is the root for "sugarcane," from AT *(n)tobos, which appears to be of great antiquity in MK although not found in Munda; note the strange "fragmentation" of the root, as shown above, including a remnant *b[u]s in Aslian which preserves the final *-s. We come now finally to the one cultural item which is represented, albeit with semantic shift, in Munda, viz. AT *lu[y]aŋ "copper/brass," yielding PM *luaŋ "iron," the final piece in the puzzle (the "missing" *y*) being supplied by Mon *sluy* "copper" (cf. *slāk* "bronze"),[29] from *s/luy[aŋ]. Thus it appears that the "culture word" of greatest antiquity in all Southeast Asia designated the very metal (copper/bronze) that was probably first produced in history by the people (AT-speaking) of this region.

We believe that the answer to the problem posed at the outset of this paper is as follows: AT and AA do not have a core vocabulary in common, despite the morphological similarity of the two language stocks, hence the idea of an "Austric" super-stock must be abandoned. There are a number of lexical agreements, however, and these are best explained by postulating that a mainland branch of AT, now extinct, became "substratum-ized" by AA, yielding up certain roots in the process. Two of the basic roots involved, those for "dog" and "left (hand)," are precisely the pair (*perro, izquierdo*) which the "Iberian" substratum passed on to the conquering Romans in Spain, while the word *dog* itself, apparently of non-IE origin, has survived a series of upheavals in Great Britain to emerge triumphantly in modern English. The left side of the body is endowed with various magical properties (cf. French *gauche*, a Germanic word ousting Old French *senestre*<Latin *sinister*), and the

body parts involved above are closely connected with "spirit life": "hair (strength)," "eye (evil)," "blood (life/soul)," "breast (mother)," etc. The words for "eye" and "day/sun" probably traveled together as a pair ("sun"="eye of the day"), with reference again to an object (the sun) of vast magical properties. We can visualize a conquered group passing on much of its esoteric (cult) learning to its conquering masters, along with certain cult "paraphernalia" in the form of lexical items.

The relationship of this "substratumized" AT group, which we shall label AT-sub., to other branches of AT is of some interest. Lexically it stands closest to AN, which has cognates for all the main forms represented here, including "hair" (AN °*busuk*). Like the other mainland branches of AT, this AT-sub. branch showed a tendency to reduce to monosyllables, as in "hair" and "eye," yet had apparently retained some disyllabic forms, as in "blood," "copper," and "sugarcane" (to account for the various forms found in AA). Specifically, AT-sub. reduced AT °*mapla* "eye" by fore-stress and retroflexing (>°*maṭ*), followed by centralization of the vowel (>°*mət*), the latter development not found elsewhere in AT. The indicated semantic shifts: "twin/double">"two" and "light/shine">"sun/day" are encountered elsewhere in AT, but a third shift: "copper">"iron," which appears to be unique, represents a development within Munda itself, after separation from the ancestral AA-speaking people, as proved by Mon *sluy* "copper," retaining the earlier meaning. The following diagram represents our present view of the relationships involved:

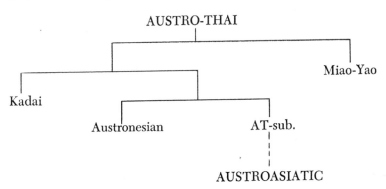

With Austro-Thai and Austroasiatic in place, it can be seen that the three language stocks of Southeast Asia show a line of primary cleavage dividing one of these stocks (ST) from the other two (AT, AA). Along this line, or within the region of linguistic separation that it implies, there developed an early transitional zone, with areal diffusion from ST to the two AT substocks (Kadai and MY) remaining on the mainland as well as to the Viet-Muong group, situated peripherally with reference to the parent AA stock. The principal language features involved here can be tabulated as follows:

The above table clearly shows the effect of areal diffusion from ST at a very early period into the transitional zone (enclosed in heavy lines), with transformation of the mainland AT substocks into essentially monosyllabic, tonal languages showing secondary aspiration of stops (in initial position), with less marked influence on features such as nasal/orals and postvelars (both lacking in ST). Viet-Muong, not included in the table, underwent closely similar changes, also at an early period. The basic two-tone scheme of ST, which early (second to first millennium B.C.) developed a third sandhi tone in Chinese, was diffused in this form, along with certain cultural loanwords, to Kadai and MY (see *Introduction*). Another basic feature of ST, the lack of final *-*h* (only final *-*ø*=vocalic final, without alternation with final -*?*), apparently also influenced the loss of this final in Kadai and MY, although within the AN substock final *-*h* was also lost in IN (and Tsouic, but maintained in Atayalic and East Formosan). Later, with the widespread unvoicing of initial stop consonants, the Kadai and MY languages paralleled ST languages in reflecting this change in various *tonal* phenomena, thus substituting one kind of glottal feature (tone production) for another (voicing). Austroasiatic, which shows a basic contrast between final glottal stop (-*?*) and continuant (-*h*), reflects the unvoicing in various *register* phenomena, which can be viewed as fundamentally another kind of glottal feature: *constricted* (glottal stop) vs. *expanded* (glottal spirant continuant = *h*), a distinction secondarily transferred to that of tongue-root position.[30] This serves to explain the strik-

AUSTRO-THAI

Sino-Tibetan	Kadai	Miao-Yao	Austronesian	Austroasiatic
syllables 1	syllables 1 (+2)	syllables 1	syllables 2 (+1,3)	syllables 2/1
nasal/orals lacking	nasal/orals (>nasals) (>stops)	nasal/orals {initial {medial	nasal/orals {initial {medial	nasal/orals medials only
velars only	postvelars	postvelars >velars	postvelars	postvelars
secondary aspiration	secondary aspiration	secondary aspiration	no secondary aspiration	no secondary aspiration
final *-ø only →	final *-ø only →	final *-ø only →	final *-ø (~final *-h) →	final *-ø/? ~final *-h →
unvoicing: tones	unvoicing: tones	unvoicing: tones	unvoicing: no change	unvoicing: registers
basic tones 2 (>3)	basic tones 3	basic tones 3	basic tones lacking	basic tones lacking

(The Kadai and Miao-Yao columns are enclosed in a box labeled AUSTRO-THAI.)

ing contrast along the primary cleavage line (PCL) in South-east Asia between tone and register phenomena, tying them in with a basic segmental feature (absence or presence of final *-h).

In addition to the features of the early transitional zone (ETZ), as shown in the table, later areal factors have also been at work, e.g. in the reduction of the isolated (from AN) Chamic languages to largely or even (Rade) completely monosyllabic speeches; note also a similar monosyllabicizing trend in the AA languages, with the Mon-Khmer group regularly reducing the CVCV(C) pattern to CCV(C). Khasi shows secondary as-piration, apparently under the influence of the surrounding TB languages, while at least two of the Palaung-Wa languages (Danaw, Riang) have developed a two-tone system as a result of unvoicing, again in keeping with the TB pattern. Finally, as an exception to the general rule that areal factors in South-east Asia have operated in the ST>AA direction, one Southern Burmese-Lolo language (Akha) has developed a register system very much like that of the neighboring AA languages.

NOTES

[1] This is a revised version of a paper presented at the First International Conference on Austroasiatic Linguistics (FICAL), Honolulu, Hawaii, January 1973.

[2] Abbreviations: AA Austroasiatic; Asl. Aslian; Bahn. Bahnar; Da. Danaw; FICAL (see Note 1); Gu. Gutob; *IPLS Indo-Pacific Linguistics Studies* (G. B. Milner and E. J. A. Henderson, eds.), Part 1, Amsterdam, North Holland Publishing Company, 1965; Ju. Juang; Kh. Kharia; Khm. Khmer; Khs. Khasi; Ku. Kurku; MK Mon-Khmer; MM Middle Mon; Mu. Mundari; Nic. Nicobarese; OM Old Mon; PAA Proto-Austroasiatic; Pal. Pa-laung; PM Proto-Munda; PMK Proto-Mon-Khmer; PNB Proto-North-Bahnaric; PW Palaung-Wa; Ri. Riang; Sa. Santali; SM Spoken Mon; St. Stieng.

[3] R. O. Windstedt, "Lexicographical Coincidences in Khasi

and Malay," *Journal of the Straits Branch of the Royal Asiatic Society* (1917): 251-60.

⁴ H. K. J. Cowan, "Aantekeningen betreffende de verhouding van het Atjehsch tot de Mon-Khmer talen," *BTLV 104* (1948): 429-514.

⁵ F. B. J. Kuiper, "Munda and Indonesian," in *Orientalia Neerlandica*, Leiden, A. W. Sijthoff's Uitgerverschmaatschappij, 1948.

⁶ H. J. Pinnow, "Über den Ursprung der voneinander abweichenden Strukturen der Munda und Khmer-Nikobar-Sprachen," *Indo-Iranian Journal 4* (1960): 81-103.

⁷ R. Shafer, "Études sur l'austroasien," *BSLP 48* (1952): 111-58.

⁸ H. J. Pinnow, *Versuch einer historischen Lautlehre der Kharia-Sprache*, Wiesbaden, Otto Harrassowitz, 1959.

⁹ D. Thomas and M. Smith, "Proto-Jeh-Halǎng," *Zeitschrift für Phonetik, Sprachwissen und Kommunikationsforschung 20* (1967): 157-75.

¹⁰ K. D. Smith, *A phonological reconstruction of Proto-North-Bahnaric*, Santa Ana, Calif., Summer Institute of Linguistics, 1972.

¹¹ L. C. Thompson, *Proto-Viet-Muong phonology*, paper presented at FICAL, 1973; also M. A. and M. E. Barker, "Proto-Vietnamuong (Annamuong) final consonants and vowels," *Lingua 24* (1970): 268-85.

¹² G. Benjamin, *Austroasiatic subgroupings and prehistory in the Malay Peninsula*, University of Singapore, Department of Sociology, Working Papers, 1972; presented at FICAL, 1973.

¹³ H. L. Shorto, "The structural patterns of Northern Mon-Khmer languages," in H. L. Shorto, ed., *Linguistic Comparisons in South East Asia and the Pacific*, London, 1963.

¹⁴ H. L. Shorto, *The vocalism of Proto-Mon-Khmer*, paper presented at FICAL, 1973.

¹⁵ H. L. Shorto, *A dictionary of the Mon inscriptions from the sixth to the sixteenth centuries*, London, Oxford University Press, 1971.

¹⁶ E. J. A. Henderson, "Final -*k* in Khasi: a secondary phonological pattern," in *IPLS* (1965): 459-66.

¹⁷ G. H. Luce, "Danaw, a dying Austroasiatic language," in *IPLS* (1965): 98-129.

490 *Austro-Thai*

[18] W. Smalley, *Outline of Khmu? structure*, New Haven, AOS, 1961.

[19] A. Haudricourt, "L'origine des tons en vietnamien," *JA 242* (1954): 69-82.

[20] R. J. Wilkinson, "A vocabulary of Central Sakai," *Papers on Malay Subjects: 2d series, no. 3*, Kuala Lumpur, 1915.

[21] A. Zide, *Sora FF and CF forms*, paper presented at FICAL, 1973.

[22] S. Bhattacharya, "Some Munda etymologies," in N. H. Zide, ed., *Studies in Comparative Austroasiatic Linguistics*, The Hague, Mouton, 1966.

[23] A. Haudricourt, "The limits and connections of Austroasiatic in the Northeast," in N. H. Zide, ed., *Studies in Comparative Austroasiatic Linguistics*, The Hague, Mouton, 1966.

[24] P. Guilleminet, *Dictionnaire bahnar-français*, Paris, EFEO, 1959-63.

[25] R. K. Headley, Jr., *Some sources of Chamic vocabulary*, paper presented at FICAL, 1973.

[26] N. Zide, "Gutob-Remo vocalism and glottalised vowels in Proto-Munda," in *IPLS* (1965): 43-53.

[27] H. J. Pinnow, "Personal pronouns in the Austroasiatic languages: a historical study," in *IPLS* (1965): 3-42.

[28] H. L. Shorto, "The word for 'two' in Austroasiatic," in J. M. C. Thomas et Lucien Bernot, eds., *Langues et techniques, nature et société, Vol. 1, Approche linguistique, Etudes présentées à André Haudricourt*, Paris, Editions Klincksieck, 1972.

[29] Mon *slāk* "bronze" appears to be isolated, the resemblance to AT *(m)baxliaq* "iron" (~"metal/copper" in Atayal) probably being coincidental; the initial cluster (*sl-*) perhaps served as a model for *sluy* "copper," both from an earlier prefixed/compounded form.

[30] See the discussion in K. J. Gregerson, *Tongue-root and register in Mon-Khmer*, paper presented at FICAL, 1973.